简明英汉对照版

世界运河辞典

A CONCISE ENGLISH-CHINESE
DICTIONARY OF WORLD CANALS

主编 魏向清 郭启新 邓 清　　　　　副主编 耿云冬 徐海江 孙文龙 刘润泽

南京大学出版社

编委会（按姓氏汉语拼音排序）：

邓　清　耿云冬　郭启新　李宏明　刘润泽　刘韶方　卢华国　乔丽婷　孙文龙
魏向清　徐海江　徐洪喜　张淑文　赵连振

项目助理（按姓氏汉语拼音排序）：

卜云峰　郭丹东　李　丹　于振平　袁天准　赵　静　朱　慧

编译人员（按姓氏汉语拼音排序）：

陈佳缘　陈梦瑶　陈思奇　陈心怡　陈秀芬　窦雨洁　段心雨　樊昕阳　方晨堃
方　婷　关颖怡　管艺添　郭　俊　黄文婧　江　珊　鞠银河　李雪妍　李玥佳
李子龙　祁梦雪　桑雯丽　申鹏飞　石忠灵　孙家磊　孙晓威　唐文晴　滕静雅
田宇健　万慧婷　王雯婕　王　鋆　王　宇　王钰靓　魏　薇　魏　玮　吴佳怡
武依伟　夏健鑫　徐妍桐　叶一诺　余沚娟　张洁婷　张　璐　张小于　赵敏敏
周昊瑾　周　宇　朱星妍

审校人员（按姓氏汉语拼音排序）：

戴拥军　董晓娜　冯雪红　龚琪峰　胡　叶　黄鑫宇　江　娜　李晓丽　梁鹏程
刘性峰　刘谕静　秦　曦　权循莲　沈家豪　王　静　吴尹清　吴　洲　杨　燕
叶　莹　殷　健　尹婵杰　郑　洁　朱　军

FOREWORD　序言

生命因水运而生，文明因江河而兴。纵观全世界，人类生命的缘起与文明的演化均离不开水的运化和江河的哺育。古今中外，运河承担着航运、灌溉、供水、排涝等主要功能，运河的修建是人类保护自然、利用自然，追求人与自然和谐共生的伟大社会实践。千百年来，世界各地的劳动人民凭借其生活智慧与顽强意志，于一凿一锤之间，完成了一个又一个伟大的运河工程，孕育了开拓进取、不畏艰难的运河精神，更创造了绵延不绝、生生不息的运河文化。

运河是人工开凿的水道，它连通着不同的水路，构建出四通八达的宏阔水网，使人类自然交通与人文交流都更为顺畅。在中国，纵贯南北的大运河连通了东部的五大水系和众多河湖，加强了运河沿线城镇多方面的联系和交流，可谓是推进国家和社会不断发展的"运河力"。在世界各大洲，诸多跨国运河的开凿实现了很多国家与地区间的互联互通，堪称以运河为媒介的区域一体化实践探索。而在大洲和大洋之间，诸如苏伊士运河、巴拿马运河等国际航道不仅为国际远洋航行提供了节约时间、资源和成本的捷径，而且切实影响到全球经济一体化进程和政治多极化态势。事实表明，全球各地各类运河的修建与利用串联起了整个世界，世界运河的发展历史正是人类由封闭、隔绝不断走向开放、交融的独特而真实的全球化过程。

运河是人类文明的摇篮，它见证了世界各国运河沿岸人民的生活变迁与发展，衍生出一幅幅动人的运河文化生活图景。这其中，不仅有人们开凿运河时设计线路的审时度势，利用运河时改造闸坝的开拓创新，而且还有管理运河时维护生态的与时俱进。世界运河城镇与乡村所创造的运河文明与文化，既极具普遍共性又富含文化特色，在人类文明史的画卷中留下了独特的印记，成为全人类值得珍藏的宝贵文化记忆与精神财富。正因为此，包括中国大运河在内的6条运河被联合国教科文组织列为世界文化遗产。

然而，自工业革命以来，以公路和铁路为主的现代交通运输方式，在很大程度上冲击并替代了运河传统的航运模式，运河文明因此也曾一度黯然失色、风光不再。世界范围内，运河的保护、传承与发展状况不容乐观：工业污染物和生活废弃物所带来的大量污染排放，破坏了运河水体及周边的生态环境，曾经"碧波如镜""鱼翔浅底"的运河，如今面临着化为一潭死水的风险，甚至有些运河因缺乏管理与维护，趋于干涸和湮没。世界范围内的运河保护、传承与发展面临前所未有的挑战，这是世界各国人民所面临的共同问题，需要各国人民共同面对。

历史和现实都告诉我们，运河在促进交通、助推经济、发展文化等方面都起到了不可忽视的重要作用。没有运河，就不可能有人类今天的灿烂文明，不关爱运河，也将丧失人类未来的可持续发展。而既往人类运河实践所留给我们的精神财富与文化遗产更无法承继与发扬光大。这些都迫切地要求我们对世界范围内运河的现状更加关注，更加重视，并积极为世界运河的未来发展思考前行的方向。

2009年，世界运河历史文化城市合作组织（英文简称WCCO）在享誉世界的中国大运河河畔的历史文化名城——扬州应运而生。作为中国运河领域唯一的国际性社会组织和世界运河领域重要的国际性社会组织，WCCO一直保持对世界运河、运河城市与运河文化的深切关注，并一直致力于推动世界运河城市之间的经验共享和交流合作，从而促进世界运河的可持续发展和运河城市的共同繁荣。自2007年起，扬州便开始举办世界运河城市论坛，15年来，论坛涵盖了"运河城市的可持续发展""运河城市历史文化遗产保护和传承""一带一路框架下互联互通的运河旅游业"等重要主题，邀请世界各地同仁多维度、多层次地探讨了在当今世界保护运河遗产、开发运河资源和传承运河精神的有效途径。

多年来，WCCO秘书处深感世界运河相关资料与知识的系统梳理是保护、传承与利用好人类运河，有效开展运河相关交流与合作的重要前提。于是，2017年，WCCO秘书处与南京大学双语词典研究中心联合编译出版了《世界运河名录（英汉对照简明版）》。这是中国乃至全世界范围内对人类运河现状的首次较为系统全面的汇集与整理，填补了世界运河辑录工作的空缺。这项工作有着非常积极的开拓性意义与价值。

几年过去了，在中国，从国家层面到地方各级政府和社会各界，运河文化受到了越来越多的关注，运河事业也如火如荼地向前发展。可以说，在世界运河保护、传承与利用方面，中国正以自身的积极实践与经验智慧给出"中国方案"，做出"中国贡献"。2017年2月，中共中央总书记、国家主席习近平在北京通州区调研时指出，"保护大运河是运河沿线所有地区的共同责任"。2019年2月，中共中央办公厅、国务院办公厅联合印发《大运河文化保护传承利用规划纲要》，强调要"加强国际交流与合作，构建区域互动合作机制；充分挖掘大运河文化丰富内涵和独特价值，讲好'运河故事'"。

2020年11月13日，习近平总书记到扬州运河三湾生态文化公园调研，指出："要保护好大运河，使运河永远造福人民。"2021年6月16日，扬州中国大运河博物馆开馆，在将实物展示和数字技术结合起来，阐释中国大运河文化发展的同时，专门设立"世界知名运河与运河城市"专题展厅，未来也将邀请更多世界运河城市参展。显然，在对世界遗产运河"中国大运河"的保护、传承与利用的过程中，中国所做的工作是具有引领性的。《世界运河辞典》的编纂工作，也是中国对于世界运河保护、传承与利用所做的开创性贡献。

《世界运河辞典》是WCCO秘书处与南京大学双语词典研究中心再度携手合作的重要科研成果。在2017年版的《世界运河名录》基础上，合作双方共同组织学术力量，首次以更丰富的条目、更充实的内容、更专业的要求来系统介绍世界各地的主要运河，从而进一步推广世界运河文化，传播世界运河知识。该辞典是目前世界上收录运河条目最多的专题百科类英汉双语工具书，共收录世界范围内已知运河约1 100条，总篇幅约100万字，是世界范围内同类辞书中填补空缺的作品。在《世界运河辞典》的编纂过程中，WCCO秘书处表现出的远见卓识值得肯定，但更值得钦佩的是具体承担编纂工作的南京大学双语词典研究中心和南京大学外国语学院翻译硕士教育中心的硕博青年科研团队。他们克服了时间紧、任务重和压力大等种种困难，通过不懈努力，出色地完成了这项光荣而艰巨的编纂任务。我深信这本《世界运河辞典》将会受到大家的喜爱，成为运河管理者、研究者、爱好者的一本工具书。

今年，恰逢中国共产党成立100周年，这本《世界运河辞典》是为党的百年华诞献上的一份特别礼物。我衷心期待，世界各国的运河管理者、研究者、爱好者携起手来，共同关心运河保护传承利用事业，推动运河可持续发展，扩大运河人文交流，共建人类命运共同体。

单霁翔

2021年9月

EDITORS' PREFACE 编者前言

2017年7月，《世界运河名录》正式出版。作为"2017世界运河城市论坛"10周年纪念出版物，这本小书的问世，意义并不寻常。它首次借助英汉双语辞书编纂的独特形式，向中外读者初步勾勒出人类运河世界图景的简约轮廓。2021年7月，时隔近5年，《世界运河辞典》又将付梓。相比于《世界运河名录》的编纂而言，这部冠名"辞典"的编纂也更不寻常。从"名录"到"辞典"的升级过程，不仅仅是从500到近1 100条目收录数量的翻倍，更意味着编纂难度在专业性、丰富性以及规范性方面要求的叠加。尽管这部运河专题辞书的编纂定位是世界主要运河的历史文化知识普及，而非科学意义上的运河专业知识集成与组织，但限于自身的知识与经验，加上时间与人力的因素，《世界运河辞典》的编纂过程中，我们始终感觉如履薄冰，难度与责任的双重压力远超乎预期。

"看似寻常最奇崛，成如容易却艰辛。"面对着眼前即将付印的终稿清样，不禁感慨良多。这次知难而进、迎难而上的《世界运河辞典》编纂之旅，或许也正是我们充分认识人类运河实践壮举之艰辛伟大的最好路径。在《世界运河辞典》编纂中勉力拼搏的短短数月，我们不仅更为深刻地体察到不同时期、不同民族或种族的人们开凿和利用运河过程中所表现出的生活智慧与顽强意志，而且更领略到世界运河历史文化知识领域的宏阔与深邃。在世界范围内，尽管各国各地运河开凿的历史渊源不尽相同，运河沿线两岸呈现的自然风貌各有特色，运河利用与完善的文化记忆丰富多样，但从根本上说，世界运河开凿和利用的历史长河中始终贯穿着一条清晰的精神线索，那就是开拓创新与坚忍不拔。正是在这种"运河精神"的不断鼓舞之下，《世界运河辞典》渐渐也呈现出它应有的基本形态，而其背后所蕴含的编纂团队的艰苦努力与辛勤劳动早已融入运河条目的字里行间。

在整个项目实施过程中，我们切实经历了从"无"到"有"的几方面不懈的努力。首先，从"无本"到"有本"。这本《世界运河辞典》的编译应是真正意义上编纂加翻译的过程。由于并无现成的文本，我们只能依据世界运河历史文化城市合作组织（以下简称"世界运河城市合作组织"）专家汇集的运河条目基础清单，面向各类纸质和电子来源的相关知识信息进行多次核查、比较和筛选，将大量碎片化的运河知识进行梳理与整合，撰写初稿后再不断打磨和优化，直至最终定稿。其次，从"无序"到"有序"。根据世界运河城市合作组织秘书处提供的运河基础清单，我们对其中大量非通用语种的运河条目形式进行了有序的转译，即从多种非通用语种转为英语的译写工作。与此同时，大量国外运河名称并无汉译先例或定译可参照，必须要解决外语运河名称汉语首译定名的问题。这两项工作的繁杂与困难程度可想而知，但鉴于英汉辞典的专业性要求，这些环节必不可少，这些难题也必须要解决。为此，我们编纂团队成员攻坚克难，查阅无数资料，并请教外语专家，不断纠正偏误，摸索规律，直至最终定稿。第三，从"无知"到"有知"。作为英汉双语辞书的专业研究机构，尽管我们之前有过较为丰富的双语语文辞书编纂经验与专业素养，但对于这本辞典所要求的专业类百科性知识积累却差距较大，虽然有先前《世界运河名

录》编译的基础，也难免左支右绌。然"无知者无畏"，我们鼓足勇气，发挥团队协作的优势，群策群力，解决了一个又一个的难题，直至最终定稿。如今，虽然读者无法从最终的辞典文本中看到这些倾力付出，亦如运河边驻足的游客通常也无法从平静的水面看到昔日的那些波澜壮阔一样。但这些宝贵的辞典编纂集体记忆无疑已经凝结成一种敢于挑战、不怕困难的"运河辞典精神"，值得我们共同珍藏。

《世界运河辞典》编纂项目的开展，正值全球新冠病毒肆虐期间。一方面，我们焦虑于全球各国疫情相互影响的严峻现实，而另一方面，我们沉浸于世界运河互联互通的历史与文化记忆之中，感叹人类运河的共同经验所赋予人类命运共同体建设独特的思想给养。更为重要的是，《世界运河辞典》出版之年，喜逢中国共产党建党100周年，我们的工作或许可以作为积极践行党的人类命运共同体建设理念的实际行动。习近平总书记在2017年中国共产党第十九次全国代表大会上的报告中曾呼吁，"各国人民同心协力，构建人类命运共同体，建设持久和平、普遍安全、共同繁荣、开放包容、清洁美丽的世界"。在构建人类命运共同体的内涵之中，特别要尊重世界文明和文化的多样性，致力于建设开放包容的世界。《世界运河辞典》的编纂工作正是这一宗旨的积极体现，我们所有参编团队成员应该都对这项工作的投入有着共同的理解。希望这本"世界运河城市论坛"15周年的献礼之作，也能为党的百年华诞献上一份我们辞典人的心意。

最后，我们也特别感谢世界运河历史文化城市合作组织秘书处的领导和同事们，感谢相关中外运河专家以及所有给予我们无私帮助的学界朋友们，没有大家的共同努力，这项"从无到有"的辞书成果不可能这么快与大家见面。当然，我们也深知，由于种种主客观因素，《世界运河辞典》的编纂工作并不尽如人意，疏漏失误在所难免。我们也衷心希望广大专家和读者给予我们宝贵的意见或建议，帮助我们今后进一步提高与完善。事实上，按照我们的最初设想，此次《世界运河辞典》纸质版的编纂是未来"世界运河历史文化多语种知识库"构建的框架性基础工作，为今后该专题动态知识库的建设提供基本条件。在当今大数据时代和信息社会，融媒体辞书的编纂与应用已成新常态，我们当与时俱进，继续砥砺前行。

南京大学双语词典研究中心

《世界运河辞典》编委会

2021年7月

1. 本辞典共收录世界范围内主要运河条目近1 100条。辞典提供运河的英语名称及其汉语译名，运河词头的英语名称和汉语译名用黑体字标注。

1.1 本辞典收录英语国家运河及其他国家运河的通用英语名称，如：

Manchester Ship Canal	曼彻斯特通海运河
Morris Canal	莫里斯运河
Nicaragua Canal	尼加拉瓜运河
Oswego Canal	奥斯威戈运河
Panama Canal	巴拿马运河

1.2 本辞典收录的非英语国家运河的名称主要源于荷兰语、法语、德语等，经转写后以英语拼写的形式收录（详情请见附录四），如：

Burumervaart（荷兰语）	Burum Canal	布鲁默运河
Ganzendiep（荷兰语）	Ganzen Canal	汉森运河
Haut Rhône（法语）	Upper Rhône	罗讷河上游运河
Obere Spree-Wasserstraße（德语）	Upper Spree Waterway	施普雷河上游航道

2. 本辞典全部条目按照运河名称英文拼写的字母顺序排列；空格、连字符等不参与词目排序。若首字母相同，则按第二个字母顺序排列，以此类推，如：

Beverlo Canal	贝弗洛运河
Bijlands Canal	白兰茨运河
Bijleveld Canal	拜勒费尔德运河
Bío-Bío Canal	比奥–比奥运河
Birmingham and Fazeley Canal	伯明翰–费兹利运河

3. 本辞典中运河名称的汉语译名原则上采用音译，部分译名视具体情况采用意译或沿用约定俗成的译名，如：

Adams Creek-Core Creek Canal	亚当斯溪–科尔溪运河
South Hadley Falls Canal	南哈德利福尔斯运河
Clubfoot Creek-Harlow Creek Canal	马蹄–哈洛运河

4. 本辞典收录的运河条目均包含英语简要信息及其相应的汉语翻译，分左右两栏并置呈现。其中英语信息以蓝色字体放置于左栏，相应的汉语译文以黑色字体置于右栏。

Aar Canal	**阿尔运河**
A canal located in South Holland Province, the Netherlands. Constructed in 1825, the Aar Canal	荷兰南荷兰省运河。阿尔运河于1825年开凿，全长11千米，其源头

5. 每个运河条目内的信息涵盖运河概况（含地理方位、长度、宽度、深度和载重能力等基本信息，以及起点和终点等连通信息）、历史沿革（含开凿与竣工、通航及变迁等）、现状（含运河的归属与管辖、用途等）以及涉及申报或入选各类遗产名录情况等相关信息，如：

Halden Canal

A canal located near Halden, Norway. The Halden Canal has a length of 80 kilometres, running from Skulerud in the north to Tistedal in the south. It was constructed between 1852 and 1860 for the purpose of transporting timber. The canal has 4 locks to control the water, which can allow the passage of boats within 24 metres in length, 6 metres in width and 1.6 metres in draught. The Strømsfoss and Ørje locks were constructed between 1857 and 1860. Today, the Halden Canal is mainly used for recreation. As a cultural heritage, the canal is under proper protection, attracting many people to swim, fish, cycle and walk along the route.

哈尔登运河

挪威近哈尔登市运河。哈尔登运河全长约80千米，从斯屈勒吕自北向南流向蒂斯特达尔。运河于1852—1860年间开凿，旨在运输木材。哈尔登运河上建有4座船闸，用以调控水位，可容最长24米、最宽6米、吃水深度1.6米以内的船舶通航。运河上的斯特姆弗斯船闸和厄里耶船闸建于1857—1860年间。如今，哈尔登运河主要用于休闲娱乐。运河作为一处文化遗迹受到了良好保护，吸引众多游客在沿线游泳、垂钓、骑行和散步。

6. 本辞典收录部分运河的别名、旧称等亦称信息, 较为知名的亦称信息在辞典正文中以参见条目的形式呈现, 将所要参见的信息指向主条目。英文信息栏(左栏)用"see"标注, 中文信息栏(右栏)用"见"标注。

Neukölln Canal	**新克尔恩运河**
An inland canal located in Berlin, Germany. Also known as Neukölln Ship Canal. The Neukölln	德国柏林市内陆运河。亦称新克尔恩通海运河。新克尔恩运河长

Neukölln Ship Canal	**新克尔恩通海运河**
An inland canal located in Berlin, Germany. See Neukölln Canal.	德国柏林市内陆运河。见新克尔恩运河。

7. 本辞典收录部分经运河化改造的自然河流, 在辞典正文中用两个波浪号(≈)进行标注。

Aa River≈	**阿河**
A canalized coastal river located in the north of France. The Aa River flows from Artois Hills to the North Sea, with a total length of about 93 kilometres. It is divided into two sections. The first section starts	法国北部沿海运河化河流。阿河源于阿图瓦山, 最终注入北海, 全长约93千米。阿河分为两个河段, 第一河段源于阿图瓦山, 流至圣

8. 除正文外，本辞典还包括4个附录和6个索引。附录包括：《世界知名运河组织介绍》《历届世界运河名城博览会概览（2007—2020）》《世界主要运河城镇概览》和《世界运河多语名称对照表》。索引包括：《英文世界运河条目》《中文世界运河条目》《英文洲别世界运河条目》《中文洲别世界运河条目》《英文国别世界运河条目》和《中文国别世界运河条目》。此外，本辞典还附有参考文献，包括运河知识和研究相关的部分文献和网址，以飨读者。

CONTENTS 目 录

A CONCISE ENGLISH-CHINESE DICTIONARY OF WORLD CANALS

Aar Canal

A canal located in South Holland Province, the Netherlands. Constructed in 1825, the Aar Canal has a total length of 11 kilometres. Originating from Amstel, it runs through the Geerpolder, passes Papenveer, continues eastwards and finally flows into the Old Rhine.

阿尔运河

荷兰南荷兰省运河。阿尔运河于1825年开凿，全长11千米，其源头是阿姆斯特尔河，流经吉尔圩田和帕彭费尔后，继续东流，最终汇入旧莱茵河。

Aa River

A canalized coastal river located in the north of France. The Aa River flows from Artois Hills to the North Sea, with a total length of about 93 kilometres. It is divided into two sections. The first section starts from its source in the Artois Hills to Saint Omer while the second section is a navigable waterway, covering a length of 29 kilometres and connecting the Calais Canal and the Bourbourg Canal. Due to siltation and industrial pollution, the section from Saint Omer down to the junction with the Dunkirk-Escaut Canal has been unnavigable since the 1970s.

阿河

法国北部沿海运河化河流。阿河源于阿图瓦山，最终注入北海，全长约93千米。阿河分为两个河段，第一河段源于阿图瓦山，流至圣奥梅尔镇。第二河段是一条通航水道，全长29千米，连通加莱运河和布尔堡运河。自20世纪70年代起，由于泥沙淤积和工业污染，从圣奥梅尔到与敦刻尔克—埃斯科运河交界处的河段已无法通航。

Aberdare Canal

A canal located in Glamorganshire, Wales, the United Kingdom. With a length of 10.86 kilometres, the Aberdare Canal connects Aberdare with the Glamorganshire Canal. Since its opening in 1812, the canal had been used for transporting ore and coal for almost 65 years. With the emergence of railway transport, the water navigation fell into de-

阿伯德尔运河

英国威尔士格拉摩根郡运河。阿伯德尔运河全长10.86千米，连接阿伯德尔郡与格拉摩根郡运河。自1812年通航后，该运河用以运输铁矿石和煤炭长达近65年。然而，随着铁路运输的出现，水运行业开始衰退。阿伯德尔运河的运营

cline. The income of operating the canal could not cover its running expenses while the maintenance costs kept increasing. Under such circumstances, the canal had to be closed in 1900. With the authorization of an act approved by the Parliament in 1924, it was taken over by the Aberdare Urban District Council and the Mountain Ash District Council, after which it was reopened.

几乎入不敷出，维护费用也不断增加。到1900年运河被迫关闭。1924年，经英国议会法案授权，阿伯德尔运河被阿伯德尔城区与芒廷阿什区当地政府接管，之后又重新开放。

Adams Creek-Core Creek Canal

亚当斯溪-科尔溪运河

A canal located in North Carolina, the United States. Built in 1911, the Adams Creek-Core Creek Canal is 12.1 kilometres long. This sea-level canal runs between Pamlico Sound and the ocean port of Beaufort as a part of the Atlantic Intracoastal Waterway. Besides its navigation purpose, the Adams Creek-Core Creek Canal is also a fishing resort.

美国北卡罗来纳州运河。亚当斯溪-科尔溪运河1911年开凿，全长12.1千米。该运河与海平面等高，位于帕姆利科湾和博福特海港之间，是大西洋沿海航道的一部分。除作航道之用外，亚当斯溪-科尔溪运河也是一处钓鱼胜地。

Adelphi Canal

阿德尔菲运河

A privately owned canal located in Duckmanton, England, the United Kingdom. Starting from an ironworks, the Adelphi Canal ends near the junction of Tom Lane and Staveley Road. It was 800 metres in length, disconnected from any other waterway. The canal was built in 1799 to transport goods from the Adelphi Ironworks by the Smith family. The canal was supplied with water pumped from the mine by an engine. The Adelphi ironworks and the start of the canal were located just to the north of the current Arkwright Town. Recent mining expansion has made the surrounding area a vast

英国英格兰达克曼顿私有运河。阿德尔菲运河始于一家钢铁厂附近，终于汤姆路与斯塔韦利路交界处，全长800米，未与其他航道相通。该运河由史密斯家族于1799年修建成，用以运送阿德尔菲钢铁厂货物，水源由一台发动机从矿井中抽水供给。阿德尔菲钢铁厂和运河的起点位于现今阿克莱特镇北部，但近来由于采矿业的扩张，此处已成为大片露天矿区，运河和钢铁厂几乎难觅踪迹。

opencast mining site, leaving little trace of the canal and the ironworks.

Aduard Canal

A canal located in the province of Groningen, the Netherlands. The 12-kilometre-long Aduard Canal has been of great significance for the drainage and flood control of the local area for centuries. The canal is a continuation of the Peizer Canal, which starts from the Hoen Canal near Hoogkerk and finally flows out via two stream arms in the Reit Canal near Aduardzijl. The construction began around 1415. The canal was excavated to supplement the Kliefsloot Canal and the Peizer Canal for the purpose of sufficient drainage. Later, the lock complex on the Aduard Canal was expanded several times to improve the drainage system. A cross-province road was built over the canal around 1840. In the 1930s the Aduard Canal was traversed by the new Van Starkenborgh Canal.

爱德华德运河

荷兰格罗宁根省运河。爱德华德运河全长12千米，几个世纪以来，对当地排水防洪工作至关重要。该运河是派泽运河的延伸，始于霍赫凯尔克镇附近的霍恩运河，随后分成两条支流，最终并入爱德华德宰尔村附近的哈伊特运河。运河1415年前后开凿，当时是为了促进克里夫斯洛特运河和派泽运河充分排水。此后，为改善排水系统，运河上的船闸群历经多次拓建。1840年前后，运河上修建了一条跨省道路。20世纪30年代，新开凿的范斯塔根博尔赫运河横穿爱德华德运河。

A.G. Wildervanck Canal

A canal located in the province of Groningen, the Netherlands. The A.G. Wildervanck Canal runs from Zuidbroek to Wildervanck, covering a total length of about 32 kilometres. The canal was built in the late 1950s, and used as a navigable waterway, then extended in the 1980s, with a branch from Veendam to the Mussel Canal to drain off excess rainwater and supply water to the IJssel Lake in the dry season.

维尔德万克运河

荷兰格罗宁根省运河。维尔德万克运河自泽伊德布鲁克流至维尔德万克，全长约32千米。该运河于20世纪50年代后期开凿，曾被用作通航水道。20世纪80年代，维尔德万克运河经扩建，新增一条从芬丹流向米瑟尔运河的支流，用以排放过量雨水，且旱季可向艾瑟尔湖供水。

Aire and Calder Canal

A canal located in West Yorkshire of England, the United Kingdom. Also called Aire and Calder Navigation. The 55-kilometre-long Aire and Calder Canal has 16 locks in total. The year 1704 witnessed the first improvement to the rivers above Knottingley, when the Aire and the Calder were made navigable to Leeds and Wakefield respectively because of the construction of 16 locks. With the deepening of water, locks were reconstructed several times in order to allow larger boats to pass through. The opening of the Selby Canal in 1778 made the Aire below Haddlesey bypassed. Since 1826, a canal connecting Knottingley with the new town located in Goole created a much more convenient route to River Ouse. In 1905, the New Junction Canal was built so as to connect the system with River Don Navigation.

艾尔-科尔德运河

英国英格兰西约克郡运河。亦称艾尔—科尔德航道。艾尔—科尔德运河长55千米，共建有16座船闸。1704年，诺廷利郡的上游河段经过首次修整，新修建的16座船闸使通往利兹和韦克菲尔德的艾尔河与科尔德河可以通航。随着河道不断拓深，为确保大型船只顺利通行，船闸也历经数次改造。1778年，塞尔比运河通航，船只不必再绕道哈德尔赛之后的艾尔河段。1826年起，新修的一条运河连接了诺廷利和古尔的新镇，使通往乌斯河的航运更为便利。1905年，连通艾尔—科尔德运河与唐河航道的新交界运河建成。

Aire and Calder Navigation

A canal located in western Yorkshire of England, the United Kingdom. See Aire and Calder Canal.

艾尔-科尔德航道

英国英格兰西约克郡运河。见艾尔—科尔德运河。

Aire Canal

A canal located in France. As a part of the Dunkirk-Escaut Canal, the Aire Canal links the Neufossé Canal to the Deûle Canal. It is 39 kilometres in length with only 1 lock in Cuinchy. The plans of constructing the canal could date back to 1271, and in 1825, the construction was commissioned.

艾尔河运河

法国运河。艾尔河运河连通诺福塞运河和德勒运河，是敦刻尔克—埃斯科运河的组成部分，全长39千米，仅在屈安希市建有1座船闸。该运河的修建计划可追溯至1271年。1825年运河被委托修建。第一次世

During World War I, the canal served as a barrier against German troops' attack. The Aire Canal originally passed through the centre of Béthune, and the waterway was later rectified and enlarged. The canal was widened in 1968. One part of this old canal was closed in the 1970s, but some structures remained. Some of the banks between the Aire Canal and the water station were demolished to give way to a leisure base and were renovated in 2012. The Aire Canal is currently under the ownership of the France Waterways (Voies Navigables de France, VNF). It is an important habitat for variable fish populations like bream, rudd and pike.

界大战期间，艾尔河运河充当了阻止德军进攻的屏障。艾尔河运河最初流经贝蒂讷市中心，后经修整和拓展后航道变宽。1968年，该运河被拓宽。艾尔河运河历史悠久，20世纪70年代部分河段关闭，但仍保留了一些运河设施。艾尔河运河和供水站之间部分河堤曾被拆毁，建起休闲度假基地。2012年，这些河堤得以修复。如今，艾尔河运河的所有权归法国航道管理局所有。该运河是欧鳊、赤睛鱼、狗鱼等多种鱼类的重要栖息地。

Aisne

埃纳河

A canalized river located in the northeast of France. The Aisne originates from the forest near Saint Mene Ould, Marne, and finally flows into the Oise in Compiegne, with a total length of 356 kilometres. It mainly flows through Wuziye, Lethelleux, and Soisson. In the Roman period, the Aisne was named Axona. The canalization project began in 1836 and was completed in 1841, then it was opened two years later. The navigable waterway is 57 kilometres long. The maximum capacity of its commercial transportation for a barge is of 220 tonnes. The recreational traffic is mainly carried out by private vessels. In 57 BC, the Romans and Berghes fought near the Axona River. It was a commercial waterway in the Gallo-Roman period. During World War I, there were three battles of Aisne that ever happened in the Aisne valley.

法国东北部运河化河流。埃纳河始于马恩省圣梅内乌尔德附近的森林，最后汇入贡比的涅瓦兹河，全长356千米。埃纳河流经的主要城市有武济耶、勒泰勒和苏瓦松。罗马时期，埃纳河被称作艾克桑那河。埃纳河于1836年进行运河化改造，1841年竣工，1843年开始通航，可通航水道长57千米，允许驳船和游船通行，驳船最大承载量不超过220吨，游船以私人船只为主。公元前57年，罗马人和伯吉斯人曾在艾克桑那河附近交战。高卢—罗马时期，艾克桑那河是一条商业航道。第一次世界大战期间，埃纳河谷发生了三次埃纳河战役。

Aisne Lateral Canal

A canal located in northern France. As a part of the Aisne, the Aisne Lateral Canal runs for 51 kilometres and has 8 locks. It connects Old Asfeld to Condé-on-Aisne. The lateral canal is also linked with the Aisne-Marne Canal at Berry-au-Bac and with the Aisne-Oise Canal at Bourg-et-Comin. The canal was opened in 1841 and reconstructed after World War II. As a vital hub in the waterway network, the canal is responsible for both north-south and east-west traffic.

Aisne-Marne Canal

A canal located in northeastern France. The Aisne-Marne Canal, linking the Aisne and the Marne valleys, starts from Berry-au-Bac and ends in Condé-sur-Marne. It is 58.1 kilometres long and has 24 locks. The construction work began in 1841 and was completed in 1866. The reason for the construction of the canal is to directly connect the Paris-Strasbourg fluvial artery to the northern regions of France. Having been entirely destroyed during World War I, the canal was rebuilt and is now managed by the France Waterways (VNF).

Albemarle and Chesapeake Canal

A canal located in Virginia, the United States. The Albemarle and Chesapeake Canal mainly flows through North Carolina with a total length of 321.9 kilometres. The original canal was 12.1 metres wide

埃纳旁侧运河

法国北部运河。埃纳旁侧运河为埃纳河一部分，全长51千米，河上共建有8座船闸，连接老阿斯费尔德镇和埃纳河河畔的孔代镇。该运河与埃纳—马恩运河在贝里欧巴克镇交汇，与埃纳—瓦兹运河在布尔—科曼镇交汇。埃纳旁侧运河于1841年开放通航，第二次世界大战后重建，是重要的航运枢纽，用以承担南北方向和东西方向的航运。

埃纳－马恩运河

法国东北部运河。埃纳—马恩运河始于贝里欧巴克镇，连接埃纳河河谷和马恩河河谷，终于埃纳河河畔的孔代镇，全长58.1千米，河上共建有24座船闸。该运河于1841年开凿，1866年竣工，开凿该运河的目的是直接连通巴黎—斯特拉斯堡河流干道与法国北部地区。第一次世界大战期间，运河遭到完全破坏，后又得以重建。如今，埃纳—马恩运河由法国航道管理局管理。

阿尔伯马尔－切萨皮克运河

美国弗吉尼亚州运河。阿尔伯马尔—切萨皮克运河主要流经北卡罗来纳州，全长321.9千米。该运河原宽12.1米，深约2.4米，后经疏

and roughly 2.4 metres deep. It was later dredged and maintained to achieve a draught of 4 metres. The bottom width of the present waterway varies from 27.4 metres to 91.4 metres. The construction of the canal began in October 1856. The first vessel passed through the canal in January 1859. During the American Civil War, nearly 9,000 ships had transited the canal. After the war, almost all trade between Albemarle Sound and Norfolk was carried out by waterway. The traffic on the Albemarle and Chesapeake Canal continued to increase. In 1973, the guard lock on the canal was rebuilt, which effectively controlled the ebb and flow of the tidewater east and west of the Elizabeth River and regulated the fresh water from the North Landing River. In 1912, the United States government acquired the Albemarle-Chesapeake Canal and renovated it, first removing the guard lock and then, in 1932, rebuilding a steel and concrete guard lock of about 183 metres in height, which has remained in use ever since. Between 1970 and 1979, the commerce on the Albemarle and Chesapeake Canal averaged roughly 1.4 million tonnes annually. By the early 2000s, the canal was used largely by pleasure craft as a part of the Intracoastal Waterway. Today, the canal is maintained and operated by the United States Army Corps of Engineers and is a part of the well-traveled Atlantic Intracoastal Waterway.

浚，河底拓宽为27.4—91.4米，通行船只的吃水深度可达4米。阿尔伯马尔—切萨皮克运河于1856年10月开始修建。1859年1月，该运河首次通航。美国南北战争期间，其通行量接近9 000艘船只。战后，由于阿尔伯马尔湾和诺福克郡之间几乎所有贸易都是通过水路进行，阿尔伯马尔—切萨皮克运河上的通航量持续增加。1973年，运河上的潮汐船闸重修，之后能有效调控伊丽莎白河东及河西涨落的潮水和来自北兰丁河的淡水。1912年，美国政府收购阿尔伯马尔—切萨皮克运河并对其进行了改造，先是拆除原有潮汐船闸，到1932年，又重新修建了一座高度约为183米的钢筋混凝土潮汐船闸，一直沿用至今。1970—1979年间，阿尔伯马尔—切萨皮克运河年均贸易量约为140万吨。21世纪初，该运河已是沿海航道的一部分，基本用于游船通行。如今，阿尔伯马尔—切萨皮克运河由美国陆军工程兵团维护和运营，是热门旅游线路大西洋沿海航道的一部分。

Albert Canal

A canal located in the northeast of Belgium. With a total length of 129.5 kilometres, the Albert Canal

阿尔贝特运河

比利时东北部运河。阿尔贝特运河连通默兹河和斯海尔德河，从列

links the Meuse River with the Schelde River. It runs from Liège to Antwerp, with 6 locks built to overcome the difference in elevation of about 56 metres. The canal was named after Albert I (1875—1934) of Belgium. The construction of the canal was started in 1930. Successfully shortening the traffic time between Antwerp and Liège from 7 days to 18 hours, the Albert Canal was put into use for the first time in 1939 and came into service intensively only after 1946. During World War II, the canal had served as a defence line of Belgium. Initially with a bottom width of 24 metres, the Albert Canal was navigable by ships of 2,000 tons with a draught of 2.7 metres. Then in 1960, it was extended and now 9,000-ton vessels with a draught of 3.4 metres can pass through the channel. The canal undertakes the transportation of various kinds of goods. In 2002, it has carried 43 million tons of cargo, making up over half of Belgium's total waterborne freight volume. Today, with well-paved roads on both sides, the Albert Canal is also a popular leisure and cycling destination for people to enjoy picturesque scenery, especially around Lanaken and Maasmechelen.

日市流往安特卫普市，全长129.5千米，水位落差达56米，运河上建有6座船闸。阿尔贝特运河得名于比利时国王阿尔贝特一世（1875—1934），1930年开凿。该运河可将往返列日和安特卫普两地的时间从7天缩减至18小时，于1939年通航，但由于第二次世界大战的爆发，阿尔贝特运河直到1946年才开始频繁使用。第二次世界大战期间，该运河还曾作为比利时的军事防线。最初，阿尔贝特运河的底部宽度为24米，可容纳重2 000吨、吃水2.7米的船舶通航。1960年扩建后，可容纳9 000吨级、吃水3.4米的船只通行。该运河承担各类货运功能，2002年，货物运载总量达4 300万吨，占比利时水路货运总量的一半以上。如今，阿尔贝特运河两岸道路平坦，风景如画，尤其是拉纳肯和马斯梅赫伦沿岸，已成为颇受欢迎的休闲度假与骑行胜地。

Aldebaran Canal

阿尔德巴伦运河

A canal located in Los Angeles, California, the United States. The Aldebaran Canal is a part of the series of the Venice Canals funded by Abbot Kinney, a tobacco millionaire and real estate developer in the early 1900s. By the late 1920s, due to the rise of Los Angeles car culture, many of the Venice Canals were filled in and paved to create roads

美国加利福尼亚州洛杉矶市运河。阿尔德巴伦运河是威尼斯运河网中的一条运河。威尼斯运河网由烟草富豪和房地产开发商阿博特·金尼20世纪初出资修建。20世纪20年代末，洛杉矶汽车文化盛行，为了修建可供汽车行驶的公

for driving. The Aldebaran Canal, therefore, was changed into a road named as Market Street.

路, 威尼斯运河网中的多条运河被回填。阿尔德巴伦运河因此被改造为"市场大街"。

Alexandra Canal (Australia)

亚历山德拉运河（澳大利亚）

A canal located in New South Wales, Australia. The Alexandra Canal derived its name from Princess Alexandra. Constructed from 1887 to 1900 on the site of salt marsh, the canal is the first inbound waterway in Sydney. It is 4 kilometres long, and its width increases from 60 metres to 80 metres at the mouth. As one of the only two navigable canals in New South Wales, the Alexandra Canal has 5 tributaries, flowing from the inner Sydney suburb of Alexandria to the Cooks River at Tempe. The Alexandra Canal meets the need of transporting goods for nearby brickworks, woolen mills, tanneries and foundries.

澳大利亚新南威尔士州运河。亚历山德拉运河得名于亚历山德拉公主。该运河为悉尼第一条回航运河, 1887—1900年间开凿, 由原先的盐沼改造而来。运河全长4千米, 宽60米, 在入海口处宽度增至80米。作为当地仅有的两条通航运河之一, 亚历山德拉运河有5条支流, 由亚历山德拉的内悉尼郊区流至坦普的库克斯河。亚历山德拉运河主要运输附近砖厂、毛纺厂、皮革厂和铸造厂的商品。

Alexandra Canal (Singapore)

亚历山德拉运河（新加坡）

A canal located in central Singapore. The Alexandra Canal is 1.2 kilometres long. It is one of the upper reaches of the Singapore River, extending from Tanglin Road to Delta Road and Prince Charles Crescent. In order to improve the structural condition of the canal and to alleviate flooding, the government rebuilt the Alexandra Canal between Tanglin Road and Kim Seng Road from 1997 to 2008. Currently, the canal is a recreational facility, which is included in the Active, Beautiful and Clean Water Programme supervised by the Public Utilities Board of

新加坡中部运河。亚历山德拉运河全长1.2千米, 为新加坡河上游一河段, 从东陵路延伸至德立达路及查理士太子湾。为改善亚历山德拉运河结构, 减轻流域内洪灾影响, 新加坡政府于1997—2008年间重修了东陵路至金声路的运河河段。如今, 亚历山德拉运河已成为一处休闲娱乐场所, 被纳入新加坡公用事业局负责的"活力、美丽和清洁水域"项目。亚历山德拉运

Singapore. The canal also boasts bioretention ponds that function as natural filters to purify water flowing into the waterway.

河还有生态滞留地，这些沼泽地起到自然过滤器的作用，可以清除杂质，净化汇入运河的水流。

Alexandria Canal

A canal located in the United States. Formerly known as Sheas Creek. The Alexandria Canal is an adapted artificial waterway, connecting the city of Alexandria to Georgetown in the District of Columbia. It stretches 4.5 kilometres from its southern point at the Cooks River to the north near Huntley Street, Alexandria. Its banks are made by dry sandstones. In 1830, merchants from Alexandria proposed linking their city to Georgetown to capitalize on the Chesapeake and Ohio Canal. The Congress granted a charter to the Alexandria Canal Company in the same year. The construction began in 1833 and was completed in 1843. The Alexandria Canal was a major reason for the economic rebirth of the city during the middle of the 19th century. Trade had increased and the town's importance as a port grew because of the canal. It also played a seminal role in the evolution of the industrial utilization and development of the local land. Aesthetically, it is a major landmark and dramatic component of the industrial landscape of the area, particularly when it is viewed from the Ricketty Street Bridge and along the Airport Drive.

亚历山大运河

美国运河。旧称谢伊斯河。亚历山大运河连接亚历山大市和哥伦比亚特区乔治敦，是一条经过改造的人工航道。该运河始于其南端的库克河，向北延伸4.5千米，终于亚历山大市附近的亨特利街。亚历山大运河堤岸由倾斜的干砂岩构成。1830年，亚历山大市的商人提议把该城与乔治敦连接起来，方便利用切萨皮克—俄亥俄运河来获得商机。同年，国会授予亚历山大运河公司特许经营权。亚历山大运河于1833年开凿，1843年竣工。该运河是19世纪中叶亚历山大市经济复苏的主要原因。运河通航后，亚历山大市贸易量增加，其作为港口城市的重要性也得到提升。此外，亚历山大运河对当地及附近郊区用地情况和工业发展起到了开创性作用。从美学角度而言，该运河是该地区工业景观的标志性建筑，特别是从里基蒂街大桥和机场大道的角度看过去，尤为如此。

Al-Gharraf River

An ancient canal located in Iraq. Also called Shaal

阿尔-盖拉夫河

伊拉克古运河。亦称夏尔盖拉夫河

Gharraf or Hayy River. The Al-Gharraf River, 230 kilometres long, links the Tigris at Kut al Amara with the Euphrates east of Nasiriyah. In World War I, several fierce military actions were aimed at it during the besiegement of Kut from December 1915 to April 1916. The Al-Gharraf River was close to the battlefields of the Battle of Hanna and the Battle of Dujaila when the forces of the Ottoman Empire and those of the British Empire were in combat. The British were determined to defend Kut because the canal was viewed as a potential means for the Turks or the Anglo-Indian Force to transport troops between the Tigris and the Euphrates.

或海伊河。阿尔—盖拉夫河长230米，连通库特艾尔阿玛拉境内的底格里斯河与纳西尔米耶东部的幼发拉底河。第一次世界大战期间的库特之围（1915年12月—1916年4月）中，阿尔—盖拉夫河曾是多次军事行动激烈争夺的目标之一。在奥斯曼帝国与大英帝国之间发生的系列战争中，汉娜之战与杜佳拉之战均发生于该运河附近。英国军队坚守库特，他们认为该运河可作为在底格里斯河和幼发拉底河之间运输部队的通道。

Ålkistan

A canal located in northern Stockholm, Sweden. The Ålkistan, linking up with Lilla Värtan and Lake Brunnsviken, marks the boundary between the northern areas of Solna and Djurgården. The canal was constructed in 1863 under the order of King Charles XV. During the construction, the silted watercourse was dredged, and thus the water level of Lake Brunnsviken was lowered by 2 metres. Over the canal, there lay a wooden bridge which was 6.5 metres in width and later was replaced by a bridge with a width of 23 metres in 1937. During the dry season, the navigation limit for vessels is 4 metres in width and 1.6 metres in draught.

阿尔希斯坦运河

瑞典斯德哥尔摩北部运河。阿尔希斯坦运河连通瓦尔坦海峡和布鲁内斯维肯湖，并将索尔纳区北部与尤尔格丹北部分隔开来。1863年，国王查尔斯十五世下令开凿阿尔希斯坦运河。修建过程中，原本被淤泥堵塞的河道得以疏通，布鲁内斯维肯湖水位因此下降2米。运河上曾建有一座6.5米宽的木制桥梁，1937年被一座23米宽的新桥取代。旱季时节，阿尔希斯坦运河能够通航宽度小于4米、吃水深度低于1.6米的船只。

Alkmaar-Kolhorn Canal

An inland canal located in the province of North

阿尔克马尔-科尔霍恩运河

荷兰北荷兰省内陆运河。亦称奥

Holland, the Netherlands. Also called Omval-Kolhorn Canal. The Alkmaar-Kolhorn Canal is 24.6 kilometres long and runs from the North Holland Canal near Omval to the Kolhorn River near Kolhorn. There are 2 locks and 19 bridges on it. The canal is an important local waterway for commercial shipping. According to the West Frisian Canal Plan, it was constructed between 1935 and 1938 to connect Alkmmar with Kohorn. It was increased considerably due to the reconstruction in 2015 and the depth is around 1.8 metres. With clear water, fish stocks are good here and it is known for large carps. With beautiful reed borders, there is a lot of recreational sailing in summer.

姆瓦尔—科尔霍恩运河。阿尔克马尔—科尔霍恩运河全长24.6千米,建有2座船闸和19座桥梁,自奥姆瓦尔附近的北荷兰运河流至科尔霍恩镇附近的科尔霍恩河。该运河是当地重要商业航道。根据西弗里斯兰运河计划,阿尔克马尔—科尔霍恩运河于1935—1938年间开凿,旨在连接阿尔克马尔市和科尔霍恩镇。2015年重建后,该运河大幅度加深,深度约1.8米。阿尔克马尔—科尔霍恩运河的河水干净无污染,鱼类资源丰富,尤以大鲤鱼闻名。运河沿岸长有美丽的芦苇,夏季有许多休闲帆船活动。

Allegheny River

阿勒格尼河

A canalized river located in the northeastern United States. The Allegheny River, a major tributary of the Ohio River, has a total length of 523 kilometres. It arises in Pennsylvania, flows northward into New York and southward into Pennsylvania again to join the Monongahela River, which is in the middle of Pittsburgh. The beginning of the Ohio River is where the Allegheny and the Monongahela converge. During the 19th century, the Allegheny River was developed into an essential waterway of navigation, especially for the coal transport in the Ohio Valley. The lower part of the river still serves as a crucial means of commercial transportation today. In 1965, the Kinzua Dam was constructed to control flood in northwestern Pennsylvania, sponsored

美国东北部运河化河流。阿勒格尼河为俄亥俄河主要支流,全长523千米,始于宾夕法尼亚州,向北流经纽约,再向南流回宾夕法尼亚州,与匹兹堡中部的莫农加赫拉河汇合,俄亥俄河正是源于此处。在19世纪,阿勒格尼河是重要的航运通道,主要服务于俄亥俄河谷地区的煤炭运输,至今,阿勒格尼河下游河流仍是重要的商业运输通道。1965年,为控制宾夕法尼亚州西北部洪水,联邦政府拨款修建了金祖亚大坝及阿勒格尼水库。如今,阿勒格尼水库的一部分已成为阿勒格尼国家休闲景区著名景点。

by the federal government. This led to the creation of the Allegheny Reservoir, a part of which belongs to the Allegheny National Recreation Area now.

Aller Canal

A canal located in the states of Saxony-Anhalt and Lower Saxony, Germany. The Aller Canal is 18 kilometres long. The construction of the canal began in 1860 and was completed in 1863. Nearly straight, the canal can carry water from the Aller River more quickly than the river itself, thus protecting agricultural land from flooding by the Aller River.

Aller River

A canalized river located in the states of Saxony-Anhalt and Lower Saxony, Germany. With a total length of 215 kilometres, the Aller River is the largest eastern tributary of the Weser. The last segment of the river, 117 kilometres in length, shapes the Lower Aller federal waterway. In the 1960s, the Aller River was widened, straightened and dammed to control the flood. Several source streams of the Aller River run from the northeast side of the Hohes Holz. The southernmost tributary of the Aller River is the Eggenstedt tributary. The nearest residential regions in the source area are Helmstedt and Magdeburg, which are 20 kilometres northwest and 25 kilometres east respectively. The 30-kilometre-long segment from the Oker to Celle is called the Middle Aller River. In this section, the water is so strong that barrages are built to control

阿勒尔运河

德国萨克森—安哈尔特州和下萨克森州运河。阿勒尔运河于1860年开凿，1863年完工。该运河全长18千米，几乎是笔直的，其水流速度比阿勒尔河自身流速快很多，从而保护农业用地不被来自阿勒尔河的洪水淹没。

阿勒尔河

德国萨克森—安哈尔特州和下萨克森州运河化河流。阿勒尔河是威悉河东部最大支流，全长215千米，其最后长达117千米的河段构成下阿勒尔联邦航道。20世纪60年代，为抵御洪水，人们对阿勒尔河进行拓宽和取直，并建筑堤坝使其得以加固。阿勒尔河源头的几条溪流均从霍赫斯霍尔茨海峡的东北方向流出，最南端是埃根斯泰特支流。距离河源最近的居民区是黑尔姆施泰特和马格德堡，分别位于河源西北20千米处和其东25千米处。从奥克河到策勒的河段被称作中阿勒尔河，全长30千米。中阿勒尔河水流强劲，人们修建拦河坝以抗洪，同时也可

it and the waterpower is available when weirs are used. The segment referred to as the Lower Aller River starts from Celle. Running for 120 kilometres to the Weser, this navigable section is designated as a federal waterway. After passing through the hills of Saxony-Anhalt, the Aller River meanders at the Wolfsburg area towards the Aller glacial valley, an ice age drainage channel. This valley was formed in the period of penultimate ice age nearly 200,000 years ago, transferring melt water into the North Sea from the ice sheet. The current course of the Aller River does not conform to what it was centuries ago, as the quantities and materials of water being transferred have made a difference in changing the size and location of the streams. Erosion, climate change and other factors also have an impact on it. Nowadays, the section of the Aller valley from Celle to Verden is primarily used as grassland. The depression region of the Aller River provides a suitable environment for animals and plants there. The landscape is featured with potholes, copses and clumps of bushes.

进行水力发电。下阿勒尔河始于策勒，一直延伸到威悉河，全长120千米，被用作联邦航道，可通航至温森。阿勒尔河穿过萨克森－安哈尔特山丘，蜿蜒流过沃尔夫斯堡地区，直至阿勒尔冰川山谷。阿勒尔冰川山谷形成于近20万年前倒数第二个冰川时代，融化后的雪水经阿勒尔冰川山谷流至北海。几个世纪以来，阿勒尔河的水量和水质发生了很大改变，河流的大小、位置也都随之改变，目前，阿勒尔河的河道流向与数个世纪之前也不尽相同。这其中还有自然侵蚀、气候变化以及其他影响因素。如今，从策勒到费尔登的阿勒尔河谷地区已成为一片草地。阿勒尔洼地树林繁茂，灌木丛生，为当地动植物提供了良好的生存环境。

Almelo-De Haandrik Canal

阿尔默洛－德·汉德里克运河

A canal located in Overijssel Province, the Netherlands. The Almelo-De Haandrik Canal is 34 kilometres long and serves as a side branch of the Overijssel Canal. It was excavated in the middle of the 19th century with the aim of supplying water for the Overijssel Canal. By 1855, it had been built from Vroomshoop to Almelo and by 1856 the excavation from Vroomshoop to De Haandrik was

荷兰上艾瑟尔省运河。阿尔默洛－德·汉德里克运河为上艾瑟尔运河支流，全长34千米。该运河于19世纪中期开凿，为上艾瑟尔运河供水。1855年弗罗姆斯霍普至阿尔默洛的河段竣工，1856年弗罗姆斯霍普至德·汉德里克河段完工。运河通航后，泥煤运输船只可经由这

completed. The Almelo-De Haandrik Canal is of vital importance for the development of its adjacent areas, especially after peat began to be shipped to elsewhere of the country through this channel. The side branch from the Twente Canal to Almelo, which was extended and deepened for several times after its opening in 1938, provided even more convenience for the transport on the Almelo-De Haandrik Canal. Being connected to the Twente Canal, the Almelo-De Haandrik Canal becomes a rather busy route compared with other canals of the Overijssel Canal System that have been non-navigable since the 1960s. There are two locks on the canal and nowadays it is accessible for boats up to 700 tons.

条航道至荷兰其他地区, 对运河周边城市的发展发挥了重要作用。1938年, 特文特运河至阿尔默洛的旁侧河段通航, 后又经历多次延长和加深, 使阿尔默洛—德·汉德里克运河的交通运输更为便利。连通特文特运河后, 该运河的航运愈加繁忙。与此同时, 上艾瑟尔省运河网中的其他一些运河自20世纪60年代起就已停用。阿尔默洛—德·汉德里克运河上共有2座船闸, 目前, 可供最大载重量700吨的船只通行。

Altair Canal

阿尔泰运河

A canal located in Los Angeles, California, the United States. The Altair Canal is a part of the series of the Venice Canals. In the early 1900s, the Venice Canals were excavated under the direction of Abbot Kinney, a tobacco millionaire and real estate developer, who funded to build a "Venice of America" in South California. By the late 1920s, due to the rise of Los Angeles car culture, many of the Venice Canals were filled in and paved to create roads for driving. The Altair Canal was one of them.

美国加利福尼亚州洛杉矶市运河。阿尔泰运河是威尼斯运河网的一条运河。20世纪初, 为打造美国加州版威尼斯, 烟草富豪和房地产开发商阿博特·金尼出资修建了南加州威尼斯运河网。20世纪20年代末, 由于洛杉矶汽车文化盛行, 为了修建可供汽车行驶的公路, 威尼斯运河网中的多条运河被回填。阿尔泰运河为其中之一。

Amstel-Drecht Canal

阿姆斯特尔-德雷赫特运河

A canal located in the province of North Holland, the Netherlands. The Amstel-Drecht Canal is the

荷兰北荷兰省运河。阿姆斯特尔—德雷赫特运河连通德雷赫特河、

waterway that connects the river Drecht and the Aar Canal with the Amstel. With a total length of 25.6 kilometres, the waterway partly forms the boundary between the Dutch provinces of North Holland, South Holland and Utrecht. On the west side, the Drecht connects the Braassem Lake and the Ring Canal of the Haarlemm Lake via the Oude Wetering. On the south side, the Aar Canal connects with the Old Rhine at Alphen-on-Rhine. The construction of the Amstel-Drecht Canal began around 1825, when King William I hoped that large ships could be able to travel between the provinces of North Holland and South Holland. The western section of the canal, starting at the Aar Canal and flowing into the Kromme Mijdrecht near Uithoorn, was once a part of the Drecht River. The Amstel originally started at the confluence of the Drecht and the Kromme Mijdrecht, just southwest of Uithoorn. Due to the construction of the Amstel-Drecht Canal, the section between Uithoorn and Ouderkerk-on-the-Amstel became a part of this canal. The northeastern section of the canal starts at the Kromme Mijdrecht along Uithoorn, and flows to Ouderkerk of Amstel. Between Uithoorn and Ouderkerk, the Waver River joins the Amstel-Drecht Canal from the east, a stretch of approximately 10.5 kilometres that was once a part of the Amstel River. The Amstel-Drecht Canal is managed by the Amstel, Gooi, and Vecht Water Board.

阿尔运河和阿姆斯特尔河，全长25.6千米，部分河段成为北荷兰省、南荷兰省和乌特勒支省的边界。在西边，德雷赫特河与布拉斯梅湖和哈莱默湖的环形运河经旧韦特灵河相连通。在南边，阿尔运河连通莱茵河畔阿尔芬的旧莱茵河。阿姆斯特尔—德雷赫特运河大约修建于1825年，当时国王威廉一世希望大型船只能够通行于北荷兰省与南荷兰省之间，故提议开凿这条运河。阿姆斯特尔—德雷赫特运河西部的河段原属于德雷赫特河的一部分，始于阿尔运河，流向奥特霍伦镇附近的克罗梅迈德雷赫特河。阿姆斯特尔河最早始于奥特霍伦镇西南部，处在德雷赫特河与克罗默迈德雷赫特河的交汇处。自阿姆斯特尔—德雷赫特运河修建之后，奥特霍伦镇与阿姆斯特尔河畔奥德科克安德之间的河段就一并归属该运河。阿姆斯特尔—德雷赫特运河东北端起于克罗默迈德雷赫特河，途经奥特霍伦镇，流向奥德科克安德阿姆斯特尔镇。瓦弗河在奥特霍伦镇到奥德科克镇之间流动，自东汇入阿姆斯特尔—德雷赫特运河，这一河段约长10.5千米，曾是阿姆斯特尔河的一部分。阿姆斯特尔—德雷赫特运河由阿姆斯特尔、霍伊和费赫特水务局共同管理。

Amsterdam Canals

A series of canals located in Amsterdam, the Netherlands. The system of Amsterdam Canals is over 100 kilometres long, comprised of 3 main canals, namely, Heren Canal, Prinse Canal and Kaiser Canal, which were excavated in the 17th century during the Dutch Golden Age. The canals form concentric belts around the city, known as the Canal Ring. The construction work went from west to east. The excavation of the northwestern sector was started in 1613 and completed around 1625. The southern sector was built after 1664 and the construction work went slowly because of the economic depression. The eastern part covered the area between the Amstel River and the IJ Bay. This 17th-century canal ring was inscribed on the UNESCO World Heritage List in 2010, which earns Amsterdam the fame as the Venice of the North. The canal system of Amsterdam is regarded officially as a symbol of the prosperous economy and culture of Amsterdam during the Dutch Golden Age, which is unique among all the canals around the world. Now the canals in Amsterdam are used as the main medium of transportation around the city.

Amsterdam-Rhine Canal

A canal located in the Netherlands. The Amsterdam–Rhine Canal was built to connect the capital city of Amsterdam to the main shipping artery of the Rhine. With a total length of approximately 72 kilometres, a width of 100 to 120 metres, and a

阿姆斯特丹运河网

荷兰阿姆斯特丹运河网。阿姆斯特丹运河网全长100多千米，由3条主要运河构成，即绅士运河、王子运河和皇帝运河。这些运河修建于17世纪荷兰"黄金时代"，运河围绕城市形成了同心形运河带，即阿姆斯特丹运河环带。该运河带的修建由西向东推进，西北段1613年开始修建，1625年前后建成；南段修建于1664年之后，但由于经济萧条，进展缓慢；东段覆盖阿姆斯特尔河和艾湾之间的区域。建于17世纪的阿姆斯特丹运河带2010年被联合国教科文组织列入世界遗产名录，为阿姆斯特丹市赢得了"北方威尼斯"的美誉。阿姆斯特丹运河网是荷兰黄金时代经济繁荣和文化发展的重要体现，在全世界范围内独一无二。如今，该运河带已经成为阿姆斯特丹市环城交通的主要方式。

阿姆斯特丹-莱茵运河

荷兰运河。阿姆斯特丹—莱茵运河连接荷兰首都阿姆斯特丹和航运主干线莱茵河，大体为东南流向，途经乌特勒支市，在迪尔斯泰德的韦克与莱茵河支流莱克河交汇，汇

depth of 5.5 to 9 metres, the canal follows a generally southeasterly direction as it goes through the city of Utrecht towards Wijk at Duurstede, where it intersects the Lek branch of the Rhine and then continues to the river Waal. On the canal, there are 37 bridges, 2 tunnels, 1 crossing point and 4 locks. The canal was excavated between 1931 and 1952. Back then, the Merwede Canal built in 1892 failed to meet the increasing shipping requirements, and the government resolved to build the Amsterdam-Rhine Canal in 1931 and made it the connection between Amsterdam and the Rhine. However, the economic crisis and World War II slowed down the construction. The section between Utrecht and the Lek Canal was put into use on 5 August 1938. It was not until 21 May 1952 that the entire canal was opened. The canal was then widened from 1965 to 1981. The Amsterdam-Rhine Canal is one of the busiest canals in the world and an important waterway between Amsterdam port and Ruhr region in Germany. Around 100,000 inland barges navigate the Amsterdam–Rhine Canal each year.

入瓦尔河。该运河全长约72千米，宽100—120米，水深5.5—9米，运河上共建有37座桥梁、2个隧道、1个渡口和4座船闸。荷兰政府于1931—1952年间开凿阿姆斯特丹—莱茵运河。当时，建于1892年的梅尔韦德运河已经不能满足日益增长的航运需求，1931年，荷兰政府通过开凿阿姆斯特丹—莱茵运河的决议，希望以此来提升阿姆斯特丹市和莱茵河之间的航运能力。后因经济危机和第二次世界大战影响，阿姆斯特丹—莱茵运河水利工程久被搁置。1938年8月5日，乌特勒支省至莱克运河段通航。1952年5月21日，阿姆斯特丹—莱茵运河全段开通。1965—1981年期间，该运河进一步拓宽。阿姆斯特丹—莱茵运河是世界上航运业务最繁忙的一条运河，也是阿姆斯特丹港与德国鲁尔河地区的重要通道。每年大约有10万艘内河驳船在此航行。

Ancient Guijiang-Liujiang Canal

古桂柳运河

An inland canal located in southern China. The Ancient Guijiang-Liujiang Canal is about 15 kilometres in length, linking the Lijiang River with the Liujiang River. The canal starts from Huixian Town of Lingui District and it is divided into two tributaries, the East Tributary and the West Tributary. The East Tributary links the Liang-

中国南部内陆运河。古桂柳运河全长约15千米，始于临桂区会仙镇，连通漓江和柳江，由东西两条支流组成。东支流与良丰河在桂林市郊雁山镇社门岭处汇合，注入漓江；西支流向西流经四塘镇达苏桥，与洛清江汇合后注入柳江。古

feng River at Shemenling of Yanshan County, Guilin City, and flows into the Lijiang River; the West Tributary passes through the Dasu Bridge in Sitang Town, merges into the Luoqing River, and finally empties into the Liujiang River. The canal was excavated in 692 AD, the third year under Empress Wu Zetian's reign. In the Qing Dynasty (1616—1911), the government carried out three major renovations, removing 386 rocks that hindered the navigation and constructing several auxiliary facilities. The canal then became navigable all year round. In modern times, several parts of the waterway between Guilin and Liuzhou were blocked because of sedimentation and inordinate fish farming. Today, the canal has undergone an overhaul and become a famous tourist spot.

桂柳运河开凿于武则天长寿元年（公元692年）。清代官府曾三次对其大规模修缮与疏浚，凿去碍航之石386处，增建附属设施，此后，该运河四季可通航。到了近代，因泥沙沉积和滥围鱼窖而致河道淤塞，桂林至柳州段航道多处被阻断航。如今，古桂柳运河情况已得到大幅度改善，成为著名景点。

Apeldoorn Canal

阿珀尔多伦运河

A canal located in Gelderland, the Netherlands. The Apeldoorn Canal is a branch of the Ijssel River which is a distributary of the river Rhine. It starts at Hattem and drains into the Ijssel River in Dieren with a total length of 52 kilometres. The construction of the whole canal spanned over 40 years, with the northern part between Hattem and Apeldoorn built from 1825 to 1829 and the southern part between Apeldoorn and Dieren built from 1858 to 1869. For the purpose of developing trade and industry in Apeldoorn, the canal was excavated to make up for the disadvantageous lack of river connection. After the boom in rail and road transport, the importance of the canal rapidly declined. The

荷兰海尔德兰省运河。阿珀尔多伦运河为艾瑟尔河支流，而艾瑟尔河又是莱茵河支流。阿珀尔多伦运河始于哈特姆市，在迪耶伦市汇入艾瑟尔河，全长52千米。该运河的修建历时40多年，运河北段，即哈特姆市和阿珀尔多伦市之间的部分建于1825—1829年间；运河南段，即阿珀尔多伦市和迪伦市之间的部分建于1858—1869年间。开凿阿珀尔多伦运河的目的是促进阿珀尔多伦地区的贸易和工业发展，弥补缺少水运的劣势。随着铁路和公路运输的快速发展，阿珀

northern part was closed in 1962, and the southern part in 1972. Nowadays, the canal is no longer navigable. Bridges and locks are all closed. Currently, it is a place for sightseeing.

尔多伦运河的重要性迅速衰退。1962年，该运河北段关闭，1972年南段关闭。如今，由于河上桥梁关闭，船闸无法操作，阿珀尔多伦运河已不再通航，成为一处旅游观光景点。

Appomattox Canal

A canal located in Virginia, the United States. The Appomattox Canal, excavated in 1816 with a length of 8.9 kilometres, was reconstructed in 1830 by John Couty with a total of 17 locks. It was converted into the bed of the Seaboard Airline Railroad in 1908. Moreover, the Appomattox River is the main waterway of the Upper Appomattox as well as a tributary of the James River. Though the canal system was no longer in use since 1890, people today can see the remains of the navigable aqueduct and other stone work on the Appomattox River and Heritage Trail in Petersburg, Virginia.

阿波马托克斯运河

美国弗吉尼亚州运河。阿波马托克斯运河全长约8.9千米。该运河于1816年开凿，1830年由约翰·库蒂重建，共建有17座船闸。1908年，这条运河被改建为海滨航空铁路的路基。此外，阿波马托克斯运河是阿波马托克斯河上游河道的主要航道，同时也是詹姆斯河的一条支流。虽然阿波马托克斯河运河网从1890年起停用，但今天人们仍然可以在弗吉尼亚州彼得斯堡市的阿波马托克斯河和文化古迹上看到可通航的渡槽和其他石建工程的痕迹。

Appomattox River Navigation⁼

A canalized river located in Virginia, the United States. The Appomattox River Navigation was named after Appomattocs Indian, a tribe inhabiting along its lower reaches in the 17th century. It has a total length of 253 kilometres and a basin area of about 3,480 square kilometres. It was modified for transportation around 1745 and was used for

阿波马托克斯河航道

美国弗吉尼亚州运河化河流。阿波马托克斯河航道因17世纪在该河下游沿岸居住的阿波马托克斯印第安部落而得名。航道全长253千米，流域面积约3 480平方千米。阿波马托克斯河航道于1745年前后改建，此后用作货运航道达100

transportation and shipping goods for over 100 years. The protection of the Appomattox River Navigation was inscribed in law by the Virginia State Assembly. The river is divided into the Lower Appomattox and the Upper Appomattox. The Lower Appomattox flows in an easterly direction across the Piedmont and Coastal Plain of south-central Virginia from the Brasfield Dam at Lake Chesdin to its confluence with the James River in Hopewell. The Upper Appomattox has a navigable length of about 200 kilometres, equipped with locks. Its construction began in 1795 and was first completed in 1807. There are four bypass canals around mill dams, each with locks to adjust for topographic relief. The Lower Appomattox is now a scenic river in Virginia.

多年。当时，弗吉尼亚州议会曾通过立法来保护阿波马托克斯河航道。阿波马托克斯河航道分为上游河道和下游河道，下游河道从切斯丁湖的布拉斯菲尔德大坝起向东，与霍普韦尔的詹姆斯河交汇，流经弗吉尼亚州中南部的皮埃蒙特和海岸平原。上游河道则为通航河道，长约200千米，设有船闸。该航道1795—1807年间修建，在工坊水坝周围有4条绕行运河，每一条运河上均建有适应地起势起伏变化的船闸。如今，阿波马托克斯河航道的下游河道已成为弗吉尼亚州一条观光河。

Arabian Canal

阿拉伯运河

An inland canal under construction located in Saudi Arabia. The Arabian Canal is designed to be 75 kilometres in length, 150 metres wide and 6 metres deep, which is navigable for yachts up to 40 metres long. As planned, it will start from Dubai Waterfront in Jebel Ali to the east of the Dubai World Central Development and then flow back to the Palm Jumeirah. To date, only Phase 1 of the Arabian Canal has started, that is, the construction at the Dubai Marina, while the rest of the plan has not been implemented. According to the original plan, the construction of the canal would be completed in 2012, but it was stopped in 2009. If completed, it would require the excavation of 1.1 billion cubic me-

沙特阿拉伯在建运河。阿拉伯运河设计长度为75千米，宽度为150米，深度为6米，可容纳40米长游艇通行。阿拉伯运河始于阿里山港口的迪拜滨水区，流向迪拜世界中心开发区东部，再回流至朱美拉棕榈岛。迄今为止，仅运河第一阶段挖掘工作启动，即迪拜码头附近的工程，其余大部分修建项目尚未动工。按照最初计划，该运河将于2012年竣工，但从2009年起，运河修建工程被搁置。预计整个运河项目完成之时，将要挖出11亿立方米泥沙。阿拉伯运河修

tres of soil. The canal itself was projected to cost 11 billion dollars. It also called for 50 billion dollars to be spent on constructing a new "city" within the city, which would take 20,000 hectares of land in the south bank of the channel. The canal was designed to be fully navigable, with locks on each end for tidal control.

建预计要花费110亿美元。同时，迪拜将依托运河南岸2万公顷滨水区修建"城中城"，预计投资500亿美元。阿拉伯运河是为实现全程通航而修建，运河两端建有水闸以调控潮汐。

Ara Canal

A canal located in South Korea. The Ara Canal runs from the port city Incheon to the capital Seoul, linking the Han River to the Yellow Sea. The main canal covers a total length of 18 kilometres with a width of 80 metres and a depth of 6.3 metres. The construction of the canal commenced in 2009 and was completed in 2012. The canal is built to offer flood control and leisure activities. In history, Choe I (1166—1249), son of Choe Chung-heon, once attempted to excavate a canal in the Goryeo period (918—1392). But the attempt failed due to technical obstacles. Later, one of the Chosun kings also tried but failed again. In the summer of 1987, there was a flood in the Incheon area, resulting in 6,000 victims. To solve this problem, the Gulpocheon waterproofing work was initiated, along with a five-year survey conducted by the government. In 1995, the Ara Canal Project was planned and controversy ensued over the next two decades. Discord lingered on even during the Ara Canal Project period. Nowadays, there are ports and bridges on the main canal, and people can enjoy the promenade along the canal.

京仁运河

韩国运河。京仁运河自港口城市仁川流向首都首尔，并连通汉江与黄海，其主体部分长18千米，宽80米，水深6.3米。该运河于2009年开凿，2012年竣工，兼具防洪和休闲两大功能。高丽王朝时期（918—1392），崔忠献之子崔瑀曾试图修建运河，终因技术困难未果。此后，朝鲜王朝君主再次尝试修建运河，也以失败告终。1987年夏季，仁川地区发生洪灾，6 000余人受灾。为解决这一问题，韩国政府开始修建浦川防洪工程，同时进行为期5年的调查研究。1995年，韩国政府开始筹划京仁运河项目，但随之而来的又是长达20年的争议。争议在京仁运河修造期间也未中止。目前，京仁运河的主河段上建有港口、桥梁，人们可以在河岸景观道上漫步观光。

Arbury Canals

A system of private canals located in the Arbury Estate, Warwickshire, England, the United Kingdom. The Arbury Canals start from the Seeswood Pool and link up with the Coventry Canal. The entire system is approximately 10 kilometres long and has 13 locks. Constructed by Sir Roger Newdigate between 1764 and 1795, the Arbury Canals consisted of 7 sections, respectively named as the Griff Hollows Canal, the Seeswood Canal, the Communication Canal, the Arbury Lower Canal or Griff Canal, the Coventry Wood Canal, the Arbury High Level Canal, and the Coton Lawn Canal. The Griff Hollows Canal was disconnected from the other 6 canals. Sir Richard Newdigate constructed 3 small canals to transport coal from the outlying pits between 1700 and 1711. Later, Sir Roger Newdigate, his son, decided to combine them into a larger system. The construction was started on his estate in 1764, and an 8.9-kilometre-long waterway had been completed by 1795. The estate system continued to run until 1812, but then it gradually became less used, and by 1819 the upper reaches were no longer in operation. From that year, only the Communication Canal linking directly with the Coventry Canal remained navigable. Today a few traces of the canal can be spotted within the Arbury Estate.

Arbury High Level Canal

A private canal located in the Arbury Estate,

阿伯里运河网

英国英格兰沃里克郡阿伯里庄园私有运河网。阿伯里运河网从西斯伍德水塘连接到考文垂运河,全长约10千米,共建有13座船闸。罗杰·纽迪盖特爵士于1764—1795年间修建了阿伯里运河网。该运河网一共分为7段,每段单独命名,包括格里夫霍洛斯运河、西斯伍德运河、交通运河、阿伯里下运河(又称格里夫运河)、考文垂伍德运河、阿伯里上运河以及科顿劳恩运河,其中格里夫霍洛斯运河未与其他6段运河相连。1700—1711年间理查德·纽迪盖特爵士修建了3条小型运河用来输送偏远地区的煤炭。此后,其子罗杰·纽迪盖特爵士决定把这些小型运河合并成一个更大的运河网,并于1764年开始在其庄园开展运河网修建工作。到1795年,庄园内修建了约8.9千米航道。直至1812年,该运河网一直都在使用,但此后逐渐停用。到1819年时,阿伯里运河上游河段已无法通航,仅有与考文垂运河直接相连的交通运河仍可通航。如今,在阿伯里庄园,仍可见运河网的少许遗迹。

阿伯里上运河

英国英格兰沃里克郡阿伯里庄

Warwickshire, England, the United Kingdom. The Arbury High Level Canal, one section of the Arbury Canals, is 2, 291 metres in length. Since it was opened for navigation in 1764, it was the earliest among the seven sections of the Arbury Canals. Besides, a survey was conducted during that year to establish how it could be incorporated into a larger system. In 1773, the canal was linked to Garden Pool by a lock. In 1775, the construction of a staircase of two locks and a single lock allowed boats to reach Hall Pool.

园私有运河。阿伯里上运河全长2 291米，为阿伯里运河网7段中最早开凿的运河。1764年，阿伯里上运河通航，同年，人们对阿伯里上运河进行调研，以确定将其纳入修建更大运河网的方案。1773年，阿伯里上运河通过1座船闸与花园池相连接。1775年，该运河上修建了2座梯级船闸和1座单厢船闸，使船只得以通航至会堂池。

Arbury Lower Canal

阿伯里下运河

A private canal located in the Arbury Estate, Warwickshire, England, the United Kingdom. Also called Griff Canal. The Arbury Lower Canal, about 1.5 kilometres long, was one section of the Arbury Canals. The canal was connected with the Communication Canal at the beginning. A great part of the Canal was in use by 1771. In 1793, a new branch canal was built to link the canal to the road from Arbury to the main turnpike road. At the end of the branch canal, there was a wharf on which a tramway linked it to coal pits.

英国英格兰沃里克郡阿伯里庄园私有运河。又称格里夫运河。阿伯里下运河全长约1.5千米，是阿伯里运河网的一段，其起点处与交通运河相连。1771年之前，阿伯里下运河大部分河段可通航。1793年，新建的一条支渠将阿伯里下运河和一条连接阿伯里地区和主要收费公路的小路连接在一起。该支渠的终点处建有码头，码头上有通向煤矿的有轨车道。

Ardennes Canal

阿登运河

A summit-level canal located in northern France. The Ardennes Canal was built between the river valleys of the Aisne and the Meuse. The canal begins at the village of Pont-à-Bar in the Dom-le-Mesnil commune and ends at the commune of Old

法国北部越岭运河。阿登运河修建于埃纳河和默兹河河谷之间。该运河始于东勒梅尼勒镇的旁达巴村，终于老阿斯费尔德镇，连通默兹河和埃纳旁侧运河。阿登

Asfeld, linking the Meuse Canal and the Aisne Lateral Canal. It has a length of 87.8 kilometres with 44 locks, including 37 on the Aisne side and 7 on the Meuse side, and a tunnel to Saint Aignan. The canal is characterized with two distinct parts and two series of locks. The first part is 39 kilometres long, which connects Pont-à-Bar to Semuy and stretches from the Meuse to the Aisne River at the junction to the Vouziers Branch. The second part begins at Vouziers and continues to reach Semuy, running parallel to the Aisne. The initial canal proposals in the region dated from 1684, but did not proceed for the following one hundred years until the subsequent Interior Minister Jean-Antoine Chaptal consented to carry out the construction. The Ardennes Canal was open between 1827 and 1835 and was modernized between 1842 and 1846 when a reservoir and the artificial Lake Bairon came into existence. In 2018, the collapse of the Lock 21 led to the closure of the canal. The lock was repaired in 2020 and reopened in 2021.

运河全长87.8千米，共建有44座船闸，其中37座位于埃纳河河段，7座位于默兹河河段，运河下建有一条隧道，通往圣艾尼昂镇。该运河分为两个独立部分，建有两套船闸体系。第一部分长39千米，连接旁达巴村和瑟米村，从默兹河一直延伸到与武济耶支流交汇处的埃纳河。第二部分从武济耶镇流至瑟米村，与埃纳河平行。该地区早期的运河修建计划可追溯至1684年，但在此后的100多年间没有进展。法国内政部长让—安托万·沙普塔尔上任后，运河修建工作才得以推进。1827—1835年间，阿登运河通航。1842—1846年间，人们对其进行了现代化改造，修建了水库和拜隆人工湖。2018年，因第21号船闸坍塌，阿登运河被关闭。2020年，船闸重修，2021阿登运河恢复通航。

Aremberger Canal

A canal located in Overijssel Province, the Netherlands. The Aremberger Canal has a total length of about 6 kilometres, connecting the Zwarte Water at Zwartsluis with the Beulaker and Belterwijde. It was constructed around 1560 and was primarily used for the drainage of the hinterland of Zwartsluis. The canal also played an important role in peat extraction. As no movable bridges were built on the canal, only relatively small ships with lowered masts

阿伦贝赫尔运河

荷兰上艾瑟尔省运河。阿伦贝赫尔运河全长约6千米，在兹瓦特斯勒伊斯市境内连通兹瓦特河与贝尔特瓦德湖。运河1560年前后开凿，主要用于兹瓦特斯勒伊斯市腹地的排水，对于泥炭开采也十分重要。运河上未建可移动式桥梁，只可通行体积相对较小且桅杆较低的船只。阿伦贝赫尔运河曾建有2

could navigate on the Aremberger Canal. The canal had two locks, the Aremberger Lock in Zwartsluis and a lock to the north at the Veneweg which no longer exists.

座船闸, 一座是位于兹瓦特斯勒伊斯市的阿伦贝赫尔船闸, 另一座船闸位于运河北部威尼韦赫, 现已不复存在。

Arkansas River Navigation System

阿肯色河航运网

A navigation system located in the middle-south of the United States. Fully called McClellan-Kerr Arkansas River Navigation System (MKARNS). The Arkansas River Navigation System starts from the Catoosa Port in Tulsa, Oklahoma, and extends southeastwards to the Mississippi River. It is 767 kilometres in length, 75 metres in width and 2.7 metres in depth, with 17 locks and dams. The construction of the navigation system began in 1964 with the authorization of the American national congress and was completed in 1971. It helps with not only the control of the recurrent flooding of the Arkansas River, but also the provision of a navigable waterway. This navigation system is used for the transportation of agricultural products, timber, oil, coal and other materials in this area all the year round. Meanwhile, it also brings many benefits to the lower reaches of the Arkansas River, including water supply, hydropower generation, leisure and entertainment. A large number of jobs have actually been created for the local people, which promote greatly the development of the local economy.

美国中南部航运网。全称麦克莱伦—克尔阿肯色河航运网。阿肯色河航运网始于俄克拉荷马州塔尔萨的卡托萨港, 向东南方向延伸至密西西比河, 全长767千米, 宽75米, 深2.7米, 建有17座船闸和水坝。1964年, 经美国国会批准, 阿肯色河航运网工程开建, 1971年竣工。建成后的阿肯色河航运网不仅有效解决了阿肯色河定期泛滥的问题, 而且还提供了可供航运的水道, 常年用于该地区农产品、木材、石油和煤炭等物资的运输。与此同时, 该航运网还为阿肯色河下游地区带来包括水资源供应、水力发电以及休闲娱乐等诸多益处, 为当地民众创造大批就业岗位, 极大地推动了当地经济的发展。

Arles-Bouc Canal

阿尔勒-布可运河

A canal located in southern France. See Arles-Fos Canal.

法国南部运河。见阿尔勒—福斯运河。

Arles-Fos Canal

A canal located in southern France. Also called Arles-Bouc Canal. The Arles-Fos Canal has a total length of 31 kilometres, connecting the Rhône near Arles and Fos-sur-Mer. There is a lock constructed on it. The construction of this canal began in 1804, and it was put into use in 1834. It is now divided into two parts by the Fos. The 30-kilometre-long upstream section is practically rectilinear and un-crowded except for the first two kilometres near the port of Arles. The downstream part is frequented by big barges. A new canal, called the Rhône-Fos Canal, connects the downstream part to the great Rhône at Barcarin. There are drawbridges across the canal, one of which is the Langlois Bridge, the one painted by Vincent van Gogh in 1888. Today, the Arles-Fos Canal is almost unnavigable due to insufficient basic maintenance although there is no official injunction. It serves as a dockyard to provide ship-related services.

阿尔勒－福斯运河

法国南部运河。亦称阿尔勒－布可运河。阿尔勒－福斯运河连接靠近阿尔勒市附近的罗讷河和滨海福斯市，全长31千米，建有1座船闸。运河于1804年开始修建，1834年投入使用。阿尔勒－福斯运河今以福斯镇为界一分为二。上游河段长30千米，除了与阿尔勒港口相通的前两千米航道，其他部分几乎笔直，来往船只不多。下游河段部分常有大型驳船通过。新建的罗讷－福斯运河将阿尔勒－福斯运河的下游河段与巴卡罕境内的罗讷河连接起来。阿尔勒－福斯运河上架设多座吊桥，其中包括梵·高1888年所绘的朗格卢瓦桥。如今，尽管没有正式的禁行令，但由于缺乏基本维护，阿尔勒－福斯运河已几乎无法通航，仅作为船坞提供与船舶有关的服务。

Army Canal

A canal located in Iraq. The Army Canal links the Tigris and Diyala rivers. It is 25 kilometres in length, running southwards from Adhamiyah at northeastern Baghdad to Rustimiyah at southeastern Baghdad. The canal was constructed in 1959. It functions as the western boundary of the Sadr City, and a highway runs parallel to its course. It became stagnant water due to the rising sludge, low water

军队运河

伊拉克运河。军队运河连通底格里斯河与迪亚拉河，全长25千米，从伊拉克首都巴格达东北部的阿德哈米亚向南流至巴格达东南部的拉斯蒂米亚。运河1959年开凿，为萨德尔城的西部边界，有一条高速公路与河道平行。由于淤泥沉积、水位过低以及维护不力等问

levels and inadequate maintenance.

题，军队运河已成为死水。

Arnot Canal

阿诺特运河

An abandoned canal located in New York and Pennsylvania, the United States. See Junction Canal.

美国纽约州和宾夕法尼亚州废弃运河。见交界运河。

Asagny Canal

阿萨格尼运河

A canal located in Abidjan, Côte d'Ivoire. The Asagny Canal, 18 kilometres in length, was excavated in 1923. Located at the western end of the Ebrié Lagoon, it is still navigable. It runs across the Azagny National Park, connecting the Bandama River and the Grand Lahou lagoon, and finally reaches the Atlantic Ocean.

科特迪瓦阿比让市运河。阿萨格尼运河全长18千米，于1923年开凿。运河位于埃布里耶潟湖西端，现仍可通航。阿萨格尼运河穿过阿萨格尼国家公园，连接邦达马河和大拉乌潟湖，最终注入大西洋。

Ashby Canal

阿什比运河

A canal located in the United Kingdom. The Ashby Canal links the mining district around Moira, which is just outside the town of Ashby de la Zouch, with the Coventry Canal at Bedworth in Warwickshire. The Ashby Canal is 50 kilometres long, which was constructed in 1794 and opened in 1804. A number of tramways were built at its northern end to transport collieries. The canal was taken over by the Midland Railway Company in 1846. It remained profitable until the 1890s but then declined steadily. Around 14 kilometres of the canal passed the Leicestershire coalfield and suffered from subsidence, which resulted in a progressive closure of this section from Moira, southwards to

英国运河。阿什比运河连接阿什比·德·拉·祖什镇外莫伊拉周边的采矿区以及沃里克郡贝德沃思的考文垂运河，全长50千米。运河于1794年开凿，1804年通航，其北端建有多条运输煤矿石的有轨电车轨道。1846年，米德兰铁路公司接管阿什比运河，19世纪90年代前一直保持盈利，此后效益持续下滑。约有14千米的运河河段穿过莱斯特郡煤田，地面下陷严重。自莫伊拉向南到斯纳尔斯通的运河河段于1944年、1957年和1966年先后停运，仅剩35千米长的运河河段可

Snarestone, in 1944, 1957, and 1966, leaving only 35 kilometres navigable. The abandoned section was restored later. An isolated section near Moira Furnace and the visitor centre of National Forest was opened between 1999 and 2005. The stretch between Carlton Bridge, north of Market Bosworth, and Turnover Bridge, north of Snarestone was recognized as a biological area with a special scientific research value in Leicestershire in 1989, covering an area of 154,000 square metres. There are many aquatic plants and invertebrates, among which submerged plants are of particular interest.

通航。后来，废弃的运河河段又得到修复。邻近莫拉伊熔炉和国家森林公园游客中心的一段相对独立的运河河段于1999—2005年间开通。1989年，在马基特博斯沃思北部卡尔顿桥和斯纳尔斯顿北部特恩欧沃桥之间的水域被认定为莱斯特郡具有特殊科学研究价值的生物区，面积为154 000平方米。该区域有多种水生植物和无脊椎动物，其中沉水植物尤其引人关注。

Assinie Canal

A canal located in Côte d'Ivoire. Named after the ancient river of Assinie, the Assinie Canal was excavated in 1931 with a total length of 48 kilometres. It allows navigation from the lagoon of Aby to the Atlantic Ocean.

阿西尼运河

科特迪瓦运河。阿西尼运河因古阿西尼河而得名，1931年开凿，全长48千米，是船只从艾比潟湖驶往大西洋的航道。

Atlantic Intracoastal Waterway

An intracoastal waterway located in the United States. The Atlantic Intracoastal Waterway (AIWW) extends from Norfolk, Virginia to Key West, Florida, running along the east coast of the United States. The AIWW, about 1,770 kilometres in length, is comprised of natural inlets, saltwater rivers, bays, sounds and artificial canals. It joins the Gulf Intracoastal Waterway. They combine to form the 4,800-kilometre-long Intracoastal Waterway which flows through most of the Eastern Seaboard.

大西洋沿海航道

美国沿海航道。大西洋沿海航道从弗吉尼亚州的诺福克延伸至佛罗里达州的基韦斯特市，全长约1 770千米，包括自然水湾、咸水河、海湾、海峡及人工运河。大西洋沿海航道与墨西哥湾沿海航道相连，流经美国东海岸大部分地区，形成长约4 800千米的美国沿海航道。该沿海航道连通数条通航河流，船舶可由此驶进密西西

The Intercoastal Waterway connects to some navigable rivers where ships can get access to the inland ports of rivers, such as the Mississippi River, the Alabama River, the Savannah River, and the Connecticut River. In 1919, the United States Congress approved the construction of the AIWW, which was completed in 1940. In 1999, the Atlantic Intracoastal Waterway Association (AIWA), a national non-profit organization, was established. Its mission is to obtain funding and support to maintain the AIWW. Nowadays, the United States Army Corps of Engineers undertakes the maintenance of the AIWW. This part of the Intracoastal Waterway is a commercial marine highway, allowing ships to transport goods to Virginia, North Carolina, South Carolina, Georgia, and Florida. The AIWW plays an important role in commerce, military affairs, recreation and dredging industry, creating billions of incomes from these sectors annually.

比河、亚拉巴马河、萨凡纳河、康涅狄格河等河流的内陆港口。1919年，美国国会批准修建大西洋沿海航道。1940年，运河工程竣工。1999年，美国非营利性质机构大西洋沿海航道协会成立，其主要任务是争取赞助和支持，用于维护大西洋沿海航道。如今，美国陆军工程兵团负责该航道的维护。大西洋沿海航道是一条海上商业高速公路，航道可将货物运输到弗吉尼亚州、北卡罗来纳州、南卡罗来纳州、佐治亚州和佛罗里达州。大西洋沿海航道在商业、军事、休闲、疏浚工程产业等方面发挥重要作用，每年在这些方面的收入高达数十亿美元。

Augusta Canal

奥古斯塔运河

A canal located in Georgia, the United States. The Augusta Canal is 20.9 kilometres long and stands as one of the most successful industrial canals in the southern part of the United States. It was built in 1847, originally serving as the main source of water, power and transportation for Augusta. In 1875, it was further extended. In the 1920s and 1930s, after several floods, a spillway was constructed along the canal. In 1996, it is designated by the Congress as a National Heritage Area. Today, it is a principal source of drinking water in Augusta and is a cen-

美国佐治亚州运河。奥古斯塔运河全长20.9千米，为美国南方最成功的工业运河之一。运河1847年开凿，最初旨在为奥古斯塔市提供水源、电力与交通运输通道。1875年，奥古斯塔运河拓宽加深。20世纪20—30年代，因多次受洪水侵袭，运河上修建了泄洪道。1996年，美国国会将该运河列入国家遗产名录。如今，奥古斯塔运河是奥古斯塔市的主要饮用水源，也是

trepiece of the city. The canal is currently famous for its outstanding recreational facilities.

这座城市的中心。如今运河以其出色的休闲娱乐设施而著称。

Augustów Canal

奥古斯图夫运河

A cross-border canal located in central Europe. The Augustów Canal, running from the Podlaskie Voivodeship of northeastern Poland to the Grodno Region of northwestern Belarus, links two major rivers, the Vistula River and the Neman River. The canal is 101.2 kilometres in length, consisting of 18 locks. It allows the passage of vessels up to 40 metres in length, 5 metres in width, with a capacity of up to 10 tons of cargo. The Augustów Canal was constructed between 1823 and 1839 to bypass Prussian territory and link the centre of the Kingdom of Poland with the Baltic seaport of Ventspils. The canal remained, after its completion, an important local waterway for commercial shipping. Since the completion of its construction, the canal has been seen as a technological marvel, with many sluices contributing to its aesthetic appeal. The canal began to decline in importance when the rail network replaced it as the major means of transporting goods in the second half of the 19th century. World War I and the Polish-Soviet War brought about some damages to the canal, but it was rebuilt by the Second Polish Republic during the early 1920s. World War II witnessed the destruction of a number of locks and weirs of the canal. After the war, the Polish part of the canal has been rebuilt. The canal became a tourist attraction for the first time between the two world wars. The canal on the section

欧洲中部跨国运河。奥古斯图夫运河连通维斯图拉河和尼曼河,自波兰东北部的波德拉谢省流至白俄罗斯西北部的格罗德诺州。运河全长101.2千米,有18座船闸,可供长达40米、宽达5米、最大载重量10吨的货船通行。运河于1823—1839年间修建,目的是绕过普鲁士领土,连接波兰王国的中心地带与波罗的海港口文茨皮尔斯。奥古斯图夫运河修建后一直是当地用于商业运输的重要内河航道。运河完工后被专家视为技术奇迹。运河之上船闸林立,风景独特。19世纪后半叶,铁路运输成为主要货运方式后,奥古斯图夫运河的商业运输功能逐步被取代,开始走向衰退。第一次世界大战和波苏战争曾对运河造成一些破坏。20世纪20年代早期,波兰第二共和国对该运河进行修复。第二次世界大战中,奥古斯图夫运河的许多闸坝遭到破坏。战后,波兰境内的运河段得到修复。在两次世界大战之间,奥古斯图夫运河首次成为旅游景点。1968年,根据波兰文化艺术部决议,自奥古斯图夫至波兰边境的运河段及其基础设施被列为一

from Augustów to the state border was declared a monument of Technology Class 1 according to the decision of the Polish Ministry of Culture and the Arts in 1968. The infrastructure includes locks, dams, bridges, housing banks, building maintenance services, ecological environment, landscape and plant. Later in 1979, the entire canal was registered as a monument. The Augustów Canal is now a protected zone proposed by Poland and Belarus for its inscription onto the World Heritage List of UNESCO. At present, it is used as one of the most beautiful kayak trails in Poland. Inland waterway vessels may also go down the canal.

级技术遗迹, 包括运河的船闸、堤坝、桥梁、护岸、建筑维护设施、生态环境、自然景观和植被。1979年, 奥古斯图夫运河全段被列为历史遗迹。目前, 波兰和白俄罗斯两国政府倡议并已将该运河列为保护区, 并共同申请将其列入联合国教科文组织世界遗产名录。奥古斯图夫运河现被用作比赛航道, 是波兰最美的皮划艇赛道之一。内河航运船只也可通行。

Aveiro Canals

A group of canals located in Aveiro in northwestern Portugal. The Aveiro Canals includes the Central Canal, the Côjo Canal, the Saint Roque's Canal, the Pyramid Canal and so on. These canals along the lagoon south of Porto had been a harbour for ships in the 16th century. The port, however, was closed in 1575 as a result of the silted lagoon. By 1808, a canal was excavated to divert water from the Atlantic, which made the Aveiro Canals navigable again. In the 19th century, the government pushed forward the construction of canals which gradually formed the Aveiro canal system. Aveiro is known as the Venice of Portugal, with a series of canals running through its city centre. The Central Canal is the main canal of the city. It goes through the very city centre, connecting most of the important spots of culture and leisure. The Côjo Canal environs offer

阿威罗运河网

葡萄牙西北部阿威罗市运河网。阿威罗运河网由中部运河、科约运河、圣罗克运河、金字塔运河等组成。16世纪时, 波尔图以南潟湖沿岸运河曾是船队停泊的港口。1575年, 泥沙淤塞潟湖, 造成河口封堵、港口停用。直到1808年, 人们开凿出一条运河, 从大西洋引入海水, 阿威罗运河网才恢复通航。19世纪, 当地政府不断推动运河建设, 逐步修建成阿威罗运河网。阿威罗被称为 "葡萄牙的威尼斯", 其市中心有一系列运河穿过。中部运河是该市的主要运河, 刚好流经市中心, 连接起大多数重要的文化与休闲景点。科约运河周边地区是阿威罗市风景最优美的地

some of the best views of Aveiro. The Saint Roque's Canal is at the northeast border of Aveiro, and the Pyramid Canal is named after two pyramids built in 1780 that were once the symbol of the city's entrance. The area along the canals gradually became the centre of fishery industry, salt-making industry and porcelain-making industry, bringing Aveiro increasing prosperity. The Aveiro canals crisscross the city, radiating from Praça Humberto Delgado in the centre of the city to the Atlantic Ocean. Recently, this picturesque city has become one of the most visited locations in Portugal. Its fame is partly due to the lovely canals.

区。圣罗克运河位于阿威罗的东北边界。金字塔运河因两座建于1780年的金字塔命名,它们曾是这座城市的门户象征。运河沿岸地区逐渐发展成为渔业、制盐业和制瓷业中心,阿威罗市日趋繁荣。运河在阿威罗纵横交错,从市中心的汉贝托·德尔加多广场向外辐射,一直延伸到大西洋。近年来,风景如画的阿威罗已成为葡萄牙接待游客最多的城市之一,这在一定程度上得益于其美丽的运河网。

Baflo-Mensingeweer Canal

A canal located in Groningen Province, the Netherlands. The Baflo-Mensingeweer Canal, 150 kilometres northeast of Amsterdam, has an elevation of —2 metres. It is 4 kilometres long, with a maximum draught of 1.2 metres and 4 bridges built on it. The maximum speed of the current is 6.6 kilometres per hour.

Bahr Yussef

A canal located in Egypt. Formerly called Great Canal, or the canal of Moeris. The Bahr Yussef is 15 kilometres long and 5 metres deep, linking the Lake Moeris with Faiyum. The canal is named after the prophet Yusuf in the Koran. It was built during the Amenemhat III period (reigned 1818 BC—1770 BC). In the ancient times, the waterway was a branch of the Nile and formed a lake called Lake Moeris to the west of the Nile. Two dams were built over the Bahr Yussef to control the flow into Lake Moeris and out of the Nile. The canal was enlarged in the 12th Dynasty. In about 230 BC, the channel's importance had declined with the surrounding area gradually undergoing transformation. Nowadays, the canal still exists and continues to deliver water from the Nile to the Birket Qarun, a smaller form of Lake Moeris in modern times which is in parallel with the Nile.

Baillie-Grohman Canal

An abandoned canal located in British Columbia,

巴夫洛-门辛赫韦尔运河

荷兰格罗宁根省运河。巴夫洛-门辛赫韦尔运河位于阿姆斯特丹东北方向150千米处，低于海平面2米。运河总长4千米，最大吃水深度1.2米，共建有4座桥，水流速度最高可达每小时6.6千米。

尤瑟夫运河

埃及运河。旧称大运河或摩里斯运河。尤瑟夫运河全长15千米，深5米，连接摩里斯湖与法尤姆绿洲。尤瑟夫运河以《古兰经》中先知约瑟夫的名字命名，开凿于阿蒙涅姆赫特三世时期（公元前1818—公元前1770年在位）。古时该运河为尼罗河支流，并在尼罗河以西形成摩里斯湖。尤瑟夫运河上建有两座大坝，用以控制摩里斯湖进水量和尼罗河出水量。运河在第十二王朝时期扩建。公元前230年左右，由于周围地区形势逐渐发生改变，运河不再受重视。如今，尤瑟夫运河仍在发挥作用，将尼罗河的水引入与其流向相同的卡伦湖，即缩小的当代摩里斯湖。

贝利-格罗赫曼运河

加拿大不列颠哥伦比亚省废弃运

Canada. The Baillie-Grohman Canal connects the Columbia Lake and the upper Kootenay River. Upon its completion, the canal was about 2 kilometres long and 14 metres wide, with a lock about 30 metres in length and 9 metres in width. The construction of the Baillie-Grohman Canal was initiated by William Adolf Baillie-Grohman, an English adventurer, hence the name. In 1887, the construction of the Baillie-Grohman Canal began, and was completed in 1889. The canal was built to connect the Columbia Lake with the upper Kootenay River, which were only around 1.8 kilometres apart. The canal was expected to allow the upstream water of the Kootenay River to be diverted to the Columbia Lake, thus relieving floods downstream and boosting the local economy. The canal had only been used 3 times, the last of which was in 1902 when the steamer North Star went through the canal. The lock of the canal was destroyed because the steamer was too large to get through. Since then, no more ships passed through the Baillie-Grohman Canal. The remaining canal and the lock, flooded and gradually silted, can still be seen today.

河。贝利—格罗赫曼运河连通哥伦比亚湖和库特内河上游。运河初建成时全长约2千米，宽约14米，有一座长约30米、宽约9米的船闸。贝利—格罗赫曼运河由英国冒险家威廉·阿道夫·贝利—格罗赫曼提议修建，运河由此得名。贝利—格罗赫曼运河1887年开凿，1889年完工。运河连接相距仅1.8千米的哥伦比亚湖与库特内河上游，期望将库特内河上游的河水引至哥伦比亚湖，从而减少下游洪灾发生，同时促进当地经济发展。运河仅通航3次便遭废弃，最后一次通航是在1902年。当时，"北极星号"轮船由此通行，由于轮船体积过大，船闸遭损毁。此后，贝利—格罗赫曼运河停止通航。运河和船闸的残留部分受洪水侵蚀，逐渐被淤泥堵塞。如今运河的部分遗迹仍然可见。

Baïse

A canalized river located in south-western France. As the left tributary of the Garonne, the Baïse River originates from the foothills of the Pyrenees and flows northwards into the Garonne near Aiguillon. It is 65 kilometres in length with 21 locks. The maximum draught upstream is 1.2 metres, and 1.5 metres downstream at the junction with

巴伊斯河

法国西南部运河化河流。巴伊斯河是加龙河左岸支流，源于比利牛斯山山麓，向北流至艾吉永附近，汇入加龙河。巴伊斯河全长65千米，有21座船闸。上游最大吃水深度1.2米，下游与加龙运河交汇处最大吃水深度1.5米。法国国王亨利

the Garonne Canal. King Henry IV of France and Napoleon both considered the canalization of the Baïse River a feasible project. In 1808, the project was started. It was completed several years later. In 1954, the canalized river was closed, becoming the private property of the riparian residents. In the early 1990s, the two departments in France, Lot-et-Garonne and Gers, invested over 10 million euros in restoring the waterway. Nowadays, the canalized Baïse is a popular route for cruising.

四世和拿破仑都认为将巴伊斯河改建为运河的计划可行。1808年运河化工程启动，几年后竣工。1954年，巴伊斯河停航，成为河岸居民的私有财产。20世纪90年代初，洛特—加龙省和热尔省投入逾1 000万欧元修复该航道。如今，巴伊斯河是十分受欢迎的游船航道。

Balgzand Canal

巴尔赞德运河

An inland canal located in North Holland Province, the Netherlands. The Balgzand Canal flows from the Amstel Lake to the North Holland Canal. It is 9.5 kilometres in length, with a lock set up along its route. The construction of the canal was started in 1924 and it was opened in 1927. Now it is mainly used for transportation and drainage.

荷兰北荷兰省内陆运河。巴尔赞德运河从阿姆斯特尔湖流入北荷兰运河，全长9.5千米，建有1座船闸。该运河1924年开凿，1927年通航。目前，巴尔赞德运河主要用于航运和排水。

Ballinamore and Ballyconnell Canal

巴利纳莫尔—巴利康奈尔运河

A cross-border canal located in Europe. See Shannon-Erne Waterway.

欧洲跨国运河。见香农—厄恩航道。

Bambawali-Ravi-Bedian Canal

班巴瓦利—拉维—白地安运河

A canal located on the east side of the city of Lahore, Punjab, Pakistan. Also simply named as the BRB Canal. The Bambawali-Ravi-Bedian Canal is 8 kilometres long, 45 metres wide and 5 metres deep. The canal starts from the Upper Chenab Ca-

巴基斯坦旁遮普省拉合尔市运河。简称班拉白（BRB）运河。班巴瓦利—拉维—白地安运河全长8千米，宽45米，深5米，自上奇纳布运河流至萨特莱杰河。20世纪50

nal and ending at the Sutlej. It was constructed by Pakistan in the 1950s. The canal has boosted the agricultural development of the area. It also has an extension canal, the Lahore Canal, which runs westwards from Jallo Mor to Thokar Niza Baig.

年代，巴基斯坦开凿了该运河。班拉白运河的修建促进了当地的农业发展。拉合尔运河为其扩建运河，从贾洛摩尔市向西流向托卡尔尼撒白市。

Bandak-Nordsjö Canal

班达克－诺德斯约运河

A canal located in southern Norway. The Bandak-Nordsjö Canal, the longer part of the Telemark Canal, extended from Nordsjö Lake through the Flåvatn and Kviteseidvatn lakes to the Bandak Lake. In 1891, the Bandak-Nordsjö Canal running towards Dalen was completed. It was opened in 1892 by the Minister of Labour Hans Hein Theodor Nysom. Regarded as the eighth wonder in Europe, the Bandak-Nordsjö Canal was mainly used for transporting goods and passengers as well as guarding against flooding. In addition, the Bandak-Nordsjö Canal was listed as a National Cultural Heritage in June 2017.

挪威南部运河。班达克—诺德斯约运河为泰勒马克运河较长的一段，源于诺德斯约湖，流经弗洛瓦特恩湖、克维特塞德特恩湖，最终注入班达克湖。1891年，通向达伦市的班达克—诺德斯约运河竣工。1892年，挪威劳工部长汉斯·海因·西奥多·尼索姆宣布该运河正式通航。班达克—诺德斯约运河号称欧洲"第八大奇迹"，主要用于航运和防洪涝。2017年6月，班达克—诺德斯约运河被列入挪威国家文化遗产名录。

Banjir Canal

班吉尔运河

A canal system located in Jakarta, Indonesia. See Jakarta Flood Canal.

印度尼西亚雅加达运河网。见雅加达泄洪运河。

Banjir Kali Malang Canal

班吉尔卡利玛琅泄洪运河

A canal located in Jakarta, Indonesia. See West Flood Canal.

印度尼西亚雅加达运河。见西泄洪运河。

Bảo Định Canal

A canal located in the Mekong Delta in Vietnam. Also called Vũng Gù Canal in some places. The Bảo Định Canal runs from the Vàm Cỏ Tây River at Tân An to the Tiền River at Mỹ Tho. It was firstly improved in the reign of Nguyn Phúc Chu (1675—1725). During the reign of Gia Long (1762—1820), it was substantially deepened and extended by 9,000 workers, thereby connecting the Vàm Cỏ Tây river and the Tiền River in 1819.

保定运河

越南湄公河三角洲运河。某些地方亦称其为万古运河。保定运河始于新安，自万古河流经美荻，注入前河。越南南北朝阮福凋执政期间（1675—1725），保定运河首次改造。嘉隆皇帝在位期间（1762—1820）又征用9 000名劳工对运河进行大规模扩建，加深拓宽河道。1819年，保定运河连通了万古河与前河。

Barisal Canal System

An integrated waterway network of dozens of small canals and rivers located in the Ganges Delta, Bangladesh. Starting at Banaripara, the Barisal Canal System passes through Uzirpur, Shikarpur, Udaypur, Sharupkathi, Pirojpur and Jhalikathi. The canal system was established in the 18th century, and was enlarged in the 19th century. Apart from irrigation, transportation and drainage control, it also serves as a tourist destination, and is regarded as the "Venice of the East". However, due to the lack of proper maintenance as well as the encroachment of private and commercial constructions, the waterways have been narrowing and disappearing. The municipal government is now taking effective measures to tackle with these problems.

博里萨尔运河网

孟加拉国恒河三角洲地区运河网。博里萨尔运河网由数十条狭小运河及河流组成，始于巴拿利帕拉，流经乌济尔布尔、希卡尔布尔、乌代布尔、沙鲁普卡提、比罗杰布尔和吉哈利卡提等地。博里萨尔运河网18世纪开凿，19世纪扩建，兼具灌溉、航运和排水功能，同时还是一处著名景点，被誉为"东方威尼斯"。但因维护不善，再加上私人建筑和商业建筑侵占航道，运河逐渐变窄，濒临消失。目前，当地市政府正采取有效措施来解决上述问题。

Barkley Canal

A canal located in Kentucky, the United States. The Barkley Canal connects Lake Barkley and the Kentucky Lake. It is nearly 3.2 kilometres in length with a bottom width of 122 metres. It is a free-flowing waterway in the nation. The Barkley Canal, named after the 35th vice president of the United States, Alben William Barkley, was constructed in the late 1950s when the Barkley Dam construction project was started. The Barkley Dam brought the two lakes to the same water level to facilitate shipping. The strip of land between Lake Barkley and the Kentucky Lake forms the "Land between the Lakes National Recreation Area". It is a complex for boating, fishing, camping and other outdoor activities.

巴克利运河

美国肯塔基州运河。巴克利运河连通巴克利湖和肯塔基湖，全长近3.2千米，底宽122米，是美国的一条无闸坝航道。巴克利运河以美国第35任副总统阿尔本·威廉·巴克利的姓氏命名。运河于20世纪50年代末巴克利大坝项目建设期间开凿，目的是将巴克利湖和肯塔基湖调节到同一水位线，便于航运。这两个湖泊之间的狭长地带被称为"湖滨国家休闲区"，可进行划船、钓鱼、野营等户外活动。

Barnsley Canal

A canal located in England, the United Kingdom. The Barnsley Canal is 23.3 kilometres in length and has 20 locks. The canal runs from the Barnby Basin through Barnsley, South Yorkshire, to a junction with the Aire and Calder Navigation. It was constructed from 1793 and fully opened in 1802. The early 1790s saw an increasing demand for coal. However, coal mines near Barnsley cannot be consumed by industries in other regions due to the lack of transport facilities. In July 1792, the Aire and Calder Canal Company planned to link Wakefield to the Barnsley mines. The construction was started on 27 September, 1793, near the junction with

巴恩斯利运河

英国英格兰运河。巴恩斯利运河全长23.3千米，有20座船闸，从巴恩比流域流经南约克郡的巴恩斯利，最后汇入艾尔—科尔德航道。该运河1793年开凿，1802年全线通航。18世纪90年代初期，用煤需求量急剧增加，但由于交通不便，巴恩斯利周边的煤矿无法将煤运往其他地区。1792年7月，艾尔—科尔德运河公司计划修建一条连接韦克菲尔德和巴恩斯利煤矿的运河。1793年9月27日，运河修建工程开工，在与艾尔—科尔德运河的交

the Aire and Calder Canal. The northern section to Barnsley was opened on 8 June 1799. However, the construction of the Barnsley-to-Barnby section did not begin until late 1798 and its opening was postponed to 1802. Despite the popularization of railways, the canal made profits until 1942. It was disused in 1953 after major breaches occurred in 1945 and 1946. It is currently abandoned, but the Barnsley Canal Consortium proposed to restore and reopen it.

Bata Canal

A canal located in the Czech Republic. The Bata Canal is about 52 kilometres long, more than half of which (about 27 kilometres) belongs to the Morava River, and 33 bridges cross over the waterway. The water level difference between different parts is 18.6 metres, with 14 locks overcoming the difference along the route. The construction of the Bata Canal was started on 16 October 1934 and completed in the autumn of 1938. It was jointly funded by the Bata Shoe Organization and the Czechoslovak government. The immediate reason to build the canal was to meet the demand to transport lignite from the mine in Ratíškovice to the Otrokovice power plant. It was also an endeavour to raise the groundwater level, a necessary work during the initial phase of the planned Danube-Oder Canal project. During World War II, the Bata Canal was severely damaged, and only part of it was under repair which lasted until 1949. After that, its shipping function gradually

汇处附近开始施工。1799年6月8日，北段运河开航，可到达巴恩斯利。巴恩斯利至巴恩比的河段直至1798年年末才开始修建，开航时间则推迟至1802年。尽管面临铁路运输的竞争，巴恩斯利运河在1942年以前仍可盈利。1945—1946年间，运河河段出现巨大缺口。运河自1953年起停航至今。目前，巴恩斯利运河联合会提议修复此运河并实现复航。

巴塔运河

捷克共和国运河。巴塔运河全长约52千米，其中约27千米是摩拉瓦河河段。运河水位落差18.6米，有33座桥和14座船闸。巴塔运河工程1934年10月16日开工，1938年秋竣工，由巴塔鞋业和捷克斯洛伐克政府共同出资修建。开凿该运河，一方面是为了解决货运需求，把剌吉士果维采矿区的褐煤运到奥特罗科维采的发电站，另一方面是为了提高地下水水位，这也是多瑙—奥得运河项目初始阶段的必要工程。第二次世界大战期间，巴塔运河遭严重毁坏，仅部分河段得以修缮，修缮工作持续到1949年。此后，该运河的航运功能逐渐衰退，1972年正式停航。1995年，为满足人们的旅游需求，巴塔运河重新开航，如今已成为受欢迎的观光

weakened and it was officially abandoned in 1972. In 1995, the canal was reopened for sightseeing and is now popular as a recreational cruise route. At present, with most locks being repaired and in operation, the canal became navigable again. The extension project to the border of Slovakia is under planning.

航线。目前，运河上多数船闸已修好并正常运行，航运也已恢复。巴塔运河至斯洛伐克边境的拓建工程已进入规划阶段。

Bean Shoals Canal

An unfinished canal located in North Carolina, the United States. As a part of the Yadkin River, the Bean Shoals Canal is a stretch of shallow water, with a total length of 3.2 kilometres. This canal was designed to improve the navigation condition on the upper Yadkin River, linking the western and central regions of North Carolina to its eastern and southern parts for commercial purposes. The initial plan, as proposed by John Hixon and Hiram Jennings, two local engineers, was to build a 5-kilometre-long canal. The construction commenced in 1820 but was suspended in 1825 due to undercapitalization. It is not known if the completed 3.2-kilometre-long section had ever been put into use. In the 1890s, a railroad bed was constructed covering the remaining section of the canal. Currently, some parts of the remains of the channel can still be seen in the Pilot Mountain State Park.

比恩浅滩运河

美国北卡罗来纳州未竣工运河。比恩浅滩运河是亚德金河的一片浅水域，全长3.2千米。修建该运河是为了改善亚德金河上游的通航条件，连通北卡罗来纳州中西部与东南部，满足商业需求。最初，本地工程师约翰·希克森和海勒姆·詹宁斯提出修建一条5千米长的运河。该运河于1820年开凿，但1825年因资金不足而停工。完工的3.2千米河道是否曾投入使用已无从考证。19世纪90年代，为铺设铁路路基，比恩浅滩运河被回填。如今，派勒特山州立公园中仍可见该运河的遗存。

Beatrix Canal

A canal located in the southern Netherlands. The Beatrix Canal, excavated in 1930, is 8.4 kilometres in length. The canal was constructed to connect

贝娅特丽克丝运河

荷兰南部运河。贝娅特丽克丝运河于1930年开凿，全长8.4千米，连接埃因霍温市和威廉敏娜运河。该

the city of Eindhoven to the Wilhelmina Canal. It was named after Princess Beatrix, the newborn and also the eldest daughter of the heiress to the Dutch throne.

运河以当时刚出生的贝娅特丽克丝公主的名字命名，她是荷兰皇室王位继承人的长女。

Beaucaire Canal

A canal located in southern France. The Beaucaire Canal runs from Aigues-Mortes to Beaucaire and links the Midi Canal with the Rhône. It is 51 kilometres long, and now a part of the Rhône-Sète Canal along with the Ètangs Canal. The construction of the canal began in 1773 but the work remained suspended until 1805. The project received a new impetus because of the creation in 1808 of the Beaucaire Canal Company controlled by the Languedocien financiers. Between 1829 and 1835, the engineer Paulin Talabot was in charge of the work. The presence of this canal was of primary necessity for the development of local commerce. But the construction of the dam of Vallabrègues in 1969 gave it the final blow with the closing of the Beaucaire Lock.

博凯尔运河

法国南部运河。博凯尔运河全长51千米，自艾格莫尔特流至博凯尔，连通米迪运河和罗讷河，与埃唐运河同为罗讷—塞特运河的一部分。博凯尔运河工程1773年动工，但一直被搁置到1805年。1808年，在朗格多克地区的金融家赞助下，博凯尔运河公司成立，运河工程建设得以推进。1829—1835年间，博凯尔运河工程交由工程师波林·塔拉博负责。该运河对当地商业的发展发挥了重要作用。但1969年瓦拉布雷格水坝修建，博凯尔船闸关闭，这是对博凯尔运河的最后一击。

Beauharnois Canal

A canal located in southwestern Quebec, Canada. The Beauharnois Canal is 24.5 kilometres in length, 8 metres in depth and 182 metres in width. In history, the Beauharnois Canal was opened in 1843 on the south side of the St. Lawrence Seaway. However, it was then replaced in 1899 by the Soulanges Canal located on the north side of the St.

博阿努瓦运河

加拿大魁北克省西南部运河。博阿努瓦运河全长24.5千米，深8米，宽182米。1843年，位于圣劳伦斯海道南侧的博阿努瓦运河通航。1899年，圣劳伦斯海道北侧的苏朗日运河建成，博阿努瓦运河遭弃用。现今的博阿努瓦运河于1929—

Lawrence Seaway. The present Beauharnois Canal was constructed from 1929 to 1932. Taking Lake Saint-Francis as the point of departure, it flows westwards, passes through Lake Saint-Louis and then turns to the northeast, bypassing a series of cities including Salaberry de Valleyfield, Beauharnois, Saint Louise de Gonzague and Saint Stanislas de Kostka. As a part of a hydroelectric development programme in Beauharnois, a dam and a power house have been built on the canal to exploit the 24-metre elevation difference between the two lakes mentioned above and generate electricity.

1932年间开凿。运河由圣弗朗西斯湖向西流经圣路易斯湖，再转而流向东北方向，毗邻多个城市，包括萨拉贝里·瓦利菲尔德、博阿努瓦、圣路易斯·贡扎加和圣斯坦尼斯拉斯·科斯特卡。博阿努瓦运河上建有1座大坝和1个发电站，是博阿努瓦水力发电项目的一部分，旨在利用圣弗朗西斯湖和圣路易斯湖两湖之间24米的水位落差发电。

Beaver and Erie Canal

An abandoned canal located near the west edge of Pennsylvania, the United States. Also called Erie Extension Canal. The Beaver and Erie Canal connected the Ohio River in the south of the state and Lake Erie in the north. This canal, with a total length of 219 kilometres, belonged to the Pennsylvania Canal system, running through five counties including Beaver County, Lawrence County, Mercer County, Crawford County, and Erie County. According to the initial proposal in 1822, the canal was designed to enlarge the transportation system within the state, connecting Philadelphia with Pittsburgh by a shipping network. At that time, this canal was seen as the rival to the Erie Canal, one of the most well-known canals in the United States. This canal had three operating divisions: the Beaver Division, the Shenango Division, and the Conneaut Division. The construction began in

比弗－伊利运河

美国宾夕法尼亚州西部废弃运河。亦称伊利扩建运河。比弗－伊利运河为南北流向，南通俄亥俄河，北入伊利湖，全长219千米，曾是宾夕法尼亚运河网的一部分，流经比弗县、劳伦斯县、默瑟县、克劳福德县和伊利县。据1822年的最初方案，该运河能够通过航运网连接费城与匹兹堡，以此扩大宾夕法尼亚州的运输系统。当时，这条运河被认为能与美国著名的伊利运河相匹敌。比弗－伊利运河共分为三部分河段，即比弗区、希南戈区和康尼奥特区河段。1831年，该运河自比弗区开始施工。比弗区河段全长50千米，延伸至珀拉斯凯。为使过往船舶尽可能避开急流和水位落差过大所带

1831, starting with the Beaver Division that ran 50 kilometres all the way to the Pulaski. A total of 17 locks and 6 dams were built on the Beaver Division to help passing ships and boats cope with rapids and abrupt elevation. The work on the Shenango Division followed in 1836, with an extension of 98 kilometres from Pulaski to the Conneaut Lake. The construction of the Conneaut Division commenced in 1838, travelling 72 kilometres further north. A private company took it over in 1843 and completed the whole project in 1844. The once busy traffic of the canal brought benefits for the local people and industries for decades. However, it was officially abandoned in 1872 for its high maintenance fees and destined failure in competing with railroads.

来的危险，比弗区共建17座船闸和6座水坝。希南戈区河段开凿于1936年，长98千米，连接珀拉斯基和康尼奥特河。康尼奥特区河段开凿于1838年，长72千米，将整个运河继续向北延伸。1843年，一家私人企业接手施工，整个工程一年后竣工。此后几十年间，比弗—伊利运河航运繁忙，当地居民和产业从中获益良多。然而，由于维护费用高昂，且不敌飞速发展的铁路，比弗—伊利运河最终于1872年被弃用。

Bederkesa-Geeste Canal

A canal located in northern Germany. The Bederkesa-Geeste Canal is 11 kilometres in length. As a part of the Elbe-Weser Waterway, it runs from Bad Bederkesa to the Geeste River with one lock at Lintig. The canal was constructed between 1858 and 1860 to boost local economic development and facilitate transportation. However, the canal was not passable until a floodgate was constructed in Geeste in 1898. High tide was also necessary for navigation on the canal. It was deepened twice between 1935 and 1937. After the improvement, barges were able to sail on the canal.

贝德凯萨－盖斯特运河

德国北部运河。贝德凯萨—盖斯特运河全长11千米，是易北—威悉航道的一部分，从巴德贝德凯萨流至盖斯特河，在林蒂希的河段上建有1座船闸。运河1858—1860年间开凿，旨在促进当地经济发展，改善交通条件。但直至1898年盖斯特河上建了防洪闸门后，运河才得以通航，且仅限于海水涨潮时段。1935—1937年间，贝德凯萨—盖斯特运河历经两次加深改造后可供驳船通航。

Beemster Belt Canal

A canal located in North Holland Province, the Netherlands. See Beemster Ring Canal.

贝姆斯特带状运河

荷兰北荷兰省运河。见贝姆斯特环形运河。

Beemster Ring Canal

A canal located in North Holland Province, the Netherlands. Also called Beemster Belt Canal. The Beemster Ring Canal has a total length of 30 kilometres. It was constructed around the wild Beemster Lake in the 17th century after the government had agreed to reclaim the Beemster polder.

贝姆斯特环形运河

荷兰北荷兰省运河。亦称贝姆斯特带状运河。贝姆斯特环形运河全长30千米。17世纪时，当地政府支持开垦贝姆斯特圩田，随后该运河围绕荒僻的贝姆斯特湖而建。

Beer Canal

A canal located in the port of Rotterdam, the Netherlands. Between the Europort and the Maasvlakte, the Beer Canal has a total length of 3.6 kilometres. Built in the early 1960s, it is a side branch of the Caland Canal. The water is up to 23 metres deep, allowing all kinds of vessels to navigate.

比尔运河

荷兰鹿特丹港区运河。比尔运河连接欧罗波特港区和马斯莱可迪港区，全长3.6千米。该运河为卡兰运河支流，20世纪60年代初期开凿，最深处达23米，可供各类船舶通航。

Bega Canal

A cross-border canal located in Europe. Crossing Romania and Serbia, the Bega Canal runs southwestwards from Timisoara in western Romania to the Serbian town of Titel. It is 114 kilometres long, with 44 kilometres in Romania and the remaining 70 kilometres in Serbia. As early as 1728, the canal had been used for the transportation of construction timber and the drainage of marshlands in the vicin-

贝加运河

欧洲跨国运河。贝加运河流经罗马尼亚和塞尔维亚两国，从罗马尼亚西部的蒂米什瓦拉向西南流至塞尔维亚境内的蒂泰尔，全长114千米，其中44千米位于罗马尼亚境内，70千米位于塞尔维亚境内。早在1728年，贝加运河就已通航，用以运输建筑木材以及周边沼泽地

ity. It was extended and repaired multiple times in the following years. In many ways, the Bega Canal has been considered a backbone of the city Timisoara. On 3 May 1910, the power plant in Timisoara, one of the oldest hydropower plants in Romania, began to produce electricity by utilizing the energy of the running water in the channel. A sluice system was built between 1900 and 1916, which contributed to the significant increase in navigation later. After World War II, the traffic through the canal took a nosedive, and the situation worsened for the absence of regular maintenance, which led to the cessation of traffic in 1958. Only after 1990 were there discussions about the rehabilitation of the Bega Canal, but no plan went into practice because of fund shortage. Dredging and restoration work began in late 2008 with a view to sustainable development of the canal. Nowadays, the Bega Canal not only provides clean drinking water but also is developing into a tourist destination known for its leisure activities and well-protected environment.

区排水。此后，该运河历经多次整修和扩建。贝加运河是蒂米什瓦拉市的重要支柱，在许多方面发挥作用。1910年5月3日，蒂米什瓦拉市水电站正式启动，利用贝加运河的水能发电，该水电站是罗马尼亚境内历史最悠久的水电站之一。1900—1916年间，贝加运河的船闸系统落成，极大地促进了航运量的增长。但在第二次世界大战后，由于运输量骤减，加之缺乏定期维护，运河于1958年停航。直到1990年，运河的维修工作才被提上议程，但由于资金不足，整修计划未能实施。2008年末，贝加运河的疏浚和维修工作正式开始，以促进该运河的可持续发展。如今，贝加运河不仅是附近城市居民饮用水的来源，还是娱乐休闲活动丰富、自然环境优越的度假胜地。

Beijing-Hangzhou Grand Canal

京杭大运河

A canal located in China. See Grand Canal (China).

中国运河。见大运河（中国）。

Belozersky Canal

别洛焦尔斯克运河

A canal located in the southwestern part of Lake Beloye in Russia. Formerly known as Mariinsky Canal. Linking the Kovzha River with the Sheksna River, the Belozersky Canal is 66.8 kilometres in length and passes the town of Belozersk. The water

俄罗斯白湖西南部运河。旧称马林斯基运河。别洛焦尔斯克运河全长66.8千米，连通科夫斯哈河与塞克斯纳河，流经别洛焦尔斯克城。该运河水位比塞克斯纳河入口高4

level of the canal was 4 metres higher than that of the Sheksna entrance and 1.8 metres higher than that of the Kovzha entrance. The construction of the Belozersky Canal was started in 1843. The Belozersk merchants contributed greatly to the initiation of this canal project. They had petitioned to Tsar Alexander I twice to permit the building of a bypass canal to avoid shipwrecks which happened frequently around Lake Beloye. The opening of the Belozersky Canal for navigation took place in August 1846. The canal was of great economic importance. It carried 70 percent of the total amount of waterborne freight transport at that time. In the 20th century, several rounds of repair works had been launched.

米，比科夫斯哈河入口高1.8米。运河于1843年开始修建，当地商人对该工程的启动功不可没。当时，白湖区水域多次发生沉船事件，为避免类似悲剧再次发生，商人们先后两次向沙皇亚历山大一世请求开凿一条运河绕过白湖。别洛焦尔斯克运河于1846年8月通航。该运河承载占当时水上运输总量的70%，具有重要的经济价值。20世纪时，别洛焦尔斯克运河经过多次维修。

Bereguardo Canal

A canal located in Lombardy, northern Italy. The Bereguardo Canal is 19 kilometres in length and has a difference of 24 metres in elevation, with 24 locks built to allow boats to pass through. As a part of the Navigli system, it is diverted from the Grand Canal at Abbiategrasso, heading southward to Bereguardo. It is the first canal in Europe using a series of pound locks (locks with gates at both ends) to overcome the great changes in elevation. The construction of the canal began in the first half of the 15th century by the order of Francesco Sforza I, Duke of Milan. As more modern canals were built during the 19th century, especially with the opening of the grander Pavese Canal, the Bereguardo Canal was relegated to irrigation duties.

贝雷瓜尔多运河

意大利北部伦巴第大区运河。贝雷瓜尔多运河全长19千米，水位落差24米，建有24座船闸以便船只通行。该运河是纳维利运河网的一部分，从阿比亚泰格拉索的米兰大运河分流出来，向南流向贝雷瓜尔多。贝雷瓜尔多运河是欧洲第一条使用一系列双向船闸（两端都有闸门）来处理水位落差的运河。15世纪上半叶，米兰公爵弗朗切斯科·斯福尔扎一世下令修建贝雷瓜尔多运河。19世纪后，随着更多现代运河陆续建成，尤其是更大的帕维亚运河通航后，贝雷瓜尔多运河仅用于农业灌溉。

Bergen Canal

A cross-border canal located in Belgium and France. Also called Kolme. The Bergen Canal connects Veurne in West Flanders, Belgium to Saint-Winoksbergen in Nord Department, France, with a total length of 23.7 kilometres. It dates back to the 9th century. The canal was excavated as a part of the drainage system and was later deepened, widened and converted into waterway channels. In the Middle Ages, it served as a main trade route between Veurne and Saint-Winoksbergen. In 1622, it was reinforced by Spaniards during wartime for flood prevention. The French part of the Bergen canal has been restored as an industrial canal, while the 11-kilometre-long Belgian part retains its medieval appearance and although silted up, it remains classified as a navigable watercourse by Flanders.

贝亨运河

欧洲流经比利时和法国的跨国运河。亦称柯尔梅运河。贝亨运河始于比利时西佛兰德省的弗尔讷，终于法国诺尔省的圣维诺克斯贝亨，全长23.7千米。该运河历史可追溯至9世纪，开凿运河的初衷是修建排水系统，后来才将其拓宽、加深，转化为水运通道。在中世纪，贝亨运河是弗尔讷和圣维诺克斯贝亨之间的主要贸易通道。1622年战争时期，西班牙人为防汛而加固运河。贝亨运河法国段经过整修后成为工业运河。比利时境内长达11千米的运河河段则保留了中世纪时期的外观，虽然部分河道淤塞严重，但仍然被佛兰德官方归为可航行水道。

Bergen Maas Canal

A canal located in North Brabant, the Netherlands. The Bergen Maas Canal, the main distributary of the Maas River, flows westwards from River Meuse to Amer estuary. The canal was constructed in 1904 and was officially declared open by Queen Wilhelmina in the same year. The canal is 24.5 kilometres in length and 180 metres in width. With no lock constructed on it, the canal has a maximum height of 2.1 metres above sea level. As for the transport, there are two road bridges above the Bergen Maas Canal and three car ferries free for all traffic for the benefit of people living around the area.

贝亨马斯运河

荷兰北布拉班特省运河。贝亨马斯运河为马斯河的主要支流，从默兹河向西汇入阿米尔河河口区域。运河于1904年开凿。同年，荷兰女王威廉敏娜宣布运河正式开通。该运河长24.5千米，宽180米，最高海拔为2.1米，河上未建船闸。为方便周围居民的出行，运河上建有2座公路桥和3个汽车轮渡点，均免费使用。

Bergues Canal

A canal located in northern France. The Bergues Canal flows from the town of Bergues to the port of Dunkirk in France with a total length of about 8 kilometres. The Bergues Canal is one of the oldest canals in West Flanders, with its course shown on the map as early as the 9th century. It was officially constructed in 1499 and extended respectively in 1574, 1621 and 1761. The canal has been navigable until the 1970s when the commercial traffic on the canal ceased. It was previously connected with the Basse-Colme Canal and the Haute-Colme Canal. The restoration of these canals would significantly increase the tourism potential of Bergues. Nowadays, Bergues remains a there-and-back excursion for visiting boats by the Bergues Canal. The site acquired worldwide fame in 2008. As the location for the film *Bienvenue chez les Ch'tis*, the local dialect and belfry chimes contributed to making the town a destination for tourists.

贝尔格运河

法国北部运河。贝尔格运河始于贝尔格镇，终于敦刻尔克港口，全长8千米。该运河是西佛兰德省最古老的运河之一，早在9世纪，相关地图已有记载。运河1499年开凿，1574年、1621年和1761年先后扩建。20世纪70年代前可通航，此后不再用于商业运输。贝尔格运河曾与下科尔莫运河和上科尔莫运河连通，重建这些运河段可极大提高贝尔格小镇对游客的吸引力。如今，贝尔格运河可供前往贝尔格小镇的游船短途往返。2008年，贝尔格镇成为世界知名小镇，因电影《欢迎来北方》在此取景，如今当地的方言和钟楼乐音备受游客欢迎。

Berlikum Canal

A canal located in Friesland, the Netherlands. The Berlikum Canal runs from Berlikum in a southwest direction to Ried. As a part of the Frisian waterways, it is approximately 5 kilometres in length. The Berlikum Canal meets the Van Harinxma Canal at Franeker and joins the Menaldum Canal at Leeuwarden.

贝利克姆运河

荷兰弗里斯兰省运河。贝利克姆运河始于贝利克姆，向西南方向流至里德，全长约5千米，为弗里斯兰河网的一部分。该运河与范哈林克斯马运河交汇于弗拉讷克，与莫纳杜默运河交汇于吕伐登。

Berlin-Spandau Ship Canal

A canal located in Berlin, Germany. The Berlin-Spandau Ship Canal is 12.2 kilometres long, connecting the Havel River to River Spree. The initiation of the canal project is attributed to the engineer Peter Joseph Lenné. The canal was constructed between 1848 and 1859. The Berlin-Spandau Ship Canal has successfully shortened the route from River Spree to the Oder-Havel Canal. Lying some 4 kilometres from its eastern end, River Spree, is the Westhafen, Berlin's largest port with an area of 173,000 square metres.

Berry Canal

A canal located in France. Formerly called Cher Canal or Duke Berry Canal. The Berry Canal links the Loire Lateral Canal and the Cher. It is 320 kilometres long, which is made up of 3 distinct branches that meet at Fontblisse, the Commune of Bannegon. Among the 3 branches, the second one is the longest, with a length of 142 kilometres, running from Fontblisse to Bourges, Vierzon, then Noyers-sur-Cher. The construction of this canal began around 1811 and ended in 1841 with the completion of the section from Vierzon to Noyers-sur-Cher. In 1955, the Berry Canal fell into disuse. But unlike other decommissioned canals that will remain the national or provincial property, the canal of Berry was sold by section to the communes or individuals. Now, the 15-kilometre-long section with 5 locks between Selles-sur-Cher and Noyers-sur-Cher has been restored and reopened to pleasure boats.

柏林－施潘道船舶运河

德国柏林市运河。柏林－施潘道船舶运河全长12.2千米，连通哈弗尔河与施普雷河。运河于1848—1859年间修建，项目发起人是工程师皮特·约瑟夫·莱内。该运河缩短了从施普雷河至奥得－哈弗尔运河的航程。柏林最大的港口西港距离运河东端施普雷河约4千米，总面积为173 000平方米。

贝里运河

法国运河。旧称谢尔运河或贝里公爵运河。贝里运河连通卢瓦尔旁侧运河和谢尔河，全长320千米，由汇聚于巴内贡市冯特布里塞地区的三条支流组成。其中，第二条支流最长，为142千米，始于冯特布里塞，流经布尔日、维耶尔宗，至谢尔河畔的努瓦耶。贝里运河于1811年开始修建，1841年，随着维耶尔宗至谢尔河畔努瓦耶段完工，工程全部竣工。1955年，贝里运河停航。运河停航后通常仍为国家或所在省份所有，但贝里运河被分段售给不同的市或个人。如今，贝里运河上的谢尔河畔塞勒和谢尔河畔努瓦耶之间的河段得到修复，全长15千米，建有5座船闸，修复后供游船使用。

Berry's Canal

A canal located in Australia. The Berry's Canal, as the first Australian transport canal, is 191 metres in length, connecting the Shoalhaven River with the Crookhaven River. The construction was conducted under the guidance of Alexander Berry, an explorer who made the first European settlement on the south coast of New South Wales in Australia. In June 1822, Berry, together with Hamilton Hume, sailed his 15-tonne cutter Blanche from Sydney 150 kilometres down the south coast to the Shoalhaven. The boat was capsized, drowning two of the men. To cope with the serious safety hazard, the two survivals decided to cut a passage along the route and it was completed in 12 days. Since then, the canal has been widened and deepened, and now becomes the real entrance to the Shoalhaven River.

贝里运河

澳大利亚运河。贝里运河是澳大利亚第一条通航运河，全长191米，连通肖尔黑文河和克鲁克黑文河。该运河由探险家亚历山大·贝里主持开凿。贝里在澳大利亚新南威尔士州南海岸建立了第一个欧洲殖民地。1822年6月，贝里与汉密尔顿·休姆乘坐重15吨的"布兰奇"号小艇从悉尼沿海岸线南下，航行150千米前往肖尔黑文市。航行过程中，贝里一行遭遇翻船事故，其中两人溺水。这一严重事故促使生还的两人决定开凿一条航道。历时12天后，运河开凿成功，此后得以拓宽和加深，如今成为肖尔黑文河真正的入口。

Besheers Canal

A canal located in the province of Groningen, the Netherlands. See Visvliet Canal.

贝希尔斯运河

荷兰格罗宁根省运河。见费斯夫利特运河。

Beukers Canal

A canal located in the province of Overijssel, the Netherlands. See Beukers-Steenwijk Canal.

布克斯运河

荷兰上艾瑟尔省运河。见布克斯—斯滕韦克运河。

Beukers-Steenwijk Canal

A canal located in the province of Overijssel, the Netherlands. Also called Beukers Canal. The Beu-

布克斯－斯滕韦克运河

荷兰上艾瑟尔省运河。亦称布克斯运河。布克斯—斯滕韦克运河长

kers-Steenwijk Canal is 14.45 kilometres in length, connecting the Meppel Canal and the Steenwijk-Ossenzijl Canal and running through Belterwijde, Beulakerwijde, Giethoorn and Steenwijk. As a busy canal, it is suitable for both commercial and recreational navigation.

14.45千米，连通梅珀尔运河和斯滕韦克—奥森宰尔运河，流经贝尔特韦德湖、伯拉克韦德湖、羊角村和斯滕韦克市。布克斯—斯滕韦克运河适合商用航运和休闲船只通行，十分繁忙。

Beuvry Canal

伯夫里运河

A disused canal located in northern France. Formerly called the Nœux Coalmine Canal. The Beuvry Canal is linked to the Dunkirk-Escaut Canal with a length of 5.3 kilometres. It was originally constructed to facilitate the development of the coal mining industry. In 1861, a French company called the Nœux Coalmine Company was permitted to build a canal whose main function was to allow the navigation and transport of goods between the Nœux Coalmine and the Aire-la Bassée Canal. However, the canal was no longer used as the local coal industry declined.

法国北部弃用运河。旧称讷克斯煤矿运河。伯夫里运河与敦刻尔克—埃斯科运河相通，全长5.3千米。该运河最初为促进煤矿业发展而开凿。1861年，法国讷克斯矿业公司获批修建该运河，主要是为实现与艾尔—拉巴塞运河之间的通航及货运。之后，随着该地区煤矿业的衰落，伯夫里运河也最终停航。

Beverlo Canal

贝弗洛运河

A canal located in Belgium. The Beverlo Canal, originating from Blauwe Kei and ending in Leopoldsburg, is a lateral canal of the Bocholt-Herentals Canal and one of the seven canals connecting the Maas with the Schelde. The Beverlo Canal is 14.8 kilometres in length with 8 bridges and no lock. The canal can be accessed freely from the Bocholt-Herentals Canal. The construction of the canal was started in 1854, and it was opened to the public in 1857 to better transport heavy military equip-

比利时运河。贝弗洛运河始于布劳韦基，终于利奥波茨堡，为博霍尔特—海伦塔尔斯运河的旁侧运河，也是连通马斯河和斯海尔德河的7条运河之一。贝弗洛运河全长14.8千米，河上共有8座桥梁，无船闸，船只可以自由通航于博霍尔特—海伦塔尔斯运河与贝弗洛运河。运河1854年开凿，1857年正式通航，以便运输重型军事装备。贝弗

ments. It now runs through many nature reserves with abundant fish resources. Nowadays, the canal is no longer an essential waterway for commercial shipping but has become a place for recreations like fishing.

洛运河流经多个自然保护区，鱼类资源丰富。如今，该运河不再是商业运输的重要航道，但已成为钓鱼等休闲活动的胜地。

Bijlands Canal

白兰茨运河

A canal located in Gelderland Province, the Netherlands. The Bijlands Canal was named after Bijlands Castle. The 3-kilometre-long canal connects Tolkamer Town with Millingen-on-Rhine Town. It was constructed between 1773 and 1776 to cut off a large bend in the Waal River for the convenience of regulating flows of water. Nowadays, the canal is vital for Rhine navigation. The area surrounding the Waal and Rhine rivers and the mostly abandoned streams are a part of the extensive nature restoration project known as Gelderse Port.

荷兰格尔德兰省运河。白兰茨运河得名于白兰茨城堡，全长3千米，连接托尔卡莫镇和莱茵河畔的米灵恩镇。该运河1773年开凿，1776年竣工，旨在通过截断瓦尔河的大弯道来调节河水流量。如今，该运河在莱茵河航运系统中发挥着重要作用。大部分已废弃的河段和瓦尔—莱茵河周围的区域共同构成海尔德斯港自然保护区的一部分。

Bijleveld Canal

拜勒费尔德运河

A canal located in Utrecht Province, the Netherlands. The Bijleveld Canal, with an entire length of 1.5 kilometres, dates back to 1413. Earl William VI permitted to excavate a canal to drain excess water from the Old Rhine to the Amstel River. Although short by itself, the canal serves as a part of the sophisticated canal systems of Utrecht. It played, historically, an essential role in drainage, transport, irrigation, defence and sewage. Today, many canals have lost their original function and were filled in to create more space for traffic and better hygiene.

荷兰乌特勒支省运河。拜勒费尔德运河全长1.5千米，其历史可以追溯至1413年。当时，威廉六世伯爵下令开凿该运河，希望将旧莱茵河多余的水排至阿姆斯特尔河。拜勒费尔德运河本身不长，与其他多条运河共同构成乌特勒支复杂的运河网，在历史上发挥过至关重要的作用。拜勒费尔德运河具有排水、船运、灌溉、城防、排污等功能。如今，为优化当地交通和卫

Fortunately, the Bijleveld Canal survived and has become a popular destination for recreation and tourism. Flowing between the countryside and the town of Kockengen, the canal offers a fantastic view for the sight-seers and travellers, with luxurious hotels and classic windmills nearby. Anglers are also welcome to the banks of the Bijleveld Canal.

生状况，很多运河都失去原先的功能并被回填成陆地，但拜勒费尔德运河还是幸运地保存下来，主要作为休闲观光之用。拜勒费尔德运河流经科肯恩城镇和郊外，沿岸自然风光绮丽，可以观赏荷兰风车，城内设有豪华酒店，很适合旅游观光，也十分适合垂钓。

Bío-Bío Canal

比奥－比奥运河

A canal located in Bío-Bío Province, Chile. The Bío-Bío Canal takes water from the Bío-Bío River south to the area of Mulchén for agricultural irrigation supplies. It is currently one of the largest irrigation canals in Chile.

智利比奥－比奥省运河。比奥－比奥运河从穆尔琴市以南的比奥－比奥河引水，用于农业灌溉。该运河目前是智利最大的灌溉运河之一。

Birmingham and Fazeley Canal

伯明翰－费兹利运河

A canal located in the West Midlands of England, the United Kingdom. As one section of the Birmingham Canal Navigations, the Birmingham and Fazeley Canal flows from the Birmingham Canal Navigations Main Line at Old Turn Junction to the Coventry Canal at Fazeley Junction. This section is 24 kilometres in length with 38 locks. The Birmingham and Fazeley Canal, along with the Coventry Canal, the Grand Union Canal and the Oxford Canal, forms a part of the Warwickshire Ring. The canal was constructed in 1784 and completed in 1789. Its purpose was to establish a link between the Coventry Canal and Birmingham and connect Birmingham to London by the Oxford Canal. The

英国英格兰西米德兰兹郡运河。伯明翰－费兹利运河为伯明翰运河航道系统的一部分，全长24千米，河上建有38座船闸。该运河始于伯明翰运河主干航道的旧转弯交汇口，在费兹利交汇口流入考文垂运河。伯明翰－费兹利运河、考文垂运河、大联盟运河和牛津运河共同构成沃里克郡的环形运河网。伯明翰－费兹利运河1784年开凿，1789年竣工，旨在连接考文垂运河和伯明翰市，进而通过牛津运河连接伯明翰市和伦敦市。目前，该运河仍可通航，可供最长约

Birmingham and Fazeley Canal is still navigable, with maximum boat dimensions of about 21 metres in length and 2.1 metres in width. It links urban and rural landscapes. The Birmingham and Fazeley Canal starts at the Gas Street Basin, in the centre of Birmingham's shopping and cultural districts, stretching out into the green and serene Midlands countryside. In the full blossom of industrial development, the Birmingham and Fazeley Canal was shut away from the city behind high walls. However, in the 1980s, it was regenerated as a green haven for local people, with new access points and the towpath resurfaced for walking or cycling.

Birmingham Canals

A canal system located in England, the United Kingdom. Currently known as Birmingham Canal Navigations Main Line. The project of Birmingham Canals was originally conceived in 1767. At that time, a number of renowned Birmingham business people proposed to construct a canal from Birmingham to the Staffordshire and Worcestershire Canal (often called Staffs and Worcs Canal) near Wolverhampton, taking in the coalfields of the Black Country. They authorized James Brindley, the canal engineer, to design a route. In 1768, an act of Parliament was passed to allow the building of the canal and Brindley was appointed engineer. In 1772, the Birmingham Main Line Canal was joined with the Staffordshire and Worcestershire Canal at Aldersley Junction. The canals measured about 56.3 kilometres, with deviations to factories

21米、最宽约2.1米的船只通行。伯明翰—费兹利运河连接城市与乡村地区，运河的一端位于伯明翰市中心的加斯街码头，附近为购物街区和文化街区，另一端连接绿意盎然、宁静平和的米德兰兹乡间地区。在工业发展全盛期，伯明翰—费兹利运河被高墙隔绝在城市之外。然而，在20世纪80年代，伯明翰—费兹利运河开通了新入口，并且周围重新铺设了人行道和自行车道，成为当地居民的绿地天堂，运河因此重获新生。

伯明翰运河网

英国英格兰运河网。现称伯明翰运河主干航道。该运河工程最早酝酿于1767年。当时，伯明翰一些有声望的富商提议开凿一条运河，自伯明翰起，经黑乡产煤区，直至伍尔弗汉普顿附近的斯塔福德郡—伍斯特郡运河。运河工程师詹姆斯·布林德利被授权设计航线。次年，运河修建获得议会法案批准，布林德利被任命为设计师。1772年，伯明翰主干航道于阿尔德斯利与斯塔福德郡—伍斯特郡运河连通，运河长约56.3千米，有多条水渠连接黑乡和伯明翰的工厂与煤矿。伯明翰运河修成后最初取得巨大成功，但存在的一个突出问题是无法充分保证斯梅西克高地

and mines in the Black Country and Birmingham. The original Birmingham Canal was extremely successful, but there was a problem with supplying sufficient water to the Smethwick Summit. A straighter "New Main Line" canal was completed in 1838, which shortened the route from Birmingham to Wolverhampton. As time passed on, the railway took most of the traffic away from the canals. The role of the Birmingham Canals as a vital transportation hub was weakened. Currently, the previously derelict canal area has been transformed with Brindley Place, National Indoor Arena, International Convention Centre and canal-side apartments. The canal environs become a leisure resort attracting millions of tourists every year. The Birmingham Canals are promoting local economic development in a new way.

的供水。1838年，一条更直的"新干线"运河修成，缩短了伯明翰与伍尔弗汉普顿之间的航线。随着时间的推移，铁路运输逐渐取代运河航运，伯明翰运河网作为重要交通枢纽的地位日渐衰弱。如今，曾经破败的运河区建筑林立，建有布林德利广场、国家室内体育馆、国际会议中心以及沿岸公寓。伯明翰运河网周边地区每年吸引成千上万游客前来观光，运河正以新的方式促进当地经济发展。

Black River Canal

布莱克河运河

A canal located in northern New York, the United States. The Black River Canal connects the Erie Canal with the Black River, starting in Rome near the Erie Canal and flowing northward till its confluence with the Black River which empties into the Lake Ontario. It serves as a part of the waterway that traverses the diverse geography of New York State and links the East Coast to the Great Lakes. The Black River Canal was often considered an engineering marvel in the 19th century, with 109 locks set along the 56-kilometre-long route to negotiate a rise and fall of about 328 metres. The project to construct this canal was proposed in 1828 and officially initiated in 1837 after numerous sur-

美国纽约州北部运河。布莱克河运河连通伊利运河和布莱克河，南起伊利运河河畔的罗马镇，一路向北，与通往安大略湖的布莱克河交汇，为跨越纽约州并连接美国东海岸和五大湖航道体系的一部分。布莱克河运河在19世纪被视为一个工程奇迹，56千米的河道建有109座船闸来调节328米的水位落差。1828年，开凿布莱克河运河的设想被提出。经过多次调研后，该运河1837年正式开凿。运河修建工程虽然在19世纪40年代被搁置过几年，最终还是于1855年按计划

veys. In 1855 the entire planned length was finished despite the unexpected suspension in the 1840s. The canal had brought a wave of prosperity to the Black River Valley. Large quantities of timber and farm products were shipped and sold outside the region. Warehouses, shipping houses, hotels and foundries sprang up in villages along the canal. For more than half a century, the Black River Canal has played a significant role in the development of the northern New York countryside. However, due to the decreased productivity of wood and the threat from railroad transportation in the beginning of the 20th century, business along the canal drastically declined, followed by its abandonment in the 1920s. Though abandoned now, the remnants of the Black Canal still serve as an active part of the modern Erie Canal. Its reservoir system keeps functioning well during times of drought. The Boonville Black River Canal Museum has been constructed to preserve and display the rich historical legacy of the Black River Canal with an extensive collection of photographs and artefacts.

完成。布莱克河运河的开凿为布莱克河谷地区带来了一时的繁荣。大宗木材和农产品通过该水路销往外地，运河沿岸村庄也出现不少货仓、运输商行、旅店和铸造厂。在半个多世纪里，布莱克河运河极大地促进了纽约州北部乡村地区的发展。但进入20世纪之后，由于木材产量下降，加之铁路运输的发展，布莱克运河带来的商业效益显著下降，20世纪20年代正式停航。目前，布莱克河运河尽管处于废弃状态，但其遗留河段作为伊利运河的一部分，仍发挥着积极作用，其水库系统在干旱时期可派上用场。布恩维尔布莱克运河博物馆陈列着相关的历史照片和器物，展现了该运河丰厚的历史遗产。

Blackstone Canal

A canal located in the United States. Linking Worcester, Massachusetts, to Providence, Rhode Island, the Blackstone Canal begins at Mill Creek, follows the course of the Blackstone River, and runs down into the Moshassuck Valley. It is about 74 kilometres in length and 10 metres in width. A series of 49 locks were set up to raise and lower barges to negotiate a 137-metre elevation difference. As early as

布莱克斯通运河

美国运河。布莱克斯通运河始于米尔克里克，沿布莱克斯通河河道流入莫沙斯克河谷地区，连接马萨诸塞州伍斯特和罗得岛州普罗维登斯。运河长约74千米，宽约10米，沿线建有49座船闸帮助驳船克服上下游137米水位落差。早在1796年，一位名叫约翰·布朗的富

1796, a prosperous merchant named John Brown first attempted to build a canal along the Blackstone River. However, this plan was blocked by its business competitors, Boston businessmen. In the 1820s, when the Industrial Revolution began in New England, Edward Carrington, another prosperous merchant, managed to construct the canal. The construction began in 1825, and the canal was opened three years later. It only took two days to travel through the canal from Worcester to Providence by shipping. As a cheaper means to transport goods than the turnpikes, the canal boosted the trade and industry in Worcester and the Blackstone Valley. However, the navigation is often plagued by sporadic flooding, insufficient water level in summer and ice in winter. After Boston merchants opened the Providence and Worcester Railroad to recapture the trade, the Blackstone Canal was closed in 1848. Now, parts of the canal have been blocked and some of the restored sections are listed on the National Register of Historic Places.

商就曾尝试在布莱克斯通河沿岸组织修建一条运河, 但在其商业竞争对手波士顿商人们的阻挠下, 这一计划被搁置。19世纪20年代, 正值新英格兰地区工业革命开展之时, 另一位富商爱德华·卡林顿成功组织修建了这条运河。运河1825年开凿, 并于3年后正式通航。从伍斯特坐船到普罗维登斯只需两天时间, 且运送货物比陆路运输更便宜, 进而促进了伍斯特和布莱克斯通河谷地区的商品贸易和工业发展。但因夏季洪水频发或水位过低、冬季河上结冰等问题, 布莱克斯通运河的通航时常受阻。1848年波士顿商人开通伍斯特和普罗维登斯之间的铁路之后, 布莱克斯通运河遭废弃。运河废弃后, 部分河段阻塞, 现有修复的部分中有一些被列入美国国家历史遗迹名录。

Bladder Canal

布莱德运河

A canal located in the Netherlands. The Bladder Canal is a part of the Oranje Canal, linking the Oranje Canal with the Verlendge Hoogeveense Canal. In 1853, the construction began from the Oranje Canal, and moves onwards to the sections through Drenthe and those in Nieum Dordrecht. The project was completed five years later. It was named after its superintendent, Bladder. The Bladder Canal benefited the peat complexes in South-

荷兰运河。布莱德运河是奥拉涅运河的一部分, 连通奥拉涅运河和乌特勒支—霍赫芬运河。运河1853年开凿。修建工程始于奥拉涅运河河段, 之后推进至德伦特省河段, 再到新多德雷赫特河段, 历年5年竣工。运河因时任运河管理人的布莱德而得名。布莱德运河通航期间, 为德伦特省东南部的泥炭

east Drenthe.

厂提供了便利的交通条件。

Blankenberg Canal

布兰肯贝赫运河

A canal located in West Flanders, Belgium. The Blankenberg Canal is 13 kilometres in length, linking the Bruges-Ostend and the North Sea. It was a small and non-navigable canal, mainly used for agricultural irrigation for areas near the North Sea and the port of Blankenberg. In the past, it has occupied a significant position in farming. In 2005, a project was initiated in the section of the municipality of Uitkerke with the aim of natural reservation. The concrete banks were replaced by smooth slopes. Besides, canes were planted to provide improved protection against erosion and created a habitat for those species that disappeared during intensive agriculture. Today, paths around the canal are paved for cyclists and walkers.

比利时西佛兰德省运河。布兰肯贝赫运河全长13千米，连接布鲁日—奥斯坦德和北海。该运河较短，不通航，过去主要用于北海和布兰肯贝赫港口地区的农业灌溉，对农业发展意义重大。2005年，为恢复厄伊特凯尔克自治州区段运河的自然生态，厄伊特凯尔克市政当局实施了一项工程，将混凝土河堤改成平缓斜坡，再种植一些甘蔗，这样既可以提高堤坝的抗冲蚀能力，也可为那些在密集耕作时期曾一度消失的生物打造栖息地。如今，布兰肯贝赫运河沿岸铺设了道路，便于自行车爱好者和行人通行。

Blaton-Aat Canal

布拉通-艾特运河

A canal located in Belgium. The Blaton-Aat Canal is 22.5 kilometres in length, running from the Nimy-Blaton-Péronnes Canal to Dender. The canal also links Blaton with Aat, with a total height difference of 56 metres. The difference is overcome by 21 locks, 10 upwards on the Blaton-Stambruges route, reaching the summit, and 11 down on the Beloeil-Aat route. This canal played a significant role in transportation in the years before World War I, when around 1-million-ton freight, mainly coal, was transported yearly. However, it has been dormant

比利时运河。布拉通—艾特运河全长22.5千米，连接布拉通和艾特，始于尼米—布拉通—佩隆内斯运河，终于丹德河。布拉通和艾特之间水位落差为56米，落差通过21座船闸来调节，其中10座船闸建于布拉通至斯坦布鲁日的河段，通至运河最高处，另外11座船闸建于贝莱尔—艾特河段。第一次世界大战之前，布拉通—艾特运河一直发挥着重要的交通运输功能，当时年货

for a long time and was not used for transportation during the last 20 years.

运量高达100万吨，其中主要是煤炭运输。但近20年来，该运河已不再用于交通运输。

Blavet Canal

A canal located in France. The Blavet Canal is connected with the Nantes-Brest Canal at Pontivy and runs to Hennebont with a length of 60 kilometres. In 1802, Napoleon gave the order to construct the canal to provide access to the town of Pontivy for its strategic military importance. The construction began in 1804 and ended in 1825. A comprehensive rehabilitation project was carried out between 2002 and 2005, and now the canal is again fully operational.

布拉韦运河

法国运河。布拉韦运河与南特—布雷斯特运河在蓬蒂维镇交汇，最终流至埃讷邦市，全长60千米。1802年，为连接战略重镇蓬蒂维，拿破仑下令开凿该运河。运河1804年开凿，1825年竣工。2002—2005年间，布拉韦运河全面升级改造，现已完全恢复通航。

B. L. Tijdens Canal

A canal located in the east of Groningen, the Netherlands. Also called United Canal. The B.L. Tijdens Canal is named after Boelo Luitjen Tijdens, a Dutch politician who initiated the construction of this canal. The canal is about 15.5 kilometres long, and it starts from the Ruiten-Aa Canal and the Mussel-Aa Canal to the Westerwoldse River. The canal was used for cargo shipping in the past, but since 2005 it has allowed access for pleasure craft. The primary function of the canal is the drainage of Westerwolde. The B.L. Tijdens Canal was a part of the canalization plan for Westerwolde, which suffered tremendously from flooding in the early 20th century due to the excessive cultivation and digging peat resources of the Bourtange Swamp. Surplus

蒂登运河

荷兰格罗宁根省东部运河。亦称联合运河。蒂登运河得名于该运河工程的重要发起人荷兰政治家布洛·勒伊琴·蒂登。运河全长约15.5千米，始于吕滕—阿河运河和米瑟尔—阿河运河，终于韦斯特沃尔德河。蒂登运河曾用于货运，2005年起允许游船通行。蒂登运河作为韦斯特沃尔德运河规划的一部分，其主要功能是满足韦斯特沃尔德市的排水需求。早前，由于过度耕种和开挖布尔唐赫沼泽的泥炭资源，韦斯特沃尔德在20世纪初遭受洪灾之苦。蒂登运河修建后，可将多余的水迅速排出。在该

water could be drained quickly with the construction of canals. A lock was built on the canal, namely, the Vriescheloo Lock. At this lock, a monument was erected for Boelo Luitjen Tijdens.

运河的弗里斯切洛船闸上竖立着布洛·勒伊琴·蒂登纪念碑。

Blyth Navigation

A canal located in Suffolk, England, the United Kingdom. The Blyth Navigation is 11 kilometres in length and has 6 locks, stretching from Halesworth to the North Sea at Southwold. The construction began in 1757 and was completed in 1761. In the early 19th century, the construction of embankments reclaimed the salt flats below the Blythburgh Bridge. The project resulted in the deposition of silt and thus the deterioration of the navigation condition of Southwold Harbour. In 1879, the Southwold Railway came into service, impacting the traffic on the Blyth Navigation. In 1884, the Commissioners claimed that the Blyth Navigation was no longer profitable, and the maintenance would not continue. In 1894, the Commissioners voted to ask the Board of Trade for a warrant to abandon the navigation. The canal was used occasionally until 1911. The abandonment took effect in 1934. Though sporadic efforts have been made to restore the canal, it has never been reopened for navigation since then.

布莱斯航海运河

英国英格兰萨福克郡运河。布莱斯航海运河全长11千米，始于黑尔斯沃思，在绍斯沃尔德注入北海，航道上建有6座船闸。运河1757年开凿，1761年竣工通航。19世纪早期，因在布莱斯堡桥下的盐滩上修建河堤，运河中泥沙沉积，导致绍斯沃尔德港口通航条件恶化。1879年，绍斯沃尔德铁路开通，极大地冲击了布莱斯航海运河的航运业务，运河使用率明显下降。1884年，该运河理事会宣称布莱斯航海运河已不再盈利，并计划停止该运河的常规维护。1894年，运河理事会投票表决，请求贸易委员会授权弃用该运河。1911年以前，布莱斯航海运河上偶有船只通行。1934年，该运河正式停航。虽然陆续有人提议对布莱斯航海运河进行整修，但运河一直未能恢复通航。

Bobota Canal

A canal located in Croatia. The Bobota Canal is 50.7 kilometres in length. The construction of the canal was started in the early 19th century. It has

博博塔运河

克罗地亚运河。博博塔运河全长50.7千米，19世纪初开凿。运河对周边地区的灌溉和住地防洪发挥

a critical role in irrigation and flood protection for settlements in the nearby regions. For this reason, it is ranked in the first-class channels in Croatia. Teeming with quality fish resources, the canal produces about 1,500 kilogrammes of fishes annually.

重要作用，被列为克罗地亚一级航道。博博塔运河中有丰富优质的鱼类资源，年产量近1.5吨。

Bocholt-Herentals Canal

A canal located in Limburg and Antwerp provinces, Belgium. Also called Maas-Schelde Canal. The Bocholt-Herentals Canal is 59 kilometres in length constructed with 7 locks, linking the South Willems Canal with the Albert Canal and the rivers Meuse and Schelde. The predecessor of the canal was the Grand North Canal (1810), of which only a few stretches were constructed. The construction was started in 1843 under the direction of the engineer Kümmer and finished in 1846. The enlargement project was started in 1928 with the discovery of shale coal deposits. The canal was used for shipping and irrigating the dry Kempen region. The canal's role in transportation was reduced later with the completion of the Albert Canal that had a larger shipping capacity. Now, the Bocholt-Herentals Canal is popular for cycling.

博霍尔特-海伦塔尔斯运河

比利时林堡省和安特卫普省跨境运河。亦称马斯—斯海尔德运河。博霍尔特—海伦塔尔斯运河全长59千米，河上建有7座船闸，连通南威廉斯运河与阿尔贝特运河，也连通默兹河与斯海尔德河。博霍尔特—海伦塔尔斯运河的前身是1810年开凿的北方大运河，但该运河仅开凿几段即终止。1843年，博霍尔特—海伦塔尔斯运河在工程师库默尔的指导下开凿，1846年竣工。1928年，由于页岩煤矿床被发现，运河得以拓宽，用于航运和灌溉干旱的肯彭地区。后来，由于修成了航运能力更强的阿尔贝特运河，博霍尔特—海伦塔尔斯运河的航运功能被削弱。如今，该运河河岸成为自行车骑行胜地。

Boeung Trabek Canal

A canal located in Phnom Penh, Cambodia. Also called Boeung Trabek Sewage Canal. The Boeung Trabek Canal runs from the city centre to the

万谷德罗贝运河

柬埔寨金边运河。亦称万谷德罗贝排污运河。万谷德罗贝运河始于金边市中心，终于南部郊区，流

southern outskirts and cuts through 30 city blocks. Built between 1943 and 1958, the canal was initially designed for the service of a city of 500 thousand people. However, it is now under severe strain because the population has approached over two million. Residents face urgent health and safety threats of severe water pollution and chronic flooding resulting from the choked channel. The government has relocated about 400 households along the banks.

经30个街区。该运河修建于1943—1958年间，主要目的是满足当时金边市50万人口的生活需求。如今，金边人口已增长至200多万，这使得万谷德罗贝运河不堪重负。废弃物排放导致运河严重污染，由于河道常年堵塞，运河丧失了排洪抗灾功能，当地居民的健康和安全受到严重威胁。目前，当地政府已搬迁安置沿岸约400户居民。

Boeung Trabek Sewage Canal

万谷德罗贝排污运河

A canal located in Phnom Penh, Cambodia. See Boeung Trabek Canal.

柬埔寨金边运河。见万谷德罗贝运河。

Boghra Irrigation Canal

波哥拉灌溉运河

A canal located in Helmand Province, Afghanistan. The Boghra Irrigation Canal is 155 kilometres in length, conveying water from the Helmand River and the Arghandab Valley to cultivated fields. In the 1950s, this waterway was constructed, and it is now under the maintenance of the Helmand and Arghandab Valley Authority.

阿富汗赫尔曼德省运河。波哥拉灌溉运河全长155千米，将赫尔曼德河与阿尔甘达卜河谷的水引向农田。20世纪50年代，运河开凿。波哥拉灌溉运河今由赫尔曼德省与阿尔甘达卜河流域当局管理。

Boicelli Canal

博采里运河

A canal located in Emilia-Romagna, Italy. The Boicelli Canal is 5.5 kilometres long. As a part of the Waterway of Ferrara, it flows from south to north and links the Po di Volano and the Po. It has an elevation of 4 metres.

意大利艾米利亚—罗马涅大区运河。博采里运河长5.5千米，是费拉拉航道的一部分，自南向北流动，连通波河博拉诺支线运河与波河。博采里运河海拔高度为4米。

Boko-Zowla Canal

A canal located in southeastern Togo. The Boko-Zowla Canal has a total length of 5 kilometres, connecting the Boko River with Lake Zowla. Most of Lake Zowla's water is fed by the Boko River, which originates from east Togo, somewhere near the border with Benin. Regions near the Boko River once enjoyed a thriving fishing economy, but it gradually declined with the population increase. The expanding population, along with the overuse of soil and chemical fertilizers in agriculture, ultimately led to silt build-up and grass invasion along waterways. Meanwhile, residents there constantly suffered from flooding. The World Bank then involved the Boko-Zowla Canal in the Integrated Disaster and Land Management project (IDLM). The Global Facility for Disaster Reduction and Recovery (GFDRR) and Global Environment Facility (GEF) of the World Bank provided total financial support of $90,000 to back up the dredging and cleaning of the Boko-Zowla Canal. Aided by the technical guidance from local agencies, this project officially commenced in November 2010 and was accomplished in early 2014. The local residents have devoted themselves to this labour-intensive project as well. Their effort has paid off. Floods were significantly reduced; fishing and agricultural activities went back to normal. This project has exerted significant influence upon not only local people's lives but also the surrounding environment.

博科－祖拉运河

多哥共和国东南部运河。博科－祖拉运河连通博科河与祖拉湖，全长5千米。博科河发源于多哥东部靠近贝宁边境之处，为祖拉湖重要水源。博科河流域渔业一度非常兴旺，但随着人口增长，出现土地过度开垦、滥用化肥等农业问题，最终河流堵塞，河道水草疯长，当地渔业也随之衰落。此外，当地居民还时常遭受洪水侵袭的困扰。为解决这些问题，世界银行将博科－祖拉运河的疏浚清理工程列入综合灾难与土地管理项目。

"全球减灾与恢复"基金及"全球环境"基金为该项目提供共计9万美元的资金支持。在当地相关机构的技术指导下，运河疏浚清理项目于2010年11月正式开始，2014年初全部清理完毕。在此过程中，当地居民也积极加入疏浚工作，并取得了积极成效。运河疏通后，洪水不再频发，渔业和农作也随之恢复正常。博科－祖拉运河的疏浚清理项目极大地改善了当地人的生活和生存环境。

Bols Canal

A canal located in the province of Friesland, the Netherlands. See Harlingen Canal.

Bolswarderzeil Canal

A canal located in the province of Friesland, the Netherlands. See Wijmerts Canal.

Bolsward Trek Canal

A canal located in the province of Friesland, the Netherlands. With a total length of 22 kilometres, the Bolsward Trek Canal starts in Bolsward, flows towards the northeast and joins the Van Harinxma Canal. The construction of the canal began in 1638 to connect several existing waterways.

Bossuit-Kortrijk Canal

A canal located in the south of West Flanders Province, Belgium. The Bossuit-Kortrijk Canal is 15.4 kilometres long and connects the Schelde with the Leie. It is mainly used to transport raw materials and functions as an essential link in the Flemish and European waterways network. In 1857, a company was founded to construct the canal to transport raw materials from Écaussinnes, Soignies and Tournai by waterway without making a detour of 138 kilometres to Ghent. The original plan included constructing 18 bridges, 11 locks, a pumping station and a 611-metre-long tunnel in Moen. In 1860, the

博尔斯运河

荷兰弗里斯兰省运河。见哈灵根运河。

博尔斯瓦德宰尔运河

荷兰弗里斯兰省运河。见韦默尔茨运河。

博尔斯瓦德拖船运河

荷兰弗里斯兰省运河。博尔斯瓦德拖船运河全长22千米，始于博尔斯瓦德，东北流向，汇入范哈林克斯马运河。该运河1638年开凿，目的是连通当时已有的数条航道。

博斯奥特－科特赖克运河

比利时西佛兰德省运河。博斯奥特－科特赖克运河全长15.4千米，连通斯海尔德河和莱厄河，主要用以运输原材料，是佛兰德和欧洲航道网中的重要航道。1857年，为避免从根特市绕道138千米，直接通过水路从埃考辛斯尼市、苏涅尼市和图尔奈市运输原材料，成立了挖掘新运河的公司。最初计划在穆恩村建造18座桥、11座船闸、1个泵站和1条611米长的隧道。1860年，运河竣工，次年2月7日通

construction was finished. On 7 February 1861, the canal was opened for its first navigation. The level of the canal is artificially maintained by a pumping station in Bossuit. Only ships under a draught of 1.8 metres and a mass of 300 tons were allowed on the canal. The numerous locks, the narrow tunnel and the limited draught highly restricted the canal from being fully capitalized on. In the 1970s, the section between Bossuit and the Kortrijk-Harelbeke industrial area was modernized, making it accessible for ships up to 1,350 tons. From the 20th century, 3 locks in Kortrijk were classified as national industrial heritage and began to be protected. Today, Seine Schelde Vlaanderen proposed a reconstruction project to adapt the canal for future needs, allowing larger ships to navigate between the industrial area Kortrijk-Harelbeke and the Leie. The project is currently in the research phase.

航。运河水位由博斯奥特市的泵站人工维持,且只能通航吃水深度最大1.8米、重量不超过300吨的船舶。因船闸众多、通道狭窄和吃水深度有限,该运河的功能不能充分发挥。20世纪70年代,博斯奥特市到科特赖克—哈勒尔贝克工业区的航道进行了现代化改造,可通航1 350吨的船舶。20世纪以来,位于科特赖克市的3座船闸被列为比利时国家工业遗产并受到保护。如今,为使运河满足未来需求,更大的船舶得以在科特赖克—哈勒尔贝克工业区和莱厄河的航道通行,佛兰德省塞纳斯海尔德项目提出运河改造计划,该计划目前正处于调研阶段。

Boter Canal

伯特运河

A canal located in the province of Groningen, the Netherlands. With a length of 25 kilometres, the Boter Canal connects the port of Uithuizen with the Van Starkenborgh Canal. Its name is presumably owed to its history of transporting milk products. The canal was built in the 17th century, with a maximal utilization of those then existing waterways. The oldest part, from Bedum to Groningen, which had been invariably referred to on maps as the Cleisloot, dates back to 1625. In 1660, it was extended to Kantens. Most of the sections were filled in the 20th century.

荷兰格罗宁根省运河。伯特运河全长25千米,从厄伊特赫伊曾港口一直延伸至范斯塔肯博赫运河。据说该运河因其曾用于奶制品运输而得名。伯特运河于17世纪开凿,最大限度地利用当时已有的航道。其中从贝杜姆到格罗宁根的这段航道最为古老,其历史可追溯至1625年,地图上一直称之为"克雷索鲁特"。1660年,这一河段扩延至坎滕斯。20世纪时,伯特运河大部分河段均被回填。

Bourbourg Canal

A canal located in northern France. The Bourbourg Canal connects the river Aa with the port facilities of Dunkirk in the Nord department. It is 21 kilometres long and has 3 locks. Its route can be divided into three sections: the western section, between the valley of the Aa and the high-capacity waterway of Dunkirk-Schelde; the middle section, as a part of the Dunkirk-Schelde, a commercial shipping route; the eastern section, between Spycker and the port of Dunkirk. In 1670, Louis XIV issued a decree to build the canal. In 1679, the construction of this canal began with Vauban as its engineer.

Brandenburg City Canal

A canal located in the state of Brandenburg, Germany. The Brandenburg City Canal is 4 kilometres long. It starts at the upstream of the river Havel and finally flows back towards the lower level of the river. As its name would indicate, its entire length lies in the city of Brandenburg an der Havel. Currently, due to its limited size, what remains on the canal is primarily leisure traffic.

Brault Maritime Canal

A canal located in the Charente-Maritime department of France. See Marans Ship Canal.

布尔堡运河

法国北部运河。布尔堡运河连接阿河和诺尔省的敦刻尔克港口，全长21千米，河上建有3座船闸。该运河航道可分为3段：西段连接阿河河谷和承载量巨大的敦刻尔克—斯海尔德运河；中段是敦刻尔克—斯海尔德商运航道的一部分；东段连接斯皮凯和敦刻尔克港口。1670年，路易十四下令修建布尔堡运河。1679年，运河工程开始动工修建，由沃邦担任工程师。

勃兰登堡市运河

德国勃兰登堡州运河。勃兰登堡市运河全长4千米，始于勃兰登堡哈弗尔河上游，最终流回哈弗尔河下游水域。如其名所示，该运河全段位于哈弗尔河畔勃兰登堡市市区内。限于运河规模，如今运河上主要通行观光船只。

布劳特通海运河

法国滨海夏朗德省运河。见马朗通海运河。

Brecknock and Abergavenny Canal

A canal located in South Wales, the United Kingdom. The Brecknock and Abergavenny Canal was 56.3 kilometres in length with 6 locks. It started from Pontymoile and ended at a basin in Brecon. It was firstly proposed in 1792 and constructed from 1795 to 1799. The Brecknock and Abergavenny Canal was opened in stages between 1797 and 1812. In 1865, it was acquired by the Monmouthshire Canal. Now the canal is mainly for water transport and leisure use.

布雷克诺克－阿伯加文尼运河

英国南威尔士运河。布雷克诺克－阿伯加文尼运河全长56.3千米，河上建有6座船闸。该运河始于庞蒂米尔区，最终抵达布雷肯的一处内湾。运河开凿的设想最早于1792年提出，1795—1799年间开凿，1797—1812年间分期通航。1865年，该运河并入蒙茅斯郡运河。如今，布雷克诺克－阿伯加文尼运河主要供水运和休闲娱乐之用。

Bree Canal

A canal located in the Netherlands. Originally designed to flow from Gouda to Bodegraven, the Bree Canal was probably excavated between 1340 and 1350. The village Reeuwijk Bridge sprang up along the canal and gradually developed into an essential centre for peat extraction. Today, replaced by road transportation, the Bree Canal has lost its importance as a crucial route between Gouda and Bodegraven. The adjusted canal runs northward from the end of the Karnemelk Trench along the Steijnkaden and the Oostboezemkade. Along the canal are many shops, parks, schools, recreational areas and clubs, instilling modern air in the medieval canal.

布里运河

荷兰运河。布里运河1340—1350年间开凿，最初设计的路线是从豪达市流向博德赫拉芬市。布里运河修成之后，一个名叫雷韦克桥的村庄沿河发展起来，之后成为重要的泥炭开采中心。布里运河曾经是豪达市和博德赫拉芬市之间的核心通道，如今，这一地位已被陆路运输取代。该运河航道调整后，从卡纳梅尔克渠的一端出发，沿施泰因加登镇和奥斯特波则姆卡达大街一路向北。布里运河沿岸分布着众多商店、公园、学校、俱乐部和其他休闲区域，为这条源于中世纪的运河注入现代感。

Briare Canal

A canal located in France. The Briare Canal is one of the oldest French canals. As a part of the Bourbonnais route, the Briare Canal is 57 kilometres in length, linking the Loire and Seine valleys. The canal is equipped with 36 locks and 9 reservoirs. Because of the shortage of water in the reservoirs and the Loire valley, the Briare Canal was annually closed for 2 to 3 months. Supported by Henry IV, the construction of the canal was started in 1604 with the aim to promote the grain trade and reduce food shortage. The construction was completed in 1642. Apart from being a channel to support trades in timber and coal, the canal was also known for its flourishing wine business in history. By the mid-18th century, about 500 wine barges had worked on the canal to bring wine from the vineyards of Burgundy and Languedoc to northen cities, and they were all hauled manually. The canal was purchased by the State in 1860. It was then decided it should be linked with the Loire Lateral Canal. For this purpose, the Briare Aqueduct, the longest metallic canal bridge in Europe, was constructed over the Loire in Briare between 1890 and 1896 by the engineer Abel Mazoyer. The impressive aqueduct is 11.5 metres in width and 662.7 metres in length, constructed on 14 piers, which support a single metal beam carrying a trough with more than 13,000 tonnes of water, 2.2 metres deep and 6 metres wide allowing boats with a 1.8 metres draught to cross.

布里亚尔运河

法国最古运河之一。布里亚尔运河是波旁奈依运河航线的一部分,全长57千米,连接卢瓦尔河谷和塞纳河谷。运河上建有36座船闸,9座水库。每年水库和卢瓦尔河谷缺水时,布里亚尔运河就会进入2—3个月的闭航期。1604年,为了应对食物短缺问题,促进粮食贸易,在亨利四世的支持下,布里亚尔运河开始修建,1642年竣工。历史上除运输木材和煤炭,运河上的葡萄酒航运业务也曾很红火。至18世纪中期,共计约有500只人工拖运驳船专门将来自勃艮第和郎格多克地区的葡萄酒运至北方城市。1860年,布里亚尔运河被政府收购。1890—1896年间,为连通卢瓦尔旁侧运河,工程师埃布尔·玛泽耶主持在布里亚尔的卢瓦河上建立布里亚尔渡槽。渡槽宽11.5米,长662.7米,建在14个石墩上,石墩支撑着金属横梁,其上架设水槽,水槽中的水重13 000余吨,深2.2米,宽6米,可容吃水深度1.8米的船只通行。

Bricktown Canal

A canal located in Oklahoma, the United States. The Bricktown Canal is a short waterway with a length of 1.6 kilometres. Completed and opened in 1999, the canal was first improved in 2004 and then in 2013. The construction of the canal cost about 23 million dollars. Now, it is maintained by Oklahoma City Parks and Recreation Department. The city used to clean up the canal once in five years, but they now plan on it once every three years. The canal serves as an integral part of downtown Oklahoma City both for locals and visitors. It boasts numerous restaurants, shops as well as hiking and bicycling trails along the bank. People can also take a water taxi to enjoy the scenery and various activities there. The canal plays a pivotal role in enhancing local economy and tourism. In 2019, a series of activities were held to celebrate the 20th anniversary of the canal. Nowadays, various programmes and plans are in the pipeline along the canal.

布里克敦运河

美国俄克拉荷马州运河。布里克敦运河河道较短，全长约1.6千米。运河于1999年竣工通航，累计投入约2 300万美元，后于2004年修缮，并于2013年再次修缮。布里克敦运河目前由俄克拉荷马市公园和休闲局负责日常管理。此前，俄克拉荷马市每五年对运河进行一次疏浚，现在计划每三年一次。对于当地居民和前来参观的游客来说，布里克敦运河都是俄克拉荷马市中心不可或缺的重要部分。运河沿岸有许多餐馆和商店，同时也是人们徒步健身和骑行的理想路线。人们还可以乘坐水上出租船去欣赏沿岸美景，参加丰富的活动。布里克敦运河对促进当地经济及旅游业的发展功不可没。2019年，当地居民举办了一系列活动来庆祝运河开凿20周年。目前，布里克敦运河沿岸仍有大量建设项目正在进行。

Bridgewater Canal

A privately-owned canal located in northwestern England, the United Kingdom. Linking Runcorn, Manchester and Leigh, the Bridgewater Canal is 66 kilometres in length. With the aim of shipping coal from the mines in Worsley to Manchester, Francis Egerton, the 3rd Duke of Bridgewater, authorized

布里奇沃特运河

英格兰西北部私有运河。布里奇沃特运河全长66千米，连接朗科恩镇、曼彻斯特市和利镇。早前为了把煤从沃斯利镇运至曼彻斯特市，第三代布里奇沃特公爵弗朗西斯·埃杰顿授权开凿该运河。1761

the construction of this canal. In 1761, the section from Worsley to Manchester was put into service. In the next year, the canal was extended from Manchester to Runcorn, and before long the section from Worsley to Leigh was also constructed. The Bridgewater Canal stands as a crucial linkage within a network of waterways. It is linked to the Rochdale Canal in Manchester, the Trent and Mersey Canal at Preston Brook, southeast of Runcorn, the Leeds and Liverpool Canal at Leigh and the Manchester Ship Canal at Cornbrook via a lock. Due to the success of the Bridgewater Canal, a large number of canals were constructed in Britain at that time, which was referred to as "canal mania." Later, despite the fierce competition from the Liverpool and Manchester Railway and the Macclesfield Canal, the Bridgewater Canal keeps being navigable all the time. It is one of the few canals in Britain that are not under a state ownership. The canal has been allowing the passage of pleasure craft since 1952. The Bridgewater Canal is now viewed as an integral part of the Cheshire Ring network of canals.

Bridgwater and Taunton Canal

An inland canal located in the southwest of England, the United Kingdom. The Bridgwater and Taunton Canal is 23.3 kilometres in length, with 7 locks. The canal links River Tone to River Parrett, passing through the unique lowland areas of Somerset. The canal was constructed from 1822 and opened in 1827. Later in 1837, a further act was issued authorising its extension from Huntworth to

年，沃斯利镇至曼彻斯特市河段开通，次年，该运河扩建至朗科恩镇，不久之后，沃斯利镇至利镇的河段也得到修建。布里奇沃特运河位置优越，连通诸多航道，如在曼彻斯特市对接罗奇代尔运河，在朗科恩镇东南部的普雷斯顿布鲁克村与特伦特—默西运河相连，在利镇与利兹和利物浦运河相交，同时还通过科恩布鲁克村的船闸连接曼彻斯特通海运河。布里奇沃特运河的成功开凿引发了所谓的"运河热"现象，英国其他地方纷纷效仿。后虽面临来自利物浦至曼彻斯特铁路以及麦克尔斯菲尔德运河的激烈竞争，布里奇沃特运河一直保持通航。该运河是英国少数没有国有化的运河之一。自1952年以来，该运河一直允许游艇航行。如今，布里奇沃特运河已是柴郡运河网必不可少的组成部分。

布里奇沃特－汤顿运河

英国英格兰西南部内陆运河。布里奇沃特—汤顿运河全长23.3千米，流经萨默塞特独特的低洼地带，连通托恩河与帕雷特河，沿线建有7座船闸。该运河1822年开凿，1827年通航。1837年经新法案批准，运河从亨特沃思延伸至布里奇沃特。1907年，运河上的商业航运终止。

Bridgwater. The year 1907 witnessed the cessation of commercial traffic on the canal. During World War II, the Bridgwater and Taunton Canal served as one of the major defence lines. In 1962, the canal became one of the first canals to commercially carry potable water for Wessex Water. At present, the canal is still used for the transport of drinking water for people in Bridgwater. It also helps to relieve the local flood. In winter, it takes water from River Tone at Taunton and discharges it into the Parrett. Nowadays, the canal has been fully restored by British Waterways and its infrastructure is well preserved.

第二次世界大战期间，布里奇沃特—汤顿运河还充当了一条主要防线。从1962年开始，该运河根据商业协议向威塞克斯水务公司输送饮用水。如今，布里奇沃特—汤顿运河仍然为布里奇沃特市运送饮用水。洪水到来时，运河还可泄洪。冬季可通过该运河将汤顿市托恩河的河水排入帕雷特河。目前，在英国航道局的主持下，布里奇沃特—汤顿运河已经得到完全修复，其基础设施也保存良好。

Bridoire Canal

布里多瓦运河

A canal located near the western shore of France. See Charente-Seudre Canal.

法国西部海岸运河。见夏朗德—瑟德尔运河。

Briegden-Neerharen Canal

比利赫登－尼尔哈伦运河

A canal located in the province of Limburg, Belgium. The Briegden-Neerharen Canal, with a length of 4.8 kilometres and a total elevation difference of 20 metres, originates from Briegden, ends at Neerharen and connects the Albert Canal to the South Willems Canal. The canal, constructed between 1930 and 1934, had two functions. Firstly, it served as a water-supply channel for the Kempen canals. Kempen is located in northeastern Belgium and southeastern Netherlands, and the Kempen canals refer to the 7 canals built between 1820 and 1940 in the Belgian part of Kempen. The canal made the water supply for the Kempen canals independent

比利时林堡省运河。比利赫登—尼尔哈伦运河全长4.8千米，总落差20米，始于比利赫登镇，止于尼尔哈伦镇，连通阿尔贝特运河和南威廉斯运河。运河建于1930—1934年间，具有两个主要功能。首先，比利赫登—尼尔哈伦运河是肯彭运河网的供水通道。肯彭地区位于比利时东北部和荷兰东南部，肯彭运河网由比利时在该地区1820—1940年间所开挖的7条运河组成。比利赫登—尼尔哈伦运河的建成使得肯彭运河网摆脱了

from the Netherlands. Secondly, the canal served as a military defence structure. Several bunkers were built and 8 of them can still be seen today. Nowadays, there are 2 locks over the Briegden-Neerharen Canal, both of which are 55 metres in length and 7.5 metres in width, dealing with an elevation difference of 8.4 metres and 8.8 metres respectively.

对荷兰供水的依赖。其次, 比利赫登—尼尔哈伦运河曾是一个军事防御设施, 沿河建有多个掩体, 其中8个掩体至今仍然可见。如今, 运河上建有2座长55米、宽7.5米的船闸, 分别应对8.4米和8.8米的水位落差。

Brienne Canal

布里耶纳运河

A canal located in the centre of Toulouse, Haute-Garonne, France. Also called Saint-Pierre Canal. The Brienne Canal connects the Garonne with the Midi Canal and has an approximate length of 1.6 kilometres and 2 locks. It serves as a feeding channel for the Garonne Canal. Authorized by the government of Languedoc in 1760, the construction of the canal was started in 1765 and finished in 1775. The name Brienne Canal is in honour of Etienne Charles de Loménie de Brienne (1727—1794), archbishop of Toulouse. When the canal was finished, the Ponts-Jumeaux (Twin Bridges) were erected. Eighty-one years later, the Twin Bridges became "triple bridges" but retained its original name.

法国上加龙省图卢兹市中心运河。亦称圣皮埃尔运河。布里耶纳运河连通加龙河和米迪运河, 全长约1.6千米, 有2座船闸, 为加龙运河的引水运河。1760年, 朗格多克联合政府决定开凿布里耶纳运河, 工程于1765年开始, 1775年竣工。运河取名布里耶纳, 是为纪念图卢兹大主教艾蒂安—夏尔·德·洛梅尼·德·布里耶纳(1727—1794)。布里耶纳运河建成后, 修建了一座双子桥, 即瑞莫桥。81年后, 尽管双子桥变成了"三子桥", 但仍沿用原名。

Bristol Feeder Canal

布里斯托尔引水运河

A canal located in Bristol of England, the United Kingdom. The Bristol Feeder Canal, links the Floating Harbour in the west with the river Avon in the east. The canal expands from Netham Lock to Totterdown Basin. At present, along the canal, remains of industrial warehouses can still be seen.

英国英格兰布里斯托尔市运河。布里斯托尔引水运河从那萨姆船闸一直延伸至托特当内湾, 东段与埃文河相通, 西段与浮动港相通。布里斯托尔引水运河沿岸还留存着从前的工业厂房遗迹。

Brittany's Canal System

A canal system located in Brittany, northwestern France. The Brittany's Canal System mainly includes the Nantes-Brest Canal, the Aulne River and the Blavet River. The Nantes-Brest Canal connects the two seaports of Nantes and Brest through inland Brittany. It was built in the early 19th century, with a total length of 385 kilometres and 238 locks. The Aulne River is 144 kilometres long, and is one part of the Nantes-Brest Canal. The Blavet River flows from central Brittany and flows into the Atlantic Ocean on the south coast near Lorient. It is 148.9 kilometres in length, connects with the Nantes-Brest Canal at Pontivy, and flows to Hennebont. Brittany began constructing its waterway network in 1538 when it decided to enhance navigation on the river Vilaine. The project for a canal throughout the province was put forward by an inland naviga-tion commission convoked in 1783. When Brest was blocked by the English fleet, Napoleon decided to build the canal to provide a safe inland link be-tween the two largest military ports of the French Atlantic front. The Nantes-Brest Canal was closed as a through route in 1920 but is still navigable over a part of its length. In addition, the Blavet River is canalized for most of its length, which has little recreational traffic because of the great number of locks in the watershed part of the Nantes-Brest Canal between Pontivy and Rohan, and the obstacle of Guerlédan Dam to the west. Today, boats from Nantes via Redon have to take the Blavet Canal to reach the ocean near Lorient.

布列塔尼运河网

法国西北部布列塔尼大区运河网。布列塔尼运河网主要包括南特—布雷斯特运河、奥讷河和布拉韦河。南特—布雷斯特运河位于布列塔尼大区的内陆地区，连接南特和布雷斯特两个城市的海港。该运河修建于19世纪早期，全长385千米，共建有238座船闸。奥讷河全长144千米，属于南特—布雷斯特运河的一部分。布拉韦河的起点位于布列塔尼大区中部，全长148.9千米，在蓬蒂维市与南特—布雷斯特运河交汇后流向埃讷邦市，在洛里昂市附近的南海岸注入大西洋。1538年，布列塔尼大区决定改善维莱讷河的航运状况，因此开始发展全区的运河系统。1783年，布列塔尼的内陆航运委员会提出修建运河网的计划。后来，布雷斯特遭到英国舰队封锁，拿破仑决定修建运河，目的是在法国大西洋前线两个最大的军事港口之间开设一条安全的内陆航运通道。南特—布雷斯特运河于1920年起不再用作航线，但部分河段仍然可通航。布拉韦河的大部分河段都已修建成通航的运河。由于蓬蒂维和罗昂之间的南特—布雷斯特运河分水部分有多处船闸，且西面受阻于盖尔莱当大坝，布拉韦河很少供娱乐休闲船只通行。如今，从南特出发、经由雷登的船只必须通过布拉韦河的运河河段才能到达洛里昂，抵达大西洋。

Brittany's Siberia   布列塔尼的西伯利亚

A canal located in northern France. See Nantes-Brest Canal.

法国北部运河。见南特—布雷斯特运河。

Britz Branch Canal   布里茨支线运河

A canal located in Berlin, Germany. See Britz Canal.

德国柏林运河。见布里茨运河。

Britz Canal   布里茨运河

A canal located in Berlin, Germany. Formerly called Britz Branch Canal. The 3.4-kilometre-long Britz Canal has no lock. Built between 1900 and 1906, it shortens the route for shipping from the Teltow Canal and the Neukölln Ship Canal to the Spree River. Standing on its way are several inner-city ports.

德国柏林运河。旧称布里茨支线运河。布里茨运河于1900—1906年间开凿，全长约3.4千米，未设船闸。布里茨运河修建后缩短了从泰尔托运河和新克尔恩通海运河到施普雷河的航程。沿布里茨运河设有多个内城港口。

Brouage Canal   布鲁瓦日运河

A canal located in Charente-Maritime, France. The Brouage Canal connects the city of Brouage with the Bridoire Canal and runs across an area of ancient salt marshes. It is 2 kilometres in length and has one lock. The construction began in 1782 and was completed in 1807. Originally, the Brouage Canal connected Brouage with Rochefort. It was extended during the Second Empire (1852—1870)

法国滨海夏朗德省运河。布鲁瓦日运河连接布鲁瓦日和布里多瓦运河，流经一片古盐沼地，全长2千米，其上建有1座船闸。该运河1782年开凿，1807年竣工。最初，布鲁瓦日运河连接布鲁瓦日市和罗什福尔市。法兰西第二帝国时期（1852—1870），运河延伸至马雷

to Marennes. Although the canal is now decommissioned, it is better maintained than some channels in service.

Bruche Canal

A canal located in eastern France. The Bruche Canal connects Soultz-les-Bains to the city of Strasbourg. It is 20 kilometres in length and has 11 locks. The construction was started in 1682 by the designer Vauban. The canal made it possible to bring to Strasbourg the sandstone from quarries of Soultz-les-Bains. These stones were necessary for constructing the bastion of the city, which was intended to defend the new frontier of the kingdom on the Rhine. In 1957, the canal was formally closed as the bridges damaged during World War II were insufficiently rebuilt.

Bruges-Ostend Canal

A canal located in Flanders Province, Belgium. The Bruges-Ostend Canal is 24.6 kilometres in length, running from Bruges to Ostend and linking the North Sea to Belgian interior. In Bruges, the canal met with three other canals, the Damme Canal, the Ghent-Bruges Canal and the Baudouin Canal. The construction work began in 1618 and was completed in 1623. Since the 1760s, this waterway had been mainly used for navigation and drainage for polders. From 1795 to 1830, it became unnavigable for lack of maintenance. Then in the 1960s, the Belgian government repaired and widened it. Today, it

讷市。目前，布鲁瓦日运河虽已停航，但比某些尚在通航的运河维护得更好。

布鲁基运河

法国东部运河。布鲁基运河连接索兹莱斯班和斯特拉斯堡市，全长20千米，其上建有11座船闸。1682年，设计师沃邦带领人们开凿运河。布鲁基运河开通后，大量砂岩可从索兹莱斯班的采石场运往斯特拉斯堡，用以建造位于莱茵河畔的边境防御堡垒。因第二次世界大战期间被摧毁的桥梁未能完全修复，布鲁基运河于1957年正式停航。

布鲁日－奥斯坦德运河

比利时佛兰德省运河。布鲁日－奥斯坦德运河全长24.6千米，始于布鲁日市，流向奥斯坦德市，连通北海与比利时内地，与达默运河、根特－布鲁日运河、博杜安运河等3条运河交汇于布鲁日市。布鲁日－奥斯坦德运河于1618年开凿，1623年完工。18世纪60年代以来，运河主要作用是通航和圩田排水。1795—1830年间，运河由于缺乏维护而无法通航。到了20世纪60年代，比利时政府修复并拓宽了运

is navigable for vessels up to 2,000 tons (Class IV) and occupies a significant position in the transportation between Bruges and Ostend.

河。如今, 布鲁日—奥斯坦德运河可供最大载重量达2 000吨（即四级）的船舶通行, 这对布鲁日和奥斯坦德两个城市间的交通运输意义重大。

Bruges-Sluis Canal

布鲁日－斯勒伊斯运河

A cross-border canal located in Europe. Also known as Damme Canal. The Bruges-Sluis Canal is about 15 kilometres long, linking Bruges in Belgium with Sluis, a border town in the Netherlands. It was excavated on the orders of Napoleon Bonaparte, and hence also called Napoleon Canal. This tree-lined canal is a popular cruising route to see the beautiful city of Bruges.

欧洲跨国运河。亦称达默运河。布鲁日—斯勒伊斯运河全长约15千米, 连接比利时的布鲁日市与荷兰的斯勒伊斯镇。该运河受拿破仑之命修建, 故又称拿破仑运河。布鲁日—斯勒伊斯运河两岸绿树成荫, 风景优美, 是布鲁日的热点观光路线。

Brugge-Zeebrugge Canal

布吕赫－泽布吕赫运河

A canal located in Belgium. The Brugge-Zeebrugge Canal is 12 kilometres long and 7 metres deep, with its width ranging from 20 metres to 110 metres. The canal has one lock. It joins the North Sea in Zeebrugge, and the Gent-Oostende Canal in Brugge, thus connecting Brugge with the North Sea. In the 9th century, Brugge was a Viking settlement downstream of the Rhine River, and soon became an important international port because of its geographical proximity to the North Sea. In the 14th century, it became one of the largest commercial ports in Europe. In 1896, a large-scale dredging programme was carried out here, which was finished in 1907, known as Brugge-Zeebrugge Canal. It runs

比利时运河。布吕赫—泽布吕赫运河全长12千米, 深7米, 最窄处为20米, 最宽处110米, 建有1座船闸。运河于泽布吕赫商港与北海相接, 于布吕赫市与根特—奥斯坦德运河相通, 从而将布吕赫市与北海连接。早在9世纪时, 这里起初是维京人沿莱茵河而下建立的村落。得益于毗邻北海的区位优势, 布吕赫市很快发展成为重要的国际港口。14世纪时, 布吕赫已经成为欧洲最大的商业港口之一。1896年, 一项大规模疏浚工程在此展开, 由此修建成今日的布吕赫—泽

through the entire port area of Brugge-Zeebrugge and connects the Zeebrugse outer harbour with the Brugge inner harbour. It also offers Zeebrugge an inland shipping connection via the Bruges Ring Canal and the Ghent-Bruges Canal. The canal successfully restored Brugge's role as an ocean port in ancient times. In 1953, the canal was renamed the Boudewin Canal, two years after the visit by King Baudouin. Serving as a commercial waterway, the Brugge-Zeebrugge Canal is currently a part of the Waterways of Mainland Europe.

布吕赫运河。运河贯穿布吕赫—泽布吕赫的整个港口区域，1907年通航，连接泽布吕赫外港与布吕赫内港。该运河通过布鲁日环形运河和根特—布鲁日运河，还为泽布吕赫提供了内河航运渠道。布吕赫—泽布吕赫运河修建后，布吕赫市旧时的海洋港口地位得以恢复。1953年，即鲍德温国王访问该运河的两年后，运河更名为鲍德温运河。如今，布吕赫—泽布吕赫运河作为一条商业航道，是欧洲大陆航道网的一部分。

Brunswick-Altamara Canal

不伦瑞克–阿尔塔马哈运河

A canal located in Georgia, the United States. The Brunswick-Altamara Canal is 19.3 kilometres long, connecting the Altamaha River and the city of Brunswick. The proposal of building this canal dates back to 1798. However, the construction was not started until 1836. The project, costing about $450,000, was not completed until the year 1854 due to the financial crisis. The canal was designed to facilitate overland and coastal trade; yet by that time, railway, which was proven to be a far more efficient transportation means, was also built and came into operation. The Brunswick-Altamara Canal was closed in 1860 and gradually fell into abandonment since then.

美国佐治亚州运河。不伦瑞克—阿尔塔马哈运河全长19.3千米，连接阿尔塔玛哈河和佐治亚州的不伦瑞克市。开凿不伦瑞克—阿尔塔马哈运河的提议始于1798年，而实际修建工作于1836年才启动。因工程资金不足，运河直到1854年才竣工并开通，耗资约45万美元。起初，修建运河旨在改善陆路和海岸的货运状况，但由于运河完工时当地已新修了铁路且其运货效率更高，不伦瑞克—阿尔塔马哈运河开通后不久即失去航运价值。1860年运河被迫停航，后来逐渐废弃。

Brussels Canal

A canal located in Belgium. The Brussels Canal is the waterway between the northernmost part of the Brussels Charleroi Canal and the southernmost part of the Brussels-Schelde Maritime Canal. The two canals meet at the Sainctelette area. The Brussels Canal itself is the border between Molenbeek and the city of Brussels. Before the 19th century, the Willebroek Canal was constructed along the western part of the defensive walls of Brussels. Boats could reach the Brussels Port through a series of locks. At present, in the suburbs of Brussels and outside the city, the river Senne still can be seen, but within the city, it mainly runs underground along the west side of the inner ring road, so the river also flows along the Brussels Canal. There are several turning basins in the urban course of the Brussels Canal.

布鲁塞尔运河

比利时运河。布鲁塞尔运河连接布鲁塞尔—沙勒罗瓦运河的最北端与布鲁塞尔—斯海尔德通海运河的最南端，二者在圣科莱特地区交汇。布鲁塞尔运河是莫伦贝克小镇与布鲁塞尔市区的分界线。19世纪前，维勒布鲁克运河沿布鲁塞尔防御墙西段而建，船只通过一系列船闸能到达布鲁塞尔港口。目前，在布鲁塞尔市郊以及城外还可以看到深讷河，但城区内的深讷河主要顺着西侧的内环路从地下流过，其流向与布鲁塞尔运河相同。布鲁塞尔运河的城区航道建有多个回船池。

Brussels-Rupel Canal

An old canal located in Belgium. Also known as Brussels-Rupel Maritime Canal. The Brussels-Rupel Canal runs from Brussels to the Rupel River. In 1997, it was extended to the Schelde.

布鲁塞尔－鲁佩尔运河

比利时古运河。亦称布鲁塞尔—鲁佩尔通海运河。布鲁塞尔—鲁佩尔运河从布鲁塞尔市流向鲁佩尔河。1997年，该运河延伸至斯海尔德河。

Brussels-Rupel Maritime Canal

An old canal located in Belgium. See Brussels-Rupel Canal.

布鲁塞尔－鲁佩尔通海运河

比利时古运河。见布鲁塞尔—鲁佩尔运河。

Brussels-Schelde Sea Canal

A canal located in the city of Brussels, Belgium. Also called Willebroek Canal, or Brussels-Willebroek Canal. The Brussels-Schelde Sea Canal connects Brussel with the Schelde River. Cities along its course include Brussels and Willebroek, where the confluence of the canal and the Rupel River forms. It is 28 kilometres in length, up to 30 metres in width, and 2 metres in depth, with 4 locks to overcome the 14-metre altitude difference. The canal is one of the oldest canals in Belgium and even in Europe. It plays a vital role in oil transportation for Brussels, occupying 30% to 50% of its annual traffic. With 7.7 million tons of goods transported through the canal every year, the Port of Brussels is recognized as the second inland port in Belgium right after the Port of Liège. The construction of the canal was started in 1550 and it took 11 years to complete. Although it was permitted by Philip the Good in 1436, the work was not initiated until Mary of Hungary agreed to begin construction in 1550. The section in Brussels was reconstructed to link the Brussels–Charleroi Canal, which was opened up in 1832, to create a direct channel between the Port of Antwerp and the industrial area of Charleroi. From 1900, the canal began to be modernized. It hosted the rowing events in the 1920 Summer Olympics. In 1965, the canal was upgraded again, with its width broadened from 30 metres to 50 metres and 2 new locks constructed, which enabled the canal to flow directly to the Schelde. In 1974 the annual transport volume had

布鲁塞尔-斯海尔德通海运河

比利时布鲁塞尔运河。亦称维勒布鲁克运河或布鲁塞尔—维勒布鲁克运河。布鲁塞尔—斯海尔德通海运河连接布鲁塞尔市和斯海尔德河，途经布鲁塞尔及维勒布鲁克等城市，在维勒布鲁克市与鲁佩尔河交汇。运河全长28千米，宽达30米，深可达2米，沿线建有4座船闸，用以调节高达14米的水位落差。布鲁塞尔—斯海尔德通海运河是比利时乃至欧洲最古老的运河之一。运河对布鲁塞尔的石油供应起着重要作用，承担了其年度运输量的30%—50%。每年通过该运河运输的货物达770万吨，布鲁塞尔港因此成为比利时第二大内陆港，仅次于列日港。运河于1550年开凿，历时11年完成。虽然早在1436年运河修建工程就得到了"善良的"菲利普的批准，但直到1550年匈牙利女王玛丽亚同意后，运河才得以开凿。后为连接1832年开通的布鲁塞尔—沙勒罗瓦运河，运河的布鲁塞尔河段经过改建，从而在安特卫普港和沙勒罗瓦工业区之间开辟了一条直通航道。1900年起，运河开始现代化改造。1920年夏季奥运会期间，运河上还举办了赛艇比赛。1965年，运河再次升级改造，从30米拓宽到50米，并新建了2座船闸，使运河能够直接流

increased to 14.4 million tonnes.

向斯海尔德河。1974年，运河运输量曾高达1 440万吨。

Brussels-Willebroek Canal

布鲁塞尔-维勒布鲁克运河

A canal located in the city of Brussels, Belgium. See Brussels-Schelde Sea Canal.

比利时布鲁塞尔市运河。见布鲁塞尔—斯海尔德通海运河。

Buckingham Arm

白金汉河湾运河

A canal located in England, the United Kingdom. The Buckingham Arm, 17 kilometres long, flows from Cosgrove, Northamptonshire to Buckingham. It was constructed as an arm of the Grand Junction Canal and it has 2 locks. The canal was built in two separate stages, which began in 1793 and 1794 and ended in 1800 and 1801 respectively. By the 1850s, the competition from railway transportation had affected the operation of the canal. Meanwhile, the canal also suffered from the problems of siltation which was compounded by the disposal of the sewage of Buckingham Corporation. This made the navigation condition deteriorate. In 1890, the Grand Junction Company appealed to legal action to stop the dumping of sewage into the canal. This, however, failed to reduce the momentum of trade decline via the canal. The upper section was claimed to be "barely navigable" by Bradshaw's Guide of 1904. It gradually fell into disuse from 1932 and was thoroughly abandoned in 1964. Today, the canal is closed, with two short sections repaired in 2013, including a short span of about 200 metres running from the junction with the Grand Union Canal at

英国英格兰运河。白金汉河湾运河全长17千米，从北安普敦郡的科斯格罗夫村流至白金汉郡，建有2座船闸。该运河为大连通运河支流，分两个阶段修建，分别于1793和1794年开凿，于1800和1801年竣工。19世纪50年代，来自铁路运输业的竞争使得运河航运备受冲击。同时，因流入运河的水夹带泥沙，淤泥沉积导致通航困难。白金汉公司还将该运河作为污水处理点，使这一问题愈加恶化。1890年，大连通公司采取法律行动，禁止污水排入运河，但这并未改变运河贸易量减少的趋势。在1904年的《布拉德肖铁路指南》中，白金汉河湾上游被定性为"几乎无法通航"。自1932年起，该运河逐步被废弃，1964年彻底停航。目前，白金汉河湾运河处于封闭状态，仅有两处河段在2013年得到修复，分别是400米长的白金汉河段以及另一长约200米的河段，此河段自科斯

Cosgrove to the west towards the A5 dual carriageway and a 400-metre span at Buckingham.

格罗夫大联盟运河交汇处向西沿A5双车道公路方向流动。

Bugsworth Basin

巴格斯沃斯内湾运河

A canal located in England, the United Kingdom. Situated at the terminal of the Peak Forest Canal, the Bugsworth Basin was previously a prosperous junction with the Peak Forest Tramway for the transportation of limestone and burnt lime. In 1968, the restoration of the Bugsworth Basin began. With the help of Waterway Recovery Group (WRG) and many locals, volunteers of the Inland Waterways Protection Society (IWPS) repaired parts of this important site for over three decades. In 1992, the IWPS gained a 50-year lease which allowed them to restore, manage and operate the canal basin. On the Easter of 1999, the basin was reopened and the use of the canal increased substantially. However, the walls along the canal collapsed afterwards, which brought about major leaks, hence the closing of the basin again in October 1999. Later, a 1.2-million-pound restoration project was conducted by British Waterways in collaboration with the IWPS, which was intended to transform this industrial heritage site as a tourist centre. On 26 March 2005, the Bugsworth Basin was officially reopened.

英国英格兰运河。巴格斯沃斯内湾运河位于皮克福里斯特运河终点，曾是繁忙的皮克福里斯特电车枢纽站，用来运输石灰石和煅石灰。巴格斯沃斯内湾运河的修复工作始于1968年。内陆运河保护协会志愿者在运河修复小组和许多当地人士协助下，用了30多年时间，修复了这个重要站点的部分河段。1992年，内陆运河保护协会获得了50年租约，可以修复、管理和经营该内湾运河。1999年复活节，巴格斯沃斯内湾运河重新开放通航，航运量大幅增加。1999年10月，因堤岸崩塌，出现多处缺口，运河再次被关闭。此后英国水务局与内陆运河保护协会合作，耗资120万英镑修复该运河，旨在将这一工业时代遗址发展成为旅游中心。2005年3月26日，巴格斯沃斯内湾运河正式重新通航。

Buiten Ring Canal

布登环形运河

A canal located in southeastern Friesland, the Netherlands. With a total length of 9.1 kilometres, the Buiten Ring Canal is a part of the small boat sailing

荷兰弗里斯兰省东南部运河。布登环形运河全长9.1千米，是小型船只航行路线"泥炭路线"的一

route called the Peat Route, which is designed to unfold the history of peat cutting before people's eyes. On the north side of the canal is the De Deelen Nature Reserve, and the whole area is covered with low hedgerows and grasses.

部分，运河展现了整个泥炭挖掘的历史。运河北侧是德伦自然保护区，整个区域被低矮的树篱和草丛覆盖。

Burgundy Canal

勃艮第运河

A canal located in Burgundy, central eastern France. The Burgundy Canal flows from Migennes to Saint-Jean-de-Losne and connects the river Yonne with the river Saône. It is 242 kilometres in length and has 189 locks. The canal allows ships with a draught of fewer than 1.8 metres and a speed below 6 kilometres per hour. Many fixed bridges were built on the canal, about half of which are located around these locks. In 1773, Louis XV issued an edict to build the canal. In 1777 the construction was started. In 1832, the entire canal was opened, but its essential feeder reservoirs were not completed until 1840. Without passage of commercial ships, now the canal is a popular route for hotel barges and a tourist attraction with spectacular scenery.

法国中东部勃艮第大区运河。勃艮第运河自米热纳流至圣让德洛斯恩，连通约讷河和索恩河，全长242千米，共建有189座船闸。该运河可供吃水深度不超过1.8米、航速不超过每小时6千米的船只通行。运河上修建了多处固定桥梁，其中约有一半建于船闸处。1773年，路易十五下令修建勃艮第运河。1777年，运河动工修建，1832年全线通航，但其重要引水水库直到1840年才全部建成。如今，勃艮第运河不通商船，成为酒店驳船的热门路线，也是一处风景秀丽的旅游景点。

Burum Canal

布鲁默运河

A canal located in Friesland, the Netherlands. Also called Schipsloot. With a length of 1.3 kilometres, the Burum Canal serves as an important water channel, connecting the village Burum with the south of the Lauwers. It was excavated in the low moor area in the 17th century.

荷兰弗里斯兰省运河。亦称史基浦斯运河。布鲁默运河全长1.3千米，是连接布鲁姆村和劳沃斯河南部的重要航道。布鲁默运河位于低沼泽地区，开凿于17世纪。

Bützow-Güstrow Canal

A canal located in Mecklenburg-Vorpommern, Germany. The Bützow-Güstrow Canal flows 14 kilometres, connecting the Nebel River with the Warnow River. It is of an average width of around 20 metres and a depth of approximately 1.5 metres, accessible to ships of up to 150 tons. The two locks, Wolken and Zepelin, combine to overcome a difference in water level of about 4 metres. In history, 7 bridges have been built on the canal. Among them, the repaired drawbridge near Lüssow is of monumental significance. It stands as the evidence of the technology of the late 19th century. The specific plan to build a canal connecting Rostock and Berlin dates back to 1873. The construction began in 1894. Two years later, the canal was opened officially. In 1914, the freight volume reached its peak of 12,500 tonnes. Then it dropped drastically because of the war. Now the canal functions only as a tourism line.

比措-居斯特罗运河

德国梅克伦堡—前波美拉尼亚州运河。比措—居斯特罗运河连通内贝尔河和瓦尔诺河，全长14千米。河道平均宽度为20米左右，水深约1.5米，可供150吨级轮船航行。运河上建有2座船闸，即沃尔肯船闸和齐普林船闸，用来调节约4米的水位落差。另外，运河上曾建有7座桥，其中吕索夫附近有一座折叠桥修缮后保存至今，该桥是19世纪后期建桥技术杰作。早在1873年，政府便提出连接罗斯托克市和柏林的运河修建计划。运河1894年开凿，1896年正式开通。通航后，运河货运量于1914年达到顶峰，约为1.25万吨。此后，运河货运量因战乱而开始急剧下降。如今，比措—居斯特罗运河仅作为一条水上游览航线供游客使用。

Bydgoszcz Canal

A canal located in Poland. The Bydgoszcz Canal runs through Bydgoszcz and Nakło, and links the Vistula River with the Oder River. It is 24.7 kilometres in length, with 6 locks overcoming the difference in elevation between its ends. Commanded by Frederick II, king of Prussia, the construction of this canal was started in 1772 and finished in 1775. The Bydgoszcz Canal has been inscribed on the Kuyavian-Pomeranian Province Heritage List on 30 November 2005.

比得哥什运河

波兰运河。比得哥什运河位于彼得哥什市与纳科市之间，连通维图拉河与奥得河。运河全长24.7千米，其上建有6座船闸，用以调节水位落差。1772年，普鲁士国王弗雷德里克二世下令开凿比得哥什运河，1775年竣工。2005年11月30日，比得哥什运河被纳入库亚维—波美拉尼亚省遗产名录。

Bystroye Canal

A deep-water canal located in the Danube Delta in Ukraine. The Bystroye Canal passes through the tributaries of Kiliya and Old Istanbul, and runs eastwards into the Black Sea. Most of the time, the canal flows along the Romania-Ukraine border, which stretches along the Danube. The navigational course along the natural channel is 172.4 kilometres long, complemented by a 3.4-kilometre-long artificial channel. It is an all-weather and two-way waterway which is accessible to vessels up to 5.9 metres in draught. The Bystroye Canal was one of the main waterways of Ukraine until 1959 when it became unnavigable due to silting. In 2004, Ukraine decided to reconstruct the canal and restore its own deep-water route from the Danube to the Black Sea as an alternative to the Romanian Sulina Canal. The project was officially launched in August 2004, though discordant voices existed from some environmentalists who believed that it could seriously harm the unique ecosystem of the Danube Biosphere Reserve. Joint efforts have been made from various sides (including WWF, EU, and the Ukrainian government) to keep the balance between the economic need and the ecological integrity. The cost of passage through the canal to the Black Sea is 40% lower than that of the Romanian Sulina Canal.

Bystry Canal

A canal located in Podlaskie Province of northeastern Poland. As a branch channel of the Augustów

比斯特耶运河

乌克兰多瑙河三角洲地区深水运河。比斯特耶运河流经多瑙河三角洲的分支河流基利亚和旧伊斯坦布尔，向东注入黑海。运河的大部分河段沿着多瑙河的走向，同罗马尼亚—乌克兰边界重合。比斯特耶运河拥有天然航道172.4千米，加上人工航道3.4千米，全天候可容吃水深度达5.9米的船只双向通行。1959年以前，该运河是乌克兰主要航道之一，后由于淤积严重而无法通航。2004年，乌克兰政府决定重修该运河，放弃罗马尼亚苏利纳运河而开辟一条从多瑙河到黑海、属于本国的深水路线。同年8月，当地政府宣布重建项目开工。该项目也引发了一些争议，部分环保主义人士认为，运河重修将严重损害多瑙河生物保护区独特的生态系统。随后，在运河重修过程中，世界自然基金会、欧盟和乌克兰政府通力合作，在多方共同努力下保持了经济发展需要和生态完整性之间的平衡。相比于罗马尼亚苏利纳运河的通航费用，经此运河通往黑海费用可节省40%。

贝斯特雷运河

波兰东北部波德拉谢省运河。贝斯特雷运河是奥古斯图夫运河的

Canal, the Bystry Canal flows into the north side of the Sajno Lake and connects with the Netta River. It is 3.2 kilometres long with 2 locks. The canal was previously built to empty excess water from the Augustów Canal. Its construction was started in 1834 and finished in 1835. Along the beginning section of the canal, there are some houses with small private docks for boats and fishing. After about 200 metres, the waterway deepens to 50-60 centimetres. Then, the channel passes through the forest area covered by spruce, pine, alder and willow trees. After running a total of 2 kilometres, the Bystry Canal joins the Sajno Lake. Now, it is an ideal fishing spot.

一条支流, 流入萨伊诺湖的北部, 与内特河相连。运河全长3.2千米, 设有2座船闸。修建运河最初是为了引流奥古斯图夫运河过多的河水。运河1834年开凿, 1835年竣工。在运河起始段, 沿河会看到一些房屋和供船停泊和捕鱼的小型私人码头。约200米后, 运河河道加深至50—60厘米, 之后流经有云杉、松树、桤木和柳树覆盖的林区。流动2千米后贝斯特雷运河注入萨伊诺湖。如今, 运河是理想的垂钓场所。

Cabrillo Canal

A canal located in Los Angeles, California, the United States. The Cabrillo Canal was one of the series of Venice Canals. In the early 1900s, in order to build a Venice of America in South California, the series of Venice Canals were excavated under the direction of Abbot Kinney, a tobacco millionaire and real estate developer. In the mid-1920s, the California State Superior Court overturned "to be held as public waterways forever" deed clause, and between 1926 and 1927, many of the canals were filled in to provide roads to bring traffic to the pier. The Cabrillo Canal was one of them, and is now the Cabrillo Avenue.

Caen Canal

A canal located in Calvados, France. The Caen Canal connects the port of Caen to the port of Ouistreham on the English Channel. It has a length of 14 kilometres, a current depth of 10 metres, a width of about 200 metres in the dock of Calix, and 2 locks, one of which at the mouth of the canal is accessible to ships of more than 200 metres in length. In the 17th century, various construction projects were put forward in response to the complaints from Caen traders, but the canal project at that time was not carried out due to financial reasons. In 1811, Napoleon I inspected the city himself and decided on the construction of the canal. The work was taken over by the engineer Pattu, whose plan was authorized in 1837. The actual construction of the canal, however,

卡布里约运河

美国加利福尼亚州洛杉矶市运河。卡布里约运河为美国威尼斯运河网中的一条运河。20世纪初，为打造美国南加州版"威尼斯"，烟草富豪和房地产开发商阿博特·金尼出资修建了威尼斯运河网。20世纪20年代中期，加州高级法院否决了有关运河"永久用作公共航道"的条款。1926—1927年间，为将公路延伸到码头，包括卡布里约运河在内的多条运河被回填，卡布里约运河成为如今的卡布里约大道。

卡昂运河

法国卡尔瓦多省运河。卡昂运河连接卡昂港口和英吉利海峡的乌伊斯特勒昂港口，全长14千米，目前深度为10米，卡利码头处宽度达200米，沿线设有2座船闸，其中运河河口的船闸可供长度超过200米的船只通行。17世纪时，因卡昂商人对当时的运输条件不满，该市提出多项运河修建规划。但由于资金问题，卡昂运河项目一直被搁置。1811年，拿破仑一世到卡昂视察，决定开凿卡昂运河。运河工程由工程师帕图负责，他的方案于1837年获得批准。然而，运河直到1844年才开工。几经拖延，卡昂运

was not started until 1844. The Caen Canal was opened in 1857 and further deepened in 1877 from 4.5 metres to 5.2 metres. In 1922, the depth reached 6.1 metres. During the early stage of the Battle of Normandy, the Caen Canal was regarded as strategically important for its location on the eastern flank of the allied beachhead area. Today, the canal is used by both merchant ships and passenger ships.

河1857年终于通航。1877年，该运河从4.5米加深到5.2米。1922年，运河深度又增至6.1米。诺曼底战役早期，卡昂运河位于盟军滩头堡东翼，具有重要的战略意义。如今，该运河上商船和客船均可通行。

Calais Canal

加莱运河

A canal located in northern France. The Calais Canal connects the Aa River to the Strait of Dover and runs from Le West to Calais. It is 30 kilometres in length and has 3 locks. The construction of this canal was started in the late 17th century and it was put into service in 1758. The Calais Canal is now still operational for commercial use, and has been upgraded to allow the navigation of barges of up to 600 tonnes.

法国北部运河。加莱运河连通阿河和多佛尔海峡，从乐维斯特市流至加莱市，全长30千米，建有3座船闸。该运河于17世纪末期开凿，1758年通航。如今，加莱运河上依旧有商船通行，扩建后可承载总重达600吨的驳船。

Caland Canal

卡兰运河

A canal located in South Holland Province, the Netherlands. The Caland Canal has a length of 20 kilometres and an elevation of 1 metre, and is near the Maeslant Barrier. It runs parallel to the New Waterway Canal from Hornof Holland and provides access to the industrial areas in the Europort. The Caland Canal was named after Pieter Caland, the engineer-director during the relocation of the Maas estuary by excavating the New Waterway Canal. It was extensively redeveloped in 2018, includ-

荷兰南荷兰省运河。卡兰运河长20千米，海拔为1米，靠近马仕朗大坝。该运河始于荷兰角港，与新航道运河平行，连接欧罗波特港工业区。卡兰运河得名于总工程师彼得·卡兰，他曾主持修建新航道运河，改变了马斯河原河口的位置。2018年，卡兰运河进行大范围整修，包括修建新的船舶液化天然气加气泊位，并新建7个内陆船舶

ing the installation of a new liquified natural gas bunkering berth and 7 new berths for inland vessels.

泊位。

Caledonian Canal

A canal located in Scotland, the United Kingdom. The Caledonian Canal, running from northeast to southwest, connects the east coast with the west coast. It is 97 kilometres in length with 29 locks, 4 aqueducts, and 10 bridges. Only one third of the whole section is man-made, and the rest is formed by Loch Dochfour, Loch Ness, Loch Oich, and Loch Lochy. It enables wooden sailing ships to go safely from the northeast to the southwest of Scotland instead of taking the route around the north coast via Cape Wrath and the Pentland Firth. Authorized by the Parliament in July 1803, the canal was designed and constructed later by Thomas Telford, a Scottish engineer, and opened in 1822, 12 years later than expected. Although the draught was finally reduced from 6.1 metres to 4.6 metres to save money, the actual cost (£910,000) still almost doubled the estimate (£474,000). The ownership of the canal was first transferred to the Ministry of Transport in 1920, and then passed to the British Waterways in 1962. As an ancient monument and a tourist attraction with beautiful scenery, the canal attracts more than 1 million visitors every year by providing a place for many leisure activities.

喀里多尼亚运河

英国苏格兰运河。喀里多尼亚运河自东北流向西南，连通苏格兰东海岸与西海岸，全长97千米，共设29座船闸、4座渡槽与10座桥梁。该运河仅有三分之一河段为人工航道，其余部分由多赫富湖、尼斯湖、奥伊赫湖以及洛希湖组成。木帆船可经喀里多尼亚运河从苏格兰东北部安全抵达西南部，而不必绕过北海岸的拉斯角与彭特兰海峡。1803年7月，经英国议会授权，喀里多尼亚运河由苏格兰工程师托马斯·泰尔福负责设计和修建工作。1822年该运河通航，比预期晚了12年。为削减开支，运河吃水深度从计划的6.1米最终降至4.6米，但总花费91万英镑仍比预算47.4万英镑超出近一倍。1920年，喀里多尼亚运河所有权被转让给英国交通部，1962年又转给英国河道局。喀里多尼亚运河是古迹工程和风景优美的旅游景点，每年都会吸引100多万名游客到此游览。

Caloosahatchee River

A canalized river located in Florida, the United

克卢瑟哈奇河

美国佛罗里达州运河化河流。克卢

States. As a part of the Okeechobee Waterway, the Caloosahatchee River is approximately 108 kilometres in length and serves as the boundaries of three adjacent cities: the city of Fort Myers, the city of Cape Coral, and the city of Labelle. It is connected to Lake Okeechobee via the Okeechobee Canal and stretches southwest towards the Gulf of Mexico through the San Carlos Bay at Sanibel Island. The low course of the river forms a tidal estuary, which is the habitat for many species. The river was firstly altered by the Calusa Indians who constructed shallow canals to connect it to Lake Okeechobee for ease of travel and trade. The Europeans arrived in the 19th century and carried out several expansions of the river for the purpose of mitigating the catastrophic floods and improving the navigation. As a link between Lake Okeechobee and the ocean, the health and vitality of the river are largely dependent on those of Lake Okeechobee. The waste water from the lake discharged into the river continuously and its ecological environment suffered a lot. In 2006, the Caloosahatchee River is nominated by American Rivers as one of the Ten Most Endangered Rivers in the United States. The state government and a number of social groups are now making efforts to facilitate its recovery.

瑟哈奇河全长约108千米，为奥基乔比航道的一部分，同时也是迈尔斯堡市、开普科勒尔市和拉贝尔市三座相邻城市的天然分界线。该河流通过奥基乔比运河与奥基乔比湖相通，流经萨尼伯尔岛的圣卡洛斯湾后，向西南方向延伸汇入墨西哥湾。河流的下游形成一个潮汐河口，许多物种栖息于此。卡卢萨印第安人是克卢瑟哈奇河的首批改造者，他们开凿运河连通奥基乔比湖，使出行与贸易更为便利。19世纪到达此地后的欧洲人为进一步减轻洪涝灾害，提升克卢瑟哈奇河的运载能力，先后对该河进行了数次扩建。克卢瑟哈奇河作为奥基乔比湖与海洋之间的连接通道，水文状况在很大程度上受奥基乔比湖的影响。后来，由于奥基乔比湖排放废水，运河的生态环境遭到严重破坏。2006年，克卢瑟哈奇河被美国河流协会列为美国十大濒危河流之一。目前，佛罗里达州政府与一些社会团体正努力修复其生态环境。

Cal-Sag Channel

卡尔-萨格航道

A channel located in Illinois, the United States. See Calumet-Sag Channel.

美国伊利诺伊州航道。见卡柳梅特-萨格航道。

Calueque-Oshakati Canal

A cross-border canal located in Africa. The Calueque-Oshakati Canal is 154 kilometres long. According to the Namibia Water Master Plan of 1974, the canal was constructed to convey drinking water from the Kunene River in Angola to north-central Namibia, meeting the national water needs. Four water plants were built along the canal to purify and distribute water and 4,000 kilometres of pipelines radiate out from water plants to supply surrounding villages, allowing both people and livestock to make free use of the water. The water is also used for irrigation and domestic purposes, benefiting more than 800,000 people in northern Namibia. Until the first decade of the 21st century, the transmitted water from the Kunene River was clean and unpolluted. With the rapid population growth and the proliferation of livestock, increasing pressure has been exerted on the water supply. Large demand for water in agriculture, commercial sectors and perished infrastructure have caused severe water pollution, leading to high cost of maintenance and purification of the canal. In November 2018, authorities of Namibia and Angola inaugurated the Calueque-Oshakati Cross-Border Drinking Water Supply Project to upgrade the existing water supply channel, the Calueque-Oshakati Canal. In addition to the cooperation between Angola and Namibia, this joint project is supported by the European Union with the finance of €2,400,000 for the pre-feasibility study through the EU-Africa Infrastructure Trust Fund (EU-AITF).

卡卢埃克-奥沙卡蒂运河

非洲跨国运河。卡卢埃克—奥沙卡蒂运河全长154千米，根据纳米比亚1974年水利总计划而修建，目的是把安哥拉库内内河的饮用水运输到纳米比亚中北部地区，以满足纳米比亚的用水需求。卡卢埃克—奥沙卡蒂运河沿岸共建有4个水厂，可用于水资源净化和调配，另外还建有总计4 000千米长的水管，以连接水厂和周边村庄，方便居民和牲畜自由用水。运河还用作农业灌溉和家庭用水来源，造福纳米比亚北部80多万人口。在21世纪第一个10年之前，引自库内内河的水干净无污染。然而，随着人口急速增长和牲畜大量繁殖，供水需求也越来越大。农业、商业大量用水以及基础设施老旧造成严重水污染，导致维护和净化运河水资源耗费大量的财力。2018年11月，为促进现存饮用水供应水道卡卢埃克—奥沙卡蒂运河基础设施的进一步升级改造，纳米比亚政府和安哥拉政府正式启动建设卡卢埃克—奥沙卡蒂跨国饮用水供应项目。这一联合项目还获得欧盟的支持，通过欧盟—非洲基础设施信托基金，欧盟资助了240万欧元用于项目实施前的可行性研究。

Calumet-Sag Channel

A channel located in Illinois, the United States. Also called Cal-Sag Channel. The Calumet-Sag Channel is 26 kilometres in length and extends from its junction with the Chicago Sanitary and Ship Canal (CSSC) in Sag Bridge and joins the Little Calumet River in Blue Island. The waterway, along with the CSSC, forms the Chicago Area Waterway System (CAWS) which connects the Mississippi River Basin and the Great Lakes. The excavation of the original Calumet-Sag Channel was completed in 1922 after a period of 11 years. It was constructed to shift the flow of the Calumet Rivers and transfer pollution away from Lake Michigan to the CSSC. The Calumet-Sag Channel once served as a watercourse for barge traffic in the heavy industry zone in southern Chicago. From 2006, it was used more as a conduit for wastewater from southern Cook County into the Illinois Waterway. The water then became heavily polluted from industry and other waste. Signs were posted on the shoreline warning people not to drink, swim in or even touch the Calumet-Sag Channel's water. The pollution of the channel has now been greatly improved with the continuous efforts of the government.

Cambridgeshire Lodes

A system of man-made waterways located in eastern England, the United Kingdom. The Cambridgeshire Lodes connect River Cambridge and River Great Ouse, and consists of 7 waterways:

卡柳梅特－萨格航道

美国伊利诺伊州航道。亦称卡尔－萨格航道。卡柳梅特－萨格航道全长26千米，自萨格桥至布卢岛，先后同芝加哥环境卫生与通海运河及小卡柳梅特河交汇。该航道同芝加哥环境卫生与通海运河一起形成联通密西西比河流域和五大湖的芝加哥地区航道网。修建卡柳梅特－萨格航道的目的是改变卡柳梅特河的流向，从而将污染物从密歇根湖转移至芝加哥环境卫生与通海运河。运河工程耗时11年，最终于1922年竣工。卡柳梅特－萨格航道曾是芝加哥南部重工业区的驳船运输航道。从2006年开始，该航道更多用作从库克县南部到伊利诺伊航道的废水排放沟渠。由于该航道河流污染严重，政府在河边专门竖立了警示牌，禁止在此游泳、饮用甚至接触河水。目前，在政府不断努力下，卡柳梅特－萨格航道的污染状况已得到有效治理。

剑桥郡运河网

英国英格兰东部人工航道网。剑桥郡运河网连接剑桥河和大乌斯河，包括7条运河：博蒂舍姆运河、斯沃弗姆巴尔别克运河、里奇运

the Bottisham Lode, the Swaffham Bulbeck Lode, the Reach Lode, the Burwell Lode, the Wicken Lode, the Monk's Lode, and the Soham Lode. The Bottisham Lode is about 4 kilometres long, joining River Cambridge. It passes a mill which has been restored by the National Trust. It allowed the passage of small ships in the 19th century but was closed around 1900. A pumping station was built at the entrance in 2001. Currently, the Bottisham Lode remains unnavigable. The Swaffham Bulbeck Lode is 5.5 kilometres long and also joins River Cambridge. It was cleared to accelerate the drainage by the commissioners of the Bedford Level. After the construction of railways in the area, the Swaffham Bulbeck Lode was much less used and only a stretch of 3.2 kilometres is now navigable. The Reach Lode is 4.8 kilometres long, joining River Cambridge at Upware and flowing to the village of Reach. The Upware Lock on the waterway allowed the passage of ships up to 14 metres in length. The waterway is deepened for the subsidence of surrounding land, and in some section the depth reaches 3 metres. Currently, the embankments have been strengthened. The present Burwell Lode was canalized in the mid-17th century. Its width varies from 12 metres to 14 metres. The current waterway allows the passage of ships up to 19 metres in length. The Wicken Lode is about 2.4 kilometres long and can only allow small ships to pass through. The waterway was mainly used to transport peat from Burwell Fen in the 19th century. The Wicken Fen near the waterway is one of the oldest nature reserves in England. A bank of the Monk's Lode

河、伯韦尔运河、芒克斯运河、威肯运河和索厄姆运河。博蒂舍姆运河长4千米，连通剑桥河。该运河流经一间工坊，该工坊现已被英国国家信托基金会修复。19世纪时，博蒂舍姆运河可通行小型船只，1900年前后停航。2001年运河入口处建了一座泵站。目前，该段运河仍不通航。斯沃弗姆·巴尔别克运河长5.5千米，也与剑桥河相连。为了加快排水，贝德福德平原的地方长官曾疏浚运河。该地区铁路建成后，运河使用频率大大降低，目前只有3.2千米仍可通航。里奇运河长4.8千米，在阿普韦尔村与剑桥河汇合，流向里奇村。运河上的阿普韦尔船闸可通行长度不超过14米的船只。由于运河两边地面下沉，运河需要加深，部分河道深达3米，现已对河堤加固。伯韦尔运河修建于17世纪中期，宽12—14米，可供长度不超过19米的船只通行。威肯运河长2.4千米，仅供小型船只通行。19世纪时，该运河主要用以运输伯韦尔沼泽地的泥煤。运河附近的威肯沼泽地是英格兰最古老的自然保护区之一。芒克斯运河的一侧河岸是剑桥和伊利之间的国家自行车网络11号公路的一部分。国家信托基金会在芒克斯运河附近开凿了一条新航道，即威肯运河，可为威肯沼泽供水。索厄姆运河建于18世纪末，

is a part of the National Cycle Network, route 11, between Cambridge and Ely. A new channel, namely, the Wicken Lode, has been built by the National Trust near the Monk's Lode to provide water for the Wicken Fen. The Soham Lode is 11 kilometres long and connects River Great Ouse. It was canalized around the late 18th century for flood prevention in the Soham region. The waterway was also used to transport corn, coal and timber. It was closed around 1990.

长11千米，连接大乌斯河，主要用于索厄姆地区的防洪工作，也曾运输谷物、煤和木材。该运河于1990年前后停航。

Canal of Alexandria

亚历山大运河

A canal located in Al Buhayrah, Egypt. See Mahmoudiyah Canal.

埃及布海拉省运河。见马赫穆迪亚运河。

Canal of Hope

希望运河

A canal located in Japan. See Lake Biwa Canal.

日本运河。见琵琶湖运河。

Canaveral Barge Canal

卡纳维拉尔驳船运河

A canal located in southern Titusville, Florida, the United States. The Canaveral Barge Canal is 9.7 kilometres in length and 3.7 metres in depth, linking the Atlantic Ocean with the Indian River across northern Merritt Island. The canal allows vessels to transverse Merritt Island between the Atlantic Ocean and the Indian River Intracoastal Waterway. It also provides access for barges transporting crude oil to the two power plants south of Titusville, Florida.

美国佛罗里达州南泰特斯维尔运河。卡纳维拉尔驳船运河长约9.7千米，深3.7米，横穿梅里特岛北部，连通大西洋与印第安河。来往船只可通过该运河穿过梅里特岛，从大西洋驶入印第安河沿海航道。同时，运输原油的驳船还可经此运河到达佛罗里达州泰特斯维尔市南侧的两处发电厂。

Canso Canal

A canal located in the eastern side of the Canso Causeway, Canada. The Canso Canal separates the Cape Breton Island from the mainland of Nova Scotia. It is 24 metres in width, 570 metres in length, with a minimum depth of 9.8 metres. There is a lock on it, equipped with double sets of sector gates at each end to manage different tide levels. The canal cuts through the causeway in its southeastern part, where a 94-metre-long swing bridge named Canso Canal Bridge is constructed, connecting the Trans-Canada Highway and a railway line. As a short link for maritime shipping through Canso Strait, the canal was constructed from 1953 to 1955. Owned by the government of Canada under the Department of Fisheries and Oceans, the canal is currently managed by the Canadian Coast Guard. Serving mainly for commercial transportation, the Canso Canal is open for approximately 254 consecutive days every year on a 24-hour basis under ice free conditions. According to the statistics, in 2015, the Canso Canal saw a traffic of about 2,069 ships carrying an average gross tonnage of 1,878,480.

Cape Cod Canal

A canal located in Massachusetts, the United States. The Cape Cod Canal is 28 kilometres in length with its dredged branches and 152 metres in width, with a minimum depth of 9 metres. It forms a part of the Atlantic Intracoastal Waterway, and joins the Cape Cod Bay with the Buzzards Bay. The canal

坎索运河

加拿大坎索堤道以东运河。坎索运河为新斯科舍省与布雷顿角岛的界河，长570米，宽24米，水深至少9.8米，运河上建有1座船闸，船闸每端配备两套扇形闸门，以适应不同的潮位。该运河在东南方向穿过坎索堤道，此处建有1座平旋桥，名为"坎索运河桥"，桥长94米，连接加拿大横贯公路和一条铁路。坎索运河是经坎索海峡的海上运输便捷通道，修建于1953—1955年间，归加拿大渔业和海洋部所有，目前由加拿大海岸警卫队负责管理。在无冰条件下，坎索运河每年持续运营约254天，且24小时通航，通航船只以商用船为主。据2015年统计数据，每年平均有2 069艘船只（平均总吨位为1 878 480吨）通过坎索运河。

科德角运河

美国马萨诸塞州运河。科德角运河包括其疏浚的支流总长达28千米，宽152米，最浅处为9米。该运河是大西洋沿海航道的一部分，连接科德角湾和巴泽兹湾，穿过科德角狭长的地峡。运河潮汐相

passes through the narrow isthmus of Cape Cod. There are considerable tidal movements. Nevertheless, no lock has been found on the canal. The canal was constructed in 1909 and put into operation in July 1914. After the construction of the canal, via the East River, Long Island Sound and the canal, the distance for waterborne traffic between New York City and Boston was cut by more than 120 kilometres. The canal helped to avoid the dangerous and windy voyage around the cape. As a free waterway, the Cape Cod Canal witnesses frequent navigation of both recreational and commercial vessels. Anglers, in-line skaters, bicyclists, and walkers can make use of the service roads on both sides of the canal. Besides, whales and dolphins, including critically endangered North Atlantic right whales, can be found in the canal.

当频繁, 但河上未建船闸。科德角运河于1909年开凿, 1914年7月投入使用。运河通航后, 经由东河、长岛海峡和科德角运河航线, 纽约至波士顿的水上交通距离缩短了120多千米, 同时避开了科德角周围原先危险、多风的航程。科德角运河免费通行, 河上的娱乐船只和商业用船往来如织。运河两旁的小道方便人们钓鱼、轮滑、骑自行车和散步等。另外, 科德角运河也是鲸鱼和海豚的栖息地, 其中包括极度濒危的北大西洋露脊鲸。

Cape May Canal

开普梅运河

A canal located at the southern tip of Cape May County, New Jersey, the United States. The Cape May Canal links Cape May Harbour to the Delaware Bay with a length of 5.4 kilometres. In early 1942, several American ships were sunk by German U-boats. In order to provide a protected route to avoid attack from German U-boats, the canal was constructed by the United States Army Corps of Engineers after many unfulfilled plans, and it became a part of the Intracoastal Waterway. The canal improved the infrastructure of Cape Island. There are 3 bridges over the Cape May Canal, namely Route 109, Route 162, and the railroad

美国新泽西州开普梅县南端运河。开普梅运河连接开普梅港和特拉华湾, 全长5.4千米。1942年初, 几艘美国船只被德国U型潜水艇击沉。随后, 为了开辟一条免受德国U型潜水艇袭击的安全航道, 美国陆军工程兵团经多次规划后开凿了开普梅运河。该运河为大西洋沿海航道的一部分, 改善了开普岛的基础设施状况。运河上有3座桥, 分别为109号路桥、162号路桥和开普梅海滨线铁路平旋桥。每逢夏季, 运河上游船如织。

swing bridge of the Cape May Seashore Lines. The canal is used heavily by recreational boats during summers.

Carillon Canal

A canal located in Quebec, Canada. The Carillon Canal is 100 kilometres from Montreal and 130 kilometres from Ottawa. Being a part of the Ottawa River canal network, it was constructed from 1830 to 1833 and put into use in 1833. In 1812, for military purposes, several canals were constructed on the Ottawa River to facilitate navigation, including the Grenville Canal and the Carillon Canal. The construction of these canals bypassed the swift currents of the Ottawa River, especially the Long Sault section, thus improving navigation conditions. Completed in 1843, the entire Ottawa River canal network boasted 11 locks, each measuring 41 metres in length, 10 metres in width, and only 1.5 metres in depth at the threshold. All sizes were designed initially for military use and not suitable for commerce. Although it was built out of military purposes, the Carillon Canal served for commercial activities from the very beginning, with forestry as the main business. Between 1873 and 1882, the Grenville and Carillon canals were expanded at the request of local merchants. From 1959 to 1963, the construction of the Carillon hydroelectric dam and a modern 20-metre high lock further transformed the canal network. The dam raised the level of the Carillon Canal by about 19 metres and the Glenville Canal by around 2.7 metres. With a higher

卡里隆运河

加拿大魁北克省运河。卡里隆运河距蒙特利尔100千米，距渥太华130千米，为渥太华河运河网的一部分。该运河修建于1830—1833年间，1833年投入使用。1812年，出于军事需要，渥太华河上开凿了多条运河以保证通航，包括格伦维尔运河和卡里隆运河。这几条运河绕开了渥太华河、特别是朗苏段的急流，航运条件得以改善。1843年，渥太华河运河竣工，共建有11座船闸。各座船闸长41米，宽10米，船闸门槛水深仅1.5米。所有尺寸最初均按军事用途设计，不适合商用。尽管如此，卡里隆运河从开通伊始就服务于商业运输，主要涉及木材和林产品。1873—1882年间，格伦维尔运河和卡里隆运河应当地商人要求进行了扩建。1959—1963年间，卡里隆堤坝式水电站和一座高20米的现代化船闸相继建成，进一步完善了运河网。水坝将卡里隆运河与格伦维尔运河的水位分别抬升约19米和2.7米。水位升高后，朗苏段的湍急水流趋于平缓。1929年，卡里隆运河被列入加拿大国家历史遗址

water level in this section, the rapids in the Long Sault have been visibly reduced. In 1929, the Carillon Canal was recognized as a National Historic Site of Canada, along with the surrounding monuments including the remains of lock No.1, the jetty of the second canal, and the Carillon Barracks (now a regional museum). The Carillon Canal now has become a popular recreational place, annually attracting more than 20,000 boat enthusiasts and over 30,000 tourists.

Carondelet Canal

A canal located in New Orleans, Louisiana, the United States. Also known as Old Basin Canal. The Carondelet Canal is 5.8 kilometres in length. Initially, the canal was 2.58 kilometres in length, from Bayou St. John to New Orleans inland, connecting with Lake Pontchartrain. In June 1794, Baron de Carondelet (whose name the canal also bore), the Governor of Louisiana, ordered the construction of a canal to improve the local drainage system, hence the name. Then after two years of widening and deepening, the canal was officially opened in 1796 with dual functions of drainage and shipping. After Carondelet was transferred away from Louisiana, the canal was left out of use. It didn't once again become a key shipping channel until the establishment of the Orleans Navigation Company in 1805 and the importance was attached to the canal by Mayor of New Orleans, James Pitot. The shipping conditions of the canal were then visibly improved. In the 1830s, merchants competed for business

名录。除运河外，运河周边的历史遗迹还包括一号船闸的遗址、第二条运河的防波堤和卡里隆兵营遗址（目前为当地的一个博物馆）等。卡里隆运河现已成为热门游览胜地之一，每年吸引2万多名划船爱好者及3万多名游客。

卡龙德莱特运河

美国路易斯安那州新奥尔良市运河。亦称旧内湾运河。卡龙德莱特运河全长5.8千米。1794年6月，运河由时任路易斯安那州州长的卡龙德莱特男爵为改进当地排水系统下令开凿，运河故此得名。运河最初长仅2.58千米，从圣约翰河口流至新奥尔良市，与庞恰特雷恩湖相通。经过两年的拓建改造后，1796年运河正式开通，兼具排水和航运双重功能。由于卡龙德莱特州长调离路易斯安那州，卡龙德莱特运河一度停用。运河能够再次成为重要的航运线路得益于两个重要原因：其一是1805年奥尔良航运公司的成立，其二是新奥尔良市新任市长詹姆斯·皮托对运河的重视。卡龙德莱特运河的通航环境与条件此后得到前所未有的改善。19世纪30年代，为应对更加

activities and constructed a deeper and wider New Basin Canal, distinguished from the Old Basin Canal, the colloquial name of Carondelet Canal. The New Basin Canal ran directly from Lake Pontchartrain to the new prosperous area of America. By the time of the American Civil War, it had carried more than twice the freight as the Carondelet Canal did. Nevertheless, there were many merchants and commercial institutions along the Carondelet Canal, the old economic centre, which maintained its operation until the early 20th century. After World War I, the use of the Carondelet Canal continued to decline and later it was declared unnavigable. New Orleans bought the canal in 1924 and began filling it the following year. In the 1990s, it was gradually transformed into a linear park and bicycle path. It is now a corridor from City Park to the vicinity of Armstrong Park, standing as a component of the Laffitte Greenway.

激烈的商业竞争，人们修建了更深更宽的新内湾运河。为加以区分，民间把卡龙德莱特运河称为"旧流域运河"。新内湾运河从庞恰特雷恩湖直接通向美国新兴繁荣地带，截至美国南北战争前，其货运量是卡龙德莱特运河的两倍多。然而，卡龙德莱特运河作为旧时的经济中心，沿线仍有不少商人和商业机构，因此一直运营至20世纪初期。第一次世界大战后，卡龙德莱特运河的使用率逐步降低，直至停航。1924年，新奥尔良市收购卡龙德莱特运河，次年开始回填工作。20世纪90年代，该运河已逐步改造成带状公园和自行车道。现在，卡龙德莱特运河已改建为一条廊道，从城市公园到阿姆斯特朗公园附近，这也是拉菲特绿廊的一部分。

Castile Canal

A canal located in the north of Spain. The Castile Canal stretches 207 kilometres and runs through the provinces of Burgos, Palencia and Valladolid. The width of the canal ranges from 11 metres to 22 metres, while its depth from 1.8 metres to 3 metres. Its overall layout is of an inverted Y shape. The southern section is 54 kilometres in length and has 18 locks. It is followed by the 78-kilometre-long Campos section running all the way to the Medina de Rioseco in Valladolid. The 75-kilometre-long

卡斯蒂利亚运河

西班牙北部运河。卡斯蒂利亚运河流经布尔戈斯、帕伦西亚和巴利亚多利德三省，全长207千米，宽度在11—22米之间，深度在1.8—3米之间，整体像一个倒Y字形。运河南段长54千米，河上建有18座船闸。德坎波斯段，即运河的中间段，全长78千米，向北一直延伸到巴利亚多利德的梅迪纳德里奥塞科。该运河的北段从阿拉尔德尔

northern section runs from Alar del Rey to Ribas de Campos in Palencia, with a total of 24 locks on this section. The construction of the Castile Canal took almost a century, from 1753 to 1849. The project was planned by the Marqués de la Ensenada during Fernando VI's reign in order to transport grain from the fertile farmland to the port of Santander. However, the plan was shelved during the Independence War of Spanish America. During the two decades following the completion of the project, the canal was actively involved in transportation activities. In 1959, the navigation on the canal was suspended when railroads were constructed in northern Spain. Then after 30 years of suspension of navigation on the canal, the Duero hydrographic confederation approved to resume the navigation. In 1991, the Castile Canal was declared Heritage of Cultural Interest.

雷伊延伸至帕伦西亚的里瓦斯德坎波斯，长75千米，运河上建有24座船闸。卡斯蒂利亚运河的修建从1753年一直持续至1849年，历时近100年。为方便将谷物从肥沃的农田运往桑坦德港口，费尔南多六世国王统治时期的恩塞纳达侯爵提出开凿卡斯蒂利亚运河的计划。然而由于西班牙属美洲殖民地独立战争爆发，该计划被长期搁置。运河开通之后的20年是其运营繁荣期。后来，随着铁路运输业在西班牙北部的发展，运河最终于1959年暂停通航。30年后，杜罗航道联合会批准卡斯蒂利亚运河恢复通航。1991年，卡斯蒂利亚运河被列为西班牙文化遗产。

Cayuga-Seneca Canal

卡尤加-塞内卡运河

A canal located in New York, the United States. The Cayuga–Seneca Canal, a part of the New York State Canal System, connects the Erie Canal to the Cayuga Lake and the Seneca Lake, stretching for approximately 32 kilometres long. It is the shortest in the New York State Canal System. There is at present a total of 4 single-chamber locks on the Cayuga-Seneca Canal, each being 100 metres in length and 13.7 metres in width. With a minimum water depth of 3.7 metres, the channel is accessible to ships up to 91 metres in length and 13.3 metres in width. The canal has been an economic power-

美国纽约州运河。卡尤加-塞内卡运河连通伊利运河与卡尤加湖和塞内卡湖，长约32千米，为纽约州运河网中最短的运河。运河上共建有4座长100米、宽13.7米的单闸室船闸。航道水深超过3.7米，可供长度不超过91米、宽度低于13.3米的船只顺利通行。卡尤加-塞内卡运河一直是滑铁卢和塞内卡福尔斯地区经济发展的推动力。运河的开凿历经了几个阶段。1821年，该运河首次通航，当时共建有8座

house for the area of Waterloo and Seneca Falls. The construction of the Cayuga-Seneca Canal was carried out in several stages. In 1821, it was put into use for the first time, with 8 locks then, connecting the Seneca Lake only to the Seneca River Outlet at the Cayuga Lake. In 1825, the canal was enlarged to meet the demand of locals. Extended for 20.1 kilometres, it was then connected to the Erie Canal, with 4 new locks added. The canal was officially put into use again in 1828. Afterwards, dams were rebuilt and movable gates were added. At the same time, its neighbourhood grew into a major industrial area. When New York State created the New York Barge Canal System in 1918, the Cayuga-Seneca Canal locks were modified and finally the present-day 4 modern concrete locks were in place from east to west. Nowadays, the Cayuga-Seneca Canal is famous for its unique experience of inland water and deep-lake cruising and convenient access to New York's premier wine region.

船闸,连接塞内卡湖和卡尤加湖的塞内卡河出口。1825年,为满足当地人的航运需求,该运河扩建,延长20.1千米,新建4座船闸,并连通伊利运河。改造后,官方于1828年再次宣布卡尤加—塞内卡运河通航,之后,政府又重建水坝,并增设可移动闸门,其周边地区逐渐发展成为重要的工业区。1918年,纽约州政府建设纽约州驳船运河网,卡尤加—塞内卡运河上的船闸得以修缮,自东而西共建有4座现代化的船闸。如今,该运河因其独特的观光体验而闻名,人们可乘船游览湖光水色,还可造访纽约州的顶级葡萄酒产区。

Cazaux-Teste Canal

A canal located in the region of Aquitaine, France. The Cazaux-Teste Canal has a length of 20 kilometres, linking the Cazaux Lake with the Arcahon Basin. It was excavated between 1835 and 1840. The canal is a tree-shaded waterway and is a popular cruising site nowadays. There are many small motor boats on the canal.

卡佐泰斯特运河

法国阿基坦大区运河。卡佐泰斯特运河全长20千米,连通卡佐湖和阿卡雄湾。运河修建于1835—1840年间。运河两侧绿树成荫,为乘船巡游的热门目的地。运河上经常会有很多小型摩托艇游弋。

Central Canal (Belgium)

A canal located in Belgium. The Central Canal connects the Meuse and the Schelde with a total length of 20.9 kilometres. Between Thieu, Le Rœulx and Houdeng-Goegnies, La Louvière, there is one section of the canal course, with a distance of just 7 kilometres but a height difference of 66 metres, which was overcome by 4 hydraulic ship elevators equipped by the hydraulic engineer Edwin Clark. The first and highest of these elevators at Houdeng-Goegnies was opened on 4 June 1888, and in 1917 the remaining 3 lifting devices came into service. These 4 hydraulic ship lifts, replaced since 2002 by the new ship lift called Strépy-Thieu, are now on the UNESCO World Heritage List because of their architectural and historical value. As once the tallest ship elevator in the world, this new lift overcomes the difference in level of 73.15 metres between the upstream and downstream reaches and also enables the navigation of ships up to 1,350 tonnes. Now the 4 old elevators are still operating for the purpose of tourism.

中部运河（比利时）

比利时运河。中部运河连通默兹河与斯海尔德河，全长20.9千米，其中一段在勒罗尔克斯的蒂厄与拉卢维耶尔的乌当—乔治涅斯之间，长仅7千米，却有66米的水位差，后来水力学工程师埃德文·克拉克用4个液压升船机解决了这一问题。第一架（也是最高的）升船机位于乌当—乔治涅斯，1888年6月4日对外开放，其余3架升船机于1917年投入使用。这4架液压升船机在2002年被斯特勒比—蒂厄升船机取代，但因其自身的建筑和历史价值而被列入联合国教科文组织世界遗产名录。新建的升船机曾经是世界上最高的升船机，解决了上游和下游河段73.15米的水位落差问题，同时能容纳1 350吨位的船只通行。目前，4架旧式升船机仅在游客参观时运行。

Central Canal (Portugal)

A main canal located in Aveiro, Portugal. The Central Canal runs through the centre of Aveiro, connecting most of the spots important for culture and leisure, such as shops, restaurants, museums, and so on. Today, it is a part of the usual itineraries of Moliceiro tours.

中部运河（葡萄牙）

葡萄牙阿威罗区主要运河。中部运河流经阿威罗市中心，连接商店、餐馆和博物馆等大部分重要的文化和休闲场所。如今，该运河是乘坐摩里西罗船观光的常规行程的一部分。

Central Canal (the United States)

A canal located in Indiana, the United States. Also known as Indiana Central Canal. The Central Canal was not finished with only 12.9 kilometres in length. It was initially designed to be 476 kilometres in length, connecting the Wabash and Erie Canal to the Ohio River, as well as facilitating interstate commerce. The year 1836 witnessed the initial construction of the canal. However, due to the lack of funding, the project was suspended in 1839. Despite its incompleteness, the Central Canal once boosted the local economy by drawing labourers to the area, increasing the population and creating new industries. In 1971, the Indiana Central Canal was declared an American water landmark, which was designated by the American Water Works Association. In the 1980s, an initiative of restoring the canal was put forward in Indianapolis. A part of the canal was included in the White River State Park, and the Canal Walk, based on the former towpaths, was paved in 2001. In 2004, the Canal and White River State Park was enlisted as one of the city's 6 cultural districts, because it provided an opportunity for people to learn about Indiana's past, present and future. Now, the Central Canal still flows and carries two thirds of the water supply in Indianapolis.

Central France Canal

A canal located in Digoin, France. Formerly known as Charollais Canal. The Central France Canal flows from Digoin, where it joins the Loire Lateral

中部运河（美国）

美国印第安纳州运河。亦称印第安纳州中部运河。中部运河仅建成12.9千米。据最初规划，建设长度达476千米，连接沃巴什—伊利运河和俄亥俄河，旨在促进州际贸易。运河1836年开凿，1839年由于缺少资金而停工。尽管如此，中部运河仍在当地的经济发展中发挥重要作用，如汇集劳动力、促进当地人口增长以及新产业的兴起。1971年，美国水务协会将中部运河指定为美国水务地标。20世纪80年代，中部运河修复工程在印第安纳波利斯市展开，运河的一部分被纳入怀特河州立公园。2001年，人们以原有的纤道为基础，修建了运河步行道。2004年，中部运河及怀特河州立公园被列为该市6个文化区之一，成为外界了解印第安纳州历史、现状和未来发展的窗口。如今，已开凿河段仍在使用，满足了印第安纳波利斯市三分之二的用水需求。

法国中部运河

法国中东部迪关运河。旧称沙罗勒运河。法国中部运河自迪关汇入卢瓦尔旁侧运河，东南流向，在

Canal, and heads southeast to the Saône at Chalon-sur-Saône. It is 112.1 kilometres in length, with a maximum authorized draught of 1.8 metres. The construction of the canal was first proposed when King Francis I was in power during the 16th century. It was not until 1783 when Émiland Gauthey, the chief engineer of Burgundy, was authorized to construct the canal, which was later opened in 1792. As one of the technical wonders of its times, the Central France Canal was the first water route from the Loire to the Rhône River, and also the first inland route from the English Channel to the Mediterranean. The canal was accessible to ships sailing south from northern France, connecting waterways in southern, central and western France to transport goods. Between 1880 and 1900, the canal was largely remodeled to meet French inland waterway standards, and the number of locks was reduced from 80 to 61 (35 in Chalon and 26 in Digoin). Within 20 years of its opening, a number of villages had sprung up along the canal banks. With the coal mining industry prospering from 1833 in Montceau-Les Mines, a large supply of shipping was brought in. Until 1936, 1.622 million tonnes of coal from the Mines had been shipped on the canal. By the 1980s, coal shipments had fallen sharply and the Montceau-Les Mines were closed in 2000. At present, the Central France Canal is devoted to tourism instead of commercial transport. The canal meanders through wooded countryside and offers stunning views for visitors along the towpaths, on hotel barge cruises or canal boats.

索恩河畔沙隆附近汇入索恩河，全长112.1千米，最大吃水深度为1.8米。早在16世纪，国王弗朗索瓦一世当政时就提出开凿该运河的设想。直至1783年，勃艮第首席工程师埃米朗·戈泰获得授权负责该运河的开凿，运河项目才进入具体实施阶段，1792年运河通航。法国中部运河是当时的水利工程技术奇迹之一，是首个连通卢瓦尔河和罗讷河的水上通道，也是首条从英吉利海峡通往地中海地区的内陆航线。运河连通法国南部、中部与西部的航道，货船可由法国南部驶向北部地区。1880—1900年间，法国中部运河按照内陆航道标准进行大规模整改，船闸数量由原先的80座缩减为现在的61座，其中沙隆35座，迪关26座。运河开通的20年间，沿河两岸的村庄数量迅速增加。自1833年起，运河沿岸蒙索莱米讷煤矿的开发带来大量的航运货源。至1936年，煤矿区所产的162.2万吨煤炭皆经由该运河运出。20世纪80年代，煤炭运输量急剧下降。2000年，蒙索莱米讷煤矿关闭。目前，运河主要发展旅游业，不再用作商业航运。运河从树木繁茂的乡村蜿蜒穿行，沿岸景色宜人。游客可沿纤道散步或骑行，也可乘坐由驳船改造的酒店游船或租借自驾船游览运河风光。

Chain of Rocks Canal

A canal located in the United States. The Chain of Rocks Canal is 13.5 kilometres long, connecting Minneapolis to New Orleans and the Gulf of Mexico. On the upper Mississippi River, there was a chain of rock ledges extending for more than 27 kilometres on the northeast side of Saint Louis, making it dangerous to navigate. In 1947, the United States Army Corps of Engineers began construction on what would become known as the Chain of Rocks Canal to bypass this area. In 1953, the canal was opened. The construction of the Chain of Rocks Canal led to the founding of America's Central Port. Without the canal, the Mississippi River would not be the strategic asset it is today.

岩石链运河

美国运河。岩石链运河全长13.5千米，连接明尼阿波利斯和新奥尔良及墨西哥湾。在密西西比河上游，圣路易斯东北侧，有一连串的岩壁，延伸超过27千米，严重影响航行。1947年，美国陆军工程兵团开始修建岩石链运河，以绕过这一地区。该运河于1953年通航。中部港口因岩石链运河而得以修建。密西西比河也因这条运河成为战略资产。

Chambly Canal

A canal located in the province of Quebec, Canada. The Chambly Canal is 20 kilometres in length and runs along the Richelieu River, passing many cities including Saint-Jean-sur-Richelieu, Carignan and Chambly. It links the Saint Lawrence River with the Hudson River. The construction of the canal was started in 1831 and it was opened in 1843. Before World War I, the Chambly Canal served as a major trading waterway for the frequent commercial communication between the United States and Canada. After World War I, the merchandise trade declined and the sightseeing tour replaced the commercial traffic on the canal in the 1970s. On this canal lie 10 bridges and 9 locks, among which a bridge and

尚布利运河

加拿大魁北克省运河。尚布利运河全长20千米，沿黎塞留河流经多座城市，包括黎塞留河畔圣让、卡里尼昂和尚布利郊区，连通圣劳伦斯河与哈德孙河。该运河1831年开凿，1843年开通。第一次世界大战前，美国和加拿大之间贸易往来频繁，尚布利运河曾是双方贸易的主要水上运输通道。第一次世界大战后，运河贸易往来渐少。20世纪70年代，尚布利运河的航运功能被游览观光功能取代。运河之上建有10座桥梁和9座船闸，其中1座桥梁和8座船闸仍靠手动操控。目

8 locks are still operated manually. It is currently a National Historic Site of Canada, providing people with leisure and entertainment.

前，尚布利运河已成为加拿大国家历史遗址，供人们休闲娱乐。

Champagne-Burgundy Canal

香槟－勃艮第运河

A canal located in northeastern France. Formerly called Saône-Marne Canal. The Champagne-Burgundy Canal connects the towns of Vitry-le-François and Maxilly-sur-Saône, with a total length of 224 kilometres. Built in 1880, the canal was an extension of the former canal of the Haute Marne, and was opened in 1907. The canal has 114 locks and 2 tunnels. At Vitry-le-François, it connects with the Marne-Rhine Canal and crosses the Langres plateau before flowing down the Vingeanne Valley to connect with the Upper Saône at Heuilley-sur-Saône. The canal serves as one of the principal waterway routes across central France between Paris and Lyon. Recently, it took the present name Champagne-Burgundy Canal in order to promote tourism. It has been tidied up in the last few years and there are lots of places of interest along the way.

法国东北部运河。旧称索恩－马恩运河。香槟－勃艮第运河连接维特里－勒弗朗索瓦和索恩河畔马克西利，全长224千米。该运河于1880年开凿，为原先马恩运河上游延伸工程，1907年通航，共建有114座船闸和2个隧道。该运河在维特里－勒弗朗索瓦与马恩－莱茵运河相通，横跨朗格勒高原，随后流入万雅讷河谷，最终在索恩河畔厄伊莱汇入索恩河上游。香槟－勃艮第运河横跨法国中部，是连接巴黎和里昂的主要航道之一。为提升旅游业，运河更名为现名"香槟－勃艮第运河"。近几年来，香槟－勃艮第运河得到有效治理，沿岸风景绮丽。

Champlain Canal

尚普兰运河

A canal located in New York, the United States. The Champlain Canal connects the south end of Lake Champlain and the Hudson River, running from Waterford through Fort Edward to Whitehall. As the second longest canal in the New York State Canal System, it is 98 kilometres in length. After its initial construction, the canal was only 19

美国纽约州运河。尚普兰运河连通尚普兰湖的南端与哈德孙河，始于沃特福德，流经爱德华堡，终至怀特霍，全长98千米，为纽约州运河网中的第二长运河。建成初期，尚普兰运河仅19千米长，后历经数次扩建。开凿该运河的设想始于

kilometres in length and was enlarged many times thereafter. The intention of excavating the canal was traced back to 1812 and the construction was authorized in 1817. In 1819, the section from Fort Edward to Lake Champlain was opened. In 1823, it was linked to the Erie Canal via the Hudson River. The Champlain Canal is a convenient waterway for transportation. It is also famous for the locks constructed on it. There are in total 11 locks on the canal functioning well nowadays. The canal is now listed as one of the National Register of Historic Places of the United States.

1812年，1817年运河开凿计划得以批准实施。1819年，爱德华堡至尚普兰湖的运河河段竣工并通航。1823年，尚普兰运河又通过哈德孙河连通伊利运河。该运河片区水上交通系统非常完善，共建有11座知名度较高的船闸，至今功能完好。目前，尚普兰运河已被列入美国国家历史遗迹名录。

Chaogou Canal

A tidal canal located in Nanjing, Jiangsu Province, China. Also known as Chengbeiqian Moat or Chengbeigou Canal. The Chaogou Canal was connected to the Yundu Canal, the Pearl River, and the Qingxi River in the west, south, and east respectively. It also linked the Qinhuai River System with the Jinchuan River System. In ancient times, the canal was connected to the Xuanwu Lake, introducing water flow from the Yangtze River to the inner city. The canal was named Chaogou since "chao" in Chinese refers to river tide. The Chaogou Canal was an important man-made waterway completed in the Wu State during the Three Kingdoms Period (220—280 AD). In the Six Dynasties Period (222—589 AD), it served as a vital waterway for Jiankang City (present-day Nanjing) in terms of balancing the water flow and facilitating transport in the city. In the Sui Dynasty (581—618 AD), Yang Jian, the first

潮沟

中国江苏省南京市潮汐运河。亦称城北堑或城北沟。潮沟西接运渎，南连珍珠河，东连青溪，将南京城内的两大水系秦淮河和金川河连为一体。在古代，潮沟北通玄武湖，将长江江潮引入南京城。

"潮"在汉语中指江潮，故名潮沟。三国时期，潮沟是吴国开凿的一条重要人工航道。六朝时期，潮沟是建康城（今南京）的一条重要航道，对维持建康城内的水流量平衡和水路运输具有重要作用。隋朝时期，隋炀帝对建康城进行平荡耕垦，昔日繁华的建康城沦为农田，潮沟也失去了往日的地位和作用。大约到了五代十国时期，潮沟大部分河道逐渐堵塞。明朝时期，潮沟北与玄武湖相接之处设置了

emperor of Sui, ordered to turn the city into a huge farmland and the canal fell into oblivion. During the Five Dynasties and Ten Kingdoms Period (907—979 AD), most part of the water course silted up. In the Ming Dynasty (1368—1644), a bronze tube and the Wumiao Lock were set in the place where the Chaogou Canal joined the Xuanwu Lake in the North. In the Qing Dynasty (1616—1911), the canal was reconnected to the Jinxianghe River as the water was introduced to the pond in front of the Jiangning School, a well-known institute of higher education in the Ming Dynasty and flowed westwards through the Wenqu River. The course of the Chaogou Canal is connected to the Xuanwu Lake in the north and the Chengbeiqu River in the south. The eastern course connected to the Qingxi River has disappeared. The western course started from the southern foot of the Arctic Pavilion Mountain to the northern tip of today's Jinxianghe River Road, which is connected to the underground section of the Jinxianghe River.

铜涵管，并建有武庙闸。清朝时期，潮沟之水引入江宁府学（明朝知名学府）前的泮池，再通过文曲河西流，与进香河重新连为一体。潮沟北与玄武湖相连、南与城北渠相接。与青溪相连的东段潮沟如今已不复存在。西段河道大致沿北极阁南麓至进香河路北端，与进香河地下河段相接。

Charente-Seudre Canal

夏朗德－瑟德尔运河

A canal located on the western shore of France. Also called Bridoire Canal. The Charente-Seudre Canal links the Charente River at Rochefort with the Seudre River at Marennes. It is 27 kilometres in length and has 5 locks. The construction of the canal had been started since 1700 and was finally completed in 1862. The canal was decommissioned in 1926.

法国西部海岸运河。亦称布里多瓦运河。夏朗德－瑟德尔运河在罗什福尔连接夏朗德河，在马雷连接瑟德尔河，全长27千米，建有5座船闸。该运河于1700年开凿，1862年完工，后于1926年停航。

Charleroi-Brussels Canal

A canal located in Belgium. Also called Charleroi Canal. As a part of the north-south axis of water transport in Belgium, the Charleroi-Brussels Canal is 65 kilometres in length, running from Charleroi in the south to Brussels in the north. During the reign of Philip the Good, Duke of Burgundy (1396—1467), the idea of building a waterway to serve the cities of Hainaut was put forward. However, due to diverse factors such as the outbreak of war, high expenses and public protest, the project was hampered until 1827 when William I of the Netherlands reigned. At that time, the industrial revolution witnessed an increasingly important role of coal mining in economy. The Sambre and Marne valleys were quite rich in coal, which entailed the need to excavate the canal. The construction began in 1827 and was finished 5 years later. The navigation capacity of the canal back then was only 70 tonnes. It was later enlarged to 1,350 tonnes in 1933. The last major improvement to the canal was building an inclined plane at Ronquières, which is regarded as a masterpiece of civil engineering. There were two prominent trade routes along the waterways. One was from the Rhineland to Flanders and the other from Antwerp to Wallonia. The routes have promoted trade and economy around the canal and the process of urbanization.

沙勒罗瓦－布鲁塞尔运河

比利时运河。亦称沙勒罗瓦运河。沙勒罗瓦－布鲁塞尔运河是比利时南北水运轴的一部分，全长65千米，自南向北由沙勒罗瓦流至布鲁塞尔。在勃艮第公爵，"善良的"菲利普统治期间（1396—1467），就提出要开凿一条航道，为埃诺省几座城市提供航运服务。然而，因战乱、成本高昂、民众抗议等因素，该项目一直未启动，直到1827年威廉一世在位时才得以实施。当时，工业革命使得煤炭在经济中的作用日益重要。桑布尔河和马恩河谷煤炭资源相当丰富，运河开凿计划终于在1827年得以通过。同年，运河开凿工作启动，5年后竣工。起初，运河所能承载的船舶最大吨位仅有70吨，后在1933年扩大至1 350吨。该运河最后一次重大改进是在隆基耶尔增加的一个斜面升船机，堪称土木工程杰作。沙勒罗瓦－布鲁塞尔运河沿线有两条主要贸易路线：一条从莱茵兰到佛兰德斯，另一条从安特卫普到瓦隆，极大地促进了当地贸易和经济的发展，加快了城市化进程。

Charleroi Canal

A canal located in Belgium. See Charleroi-Brussels Canal.

Charlottenburg Canal

A canal located in Berlin, Germany. The Charlottenburg Canal runs north from River Spree until it passes under the railway bridge where it turns east to the south of the Westhafen Canal. Built between 1848 through 1859, the Charlottenburg Canal was 3.2 kilometres in length but what is left now is only 1.7 kilometres long. Currently, the canal still connects the Westhafen Canal and River Spree as well as the Landwehr Canal. Meanwhile, it also connects River Spree in Charlottenburg with the Berlin-Spandau Ship Canal.

Charnwood Forest Canal

A freshwater canal located in central England, the United Kingdom. Also called Forest Line of the Leicester Navigation. The Charnwood Forest Canal runs approximately 12 kilometres long, linking the village of Thringstone with the village of Nanpantan in the southwest of the town of Loughborough. It is named after the Charnwood Forest in northwestern Leicestershire. Constructed by the Leicester Navigation Company, the project was finished in 1794. The canal was mainly used for transporting coal. By the 1830s, a convenient railway network had been established in the region and the canal was almost

沙勒罗瓦运河

比利时运河。见沙勒罗瓦—布鲁塞尔运河。

夏洛滕堡运河

德国柏林市运河。夏洛滕堡运河自施普雷河向北穿过铁路大桥，并由此朝东流向韦斯特哈芬运河之南。该运河于1848—1859年间开凿，当时全长3.2千米，如今仅留存1.7千米。目前，夏洛滕堡运河成为韦斯特哈芬运河与施普雷河、兰韦尔运河之间的纽带。同时，该运河还连接夏洛滕堡的施普雷河与柏林—施潘道通海运河。

查恩伍德森林运河

英国英格兰中部淡水运河。亦称莱斯特郡森林航道。查恩伍德森林运河连接斯林斯通村和拉夫伯勒镇西南部的南潘滕村，全长约12千米，得名于莱斯特郡西北部的查恩伍德森林。该运河的开凿工作由莱斯特航海公司承担，1794年竣工通航，主要用于煤炭运输。19世纪30年代，由于便捷的铁路网已经覆盖该地区，查恩伍德森林运河几近废弃。1846年，查恩伍德森林运河正式停航。

disused. In 1846, the Charnwood Forest Canal was officially declared out of use.

Charollais Canal

A canal located in Digoin, France. See Central France Canal.

沙罗勒运河

法国迪关运河。见法国中部运河。

Chelles Canal

A canal located in France. Also called Vaires Canal. The Chelles Canal runs parallel to the Marne River, linking the Marne River in Neuilly-sur-Marne with the Marne River in Vaires-sur-Marne. It is 8.5 kilometres long. The canal is named so because it crosses the southern part of the town of Chelles. The construction of the canal was started in 1848 when the government of the French Second Republic (1848—1851) created the National Workshops to provide jobs for the unemployed after the Revolution of 1848. Due to the lack of funding, the construction was abandoned shortly afterwards and was resumed under the Second French Empire (1852—1870). The canal was opened in 1865.

谢勒运河

法国运河。亦称威尔运河。谢勒运河与马恩河平行，从马恩河畔讷伊流至马恩河畔韦尔，两端皆与马恩河交汇，全长8.5千米。该运河因其流经谢勒镇南部而得名。该运河于1848年开凿，彼时，法兰西第二共和国（1848—1851）成立了国家工场，旨在为一八四八年革命后的失业者提供工作机会。但由于资金不足，该运河工程动工不久后便停工，后于法兰西第二帝国期间（1852—1870）续建。1865年，谢勒运河建成通航。

Chelmer and Blackwater Navigation

A canal located in southeastern England, the United Kingdom. As the canalized part of River Chelmer and River Blackwater, the Chelmer and Blackwater Navigation runs roughly eastwards from Chelmsford to the Heybridge adjacent to Maldon. The canal is 22 kilometres long and has 12 locks, 6

切尔默－布莱克沃特运河

英国英格兰东南部运河。切尔默－布莱克沃特运河由切尔默河和布莱克沃特河的部分河段改造而成，自切姆斯福德市向东流至莫尔登镇附近的海布里奇村。运河全长22千米，建有12座船闸、6座桥梁

bridges as well as several flood gates, allowing the passage of ships up to 18.3 metres in length and 4.9 metres in width. The construction was started in 1793 and finished in 1797. It was mainly used for the transportation of cargoes such as coal, bricks, timber, grain and flour. By 1972, the Chelmer and Blackwater Navigation was no longer used for cargo transportation. It then gradually developed into a recreational and leisure site. Currently, the canal is still owned by the Company of Proprietors of the Chelmer and Blackwater Navigation Ltd., but is run by the Essex Waterways Ltd., a subsidiary of the Inland Waterways Association.

和若干防洪闸门，可供长度不超过18.3米、宽度不超过4.9米的船只通航。切尔默—布莱克沃特运河于1793年开凿，1797年竣工，当时主要用以运输煤炭、砖、木材、谷物和面粉等货物。至1972年，切尔默—布莱克沃特运河不再用于货物运输，后逐渐用于娱乐休闲。目前，该运河所有权仍属于切尔默—布莱克沃特运河有限公司，但主要由内陆运河协会的子公司艾塞克斯运河有限公司负责运营。

Chemung Canal

希芒运河

A disused canal located in New York, the United States. The Chemung Canal was 32.2 kilometres long, 1.2 metres deep, 12.8 metres wide at the surface and 7.9 metres wide at the base. Its artery linked the Seneca Lake with the Chemung River, with a navigable feeder canal that stretched from Horseheads to Corning. With 49 locks, it chiefly functioned as a freight canal. Encouraged by the construction of the Erie Canal in New York in 1825, many communities longed for new canal systems to promote the local economy. In 1830, a total of $300,000 was appropriated by the state government for the construction of the Chemung Canal. The project was started in 1830 and completed in 1833. The construction faced many difficulties due to the elevation drop of over 122 metres, loose soil and a huge swamp in the north of Elmira. On

美国纽约州弃用运河。希芒运河长32.2千米，深1.2米，水面宽12.8米，河底宽7.9米。该运河主干连通塞内卡湖和希芒河，二者之间建有一条可通航的引水运河，从纽约州的霍斯黑兹镇延伸至科宁市。希芒运河上共建有49座主要用于货运的船闸。1825年，纽约州伊利运河建成后，其他地方的民众受到鼓舞，希冀修建新的运河网以促进地方经济发展。1830年，纽约州政府拨款30万美元用以开凿希芒运河。该运河1830年开凿，1833年竣工。运河修建过程中遇到许多难题，主要包括如何处理超过122米的水位落差、土壤疏松以及埃尔迈拉县北部大片沼泽地的问

completion, the Chemung Canal served as a link between the Susquehanna River Watershed and the Erie Canal System, facilitating the navigation of barges from Pennsylvania and the south of New York. It was also a trade route through which goods from all over the world could be imported into the local cities, which boosted the development of business and economy in this area. Afterwards, a variety of factors led to the disuse of the canal. On the one hand, its maintenance was expensive owing to the damage by seasonal flooding and dry periods every year. On the other hand, the normal navigation was limited by the poor drainage of the canal as well as the wooden locks that were far from being durable. Meanwhile, the emergence of the railway also induced the dereliction of the canal. The Chemung Canal was finally abandoned in 1878. Nowadays, the section of the canal from the north of Montour Falls to Watkins Glen, which was once widened, is still in use as a part of the Barge Canal System. Portions of former towpaths were transformed into the current Catharine Valley Trail.

题。竣工后，希芒运河成为萨斯奎汉纳河流域和伊利运河网的纽带，带动了宾夕法尼亚州和纽约州南部航运业的发展。作为贸易通道的希芒运河将世界各地的商品运送到运河沿岸城市，促进了当地的经济发展与商业繁荣。后来，多种因素导致该运河航运业务日渐衰退。一方面，每年受季节性洪水和枯水期影响，运河维护费用高昂；另一方面，运河排水不畅，且木质船闸的耐用性不强，影响了正常的航运效率。此外，铁路的出现进一步加速了希芒运河的衰落。1878年，希芒运河终被废弃。如今，该运河从蒙图尔福尔斯以北到沃特金斯格伦的河段拓宽后，仍是纽约州驳船运河网的一部分。旧日的几条纤道已被改建为现在的卡特琳山谷步道。

Chenango Canal

希南戈运河

A canal located in central New York, the United States. The Chenango Canal starts at Binghamton in the south and ends at Utica in the north, with a south-to-north span in New York. It connects the Susquehanna River to the Erie Canal. The canal is 156 kilometres long, 1.2 metres deep in average, 12.8 metres wide on the surface and 7.9 metres wide at the bottom. There were once 12 dams and 19 aq-

美国纽约州中部运河。希南戈运河南起宾厄姆顿市，北至尤蒂卡市，从南至北穿过美国纽约州，连通萨斯奎汉纳与伊利运河。运河全长156千米，平均深度为1.2米，河面宽12.8米，河底宽7.9米。运河上曾建有12座大坝和19座渡槽。希南戈运河开凿于19世纪中

ueducts across the river. The Chenango Canal was built in the mid-19th century. When the Erie Canal was opened in 1825, the Great Lakes and Hudson River were connected to the port of New York City, facilitating the trade and business in New York State. To ship coals from Pennsylvania to the Erie Canal, 9 leaders of the Chenango Canal Committee spent 19 years lobbying for the construction of Chenango Canal. In 1833, this proposal was authorized by the New York Legislature. The construction began in 1834. It was designed by an American civil engineer John B. Jervis and mainly constructed by the immigrant labourers from Ireland and Scotland. When finished in 1836, this canal cost a total of $2.5 million. The canal was special since it was fed by the reservoir system, and this feeding method had never been used in America before. The Chenango Canal facilitated the transportation of goods in this area, and also boosted local tourism and entertainment. In 1878, the canal was closed due to high maintenance fees. Nowadays, the Chenango Canal is home to a variety of wild life, including ducks, geese and blue herons. In order to preserve and promote the area for the benefits of the public, the Chenango Canal Association launched the Chenango Canal Project, which includes efforts such as transforming the towpath into an 8-kilometre-long walkway, establishing a canal museum, and building a deck for fishing and sightseeing.

叶。1825年，伊利运河开航，连通了五大湖和哈德孙河到纽约港的航道，促进了纽约州商贸业的发展。为将宾夕法尼亚州的煤炭运送到伊利运河，希南戈运河委员会9位倡导人耗费19年时间向议员们游说修建希南戈运河。1833年，这项议案终获纽约州议会批准。运河修建工程于1834年开始，1836年竣工，共耗资250万美元。希南戈运河由美国土木工程师约翰·杰维斯设计，爱尔兰和苏格兰移民是开凿运河的主要劳动力。运河的一个特殊设计是通过水库系统向运河供水，这也是美国运河工程中首次使用此种方法。运河通航后为当地的货物运输提供了便利，同时带动了当地旅游业和娱乐业的发展。1878年，由于航运维护费用高昂，希南戈运河停用。如今，希南戈运河已成为野鸭、大雁和蓝鹭等野生动物栖息地。为保护运河遗址并促进当地建设，希南戈运河协会实施了运河改建项目，改建8千米纤道为步道，并建成运河博物馆以及垂钓观光两用观景台。

Chengbeigou Canal

城北沟

A tidal canal located in Nanjing, Jiangsu Province,

中国江苏省南京市潮汐运河。见

China. See Chaogou Canal.

潮沟。

Chengbeiqian Moat

A tidal canal located in Nanjing, Jiangsu Province, China. See Chaogou Canal.

城北堑

中国江苏省南京市潮汐运河。见潮沟。

Cheonggyecheon Stream

An inland canal located in Seoul, South Korea. The Cheonggyecheon Stream flows from west to east through downtown Seoul and connects the Han River by Jungnangcheon. It is 10.92 kilometres in length, and the basin area covers 50.96 square kilometres. During the Joseon Dynasty (1392—1910), the stream was named Gaecheon (literally excavation of rivers). It refers to the projects aimed for the improvement of the conditions of the stream at that time. These improvement projects were carried out every two to three years, including clearing and widening the riverbed, building dams and bridges to prevent flooding, etc. After the Korean War, the Cheonggyecheon Stream became home to many of the refugees who poured into Seoul to make ends meet. The dirty wooden sheds that stood along the river and the sewage discharged there worsened the pollution. The economic strength of Korea at that time only allowed covering the stream as a way to solve the problem. In the 1970s, the Cheonggyecheon Stream was finally covered by an elevated highway, which was 5.6 kilometres long and 16 metres wide. The highway provided great convenience for people but polluted the environment with the

清溪川运河

韩国首尔内陆运河。清溪川运河自西向东穿过首尔城区，经中浪川与汉江相连，全长10.92千米，流域面积50.96平方千米。朝鲜王朝时期（1392—1910），这条溪流称作"开川"，意为开凿河川，也就是当时的河流整治。为防止洪水泛滥，每2—3年对该运河进行一次整治，包括清理和拓宽河床、建水坝和桥梁等。朝鲜战争后，大量难民涌入首尔，在沿河而建的肮脏木棚里艰难度日，排放的污水加剧了清溪川的污染。就当时的经济实力而言，解决污染的唯一办法就是掩埋河流。20世纪70年代，一条长5.6千米、宽16米的高架公路建于清溪川运河之上。虽然高架公路给人们提供了诸多便利，但大量汽车排放的尾气和产生的噪音也严重污染了周围环境。2003年7月，在时任首尔市长李明博的推动下，韩国政府发起了一项环境治理项目，主要措施包括拆除高架公路、重新开凿河道、分置清水和污水管道以保

exhaust gas and noise generated by the large number of cars passing by. A restoration project was carried out in July 2003 under the promotion of then Seoul Mayor Lee Myung-bak. Under this project, the elevated highway was removed, the river was re-excavated, and the water and sewage pipes were separated to keep the water clean. The project cost 900 billion won and was completed in September 2005. With ten fountains, a square and a cultural hall, the Cheonggyecheon Stream attracted 62 million visitors in two years after its restoration, serving as a place for leisure and recreation in downtown Seoul.

持水质清洁。该项目耗资9 000亿韩元,于2005年9月完工。整治后的清溪川运河建有广场、文化馆和10个喷泉,两年时间里就吸引了6 200万游客,成为首尔市中心新的休闲娱乐场所。

Cher≈

A canalized river located in central France. As a tributary of the Loire River, the total length of the Cher is 367.8 kilometres and the area of the Cher basin covers 13,718 square kilometres. It originates from the west of Massif Central, flows northwest and joins with the Loire River at Villandry. The average yearly runoff of the Cher is 104 cubic metres per second. In the 19th century, a 130-kilometre-long part of the river, i.e., from Tours to Vierzon, was canalized. It served as one part of the river network that connected Tours to Nevers. Nowadays, the Cher only has 54 kilometres of navigable waterway for boats with a maximum draught of 80 centimetres. Local councils once planned to restore the navigation of the whole 130-kilometre-long canal, but had to give up as the weirs between Saint Aignan and Montrichard were removed. The French

谢尔河

法国中部运河化河流。谢尔河是卢瓦尔河支流,全长367.8千米,流域面积13 718平方千米。该河始于中部高原西部,西北流向,在维兰德里汇入卢瓦尔河,年均流速为每秒104立方米。19世纪时,从图尔市到维耶尔宗市的一段130千米的河道被改建为运河,成为连接图尔市与讷韦尔市河运网的组成部分。如今,谢尔河仅有54千米可通航,可容最大吃水深度为80厘米的船只。当地议会曾计划将130千米的整条运河航道全线复航,但由于圣艾尼昂市和蒙特里夏尔市之间的堰坝被移除而未能实现。另外,法国政府为保护迁徙的鱼类也反对复航。谢尔河两岸文化和

government also opposed the restoration to protect migrating fish species. Many cultural and historical sites stand alongside the Cher, and one of the most famous is the Château at Chenonceaux.

历史遗迹林立，其中最著名的是舍农索城堡。

Cher Canal

谢尔运河

A canal located in France. See Berry Canal.

法国运河。见贝里运河。

Chesapeake and Delaware Canal

切萨皮克－特拉华运河

A canal located in Delaware State, the United States. Also called C&D Canal. The name of the canal reflects the names of the two water bodies that it connects, i.e., the Delaware River with the Chesapeake Bay. The Chesapeake and Delaware Canal divides Delaware State into northern and southern parts. It is 22.5 kilometres in length, 137.2 metres in width and 10.7 metres in depth. It is one of the few fully sea-level shipping canals in the world. The canal is under the management of the United States Army Corps of Engineers, Philadelphia District. Early in the 17th century, settlers on the American continent realized the importance of building a waterway system. In the mid-17th century, a mapmaker called Augustine Herman found that the Delaware River and the Chesapeake Bay could easily be connected, as there was only a small strip of land between the two. After several decades, the Americans put this proposal into action in 1804. However, the work was suspended due to the lack of funding. In 1829, the canal was finally opened to the public. It cost 2.5 million dollars and was listed

美国特拉华州运河。亦称切特运河。运河之名反映了它连接的两大水域：特拉华河与切萨皮克湾。切萨皮克－特拉华运河将特拉华州分为南北两部分，全长22.5千米，宽137.2米，深10.7米。该运河是世界上为数不多的完全海平式通海运河，由美国费城的陆军工程兵团管理。早在17世纪初，美洲大陆移民就已经意识到修建运河网的重要性。17世纪中叶，一位名叫奥古斯丁·赫尔曼的地图绘制员发现，特拉华河和切萨皮克湾之间仅相隔很小的一块陆地，易于连通。几十年以后，这一提议由美国人于1804年最终付诸实施。不过，由于资金缺乏，这项工程曾一度搁置。直到1829年，运河才竣工通航，总造价高达250万美元，为当时修建费用最昂贵的运河之一。切萨皮克－特拉华运河将费城和巴尔的摩港之间的贸易路程缩短了近483

as one of the most expensive canals at that time. The Chesapeake and Delaware Canal shortens the trade routes between Philadelphia and the Port of Baltimore by about 483 kilometres. In 1919, the canal was purchased by the United States government and several expansions of the canal were conducted by the United States Army Corps of Engineers over the years. To this day, the canal is still in use for business and improvement projects are conducted continuously. It transports about 40% of all vessels that come into the Port of Baltimore. The Chesapeake and Delaware Canal is listed on the National Register of Historic Places, and designated as a National Historic Civil Engineering and Mechanical Engineering Landmark. A C&D Canal Museum is established to illustrate the history and operation of this canal.

千米。1919年,运河被美国政府购买,多年来,美国陆军工程兵团对该运河进行了几次扩建。时至今日,切萨皮克—特拉华运河仍作商用,并且在不断维护和修缮,承运了约40%进入巴尔的摩港的船只。切萨皮克—特拉华运河被列入美国国家历史遗迹名录,也被列为国家历史土木工程和机械工程地标。为展示运河的历史和通航情况还修建了切特运河博物馆。

Chesapeake and Ohio Canal

A disused canal located in the northeast of the United States. Connecting the Alexandria Canal and the Goose Creek and Little River Navigation in Virginia, the Chesapeake and Ohio Canal was 296.9 kilometres long and ran from Georgetown, Washington, D.C. to Cumberland, Maryland. Due to a huge difference in water levels of 184 metres, the canal was equipped with 74 locks, 11 aqueducts, along with more than 240 culverts for smaller streams. The width of the canal also varied with different sections. The canal accommodates vessels of a maximum of 27 metres in length and 4.4 metres in width. The plan to build the canal can

切萨皮克-俄亥俄运河

美国东北部废弃运河。切萨皮克—俄亥俄运河全长296.9千米,自华盛顿特区的乔治敦流向马里兰州的坎伯兰郡,连通弗吉尼亚州的亚历山大运河和古斯河—利特尔河航道。运河水位差达184米,共建有74座船闸及11座渡槽,在小的河段上开凿了240多个涵洞。切萨皮克—俄亥俄运河各河段宽度不同。运河可通航船只的最大尺寸为27米长,4.4米宽。开凿该运河的设想最早由总统乔治·华盛顿在独立战争后提出,1825年3月在詹姆

be traced back to the idea of George Washington after the American War of Independence, which was finally materialized by President James Monroe in March, 1825 when he signed the bill and authorized the construction of the canal. With favourable conditions of free taxation, the canal company was supposed to build 160 kilometres available in five years, and to complete the project in 12 years. The construction was started in 1828. Because of the competition from the Erie Canal, the canal company stopped the project. In the 1840s, the canal had to face fierce competition from the railroad. In 1938, the canal was purchased by the United States government. Formerly, the canal functioned mainly for the transportation of coals from the Allegheny Mountains, whereas in 1971, the canal was renovated as the Chesapeake and Ohio Canal National Historical Park. Now, it attracts many tourists to pay a visit.

斯·门罗总统任内得以落实。门罗总统签署了批准开凿切萨皮克—俄亥俄运河的法案。运河公司享受免纳税的优惠政策，在5年内建成160千米运河并投入使用，且在12年内完成所有的开凿工作。1828年，运河工程动工，但由于伊利运河带来的竞争压力，运河公司终止了切萨皮克—俄亥俄运河开凿工程。19世纪40年代，运河与铁路竞争激烈。1938年，美国政府收购了切萨皮克—俄亥俄运河。该运河之前主要用于运输阿勒格尼山脉的煤炭。1971年，运河被改建为切萨皮克—俄亥俄运河国家历史公园，吸引了众多游客。

Chesterfield Canal

A canal located in England, the United Kingdom. Also called Cuckoo Dyke. The term "cuckoo" is believed to originate from the comments on the boatmen on the Chesterfield Canal in the 19th Century. They were deemed as mad (cuckoo) for sailing narrow craft, which were unique to the canal, on the wild river. The Chesterfield Canal meanders from River Trent at West Stockwith to Chesterfield with a length of 73.3 kilometres and 65 locks. Currently, only the section between West Stockwith and the eastern end of Norwood Tunnel is navigable, which

切斯特菲尔德运河

英国英格兰运河。亦称疯人堤。

"疯人"是19世纪时人们对切斯特菲尔德运河的船夫的评价。船夫驾驶着该运河独有的狭长小船在汹涌的河水上来往，被认为是一种疯狂的举动。切斯特菲尔德运河自位于西斯托克威斯的特伦特河蜿蜒流向切斯特菲尔德，全长73.3千米，共建有65座船闸。目前，仅西斯托克威斯至诺伍德隧道东端的河段可通航，可通航河段长50.9

is 50.9 kilometres long with 46 locks. The Chesterfield Canal was constructed under the direction of the engineer James Brindley, and was officially opened in 1777. It played a vital part throughout the 19th century. Apart from coal, it also carried cargoes like agricultural goods, iron, pottery and ale. Among them, the most famous one was the 250,000 tons of stone from local quarries, which was used later to build the House of Parliament in the United Kingdom. The last recorded commercial cargo was in the 1960s. With the campaigners' efforts, the Transport Act 1968 reclassified canals with regard to their usage status, and allowed a sizeable section between Stockwith and Worksop to remain navigable. By this time restoration efforts were already in progress. In 1976, the Chesterfield Canal Society was formed, which is now known as the Chesterfield Canal Trust.

千米, 有46座船闸。切斯特菲尔德运河在工程师詹姆斯·布林德利的指挥下开凿, 1777年正式通航。该运河在整个19世纪发挥了重要作用, 除运输煤炭外, 还输送各种农产品、铁、陶器和麦芽啤酒等货物。其中最出名的货运物资应属当地采石场的25万吨石头, 它们被用于建造英国议会大厦。据记载, 自20世纪60年代后, 该运河不再用于商业货运。1968年, 在众多运河工程推动者的努力下, 英国《运输法》根据使用状况对运河重新分类, 允许西斯托克威斯到沃克索普市之间的一大段河道继续通航。此后, 切斯特菲尔德运河开始重建。1976年, 切斯特菲尔德运河协会成立, 后更名为切斯特菲尔德运河信托基金会。

Chicago Drainage Canal

芝加哥排污运河

A canal located in northeastern Illinois, the United States. See Chicago Sanitary and Ship Canal.

美国伊利诺伊州东北部运河。见芝加哥环境卫生与通海运河。

Chicago Sanitary and Ship Canal

芝加哥环境卫生与通海运河

A canal located in northeastern Illinois, the United States. Also called Chicago Drainage Canal. Connecting the Chicago River with the Des Plaines River, the Chicago Sanitary and Ship Canal is about 48 kilometres in length, with a minimum width of 50 metres and a minimum depth of 2.7 metres.

美国伊利诺伊州东北部运河。亦称芝加哥排污运河。芝加哥环境卫生与通海运河连通芝加哥河与德斯普兰斯河, 全长约48千米, 最窄处50米, 最浅处2.7米, 建有2座船闸。开凿该运河的主要目的是处

There are 2 locks on the canal. It was primarily built to dispose of the city's sewage, most of which had previously been dumped into the Chicago River and ultimately polluted the Michigan Lake, the source of the city's drinking water. The Chicago Sanitary and Ship Canal was also constructed to replace the shallow and narrow Illinois and Michigan Canal which connected the Michigan Lake with the Mississippi to allow much larger ships to navigate up and down the canal. The canal was opened in 1900 and was later extended from Lockport to Joliet during the years between 1903 and 1907. The excavation reversed the flow of the Chicago River so that it flew out of the Michigan Lake. In 1999, the canal was acclaimed as a Civil Engineering Monument of the Millennium by the American Society of Civil Engineers. In 2011, it was listed on the National Register of Historic Places.

理城市的污水排放问题。运河建成前，芝加哥市大部分污水被排入芝加哥河，最后流入并污染了该市的饮用水源密歇根湖。此外，开凿芝加哥环境卫生与通海运河也为了使更大的船只能够航行其上，以取代连通密歇根湖和密西西比河的伊利诺伊—密歇根运河，该运河浅而窄。芝加哥环境卫生与通海运河于1900年通航，并于1903年至1907年扩建，自洛克波特延伸至乔利埃特。该运河开凿后改变了芝加哥河的流向，河水不再注入密歇根湖。1999年，美国土木工程协会赞其为"千禧年土木工程里程碑"。2011年，芝加哥环境卫生与通海运河被列入美国国家历史遗迹名录。

Chichester Canal

奇切斯特运河

A canal located in England, the United Kingdom. The Chichester Canal originates in the south of the historic city Chichester and empties into the Chichester Harbour. The total length of the canal is about 6.4 kilometres with 2 locks on it. The Chichester Canal is actually a part of the larger Portsmouth and Arundel Canal which runs from Ford to the Portsmouth Harbour. It was excavated in 1819 and opened in 1822. A century later, it was abandoned in 1928. In 1953, the Chichester Canal was purchased by the West Sussex County Council. From the 1980s, the restoration of the canal was started.

英国英格兰运河。奇切斯特运河始于历史名城奇切斯特市南侧，止于奇切斯特港，全长约6.4千米，建有2座船闸。奇切斯特运河是朴次茅斯—阿伦德尔运河的一段，后者从福特镇流向朴次茅斯港。运河于1819年开凿，1822年正式通航，1928年被弃用。1953年，西萨塞克斯郡议会收购了该运河所有权。自20世纪80年代起，奇切斯特运河修复工作启动。从运河港池到唐宁顿交叉口的4千米航段已由

Now the 4-kilometre-long section from the Canal Basin to the Donnington crossing has been restored by the Chichester Ship Canal Trust. There a daily boat service is provided from February to October, and Charter boat trips are available throughout the year. The Trust also offers rowing boat rentals and issues licenses for fishing, canoes and paddle boards. Today the Chichester Canal is an important aquatic and terrestrial habitat for wildlife and is listed as a Site of Nature Conservation Importance (SNCI).

奇切斯特通海运河信托基金会修复，每年2—10月提供日常航运服务，全年提供租赁游船服务。该基金会还提供划艇租赁，并办理钓鱼、皮划艇和冲浪板许可证服务。如今，奇切斯特运河还是水陆野生动物的重要栖息地，已被列为英国的自然保护区。

Christian Port Canal

克里斯钦港运河

A canal located in the Christiana community of Copenhagen, Denmark. The Christian Port Canal divides the community into two parts, runs from northeast to southwest. In the end it comes to an abrupt turn to the right and flows into the main harbour at the north of the Langebro Bridge. It is known as a relaxed place with many boats and houseboats. A cruise through the canal is one of the highlights of Copenhagen sightseeing tours. At the northern mouth of the Christian Port Canal, the plan of a bridge is conceived to enable the public to have an easy access to the Copenhagen Opera House and Holmen in general. At the other end, another pedestrian and bicycle bridge is in the blueprint.

丹麦哥本哈根市克里斯钦港社区运河。克里斯钦港运河将该社区一分为二，自东北流向西南方向，在南段尽头急转向右注入长桥北边的主港口。该运河是休闲胜地，提供大量船只和船屋，泛舟其上是哥本哈根旅游必玩项目之一。为方便人们前往哥本哈根戏剧院和霍尔门岛，克里斯钦港运河北河口处计划建造一座大桥。在运河南端，一座供自行车与行人通行的桥也被列入规划。

Chute-à-Blondeau Canal

许特布隆多运河

An abandoned canal located in southeastern Canada. The Chute-à-Blondeau Canal, situated upriver from the Carillon Canal, was about 260 metres in

加拿大东南部废弃运河。许特布隆多运河位于卡里隆运河上游处，长约260米，建有1座船闸，是渥太

length and equipped with one lock, the shortest among the three military canals of the Ottawa River, the other two being the Carillon Canal and the Grenville Canal. After the War of 1812, the British government financed the construction of these three canals to provide an alternative military supply route to Kingston, replacing the Saint Lawrence, which was vulnerable to attacks of the United States army. Excavated through rocks, the Chute-à-Blondeau Canal was constructed by the Royal Engineers between 1819 and 1833. Along with other two canals, the Chute-à-Blondeau Canal was used to transport British troops and supplies during the war with the United States. After being transferred to the Canadian government in 1857, the canals were less used for military purpose but served more as commercial channels for the trade along the Ottawa River. They became important links between Montreal, Bytown and Kinston. The canals were then enlarged to accommodate larger vessels between 1873 and 1882, during which the Chute-à-Blondeau Canal gradually became disused. When a new dam was built on the Carillon Canal, the Chute-à-Blondeau Canal was finally discarded. In 1963, the canal was thoroughly submerged with the construction of the modern hydraulic plant.

华河上3条军用运河中最短的一条，其他2条分别是卡里隆运河和格伦维尔运河。1812年战争后，英国政府出资修建上述3条运河，作为通往金斯顿市的军用航道，取代易受美国军队袭击的圣劳伦斯河。许特布隆多运河从岩石道路中间开凿，由英国皇家工兵部队于1819—1833年间修建。此后英军与美军交战时期，这3条运河用来运送英方军队和物资。1857年，这些运河被移交给加拿大政府管理，逐渐转为商用，成为渥太华河沿线贸易往来的货运通道，可以连接蒙特利尔市、拜城和金斯顿市。1873—1882年间，为使更大规模的船只通行，这3条运河被拓宽。这期间，许特布隆多运河的使用逐渐减少。等到卡里隆运河上的新水坝建成后，许特布隆多运河最终被废弃。1963年，随着现代水电站建成，许特布隆多运河被彻底淹没于水下。

City Canal

城市运河

A canal located in England, the United Kingdom. The City Canal serves as a bridge between the 2 reaches of River Thames. It is 1,130 metres in length with a surface width of 53 metres and a

英国英格兰运河。城市运河连通泰晤士河的2个河段，全长1 130米，河面宽53米，深14米。运河上建有2座长59米、宽14米的船闸。

depth of 14 metres. There are 2 locks on the canal, both of which are 59 metres in length and 14 metres in width. Authorized by the West India Docks Act of 1799, the canal was constructed from the Limehouse Reach to the Blackwall Reach. In the 1920s, it was stated that the South Dock should be connected to the West India Import and Export docks, as well as the Millwall Dock. Later in 1931, for this purpose, three new passages linking the three docks were excavated and a new lock at the South Dock east entrance was built. Nowadays, the City Canal has been reconstructed. The original route of the canal across the Isle of Dogs in London no longer exists. The South Dock, as the furthest point upstream for ships to turn around, plays a regular host to medium-sized military vessels visiting London.

1799年,《西印度港区法案》授权伦敦城市公司在莱姆豪斯河段到布莱克沃尔河段之间开凿一条运河。20世纪20年代,人们决定连接南码头、西印度进出口码头以及米尔沃尔码头,随后便在南码头东入口处开始修建1座新船闸,并开凿3条航道来连接这3座码头,1931年竣工。如今,城市运河得以重建。最初穿越伦敦道格斯岛的运河线路已不复存在。在上游河段,南码头是供船只调头的最远端,如今主要通行巡查伦敦的中型军用船只。

Clignon Canal

A canal located in northern France. The Clignon Canal links the Ourcq Canal with Montigny-l'Allier. It is 1.2 kilometres in length and has no lock.

克利尼翁运河

法国北部运河。克利尼翁运河连接乌尔克运河和蒙蒂尼—阿列市,全长1.2千米,未建船闸。

Clinton and Kalamazoo Canal

An uncompleted canal located in Michigan, the United States. The Clinton and Kalamazoo Canal was designed to link Lake St. Clair with Lake Michigan. The canal was planned to be 347.6 kilometres in length and 20 metres in width, starting from the banks of the Clinton River to the mouth of the Kalamazoo River, hence the name of the

克林顿—卡拉马祖运河

美国密歇根州未完工运河。克林顿—卡拉马祖运河原计划连通圣克莱尔湖和密歇根湖,原定长度约347.6千米,宽20米,始于克林顿河浅滩,终于卡拉马祖河河口,运河由此得名。1837年时,密歇根州森林和沼泽密布,通往美国内

canal. In 1837, Michigan was a land of forests and swamps, which made it extremely difficult to get inland. To improve the state of transportation, the Internal Improvement Act was passed for the construction of 3 railroads and 2 canals. The Clinton and Kalamazoo Canal was on the list. The construction of this canal was started in 1838. In 1843, the project was left unfinished at Rochester due to financial problems, and only a section of 20.9 kilometres was completed. The failure of the project was directly in association with the Panic of 1837 during which the major New York financial institutions that had supported the canal went bankrupt. When the project ran out of money, no further funds were raised, and then it was declared a failure in 1844. The other cause of the termination of the construction lay in the fact that this canal was not deep and wide enough for heavy cargo ships. The completed parts of the canal turned out to be of little use. After the project ended, the Clinton and Kalamazoo Canal soon became unsuitable for navigation. For many years, the water from the canal was used to provide electricity for several mills nearby. In 1972, the canal was listed as one of the National Register of Historic Places. The remains of the canal can be seen in some parks along the canal route today.

陆地区的交通极为不便。为改善交通状况，政府通过了《内部改进法案》，批准修建3条铁路和2条运河，其中就包括克林顿—卡拉马祖运河。克林顿—卡拉马祖运河于1838年开凿，但到了1843年，由于资金不足，运河工程在罗切斯特市附近中止，此时仅建成20.9千米。1837年经济大恐慌是该运河项目流产的直接原因。在这场金融危机中，作为资金源的几家纽约金融机构全部破产。工程资金耗尽，又未能筹得新款，1844年该运河项目宣告终止。运河停建的另一个原因是运河深度和宽度不足，大型货船无法通行，已修河段几乎无法通航。工程终止后，克林顿—卡拉马祖运河也逐渐不再适合航运。多年来，该运河河水用来为附近的工坊供电。1972年，克林顿—卡拉马祖运河被列入美国国家历史遗迹名录。如今，在运河边的几个公园里还可见到这条运河残留的河段。

Clubfoot Creek-Harlow Creek Canal

马蹄－哈洛运河

An inland canal located in Carteret, north California, the United States. The Clubfoot Creek-Harlow Creek Canal links Pamlico Sound with the ocean port of Beaufort with a length of about 9.7 kilo-

美国加利福尼亚州北部卡特雷特地区内陆运河。马蹄－哈洛运河全长约9.7千米，连接帕姆利科湾和博福特港口。1766年，北卡罗来

metres. In 1766, the Colonial Assembly of North Carolina passed an act to construct a canal to connect Clubfoot Creek and Harlow's Creek, but this plan was not carried out until 1795. The project was completed in 1827, including the construction of a tide control lock at the northern end on the Pamlico Sound to prevent the water from rushing in. Meanwhile, the lock enabled small ships to enter the Atlantic Ocean from the Pamlico Strait. For the first 3 decades, the canal was operated well, but it was abandoned in 1856 when a lock at Harlow fell into malfunction. In 1880, this canal was rebuilt and reopened as the New Berne and Beaufort Canal. In 1891, it was acquired by the government. The Clubfoot Creek-Harlow Creek Canal is now called Harlow Canal, and it is a part of the Atlantic Intracoastal Waterway.

纳州殖民地议会通过一项法案，计划开凿一条连接马蹄河和哈洛河的运河，但直至1795年该计划才启动，1827年竣工。帕姆利科湾北端建有一个挡潮闸，可防止海水倒灌河道，还可使小型船只通过船闸直接从帕姆利科海峡驶入大西洋。马蹄—哈洛运河通航后，在长达30多年的时间里运行良好。然而，在1856年，因哈洛河上一座船闸年久失修，马蹄—哈洛运河被迫暂时停用。1880年，该运河重修后再次开放，更名为新伯尔尼—博福特运河。1891年，政府出资收购了该运河。目前，马蹄—哈洛运河被称作哈洛运河，是大西洋沿海航道的一部分。

Coastal Canal

沿海运河

A summit-level canal located in Lower Saxony, Germany. See Küsten Canal.

德国下萨克森州越岭运河。见屈斯滕运河。

Colme Canal

科尔莫运河

A cross-border canal located in western Europe. The Colme Canal runs from Veurne Town, Belgium to Saint-Winoksbergen, France, connecting the Colme River and the Aa River. The 25-kilometre-long canal is built with 3 locks, two of which remain in use today. Built in the 17th century, the canal consists of 3 parts, namely, the Upper Colme Canal, the Lower Colme Canal and the Bergues Canal. It is mainly

欧洲西部跨国运河。科尔莫运河自比利时弗讷市流至法国圣维诺克斯贝亨，连通科尔莫河与阿河，全长25千米。运河上建有3座船闸，其中2座至今仍在使用。该运河修建于17世纪，包括科尔莫上游运河、科尔莫下游运河和贝尔格运河三部分河段。科尔莫运河主要用

used for alleviating the flood damage and facilitating transportation.

以减轻洪涝灾害和改善交通。

Columbia River

A canalized cross-border river located in the west of North America. The Columbia River flows from the Rocky Mountains in the south of Canada to the Pacific Ocean through the United States. It has a total length of 2,044 kilometres and a basin area of 415,000 square kilometres, with the Snake River as the largest tributary. During the Steamship Era, the far inland was reachable by sailing through the Columbia River. Since the end of the 19th century, both the public and private sectors have vigorously developed the Columbia River. In 1891, the Columbia River was dredged to improve its navigability. In the 20th century, the International Boundary Waters Treaty and the Columbia River Treaty were signed by the United States and Canada for the development of hydraulic facilities. Today, there are 14 dams on the main stem of the Columbia River, 3 in Canada and 11 in the United States, with more than 400 dams in the Columbia River Basin mainly for the purpose of irrigation and electricity generation. These dams actually meet a variety of needs and can be used for navigation, storing water, generating power, and controlling floods. It's worth noting that with the establishment of the dams, the seasonal flow of the river can be regulated to meet the needs for electricity in winters. However, the ecosystem along the waterway is also negatively influenced by the engineering, which brings about a

哥伦比亚河

北美洲西部跨国运河化河流。哥伦比亚河源于加拿大南部落基山脉，流经美国后向西注入太平洋。该河全长2 044千米，流域面积达41.5万平方千米，最大支流为斯内克河。在蒸汽船时代，早期的通航运河经由哥伦比亚河后可通往更远的内陆。19世纪末以来，政府部门和私营公司均十分重视对哥伦比亚河的开发。1891年，为了改善航运条件，相关部门对哥伦比亚河进行疏浚。20世纪，出于水利开发需要，美国和加拿大签署了《国际边界水域条约》和《哥伦比亚河条约》。目前，哥伦比亚河的主航道上共建有14座大坝，其中3座在加拿大，11座在美国。另外，在整个哥伦比亚河流域建有超过400座大坝，用于水力发电、灌溉、蓄洪和通航。该水利系统在调节哥伦比亚河季节性流量和满足冬季电力需求方面发挥着重要作用。然而，大坝的修建也给河流周边的生态环境带来一些负面影响，大坝建成后鲑鱼的数量急剧下降。

sharp decline in the number of salmons.

Columbus Feeder Canal

A canal feeder located in the United States. As the feeder of the Ohio-Erie Canal, the Columbus Feeder Canal joins the main canal at Lockbourne. With a total length of 19 kilometres, it connects Columbus, the capital of Ohio, with the Ohio-Erie Canal. In 1824, the preliminary rounds of survey for the construction of the feeder canal were started. On 30 April 1827, the groundbreaking ceremony was held in Columbus and the Granville Company was responsible for all the masonry work of the main canal and the feeder in the Lockbourne area. On 23 September, 1831, the first canal boat arrived in the canal. This channel has provided convenient transportation and water power for Columbus and Franklin County, once attracting many mills and factories clustered along the line. In 1904, the Columbus Feeder Canal was closed.

Communication Canal

A canal located in England, the United Kingdom. As a part of the Arbury Canals, the Communication Canal is 986 metres long, with a stop lock close to the junction with the Coventry Canal. The construction of the canal was between 1771 and 1773 to link a wharf near a worsted factory to the Coventry Canal. Eventually, the Communication Canal is connected to the Arbury Lower Canal, or the Griff Canal. By 1819 the upper reaches of the

哥伦布引水运河

美国引水运河。哥伦布引水运河是俄亥俄—伊利运河的引水河，与俄亥俄—伊利运河干渠部分交汇于洛克本，全长19千米，连接俄亥俄州的首府哥伦布和俄亥俄—伊利运河。1824年，哥伦布引水运河开凿前的勘察工作开始进行。1827年4月30日，引水运河开凿动工仪式在哥伦布举行，格兰维尔公司负责洛克本地区开凿干渠和哥伦布引水运河所需的石工作业。1831年9月23日，首艘运河船只抵达哥伦布引水运河。引水运河为哥伦布和富兰克林县提供了运输便利和水力资源，沿线曾一度吸引了许多工坊和工厂在此聚集。1904年，哥伦布引水运河停航。

交通运河

英国英格兰运河。交通运河全长986米，为英格兰阿伯里运河网的一部分，与考文垂运河的交汇处附近有1座节制船闸。运河1771年开凿，1773年竣工，旨在连接精纺工厂附近的码头与考文垂运河。交通运河最终与阿伯里下运河（即格里夫运河）交汇。到1819年时，阿伯里运河网上游不再通航，仅有

Arbury Canals were no longer in operation, only the Communication Canal remained navigable.

交通运河仍可通航。

Conneaut Line

The northern section of the Beaver and Erie Canal located in Pennsylvania, the United States. The Conneaut Line is 72 kilometres in length, connecting the Conneaut Lake and Erie City. In 1843, the Erie Canal Company took over the Conneaut Line from the state and completed the construction in 1844. It was the most difficult section to construct among the 3 divisions of the Beaver and Erie Canal. Engineers encountered two major problems. The first challenge was the need of building a large number of locks, and the second was the lack of large streams that were needed to form a part of the division. The elevation difference to be overcome was 155 metres and there were up to 4 locks per kilometre in the northern part of the line. The opening of the Conneaut Line in 1844 marked the completion of the Beaver and Erie Canal. In the spring of 1845 when the ice broke, the first commercial ships sailing from Ohio to Erie and Meadville began to navigate on the Beaver and Erie Canal. The development of western Pennsylvania has benefited from the navigation on the canal.

康尼奥特河段

美国宾夕法尼亚州比弗—伊利运河北部河段。康尼奥特河段全长72千米，连接康尼奥特湖和伊利市。1843年，伊利运河公司从当地州政府承接康尼奥特河段的开凿项目，1844年运河竣工。在比弗—伊利运河的三个河段中，此河段的开凿难度最大，其中有两个重大难题需要克服。其一是需要修建大量船闸，二是缺少可构成河段的大型河流。修建该河段需克服的最大水位落差高达155米，在河段北部，每开凿1千米就需修建4座船闸。1844年，康尼奥特河段开放，这标志着比弗—伊利运河正式竣工。1845年春，河面冰冻解封后，第一批从俄亥俄州驶往伊利和米德维尔的商船开始在比弗—伊利运河上航行。该运河促进了宾夕法尼亚州西部地区的发展。

Coode Canal

A canal located in the lower reach of the Yarra River, Victoria, Australia. The Coode Canal is 2 kilometres in length, 130 metres in width and 6

库德运河

澳大利亚维多利亚州亚拉河下游运河。库德运河长2千米，宽130米，深6米。1886年，为了改善轮

metres in depth. Excavated in 1886, the canal was the result of Sir John Coode's efforts to improve the accessibility of Melbourne's main river docks and was thus named after this British harbour engineer. The Coode Canal has shortened the navigation along the Yarra River and provided access for cargoes shipped to the Swanson Dock and the Appleton Dock. With this route, the dangerous tidal ebbs and inflows can be avoided. In addition, this canal ensures that the Yarra waters discharge into the river mouth, scouring the bay and reducing silt deposition.

船通往墨尔本主要码头的通航条件，英国港口工程师约翰·库德爵士规划设计了该运河，库德运河因此得名。该运河的开凿缩短了船只在亚拉河上的航行时间，并为运往斯旺森码头和阿普尔顿码头的货物提供运输通道。库德运河航道有助于船只避开危险的潮汐变化，此外还可确保亚拉河水注入河口，然后通过不断冲刷海湾有效减少淤泥堆积。

Cooper River≈

A canalized tidal river located in South Carolina, the United States. The Cooper River flows out of Lake Moultrie, and passes through cities including North Charleston, Mount Pleasant and Charleston. With a total length of 5.8 kilometres, it joins the Ashley River to form the Port of Charleston. During the American Revolution, the Cooper River and its tributaries occupied an important position in the development of Carolina's rice culture. However, in the late 19th century, the rice industry declined and the plantations remained idle in World War I. Later, the United States Navy became the primary developer in the Cooper River basin, where they built bases, shipyards and submarine stations. At the beginning of the 21st century, the Cooper River basin continued to function as the industrial centre of the Charleston area and the shipping industry there flourished. It also became one of the most polluted

库珀河

美国南卡罗来纳州运河化潮汐河流。库珀河全长5.8千米，源于莫尔特里湖，流经北查尔斯顿、芒特普莱森特、查尔斯顿等城市，与阿什利河交汇形成查尔斯顿港。美国独立战争时期，库珀河及其支流在卡罗来纳的水稻种植中占据重要地位。19世纪末期，稻作行业衰落，到第一次世界大战期间，多处种植地处于闲置状态。此后，美国海军在库珀流域建立了海军基地、海军造船厂和潜艇站，成为该地区最大的河流项目开发者。21世纪初，库珀河流域仍然是查尔斯顿地区的工业中心，其航运业十分繁荣。但由于过度开发，库珀河也成了南卡罗来纳州污染最严重的河流之一。

rivers in South Carolina due to overuse.

Coral Canal

A canal located in Los Angeles, California, the United States. The Coral Canal was one of the series of the Venice Canals. In the early 1900s, in order to build a Venice of America in South California, the Venice Canals were excavated under the direction of Abbot Kinney, a tobacco millionaire and real estate developer. The original canals were about 26 kilometres long. Kinney named the other six canals as follows: Aldebaran Canal, Altair Canal, Cabrillo Canal, Venus Canal, Grand Canal and Lion Canal. During 1926 and 1927, many of the canals were filled in to provide roads to bring traffic to the pier, and the Coral Canal was one of them. Now on the site of the Coral Canal lie the Main Street and Canal Street.

科勒尔运河

美国加利福尼亚州洛杉矶市运河。科勒尔运河为美国威尼斯运河网中的一条运河。20世纪初，为打造美国南加州版"威尼斯"，烟草富豪和房地产开发商阿博特·金尼出资修建威尼斯运河网。运河原长度约26千米。金尼将该运河网中的其他6条运河命名为阿尔德巴伦运河、阿尔泰运河、卡布里约运河、维纳斯运河、格兰德运河和莱昂运河。1926—1927年间，为将公路延伸到码头，包括科勒尔运河在内的许多运河被回填，科勒尔运河原址变成了现在的主大街和运河大街。

Corinth Canal

A tidal canal located in southern Greece. The Corinth Canal connects the Gulf of Corinth with the Saronic Gulf in the Aegean Sea, cuts through the narrow Isthmus of Corinth and separates the Peloponnese from the Greek mainland. The canal is 8 metres deep and 6,343 metres long, with a surface width of 24.6 metres and a bottom width of 21.3 metres. It allows ships passing through in one column at a time in a one-way direction. Constructed between 1882 and 1893, the Corinth Canal saves a 700-kilometre-long detour around the Peloponnese,

科林斯运河

希腊南部潮汐运河。科林斯运河连通科林斯湾和爱琴海的萨罗尼克湾，横穿狭窄的科林斯地峡，将伯罗奔尼撒半岛与希腊大陆分隔开来。运河深8米，长6 343米，河面宽24.6米，河底宽21.3米。科林斯运河为单向航道，每次仅可容纳单列船只通行。科林斯运河于1882年开凿，1893年竣工，通航后，船只不必再绕行至伯罗奔尼撒半岛，航程缩短了700千米。然而，该运

but has failed to attract the expected volume of traffic due to the narrowness of its channel and periodic closures for the recovery of the steep riverbed from the damage of mudslides. It can only accommodate ships with a maximum width of 17.6 metres and a draught of up to 7.3 metres. Larger ships have to be towed by tugs. Nowadays, the Corinth Canal is mostly used for recreational purpose, with around 11,000 ships navigating on it annually.

河的航运量并未达到预期，主要原因是航道过窄不易通航，且河床较陡易受泥石流破坏，需定期关闭整修。科林斯运河可通航船只的最大尺寸为宽17.6米，吃水深度7.3米。体积较大的船只必须使用拖船牵引。目前，该运河主要用于旅游航运，每年约有11 000艘游船通行。

Coșteiu-Chizătău Canal

库斯蒂尤－智扎塔瓦运河

A canal located in Timiș County, western Romania. Constructed between 1757 and 1758, the Coșteiu-Chizătău Canal links the Timiș River to the Bega River, and a part is the lower course of the Glavița River, a left tributary of the Bega River. The canal also has a tributary named Coștei.

罗马尼亚西部蒂米什县运河。库斯蒂尤－智扎塔瓦运河修建于1757—1758年间，连通蒂米什河和贝加河，其中部分河段为贝加河左线支流格莱维塔河的下游河段。库斯蒂尤－智扎塔瓦运河还有一条名为库斯泰河的支流。

Coton Lawn Canal

科顿劳恩运河

A canal located in Warwickshire, England, the United Kingdom. As a section of the Arbury Canal system, the Coton Lawn Canal is 1,931 metres long, running from the Arbury High Level Canal to the Rough Wood wharf. It is the final part of the Arbury Estate Canals.

英国英格兰沃里克郡运河。科顿劳恩运河全长1 931米，从阿伯里上运河一直延伸到拉夫伍德码头。该运河是阿伯里庄园运河网的一部分，也是该运河网的最后一段。

Coupure Canal

库比赫运河

A canal located in the city of Ghent in the Flemish Region of Belgium. The Coupure Canal was con-

比利时佛兰芒大区根特市运河。库比赫运河建于根特市与布鲁日市

structed between Ghent and Bruges, connecting the Ring Canal with the confluence of the Groenerei and the Saint-Annarei. During the period of disintegration, trade in the Southern Netherlands was impeded due to the disconnection of canals. To get from the Bruges-Ostend Canal to the Ghent Canal, one had to sail through Bruges. To address the issue, the Coupure Canal was excavated between 1751 and 1753 under the order issued by Maria Theresa of Austria and her minister plenipotentiary Antoniotto Botta Adorno. At the same time, the Bruges Canal and the Bruges-Ostend Canal were deepened and widened, connecting Ghent to the North Sea. After the canal was officially opened in 1753, warehouses, cotton mills and iron factories started to emerge alongside the canal. A street was built at each side of the waterway. The one on the east of the canal was named Predikherenrei, and the other on the west Coupurerei, later renamed as Coupure. The Coupure Canal used to be a busy commercial waterway, but it gradually lost its economic importance after the Ring Canal began to take its place as the main route. With a bicycle and pedestrian bridge constructed over the canal in 2002 and a small marina where a few houseboats are moored, now the canal is a recreation site.

之间，一端连接环形运河，另一端连接格罗那雷河与圣安纳雷河的交汇处。尼德兰王国分裂时期，南尼德兰的贸易因各运河互不连通而受阻，船只需穿过布鲁日市才能从布鲁日—奥斯坦德运河到达根特运河。为解决这一问题，奥地利女大公玛丽娅·特蕾莎与其全权公使安东伊奥托·博塔·阿多诺下令开凿该运河，修建时间从1751持续至1753年。与此同时，人们对布鲁日运河与布鲁日—奥斯坦德运河也进行了加深和拓宽，最终将根特市与北海连接。1753年，库比赫运河正式通航后，沿河两岸陆续建起了仓库、棉花厂和炼铁厂等。运河两边还各建有一条街道，河东为普莱迪克赫亨莱，河西为库比赫莱，后改名为库比赫。库比赫运河一度为重要商业航道，但随着多数货船开始选择环形运河航线后，该运河逐渐失去了商业价值。目前，库比赫运河多用于户外娱乐，2002年运河上建了一座天桥，供自行车与行人通行，沿岸有一座小型码头可提供游船观光服务，是休闲的好去处。

Coventry Canal

考文垂运河

A canal located in the Midlands of England, the United Kingdom. The Coventry Canal is about 61 kilometres long. It starts in the Coventry Canal Ba-

英国英格兰中部地区运河。考文垂运河全长约61千米，始于考文垂运河内湾，终于利奇菲尔德镇

sin and ends its flow 61 kilometres north of Fradley Junction in the north of Lichfield, where it joins the Trent and Mersey Canal. It runs through the towns of Bedworth, Nuneaton, Atherstone, Polesworth and Tamworth. The canal is navigable for ships with a length of up to 21.9 metres, a maximum beam height of 2.1 metres and a maximum headroom of 2 metres. The construction of the canal was started in 1768, and was opened in 1789. The Coventry Canal has been a vital trade artery for many years. In particular, it is a part of the Birmingham-London route, connecting with the Birmingham and Fazeley Canal, the Oxford Canal, and River Thames. In 1948, it was nationalized and operated first by the British Transport Board and then by the British Waterways Board. In 1957, the Coventry Canal Society was established, with the aim of promoting the proper use and maintenance of the canal, and protecting its interests. The canal acts as a base for a canoe club affiliated to the Coventry Canal Society.

北部的弗拉德利交界点以北61千米处，并在此与特伦特—默西运河汇合，流经贝多沃斯、纽尼顿、阿瑟斯通、波莱斯沃思和塔姆沃思等城镇，可容纳最大尺寸为长21.9米、梁高2.1米、净空高2米的船只通行。运河于1768年开凿，1789年通航。多年来，考文垂运河一直是重要的贸易主航道，也是伯明翰—伦敦航线的重要组成部分，与伯明翰—费兹利运河、牛津运河以及泰晤士河相通。1948年，考文垂运河被收归国有，先后由英国运输委员会与英国水务局管理。1957年，考文垂运河协会正式成立，以维护运河正常运行，并保障其相关利益。该运河同时也是考文垂运河协会皮划艇俱乐部基地。

Coventry Wood Canal

考文垂伍德运河

A canal located in Warwickshire, England, the United Kingdom. The Coventry Wood Canal is 483 metres long and is a part of the Arbury Canal system. It was operational in 1771. The locks on its both ends were completed in 1772, connecting it to the Arbury Lower Canal and the Arbury High Level Canal.

英国英格兰沃里克郡运河。考文垂伍德运河为阿伯里庄园运河网的一部分，全长483米。该运河于1771年通航，两端的船闸1772年建成，将其与阿伯里下运河和阿伯里上运河连通。

Crinan Canal

A canal located in western Scotland, the United Kingdom. The Crinan Canal, named after the village of Crinan at its western end, connects Crinan and Ardrishaig. It is 14 kilometres in length, 3 metres in depth, with 15 locks and 7 bridges, including 6 swing bridges and a retractable one. The canal was constructed in 1794, completed and opened in 1801, two years later than expected. It provided a shortcut between the industrialized region around Glasgow and the West Highland villages and islands for commercial sailing, fishing vessels, and Clyde puffers. In 1847, Queen Victoria travelled along the canal to the Scottish Highlands for a holiday, which made it a royal route as advertised by passenger steamer companies. From 1930 to 1932, new sea locks were built at both ends of the canal, making it accessible at any state of tide. In 1962, the Crinan Canal was operated by the British Waterways Board. Today the canal is a popular tourist route for leisure craft and is used by nearly 2,000 pleasure boats every year.

克里南运河

英国苏格兰西部运河。克里南运河因位于运河西端的克里南村而得名，连接克里南和阿德里希格，全长14千米，深3米，建有15座船闸和7座桥梁，其中包括6座平旋桥和1座伸缩桥。运河1794年开凿，1801年竣工并正式通航，比预期晚了2年。克里南运河的开凿使得商船、渔船以及克莱德燃煤单桅货船能够在格拉斯哥工业区与西高地村庄和岛屿之间的通行更快捷。1847年，维多利亚女王沿该运河至苏格兰高地度假，客轮公司便借机将其打造成一条皇家航线。1930—1932年间，为确保过往船只在任何潮汐状态下均能顺利通行，运河两端又建了新船闸。1962年起，克里南运河由英国水务局管理。目前，该运河是一条极受欢迎的旅游路线，每年有近2 000艘游船通行。

Criş Collector Canal

An inland canal located in Bihor County, western Romania. The Criş Collector Canal starts from the Crişul Repede near the village of Tărian, and flows into the Crişul Negru near the village of Tămaşda. The canal has a length of about 61.8 kilometres. It constitutes the main part of the drainage system between the Crişul Repede and the Crişul Negru. The

克里什集流运河

罗马尼亚西部比霍尔县内陆运河。克里什集流运河全长约61.8千米，源于塔里安村的湍克里什河，流入塔马斯达村附近的黑克里什河。湍克里什河和黑克里什河之间排水系统的主要部分正位于克里什集流运河。该运河的下游河段也称

lower reaches of the canal is also called Tămaşda Collector Canal.

作塔马斯达集流运河。

Cromford Canal

克罗姆福德运河

A canal located in England, the United Kingdom. The Cromford Canal runs from Cromford to the Erewash Canal in Derbyshire with a branch running to Pinxton. It is 23.3 kilometres in length. Its construction was authorized by the Act of Parliament in 1789 and the canal was opened in 1794. Costing twice the initial budget, the project turned out to be a financial success. For a better service for the general public, it has now been restored by the Friends of the Cromford Canal, a charitable organization. Now apart from functioning as an independent navigation channel, it is also directly connected to the High Peak Railway for transference. Moreover, the 9.7-kilometre-long section between Cromford and Ambergate is listed not only as a local nature reserve, but also a Site of Special Scientific Interest.

英国英格兰运河。克罗姆福德运河始于德比郡的克罗姆福德，注入埃里沃什运河，其中一条支流流至平克斯顿，全长23.3千米。1789年，开凿该运河的计划得到英国国会法案批准，1794年运河开放通航。虽然开凿成本高达预算的2倍，但该运河在当时仍获得巨大经济利润。为更好地服务公众，克罗姆福德运河在慈善组织"克罗姆福德运河之友"的帮助下日渐复兴。如今，除航运外，该运河还与高峰铁路相连，可直接进行货运转接。克罗姆福德至安伯格长达9.7千米的河段被划为当地自然保护区，被认定为具有特殊科学价值。

Crooked Lake Canal

克鲁克德湖运河

A disused inland canal located in New York, the United States. The Crooked Lake Canal is 12.9 kilometres in length, consisting of 28 locks, through which the canal rises a total of 82 metres. It linked the Keuka Lake and the Seneca Lake, which were two of the Finger lakes (a group of 11 long, narrow, roughly north–south lakes in New York). The name of the canal came from the winding shape

美国纽约州弃用内陆运河。克鲁克德湖运河连通芬格湖泊群（由11个整体南北向的细长湖泊组成）中的丘卡湖和塞内卡湖，全长12.9千米，建有28座船闸，湖水流经所有船闸后水位升高82米。该运河因丘卡湖蜿蜒曲折的形态而得名。丘卡湖俗称"库克"，意为"弯曲"。

of Keuka, which was called Crooked informally. In 1829, the state government authorized the proposal of constructing the canal. It was built then from 1830 to 1833, at a total cost of $157,000. Although the canal stimulated local economic development immediately after its completion, it was confronted with a series of problems during and after its construction. For example, the local people had to face water shortage throughout the construction, and it cost as high as $107,000 to replace the rotten wood locks. Besides, the shallowness of the channel was attended by the risk of flood damages. To address the problem, 2 rounds of rebuilding ensued spanning 3 years and 8 years respectively, but little effect had been achieved. Years of unprofitability forced the state government to abandon this canal in 1877. Now the Crooked Lake Canal mainly serves as a recreational spot. The modern 11-kilometre-long Keuka Outlet Trail for hiking and biking follows roughly the original route of the former canal.

1829年，纽约州政府批准修建该运河的提案，1830年开凿，1833年竣工，工程总造价15.7万美元。运河建成后，虽然的确促进了当地经济发展，但也带来一系列问题。例如，开凿期间沿河居民取水难、木制船闸替换费用高（达10.7万美元）等。后又因河道过浅，运河始终无法有效发挥防涝泄洪功能，人们又分别对该运河进行了为期3年和8年的两次改建工程，但收效甚微。长期高昂的运营成本使得纽约州政府最终在1877年弃用该运河。目前，克鲁克德湖运河主要作为一个旅游景点，沿其旧有河道建有长达11千米的丘卡湖口步道，是远足与骑行胜地。

Cross-Cut Canal

A canal located in Indiana, the United States. The Cross-Cut Canal is about 68 kilometres long, connecting the Wabash River with the West Fork of the White River. It is supplied by waters from the Eel River Feeder, as well as the Birch Creek and Splunge Creek Reservoirs. The Cross-Cut Canal was considered historically to be a part of the Wabash and Erie Canal System. It was constructed under the Indiana Internal Improvement Act in 1836, and was finally completed in 1850. The canal was in

横断运河

美国印第安纳州运河。横断运河全长约68千米，连接沃巴什河与怀特河西汊。该运河的水源补给来自伊尔河引水运河及伯奇河和斯普隆奇河水库。历史上，横断运河是沃巴什—伊利运河网的一部分，1836年据印第安纳州内部改善法案开凿，1850年竣工。该运河在1850—1861年间开放。

service from 1850 to 1861.

Cross Florida Barge Canal

An uncompleted canal located in the United States. Also known as Marjorie Harris Carr Cross Florida Greenway. The Cross Florida Barge Canal was originally planned to run from near Palatka in north Florida, the United States to the Gulf of Mexico, with a width of more than 1.6 kilometres. It was originally a project proposed by the United States Army Corps of Engineers, mainly for the benefit of barge transportation. In 1818, John Calhoun, the Secretary of War, proposed the construction of the canal in order to obtain some financial benefits to balance the economic losses caused by shipwrecks and pirates looting at sea. As an economic recovery plan, the construction of the canal began in the 1930s. In May 1933, the Canal Authority of the State of Florida was formally established. In 1935, with the authorization of President Franklin D. Roosevelt, the project received a grant of $5,000,000. However, in 1936, Michigan Senator Arthur Vandenberg challenged the validity of this project, contending that it had never been officially authorized by the Congress. Subsequently, the project was also opposed by the local state government and Florida residents, assuming that the construction of the canal might damage the natural environment. The project was finally shelved and failed to be completed on schedule. In 1990, the Congress officially deauthorized the construction of the canal, and the land was handed over to Florida as a public area for

跨佛罗里达驳船运河

美国未完成运河。亦称马乔里·哈里斯·卡尔跨佛罗里达绿道。跨佛罗里达驳船运河的原开凿计划是从美国佛罗里达州北部的帕拉特卡附近延伸到墨西哥湾,河宽超过1.6千米。该计划最初是美国陆军工程兵团拟建的一个运河项目,旨在服务于驳船运输。1818年,美国陆军部长约翰·卡尔霍恩正式提议开凿该运河,拟用以此获得的财政收益来弥补海上沉船和海盗抢掠造成的经济损失。作为当时一项重要的经济复苏计划,该运河于20世纪30年代开凿。1933年5月,佛罗里达州运河管理局正式成立。1935年,经富兰克林·罗斯福总统授权,该项目获得500万美元的政府拨款。然而,1936年,密歇根州参议员阿瑟·范登堡对该项目提出质疑,称该工程从未得到国会正式授权。随后,该项目也遭到当地州政府和佛罗里达州居民的共同反对,理由是运河的开凿可能会破坏当地自然环境。最终该项目被搁置,运河也未能如期完工。1990年,国会宣布正式取消对该运河项目授权,并将其所占土地资源一并移交给佛罗里达州,作为公共保护区和休闲区。1998年,为纪念马

conservation and recreation. In 1998, the land was officially renamed as Marjorie Harris Carr Cross Florida Greenway in memory of Marjorie Harris Carr, who founded the organization Florida Defenders of the Environment to lead the campaign against the construction of the canal.

乔里·哈里斯·卡尔（佛罗里达环境卫士组织创建人）所领导的运河开凿抗议活动，该区域正式更名为马乔里·哈里斯·卡尔跨佛罗里达绿道。

Croydon Canal

A closed canal located in the county of Surrey, England, the United Kingdom. The Croydon Canal was a 15-kilometre-long inland canal extending from Croydon to its junction with the Grand Surrey Canal at New Cross in south London, England, passing through Forest Hill, Sydenham, and Anerley. It was 10 metres in width and had a maximum depth of 1.5 metres, navigable only for barges with small loads. Excavated to facilitate the trade between London and Croydon, the canal was mainly used to transport lime, timbre, chalk and agricultural produce to London and carry coal back to Croydon, an ancient market town at that time. It was opened on 22 October 1809 and kept functional for 27 years before it was closed on 22 August 1836. Over the canal had been built a total of 28 locks, which required high maintenance costs and unfortunately led to severe traffic jams. To guarantee the water level of the canal, 2 reservoirs were also constructed, one at Sydenham and the other at South Norwood. The latter remains at present and is now known as South Norwood Lake. It turned out later that the Croydon Canal was totally an unsuccessful investment project. Its shares worth £100 at first

克罗伊登运河

英国英格兰萨里郡已停用运河。克罗伊登运河连接克罗伊登与伦敦，与萨里大运河在伦敦南部新十字地区交汇，流经福里斯特希尔、锡德纳姆与阿纳利地区，全长15千米，宽10米，最深处1.5米，仅可承载货物装载量少的驳船。开凿该运河旨在促进伦敦与克罗伊登两地之间的贸易，主要用于将石灰、木材、白垩和农产品从克罗伊登这一历史悠久的商业城镇运往伦敦，并将煤炭运回克罗伊登。克罗伊登运河1809年10月22日竣工通航，共运营27年，最终于1836年8月22日关闭停航。运河上建有28座船闸，运营费用高昂，同时还造成运河拥堵。为了保持运河水位，人们在锡德纳姆和南诺伍德各建了1座水库。其中南诺伍德水库存续至今，已更名为南诺伍德湖。事实证明，克罗伊登运河完全是一个失败的投资项目，最初价值100英镑的股票在1830年仅能卖到2先令。后来，该运河经营者抓住铁路建设的机

ended up 2 shillings in 1830. The proprietors seized the opportunity of railway construction and sold the canal to the London and Croydon Railway Company at a price of £40,250. The railway line from London Bridge to Croydon, which was opened in June 1839, was built mostly along the route of the Croydon Canal.

会，以40 250英镑的价格将其卖给了伦敦和克罗伊登铁路公司。从伦敦桥到克罗伊登之间的铁路主要沿该运河路线修建，1839年6月建成通车。

Cuckoo Dyke

疯人堤

A canal located in England, the United Kingdom. See Chesterfield Canal.

英国英格兰运河。见切斯特菲尔德运河。

Cumberland and Oxford Canal

坎伯兰-牛津运河

An abandoned canal located in Maine, the United States. The Cumberland and Oxford Canal extended from Harrison on the Long Lake to the harbour of Portland. It consisted of a natural waterway of about 48 kilometres and man-made sections of 32 kilometres. The 28 locks were 3 metres wide and 24 metres long. The canal was constructed in 1830 and opened in 1832. Its operation ceased in 1870. The canal provided the transportation of lumber from Harrison on the Long Lake to Portland. In 1978, the local division of the American Society of Civil Engineers dedicated a plaque to the canal in the historic Stroudwater Park, which is located on Congress Street at the intersection with Waldo Street.

美国缅因州停用运河。坎伯兰—牛津运河始于缅因州长湖的哈里森，终于波特兰港，其上建有28座3米宽、24米长的船闸。运河由两部分组成，分别是48千米长的天然航道和32千米长的人工航道。坎伯兰—牛津运河开凿于1830年，1832年通航，运营至1870年。通过坎伯兰—牛津运河可将木材从长湖的哈里森运往波特兰港。1978年，美国土木工程师协会缅因州分会在国会街与沃尔多街交汇处历史悠久的斯特劳德沃特公园内竖立了一块运河纪念牌匾。

Dalles-Celilo Canal

An inland canal located in Oregon, the United States. The Dalles-Celilo Canal was 13 kilometres in length, connecting the Columbia River between Oregon and Washington. Its construction was started in 1905 and completed in 1915 with the aim of coping with the rapid streams from the Columbia River. The lower end of the canal and the locks were located at Dalles Dam, and the upper end at today's Celilo Park. The canal had 5 locks with the dimension of 80.8 metres by 13.7 metres. Due to the development of the railway system, the transportation business on the canal did not flourish as expected. In 1957, with the opening of the Dalles Dam, the Dalles-Celilo Canal and its locks were submerged. The canal faced its final curtain.

Dalsland Canal

A canal located in Dalsland, western Sweden. The Dalsland Canal is 254 kilometres in length, linking Lake Vänern with the central parts of the Dalsland and lake districts in southwestern Värmland and flows across the famous Håverud Aqueduct. It was built between 1864 and 1868. Under the direction of the engineer Nils Ericson, scattered lakes around the area were utilized and only a 12-kilometre-long section of the entire canal was man-made. Flowing from Köpmannebro on Lake Vänern to Östervallskog on Lake Östen, it connects several lakes on its way, such as Lake Lelång, Stora Le, Lake Foxen, and

达尔斯－塞利洛运河

美国俄勒冈州内陆运河。达尔斯－塞利洛运河全长13千米，连通俄勒冈州和华盛顿州之间的哥伦比亚河段。运河1905年开凿，1915年竣工，修建运河目的是缓冲来自哥伦比亚河的急流。达尔斯－塞利洛运河上游位于今塞利洛公园内，下游和船闸位于达尔斯大坝所在处。整条运河上建有5座船闸，各闸长80.8米，宽13.7米。由于铁路交通的发展，该运河上的运输业并未出现人们所预期的繁荣景象。1957年，达尔斯大坝开闸泄洪，淹没了达尔斯－塞利洛运河和船闸。达尔斯－塞利洛运河的历史自此落幕。

达尔斯兰运河

瑞典西部达尔斯兰省运河。达尔斯兰运河全长254千米，连接维纳恩湖和达尔斯兰中部地区以及韦姆兰省西南部湖区，流经著名的霍沃鲁德渡槽。运河修建于1864—1868年间。在工程师尼尔斯·埃里克森的指导下，利用了周围散布的湖泊，只有12千米长的河段由人工开凿而成。达尔斯兰运河自维纳恩湖畔的雪普曼讷布鲁延伸至东湖边的东瓦尔斯库格，贯通莱隆湖、大莱湖、福克森湖和特克湖等湖泊。

Lake Töck. There are 31 locks and 17 lock stations along the canal. The maximum dimension of boats allowed is 22.8 metres long, 4.1 metres wide with a draught of 1.8 metres. The speed limit over the canal is 2.5 knots. The Dalsland Canal has become a popular tourism spot, and canoeing competitions are held every year on some of the lakes along its route.

运河沿线共建有31座船闸和17个闸站，可容长22.8米、宽4.1米、吃水深度1.8米的船只通行，最高航速2.5节（1节相当于每小时1海里或1.9千米）。达尔斯兰运河如今已成为著名的旅游景点，每年都会在其沿线湖泊上举行独木舟赛。

Damme Canal

达默运河

A canal located in Flanders, Belgium. Also called Napoleon Canal, or Bruges-Sluis Canal. The Damme Canal is about 15 kilometres long, connecting Bruges to the Dutch border town of Sluis. In 1810, the canal was initially excavated under the orders of Napoleon Bonaparte in hope that the French troops could avoid confrontation with the British Navy at sea. Following Napoleon's defeat in the Battle of Waterloo, the canal lost its strategic imperative. Its construction, under the direction of Dutch King Willem I, was later completed in 1856. The canal meets the Leopold Canal and the Schipdonk Canal at Damme. Given the level difference among the 3 canals, a siphon system was constructed. The canal remained operational until 1940 when French engineering troops toppled the siphons. Later, the canal was mainly used for recreational boating in the section between Bruges and Damme. Today, only the first 500 metres in Bruges is the navigable Class I section. The channel and its surroundings now stand as a nature reserve. The poplar-lined canal is probably the most beautiful canal in Flanders.

比利时佛兰德省运河。亦称拿破仑运河或布鲁日—斯勒伊斯运河。达默运河全长约15千米，连接布鲁日与荷兰边境小镇斯勒伊斯。1810年，拿破仑·波拿巴下令修建达默运河，意使法国部队免受英国海军袭扰。后因拿破仑兵败滑铁卢，运河失去了战略意义。之后，在荷兰国王威廉一世指挥下，达默运河得以继续修建，于1856年完工。运河在达默小镇与利奥波德运河和斯希普顿克运河连通。这三条运河有水位差，为保障通航，人们专门建造了虹吸系统。1940年，法国工兵部队摧毁了这一系统，达默运河从此停航。此后，布鲁日与达默之间的部分河段主要用于休闲娱乐，供游船通行。目前，只有位于布鲁日的前500米河段有一级通航功能，航道及周边地区的自然景观得到保护。运河两岸白杨林立，堪称佛兰德省最美运河。

Damster Canal

A canal located in the Netherlands. The Damster Canal runs through Appingedam and ends in the Ems, running 27 kilometres and connecting Groningen and the coastal town of Delfzijl. The canal can be divided into two parts, with the village of Ten Post lying in between. The western section, excavated around 1425, is a straight channel running from Groningen to Ten Post while the eastern part moves on from Ten Post to Delfzijl. The origin of the eastern part can be traced back to 1000 AD or even earlier. Back then, it was connected with the sea. Under the influence of the ebb and flow, a meander known as the Tuikwerderrak has developed near Delfzijl, which was also known as Old Ee in the 15th century. In history, the Damster Canal was once an important trade route. It has been however replaced later by the Ems Canal, which is wider and deeper. Now the Damster Canal is not used anymore for commercial navigation, but used for recreational purposes.

达姆斯特运河

荷兰运河。达姆斯特运河流经阿平厄丹，最终汇入埃姆斯河，连接格罗宁根市和代尔夫宰尔，全长27千米。运河在滕波斯特分为两个部分，滕波斯特以西河段开凿于1425年左右，始于格罗宁根市，河道笔直；东段通往代尔夫宰尔，修建于公元1000年前或更早。当时东段曾与大海相通。受水潮涨落和水流的影响，河道在代尔夫宰尔附近形成图科沃德拉克曲流，15世纪时曾被称为老埃河。达姆斯特运河历史上是一条重要的商用航线，但因水位较浅，后被更宽更深的埃姆斯运河取代。如今，达姆斯特运河不再用作商业航运，主要供游船通行。

Danube-Black Sea Canal

A canal located in southeastern Romania. The Danube-Black Sea Canal links the Danube River and the Black Sea, and it starts from Cernavodă in the west and runs towards the southeast to Poarta Albă, where it is divided into 2 sections: a southern one and a northern one. The southern section is 64.4 kilometres long, 90 metres wide, and 7 metres deep, while the northern branch is 31.2 kilometres long,

多瑙－黑海运河

罗马尼亚东南部运河。多瑙－黑海运河连通多瑙河和黑海，西起切尔纳沃德港，向东南方向流至波阿尔塔阿尔伯。运河在波阿尔塔阿尔伯分为南北两条河段。南河段为运河主航道，长64.4千米，宽90米，深7米，可容纳载重达5 000吨、长138米、吃水5.5米的船只。北河段

50 metres wide, and 5.5 metres deep. The southern section is also the main channel of the canal, allowing ships of up to 5,000 tonnes, 138 metres in length and 5.5 metres in draught. The canal was constructed in 1975, the southern branch was completed in May 1984, and the northern branch was opened in October 1987. Four locks can be found on the canal in Cernavodă, Agigea, Ovidiu and Midia. Its route circumvented the Danube Delta, which was difficult and dangerous to navigate, and provided a shorter and more convenient waterway from the Danube River to the Black Sea. Specifically, the southern branch shortened the passage from Cernavodă to Constanța by 400 kilometres. Currently, the canal is equipped with power generating facilities at both ends and it is used for irrigation and drainage as well.

长31.2千米，宽50米，深5.5米。多瑙—黑海运河1975年开凿，南河段于1984年5月竣工，北河段于1987年10月正式通航。运河上建有4座船闸，分别位于切尔纳沃德、阿吉加港、奥维迪乌和米迪亚。运河避开了不易航行且危险的多瑙河三角洲水域，并使从多瑙河通往黑海的航线更为便捷。具体而言，南河段将切尔纳沃德港与康斯坦察港之间航程缩短了400千米。目前，多瑙—黑海运河两端都建有发电设施，同时还用于灌溉和排水。

Danube-Bucharest Canal

多瑙—布加勒斯特运河

A canal located in southern Romania. Connecting the Danube with the capital Bucharest, the Danube-Bucharest Canal is 73 kilometres in length. The construction of the canal had experienced twists and turns. The earliest plan dates back to 1880. In August of 1929, the Romanian parliament authorized the construction of the canal. The plan was shelved due to a financial shortage caused by the world economic depression in the early 1930s. Then World War II kept holding back the project. In 1982, the project was proposed again. According to the new plans, the canal would have 5 locks and 4 hydroelectric plants. The actual construction of the canal did

罗马尼亚南部运河。多瑙—布加勒斯特运河连接多瑙河和首都布加勒斯特，全长73千米。运河的修建工作几经波折。早在1880年时运河开凿计划就已提出。1929年8月，罗马尼亚议会颁布法令决定修建运河，但由于20世纪30年代初发生世界经济危机，政府资金短缺，修建计划被迫中止。后第二次世界大战爆发，运河修建计划再度被搁置。1982年，运河修建计划又被重新提上议程。根据新计划，运河上将修建5座船闸和4个水电站，但直

not begin until 1986. However, it was stopped in February of 1990, with 60% finished. In 1997, the Minister of Transport declared that the government could not afford another $400 million and 4 years to complete the canal. It was not until 2005 that the mayor of Bucharest officially expressed the intention to complete the project. Eventually, the construction of the canal was jointly aided by Romanian national funds and EU Cohesion Fund as a part of the EU Strategy for the Danube Region. The project was started in 2014 and finished in 2020.

Danube-Oder Canal

An unfinished transnational canal located in Europe. The Danube-Oder Canal, situated in the Lobau flood plain of the Danube, is planned to run along the Morava River in the Czech Republic and join the Oder at the city of Kędzierzyn-Koźle in Poland with the total length of 300 kilometres and an altitude range of 124 metres. As early as the 14th century, Charles IV of the Holy Roman Empire had already conceived the idea to build a waterway between the Oder and the Danube. Further plans for this conceived waterway can be traced back to the 19th century. The construction was finally started in the 1930s. Up to 1943, only a few kilometres of the planned 40-kilometre-long channel between Vienna and Angern was actually finished. Further construction has been promoted later but was carried out at a slow pace, mainly for the environmen-

到1986年，实质性的修建工作才开始。1990年2月，多瑙—布加勒斯特运河停建，此时已完工60%。1997年，罗马尼亚交通部部长宣布，此运河工程还需耗时4年，并再耗资4亿美元，而政府已无力承担。直到2005年，布加勒斯特市长才正式表态要完成该运河的修建工作。最终，多瑙—布加勒斯特运河被列入欧盟多瑙河地区战略计划的一部分，由罗马尼亚国家基金和欧盟团结基金共同资助修建，工程于2014年开始，2020年结束。

多瑙—奥得运河

欧洲未完工跨国运河。多瑙—奥得运河位于多瑙河罗堡冲积平原，计划沿捷克共和国境内的摩拉瓦河修至波兰肯杰任科兹莱城，以连通奥得河，全长300千米，水位落差124米。早在14世纪，神圣罗马帝国皇帝查理四世即提出要修建一条可使船只从奥得河通行至多瑙河的航道。后续的修建计划可追溯至19世纪。20世纪30年代，运河终于动工修建。到1943年，原计划从维也纳到昂格恩的40千米河道只完成了几千米。之后，其他河段的修建工作陆续开展，但考虑到环境保护的因素，进展缓慢。根据欧洲多瑙—奥得—易北运河项目计划，今后，多瑙—奥得运河还

tal concerns. Nowadays, the canal is still a part of the plans to build a European Danube-Oder-Elbe Canal connecting the Elbe River.

将与易北河连通。

Danube-Tisa-Danube Canal

多瑙－蒂萨－多瑙运河

A canal system located in northern Serbia. Originally called Franz Channel. The Danube-Tisa-Danube Canal extends 929 kilometres, including canals and rivers that have been completely or partly reconstructed. On the canal network can be found 24 gates, 16 locks, 5 safety gates, 6 pumping stations, 14 cargo ports and 180 bridges. Its present name comes from the two large rivers it connects, namely the Danube and the Tisa. This hydro-engineering system has played an irreplaceable role in flood control, forestry, fishing, water supply, wastewater evacuation, tourism and so on.

塞尔维亚北部运河网。旧称弗朗茨航道。多瑙—蒂萨—多瑙运河主航道长929千米，其中包括数条局部或全面改造过的运河以及河流。运河上共建有24道闸门、16座船闸、5道安全闸门、6座泵站、14个货运港和180座桥梁。该运河现名取自其所连通的两条河流，即多瑙河和蒂萨河。多瑙—蒂萨—多瑙运河这一水利系统工程为周边地区的防洪、林业、渔业、供水、废水处理、旅游业等做出了重要贡献。

Datteln-Hamm Canal

达特尔恩－哈姆运河

A canal located in the state of North Rhine-Westphalia, Germany. Linking the Dortmund-Ems Canal with the city of Hamm, the Datteln-Hamm Canal is 47.2 kilometres in length. With an elevation difference of 6.8 metres, it is equipped with two locks, situated respectively at Hamm and Werries. At Hamm, a water exchange facility was set to refill the waterway with water from River Lippe to make up for what is lost in evaporation, infiltration and the operation of locks. When the flow rate of River Lippe drops below the expected level of 10 cubic metres per second, the facility will replenish

德国北莱茵—威斯特伐利亚州运河。达特尔恩—哈姆运河连接多特蒙德—埃姆斯运河与哈姆市，全长47.2千米。运河上建有2座船闸，一座位于哈姆市，另一座位于韦里斯，两者之间水位落差达6.8米。哈姆市安装了水交换设施，将利珀河的水注入达特尔恩—哈姆运河，以弥补因蒸发、渗透、开关船闸等造成的水量流失。一旦利珀河的流速低于每秒10立方米，该设施就会通过达特尔恩—哈姆运河为其补

the river with the water extracted from the Datteln-Hamm Canal, which then receives the provision of water from the Ruhr and the Rhine.

水，而运河流失的水量则会从鲁尔河和莱茵河得到补充。

Dazhihe Canal

A canal located in Shanghai, China. Its Chinese name "Dazhi" means the aspiration for political stability and social security. As the largest canal in Shanghai, the Dazhihe Canal is about 39.5 kilometres in length. It starts from the Huangpu River and empties into the East China Sea, flowing through the districts of Minhang and Pudong. The canal has 2 locks, one in the west end, and the other in the east. These 2 locks can prevent floods and saltwater encroachment, and keep the water level at about 2.7 metres all year round to ensure its navigability. The Dazhihe Canal serves the needs for freight transport, irrigation, flood discharge, and household refuse transport. In 1977, the Shanghai authorities decided to excavate a canal in the Pudong District to ease the pressure of flood control in the areas of Shanghai City, Jiangsu Province, and Zhejiang Province. The excavation of the Dazhihe Canal began in 1977, and the canal was opened in 1979. After its completion, the Dazhihe Canal is navigable for ships with a tonnage of 300. With the development of the Lingang Special Area of China (Shanghai) Pilot Free Trade Zone, the Dazhihe Canal becomes a part of the boundary for the Lingang Special Area of China(Shanghai) Pilot Free Trade Zone, and is presented with new development opportunities. In 2019, a new lock in the west

大治河

中国上海市运河。大治河的名称蕴含了人们希望国家政治稳定、社会安全的愿望。大治河是上海市最大的运河，全长约39.5千米，西起黄浦江，流经上海市闵行、浦东两区，向东注入东海。大治河东、西两端各建有1座船闸，用以防洪和阻止海水倒灌，同时还可控制水位，确保运河水位常年维持在2.7米左右，以保障船舶正常航行。大治河为人们的生活提供了许多便利，譬如运输货物、灌溉农田、纳潮泄洪、清运城市生活垃圾等。1977年，为减轻上海市和江苏、浙江两省汛期的洪水压力，上海市委、市政府决定在浦东地区开凿运河，同年工程启动，1979年大治河正式通航，可容纳300吨级的船只。随着中国（上海）自由贸易试验区临港新片区的建设和启动，大治河成为临港新片区的一条界河，并因此迎来新的发展机遇。2019年，大治河西枢纽的船闸工程建成并正式投入使用，新船闸可通行1 000吨级的船只，是长三角地区最大的内河枢纽船闸。未来，大治河的防洪排涝和航运功能将愈

end of the Dazhihe Canal was completed. The lock allows ships with a tonnage of 1,000 to transit and becomes the largest one in the inland waterways in the Yangtze Delta. In the future, the Dazhihe Canal will function more effectively in flood control and inland navigation and become an integral part of the high-speed waterway network in Shanghai.

发凸显, 成为上海高速水路网的重要组成部分。

Dedems Canal

A canal located in the north of Overijssel Province, the Netherlands. The Dedems Canal is 40 kilometres long, named after Baron Van Dedem, who had this canal constructed for the transport of peat. The construction work began in 1809, and was completed in 1854. After World War II, the Dedems Canal lost its importance for navigation. In the 1960s, most sections of the canal were filled in, often for the construction of roads. The N377 road partly follows the previous route of the canal. Currently, the sections respectively between Hasselt and Nieuwleusen, Dedems and Lutten, have been preserved, but they are no longer used for commercial navigation.

代德姆斯运河

荷兰上艾瑟尔省北部运河。代德姆斯运河全长40千米。运河由男爵范代德姆命人开凿, 用来运输泥炭, 运河名称由此而来。代德姆斯运河1809年修建, 1854年竣工。第二次世界大战后, 该运河的航运价值降低。20世纪60年代, 运河的大部分河段被回填, 主要用以修建公路。其中, N377号公路的一部分线路就在旧运河遗址上修建而成。如今, 哈瑟尔特和尼乌勒森之间以及代德姆斯和吕滕之间的部分河段被保留下来, 但不再用于商业航运。

Delaware and Hudson Canal

A canal located in Pennsylvania, the United States. The Delaware and Hudson Canal is 174 kilometres long, 2 metres deep and 10 metres wide, overcoming an elevation difference of 328 metres by virtue of the 108 locks on it. There are 137 bridges as well as 26 dams and reservoirs within the basin of the canal. It begins at Rondout Creek and continues

特拉华－哈得孙运河

美国宾夕法尼亚州运河。特拉华－哈得孙运河全长174千米, 深2米, 宽10米, 全程水位落差328米, 建有108座船闸。运河沿线建有137座桥梁、26座水坝和水库。运河始于朗道特溪, 蜿蜒穿过桑德堡溪谷和内弗辛克河谷后, 流至特拉

winding through the valley of the Sandburg Creek and the Neversink River to Port Jervis on the Delaware River. From there the canal runs northwest and at last joins the Honesdale. The canal was built by the Delaware and Hudson Canal Company in 1825 and opened in 1828. It was used to transport anthracite coal from the mines of the coal region in northeastern Pennsylvania to the Hudson River, and then to the market in New York City. The Delaware and Hudson Canal and the Gravity Railroad combined to constitute a system of transportation between the northeastern Pennsylvania coal fields and the ports of New York and New England. Before the canal was decommissioned in 1898, the canal system had transported millions of tons of anthracite coal. Fueled by the cheap and plentiful coal supply, the city of New York industrialized and thrived along with other eastern cities. The Delaware and Hudson Canal was abandoned in the early 20th century, and much of its body was subsequently drained and filled. The canal was listed as a National Historic Landmark in 1968. At present, the museum maintained by the Delaware and Hudson Canal Historical Society offers educational programme for the public presenting various historical inheritage of the canal.

华河上的杰维斯港，之后向西北方向延伸，最终汇入洪斯代尔河。1825年，该运河由特拉华－哈得孙运河公司开始修建。1828年运河开通后，人们将产自宾夕法尼亚州东北部煤矿区的无烟煤运往哈德孙河，随后输送到纽约市场。特拉华－哈得孙运河和重力缆车道构成了宾夕法尼亚州东北部煤田与纽约市及新英格兰地区港口群之间的运输系统。1898年特拉华－哈得孙运河停运前，共计运输数百万吨无烟煤。纽约市得益于廉价而充足的煤炭供应，加快了工业化发展进程，成为东部繁华都市之一。20世纪初，特拉华－哈得孙运河被弃用后，大部分河段的河水被排干，河道回填。1968年，运河被列为美国国家历史地标。如今，由特拉华－哈得孙运河历史协会运营的博物馆里陈列着各类运河遗产，向公众展示该运河的历史。

Delaware and Raritan Canal

特拉华－拉里坦运河

A canal located in central New Jersey, the United States. By connecting the Delaware River (its source of water) and the Raritan River, the Delaware and Raritan Canal serves as an efficient and

美国新泽西州中部运河。特拉华－拉里坦运河连通特拉华河（即运河源头）与拉里坦河，是费城与纽约市之间一条高效且可靠的水运

reliable waterway of freight transportation between Philadelphia and New York City, with the coal from the anthracite fields as the main cargo. The total length of the entire canal system was approximately 106 kilometres, including a 71-kilometre-long, 23-metre-wide and 2.4-metre-deep main section and a 35-kilometre-long, 18-metre-wide and 2-metre-deep feeder canal. At an estimated cost of $2,830,000, the construction of the Delaware and Raritan Canal began in 1830 and was completed in 1834. The canal found itself in its prime time during the 1860s and 1870s, when it was used to transport coal from Pennsylvania to New York City against the background of the Industrial Revolution, cutting miles off the previous route. With the time passing by, the importance of the Delaware and Raritan Canal declined as railroads, which were more capacious and faster, were put into use. The canal remained in operation until 1932. The section between Trenton and Bordentown was filled in to give way to various roads and railways. The Delaware and Raritan Canal was listed as the National Register of Historic Places on 11 May 1973, and a state park bearing the name of the canal was built in the following year. Now, the remains of the main canal and the feeder canal are transformed into a public space for recreation.

航线，主要运输产自无烟煤田的煤炭。这条运河全长约106千米，包括运河主航道（长71千米、宽23米、深2.4米）和引水运河（长35千米、宽18米、深2米）。运河于1830年开凿，1834年竣工，耗资约283万美元。19世纪60—70年代间，正值工业革命时期，大量煤炭经由该运河从宾夕法尼亚州运往纽约市。当时，运河迎来了航运高峰期，相对于以往线路而言，航程大为缩短。后由于铁路运载量更大、运输速度更快，特拉华—拉里坦运河航道的重要性逐渐减弱，1932年停运。此后，人们回填了托伦顿和博登敦之间的河段，铺设了公路和铁路。1973年5月11日，特拉华—拉里坦运河被列入美国国家历史遗迹名录，次年，特拉华—拉里坦运河州立公园开放。如今，该运河主航道及其引水渠遗址已改建为公园，供人游览。

Delaware and Raritan Feeder Canal

特拉华-拉里坦引水运河

A canal located in the northeast of the United States. Extending 35 kilometres, the Delaware and Raritan Feeder Canal starts from the Bull's Island

美国东北部运河。特拉华—拉里坦引水运河长35千米，从特拉华河上的布尔岛向南汇入特拉华—拉里

on the Delaware River and runs southward to the main canal's kernel section. A connection was built at Lambertville from the feeder canal to the Delaware Canal in Pennsylvania. It is navigable by small boats throughout its length.

坦运河的主干段。兰伯特维尔处修建了一河段用以连通此引水运河与宾夕法尼亚州的特拉华运河。特拉华—拉里坦引水运河全线可通行小型船只。

Delaware Canal

A canal located in Pennsylvania, the United States. Also called the Delaware Division of the Pennsylvania Canal. The Delaware Canal runs roughly parallel to the Delaware River from Easton (around where the Delaware canal connects the Lehigh Canal) to Bristol. It is about 96.9 kilometres long, 18 metres wide, and 1.5 metres deep, with 23 locks and 10 aqueducts overcoming a total fall of nearly 50 metres. In the early 1800s, the industry in America was developing drastically, but the transportation of anthracite coal to the eastern seaboard was severely hindered by the poor road condition. Back then, the Delaware River was found unsuitable for navigation for its rapids and strong currents. To address the issue and inspired by the success of the Erie Canal in New York, the Commonwealth of Pennsylvania decided to construct a 1, 932-kilometre-long canal system to bolster the progress of industrialization, and the Delaware Canal was a part of this project. The construction of the canal was started in 1827 and completed in 1832, and it experienced its most productive stage during the years prior to the Civil War. In 1858, the state sold the canal to the Lehigh Coal and Navigation Company. However, with the emergence of railroads and the decline of the

特拉华运河

美国宾夕法尼亚州运河。亦称宾夕法尼亚运河特拉华段。特拉华运河从伊斯顿（特拉华运河在该市附近与利哈伊运河交汇）流至布里斯托尔，与特拉华河的流向大致平行。运河全长约96.9千米，宽约18米，深约1.5米，河上建有23座船闸和10座渡槽，调节总落差近50米。19世纪初，美国工业化进程发展迅猛，但由于公路路况差，且特拉华河水流湍急，不适合货运，通向东海岸地区的无烟煤运输渠道因此极不畅通。为解决这一问题，宾夕法尼亚州受纽约州开凿伊利运河这一成功先例的启发，决定修建一条总长1 932千米的运河，以促进工业化发展进程，特拉华运河便是此项工程的一部分。特拉华运河1827年开凿，1832年完工。运河在美国南北战争爆发前几年迎来其鼎盛期。1858年，宾夕法尼亚州把运河出售给利哈伊煤炭与航运公司。然而，由于铁路运输兴起，同时无烟煤被其他燃料取代，利哈伊煤炭与航运公司破

anthracite as a source of fuel, the bankrupt company sold the canal back to the state for a nominal fee. The Delaware Canal remained in use until the Great Depression in the early 1930s. Most of its original aqueducts, locks and overflows have been retained, and it is preserved as the last towpath canal in the United States. In 1974, it was listed on the National Register of Historic Places. In 1978, it was designated a National Historic Landmark.

产，之后以极低的价格将运河回售给州政府。特拉华运河一直运营至20世纪30年代初美国大萧条时期。这条运河是美国最后一条纤道运河，大部分原有的水渠、船闸和排航道保留至今。1974年，特拉华运河被列入美国国家历史遗迹名录，1978年被认定为美国国家历史地标。

Delaware Division of the Pennsylvania Canal

宾夕法尼亚运河特拉华段

A canal located in Pennsylvania, the United States. See Delaware Canal.

美国宾夕法尼亚州运河。见特拉华运河。

Delfshaven Schie Canal

斯希运河代尔夫斯哈芬段

A canal located in Rotterdam, South Holland, the Netherlands. The Delfshaven Schie Canal connects the Schie to the New Maas at Delfshaven. There are 7 bridges on this canal. Along with the Delft Schie, the Rotterdam Schie and the Schiedam Schie, this canal is one of the 4 sections of the Schie Canal. These waterways were constructed in the Middle Ages as a result of the contest for the right over toll collection among the cities of Delft, Rotterdam and Schiedam. Back then, in order to levy tolls on ships that sailed on the Schie and to make its trade independent of Schiedam and Rotterdam, Delft excavated the Delft Schie Canal in 1389 and the Delfshaven Schie Canal later. In 1933, the Coolhaven was constructed to provide a better connection

荷兰南荷兰省鹿特丹市运河。斯希运河代尔夫斯哈芬段连接斯希运河（4条航道交汇处），并在代尔夫斯哈芬行政区左侧与新马斯河连通，沿线建有7座桥梁。该运河与斯希运河代尔夫特段、斯希运河鹿特丹段、斯希运河斯希丹段构成斯希运河。这4段运河是中世纪时期代尔夫特、鹿特丹和斯希丹为了争夺运河收费权而开凿的。当时，代尔夫特为了收取斯希运河的船只过路费，同时争取贸易自主权，于1389年左右先后开凿斯希运河代尔夫特段和斯希运河代尔夫斯哈芬段。1933年，为了改善斯希

between the Delfshaven Schie and the New Maas. Nowadays, the Delfshaven Schie Canal serves as a crucial shipping route between the Delft Schie Canal and the New Maas, and plays an important role in the drainage of this area.

运河代尔夫斯哈芬段与新马斯河之间的航运条件，人们又修建了库尔黑文港。如今，斯希运河代尔夫斯哈芬段是斯希运河代尔夫特段和新马斯河之间的重要航道，也是该地区重要的排水系统。

Delft Schie Canal

斯希运河代尔夫特段

A canal located in South Holland Province of the western Netherlands. Connecting the old harbour of Delft to Rotterdam and Schiedam, the Delft Schie Canal is one of the 4 waterways of the Schie Canal system along with the Delfshaven Schie, the Rotterdamse Schie and the Schiedamse Schie. In 1389, the city of Delft received permission from Duke Albert I to construct its own canal to connect the Merwede. Then, the previous waterway from Delft to Overschie was widened, and became known as the Delft Schie Canal. The canal was important for the economic development of Delft City as a trade centre for spices, porcelain and arts in the 16th and 17th centuries. Since 1893 the Delft Schie Canal had been included in an even larger project, namely, the Rhine-Schie Canal. In 2015, it was set for another round of widening.

荷兰西部南荷兰省运河。斯希运河代尔夫特段连接代尔夫特旧港口、鹿特丹市和斯希丹市，与斯希运河代尔夫斯哈芬段、斯希运河鹿特丹段和斯希运河斯希丹段构成斯希运河网的4段航道。1389年，阿尔贝特一世公爵允准代尔夫特市开凿一条连通梅尔韦德河的运河，代尔夫特至奥佛斯希的原有航道得以拓宽，被称为斯希运河代尔夫特段。16世纪和17世纪时，这条运河促进了代尔夫特市的经济发展，代尔夫特市因此成为香料、瓷器和艺术品贸易中心。斯希运河代尔夫特段自1893年起被纳入莱茵—斯希运河网。2015年，该运河被再次拓宽。

Delft Vliet Canal

代尔夫特－弗利特运河

A canal located in South Holland Province of the western Netherlands. Connecting the Rhine River and the Meuse estuary, the Delft Vliet Canal is 4.6 kilometres long. It starts at the Old Rhine near

荷兰西部南荷兰省运河。代尔夫特—弗利特运河连接莱茵河和默兹河口，全长4.6千米，是莱茵—斯希运河的一段河道。该运河始于

Leiden and joins the Delfshaven Schie Canal at Delft, as a part of the Rhine-Schie Canal. The section from Leiden to the Hoorn Bridge is now called the Vliet Canal. This waterway was excavated in 47 AD, and it partly followed the course of the Corbulo Canal built by the Romans in the first century. In the Middle Ages, the Vliet was an important trade link, as it flowed through the heart of the County of Holland. From 1891 to 1894, the Delft-Vliet was widened.

莱顿附近的旧莱茵河，在代尔夫特与斯希运河代尔夫斯哈芬段交汇。莱顿至霍恩大桥之间的河段如今被称为弗利特运河。该航道开凿于公元47年，其流向与罗马人在1世纪修建的科布洛运河部分相同。中世纪时期，弗利特河因流经荷兰郡的中心地带，成为重要的贸易纽带。1891—1894年间，代尔夫特—弗利特运河被拓宽。

De Lits Canal

德利茨运河

A canal located in Friesland, the Netherlands. The De Lits Canal is 3.8 kilometres in length and connects Rottevalle Town with the Bergum Lake. Its estimate elevation above sea level is 254 metres.

荷兰弗里斯兰省运河。德利茨运河全长3.8千米，连接罗特瓦勒镇与贝赫姆湖，海拔约254米。

Dender ~

丹德河

A canalized river located in Belgium. As a tributary of the Schelde, the Dender flows through the provinces of Hainaut, Flemish Brabant, and East Flanders. It is 61 kilometres in length, and its basin area covers 1,384 square kilometres. The canal has two branches, namely, the Western Dender and the Eastern Dender, which meet at Ath in the south and flow into the Schelde in the north. The 22-kilometre-long Western Dender takes its source near Maubray and passes through Leuzen-en-Hainaut at an altitude of about 60 to 70 metres. The 39-kilometre-long Eastern Dender rises near Jurbise at an elevation of 100 metres above sea lev-

比利时内陆运河。丹德河是斯海尔德河支流，流经埃诺省、弗兰芒布拉班特省和东佛兰德省，全长61千米，流域面积为1 384平方千米。该河有2条支线，即西丹德河和东丹德河，二者在南部的阿特交汇，向北注入斯海尔德河。西丹德河长22千米，始于莫布雷附近，流经埃诺的勒兹市，海拔在60—70米间。东丹德河长39千米，始于瑞尔比斯，海拔为100米。登德尔蒙德至阿尔斯特的河段可容纳载重达600吨的船只，上游阿尔斯特至阿特之

el. Between Dendermonde and Aalst, the Dender is navigable by vessels weighing 600 tonnes and the maximum navigation capacity is halved to 300 tonnes further upstream between Aalst and Ath. In 2014, the permissible draught went down to 1.6 metres because of siltation. The canal is mainly used by pleasure boats now.

间的河段，船只载重限度则减至300吨。2014年，由于泥沙淤积，丹德河最大吃水深度降至1.6米。如今，该河主要供游船通行。

Denison Canal

A canal located in the south of Tasmania, Australia. Linking the Frederick Henry Bay and Blackman Bay, the Denison Canal covers a full length of 895 metres, or 2.4 kilometres with its dredged approaches included. The canal has a width of 34 metres at ground level and 7 metres at low tide. The water depth ranges from 3.9 metres at high tide to 2.6 metres at low tide. The construction was started in 1905 to shorten the routes between the east coast and Hobart for fishing and trade. The Denison Canal was named after the former Governor, William Denison, and was then reportedly the second longest canal in Australia. It is now said to be the only canal still in use for shipping. The Denison Canal used to be accessible to small trade vessels, but today it only allows small fishing vessels and recreation boats to pass.

丹尼森运河

澳大利亚塔斯马尼亚州南部运河。丹尼森运河连通腓特烈亨利湾和布莱克曼湾，全长895米，加上疏浚的引水河，总长2.4千米。运河河面宽34米，落潮时减至7米；涨潮时水深达3.9米，落潮时降至2.6米。1905年，丹尼森运河开始修建，主要是为了缩短东海岸与霍巴特镇之间的航程，促进渔业与商业发展。运河得名于澳大利亚前任总督威廉·丹尼森，据说是当时澳大利亚第二长运河，如今是澳大利亚唯一一条仍通航的运河。过去，丹尼森运河可通行小型商用船只，现仅允许小型渔船和游船通行。

De Pauw Canal

A canal located in the city of Ghent, Belgium. Also called Peacock Canal. The De Pauw Canal is one of the shortest canals in the whole country, only

迪堡运河

比利时根特市运河。亦称孔雀运河。迪堡运河是比利时最短的运河之一，全长仅391米，部分河段

391 metres in length. A part of the canal was built on the northern verge of the Spanish Castle, which was on the site of the Saint Bavo's Abbey. The De Pauw Canal was constructed in 1827 and completed in 1829. It was named after Napoleon Lievin de Pauw. It used to have 2 bridges and 1 lock. The bridges have long disappeared and the lock is no longer in use.

位于圣巴沃修道院旧址的西班牙城堡北沿。迪堡运河1827年开凿，1829年竣工。该运河以拿破仑·利文·迪堡的名字命名，河上曾建有2座桥和1座船闸。如今，桥早已不复存在，船闸也已废弃。

Derby Canal

德比运河

A canal located in England, the United Kingdom. The Derby Canal flows from the Trent and Mersey Canal at Swarkestone to the Erewash Canal, connecting Derby and Little Eaton to Derbyshire. It is 23 kilometres in length. The construction was authorized by an act of Parliament in 1793 and was finally completed in 1796. With coal as its main cargo, it was more successful than other contemporary canals. When the railways appeared in 1840, the traffic on the canal declined severely. In 1964, the canal was abandoned. With the improvement of the economy in England during the 1990s, many other canals were restored successfully. In such circumstances, the restoration scheme of the Derby Canal was proposed in 1994, with the estimated cost of the main line at £17.3 million. Finally, in the middle of 2003, the project of protecting the whole canal was included in the local council's structure plans due to the great support of the Canal Trust.

英国英格兰运河。德比运河从斯沃克斯顿的特伦特—默西运河流入埃里沃什运河，连接德比、小伊顿以及德比郡，全长23千米。1793年，英国议会通过法案授权开凿该运河，1796年竣工。该运河主要运输煤炭，运营较同时期其他运河更为成功。1840年铁路开通后，运河航运量大幅下滑。1964年，运河被弃用。20世纪90年代，英国经济好转，多条运河相继得以复建。在这种形势下，复建德比运河的计划于1994年提上日程，复建主河道预计耗费1 730万英镑。2003年年中，在运河信托基金会支持下，德比运河全段的保护工程最终被纳入当地市政厅发展规划。

Desjardins Canal

A canal located in Ontario, Canada. The Desjardins Canal is a short canal excavated to provide Dundas in Hamilton, with an easier access to Lake Ontario. It was named after its promoter Pierre Desjardins. Following the American Revolutionary War, the British government looked to the interior of the Upper Canada (the predecessor of partial Ontario) as a habitat for Loyalists coming from the United States and a strategic zone to defend the possible attack from the US army in the future. In order to attract people as well as to boost the economy and support military operations, John Graves Simcoe, then Lieutenant-Governor, made efforts to facilitate transportation around the area. At that time, Richard Hatt owned a flour mill in Dundas and cleared a path through the marsh located on the waterway from Dundas to Burlington beach, which set in place the plans and facilities from which the Desjardins Canal would later emerge. After Hatt died in 1819, Pierre Desjardins, one of Hatt's clerks, also believed in the promising benefits if the access was improved and devoted himself to this project. Desjardins planned to establish a joint-stock company to raise funds and the corporation was finally approved in 1826. The construction of the canal lasted 10 years from 1827 to 1837, as it gained financial and political support solely from within Upper Canada. Dundas had been increasingly flourishing since the canal was opened as the local industries were boosted and the population drastically increased. However, the canal company was struggling

德雅尔丹运河

加拿大安大略省运河。德雅尔丹运河是一条短程运河，其开凿初衷是更为便捷地连接汉密尔顿市内的邓达斯与安大略湖。运河以其发起人皮埃尔·德雅尔丹的姓氏命名。美国独立战争后，英国政府把上加拿大内陆地区（即安大略省部分地区前身）辟为来自美国的亲英人士住所，同时将其作为一个战略区域，以提防美国军队可能发动的攻击。为了吸引人口、促进经济发展并支持军事行动，当时的总督约翰·格雷夫斯·西姆科致力于改善该地区的交通状况。当时理查德·哈特在邓达斯有一家面粉厂，他从一片沼泽中清理出了一条通道，这片沼泽是从邓达斯到伯灵顿海滩走水路的必经之地，通道为之后修建德雅尔丹运河打下了基础。1819年，哈特去世后，他先前的雇员皮埃尔·德雅尔丹也坚信，这条通道如果能够得到修缮，将会带来巨大收益，因此他全力推动这项工程。德雅尔丹计划成立一家股份公司来筹集资金，该公司最终于1826年获得批准。运河于1827年开凿，但因只获得了上加拿大的资金和政策支持，1837年才得以完工，工程耗时长达10年之久。自运河通航后，当地工业快速发展，人口急剧增加，邓达斯也

with the financial and technical issues during the operation and maintenance of the canal. Moreover, the emerging of railroads in the later years severely diminished waterways' role of transportation. The company was eventually liquidated, and the canal was turned over to the government in 1876. Although the local government tried several times to revive the canal, it was officially out of use when direct rail service to Dundas was available in 1895.

日益繁荣。然而，运河公司对运河的运营和维护深受资金和技术问题困扰。不久后，铁路的崛起也严重削弱了水路运输的作用。运河公司最终宣告破产，德雅尔丹运河于1876年移交给政府管理。虽然当地政府屡次尝试恢复运河昔日的繁盛景象，但并未奏效。1895年，直达邓达斯的铁路线路开通，德雅尔丹运河正式停用。

Dessel-Kwaadmechelen Canal

代瑟尔-克瓦德梅赫伦运河

A canal located in the province of Antwerp, Belgium. Connecting Dessel to the Albert Canal in Kwaadmechelen, the Dessel-Kwaadmechelen Canal contains a bend near the junction with the Albert Canal. In Dessel, it also connects to the Bocholt-Herentals Canal and the Dessel-Turnhout-Schoten Canal. The Dessel-Kwaadmechelen Canal is 15.7 kilometres in length with no lock. It can transit ships up to 2,000 tonnes. The construction began in 1854 and was completed in 1858. From 1972 to 1974 it had been widened from the original width of 20 metres to 60 metres.

比利时安特卫普省运河。代瑟尔—克瓦德梅赫伦运河在克瓦德梅赫伦连接代瑟尔与阿尔贝特运河，在其与阿尔贝特运河的交汇处有一个弯道。在代瑟尔地区，该运河还连通博霍尔特—海伦塔尔斯运河和代瑟尔—蒂伦豪特—斯霍滕运河。代瑟尔—克瓦德梅赫伦运河全长15.7千米，未建船闸，可通行重达2 000吨的船只。运河于1854年开凿，1858年完工。运河原宽20米，1972—1974年间被拓宽至60米。

Dessel-Turnhout-Schoten Canal

代瑟尔-蒂伦豪特-斯霍滕运河

A canal located in the province of Antwerp, Belgium. Linking Dessel with Schoten and flowing into the Albert Canal, the Dessel-Turnhout-Schoten Canal is 63 kilometres in length. The canal was built in the 19th century in two stages.

比利时安特卫普省运河。代瑟尔—蒂伦豪特—斯霍滕运河全长63千米，连接代瑟尔镇与斯霍滕镇，汇入阿尔贝特运河。运河开凿于19世纪，分为两个阶段修建，1844年开

The first stage was from 1844 to 1845, with the purpose to link Dessel and Turnhout; the other was from 1854 to 1875, when the section between Turnhout and Schoten was constructed. In the 19th century, the canal was very important for ceramics factories. After the opening of the Albert Canal in 1939, this canal's importance in economy decreased. Today, the canal is not wide enough for 2 commercial vessels to pass simultaneously. With the presence of 10 locks, it cannot provide a competitive rate compared with road transport. The general plan of the province of Antwerp is to develop the canal's recreational function.

始的是代瑟尔至蒂伦豪特一段，次年完工；1854年修建的是蒂伦豪特至斯霍滕段，1875年完工。当时这条运河对陶瓷厂十分重要。1939年，阿尔贝特运河开通后，这条运河在经济方面的重要性开始降低。如今，该运河已无法容纳2艘商船同时通航，现有的10座船闸也使运河运输无法达到与道路运输一样的速度。目前，安特卫普省的总体规划是发展代瑟尔—蒂伦豪特—斯霍滕运河的休闲娱乐功能。

Deûle Canal

德勒运河

A canal located in northern France. The Deûle Canal is 36 kilometres in length and has 4 locks, linking Bauvin with River Lys (or Leie) near the Belgian border. As a branch of the Dunkirk-Escaut Canal, the canal passes the south of Bauvin and runs along towards Douai. In the 13th century, parts of the Deûle Canal were already navigable. Entirely opened in 1693, the Deûle Canal was originally designed to link the Scarpe to the Deûle. It was connected with the Scarpe in the 17th century but not with the Lys River until a century later. Renovation was undertaken in the 19th century, extending the canal down through Lille, which saved barges from the unnecessary transfer from the Upper Deûle to the Lower Deûle.

法国北部运河。德勒运河全长36千米，共建有4座船闸，连接博万镇和邻近比利时边境的利斯河（莱厄河）。该运河是敦刻尔克—埃斯科运河支流，经博万镇南面，流至杜埃镇。13世纪时，德勒运河的部分河段便已经通航。运河于1693年全线贯通，初衷是连通斯卡尔普河和德勒河。17世纪时，德勒运河已经连通斯卡尔普河，至18世纪才连通利斯河。19世纪，德勒运河得以重修，延长至里尔，此后驳船不必再从德勒河上游转道至德勒河下游。

Devil's Canal

A canal located in Prague, the Czech Republic. Also known as Little Prague Venice. The Devil's Canal was built around the 12th century by the Knights of Malta. The canal carries water from River Vltava and runs back to Vltava, with a course of approximately 900 metres. Two medieval mills are situated on the canal.

魔鬼运河

捷克共和国布拉格市运河。亦称布拉格小威尼斯。魔鬼运河大约在12世纪时由马耳他骑士团开凿。运河从伏尔塔瓦河引水，最后又汇入伏尔塔瓦河，全长约900米。魔鬼运河上至今还保留着2座中世纪时修建的工坊。

Dieze Canal

A canal located in North Brabant Province, the Netherlands. The Dieze Canal is about 2 kilometres long. Flowing from Engelen to the Meuse River, it serves as commercial waterway. It is now considered as a CEMT (Classification of European Inland Waterways) Class IV waterway. From 1897 to 1902, the Dieze Canal was excavated for the purpose of improving regular steamboat service between 's-Hertogenbosch and Rotterdam. The Dieze Canal contains the Engelen Lock, the official name of which is Henriëttesluis. The lock allows a maximum size of 90 metres long by 12 metres beam. Due to the opening and navigation of the Máxima Canal in December 2014, the Dieze Canal no longer took on heavy shipping tasks. However, the Dieze Canal still plays an important role for shipping.

迪兹运河

荷兰北布拉班特省运河。迪兹运河全长2千米，自恩格伦流向默兹河，用作商业航道。该运河被认定为欧洲内陆四级航道，于1897—1902年间修建，旨在完善斯海尔托亨博斯和鹿特丹之间的班轮服务。迪兹运河之上有一座名为恩格伦的船闸，其官方名称为"亨利埃特船闸"，船闸可供长达90米、船幅12米的船只通行。自2014年12月马西玛运河开通后，迪兹运河不再承担繁重的航运任务，但仍然具有重要的航运功能。

Dike Canal

A canal located in northern Columbia. See Dique Canal.

戴克运河

哥伦比亚北部运河。见狄克运河。

Dique Canal

A canal located in the northern Columbia. Also called Dike Canal or Levee Canal. The Dique Canal begins from the Magdalena River in the Bolívar department and empties into the Bay of Cartgena at the town of Pasacaballos. It is currently 118 kilometres long and 75 metres wide, crossing 15 municipalities among the departments of Bolívar, Atlántico and Sucre. First built by the Spanish in the late 16th century, and rebuilt in the mid-17th century, it was the earliest and largest canal project during the colonial period. The waterway provided a convenient path to the Magdalena River and the inner area of the country. At that time only small-sized vessels could navigate it. By the end of the 18th century, the channel became nearly unnavigable. At the end of the 19th century a railroad had replaced it. The renovation work, which failed in 1923, was finally accomplished in 1952. However, the importance of the Dique Canal gradually declined with the serious sediment deposition in the Magdalena River and the monopoly of road transport. During the La Niña events in December 2010, the canal burst its banks and flooded dozens of villages. Currently, with the Autonomous Regional Corporation of the Dique (CARDIQUE) taking charge of protecting the surrounding ecosystems, the strategic ecosystems like mangrove areas around the canal are a driving force of the local development. Meanwhile, the modernization of the channel is being seriously considered to promote trade in Cartagena. In September 2012, the Permanent Delegation of

狄克运河

哥伦比亚北部运河。亦称戴克运河或莱维运河。狄克运河源于玻利瓦尔省的马格达莱纳河，在帕萨卡巴罗镇汇入卡塔赫纳湾。该运河全长118千米，宽75米，流经玻利瓦尔省、大西洋省和苏克雷省的15个城市。运河最早由西班牙人于16世纪晚期开凿，17世纪中叶得以重修。这一工程是殖民时期最早最大的运河修建工程，为通往马格达莱纳河和内陆地区提供了快捷通道。当时只有小型船只可以通行。至18世纪末，该运河几近断航，至19世纪末，被铁路取代。狄克运河于1923年改建，但收效甚微，直至1952年，工程才基本完成。由于马格达莱纳河泥沙淤积严重，同时货车运输占据垄断地位，狄克运河逐渐失去了航运价值。2010年12月，拉尼娜现象导致运河决堤，洪水摧毁了数十座村庄。如今，当地生态系统保护工作由狄克运河地区自治管委会负责，运河周边的战略生态系统，如红树林区，已成为当地发展驱动力。同时，为促进卡塔赫纳港口的贸易发展，运河现代化改造也提上了议程。2012年9月，哥伦比亚联合国常驻代表团提交申请，提议将狄克运河列入世界文化遗产候补名录。

Columbia submitted the application to incorporate the Dique Canal into the Tentative Lists of World Cultural Heritage.

Dismal Swamp Canal

A canal located in the United States. Along the eastern edge of the Great Dismal Swamp, the Dismal Swamp Canal flows between Chesapeake in Virginia and South Mills in North Carolina. With a total length of 36 kilometres, the canal is a part of the Intracoastal Waterway, which is a 4,800-kilometre-long inland waterway along the Atlantic and the Gulf of Mexico. The construction of the canal began in 1793. The canal was built from two ends to the middle, and was completed in 1805. During the American Civil War (1861—1865), the canal was severely damaged, making the navigation difficult. In 1892, renovations were launched by Lake Drummond Canal and Water Company, and the canal restored its hustle and bustle. Today, the canal is operated and maintained by the United States Army Corps of Engineers. It has been listed on the National Register of Historic Places and designated a National Civil Engineering Landmark.

迪斯默尔沼泽运河

美国运河。迪斯默尔沼泽运河位于大迪斯默尔沼泽东部地区，自弗吉尼亚州的切萨皮克流向北卡罗来纳州的南米尔斯，全长36千米，是途经大西洋与墨西哥湾沿岸地区、长达4 800千米的内陆沿海航道的一段。1793年，迪斯默尔沼泽运河修建工程启动，从运河两端并进开凿，交会于中段，1805年竣工。美国内战期间（1861—1865），运河遭到严重破坏，往来航运不便。1892年，德拉蒙德湖运河与水利公司数次主持修缮工作，迪斯默尔沼泽运河恢复了往日的忙碌景象。如今，迪斯默尔沼泽运河由美国陆军工程兵团负责运营与维护，已被列入美国国家历史遗迹名录，并被评为国家土木工程典范。

Dnieper-Bug Canal

An inland canal located in Belarus. The Dnieper-Bug Canal is the longest canal in Belarus, linking the Mukhavets River, a branch of the Bug River, and the Pina River, a branch of the Pripyat River, It was originally named the Royal Canal as the king

第聂伯–布格运河

白俄罗斯内陆运河。第聂伯—布格运河连接布格河的支流穆哈韦茨河和普里皮亚季河的支流皮纳河，是白俄罗斯最长运河。由于该运河项目由当时的国王启动，运河

initiated the project. The project was started in 1775 and completed in 1784. It forms an important section of the transportation route which connects the Baltic Sea with the Black Sea. The waterway from Brest to Pinsk is 196 kilometres long, including the 105-kilometre-long man-made waterway. The construction of the railway along the canal in the late 19th century decreased the importance of the canal. From then on, the canal was used mainly for exporting lumber to western countries by rafts. The canal fell into disuse during World War I. In 1940, the Soviet administration launched a large-scale project to reconstruct the canal. The recent years saw Belarus governments' efforts to rebuild the canal to be a Class IV inland waterway of global influence. Four sluice dams and one shipping lock have been constructed by the government. It is now navigable for vessels of 110 metres long, and 12 metres wide. It is expected that the reconstruction will continue over the next few years.

最早名为皇家运河。第聂伯—布格运河于1775年开凿，1784年竣工，是连通波罗的海和黑海交通大动脉的重要组成部分。连接布列斯特市和平斯克市之间的运河段长196千米，其中包括长达105千米的人工运河。19世纪末期，运河沿线建起了铁路，此后，运河主要用于筏运木材至西欧国家。第一次世界大战期间，该运河曾停航。1940年，苏联当局着手对运河进行大规模重修。近年来，白俄罗斯政府开始对该运河进行整修，致力于将其改造成一条具有国际影响力的四级内陆运河。目前，运河上已重建了4座蓄洪水坝和1座船闸，该船闸可容纳110米长、12米宽的船只通行。预计在未来几年内，重修工作将持续推进。

Dokkum-Ee Canal

A canal located in Friesland Province, the Netherlands. Linking Leeuwarden with Dokkum, the Dokkum-Ee Canal was excavated around the area between Burdaard and Tergracht to connect two naturally formed rivers. In the past, the outlet connecting Leeuwarden to the wider ocean was silted up while the harbour of Dokkum was still in operation. Thus, a clear pathway between the two cities was necessary and the Dokkum-Ee Canal was constructed. Later, the canal had been dredged and

多克默—埃运河

荷兰弗里斯兰省运河。多克默—埃运河连接吕伐登和多克默，最早在布尔达德和泰尔赫拉赫特之间开凿，用以连通两条自然河流。此前，吕伐登出海口淤堵，而多克默港口仍可正常运转，因此，在两个城市之间建立起一条畅通航道势在必行，多克默—埃运河应运而生。此后，历经多次疏浚和加深，该运河在弗里斯兰省北部运输原

deepened several times, and its role of transporting raw materials in the north of Friesland became increasingly important. Today the Dokkum-Ee Canal is still a very important waterway, especially for recreational shipping, as it is a part of the "Mast-Up Route" between the Frisian Lakes and the Wadden Sea. Meanwhile, when there is thick ice in winter, it is also a part of the track for the Elfstedentocht, a long-distance tour skating event on natural ice, almost 200 kilometres long.

材料的作用变得日益重要。时至今日, 多克默—埃运河仍是一条非常重要的航道, 尤其是在水上休闲方面, 它是从弗里斯兰众多湖泊至瓦登海的"立桅航线"中的一部分。冬季, 河面结出厚冰层, 运河也是十一城冰上马拉松赛道的一部分, 十一城冰上马拉松赛是一项在天然冰上举办的长距离滑冰赛, 全程近200千米。

Dokkum Trek Canal

A canal located in Friesland Province, the Netherlands. See Stroobos Trek Canal.

多克默拖船运河

荷兰弗里斯兰省运河。见斯特罗博斯拖船运河。

Dommers Canal

A canal located in Drenthe, the Netherlands. The Dommers Canal starts from the meeting point of the Stieltjes Canal and Zijtak near Zandpol, flows in an easterly direction to Amsterdamscheveld and finally reaches the village of Weiteveen. However, it is only navigable to Amsterdamscheveld, after which it is too narrow and shallow for shipping. It was named after Lodewijk Dommers, an administrator in the corporation that financed the construction of the canal. The project began in 1861 and was carried out in phases to facilitate the transportation of peat.

多默斯运河

荷兰德伦特省运河。多默斯运河始于斯蒂尔切斯运河与吉塔克河位于桑德波尔附近的交汇处, 向东流经阿姆斯特丹谢维尔德, 最后流至维特芬的村庄。运河仅可通航至阿姆斯特丹谢维尔德, 之后的河段既窄又浅, 难以通航。该运河得名于工程建设出资方管理者洛德韦克·多默斯。多默斯运河1861年开凿, 分阶段修建, 旨在为当时的泥煤运输业服务。

Dongguan Canal

A canal located in Dongguan City, Guangdong Province, China. The Dongguan Canal runs across 13 towns from Qiaotou Town to Chang'an Town and empties into the Pearl River (or the Zhujiang River). The canal, 103 kilometres in length, is the longest canal in Guangdong Province. In order to control floods and facilitate irrigation, the construction was started on 13 December 1957 and finished on 1 May 1958. The original canal was 19.5 kilometres long, stretching from the gorge of Fucheng (the present-day Dongcheng District, Dongguan), travelling westwards to the Shigu Lock in Houjie Town, and flowing into the south branch of the Dongjiang River. By connecting artificial and natural river courses, the extension project, beginning in 1971, formed a 103-kilometre-long canal which surrounds half of Dongguan City. It was enlarged for the second time in 1975 and expanded to 35 metres wide. The canal was heavily polluted and the water quality is getting better after years of restoration.

Dongyin Canal

A canal located in Dongguan City, Guangdong Province, China. Stretching for 102.6 kilometres, the Dongyin Canal is composed of some parts of the Shima River and the Hanxi River, the original Dongguan Canal, and the Shatian Artificial Channel. The construction of the canal was initiated in January 1970, and the main section was completed and put into operation in October of the same year.

东莞运河

中国广东省东莞市运河。东莞运河始于桥头镇，流经13个乡镇，在长安镇注入珠江。东莞运河全长103千米，是广东省最长的运河。为解决沿线城镇防洪排涝和农业灌溉问题，1957年12月13日，东莞运河开凿。1958年5月1日，运河竣工。最初，该运河始于附城（今东莞东城区）峡口，向西流经厚街镇石鼓船闸，注入东江南支流，全长19.5千米。1971年，东莞运河开始拓建，通过人工水渠和自然河道上伸下延，长度达到103千米，环抱半个东莞市。1975年，东莞运河第二次拓建，拓宽至35米。东莞运河曾受到严重污染，但经过多年治理，目前水质已经好转。

东引运河

中国东南部广东省东莞市运河。东引运河全长102.6千米，包括石马河和寒溪河的部分河段、原东莞运河以及沙田人工渠。东引运河项目1970年1月开始启动，同年10月，主体工程完工并投入使用。运河始于桥头镇，至长安镇注入东江（珠江水系干流之一），流经

Aiming for flood control and drainage, agricultural irrigation, and the provision of drinking water in cities and towns along the route, the canal starts from Qiaotou Town and enters the Dongjiang River (one of the mainstreams of the Pearl River System) in Chang'an Town, flowing through 15 towns or districts. Though it witnessed an all-round success from the 1970s to the 1980s, the rapid development of Dongguan's industry and the explosive growth of the immigrant population in the later years brought about a great deal of industrial waste water and domestic sewage, which were directly discharged into the canal without proper treatment and severely polluted the water. It affected nearby waterworks abstracting water from the southern tributaries of the Dongjiang River. With the intensified regulation and management by the municipal government since the late 20th century, the water quality has been continuously improving in recent years. Water pollution in a few sections has been controlled. With the help of the information technology network and the modern hydraulics measures, the comprehensive and overall enhancement will be achieved in the near future.

15个镇（区）。开凿该运河旨在解决沿线城镇防洪排涝、农业灌溉和饮用水源等问题。东引运河在20世纪70—80年代取得了良好的综合效益，但随着东莞工业快速发展和外来人口急剧增长，大量工业废水和生活污水未经妥善处理直接排入运河，污染严重，极大地阻碍了附近水厂在东江南支流取水。自20世纪末，东莞市政府加大了对东引运河水污染的整治力度，水质由此不断得到改善。近年来，一些水域的污染情况已经得到有效控制。随着信息网络技术和现代水力学方法的不断改进，东引运河的水质问题在不久的将来一定能够得到全面改观。

Doorslag Canal

多斯拉赫运河

A canal located in Utrecht, the Netherlands. The Doorslag Canal is a short connecting canal built in 1295 between the Merwede Canal and the Holland Ijssel in order to dredge the Holland Ijssel. From its confluence with the Doorslag Canal, the Holland IJssel starts to flow in two directions. Its estimate

荷兰乌特勒支省运河。多斯拉赫运河是一条连通梅尔韦德运河与荷兰艾瑟尔河的短程运河，修建于1295年，旨在疏浚荷兰艾瑟尔河。后者在与多斯拉赫运河汇合处分为两条流向不同的支流。多斯拉赫

terrain elevation above sea level is 4 metres.

运河海拔高度约为4米。

Dorset and Somerset Canal

An unfinished canal located in the southwest part of England, the United Kingdom. The main line of the Dorset and Somerset Canal connects Poole in Dorset to the Kennet and Avon Canal. To reach the Somerset coalfield at Nettlebridge from Frome, a branch was proposed and constructed in 1786. When there were any level changes to be dealt with in the initial construction, boat lifts were used rather than locks. Eventually a line from Stratton Common towards Frome was built, running for 13 kilometres and passing through Coleford and Vobster. Although the company responsible for the canal was allowed to raise money according to an act of Parliament in 1803, the construction was stopped due to the lack of funds, leaving the canal uncompleted. Today, the Dorset and Somerset Canal has several visible features. One is a bridge which was used to connect Edford to the Stratton Common road. Another is an aqueduct at Coleford, with two semicircular arches of nearly 10 metres wide and 10 metres high. Recently, the Somerset Aggregates Levy Sustainability Fund has approved of a project in support of the canal conservation.

多塞特－萨默塞特运河

英国英格兰西南部未完工运河。多塞特－萨默塞特运河的主航道连接多塞特郡的普尔镇与肯尼特－埃文运河。该运河是1786年为连接弗罗姆镇和内特尔桥的萨默塞特煤田而修建的一条支线运河。在前期建造过程中，为调整水位，施工方采用了升船机而不是船闸，最终修成了一条自斯特拉顿康芒公路通向弗罗姆的大约长13千米的河道，流经科尔福德和沃布斯特。负责建造该运河的公司经1803年议会法案批准可以筹集资金，但开凿运河的工作仍因资金短缺而未能竣工。如今还有些运河遗迹仍然可见，包括运河上曾经用来连接爱德福与斯特拉顿康芒公路的一座桥梁，还有科尔福德的一座渡槽，上有两个高与宽均接近10米的半圆拱形建筑。近年来，萨默塞特集团可持续发展基金会通过了项目提议，将为保护运河提供资助。

Dortmund-Ems Canal

A canal located in western Germany. Starting from the south of Dortmund, the Dortmund-Ems Canal comprises three different sections, namely, the

多特蒙德－埃姆斯运河

德国西部运河。多特蒙德－埃姆斯运河始于多特蒙德市南部，分为三段：第一段为人工开凿河段，

215-kilometre-long artificial part ending at Her-brum Lock near Meppen, the 45-kilometre-long route from River Ems to the Oldersum Lock, and the 98-kilometre-long artificial segment. It links the Ruhr industrial area with the North Sea near Emden, and the Rhine River with the North Sea. The canal was built between 1892 and 1899 to reduce the demand on the railway network. Also, the canal made the coal from the Ruhr area more competitive compared to the imported English kind. Two boat lifts and two locks were built to offer access to the increasing traffic and boat size. The best-known building of the Dortmund-Ems Canal is the Henrichenburg boat lift in Waltrop, which was in use until 1962 and today houses the Westflisches Industrial Museum. Owing to its strategic importance, the canal was under attack for many times during World War II. After the war, it had to be widened. As the widening programme could not be easily achieved, a new route lying parallel to the old route had to be constructed between Olfen and Münster. When the transformation was finished in 1963, the canal could accommodate ferries as large as 1,350 tonnes and the old one has not been available to shipping since then. There are a large number of port towns spreading along the canal, including Dortmund, Meppen, Emden and Münster.

长215千米，自多特蒙德流至梅彭附近的赫尔不鲁姆船闸；第二段长45千米，自埃姆斯河流至奥尔德瑟姆船闸；第三段亦为人工开凿河段，长98千米。多特蒙德—埃姆斯运河连通莱茵河与北海，也是鲁尔工业区至埃姆登附近北海区域的通道。运河1892—1899年间开凿，旨在减轻当时对铁路运输系统的依赖。此外，该运河使得鲁尔区运来的煤炭比从英国进口的煤炭更具市场竞争力。多特蒙德—埃姆斯运河上另建了2座升船机和2座船闸，以便通行数量更多、体积更大的船只。位于瓦尔特罗普处的亨利兴堡升船机是多特蒙德—埃姆斯运河上最负盛名的建筑，1962年之前一直在使用，如今该建筑已改建为威斯特法利亚工业博物馆。多特蒙德—埃姆斯运河因具有军事战略意义，第二次世界大战期间曾多次遭受攻击。战后，运河河道需要拓宽，但因有一定难度，只能在奥尔芬与明斯特之间新开凿一条与旧航线平行的航道。1963年，新航线整改完工，可容1 350吨位的货轮通航，旧航线也随之停止使用。多特蒙德—埃姆斯运河沿岸有诸多港口小镇，包括多特蒙德、梅彭、埃姆登和明斯特。

Draget Canal

A canal located in southeastern Sweden. The Draget Canal is situated on the Baltic coast of Södermanland, near Nynshamn and Landsort, connecting the island of Järflotta and the mainland. In the early 13th century, the canal was a natural strait with a water level 3 metres higher than today's. In the mid-19th century, the Sweden navy decided that this passage could be useful for small warships and thus dredged it deeper in the late 19th century. Currently, the Draget Canal is one of the narrowest passages in Sweden and also a tourist attraction for yachts less than 2 metres in draught and 4 metres in width.

德拉戈特运河

瑞典东南部运河。德拉戈特运河位于南曼兰省波罗的海沿岸，靠近尼奈斯港和兰德索尔特，连接耶尔弗鲁塔岛与内陆。在13世纪初，德拉戈特运河是一个天然海峡，其水位比现在高3米。19世纪中期，瑞典海军认为这一水运通道可为小型军舰航行提供便利，19世纪后期对河道进行了疏浚和加深。德拉戈特运河是瑞典最狭窄的河道之一，也是著名的旅游胜地，现可通行吃水深度不超过2米、宽度不超过4米的游艇。

Drecht River

A canalized river located in North Holland Province, the Netherlands. The Drecht River is 6.5 kilometres long. It originates from Old Wetering, which is connected to the junction of the Aar Canal and the Amstel River. It is now a river which can only be freely cruised by vessels with the headroom lower than 3.15 metres due to the bridge at Leimuiden. Meanwhile, the access at Leidmuiden Tolbrug is narrow and twisted, not allowing boats longer than 14 metres to pass.

德雷赫特河

荷兰北荷兰省运河化河流。德雷赫特河全长6.5千米，始于旧韦特灵，连通阿尔运河与阿姆斯特尔河。由于莱默伊登的桥梁限高，德雷赫特河仅供净空高度低于3.15米的船只通行。此外，位于莱默伊登托尔布鲁赫的入口狭窄曲折，长度超过14米的船只无法通过。

Drenthe Hoofd Canal

A canal located in Drenthe Province, the Netherlands. The Drenthe Hoofd Canal has a total length

德伦特大运河

荷兰德伦特省运河。德伦特大运河全长43.8千米，建有6座船闸，

of 43.8 kilometres and 6 locks, connecting the Meppel Canal and the Reest River in Meppel to the North Willems Canal near Assen. Built from 1767 to 1780, it flows through Drenthe and plays an important role in drainage in the central part of Drenthe Province. During the 19th and 20th centuries, it was used to transport passengers, building materials, peat, food, almost everything the population needed. During the period between 1970s and 1990s, the canal was mainly used for yachts.

在梅珀尔连通梅珀尔运河和雷斯特河,流至阿森附近连通北威廉斯运河。该运河1767—1780年间开凿,流经德伦特省,在该省中部地区的排水作业中发挥重要作用。19至20世纪期间,德伦特大运河曾用于客运及货运,运输建筑材料、泥煤、食物及人们所需的其他各种物品。20世纪70—90年代,该运河主要供游艇通行。

Dubai (Water) Canal

A canal located in Dubai of the United Arab Emirates. The Dubai (Water) Canal is a 3-kilometre-long canal which flows from the Business Bay to the Persian Gulf through Safa Park and Jumeirah. The construction work began in 2013 and was completed in 2016. The canal's width ranges from 80 metres to 120 metres, and its depth is 6 metres. It creates new public spaces and facilities with a total area of 80,000 square metres, with private marinas for boats and a trade centre at the entrance of the canal. Roads and Transport Authority built bridges over the canal for the facilitation of traffic through the Sheikh Zayed Road, Al Wasl Road and Jumeirah Road. The bridges are 8.5 metres above the water to allow boats to pass underneath.

迪拜运河

阿联酋迪拜市运河。迪拜运河全长3千米,始于迪拜商业湾,流经塞法公园和朱美拉古城,最后注入波斯湾。运河2013年开凿,2016年竣工。目前,迪拜运河最窄处80米,最宽处120米,深6米。运河修建项目为这座城市创造了总面积达8万平方米的全新公共区域,运河上有若干私人游船码头,运河入口处还有一个贸易中心。为确保谢赫扎耶德路、阿瓦斯路和朱美拉路的交通便利,迪拜交通运输局在运河上建有数座大桥,所建桥梁高出水面8.5米,河上往来的船只可畅行无阻。

Duke Berry Canal

A canal located in France. See Berry Canal.

贝里公爵运河

法国运河。见贝里运河。

Duluth Ship Canal

A canal located in eastern Minnesota, the United States. Linking Duluth Harbour with Lake Superior, the Duluth Ship Canal was constructed in 1870 and finished in 1871. Several years after the completion, the canal was put under federal supervision and maintenance. It is outlined by two 520-metre-long breakwaters, which are 91 metres apart from each other and are built of concrete set on timber and stone cribbing. This canal is navigable for ocean-going ships. Three lighthouses are pitched on the sides of the canal, namely the Duluth North Pier Light, the Duluth South Breakwater Outer Light and the Duluth South Breakwater Inner Light. At the end of the harbour, the Aerial Lift Bridge straddles the canal. There are no locks on the canal. Every year, about a thousand vessels sail from Duluth Harbour to Lake Superior through the canal.

德卢斯通海运河

美国明尼苏达州东部运河。德卢斯通海运河连接德卢斯港与苏必利尔湖，1870年开凿，次年竣工，几年后由联邦政府负责管辖和维护。运河两岸是长520米、相隔91米的两座防波堤，由混凝土筑成，以木垛和石垛支撑。运河可供海船通行，两岸矗立着3座灯塔，即德卢斯北码头灯塔、德卢斯南防波堤外灯塔和德卢斯南防波堤内灯塔。港口尽头有升降吊桥横跨运河。该运河为无船闸运河。每年大约有1 000艘船经由德卢斯通海运河往来于德卢斯港与苏必利尔湖之间。

Dunkirk-Escaut Canal

A large-scale canal located in northern France. The Dunkirk-Escaut Canal runs from Dunkirk to Mortagne-du-Nord. It is 189 kilometres in length and has 14 locks. The canal is aimed at providing a route for large commercial barges up to 143 metres long and 11 metres wide to navigate between the North Sea Harbour and the industrial towns on the Escaut, Denain and Valenciennes. The construction was started after World War II and completed in the late 1960s. It was built by connecting the 8 original canals. Almost half a century after the comple-

敦刻尔克－埃斯科运河

法国北部大运河。敦刻尔克－埃斯科运河连接敦刻尔克和北莫尔塔涅，全长189千米，建有14座船闸，是大型商船往来于埃斯科河畔的工业城镇德南和瓦朗谢讷与北海港口之间的重要航道，最大可容长143米、宽11米的商业驳船通行。该运河于第二次世界大战结束后开始修建，20世纪60年代末竣工，由原有的8条运河连接而成。2016年，敦刻尔克－埃斯科运河在开通

tion, an ambitious programme to enlarge the canal was carried out in 2016. The programme was included in the overall Seine-Schelde Waterway project, a transport infrastructure project high on the EU's list of priorities. Thirty-five bridges will be renovated to make it accessible to vessels with 3-tier containers.

近半个世纪后开始大规模扩建。扩建计划被纳入欧盟重点交通基础设施工程塞纳—斯海尔德运河修建项目。项目完工后，该运河上的35座桥梁将得到整修，可供装载三层集装箱的船只通行。

Dunkirk-Newport Canal

敦刻尔克-新港运河

A cross-border canal located in Europe. See Newport-Dunkirk Canal.

欧洲跨国运河。见新港—敦刻尔克运河。

East Canal

A canal located in northeastern France. The East Canal is 397 kilometres long. Built from 1874 to 1887, it is now composed of two parts, namely, a 272-kilometre-long northern branch connecting the Meuse River and the Moselle, and a 125-kilometre-long southern branch connecting the Moselle to the Saône. In 2003, the two branches were officially named the Meuse Canal and the Vosges Canal respectively.

东方运河

法国东北部运河。东方运河全长397千米，1874—1887年间开凿。该运河由南北两条支线运河构成。其中，北支线运河长272千米，连通默兹河与摩泽尔河；南支线运河长125千米，连通摩泽尔河与索恩河。2003年，两条支线运河分别正式定名为默兹运河与孚日运河。

Eastern Division (Pennsylvania)

A canal located in Pennsylvania, the United States. The Eastern Division has a length of 69 kilometres, flowing along the east side of the Susquehanna River between Columbia and Duncan's Island at the mouth of the Juniata River. It was opened in 1833 and 14 locks were set up, an average lift of which was 2.3 metres. The Pennsylvania state government initially planned to build a 39-kilometre-long canal from the Union Canal in Middleton to Juniata. However, in 1828, the state abandoned the original plan and chose to extend the Eastern Division 31 kilometres south, connecting it to the Philadelphia and Columbia railroad. A 609-metre-long and 2.6-metre-high dam was built to facilitate passage, forming a pool through which ships can bypass the wooden, two-tier towpath bridge at Clark's Ferry.

运河东段（宾夕法尼亚）

美国宾夕法尼亚州运河。运河东段全长69千米，沿萨斯奎汉纳河东岸，自哥伦比亚流向邓肯岛，汇入朱尼亚塔河口。1833年，运河东段通航，河上建有14座船闸，每座船闸平均升水2.3米。宾夕法尼亚州政府最初计划修建一条长39千米的运河，在米德尔顿连通联合运河和朱尼亚塔河。1828年，州政府放弃最初计划，转而将运河东段向南延伸31千米，与费城和哥伦比亚的铁路线相连。为方便船只通行，运河上修建了一座长609米、高2.6米的大坝，形成一处深潭。通过该深潭，船只可以绕过克拉克渡口上的双层木制拖链桥。

Eastern Wijtwerd Canal

A canal located in Groningen Province, the Netherlands. The canal is 2.7 kilometres long and was officially opened on 1 October 2007 with the support of the Cultural Heritage Agency of the Netherlands. Its branches include the Godlinze Canal, the Leermens Canal and the Spijkster Canal, all flowing into the Eastern Wijtwerd Canal and ultimately joining the Damster Canal.

Eastern Zhejiang Canal

A canal located in Zhejiang Province, China. Also called Hang-Yong Canal. The Eastern Zhejiang Canal is 239 kilometres long, running from Hangzhou to the Yongjiang River estuary in Ningbo City. It was first built during the Spring and Autumn Period (770 BC—476 BC). In the middle Tang Dynasty (618—907 AD), as inland shipping became increasingly busy, the canal was dredged and a new channel excavated. During the Southern Song Dynasty (1127—1279), it became an important waterway for shipping and export trades since its shipping conditions were greatly improved after several overhauls. Porcelain and other products were transported to Ningbo through the canal, and then to overseas markets through the Maritime Silk Road. It also played an important part in irrigation and postal service then. The canal transportation gradually declined in the Qing Dynasty (1616—1911). In the 1990s, the development of Ningbo Port triggered the reconstruction of the Eastern Zhejiang Canal.

东维特维德运河

荷兰格罗宁根省运河。东维特维德运河全长2.7千米。在荷兰文化遗产局支持下，运河于2007年10月1日正式通航。豪特林泽运河、利尔曼斯运河和斯皮克斯特运河3条支线运河均汇入东维特维德运河，最后与达姆斯特运河交汇。

浙东运河

中国浙江省运河。亦称杭甬运河。浙东运河全长239千米，西起杭州，东至宁波市甬江入海口。运河最早开凿于春秋时期。唐代中期，随着江南航运日益繁忙，人们对浙东运河进行疏浚并开凿了新航道。南宋时期，浙东运河经多次修缮，航运条件不断改善，成为重要的航运与对外贸易通道。瓷器等产品通过浙东运河运往宁波，再通过海上丝绸之路运往海外市场。浙东运河还曾在土地灌溉和邮政服务方面发挥过重要作用。清朝时期，运河的航运功能逐渐减弱。20世纪90年代，随着宁波港的发展扩大，浙东运河改造也提上了日程。2009年，浙东运河改造工程竣工。2013年5月，浙东运河被列为第七批国家重点文物保护单位，成为大运河项目的一部分。

In 2009, the renovation was completed. In May 2013, as a part of the Grand Canal, the Eastern Zhejiang Canal was listed in the seventh group of National Historical and Cultural Heritage.

East Flood Canal

A canal located in Jakarta, Indonesia. The East Flood Canal is 23.6 kilometres long and 100 to 300 metres wide, flowing from East Jakarta to North Jakarta. It is mainly used to divert the Ciliwung River, the Cipinang River, etc. In 1918, when Jakarta experienced its fourth catastrophic flood in the recorded history, the Dutch colonial government appointed Hendrik van Breen as the engineer in charge of constructing the Jakarta Flood Canal. In 1973, the Indonesian government, with the assistance of the Netherland Engineering Consultant (NEDECO), formulated the Master Plan for Drainage and Flood Control of Jakarta. As a part of the plan, the East Flood Canal was excavated on 22 June 2002, the 475th anniversary of Jakarta.

East Qinhuai River

A canal located in Nanjing, Jiangsu Province, China. The East Qinhuai River is about 53 kilometres in length. The Yunlianghe River, its main waterway, is about 32 kilometres long with a width of 60 to 120 metres. The two branches of the river empty into the Yangtze River in the northern part of Nanjing. Connected to the Qinhuai River, it will be used as a flood control channel. The project of dredging

东泄洪运河

印度尼西亚雅加达运河。东泄洪运河全长23.6千米，宽100—300米。运河从东雅加达省流向北雅加达省，主要用于调节芝利翁河、芝比南河等河流的水量。1918年，雅加达遭遇了有史以来第四次大洪灾，当时的荷兰殖民政府指派亨德里克·范布林负责修建雅加达泄洪运河。1973年，在荷兰工程咨询集团的协助下，印尼政府制定了《雅加达排水与防洪总体规划》。东泄洪运河作为规划内容之一，于雅加达建城475周年纪念日（2002年6月22日）开凿。

秦淮东河

中国江苏省南京市运河。秦淮东河总长约53千米，其中主航道运粮河长约32千米，河道宽60—120米。秦淮东河的两汊在南京城北部汇入长江。秦淮东河主要是作为城市泄洪通道，将与现有的秦淮河航道相通。2015年，秦淮东河疏浚工程启动，初步规划10年完

the East Qinhuai River was started in 2015 and was planned to be completed in ten years. It is the largest and most heavily invested waterway project in Nanjing since 1949. The New Qinhuai River, the East Qinhuai River and the Yangtze River can form a 100-kilometre-long waterway around Nanjing to protect it from flood.

工。该工程是南京市重大人工河工程, 为1949年以来南京市规模最大、投资最多的水利工程。秦淮新河、秦淮东河和长江将形成100多千米长的绕城水路, 守护南京城市安全。

East Singel Canal

东辛厄尔运河

A canal located in South Holland, the Netherlands. The East Singel Canal mainly flows through the city of Delft. A cast-iron pedestrian bridge was built on the canal in the Hague section in 1861, and it is now preserved as the national heritage.

荷兰南荷兰省运河。东辛厄尔运河主要流经代尔夫特市。1861年人们在运河海牙段建了一座铸铁人行桥, 这座桥现为荷兰国家级遗产。

Edinburgh and Glasgow Union Canal

爱丁堡－格拉斯哥联合运河

A contour canal located in Scotland, the United Kingdom. Also called Union Canal. The Edinburgh and Glasgow Union Canal extends from Edinburgh to Falkirk, where it joins up with the Forth and Clyde Canal. The navigable canal is estimated to be around 51 kilometres, with 2 locks equipped with boat lifts. Approved by an act of Parliament in 1817, the canal was excavated by the Edinburgh and Glasgow Union Canal Company in 1818 and opened in 1822 to transport minerals, especially coal, to Edinburgh. But the traffic declined as the Edinburgh and Glasgow Railway was opened in 1842. Passenger services on the canal ceased by 1848. It was officially closed to navigation in 1965. With the recognition of its historical and cultural

英国苏格兰等高运河。亦称联合运河。爱丁堡－格拉斯哥联合运河自爱丁堡延伸至福尔柯克, 汇入福斯－克莱德运河, 可通航河道约长51千米, 沿途建有2座带升船机的船闸。1817年, 运河开凿方案得到议会批准, 次年, 爱丁堡－格拉斯哥联合运河公司开始施工, 1822年运河竣工通航, 将矿物（尤其是煤炭）运往爱丁堡。1842年, 爱丁堡－格拉斯哥铁路通车后, 联合运河的功能日渐衰退。1848年运河客运服务中止。1965年运河停航。数十年后, 人们认识到了该运河的历史与文化价值, 在英国境内最大

value decades later, the canal was reopened in 2001 and reconnected to the Forth and Clyde Canal in 2002 under the support of the Millennium Link Project, the largest canal restoration work in the United Kingdom. Today the Union Canal is listed as a monument featuring the Falkirk Wheel, the Leamington Lift Bridge, the Prospect Hill Tunnel (the only canal tunnel in Scotland) and the Avon Aqueduct (the longest and tallest aqueduct in Scotland). The canal is now for recreational use by canoeists and rowers. It is also one of Scotland's most popular tourist attractions with millions of visitors every year.

的运河复兴计划"千禧年连通计划"资助下, 联合运河于2001年重新开放, 并于次年与福斯—克莱德运河连通。如今, 该运河已被列为文物保护遗址, 其特色景点包括福尔柯克轮、利明顿吊桥、普罗斯佩克特山隧道(苏格兰唯一的隧道)和埃文渡槽(苏格兰最长、最高的渡槽)。该运河现已成为独木舟和赛艇活动基地, 是苏格兰最著名的景点之一, 每年吸引数百万游客。

Eeklo Canal

埃克洛运河

A canal located in Eeklo, Belgium. The Eeklo Canal has a length of 1.6 kilometres, running from Eeklo to the Schipdonk Canal. The Schipdonk Canal was excavated in the bed of the Lieve Canal, which became unnavigable for the vessels to travel to Eeklo. The city was also in the risk of insufficient fresh water supply. As a result, the Council of Eeklo urged to construct the Eeklo Canal. The canal was officially opened in 1860. A marina was built in the 1990s. Now still navigable for Class I vessels, the Eeklo Canal is of less economic value.

比利时埃克洛市运河。埃克洛运河全长1.6千米, 自埃克洛市汇入斯希普顿克运河。由于斯希普顿克运河开凿于利费运河的河床上, 而利费运河上的船只无法驶入埃克洛市, 同时该市的淡水供应也无法得到保证, 因此, 埃克洛市议会敦促修建埃克洛运河。埃克洛运河于1860年正式通航。20世纪90年代, 运河上新建1个码头。目前, 埃克洛运河仍可通行一级船只, 但经济价值已减弱。

Eendrachts Canal

团结运河

A canal located in Groningen, the Netherlands. Connecting to the Hoen Canal, the Verbindings

荷兰格罗宁根省运河。团结运河连通霍恩运河、韦尔宾丁斯运河和

Canal and the North Willems Canal, the Eendrachts Canal starts from the Zoom Lake and ends in the Krabbenkreek estuary. It used to be a tidal branch of the Schelde that has been made a canal from the northern stretch of the Schelde-Rhine Canal. In 1907, the Eendrachts Canal was built in order to improve the navigability on the winding shipping route. In 1909, the canal was put into use. In the 1930s, it fell into disuse. The passage to the Krabbenkreek estuary was closed, and an additional canal was excavated to connect the Eendrachts Canal with the Krammer Lake.

北威廉斯运河，始于佐姆湖，汇入克拉本河河口。该运河曾是斯海尔德河的潮汐汊道，斯海尔德河已改造为斯海尔德—莱茵运河北部的旁侧运河。为改善弯曲航道的航运条件，团结运河修建于1907年，1909年通航。20世纪30年代，该运河被弃用。目前，通往克拉本河河口的通道已关闭，团结运河与克拉默湖之间又新修了一条连接运河。

Eglinton Canal

埃格林顿运河

A canal located in Galway, Ireland. The Eglinton Canal, named after the 13th Earl of Eglinton, a former Lord Lieutenant of Ireland, is about 1.2 kilometres long. It starts at Lough Corrib in the north, flowing into the Galway Bay in the south. The canal was constructed by the Commissioners of Public Works between 1848 and 1852. The canal has 2 locks, i.e., the Parkavera Lock and the sea lock linking the Claddagh Basin to the bay. There were once 5 hand-operated wood swivel bridges in steel frames. It was found that these bridges could be opened normally, but could not be closed safely, so the 5 swivel bridges for navigation were later replaced by fixed bridges. During the first several decades, the canal was a great navigation passage busy for transporting goods between inland Ireland and other countries. However, by 1915, due to the neglect of management and drainage problems, the

爱尔兰戈尔韦郡运河。埃格林顿运河以当时的爱尔兰总督、第13代伯爵埃格林顿的名字命名，全长1.2千米，北起科里布湖，向南注入戈尔韦湾。埃格林顿运河由公共事务局于1848—1852年间开凿，建有2座船闸，即帕卡维拉船闸和连接戈尔韦湾和克拉达湾的通海船闸。运河上曾建有5座钢架木质手动旋转桥。这些旋转桥可以正常打开，却无法安全关闭，之后全部更换成固定桥。最初几十年，运河航运繁忙，船只穿梭于爱尔兰内陆和其他国家之间运输货物。自1915年起，因疏于管理和排水问题，运河渐渐失去了通航价值。1954年，埃格林顿运河停航。如今，埃格林顿运河为戈尔韦郡著名

canal gradually lost its value in navigation. In 1954, the canal was closed. Today, the Eglington Canal is a famous tourist attraction in Galway.

的旅游景点。

Elbe-Havel Canal

A canal located in Germany. The Elbe-Havel Canal is 56 kilometres in length, running from Magdeburg on River Elbe to Brandenburg on River Havel. Since 2003, the canal has been connected to the Mittelland Canal by the Magdeburg Water Bridge, which spans over River Elbe. The Mittelland Canal provides the Elbe-Havel Canal with a connection to the west of Germany, where the waterway can continuously spread to Berlin and Poland.

易北-哈弗尔运河

德国运河。易北—哈弗尔运河全长56千米，连接易北河河畔的马格德堡和哈弗尔河河畔的勃兰登堡。自2003年开始，该运河通过易北河上的马格德堡水桥与中部运河相通，通向德国西部地区，航道由此延伸至柏林和波兰。

Elbe Lateral Canal

An inland canal located in Lower Saxony, Germany. The Elbe Lateral Canal is 115 kilometres in length from Lauenburg to Gifhorn, linking Lower Elbe and the Mittelland Canal. Before Germany was reunited, the waterway to Hamburg was cut off because ships had to pass through the German Democratic Republic. The canal was built in 1968 to restore the connection between Hamburg, the biggest sea harbour of the Federal Republic of Germany, and the inland waterways. It was opened in June 1976 but was closed in July due to a dam rupture. The canal was not reopened until June 1977. The difference in elevation between the Elbe and the Mittelland Canal is 61 metres. The waterway is connected by a lock with a 23-metre height and a

易北河旁侧运河

德国下萨克森州内陆运河。易北河旁侧运河全长115千米，从劳恩堡流向吉夫霍恩，连通易北河下游和中部运河。德国统一之前，驶向汉堡的船只必须经过德意志民主共和国，所以水路运输中断。1968年，为恢复德意志联邦共和国最大的海港汉堡港与内河水系之间的交通，易北河旁侧运河开始修建。1976年6月，运河通航。但由于大坝出现断裂，易北河旁侧运河同年7月停航，直到1977年6月才重新开放。易北河和中部运河之间水位落差达61米，二者之间通过一座高23米的船闸和一台升船机相连

ship lift with a 38-metre height, the largest ship lift in the world at that time.

通；此升船机提升高度达38米，为当时世界之最。

Elbe-Lübeck Canal

易北－吕贝克运河

A canal located in eastern Schleswig-Holstein, Germany. Also called Elbe-Trave Canal. The Elbe-Lübeck Canal is 67 kilometres in length from Lübeck to Lauenburg, linking the Elbe River and the Trave River. It has 7 locks. The interior length of each lock is 80 metres while the interior width is 12 metres. The canal was constructed to replace the Stecknitz Canal, a waterway linking these two rivers. In 1893, the Stecknitz Canal was closed to barge traffic. In 1895, the construction of the Elbe–Lübeck Canal began on the basis of the old canal's watercourse. In 1900, it was opened. The Elbe-Lübeck Canal was generally straightened, thus reducing the original length of 94 kilometres to the current 67 kilometres. Today, it still carries a substantial freight traffic and offers boat tour as well.

德国石勒苏益格－荷尔斯泰因州东部运河。亦称易北－特拉沃运河。易北－吕贝克运河全长67千米，从吕贝克流向劳恩堡，连通易北河和特拉沃河，运河上建有7座船闸，每座船闸的内长为80米、宽为12米。这条运河是为取代原连通易北河和特拉沃河的斯特克尼兹运河而开挖。1893年，斯特克尼兹运河关停了驳船运输业务。1895年，人们在原运河航道基础上，开始修建易北－吕贝克运河。1900年，运河正式通航。易北－吕贝克运河矫直后，航线由原来的94千米缩短至现在的67千米。如今，该运河仍然货运繁忙，同时也提供游船观光服务。

Elbe-Trave Canal

易北－特拉沃运河

A canal located in eastern Schleswig-Holstein, Germany. See Elbe-Lübeck Canal.

德国石勒苏益格－荷尔斯泰因州东部运河。见易北－吕贝克运河。

Elbe-Weser Waterway

易北－威悉航道

A waterway located in North Germany. Linking River Elbe and River Weser, the Elbe-Weser Waterway is 54.7 kilometres in length and runs from

德国北部航道。易北－威悉航道全长54.7千米，从奥滕多夫镇流向不来梅港，连通易北河和威悉河。

Otterndorf to Bremer Port. The waterway consists of the Hadeln Canal, the Bederkesa-Geeste Canal and River Geeste. The Hadeln Canal is a drainage channel with a length of about 32 kilometres. It was constructed between 1852 and 1855, running from the Elbe near Otterndorf to the lake near Bad Bederkesa. The length of the Bederkesa-Geeste Canal is 11 kilometres. It was built between 1858 and 1860 and deepened twice later. River Geeste runs through Lower Saxony and Bremen. The lock built in 1898 protected the river from tides but also resulted in a low water level of the channel. The storm surge barrier built at Bremer Port later greatly improved its shipping capacity. In the late 1960s, the freight traffic was particularly thriving on the Elbe-Weser Waterway, but it declined from 1973 onwards. Today it is mainly used for the navigation of sports boats and pleasure craft.

航道共分三段，分别为哈德尔恩运河、贝德凯萨—盖斯特运河和盖斯特河。第一段哈德尔恩运河长约32千米，1852年开凿，1855年竣工。该运河是一条排水渠，从奥滕多夫附近的易北河流向巴德贝德凯萨村附近的湖泊。第二段贝德凯萨—盖斯特运河长11千米，1858年开凿，1860年竣工，其后经过两次加深改造。第三段盖斯特河流经下萨克森州和不来梅，河上的船闸修建于1898年，旨在避免河流受潮汐影响，但也导致航道水位较低。不来梅港建有抵挡风暴的大坝，极大提升了盖斯特河的航运能力。20世纪60年代后期，易北—威悉航道货运繁忙，但其货运量从1973年开始下降。如今，该航道主要供各类体育和休闲用船通行。

Elbląg Canal

A canal located in Warmian-Masurian Province, Poland. The Elbląg Canal runs from Lake Druno to River Drwęca and Lake Jeziorak, with a length of 80.5 kilometres. It can carry small ships up to 50 tons in displacement, 24.5 metres in length, 3 metres in width, and 1.1 metres in draught. The canal was constructed in 1844 and opened in 1860. Damaged in World War II, it was repaired and reused in 1948. Locks and a striking system of inclines between the lakes are used to overcome an 100-metre elevation difference between its ends.

埃尔布隆格运河

波兰瓦尔米亚—马祖里省运河。埃尔布隆格运河自德鲁湖流向德尔文察河与耶焦拉克湖，全长80.5千米，可通行排水量低于50吨、吃水深度不超过1.1米、船只长宽不超过24.5米和3米的小型船只。运河1844年开凿，1860年通航。第二次世界大战期间运河遭到破坏，修复后于1948年重新通航。为克服运河首尾100米的水位落差，人们在德鲁湖和耶焦拉克湖之间修建了

Regarded as one of the Seven Wonders in Poland, it is one of the most important monuments marking the progress of technology. It now mainly serves as a tourist attraction.

船闸和完备的斜面升船机系统。埃尔布隆格运河为波兰七大奇迹之一, 是见证波兰水利工程技术进步的重要里程碑之一, 如今主要作为一处旅游景点。

Elisabethfehn Canal

伊丽莎白费恩运河

A canal located in Lower Saxony, Germany. The Elisabethfehn Canal, linking the Coastal Canal with the Leda River, has 4 locks and runs for a distance of about 15 kilometres. It has a water level of 13.5 metres and is up to 1.5 metres deep. The canal was constructed between 1855 and 1893, and it was once the northwestern part of the former Hunte-Ems Canal. After World War II, the shipping on the canal almost came to a standstill. The Elisabethfehn Canal was mainly used for the navigation of pleasure boats since the 1960s.

德国下萨克森州运河。伊丽莎白费恩运河连通沿海运河和莱达河, 全长约15千米, 共建有4座船闸, 水位为13.5米, 水深1.5米。该运河1855年开凿, 1893年竣工, 曾是洪特—埃姆斯运河的西北分支。第二次世界大战后, 伊丽莎白费恩运河航运几乎停滞。20世纪60年代以后, 运河主要供游船通行。

El Salam Canal

埃尔萨拉姆运河

A canal located in Egypt. The El Salam Canal has a total length of 242 kilometres with 87 kilometres in the west of the Suez Canal and 155 kilometres in the east side. It starts from the west of the Suez Canal and stretches to Israel and the Gaza Strip, passing Lake Manzala, El Sarow drainage, and Hadoos drainage. The El Salam Canal was constructed as a part of a project called Toshka. The project was aimed for carrying the Nile Delta drainage water to the farms on the Sinai desert.

埃及运河。埃尔萨拉姆运河全长242千米, 其中87千米位于苏伊士运河西部, 155千米位于苏伊士运河东部。该运河始于苏伊士运河西侧, 一直延伸到以色列和加沙地带, 流经曼扎拉湖、埃尔萨罗排水系统以及哈多斯排水系统。埃尔萨拉姆运河是托斯卡工程的一部分。该工程旨在把尼罗河三角洲的排水引向西奈沙漠的农场。

Ems Canal

A canal located in Groningen Province, the Neth-erlands. Flowing from the city of Groningen to Delfzijl Port, the Ems Canal is 26.4 kilometres long and 60 metres wide with one lock. It was built be-tween 1866 and 1876 and widened in 1963 with six bridges over it. The Ems Canal plays a vital role in the local shipbuilding industry and transportation. The adjustments to the embankment structures and dykes of the canal were carried out from 1993 to 1995 because the natural gas extraction caused subsidence. In 2011, the ownership, management and maintenance of the canal were transferred from Groningen to Public Works and Water Manage-ment, which started the reconstruction of the main waterway Lemmer-Delfzijl. As a busy route for goods transportation and pleasure craft, the canal was widened for the ships of Class Va. Due to the tide, the drainage of the canal was ineffective. Now it performs well as a drainage canal after its bottom was widened at least 12 metres and deepened to 5.2 metres in Groningen and 5.8 metres in Delfzijl. The current Ems Canal is used recreationally. The Groningen Student Rowing Association has been organizing the 6-kilometre-long rowing race on it since 1988.

埃姆斯运河

荷兰格罗宁根省运河。埃姆斯运河全长26.4千米，宽60米，建有1座船闸，自格罗宁根市流入代尔夫宰尔港。运河1866年开凿，1876年竣工，后于1963年拓宽。运河上建有6座桥梁。埃姆斯运河对促进当地造船业和运输业发展发挥了重要作用。由于天然气开采造成沉陷，1993—1995年间，人们对埃姆斯运河堤岸进行了修缮。2011年，运河的所有权、管理权和维护权由格罗宁根移交给公共工程与水利管理局。该管理局重修了莱默—代尔夫宰尔航道。运河作为货运和游览的重要线路，拓宽为五甲级航道。过去因受潮汐影响，运河排水效果不佳。埃姆斯运河经拓建后，河道底部拓宽了12米以上，其中位于格罗宁根的河段加深到了5.2米，位于代尔夫宰尔港的部分加深至5.8米，现已成为排水良好的运河。目前，埃姆斯运河上经常举办休闲娱乐活动。自1988年以来，格罗宁根学生赛艇协会一直在运河上举行6千米赛程的赛艇比赛。

Ems-Jade Canal

A canal located in Lower Saxony, Germany. The Ems-Jade Canal is 72.3 kilometres in length with 3 locks, running from the city of Emden to Wilhelm

埃姆斯－亚德运河

德国下萨克森州运河。埃姆斯—亚德运河自埃姆登市流向威廉姆斯港，全长72.3千米，建有3座船闸，

Port. It links the Ems River and the Jade Bay. The canal was opened in 1888 and accessible to ships with a displacement of up to 300 tonnes. Today, it is not important for freight traffic anymore, but mainly used for tourism.

连通埃姆斯河和亚德湾。该运河1888年竣工，可容排水量达300吨的船舶通行。如今，埃姆斯—亚德运河不再是重要的货运通道，主要用于旅游观光。

Ems Lateral Canal

埃姆斯河旁侧运河

A federal canal located in Lower Saxony, Germany. The Ems Lateral Canal is 9 kilometres long, 27 metres wide and 1.5 to 2 metres deep. It runs from Lower Ems at Oldersum to the Emden Harbour, running parallel to the Ems River. Constructed from 1894 to 1897, the canal was originally the final section of the Dortmund-Ems Canal, which was opened in 1899. Since 1968, the Ems Lateral Canal has become a federal waterway and it no longer belonged to the Dortmund-Ems Canal. Currently, the canal is mainly used by recreational boats and there are several small harbours along the route.

德国下萨克森州联邦运河。埃姆斯河旁侧运河长9千米，宽27米，深1.5至2米不等，从奥尔德瑟姆的埃姆斯河下游流至埃姆登港，与埃姆斯河流向平行。该运河于1894—1897年间开凿，最初是多特蒙德—埃姆斯运河（1899年启用）的末段。自1968年以来，埃姆斯河旁侧运河已成为联邦航道，不再隶属于多特蒙德—埃姆斯运河。目前，该运河沿岸建有多个小型港口，主要供游船使用。

Ems-Vecht Canal

埃姆斯–费赫特运河

A canal located in Lower Saxony, Germany. The Ems-Vecht Canal, running from River Ems to River Vechte, is 22.3 kilometres long with 2 locks. The canal was excavated in 1870 and opened in 1879. The canal was closed in 1973. Today the canal comes back to use again and is accessible to excursion boats less than 12 metres in length.

德国下萨克森州运河。埃姆斯—费赫特运河连通埃姆斯河和费赫特河，全长22.3千米，建有2座船闸。该运河1870年开凿，1879年竣工通航，1973年停航。如今，埃姆斯—费赫特运河又投入使用，可容纳长度不超过12米的游船通行。

Enfield Falls Canal

A canal located in Hartford in Connecticut, the United States. See Windsor Locks Canal.

恩菲尔德福尔斯运河

美国康涅狄格州哈特福德市运河。见温莎洛克斯运河。

English Canal

An uncompleted canal located in northern Sweden. The English Canal was expected to link the Swedish iron ore fields around Kiruna and Gällivare with Luleå and the Gulf of Bothnia. It was decided in 1863 that the waterway of the Lule River between Storbacken and Luleå was going to be canalized to join the railway to efficiently transport the ore produced in the northern iron ore fields. The Gällivare Company Limited began to work on the construction of the canal in October 1864. About 1,500 men were working on the project by 1865. But the construction was suspended in the next two years because of an economic crisis of the company and finally ended in 1867 when the company went into bankruptcy. There are some remains of the canal in Norrbotten and Swedish Lapland, standing as the architectural memorials of the canal's history.

英吉利运河

瑞典北部未完工运河。修建英吉利运河是计划将位于瑞典基律纳和耶利瓦勒附近的铁矿区同吕勒奥及波的尼亚湾相连接。1863年，人们决定将斯德贝肯至吕勒奥之间的吕勒河河段改造为运河，并同铁路运输贯通，以便更高效地运输北部矿区的铁矿石。1864年10月，耶利瓦勒有限责任公司开始修建英吉利运河。到1865年，大约有1 500名工人参与了该运河的修建。但在之后的两年里，由于耶利瓦勒公司陷入经济危机，运河修建处于停滞状态。随着耶利瓦勒公司在1867年宣告破产，运河项目也因此终止。如今，在北博滕省和拉普兰地区有几处运河遗址，这些遗址具有重要的历史纪念意义。

Ens Canal

A canal located in Northeast Polder in Flevoland Province, the Netherlands. With a length of 9.5 kilometres and an elevation of —4 metres, the Ens Canal runs southwest from the Zwolse Canal and then flows southeast along the Kamper Route, ending in a

恩思运河

荷兰弗莱福兰省东北圩田运河。恩思运河长9.5千米，水位低于海平面4米。该运河始于兹沃尔瑟运河，流向西南，继而沿着坎彭路转向东南方向，到恩思352号省道旁

turning basin along the provincial road N352 in Ens.

的回船池。

Erewash Canal

埃里沃什运河

A canal located in England, the United Kingdom. The Erewash Canal is about 19 kilometres with 14 locks. Starting from the Trent River at Trent Lock, it flows parallel to the Erewash River, then crosses the Erewash near Eastwood, and finally ends at the Langley Mill basin, thus connecting the Nottingham Canal and the Cromford Canal. It allows vessels that are 24.5-metre-long and 4.1-metre-wide to pass through. Completed in 1779, the canal was a commercial success in transporting coal especially for the Eastwood Colliery, located on a narrow plot of land between the Erewash Canal and the Nottingham Canal. This helped to keep the canal operating longer than many of its contemporary canals in the fierce competition with railways. Nevertheless, a proposal to close the canal was put forward by the British Waterways Board. In response to it, the Erewash Canal Preservation and Development Association was founded in 1968.

英国英格兰运河。埃里沃什运河全长约19千米，建有14座船闸，起于特伦特洛克的特伦特河，与埃里沃什河平行，在伊斯特伍德附近与埃里沃什河交汇，到兰利米尔流域。该运河连通诺丁汉运河与克罗姆福德运河，最大允许长24.5米、宽4.1米的船只通行。1779年埃里沃什运河竣工通航后，商业航运极为成功，运输了大量产自伊斯特伍德煤矿的煤炭，该煤矿处于埃里沃什运河与诺丁汉运河之间的狭窄地段上。面临铁路运输的激烈竞争，该运河运营时间远超同时代的其他运河。尽管如此，英国水务局仍然提议关闭该运河。鉴于此，1968年人们专门成立了埃里沃什运河保护与发展协会。

Erie Canal

伊利运河

A canal located in New York, the United States. Formerly known as New York State Barge Canal. The Erie Canal is 584 kilometres in length, 8.5 metres in bottom-width, and 1.2 metres in depth, running westwards from Albany on the Hudson River to Buffalo at Lake Erie. It links New York City with the Great Lakes and overcomes an ele-

美国纽约州运河。旧称纽约州驳船运河。伊利运河全长584千米，河底宽8.5米，水深1.2米，水位落差达150米，建有83座船闸，东起哈德孙河岸的奥尔巴尼市，西至伊利湖港口城市布法罗，将纽约市与五大湖区连通。1817年，时任纽约

vation difference of 150 metres with 83 locks. The construction of the canal was initiated by DeWitt Clinton in 1817, the then governor of New York, and was completed in 1825. The construction was considered as an engineering marvel, during which many technological challenges had been successfully addressed. For instance, a series of staircase-like locks had been built on the western side to carry boats over the rock ridge known as the Niagara Escarpment. On the eastern section, 27 locks had been constructed over a stretch of 50 kilometres to surmount a series of natural rapids. Back then, the Erie Canal was deemed as an exemplar for canals constructed afterwards throughout the United States. Upon completion, the canal was an instant commercial success. Farm produce was transported from the midwestern region to New York City at a lower cost (less than $10 per ton) while manufactured goods from eastern cities reached the market of western towns and villages. With the presence of the Erie Canal, Buffalo became a busy transshipment hub while New York City was transformed into a major commercial centre, with a noticeable surge in population. The last commercial ship transiting the canal was known as the Day Peckinpaugh in 1994. Since then, the canal has been mainly used for recreational activities. In 2000, the Erie Canal was officially designated as National Heritage Corridor by the United States Congress, in order to recognize the status of the canal system as the most influential waterway and one of the most important works of civil engineering and construction in North America. The commercial traffic on the canal resumed in

州州长的迪维·克林顿发起倡议修建该运河，1825年竣工。施工期间，人们攻克了诸多技术难题，在运河西侧修建了梯式船闸，使船只可以安全经过尼加拉陡崖，在东侧50千米的河段上修建了27座船闸来克服急流。伊利运河项目是美国工程史上的一个壮举，也是美国境内运河修建的首个标杆工程。运河开通后，很快大获成功。美国中西部地区的农产品可以每吨不超过10美元的低廉价格运往纽约市，而加工自东部城市的各类产品也可通过该运河输送至西部的乡镇。在伊利运河的带动下，布法罗市成为繁忙的转运中心，而纽约市则发展为重要的商业中心，人口也随之大幅增长。1994年，戴伊·帕金波号通过，成为当时伊利运河上最后一艘大型商船，自此以后，伊利运河主要用于观光旅游。2000年，伊利运河网作为最具影响力的河道以及北美地区最重要的土木工程，被美国国会认定为国家遗产廊道。2008年，伊利运河上的商业运输得以恢复，目前在每年的5—11月对小型船只和少量大型船只开放。

2008. It is currently open to small craft and several larger vessels from May to November every year.

Erie Extension Canal

A canal located near the west edge of Pennsylvania, the United States. See Beaver and Erie Canal.

Escaut

A canalized cross-border river located in Europe. Also called Schelde River. The Escaut begins in northern France, flows through western Belgium and the southwestern Netherlands, and empties into the North Sea. Stretching 350 kilometres long, the Escaut is an important waterway and has been made navigable from its mouth up to Cambrai in France. In France, its canalized section, completed in 1788, starts from the connection with the Saint-Quentin Canal, runs toward the industrial towns of Valenciennes and finally the Belgian border. It can be further divided into two sections of different features roughly at its junction with the Dunkirk-Escaut Canal, namely, the waterway from Cambrai to Hordain and the other from Pont-Malin to the Belgian border. The former is 13 kilometres in length and is only accessible to small ships while the latter is 46 kilometres long and boasts a high capacity. In history, locks on the Escaut have been renovated to meet the increasing need of coal transportation during the industrial revolution. From 1960s, a further round of renovation has been implemented to make this commercial chan-

伊利扩建运河

美国宾夕法尼亚州西部运河。见比弗—伊利运河。

埃斯科河

欧洲跨国运河化河流。亦称斯海尔德河。埃斯科河全长350千米，始于法国北部，流经比利时西部和荷兰西南部，最终汇入北海。埃斯科河是一条重要航道，从法国康布雷市至入海口的河段可通航。其中，位于法国境内的可通航河段始于与圣康坦运河的连接处，流经瓦朗谢讷市的工业城镇后到达比利时边境。这一河段于1788年完成改造，与敦刻尔克—埃斯科运河交汇，上下游水文条件差异较大，可分两个河段，即康布雷市至奥尔丹河段，全长13千米；马林桥至比利时边境河段，全长46千米。前者仅供小型船只通行，后者航运能力更强。工业革命期间，煤炭成为主要运输品，为满足与日俱增的航运需求，人们当时就重修过埃斯科河上的船闸。20世纪60年代以来，人们继续升级改造埃斯科河，使之达到欧洲航道标准。如今，作为一条联通巴黎

nel meet the European waterway standard. Now as a part of the route from the Paris region to northern France, Belgium and the Netherlands, heavy barges were often found on the river. On its banks in Belgium also stands the port of Antwerp, the second-largest port in Europe. Many of the factories built along its route have been demolished to give way to the attractive rural landscape.

地区、法国北部地区、比利时和荷兰的商业航道,埃斯科河上驳船众多,贸易繁忙。该河位于比利时境内的河畔有欧洲第二大港口安特卫普。运河沿岸许多工厂都已拆除,两岸乡村风光秀美怡人。

Escaut Canal

A canal located in northern France. Also called Upper Escaut Canal. The Escaut Canal runs from the Saint-Quentin Canal at Cambrai to the Sensée Canal at Bassin Rond. It is 13.7 kilometres in length and has 5 locks.

埃斯科运河

法国北部运河。亦称埃斯科上游运河。埃斯科运河在康布雷连通圣昆廷运河, 在龙德湖连通桑塞运河, 全长13.7千米, 建有5座船闸。

Espel Canal

An inland canal located in Flevoland Province, the Netherlands. The Espel Canal is 8 kilometres in length. Starting from Emmeloord, the canal first heads north, connecting with the Lemster Canal, and then flows westward through the countryside to Espel, and finally stops at N712, a provincial road in Flevoland Province. The Espel Canal was used for beet transport. In the 20th century, there was a discussion on whether it should be shut down or not.

埃斯珀尔运河

荷兰弗莱福兰省内陆运河。埃斯珀尔运河全长8千米, 始于埃默洛尔德, 先向北汇入莱姆斯特运河, 后向西穿过乡村地区流至埃斯珀尔, 最终止于弗莱福兰省的712号省道。埃斯珀尔运河曾用于甜菜运输, 20世纪时, 人们围绕是否停用该运河曾展开过讨论。

Espierres Canal

A canal located in Belgium. The Espierres Canal lies between the French border and the Escaut. With

埃斯皮埃尔运河

比利时运河。埃斯皮埃尔运河位于法国边境和埃斯科河交界处, 全

a length of 8 kilometres, the canal winds its way through the provinces of Hainaut and West Flanders and enters France. Its French extension is called the Roubaix Canal. The Espierres Canal was excavated in 1840 and was officially opened in 1843. It was constructed to connect the Deûle Canal and the Escaut as well as supply water and transport coal to the Lille-Roubaix-Tourcoing metropolitan district. The canal had contributed to the development of the local economy for more than 100 years since its completion. Benefiting from the water quality, the fishing industry prospered in the Estaimpuis and Leers-Nord sections. During World War I, the Espierres Canal was once used to transport gravel and other construction materials from the Rhine, with 30 to 40 ships sailing through it every day. Since 1950, the canal had suffered from serious pollution due to the industrial development of the towns of Roubaix and Tourcoing, with industrial waste water discharged into its tributaries. The Espierres Canal was closed to traffic in 1985. On 8 September 2000, the canal was listed in the Walloon Heritage. Supported by the EU programme Blue Links, the Espierres Canal was reopened in 2011 as a part of the Deûle-Escaut link, with recreational navigation as the major function.

长8千米,主要流经比利时的埃诺省和西佛兰德省,之后进入法国。该运河在法国境内的延伸部分称为鲁贝运河。埃斯皮埃尔运河1840年开凿,1843年正式通航,旨在连通德勒运河与埃斯科河,并为里尔—鲁贝—图尔宽城市群提供淡水和煤炭资源。运河正式通航后的100多年里,为当地的经济发展做出了重要贡献。运河在埃斯坦皮和里尔斯—诺德这一河段的水质优良,此地捕鱼业十分发达。第一次世界大战期间,埃斯皮埃尔运河运输繁忙,每天有30—40艘从莱茵河运输砾石和其他建筑材料的货船通行。1950年后,鲁贝镇和图尔宽镇的工业迅速发展,大量工业废水排入埃斯皮埃尔运河支线。埃斯皮埃尔运河1985年停航。2000年9月8日,该运河被列为瓦隆遗址。2011年,在欧盟资助的"蓝色连通"工程推动下,埃斯皮埃尔运河被纳入德勒运河—埃斯科河航线,重新开放。恢复通航后,该运河主要服务于旅游业。

Étangs Canal

埃唐运河

A canal located in southern France. The Étangs Canal has a total length of 49 kilometres, linking Sète with Aigues-Mortes. It now constitutes a section of the Rhône-Sète Canal. The canal was excavated as an effort to broaden those medieval channels exis-

法国南部运河。埃唐运河全长49千米,连接塞特港和艾格莫尔特,现为罗讷—塞特运河的一部分。该运河由前朗格多克省负责修建,旨在拓宽当时尚存的中世纪航道,

tent through and between the shallow lakes and salt marshes by the former province of Languedoc.

连接众多浅水湖泊和盐沼。

Eurasia Canal

A proposed canal located in Russia. Along the Kuma-Manych Depression, the Eurasia Canal was planned to link the Caspian Sea with the Black Sea. The canal was designed to be 700 kilometres long, as a shorter alternative along with the existing Volga-Don Canal. The idea of constructing the Eurasia Canal was put forward several times since the times of the Union of Soviet Socialist Republics (USSR) and reanimated in 2007 by the then Kazakhstan president. It was expected to strengthen the Russian and Kazakh maritime power as well as benefiting the cargo traffic between the Volga-Caspian and surrounding areas. The Eurasia Canal was expected to be a convenient, safe and efficient route for the sustainable development of Sino-European trade. According to the initial assessment, the approximate cost of the project was about $4.5 billion. The construction would last 6 to 8 years. Upon completion, the canal is projected to serve with a freight-carrying capacity up to 10,000 tonnes. The Eurasia Canal project has not been implemented by now.

欧亚运河

俄罗斯拟建运河。欧亚运河拟跨越库马—马内奇洼地地区，连接里海和黑海，规划长度为700千米，旨在提供一条比现有的伏尔加—顿河运河更短的水上运输线路。建造欧亚运河的想法源于苏联时期，2007年，时任哈萨克斯坦总统再次提议开凿该运河，意在增强俄罗斯和哈萨克斯坦的海上实力，并促进伏尔加—里海地区与周边货运贸易的发展。该运河有望促进中欧贸易可持续发展，成为一条便捷、安全、高效的航道。根据最初的评估，欧亚运河修建成本约为45亿美元，预计耗时6—8年。欧亚运河一旦建成，将有望通行万吨级货轮。但工程至今尚未动工。

Europe Canal

A canal located in Germany. See Main-Danube Canal.

欧洲运河

德国运河。见美因—多瑙运河。

Falsterbo Canal

A canal located in the Skanör-Falsterbo Peninsula, Sweden. The Falsterbo Canal is 27 kilometres in length, of which only 1,600 metres goes through the Falsterbo Peninsula, while the rest is sea channel. It connects the Baltic Sea and the Öresund, allowing ships to pass among the regions of Falsterbo, Skanör, and Ljunghusen. In the 1880s and 1890s, various attempts to construct canals in this place all failed. During World War II, the extensive mining activities of Germans at the Falsterbo reef threatened the safety of Swedish merchant ships transiting into or out of the Baltic Sea, so Sweden decided to excavate a canal between Höllviken and Ljunghusen to provide a safe passage. The Falsterbo Canal was constructed in January 1940 and allowed ship passage in August 1941. The canal contains a sluice that prevents too much water flow through it when the difference of water levels between the Baltic Sea and Öresund is too large. In earlier years the bridge over the canal was opened at the discretion of the canal master, but later the opening hours were regulated. The Falsterbo Canal is currently navigated by 15,000 ships annually, but it is practically a passage for small craft.

Farmington Canal

A canal located in the northeastern United States. See New Haven and Northampton Canal.

法尔斯特布运河

瑞典斯科讷—法尔斯特布半岛运河。法尔斯特布运河全长27千米，但仅有1 600米流经法尔斯特布半岛，其余河段则属于海上航道。法尔斯特布运河连通波罗的海和厄勒海峡，船只可经由该运河在法尔斯特布、斯卡讷和伦吉森三个地区之间航行。19世纪80—90年代，人们曾多次试图在此处开凿运河，但均以失败告终。第二次世界大战期间，德国人在法尔斯特布礁附近大规模采矿，对进出波罗的海的瑞典商船造成了安全威胁。于是，瑞典决定在赫尔湾和伦吉森之间开凿一条运河，为商船提供安全通道。法尔斯特布运河1940年1月开凿，1941年8月通航。该运河建有1座船闸，用来调节因波罗的海和厄勒海峡水位差过大时流入运河的水量。早年，法尔斯特布运河大桥的开通时间由运河管理者酌情决定，之后才逐步规范起来。目前，该运河每年通航船只数约为15 000艘，以小型船只为主。

法明顿运河

美国东北部运河。见纽黑文—北安普敦运河。

Faux-Rempart Canal

A canal located in eastern France. Also called Faux-Rempart Ditch. The Faux-Rempart Canal runs in the centre of Strasbourg. It is 2 kilometres in length and has only one lock. The canal embraces the Grand Isle with both its ends connected to River Ill. There are 13 bridges across the canal. Originally, it was a branch of River Ill. It was named after a city wall known as Faux Rempart built and fortified along its middle part in the 13th century. Between 1831 and 1832, the Faux Rempart was pulled down under the order of the Mayor Frédéric de Turckheim with the purpose of creating a broad navigation channel and boosting the river transport of the city. The Faux-Rempart Canal became navigable in 1840. Now only tour boats are officially allowed to cruise round the Grand Isle and through the historic Little France district of the city.

福−朗帕运河

法国东部运河。亦称福−朗帕护城河。福−朗帕运河位于斯特拉斯堡市中心，全长2千米，河上仅建有1座船闸。运河环绕格朗岛，两端皆与伊尔河交汇，运河上建有13座桥梁。最初，该运河为伊尔河支流。13世纪时，人们沿运河中段修建并加固了名为福−朗帕的城墙，运河名由此而来。1831—1832年间，市长弗雷德里克·德·特克汉下令拆毁福−朗帕城墙，旨在修建一条宽阔的运河，促进城市水运发展。1840年，福−朗帕运河通航。如今，官方仅允许游船经由运河环游格朗岛，穿行于市内的小法兰西历史街区。

Faux-Rempart Ditch

A canal located in eastern France. See Faux-Rempart Canal.

福−朗帕护城河

法国东部运河。见福−朗帕运河。

Fearn Canal

A canal located in Alabama, the United States. Also known as Huntsville Canal. With its source in the Big Spring in Huntsville, the Fearn Canal stretched southward for 4 kilometres along the Big Spring Branch, and went further for 16.9 kilometres to Looney's Mill, and another 4.8 kilometres to Ten-

费恩运河

美国亚拉巴马州运河。亦称亨茨维尔运河。费恩运河源于亨茨维尔市大泉溪，沿着大泉溪支流向南延伸4千米，之后的16.9千米河道直通卢尼工坊，最后延伸4.8千米进入田纳西州。据相关记载，该运

nessee. It is recorded that the depth of the Fearn Canal would accommodate boats with a capacity of 80 to 100 bales of cotton and 50 passengers. This canal was built to cut the cost of transporting cotton to the market from Huntsville, a trading centre of great significance in northern Alabama. The project was led by Dr. Thomas Fearn and four other citizens, after the Indian Creek Navigation Company obtained the authorization in 1820. The construction of this first canal in Alabama began in 1821 but proceeded at a slow pace. To divert the water from the Big Spring Creek via the Indian Creek to the Tennessee River, the company built a large number of dams and locks. In 1822, the lower part of the canal was opened. Within five years, cotton was able to be transported by water from Sivley's Mill. Eventually, in 1831, the construction was completed and the first keelboats arrived at the Big Spring. A great celebration was held for their arrival. However, the booming period of the Fearn Canal was short due to the lack of water. There was no sufficient water, except in high-water seasons, to float the keelboats. Not long after that, the local transportation was greatly improved because of the construction of railways and the use of other modern technologies. The Fearn Canal was abandoned gradually. Despite being short-lived, the Fearn Canal was universally recognized as a success since its value as a canal was realized.

河的深度可容纳装载80—100捆棉花和50名乘客的船只通行。修建费恩运河的初衷是降低从亚拉巴马州北部贸易中心亨茨维尔市到棉花市场的运输成本。1820年，在印第安河航运公司取得授权之后，托马斯·费恩博士等5人开始筹备运河的修建工作。费恩运河是亚拉巴马州第一条运河，1821年开始修建，但进展缓慢。为了将大泉溪的水引入印第安河，再流向田纳西河，印第安河航运公司修建了多座大坝和船闸。1822年，费恩运河下游通航。不到5年，人们便可以通过水路将棉花从西弗里工坊运往市场。1831年，费恩运河最终修建完工，第一批平底货船顺利抵达大泉溪，人们还为此举行了盛大庆典。然而，由于缺水，费恩运河好景不长。运河的水位除了汛期，都不足以让平底货船通行。不久以后，当地修建了铁路，加上现代技术的发展，交通状况得到了极大改善，费恩运河也因此渐遭废弃。费恩运河历史虽短，但其作为运河的价值已经实现，该运河工程也被视为成功之举。

Finow Canal

菲诺运河

A canal located in Brandenburg, Germany. Linking

德国勃兰登堡市运河。菲诺运河

Berlin with the Baltic ports, the Finow Canal is 41.3 kilometres long and runs from the Oder River to the Havel River. Constructed in 1605, the canal ranks among the most ancient European waterways. It was finished in 1620, but was destroyed shortly after completion in the course of the Thirty Years War. After years of reconstruction, the Finow Canal was reopened in 1746 under the reign of Frederick II. In the 19th century, the canal, as one of the most important Prussian waterways, has contributed greatly to the industrial development of the Finow Valley. However, at the beginning of the 20th century, another waterway was needed due to the enormously increased freight traffic. In the summer of 1914, the new Oder-Havel Canal was opened and the Finow Canal lost its economic importance.

连接柏林与波罗的海港口，全长41.3千米，自奥得河流至哈弗尔河。运河于1605年开凿，是欧洲最古老的航道之一。1620年，运河竣工后不久，即在三十年战争中遭到破坏。经过多年重修，1746年，菲诺运河在腓特烈二世统治时期又重新开放。19世纪时，菲诺运河是普鲁士最重要的运河之一，对菲诺河谷地区的工业发展至关重要。20世纪初，由于货运量大幅增加，需要另修建一条运河。1914年夏，奥得—哈弗尔运河通航，菲诺运河不再具有重要的经济价值。

Forest Line of the Leicester Navigation

莱斯特郡森林航道

A waterway located in Leicestershire, central England, the United Kingdom. See Charnwood Forest Canal.

英国英格兰中部莱斯特郡航道。见查恩伍德森林运河。

Forth and Clyde Canal

福斯－克莱德运河

A canal located in central Scotland, the United Kingdom. The Forth and Clyde Canal is a 56-kilometre-long route between Forth and Clyde at the narrowest part of the Scottish Lowlands. Designed by John Smeaton, the canal was constructed in 1765 and was not completed until 1790 due to insufficient funding. Passage boats started to run on the canal from 1783 and later it took only 3.5 hours to

英国苏格兰中部运河。福斯—克莱德运河全长56千米，为苏格兰低地最窄处福斯湾与克莱德湾之间的一条航线。该运河由约翰·史密顿设计，1765年开凿，后因资金不足，直到1790年才竣工。但自1783年起，运河上就有客轮通行，后乘快船从爱丁堡到福尔柯克仅需3.5

sail from Edinburgh to Falkirk by fast boats. Steamboats appeared on the canal in 1828. The canal became nationalized in 1948, and was operated by the British Transport Commission. In 1962, it was taken over by the British Waterways Board, and finally by the Scottish Canals. Since the maintenance cost was higher than the revenues, the canal was closed in 1963, and remained semi-derelict. To fight for its preservation, restoration, and improvement, the Forth and Clyde Canal Society was established in 1980. With its efforts, the Forth and Clyde Canal was reopened as a part of the Millennium Link Project started in 1999.

小时。1828年，运河上开始有蒸汽船航行，1948年，运河成为国有资产，由英国运输委员会管理。1962年，福斯－克莱德运河管理权移交给英国水务局，后又转至苏格兰运河管理部门。由于维修费用高于航运收益，运河于1963年关闭，并一直处于半废弃状态。1980年，为保护、重修与完善运河，福斯－克莱德运河协会成立。在该协会的努力下，福斯－克莱德运河作为1999年启动的"千禧年连通计划"的组成部分重新对外开放。

Fox-Wisconsin Waterway

福克斯－威斯康星航道

A waterway located in the northernmost tip of the United States. The Fox-Wisconsin Waterway starts from its western end at the Mississippi River at Prairie du Chien and flows up the Wisconsin River to Portage with a partial length of around 187 kilometres. It links the Mississippi basin to the Great Lakes. In Portage, ships would enter into the Upper Fox River, and eventually, the Portage Canal. Then the Fox-Wisconsin Waterway runs about 272 kilometres down the Fox River through Lake Winnebago and continues on the Lower Fox River to its eastern end at the Green Bay. The construction of the locks of the Fox River began in 1839. Finally, 17 locks were constructed, with a height of 51.5 metres rising above the Green Bay. The Upper Fox River had 9 locks, rising from the west side of Lake Winnebago to the Portage Canal, each being

美国最北端航道。福克斯－威斯康星航道西段始于普雷里德欣处的密西西比河河段，沿威斯康星河上游流至波蒂奇县，此河段长约187千米。西段连通美国北部密西西比河流域和五大湖，通航船只在波蒂奇县驶入福克斯河上游，最终进入波蒂奇运河。之后福克斯－威斯康星航道沿福克斯河方向流动约272千米，穿过温纳贝戈湖，在格林湾与福克斯河下游东端交汇。1839年，福克斯河上开始修建船闸，共建有17座船闸，使其水位高出格林湾51.5米。福克斯河上游共建有9座船闸，从温纳贝戈湖以西向上延伸至波蒂奇运河，每座船闸高约61米，宽约10.7米。19

61 metres high and 10.7 metres wide. In the mid-19th century, plentiful locks, dams, and canals were constructed, including the 3.7-kilometre-long Portage Canal between the Fox and Wisconsin Rivers. Excavated in 1838, the Portage Canal was linked to Wisconsin with 2 locks. Before the Illinois and Michigan Canal was constructed in 1848 and the railroads were fully put into use, the Fox-Wisconsin Waterway was one of the major navigation routes between the Mississippi River and the Great Lakes. Later because of two unsolved technical problems, i.e. the control of sand bars of the Lower Wisconsin and the flow of the Upper Fox River, it no longer played a substantial role and slowly fell into disuse. The Portage Canal fell into disuse in 1951, so did most of the Upper Fox River locks and dams. The lock system on the Lower Fox River from Lake Winnebago to the Green Bay was disused in 1983 to contain the upstream spread of invasive species, such as the lamprey. The Fox-Wisconsin Waterway is no longer used as a route for water transportation between the Mississippi River and the Great Lakes. Currently, the various reaches of the waterway play an important recreational role.

世纪中期, 人们在福克斯河和威斯康星河之间修建了很多船闸、大坝和运河, 其中包括长3.7千米的波蒂奇运河。波蒂奇运河于1838年开凿, 建有2座船闸, 介于福克斯河与威斯康星河之间。在1848年修建伊利诺伊—密歇根运河以及铁路运输全面兴起之前, 福克斯—威斯康星航道是连通密西西比河与五大湖之间的主要航道之一。后来, 由于威斯康星河下游的沙坝控制和福克斯河上游的流量控制这两个技术问题难以解决, 福克斯—威斯康星航道不再发挥实质性作用, 逐渐被废弃。波蒂奇运河于1951年停用, 福克斯河上游的多数船闸和大坝也逐渐停用。1983年, 为防止七鳃鳗等物种入侵福克斯河上游, 温纳贝戈湖到格林湾下游的船闸系统关闭。福克斯—威斯康星航道已不再用作密西西比河和五大湖之间的水路通道。如今, 多数河段成为大众休闲娱乐的好去处。

Franeker Canal

弗拉讷克运河

A canal located in Friesland Province, the Netherlands. The Franeker Canal is approximately 20.6 kilometres in length and about 1.6 metres in depth. The canal originates from the Van Harinx Canal in the Franeker Town and flows into the Sneek Town. It runs along the towns of Rien, Tierns, Welsrijp and Winsum.

荷兰弗里斯兰省运河。弗拉讷克运河长约20.6千米, 深约1.6米。该运河源于弗拉讷克镇, 从范哈林克斯运河流至斯内克镇, 流经里恩镇、蒂恩尔斯镇、韦尔斯里普镇以及温瑟姆镇。

Franz Channel

A canal system located in northern Serbia. See Danube-Tisa-Danube Canal.

弗朗茨航道

塞尔维亚北部运河网。见多瑙—蒂萨—多瑙运河。

Frederik Islet Canal

A canal located in the central part of Copenhagen, Denmark. The Frederik Islet Canal runs along the southwest side of Castle Islet and, together with the Slotholmens Canal, separates it from Zealand. The canal was constructed in 1681. Its history dates from the expansion of Copenhagen's West Rampart after the Assault on Copenhagen in 1659. Castle Islet then was home to the royal palace and the fleet. To protect the island, the West Rampart was expanded into the sea. The area between the rampart and the island was filled to form a place called Frederiksholm. Many historic buildings stand by the canal, such as Prince's Mansion, which now houses the National Museum, Christiansborg's riding grounds, etc.

弗雷德里克岛运河

丹麦哥本哈根中部运河。弗雷德里克岛运河沿城堡岛西南方向流动，与城堡岛运河一起将城堡岛同西兰岛分隔开来。该运河于1681年开凿，其历史可追溯到1659年哥本哈根战役后的西城墙扩建工程。城堡岛当时是皇宫和舰队所在地，为保护该岛，西城墙得以向海中扩建，城堡防御墙和岛屿之间填土后形成弗雷德里克岛。弗雷德里克岛运河沿岸有许多历史建筑物，如亲王官邸（现为国家博物馆）、克里斯蒂安堡骑马场等。

Freshwater Bayou Canal

A canal located in Louisiana, the United States. The Freshwater Bayou Canal is 32 kilometres long. It provides major shipping access from Louisiana's Intracoastal Waterway to the Gulf of Mexico.

弗雷什沃特河口运河

美国路易斯安那州运河。弗雷什沃特河口运河全长32千米，为往来于路易斯安那州海湾沿海航道与墨西哥湾之间的船只提供通航服务。

Fugan Canal

A canal located in Toyama, Japan. The Fugan Canal

富岩运河

日本富山市运河。富岩运河长4.8

is 4.8 kilometres in length and 6 metres in width, connecting Toyama City and the Toyama Port. Crisscrossed with rivers in ancient times, Toyama City was therefore called the floating city, which was afflicted with floods. Between the late 1920s and the early 1930s, the Fugan Canal was excavated as a part of the city project to foster industrial development while lessening the risk of flooding. The canal was opened in 1935 and contributed to the industrialization of Toyama City. But it only functioned about 20 years before its use was superseded by road transport. Built in the middle of the canal, the Nakajima Lock is the only lock in Japan which can elevate a passing boat 2.5 metres high to adjust to different water levels in Japan. The lock was recognized as an important national cultural inheritage in 1998. Now the Fugan Canal boasts a number of tourist attractions, with the Fugan Unga Kansui Park being the most famous local scenic spot. One section of the canal is in the downtown area that seats Toyama City Office, Toyama Municipal Government and Japan Broadcasting Corporation (NHK).

千米，宽6米，连接富山市与富山港。古时富山境内河流纵横交错，富山市被称为"漂浮的城市"，饱受洪涝灾害侵扰。20世纪20年代末至30年代初，为促进工业发展，降低洪涝风险，富岩运河被纳入富山市政工程，随后开始动工修建。1935年运河竣工通航，为富山市的工业发展做出了贡献。然而，该运河仅运营了约20年，其后，其航运业务被卡车运输取代。富岩运河中部建有中岛船闸，是日本唯一一座可适应不同水位变化、将通行船只提升2.5米高的船闸。1998年，该船闸列为日本国家级重要文化遗产。如今，富岩运河沿岸景点众多，其中，运河环水公园闻名遐迩。地处市中心的运河段两岸坐落着富山市役所、富山市政府以及日本广播协会。

Furnes Canal

弗尔讷运河

A canal located in northern France. The Furnes Canal runs from Dunkirk to the town of Veurne on the Belgian border. The canal has a total length of 13.3 kilometres. It is actually the French section of the Newport-Dunkirk Canal. The canal was constructed around 1630.

法国北部运河。弗尔讷运河连接敦刻尔克与邻近比利时边境的城镇弗尔讷，全长13.3千米。该运河实际上是新港—敦刻尔克运河的法国河段，约开凿于1630年。

Gan-Yue Canal

A cross-border canal under construction, located in Jiangxi Province (shortened to Gan) and Guangdong Province (shortened to Yue), China. The Gan-Yue Canal was designed to start from the Poyang Lake in Jiangxi, connecting the Yangtze River System and the Pearl River System. It will go up the Ganjiang River, pass through the Taojiang River, cross the watershed at the junction of Jiangxi and Guangdong, enter the Zhenshui River and finally empty into the sea along the Beijiang River at Guangzhou. The canal was projected to cost ¥ 150 billion (about $23 billion). As planned, the 1, 228-kilometre-long canal will have 16 locks and allow ships of 1,000 tonnes to navigate. During the Yongle Reign (1403—1424) in the Ming Dynasty (1368—1644), Xie Jin, a great master, had already put forward the idea of digging a canal linking the Ganjiang River and the Beijiang River for irrigation. In 1923, Sun Yat-sen also remarked on this idea in his Fundamentals of National Reconstruction. In 1958, the plan of excavating the canal was officially proposed by the local governments, and many preliminary investigations and studies were conducted since then. In 2015, this project was carried out jointly by the two provinces of Jiangxi and Guangdong. At present, about 70% of the Nanchang-Ganzhou section and Sanshui-Shaoguan section have been constructed, and the whole project is expected to be completed before 2028. Once it is finished, a north-south artery will be formed in the southern region of the Yangtze River, and the

赣粤运河

中国江西和广东两省跨境在建运河。赣粤运河计划连通长江和珠江两大水系。运河北起江西鄱阳湖，溯赣江而上，经桃江，跨江西、广东两省交界的分水岭，入浈水，后沿北江至广州出海。根据规划，赣粤运河全长约1 228千米，投资预算约1 500亿元人民币（约合230亿美元），全线设16座船闸，通航标准为1 000吨级船舶。早在明永乐年间，大学士解缙便提出开凿赣粤运河的设想，引赣江水与北江水用于农田灌溉。1923年，孙中山在《建国方略》中也曾提及修建赣粤运河的设想。1958年，多地政府正式提出开凿赣粤运河。后又经多次考察和研究，直至2015年条件成熟后，江西、广东两省携手正式启动该运河工程。目前，南昌至赣州段、三水至韶关段已完成70%左右的工程量，全线预计2028年前完工。赣粤运河工程完工后，将形成长江以南地区南北向水上交通大动脉，从长江到珠三角的船只不必再绕道东海，可缩短航程1 200多千米。我国内河航运最为发达的长江和珠江两大水系连通后，不仅能够加快长江经济带与珠江经济带的经贸往来，同时也可促进沿线城镇发展，对于开发沿线国

ships navigating from the Yangtze River to Pearl River Delta will no longer have to make a detour via the East China Sea and hence shorten the route by over 1, 200 kilometres. The connection between the two most developed river systems in China's inland navigation will not only speed up the economic exchange between the Yangtze River Economic Belt and the Pearl River Economic Belt, but also promote the development of the cities and towns along the route, which is of great significance in the utilization of the land and resources nearby.

土资源等具有重要意义。

Ganzen Canal

A canal located in Overijssel Province, the Netherlands. The Ganzen Canal, as a branch of the IJssel River, is 9 kilometres long, originating from the IJssel River near Kampen City and emptying into the Zwarte Lake. There is a ship lock named Ganzen Sluis near Kampen City. Since the mouth of the Ganzen Canal to the Zwarte Lake is not navigable, the shipping route from the IJssel River to the Zwarte Lake is via the Goot, a branch of the Ganzen Canal. The Ganzen Canal includes two parts. The first 6-kilometre-long part from the Goose Lock to the Gutter Lock is owned by Overijssel, and the second 3-kilometre-long part from the Goot to the Zwarte Lake is administered by Staatsbosbeheer, a Dutch government organization for forestry and the management of nature reserves. The fishing rights of the entire Ganzen Canal belonged to the municipality of Kampen. Since 2004, there has been a recreational bicycle ferry in the

汉森运河

荷兰上艾瑟尔省运河。汉森运河为艾瑟尔河支流，全长9千米，源于坎彭市附近的艾瑟尔河，最终注入兹瓦特湖。坎彭市附近河段上建有汉森船闸。因汉森运河通往兹瓦特湖的入口无法通航，艾瑟尔河和兹瓦特湖之间的航运路线需借道汉森运河的支流霍特河。汉森运河分为两段：第一段是从胡斯闸到胡特闸，长6千米，由上艾瑟尔省管辖；第二段从霍特湖到兹瓦特湖，长3千米，由荷兰林业与自然保护区管理组织斯塔茨博斯彼赫管辖。汉森运河全域捕鱼权归属坎彭市。2004年以来，汉森运河的第二段上有一处提供休闲运动自行车租赁的码头，渡船可往返于坎彭岛至曼杰斯瓦德之间。

second part of the canal, linking Kampereil and Mandjeswaard.

Garonne Canal

A canal located in France. Formerly known as Garonne Lateral Canal. Linking Toulouse with Castets-en-Dorthe, the Garonne Canal is 193.6 kilometres long with 53 locks. In the late 17th century, the canal was first proposed by Vauban as a continuation of the Midi Canal built by Pierre-Paul Riquet to bypass River Garonne. The construction of this canal began in 1838 and was completed in 1856. There were many bridges across the canal, most of which had been rebuilt in 1933 to facilitate the navigation of larger vessels. After larger ships could transit the canal, tourism industry has considerably developed there. Now the Garonne Canal is almost used for tourism only.

加龙运河

法国运河。旧称加龙河旁侧运河。加龙运河连接图卢兹和多尔特地区的卡斯泰昂，全长193.6千米，建有53座船闸。17世纪末，沃邦最先提议新开凿一条运河，目的是延伸皮埃尔—保罗·里凯设计的米迪运河，同时为加龙河开通旁侧航道。运河1838年开凿，1856年竣工。运河上建有多座桥梁。为方便大型船只通行，大多数桥梁于1933年进行了重建。加龙运河可通行更大吨位的船只后，极大地推动了当地旅游业的发展。如今，加龙运河仅用于旅游观光。

Geeuw Canal

An inland canal located in Friesland Province, the Netherlands. The Geeuw Canal flows between the cities of IJlst and Sneek, with a length of 4.3 kilometres. As a part of the Sneek Lake-Heeger Lake connection, the Geeuw Canal is very busy in summer. There are 5 bridges built over the canal in total, among which the Geeuw Bridge, with a height of 3 metres and a width of 9 metres, is the largest. The bridge is located just outside the downtown of Sneek. It is at that point that the City Bypass South and the canal intersected. As a replacement for this

黑伍运河

荷兰弗里斯兰省内陆运河。黑伍运河连接艾尔斯特市和斯内克市，全长4.3千米。黑伍运河为连通斯内克湖和海赫湖水路的一部分，夏季十分繁忙。运河上建有5座桥梁，其中规模最大的是黑伍桥，高3米，宽9米，紧邻斯内克市中心，连接黑伍运河和南环大道。2008年，黑伍渡槽竣工，取代了黑伍桥，并连接A7高速公路和黑伍运河。运河沿岸的著名建筑包括艾尔

bridge, the Geeuw Aqueduct was completed in 2008. The A7 highway and the Geeuw Canal now intersect here. Notable buildings along the river include the Rat Sawmill in IJlst and the Waterpoort in Sneek. The Geeuw Canal is also a part of the Elfstedentocht, a long-distance tour skating event on natural ice.

斯特市的兰特锯木厂和斯内克市的水门等。黑伍运河也是十一城冰上马拉松赛道的一部分。

Gelderse Ijssel Canal

海尔德瑟-艾瑟尔运河

A canal located in Overijssel Province, the Netherlands. The Gelderse Ijssel Canal, with a total length of 127 kilometres, runs from Westervoort to Lake IJssel through Zutphen, Deventer and Kampen. Formed by the northward diversion of the river, it is the third major tributary of the Rhine, accounting for approximately 15% of the water. The canal flows northeastwards to the Ketel Lake and then northwards to the Ijssel Lake. Its course follows the valley between the Veluwe and the Salland Ridge, forming the border between Gelderland and Overijssel. The Old Ijssel is the main tributary, which flows into the Gelderse Ijssel Canal at Doesburg. Other tributaries include Berkel and Schipbeek. The Gelderse Ijssel Canal originated between 1,500 and 2,000 years ago after a sudden natural change of the river loop. At the beginning of Roman times, the canal was not yet connected to the Rhine. In the early Middle Ages, the Gelderse Ijssel Canal was known as the Rhine Branch after the upper part of the Ijssel was reactivated. At that time, Zutphen and Deventer, among other cities, got benefits from the Gelderse Ijssel Canal. Since the 15th century,

荷兰上艾瑟尔省运河。海尔德瑟—艾瑟尔运河全长127千米, 自韦斯特福特流至艾瑟尔湖, 途经聚特芬、代芬特尔与坎彭。运河由莱茵河北向支流形成, 是莱茵河第三大分支, 约占莱茵河水量的15%, 沿东北方向注入凯特尔湖, 后向北汇入艾瑟尔河。运河沿费吕沃地区和萨兰岭之间的山谷流动, 成为海尔德兰省和上艾瑟尔省的边界。旧艾瑟尔河作为其主要支流, 在杜斯堡汇入该运河。运河其他支流包括贝克尔河和斯希普河等。海尔德瑟—艾瑟尔运河1 500—2 000年前因河道的自然变化而形成。罗马时代初期, 艾瑟尔河尚未与莱茵河相连。中世纪早期, 艾瑟尔河的上游部分重新使用, 时称莱茵河分支。聚特芬、代芬特尔等城市因此得以繁荣发展。自15世纪以来, 运河泥沙淤积, 通航能力降低。主要原因是圣伊丽莎白大洪水为瓦尔河形成了一条通海捷径,

the canal became less navigable because of silt. One major reason was that Saint Elisabeth Flood gave the Waal a shortcut to the sea, reducing the water through the Gelderse Ijssel Canal. In the 18th century, the Pannerden Canal was excavated to improve the navigability of the Gelderse Ijssel Canal, and to provide the largest possible freshwater supply in the Ijssel Lake, especially in dry times. Other projects have been carried out in order to improve the capacity and navigability of the Gelderse Ijssel Canal, such as the "Space for the River" project. Along the canal are several historical places, such as Doesburg, Bronkhorst and Hattem.

减少了海尔德瑟—艾瑟尔运河的水量。18世纪，人们开凿了潘讷登运河，以改善海尔德瑟—艾瑟尔运河的通航条件并为处于干旱期的艾瑟尔湖保障最大淡水供应量。为提升海尔德瑟—艾瑟尔运河的通航能力，"运河空间"等项目相应展开。运河沿岸杜斯堡市、布龙克霍斯特和哈特姆镇等有多处名胜古迹。

Genesee Valley Canal

杰纳西谷运河

A closed canal located in central New York State, the United States. The Genesee Valley Canal is approximately 200 kilometres in length with 106 locks and was opened from 1840 to 1878. It starts from the Erie Canal in Rochester, New York, flows south-west along the Genesee River valley to Mount Morris, Portageville, and Belfast, then runs across the country to the Allegheny River at Olean, New York. The canal has a branch, which is in parallel with the Canaseraga Creek, starting from Mount Morris and flowing to Dansville, a village in New York State. The construction of the Genesee Valley Canal was approved by the New York Legislature in 1836 with the aim of meeting the needs of settlers along the Genesee River to transport their crops north to Rochester. However, from 1842, the canal experienced a 4-year suspension because of

美国纽约州中部废弃运河。杰纳西谷运河全长约200千米，其上建有106座船闸，1840—1878年间通航。运河始于纽约州罗切斯特市的伊利运河，沿杰纳西河谷朝西南方向流向莫里斯山、波蒂奇维尔和贝尔法斯特，穿过乡村地区，在纽约奥利安汇入阿勒格尼河。该运河有一条支流，流向与卡纳塞罗加河平行，从莫里斯山流向纽约州的丹斯维尔村。1836年，纽约州议会批准开凿杰纳西谷运河，以满足沿线居民将农作物运往北边的罗切斯特市的需求。由于19世纪30年代后期纽约州财政出现困难，从1842年开始，杰纳西谷运河的开凿工作中断4年。1840年，连接罗切

the state's financial trouble in the late 1830s. The section connecting Rochester and Mount Morris was first put into use in 1840. In the autumn of 1841, the extension to Dansville was opened. Not until 1862, when the connection down to the Allegheny River at Olean was completed, the entire canal was opened. Moreover, in order to ensure sufficient water supply, several creeks were dammed to feed the canal, creating some reservoirs such as the Rockville Lake and the Oil Creek Reservoir, today known as the Cuba Lake. In 1877, the legislature confirmed that the Genesee Valley Canal would be officially closed after 1878. In 1880, the canal was sold to the Genesee Valley Canal Railroad. The construction of the railway began in 1882 and the part between Rochester and Hinsdale was in operation in the same year. However, the branch of the canal to Dansville was not used for the construction of the railroad. In the 1960s, the Genesee Valley Canal Railroad was out of service. In 1991, the Genesee Valley Greenway Project was implemented to transform the abandoned canal and railroad routes into a rail trail, which was the origin of the Genesee Valley Greenway State Park. As an important link between the Allegheny River and the Erie Canal, the Genesee Valley Canal played a significant role during the mid- and late 19th century in the economic development of the United States.

斯特市与莫里斯山的运河段首次通航。1841年秋，延伸至丹斯维尔的扩建部分开始通航。直到1862年，当该运河与奥利安的阿勒格尼河连通河段竣工后，运河才全线贯通。后为确保运河有足够水源，人们在运河沿线几条溪流上筑坝蓄水，由此形成一些水库，如罗克维尔湖和石油溪水库，后者现被称为古巴湖。1877年，纽约州议会批准杰纳西谷运河1878年之后正式关闭。1880年，杰纳西谷运河被出售给杰纳西谷运河铁路公司。该公司于1882年开始修建杰纳西谷铁路，同年，罗切斯特市和欣斯代尔村之间的铁路开始运营。但杰纳西谷运河通往丹尼斯维尔的支流河段并没有用于修建铁路。20世纪60年代，杰纳西谷运河铁路停运。1991年，纽约州政府开始实施杰纳西谷绿道项目，将废弃的运河和铁路线路改造成铁轨步道，这就是杰纳西谷绿道国家公园的起源。作为连接阿勒格尼河和伊利运河的重要通道，杰纳西谷运河对19世纪中后期美国经济发展的意义重大。

Geuzen Canal

荷森运河

A canal located in Utrecht Province, the Netherlands. The Geuzen Canal has a length of 880 metres

荷兰乌特勒支省运河。荷森运河全长880米，处于阿姆斯特丹正常

at the Normal Amsterdam Water Level. It receives the excess water of the lakes of Vinkeveen by a pumping station. It is navigable and now mainly used for drainage.

水位范围。通过泵站，该运河可存储来自芬克维恩湖泊网的多余水量。荷森运河可以通航，现主要用于排水。

Ghent-Bruges Canal

A canal located in northwestern Belgium. The Ghent-Bruges Canal is 42 kilometres in length, linking Ghent and Bruges. The surroundings around the canal are rich in vegetation and densely populated. Through the Bruges Ring Canal, the canal is connected to the Ghent-Ostend Canal and the two canals are collectively called the Ghent-Bruges-Ostend Canal. The Ghent-Bruges Canal runs along 4 historic rivers, namely the Reie, the Zuidleie, the Hoge Kale and the Kale. In the 13th century, to increase the supply of drinking water, the parts of the Reie and the Zuidleie were widened and deepened and later the section was excavated from the Zuidleie to the Hoge Kale. Despite the connection between the two cities, the canal was then only used for water supply and it was not until the 16th century when the canal was used for navigation. After the railroads developed in the 19th century, the canal gradually lost its economic importance.

根特－布鲁日运河

比利时西北部运河。根特－布鲁日运河全长42千米，连接根特和布鲁日两个城市。运河沿岸植被丰富，人口稠密。运河通过布鲁日环形运河与布鲁日－奥斯坦德运河连通，两条运河合称为根特－布鲁日－奥斯坦德运河。根特－布鲁日运河主要流经4条古老的河流，即莱伊河、南莱厄河、霍赫卡莱河以及卡莱河。13世纪，为增加饮用水供给量，莱伊河和南莱厄河河段被拓宽加深，之后人们又开凿了从南莱厄河到霍赫卡莱之间的河段。虽然两市之间已有水路连接，但当时该运河仅用于水源供给，直到16世纪才用于航运。19世纪铁路兴起后，根特－布鲁日运河逐渐丧失了经济价值。

Ghent-Bruges-Ostend Canal

A canal located in Flanders, Belgium. The Ghent-Bruges-Ostend Canal is a collective name of the Ghent-Bruges Canal and the Bruges-Ostend Canal. The canal connects three cities, namely

根特－布鲁日－奥斯坦德运河

比利时佛兰德省运河。根特－布鲁日－奥斯坦德运河是根特－布鲁日运河与布鲁日－奥斯坦德运河两条运河的合称。该运河连接根

Ghent, Bruges and Ostend.

特、布鲁日和奥斯坦德3座城市。

Ghent Canal

根特运河

A canal located in Flanders, Belgium. The Ghent Canal is at 4 metres above sea level. It is a waterway used for peat transport between Ghent and Hulst. There was a bridge across the canal in Kapellebrug. The current Stekene Canal is the only remnant of the Ghent Canal. The part from Kemzeke to Hulst was filled in.

比利时佛兰德省运河。根特运河海拔4米，连接根特市和许尔斯特市，主要用于泥炭运输。位于卡佩勒布鲁格的河段上曾建有1座桥梁。如今的斯泰克讷运河是根特运河仅存的部分河段。从克姆泽克到许尔斯特市的部分河道已被回填。

Ghent-Ostend Canal

根特－奥斯坦德运河

A canal located in the provinces of East and West Flanders, Belgium. The Ghent-Ostend Canal is about 60 kilometres in length and has 3 locks. It runs northwest from Ghent to Ostend and empties into the North Sea. As a part of the Waterways of Mainland Europe, the canal is an important commercial waterway to the seaports of Zeebrugge and Ostend.

比利时东、西佛兰德省跨境运河。根特—奥斯坦德运河全长约60千米，其上建有3座船闸。运河南起根特市，向西北流经奥斯坦德市，最后注入北海。根特—奥斯坦德运河属于欧洲大陆航道，是通往泽布吕赫和奥斯坦德港口的重要商业航道。

Ghent-Terneuzen Canal

根特－特尔纽曾运河

A cross-border canal located in the Netherlands and Belgium. Also called Sea Canal. The Ghent-Terneuzen Canal, flowing from Ghent in Belgium to the port of Terneuzen in the Netherlands, the canal is 32 kilometres in length, of which 16 kilometres lies in the Netherlands while 16 kilometres in Belgium. The average width of 140 metres and

欧洲荷兰和比利时跨国运河。亦称滨海运河。根特—特尔纽曾运河自比利时的根特市流向荷兰的特尔纽曾港，全长32千米，其中荷兰境内16千米，比利时境内16千米，平均河宽140米，水深13.5米，可通行最大吃水深度12.5米、载重量

a depth of 13.5 metres make it accessible to ships weighing up to 125,000 tons with a draught of 12.5 metres. Originally there were 5 locks available, but now only 3 remained. The construction of the canal was started in 1823 when the Dutch King William I ordered to extend the original canal, the Sasse Canal, which was opened in 1549. The project was completed in 1827, when the Netherlands and Belgium were a united country. However, vessels were prohibited to travel to and from Belgium due to the separation of Belgium from the United Kingdom of the Netherlands in 1830. This ban was not lifted until 1841. Between 1830 and 1841 there was no shipping from Terneuzen to Ghent. From 1870 to 1885, the canal was deepened to 6.5 metres at its centre, and broadened to 17 metres at its base and 68 metres at its surface. The major enlargement took place during the 20th century, especially in the early 1960s. In 1963, two new locks were built in Terneuzen, responsible respectively for inland waterway vessels and seagoing ones. Nowadays this canal is capable of accommodating ships with a 265-metre length, a 34-metre width and a draught up to 12.5 metres. The well-known Cluysen-Ter Donck Regatta was held here for many decades (1888—1954). The European Rowing Championships also took place on the canal during the 1913 Expo of Ghent. In 2015, Flanders in Belgium and the Netherlands signed a treaty for building a new lock in Terneuzen. 427 metres in length, 55 metres in width and 16.4 metres in depth, the new lock will become one of the largest locks in the world. With a greater capacity, the lock complex will benefit the

12.5万吨的货轮。运河上曾建有5座船闸，现仅存3座。1823年，荷兰国王威廉一世下令开凿运河。该运河是1549年开通的萨瑟运河的延伸河段。1827年运河工程竣工，在此期间荷兰与比利时同属尼德兰联合王国。1830年，比利时独立，往来比利时的船只被荷兰禁航，禁令直至1841年才解除。1830—1841年间，该运河在根特至特尔纽曾河段内无船只往来。1870—1885年间，根特—特尔纽曾运河加深至6.5米，底部拓宽至17米，河道表面拓宽至68米。20世纪，该运河再次扩建，尤以20世纪60年代初期的扩建规模最大。1963年，人们在特尔纽曾港新建了2座船闸，分别用于内河船舶和海洋船舶通行。如今该运河可通航船只的最大尺寸长达265米、宽34米、吃水深度12.5米。1888—1954年间，著名的科索恩—泰尔顿克赛艇大会一直在此地举办。1913年根特世博会期间，欧洲赛艇锦标赛也在该运河上举行。2015年，比利时佛兰德大区与荷兰政府签署条约，计划在特尔纽曾新建1座船闸，其闸室长为427米，宽55米，门槛水深16.4米，将成为世界上最大的船闸之一。随着运力增加，运河之上的水闸群将大大缩短船只等待放行时间，改善通行状况，从而促进荷兰、比利时和法国之间的货运，长远来看，这

freight transportation between the Netherlands, Belgium and France by shortening waiting time and improving the through-flow. As a result, it will give an economic boost to the regions of Ghent and Terneuzen and even Europe as a whole in the long run. The construction is in full swing and the lock is expected to open in late 2022.

也将促进根特和特尔纽曾地区乃至整个欧洲的经济发展。目前, 运河工程建设正全面展开, 预计将于2022年底竣工通航。

Gieselau Canal

吉塞劳运河

An inland canal located in Schleswig-Holstein, Germany. The Gieselau Canal, linking the Kiel Canal with the Eider River, is 2.9 kilometres in length and has one single lock. It was constructed from 1936 to 1937 to create a more favourable connection between the ports of the Lower Elbe and the Lower Eider. The difference in water levels between the Kiel Canal and the Eider River is overcome by a 65-metre-long and 9-metre-wide lock, which is located approximately in the middle of the Gieselau Canal. The canal is navigable for vessels up to 65 metres long, 9 metres wide and 2.7 metres in draught. Today it is primarily used by sport boats.

德国石勒苏益格－荷尔斯泰因州内陆运河。吉塞劳运河连通基尔运河和艾德河, 全长2.9千米, 其上建有1座船闸。为使易北河下游港口与艾德河下游港口间的航行更加便利, 德国于1936—1937年间开凿了该运河。在运河的中段修建有1座长65米、宽9米的船闸, 解决了基尔运河和艾德河之间的水位落差问题。该运河可通行长65米、宽9米、吃水深度2.7米的船只。如今, 吉塞劳运河上通行的船只主要用于水上运动。

Giudecca Canal

朱代卡运河

An inland canal located in Venice, Italy. The Giudecca Canal is about 4 kilometres in length, 244 to 450 metres in width, and up to 12 metres in depth, running into the San Marco Basin. As one of the major canals in the city, the Giudecca Canal divides Dorsoduro into two parts, separating the Giudecca Island from the Dorsoduro District. The canal al-

意大利威尼斯内陆运河。朱代卡运河全长约4千米, 宽244至450米不等, 深达12米, 流向威尼斯的圣马可内湾。朱代卡运河是威尼斯主要运河之一, 将多尔索杜罗区一分为二, 分隔了朱代卡岛与多尔索杜罗区。大型船只经由朱代卡运河

lows larger vessels to pass through Venice, which is inscribed on the list of the UNESCO World Heritage Cities.

可穿行世界遗产城市威尼斯。

Givors Canal

An inland canal located in Givors, France. With a total length of 20 kilometres, the Givors Canal has 42 locks, linking La Grand-Croix with Givors. Its construction began in 1761 and was completed in 1780 and put into use in December of the following year. Originally 15 kilometres in length and 1.8 metres in depth, the canal was mainly constructed for coal transportation. In 1839, it was extended to 20 kilometres long. The Givors Canal played a critical part in the development of Givors in the early industrialization, and yielded considerable profits. After the Saint Étienne-Lyon Railway, the first passenger railway in France, was built in 1833 along the same route, the canal fell into disuse. In the early 20th century, it was almost abandoned and parts were filled in. Today, all the remaining sections have almost been covered by the A47 autoroute, except for the section at Tartaras, which has been preserved as a heritage site.

日沃尔运河

法国日沃尔内陆运河。日沃尔运河全长20千米，建有42座船闸，连接大十字镇和日沃尔。运河1761年开凿，1780年竣工，次年12月正式通航，主要用于煤炭运输。运河最初长15千米，深1.8米，1839年延伸至20千米。日沃尔运河在日沃尔工业化初期产生了可观的经济效益，对日沃尔的发展意义重大。1833年，法国第一条客运专线圣埃蒂安—里昂铁路沿运河建成，日沃尔运河不再用于航运。20世纪初，该运河被废弃，部分河道被回填。如今，A47高速公路几乎覆盖了所有现存运河河段，只有塔尔塔拉的河段作为运河遗址被保留下来。

Glamorganshire Canal

An inland canal located in South Wales, the United Kingdom. The Glamorganshire Canal is about 40 kilometres long, with an elevation drop of about 165 metres, which requires 50 locks in total. It runs from Merthyr Tydfil to Cardiff. It was constructed

格拉摩根郡运河

英国南威尔士内陆运河。格拉摩根郡运河全长约40千米，落差约为165米，其上建有50座船闸，自梅瑟蒂德菲尔流向卡迪夫。运河于1790年开凿，1798年通航。如

in 1790, and opened in 1798. Today limited traces of the canal can still be found, though part of the canal is covered by the A470 trunk road (from Cardiff to Merthyr Tydfil) completed in the 1970s. Moreover, a footbridge over the canal near the Cardiff Castle is still in use, accessible to pedestrians near the Castle.

今, 运河有部分航道被建于20世纪70年代的A470主干路（从卡迪夫至梅瑟蒂德菲尔）所覆盖, 但仍可看到部分遗迹。靠近加迪夫城堡的运河人行桥仍在使用, 供城堡附近的行人通行。

Glan-y-wern Canal

A canal located in South Wales, the United Kingdom. The Glan-y-wern Canal was the predecessor of the Tennant Canal. It runs through the centre of Crymlyn Bog. Constructed in 1790, the canal used to be a transport route between a colliery and River Neath. Although there was no actual connection to rivers, it remained in use for about 20 years. In 1814, George Tennant leased the disused canal from the Earl of Jersey. He decided to upgrade it to provide a link between River Neath and the docks at Swansea. The construction was completed by the autumn of 1818. In 1839, the Glan-y-wern Canal was dredged and reopened. For a long time, the canal has received little management but most parts are still used as an open water channel.

格兰叶韦恩运河

英国南威尔士运河。格兰叶韦恩运河为坦南特运河的前身, 横穿克莱姆林沼泽中心。运河1790年开凿, 曾是一家煤矿与尼思河之间的运输通道。该运河不与其他河流相通, 通航时间约20年。1814年, 乔治·坦南特从泽西伯爵那里租下这条当时已经废弃的运河, 并进行升级改造, 意在连接尼思河与斯旺西的船埠。运河改造工程于1818年秋竣工。1839年, 格兰叶韦恩运河疏浚清理后, 重新通航。该运河虽长期疏于管理, 但其主要河段仍可通航。

Glens Falls Feeder Canal

A canal located in New York, the United States. The Glens Falls Feeder Canal is 11 kilometres long, flowing from Hudson Falls to Fort Edward and delivering water from above Glens Falls on the Hudson River to the highest point of the Champlain Canal. In 1824, a new dam was built on the

格伦斯福尔斯引水运河

美国纽约州运河。格伦斯福尔斯引水运河全长11千米, 自哈德孙福尔斯流向爱德华堡, 将哈德孙河的水经格伦斯福尔斯输送到尚普兰运河的最高处。1824年, 人们在哈德孙河上修建大坝, 与此同时格伦

Hudson River and the excavation of the Glens Falls Feeder Canal was started to connect the Hudson River with the Champlain Canal, ensuring sufficient water at its highest elevation. In 1832, the canal was further widened and deepened to accommodate large vessels. There were 14 locks on the canal, and 13 of them were within the final section, which was about 1.6 kilometres long connecting the Champlain Canal. The Lock No.14 was a guard lock at the head of the feeder canal, allowing boats to continue travelling into the Hudson River. Nowadays, the Glens Falls Feeder Canal is still in use as a water source to the Champlain Canal, a power source for mills and a recreation destination. With the maintenance continuing to the 1940s, the canal is in excellent condition. Some locks have been over-hauled for modern uses.

斯福尔斯引水运河开凿，连接哈德孙河和尚普兰运河，确保后者在海拔最高处水量充足。1832年，为满足大型船舶运输需求，人们对运河进行了拓宽加深。运河上错落分布着14座船闸，其中13座处于与尚普兰运河相通的最后1 600多米的河段内。第14号船闸是引水运河起始处的一座安全船闸，船只经此驶向哈德孙河。如今，格伦斯福尔斯引水运河仍为尚普兰运河提供水源，并为工坊提供电能，还具备休闲娱乐功能。格伦斯福尔斯引水运河维护工作持续到20世纪40年代，目前运转状况良好。为满足当代需求，人们还对运河上的部分船闸进行了大规模翻修。

Gliwice Canal

A canal located in Poland. Also called Upper Silesia Canal. The Gliwice Canal, which is 41.6 kilometres in length, 38 metres in width, and 3.5 metres in depth, has 6 locks. It links the Oder River with Gliwice in Silesian Province. It drains water from the Chodnica River, lakes and reservoirs, flows from the town of Kędzierzyn to Koźle on the Oder and empties into the port of Gliwice. The construction was started in 1935 and finished in 1939, replacing the obsolete Chodnicki Canal, which was closed in 1937. The limited speed for ships is 6 kilometres per hour, and the water level difference between its ends is 43.6 metres. It is open for 9 months every

格利维采运河

波兰运河。亦称上西里西亚运河。格利维采运河长41.6千米，宽38米，深3.5米，河上建有6座船闸。运河连接奥得河与西里西亚省格利维采市，是科迪尼卡河与其他湖泊和水库的排水运河。运河自肯杰任流向奥得河河畔的科兹莱，汇入格利维采港。格利维采运河1935年开凿，1939年竣工，用以取代1937年停航的科迪尼克运河。运河限速每小时6千米，两端水位落差为43.6米。格利维采运河每年通航9个月（3月15日—12月15日），是

year from March 15 to December 15, providing transportation between Opole Province and Silesian Province in Poland. The annual shipment of the canal reaches 700,000 tonnes. After World War II, the jurisdiction of the canal and its peripheral territories was transferred to Poland as was decided by the 1945 Potsdam Conference.

船只往返奥波莱省和西里西亚省之间的运输通道，货运量每年达70万吨。第二次世界大战后，1945年召开的波茨坦会议决定，格利维采运河及其周边区域交由波兰政府管辖。

Glory River

荣耀河

An inland canal located in Iraq. Also called Prosperity Canal. The Glory River was built in 1993 by the order of Saddam Hussein to drain and dam the marshes. Unfortunately, the Glory River converted much of the wetlands into desert. After the fall of Saddam, the locals broke down the main embankment and the water returned to the Central Marsh. However, the current salinization makes it difficult either for the reeds to grow or to water herds of buffalo. Currently many villages are depopulated because of the lack of quality water.

伊拉克内陆运河。亦称繁荣运河。荣耀河由萨达姆·侯赛因1993年下令开凿，用以排干和拦截流入沼泽地的水。但荣耀河开凿后却使很多湿地变为荒漠。萨达姆政权倒台后，当地人捣毁河坝，将水引回中部沼泽地区。然而，河水的盐化程度很高，不利于芦苇生长，水牛也无法饮用。当前，很多村落因缺乏优质水源而日渐萧条。

Gloucester and Sharpness Canal

格洛斯特-夏普内斯运河

A canal located in the west of England, the United Kingdom. Also called Gloucester and Berkeley Canal. Once the broadest and deepest canal in the world, the Gloucester and Sharpness Canal runs 26.5 kilometres. Today the canal can accommodate boats of 64 metres in length, 9.6 metres in width, 32 metres in height, and with a 3.5-metre draught at the maximum. Close to the tidal river Severn in the main part, it cuts off at a bend near Arlingham,

英国英格兰西部运河。亦称格洛斯特-伯克利运河。格洛斯特-夏普内斯运河曾是世界上最宽和最深的运河，全长26.5千米。如今，运河可通行长64米、宽9.6米、高32米、最大吃水深度为3.5米的船只。运河主河段靠近潮汐河流塞文河，在阿灵厄姆附近的一个拐弯处中断，这里曾经非常险要。格

which used to be very dangerous. At the cost of £440,000 for construction, the canal was opened in April 1827, and became nationalized in 1848. Meanwhile, the Sharpness Dock Police, which had governed the dock since 1874, was absorbed into the British Transport Police. By the middle of the 1980s, the canal was given over to pleasure cruisers except for some grain barges, and its commercial traffic gradually ceased later on.

洛斯特—夏普内斯运河于1827年4月通航，开凿费用高达44万英镑，1848年收归国有。自1874年以来，一直负责管理该运河码头的夏普内斯码头警署被并入英国运输署。20世纪80年代中期以来，该运河除通行部分运粮驳船外，主要用作游轮航线，商业运输功能日渐衰退。

Godlinze Canal

A canal located in Groningen, the Netherlands. As one of the branches of the Eastern Wijtwerd Canal, the Godlinze Canal has a length of 5.6 kilometres with an elevation of −3 metres. It originates in the village of Godlinze and flows southwest before connecting the Losdorp Canal and the Leege Canal. It continues to flow south to the northwest of the Eastern Wijtwerd Canal and joins the Leermens Canal, which further flows into the Eastern Wijtwerd Canal.

豪特林泽运河

荷兰格罗宁根省运河。豪特林泽运河为东维特维德运河分支，全长5.6千米，水位低于海平面3米。该运河始于豪特林泽村，后向西南延伸，与洛斯多普尔运河和列格运河连通后继续向南，流向东维特维德运河西北部，与利尔曼斯运河交汇，最终汇入东维特维德运河。

Gosen Canal

An inland canal located in the eastern suburb of Berlin, Germany. The Gosen Canal, linking the Dämeritz Lake and the Seddin Lake, is 4 kilometres in length, and has no lock since there is only a small water level difference between the lakes. It was named after the village Gosen at its southern end. The plan for the construction of a shipping channel between the two lakes dates back to 1872.

格森运河

德国柏林东郊内陆运河。格森运河全长4千米，连通达默里茨湖和塞丁湖。因两湖之间水位落差较小，运河上没有修建船闸。运河因其南端村庄格森而得名。1872年就有人计划在两湖之间修建货运航道。然而，直到20世纪20年代初才开始前期准备工作，后期

The preparation of the canal was started in the early 1920s. However, the work was discontinued due to hyperinflation, and the construction was not officially carried out until August 1933. The canal was opened at the end of January 1936 to provide an alternative route for the commercial shipping between Berlin and the Oder-Spree Canal during the 1936 Summer Olympics. Boats with a draught of up to 2 metres can pass through it. Now the canal is not only a link in a commercial navigation route, but also a popular destination for sightseeing.

又由于恶性通货膨胀而中断，直到1933年8月，格森运河才正式开凿，1936年1月底通航。1936年举办夏季奥林匹克运动会期间，格森运河为柏林和奥得—施普雷运河之间的商业航运提供了一条新航线。格森运河可容纳吃水2米的船只通行。现在，该运河不仅用于商业航运，也是观光胜地。

Göta Canal

约塔运河

An inland canal located in Götaland, southern Sweden. The Göta Canal is 190 kilometres in length, 7 to 14 metres in width, and about 3 metres in maximum depth. It has 58 locks, allowing vessels up to 32 metres in length, 7 metres in width, and 2.8 metres in draught to navigate. The canal is the backbone of the waterway which runs eastwards through many lakes and rivers, such as Lake Vänern, Lake Vättern, the Göta River, and the Trollhätte Canal. It links Gothenburg by the Kattegat Strait with Söderkoping on the Baltic Sea. The idea of constructing a canal across southern Sweden was proposed as early as the 16th century, but it was not put into action until three centuries later, when Baltzar von Platen, a German-born former officer in the Swedish Navy, managed to obtain the necessary financial and political backing, and organized the project. Constructed between 1810 and 1832, the canal marked the realization of the Swedish

瑞典南部约塔兰内陆运河。约塔运河全长190千米，河宽7—14米，最深处约3米。运河上共建有58座船闸，可容纳长32米、宽7米、吃水2.8米的船只通行。以约塔运河为主体的航道由西向东流经众多湖泊和河流，包括维那恩湖、韦特恩湖、约塔河及特罗尔海特运河，在卡特加特海峡附近连接滨海城市哥德堡和波罗的海沿岸城市南雪平。在瑞典南部开凿运河的设想早在16世纪就有人提出，不过直到3个世纪之后才付诸实施。德国裔瑞典海军军官波尔查·冯普拉顿争取到了必要的经济和政治支持，组织运河项目的实施。约塔运河1810年开凿，1832年竣工，实现了瑞典人通过运河连通波罗的海和大西洋的梦想。在历史上，约塔运河对

dream of connecting the Baltic Sea and the Atlantic Ocean with a canal. Historically, the Göta Canal had great significance in promoting the domestic trade of Sweden. Today, as "Sweden's blue ribbon", the canal is used partially for goods transportation and mainly for tourism and leisure, with 2 million tourists annually. The Göta Canal enjoys its fame as one of the world-renowned civil engineering works.

促进瑞典国内贸易发展发挥了巨大作用。如今, 这条运河部分河段依然用于货物运输, 但主要河段已成为旅游休闲景点, 每年接待游客大约200万人次, 被誉为"瑞典蓝丝带"。约塔运河在世界著名土木工程中也享有盛誉。

Gouwe≋

A canalized river located in South Holland, the Netherlands. The Gouwe is 14 kilometres in length with 1 lock, running through Boskoop and Waddinxveen to Gouda, where it branches with a tributary through the city of Gouda and another one into the Gouwe Canal on the city's west side. There are 3 vertical lift bridges over the canal, which span the towns of Alphen, Boskoop and Waddinxveen. For centuries, the Gouwe has been one of the primary shipping routes in the Netherlands, connecting the cities of Dordrecht, Harlem and Amsterdam. Today, the canal still plays an important role in shipping, and serves as the main drainage channel of the Rhineland region.

豪鄂河

荷兰南荷兰省运河化河流。豪鄂河全长14千米, 建有1座船闸。该河流经博斯科普和瓦丁克斯芬, 在豪达市分流, 一条流经豪达市, 另一条在豪达市西边汇入豪鄂运河。河上建有3座垂直升降桥, 横跨阿尔芬、博斯科普和瓦丁克斯芬。数个世纪以来, 豪鄂河一直是荷兰主要航运线路之一, 连接多德雷赫特、哈勒姆和阿姆斯特丹市。如今, 豪鄂河仍具有重要的航运功能, 同时也是莱茵兰地区的主要排水运河。

Gowanus Canal

A canal located in New York City, the United States. The Gowanus Canal stretches 2.9 kilometres, connected to the Upper New York Bay. Once a small creek, it was expanded to a commercial waterway under a decree by the New York Legislature

格瓦努斯运河

美国纽约市运河。格瓦努斯运河全长2.9千米, 连接上纽约湾。该运河原为纽约市一条小河, 1849年, 纽约州议会批准将其拓宽加深为商用运河。1860年和1867年,

in 1849. It was enlarged in 1860 and 1867 respectively. However, with the rapid development of the industrial sectors after the Civil War, the canal was filled with various kinds of waste, making it poorly navigable and one of the most polluted bodies of water in the United States. With the collaboration of the U.S. Environmental Protection Agency, the Gowanus Canal Conservancy and the United States Army Corps of Engineers, several restoration plans were carried out afterwards. The zoning and cleanup work came to be crucial in 2019 when the area underwent thorough changes. Now the waterway is only used for occasional shipping and daily navigation of small boats.

人们对运河进行了两次拓建。南北战争结束后，随着工业的快速发展，各种污染物排入格瓦努斯运河，使之成为美国污染最严重的水体之一，且通航能力变差。此后，在美国环境保护署、格瓦努斯运河保护协会以及美国陆军工程兵团等组织的通力合作下，人们采取一系列措施对运河进行治理。2019年，分区整治行动进入最后攻关阶段，该区域终得以彻底改观。现该运河偶尔用于航运，日常通行船只则多为小型船只。

Grand Alsace Canal

阿尔萨斯大运河

An inland canal located in eastern France. Also called Rhine Lateral Canal. The Grand Alsace Canal is 50 kilometres in length, stretching from Kembs to Vogelgrun. It is parallel to, and a few hundred metres from, the canalized Rhine on the French side. The construction of the canal began in 1932 and was completed in 1959. The canal provides hydroelectric power to one of the most heavily industrialized regions in France which it flows through. It also supplies enough water all around the year to a nuclear power plant at Fessenheim, making it unnecessary to build cooling towers. It permits more than 30,000 boats per year to travel between Basel and Strasbourg and renders the region accessible from the Rhine River, Basel in Switzerland, and the North Sea for barges of about 5,000 metric tonnes.

法国东部内陆运河。亦称莱茵旁侧运河。阿尔萨斯大运河全长50千米，始于康布，流向博赫尔格伦，与莱茵河在法国境内的运河化河段相距几百米且流向平行。该运河于1932年开凿，1959年竣工。运河流经法国工业化程度最高的区域之一，为该地区提供电力。阿尔萨斯大运河还全年为费斯内姆镇的核电站提供充足水源，电站不需另修冷却塔。得益于该运河，每年3万多船只通行于瑞士巴塞尔与法国斯特拉斯堡之间，排水量约5 000吨的驳船可从莱茵河、瑞士巴塞尔和北海进入该运河区域。

Grand Canal (China)

An inland canal located in China. Also known to the Chinese as Beijing-Hangzhou Grand Canal. The Grand Canal is the longest man-made waterway in the world, stretching over 1,797 kilometres in length from Hangzhou to Beijing, with a south-to-north journey across four provinces of Zhejiang, Jiangsu, Shandong and Hebei and two municipalities of Tianjin and Beijing. It connects China's five major river systems, i.e., the Haihe River, the Yellow River, the Huaihe River, the Yangtze River and the Qiantang River. As the longest ancient canal constructed with the largest sum of labour work in the world, the canal boasts a history of more than 2,500 years, making it one of the world's oldest canals. In the Spring and Autumn Period (770 BC—476 BC), a canal was excavated by the State of Wu to wage an attack on the State of Qi. In the Sui Dynasty (581—618 AD), a grand expansion project (historically the Suitang Canal) was initiated by the imperial court, connecting the previous waterway with Luoyang and Zhuojun (known as Beijing today). In the Yuan Dynasty (1206—1368), the part in Luoyang was abandoned so as to straighten the water route to Beijing, shortening the overall length by 700 kilometres and linking Hangzhou and Beijing with a direct south-to-north waterway for the first time, hence the name of the Beijing-Hangzhou Canal. There is also an extension part in the eastern Zhejiang, or called Hang-Yong Canal, 239 kilometres in length, which was constructed in the Spring and Autumn Period. The Grand Canal is the

大运河（中国）

中国内陆运河。亦称京杭大运河。大运河是世界上最长的人工航道，全长1 797多千米，南起杭州，北至北京，途经浙江、江苏、山东、河北四省及天津、北京两个直辖市，贯通海河、黄河、淮河、长江、钱塘江五大水系。大运河是世界上耗费人力最多、里程最长的古运河，从开凿至今历经2 500多年。春秋时期，吴国为讨伐齐国而开凿大运河。隋朝时，朝廷下令扩建，运河（史称隋唐运河）贯通至都城洛阳且连接涿郡（今北京）。元朝翻修时，大运河弃洛阳段而取直至北京，总里程缩短约700千米，首次实现了连接杭州和北京两地的南北直通水路（即京杭大运河）。大运河的扩展段为全长239千米的浙东运河（杭州至宁波），始凿于春秋，后不断拓建。中国大运河是工业革命前世界上最大规模的土木工程项目。大运河对中国南北地区的经济、文化交流与社会发展，特别是对沿线地区工农业发展发挥了巨大的推动作用。2014年，中国大运河成功入选世界遗产名录。列入保护的运河部分跨度达1 011千米，包括隋唐运河、京杭大运河和浙东运河，涵盖27处河段的58个遗产点。2019年2月，中共中央办公厅、国务院办公厅印发了《大运河

world's largest civil engineering project prior to the Industrial Revolution. It has brilliantly advanced the economic and cultural exchanges and development in the south and north of China, and of particular note is its significant role in the industrial and agricultural progress of the areas along the waterway. The Grand Canal was listed in UNESCO's World Heritage in 2014. The three parts of the canal, i.e., the Suitang Canal, the Beijing-Hangzhou Grand Canal and the Zhedong Canal, extending 1,011 kilometres in length, cover 58 heritage sites on 27 sections. In February 2019, the Guideline for Protecting, Inheriting and Making Use of the Grand Canal Culture was issued by the Chinese government. Four projects were proposed in the document, namely protecting the canal's cultural heritage, improving its water resources, building a green ecological corridor and promoting culture and tourism. It is a plan to promote the protection and inheritance of the heritage of the Grand Canal. A cultural belt will be built along the canal's existing main river course. In October 2019, the course between the Beiguan Lock and the Gantang Lock, with a length of 11.4 kilometres, was opened for pleasure boats.

Grand Canal (Ireland)

A canal located in central Ireland. The main line of the Grand Canal is 131 kilometres in length with 43 locks, connecting Dublin in the east of Ireland with River Shannon in the west. There are three additional sea-locks linking the Grand Canal Basin in

文化保护传承利用规划纲要》。纲要提出文化遗产保护展示、河道水系资源条件改善、绿色生态廊道建设与文化旅游融合提升四大工程，旨在全面促进大运河遗产保护与传承，打造大运河璀璨文化带。2019年10月，京杭大运河北关闸至甘棠闸段的11.4千米河段开放，供观光船通行。

大运河（爱尔兰）

爱尔兰中部运河。大运河主航道长131千米，其上建有43座船闸，连接爱尔兰东部的都柏林和西部的香农河。此外，在林森德的大运河内湾和受潮汐影响的利菲河之间

Ringsend with the tidal river Liffey. At present the Grand Canal begins at River Liffey in the Grand Canal Dock and flows to River Shannon with various branches, including a link to River Barrow at Athy. The idea of connecting Dublin to the Shannon was proposed as early as 1715, and the work began in 1755 and was substantially completed in 1803. Because of leakages and a dry summer, the official opening had to be delayed until the April of 1804. The famous Grand Canal Way is a 117-kilometre-long trail from the Lucan Bridge, near Adamstown, to the Shannon Harbour. Along the canal, there are various habitats for a variety of animals. It had played an important role in trade and economic development, however, it ceased navigation in 1960. Today it mainly serves as a recreational waterway. In January 2020, the Irish cabinet approved the Grand Canal Innovation District plan. The district will serve as an innovation hub which allows start-ups, multinational companies and academics to share the infrastructure and resources so that they can make joint efforts to advance technological development. The project is scheduled to finish in ten years and the first phase commenced in 2020.

建有3座通海船闸。现今的大运河源于大运河码头处的利菲河，汇入香农河，沿途有多条支流，其中有一条在阿塞与巴洛河相通。早在1715年即有人提议开凿一条连接都柏林和香农河的运河。运河于1755年开凿，1803年竣工。然而，由于出现渗漏现象，加之当年夏季干旱，大运河直到1804年4月才正式启用。著名的大运河漫步小径全长117千米，从亚当斯敦附近的卢坎大桥一直延伸到香农河港口。大运河沿线有各类动物栖息地。该运河曾促进了贸易和经济发展，但已于1960年停航。如今，该运河主要用于休闲娱乐。2020年1月，爱尔兰内阁批准打造大运河创新区。在创新区内，新兴企业、跨国公司和科研人员共享基础设施及其他资源，共同促进科技发展。该项目建设预期10年，第一阶段建设已于2020年启动。

Grand Canal (Italy)

A canal located in Lombardy, Italy. The Grand Canal is 49.9 kilometres in length, 22 to 50 metres in width, with an elevation difference of 34 metres. As the most important canal of the Navigli system, it joins the Ticino River near Tornavento (23 kilometres south of Sesto Calende), and leads to the Porta

米兰大运河（意大利）

意大利伦巴第大区运河。米兰大运河全长49.9千米，宽度22—50米，水位落差34米。该运河是纳维利运河网中最重要的航道，在托那梵托（塞斯托—卡伦代以南23千米）附近汇入提契诺河，流向米兰市提奇

Ticinese dock (also called Darsena) in Milan. The canal probably originated from a ditch excavated in 1157 between Abbiategrasso and Landriano as a military defence work. The construction began in 1177 near Tornavento but came to an immediate halt for the engineering problem. In 1258 the Grand Canal reached Milan, and the whole canal was finally navigable in 1272 when the canal at last reached the bridge of Sant' Eustorgio, today's Porta Ticinese. A single lock with vertically lifting gates was built in 1438 on the canal, which was used for transporting stone for the construction of the Milan Cathedral. In 1482, Leonardo da Vinci reconstructed the Grand Canal with another 6 locks. The canal was relegated to an irrigation channel since the 1960s. Recently the Institute for the Navigli has been campaigning for the resumption of navigation on the canal. The Grand Canal is one of the largest post-medieval engineering projects, which contributed significantly to the development of commerce, transport and agriculture. The latest renovation of the canal was completed in 2015.

内斯码头（亦称达尔森纳码头）。米兰大运河的前身可能是一条开凿于1157年的沟渠，由阿比亚泰格拉索通向兰德里亚诺，作为一项军事防御工事。1177年，人们开始在托那梵托附近开凿运河，但因遇到问题而被迫中止。1258年，大运河连通米兰。1272年，运河修至圣欧斯托焦桥（即现在的提奇内斯码头），实现全线通航。1438年，米兰大运河上修建了一座有垂直升降闸门的单厢船闸，用于运输修建米兰大教堂所需的石材。1482年，列奥纳多·达·芬奇在米兰大运河上修建了6座船闸。20世纪60年代后，该运河仅用于灌溉。近期，纳维利运河网研究院呼吁恢复该运河的通航功能。米兰大运河是中世纪以来最宏大的水利工程之一，为当时的商业、交通以及农业发展做出了巨大贡献。2015年，运河完成了新一轮修建工程。

Grand Canal (the United States)

格兰德运河（美国）

A canal located in Ohio, the United States. See Ohio and Erie Canal.

美国俄亥俄州运河。见俄亥俄—伊利运河。

Grand Canal (Venice)

大运河（威尼斯）

A canal located in Venice, Italy. The Grand Canal is 3.8 kilometres in length, with a width of 30 to 90 metres and an average depth of 5 metres, linking the

意大利威尼斯市运河。威尼斯大运河全长3.8千米，宽30—90米，平均水深5米，连接圣露西亚火车站

Venetian Lagoon near the Santa Lucia train station and the St. Mark's Basin. The Grand Canal flows across the centre of Venice. As one of the city's main waterway corridors, the canal is famous for the centuries-old buildings on the banks in Romanesque, Gothic, and Renaissance styles. In Venice, water buses and private taxis are the main vehicles for public transportation and many tourists like to ride gondola on the canal. The city's transport network is mainly built along the canal. There was only one bridge, the Rialto Bridge, before the 20th century. But now the canal has been renovated with 3 other bridges: the Barefoot Bridge, the Constitution Bridge and the Academy Bridge. People can still take a ride across the canal at the fixed points by gondola as usual in the past, but the service is not as common as it was a decade ago.

附近的威尼斯潟湖和圣马克湾。该运河流经威尼斯市中心,为威尼斯水上交通要道之一。威尼斯大运河因其两岸的建筑而闻名,这些建筑大多有几百年历史,风格各异,包括罗马式、哥特式和文艺复兴式等。在威尼斯,公共交通工具是水上巴士和私人出租车,但许多游客喜欢乘贡多拉船游览运河。全市大部分交通网络沿运河修建,20世纪以前,这条运河上只有一座雷雅托桥,现又增修了3座,分别是赤足桥、宪法桥和学院桥。如今,人们依然可以在固定地点乘坐贡多拉船到运河对岸,不过这项服务已不如10年前那样普遍。

Grand Contour Canal

等高大运河

A proposed canal located between England and Wales, the United Kingdom. The Grand Contour Canal is intended for better transport with the British canal system and sufficient water supply in England and Wales. Upon completion, it will accommodate 300-tonne barges with a width of 30 metres, a depth of 5.2 metres, and a headroom of 7.6 metres. Vertical lift locks are also planned to be set up at the 9 termini, each with a water tank of 76 metres×11 metres×4.3 metres, which will help the canal to connect the major industrial centres of London, Bristol, Southampton, Coventry, etc. The construction of the canal was first proposed in

英国拟建跨境运河,流经英格兰与威尔士。等高大运河旨在改善英国运河网络的交通运输条件,并为英格兰与威尔士提供充足水源。修建完成后,该运河可容纳宽30米、深5.2米、净空高度7.6米、排水量达300吨的驳船。等高大运河9个站点上拟设立水槽规格为76米×11米×4.3米的垂直升降闸,从而连接伦敦、布里斯托尔、南安普敦、考文垂等主要工业中心。伯纳尔先生于1943年和1953年两次提议修建等高大运河。2012年此提

1943, then in 1953 by Mr. Pownall, and received support from Boris Johnson, the Mayor of London, in 2012. However, so far the canal has not been constructed yet.

议得到时任伦敦市长鲍里斯·约翰逊的支持，不过运河工程至今尚未启动。

Grand Junction Canal

A canal located in England, the United Kingdom. The original Grand Junction Canal ran from Birmingham to London. About 220 kilometres long, the canal provides a better route from Birmingham through the Midlands to London with many branches. Constructed between 1793 and 1805, the main line bypasses the upper end of River Thames near Oxford. In 1927, the canal, along with other three Warwick canals, was purchased by the Regent's Canal Company. It has become a part of the new Grand Union Canal since 1929. Today it offers drinking water as well as leisure traffic service.

大连通运河

英国英格兰运河。大连通运河连接伯明翰与伦敦，全长约220千米。该运河支流众多，极大地改善了自伯明翰经英格兰中部地区至伦敦的运输状况。大连通运河主干河道1793年开凿，1805年竣工，绕开了牛津附近的泰晤士河源头。1927年，该运河与沃里克市的3条运河一同被摄政运河公司收购，自1929年起成为新大联盟运河的一段。如今，该运河不仅提供饮用水源，而且提供休闲观光游船服务。

Grand Korean Waterway

A proposed canal located in South Korea. Officially known as Pan-Korea Grand Waterway. The 540-kilometre-long Grand Korean Waterway is designed to connect Seoul and Pusan, the two largest cities in South Korea, and link the Han River, which flows through Seoul into the Yellow Sea, to the Nakdong River, which flows through Pusan into the Korea Strait. The canal would extend through complicated mountainous terrain. The Grand Korean Waterway project also includes a smaller canal planned to connect Seoul and neighbouring

韩国大运河

韩国拟建运河。官方亦称泛韩大运河。韩国大运河规划长度为540千米，建成后将连接韩国两个最大城市首尔和釜山。运河穿越地形复杂的山区，连通汉江（穿过首尔注入黄海）和洛东江（流经釜山入朝鲜海峡）。韩国大运河包括一条连接首尔及邻城仁川的小型运河。除提供首尔通向黄海的航道外，该运河也将促进两座城市间的经济合作，减轻交通拥堵，刺激旅

Incheon. Apart from providing Seoul with access to the Yellow Sea, the canal would facilitate economic partnerships between the two cities, lessen traffic congestion and stimulate tourism. The plan was rejected in 2008 for disagreement among citizens.

游业发展。2008年，该运河开凿计划因韩国国民反对而终止。

Grand Morin Canal

A canal located in northern France. The Grand Morin Canal connects the Grand Morin River in Saint-Germain-sur-Morin to the Meaux-Chalifert Canal in Esbly. The canal is 3.4 kilometres in length with one lock. It was constructed in 1837 and opened in 1846. The canal serves to feed the Meaux-Chalifert Canal. It has no longer been used for navigation since 1963 with the permanent closure of the lock previously serving the port of Saint-Germain-sur-Morin.

大莫兰运河

法国北部运河。大莫兰运河始于莫兰河畔圣日耳曼的大莫兰河，在埃斯布利与莫—查理菲尔运河连通，全长3.4千米，建有1座船闸。该运河是莫—查理维特运河的引水运河，1837年开凿，1846年通航。1963年，莫兰河畔圣日耳曼港口的船闸永久关闭，大莫兰运河随后停止通航。

Grand River Navigation

A system of canals located in Ontario, Canada. The Grand River Navigation boosted the industrial and commercial development in Brantford and turned it from a small village into a prosperous town. In 1832, inspired by the success of the Welland Canal, the Grand River Navigation Company was established to excavate a system of canals to expand the previous canal network, linking Brantford to Lake Erie and some important cities like Buffalo. The coming of railways in the 1850s together with mismanagement led the Grand River Navigation Company to bankruptcy. In the 1880s, the five dams and

格兰德河航道

加拿大安大略省运河网。格兰德河航道促进了布兰特福德的工商业发展，使该地从一个小村庄发展成为繁荣的城镇。受韦兰运河成功开凿的鼓舞，人们开凿了格兰德河航道。1832年，格兰德河航运公司成立，决定扩建先前的运河网络，将布兰特福德市同伊利湖以及布法罗市等重要城市相连通。19世纪50年代由于铁路的出现及公司经营不善，格兰德河航运公司宣告破产。19世纪80年代，运河上

locks built over the canal were abandoned. Some vestiges are still visible to date.

修建的5座大坝和船闸均已废弃。如今, 格兰德河航道的部分遗存依然可见。

Grand Surrey Canal

A canal located in the south of London, the United Kingdom. The Grand Surrey Canal, 4 kilometres long, was authorized for construction by an act of Parliament in 1801. Connected to the Old Kent Road in 1807, it was navigable to Camberwell in 1810, and later to Peckham in 1826. The canal was originally used to carry cargoes, especially timber, to the Surrey Commercial Docks. With the expansion of road transport after World War II, the canal started to decline in importance, a great section of which dried up in 1960, and the dock was closed in 1970. Although many parts of its route have now been turned into roadways and parks, traces of the canal can still be seen. Permitted by the Lewisham Council, "the Surrey Canal Triangle Development Framework", a multimillion-pound redeveloping scheme of the area, will be carried out in the future.

萨里大运河

英国伦敦南部运河。萨里大运河全长4千米, 1801年由英国国会法案授权开凿。1807年该运河与旧肯特路相连, 1810年通航至坎伯威尔, 1826年至佩卡姆。木材等货物通过萨里大运河运送到萨里商业码头。第二次世界大战后由于公路交通迅速发展, 萨里大运河的重要性降低。1960年, 该运河大部分航段已干涸, 码头也于1970年关闭。目前, 萨里大运河大部分航道已成为公路与公园, 但运河遗迹依稀可见。在路易舍姆市议会的批准下, 耗资数百万英镑的 "萨里运河三角区" 重建计划即将实施。

Grand Union Canal

A canal located in England, the United Kingdom. The Grand Union Canal, 452.7 kilometres long, is by far the longest merged canal in Britain, excluding the shared line with the Oxford Canal. As a part of the British canal system, its main line runs for 220 kilometres in total from London to Birmingham with 166 locks. With its branches, the canal reaches

大联盟运河

英国英格兰运河。除去与牛津运河共用的河道, 大联盟运河全长452.7千米, 为英国目前最长的合并运河。作为英国运河网中的一部分, 该运河主航道总长220千米, 从伦敦延伸至伯明翰, 有166座船闸。运河有数条支线, 流经莱斯特、斯

many cities, including Leicester, Slough, Aylesbury, Wendover, and Northampton. The canal was constructed in 1929, and extended in 1932. After being nationalized in 1948, it was transferred first to the British Transport Commission, and then to the British Waterways Board in 1962, now called the British Waterways. Despite the cessation of commercial navigation, the leisure traffic on the canal is now quite popular, including boating, fishing, walking and cycling.

劳、艾尔斯伯里、文多弗与北安普敦等城市。运河1929年开凿，1932年拓建。1948年，大联盟运河收归国有后，交由英国运输委员会管理，1962年转交给英国水务局（即今天的英国水务署）管理。目前，该运河已停止商业航运，但其沿线的休闲娱乐项目仍备受欢迎，包括游船、垂钓、步行和骑行等。

Great Bačka Canal

大巴奇卡运河

A canal located in northern Serbia. As a part of the larger Danube-Tisa-Danube Canal system, the Great Bačka Canal runs from Bezdan on the Danube River to Bečej on the Tisa River. It is 118 kilometres in length. The bed of the canal is 17 metres in width at the bottom and 25 metres at the top, and the average depth is 3 metres. The canal was excavated between 1794 and 1801. Since the second half of the 20th century, it has been suffering from serious pollution, which threatens the health of the residents along the canal. The Minister of Environment Protection of Serbia signed the Memorandum of Canal Cleaning in 2008 with a view to solving the problem.

塞尔维亚北部运河。大巴奇卡运河为多瑙－蒂萨－多瑙运河网的一部分，由多瑙河上的贝兹丹流至蒂萨河上的贝切伊。运河长118千米，河床底部宽17米，上部宽25米，平均深度3米。大巴奇卡运河开凿于1794—1801年间。自20世纪下半叶以来，运河一直存在严重的污染问题，对沿岸居民的身体健康造成了威胁。为了解决这一问题，塞尔维亚环境保护部部长于2008年签署了《运河清污治理备忘录》。

Great Lakes Waterway

五大湖水网

A system of canalized cross-border channels located in North America. Enabling navigation between the North American Great Lakes, the main parts

北美洲跨国运河化水网。五大湖水网为北美五大湖之间的航运系统，主体包括43千米的韦兰运河

of the Great Lakes Waterway include the 43-kilo-metre-long Welland Canal, bypassing Niagara Falls between Lake Ontario and Lake Erie, and the Soo Locks, bypassing the rapids of the St. Marys River between Lake Superior and Lake Huron. The waterway also includes channels between Lake Huron and Lake Erie. Along with the Saint Lawrence Seaway, it allows both ocean-going vessels and lake freighters to traverse from the saltwater outlet in the system to its far interior. The Great Lakes Waterway, often referred to simply as the "St. Lawrence Seaway", together with the St. Lawrence River, comprise a single navigable body of freshwater connecting the Atlantic Ocean to the continental interior. The Great Lakes Waterway is co-governed by Canada and the United States.

和苏船闸。韦兰运河绕开了安大略湖与伊利湖之间的尼亚加拉大瀑布,苏船闸则使船只避开苏必利尔湖与休伦湖之间圣玛丽河上的急流。该水网还包括休伦湖与伊利湖之间的一系列航道,与圣劳伦斯海道共同组成一条通航水路,使得海轮与湖上货船可在入海口和内陆之间往返。该运河网与圣劳伦斯河常被合称为"圣劳伦斯海道",构成了连接大西洋与北美内陆淡水区的唯一通航水路。五大湖水网由美国与加拿大共同管理。

Grecht Canal

赫列赫特运河

An inland canal located in Utrecht Province, the Netherlands. Connecting the Old Rhine and the Kromme Mijdrecht, the Grecht Canal is 8.5 kilometres in length. It was first excavated at the end of the 14th century in order to discharge the excess water out of the surrounding polders. The artificial watercourse ran straight through the polder of Kamerik-Mijzijde, which brought much inconvenience to the farmers in that their lands were separated by the canal. In the 15th century, it was also used as a navigation channel between the town of Woerden and Amsterdam. However, the overexploitation of the canal's shipping function has resulted in the erosion of the banks. In 1494, the

荷兰乌特勒支省内陆运河。赫列赫特运河连通旧莱茵河和克罗默迈德雷赫特河,全长8.5千米。运河开凿于14世纪末,用于周围圩田的排水。但运河河道横穿卡默里克—麦泽德圩田,将其分成两半,给农民带来诸多不便。15世纪,赫列赫特运河开始承担航运业务,连接武尔登镇和阿姆斯特丹市。因对该运河的航运功能开发过度,河岸遭侵蚀。1494年,为便于农作,农民自费在旧赫列赫特运河基础上开凿了新赫列赫特运河,同时在武尔登镇建造新船闸以改善

New Grecht Canal was constructed on the basis of the Old Grecht Canal at the farmers' own expense so as to eliminate the inconvenience caused by the former watercourse, and a new lock in Woerden was built to improve the navigation conditions. In 1987, a new and large pumping station for water drainage was put into use on the canal. Hence, the Grecht Canal is no longer used as a trade channel to the north, and only pleasure boats can be found on it.

航行条件。1987年，一座全新的大型排水泵站投入使用。之后，赫列赫特运河不再用作通往北方的贸易航道，只供游船航行。

Grenville Canal

A canal located in Quebec, Canada. The Grenville Canal is situated at the north side of the Ottawa River between Montréal and Ottawa. Its name originated from William Wyndham Grenville, the UK Prime Minister during 1806 and 1807. The original length of the Grenville Canal was 9.5 kilometres with 11 locks. The construction was undertaken by Captain Henry Vernet of the Royal Engineers. It began in 1819 and was completed in 1833. The canal, mainly for military purposes, was a part of the military canal system. It was used to bypass the rapids of the Ottawa River and transport the supplies for the armies. The canal was constructed in accordance with the military standards, which required the locks to be 41 metres long, 10 metres wide, and 1.5 metres deep, thus not navigable for commercial ships. From 1867, local businessmen demanded the government to improve the canal and it was enlarged from 1873 to 1882. The western section of the enlarged canal extended from the upstream entrance to Lock No. 9, and the eastern section from Lock No. 8 to the end

格伦维尔运河

加拿大魁北克省运河。格伦维尔运河位于蒙特利尔和渥太华之间的渥太华河段北侧，得名于1806—1807年间担任英国首相的威廉·温德姆·格伦维尔。该运河最初长度为9.5千米，其上建有11座船闸。修建工程始于1819年，1833年竣工，由英国皇家工兵团的亨利·韦尔内上尉负责。格伦维尔运河起初主要用于军事运输，是军事运河网络的一部分，旨在绕过渥太华河的急流建立水上通道，为军队运送补给。运河最初依照军事标准修建，规定船闸闸室长41米，宽10米，门槛水深1.5米，故商用船只无法通行。1867年起，当地商人要求政府修缮运河。1873—1882年间政府对运河进行了拓建，拓建后的西段从上游的入口延伸至9号船闸，东段从8号船闸延伸至下游终点。该运河是加拿大最古老的军用运河之

downstream. As one of the oldest military canals in Canada, the Grenville Canal was controlled by the federal government for over 150 years. In 1988, it was transferred to the provincial government and then to the municipality two years later. However, the Village of Grenville could not undertake the financial burden, leading to the negligence of maintenance. Currently, the canal has great tourism potential but is severely underfunded.

一，联邦政府管理长达150多年。1988年，运河管理权移交至魁北克省，两年后又移交至当地市政部门。然而，格伦维尔村因无法承担维护运河的经费，而疏于运河的修缮管理。如今，该运河虽有旅游发展潜力，但由于资金匮乏，尚未开发。

Grevelings Canal

赫弗宁斯运河

An inland canal located in Drenthe Province, the Netherlands. The Grevelings Canal is 6 kilometres long, linking the Kiel Canal and the Stads Canal, two canals in Groningen Province. The excavation of the canal was started in 1771 and completed in 1780. It was an instrumental navigation channel for peat transport from the Oostermoer. Later, it was used for the transportation of potato flour. Now, the Greveling Canal serves as a vital recreational waterway linking the waters of north Drenthe and those of east Groningen.

荷兰德伦特省内陆运河。赫弗宁斯运河连通格罗宁根省的基尔运河和斯塔茨运河，全长约6千米。运河1771年开凿，1780年竣工。赫弗宁斯运河曾是奥斯特莫尔泥煤运输的重要航道，后又用于马铃薯粉运输。如今，该运河连接着德伦特北部和格罗宁根东部水域，主要用于休闲娱乐。

Griebnitz Canal

格里布尼茨运河

A canal located in the western outskirts of Berlin, Germany. Also known as Prince Friedrich Leopold Canal. The Griebnitz Canal is 3.9 kilometres in length, linking Lake Griebnitz with Lake Großer Wann. It was built between 1901 and 1906. The canal was intended to serve recreational ships and improve the water quality of the lakes. There are 3

德国柏林西郊运河。亦称弗里德里希·莱奥波德王子运河。格里布尼茨运河全长3.9千米，连通格里布尼茨湖和大万湖。该运河修建于1901—1906年间，旨在服务于娱乐休闲船只，以及改善河流水质。运河上建有3座桥梁，无船闸。运河

bridges but no lock along the route. It is a class I federal waterway in the jurisdiction of the Berlin Waterways and Shipping Office. It is regarded by travelers as one of the most attractive canals near Berlin. The numerous rowing clubs settled in large parts of the bank are in private ownership hence inaccessible to the public.

为联邦一级航道，受柏林航道与运输局管辖。格里布尼茨运河被游客视为柏林最美运河之一。河畔有数家划船俱乐部，均为私人所有，不对公众开放。

Griff Canal

格里夫运河

A private canal located in the Arbury Estate, Warwickshire, England, the United Kingdom. See Arbury Lower Canal.

英国英格兰沃里克郡阿伯里庄园私有运河。见阿伯里下运河。

Griff Hollows Canal

格里夫霍洛斯运河

A canal located in the Arbury Estate, Warwickshire, England, the United Kingdom. As a part of the Arbury Canals, the Griff Hollows Canal is about 1.2 kilometres long, which was separated from other canals of the main system. The canal, designed for coal transportation from the Griff Hollows wharf to the Coventry Canal, was built in 1785 and opened on 29 July, 1787. The Griff Hollows Canal was used to carry coal until 1961, when the colliery at Griff was closed. In 1973, the construction of the A444 road severed the canal and made it unnavigable any longer. Today, the entrance of the Griff Hollows Canal can still be seen and the canal supplies water to the Coventry Canal.

英国英格兰沃里克郡的阿伯里庄园内运河。格里夫霍洛斯运河全长约1.2千米，为阿伯里运河网的一部分，但与该网络中的其他运河并不连通。该运河1785年开凿，1787年7月29日开通，可将煤炭从格里夫霍洛斯码头运往考文垂运河。1961年，格里夫煤矿关闭，运河停止了煤炭航运业务。1973年A444号公路修建后运河被截断，此后不再通航。如今，格里夫霍洛斯运河的入口依然可见，运河还在为考文垂运河提供水源。

Groeve Canal

An inland canal located in the province of Groningen, the Netherlands. Formerly known as Schildgroeve and Damster Canal. The Groeve Canal covers a length of 3.6 kilometres, flowing from the Schild Lake to the Appingendam Town. The construction of the canal dates back to the early 14th century to ensure the drainage from the Schild Lake to the Damster Canal. With the completion of the Ems Canal, the section of watercourse between Groeve and the Damster Canal lost its function of drainage and was used only for navigation.

赫鲁夫运河

荷兰格罗宁根省内陆运河。旧称斯希尔德赫鲁夫—达姆斯特运河。赫鲁夫运河全长3.6千米，连接斯希尔德湖与阿平厄丹镇。赫鲁夫运河于14世纪早期开凿，旨在确保斯希尔德湖的水可排入达姆斯特运河。埃姆斯运河建成后，赫鲁夫和达姆斯特运河之间的河段失去排水作用，仅用作航运通道。

Groguida Canal

A canal located in Côte d'Ivoire. The Groguida Canal has a length of 1 kilometre, connecting the two branches of the Grand-Lahou lagoon.

格罗吉达运河

科特迪瓦运河。格罗吉达运河全长1千米，连通大拉乌潟湖的两大支流。

Grootfontein-Omatako Canal

A canal located in northern Namibia. The Grootfontein-Omatako Canal is 263 kilometres in length, of which 203 kilometres is open and parabolic, and the other parts are 23 inverted siphons. The canal serves as a vital part of the Eastern National Water Carrier (ENWC), which is aimed to bring water from the Okavango River in the North to Windhoek. The construction of the canal was started in 1981 and finished in 1987. Its maximum width is 3.7 metres and maximum depth 1.65 metres. When the canal is full, its flow velocity is 0.8 metre per

格鲁特方丹–奥玛塔科运河

纳米比亚北部运河。格鲁特方丹—奥玛塔科运河全长263千米，其中包括一段长达203千米的抛物线型明渠和23处倒虹管渠。该运河为"国家东部调水项目"的重要组成部分，原计划把北部的奥卡万戈河河水输送到首都温得和克。格鲁特方丹·奥玛塔科运河1981年开凿，1987年竣工。运河最宽处可达3.7米，最深处达1.65米，在水满条件下，运河流速为每秒0.8米，最大

second and the maximum capacity is 3 cubic metres per second. The canal mainly conveys groundwater from Kombat and Grootfontein to the Waterberg Water Supply Area (WWSA). In order to alleviate water shortage in rural areas, water has been delivered from the Kombat Mine to the central areas via the canal during long-term droughts. It has an adverse effect on the environment. Owing to its steep parabolic sides, the canal has become a death trap for local wild animals. Given the fact that there are nearly 5,000 drowned wild animals each year, more people claimed that such a steep sided open canal is not an appropriate option for a country with diverse wildlife.

流量为每秒3立方米。运河的主要功能是把孔巴特和格鲁特方丹的地下水输送到瓦特贝格供水区。在久旱时节，孔巴特矿的水会通过该运河输送到中部地区，以缓解该地区农村水资源短缺问题。但另一方面，格鲁特方丹—奥玛塔科运河也对环境造成了一定的负面影响。由于河岸呈抛物线型，该运河成为当地野生动物的死亡陷阱。每年近5 000只野生动物在此溺亡，鉴于此，越来越多的人认为，在纳米比亚这样一个野生物种丰富的国家，不适合修建河岸陡峭的运河。

Grote Heekt

A drainage canal located in Groningen, the Netherlands. The Grote Heekt flows into the Damster Canal, linking the Bierum River and the New Heekt. Connecting Holwierde to Appingedam, it belongs to a watercourse system called the Heekt. The Groote Heekt might be constructed around the 9th or 10th century for the drainage of the water from the low lands near Appingedam to the north. The channel led to the sea near Hoogwatum. In the Middle Ages, the Grote Heekt was a crucial trade and shipping route with heavy traffic. In the 13th century, the estuary of the canal vanished. In the 19th and 20th centuries, large amounts of clay were extracted by the local brickworks in the streambed and banks of the Grote Heekt.

赫鲁特黑克特运河

荷兰格罗宁根省排水运河。赫鲁特黑克特运河连通比勒姆河与新黑克特运河，汇入达姆斯特运河。该运河连接霍尔维德市和阿平厄丹市，为黑克特航道系统的一部分。赫鲁特黑克特运河大约开凿于9世纪或10世纪，在霍赫沃德附近入海，阿平厄丹市附近低洼地区通过此运河向北排水。中世纪时，赫鲁特黑克特运河是一条重要的贸易运输路线，河上交通十分繁忙。13世纪时，该运河河口消失。19世纪和20世纪时，当地砖瓦厂从运河河床和河岸中挖取大量黏土作为生产原料。

Guijiang River

A canalized river located in Guangxi Zhuang Autonomous Region, China. Also called Lishui River in ancient times. It is named the Guijiang River because of the abundant osmanthus trees (gui in Chinese) at its source. The Guijiang River has a total length of 426 kilometres and a basin area of 19,288 square kilometres. The river is one of the major tributaries of the Xijiang River system, the main stream of the Pearl River Basin. Originating in the Mao'er Mountain, the highest peak in Guangxi, the river flows southwards to join the Lingqu Canal near Guilin City. It continues southwards to its confluence with the Gongcheng River at Pingle County, Guilin City. After flowing through Hezhou City, it merges into the Xunjiang River, a main tributary of the Xijiang River, at Wuzhou City. The main stream of the Guijiang River includes four sections, namely the source section, the Darong River section, the Lijiang River section and the Guijiang River section. The source and Darong River sections are the upstream which flows through mountainous regions with highlands and narrow valleys. The land on both sides of the river is fertile, which is an area of commercial grain production. The middle reach is the Lijiang River, below the confluence of the Darong River and the Lingqu Canal. The gentle current winds forward, along which are beautiful scenery featuring peaks and caves, typically representing the Guilin landscape. This section is a golden waterway for tourism. The main problem in this part is the deficiency of shipping capacity in the dry season,

桂江

中国广西壮族自治区运河化河流。古称漓水。桂江因其源头多桂树而得名。桂江全长426千米，流域面积达19 288平方千米，为珠江流域干流西江水系支流之一。桂江发源于广西第一高峰猫儿山，向南流至桂林市与灵渠汇合，之后继续向南流至桂林市平乐县与恭城河汇合，流经贺州市后，在梧州市汇入西江干流浔江。桂江干流分为河源段、大溶江段、漓江段和桂江段四段。河源段和大溶江段属河流上游，流经山地，山高谷狭。大溶江段两岸土地肥沃，是商品粮产区。大溶江段与灵渠交汇后形成的漓江段属河流中游，该河段水流平缓，河道蜿蜒，奇峰异洞，山清水秀，是桂林山水风光的典型代表，也是旅游黄金航道。漓江河段的主要问题是枯水期航运能力不足，故以青狮潭水库作为补充水源，加以桂江整治和航道疏浚，确保漓江枯水期通航顺畅。平乐县以下桂江段属河流下游，恭城河和荔浦河的汇入使该河段水量大增，水力资源丰富。该河段的开发以发电及航运为主。

so the Qingshitan Reservoir is used as a supplementary water source Regulation projects as well as waterway dredging projects are also carried out to ensure the smooth navigation of the Lijiang River in the dry season. The Guijiang River below Pingle County is the downstream. The inflow of the Gongcheng River and the Lipu River results in a great increase in water volume, thus leading to richness in hydraulic resources. The development of this section mainly focuses on power generation and shipping.

Gulf Intracoastal Waterway

A waterway located along the Gulf Coast of the United States. The Gulf Intracoastal Waterway, a part of Intracoastal Waterway, stretches more than 1,770 kilometres from Carrabelle, Florida to Brownsville, Texas. It is a man-made shallow-draught channel with a depth of 3.7 metres and a width of 38 metres, allowing barges and light-loaded vessels to travel. The idea of building the waterway system was proposed by Albert Gallatin, United States Secretary of Treasury in 1808, to meet the urgent need for inland transportation. Due to various reasons, the project was not completed until 1949. Now, the Gulf Intracoastal Waterway ranks the third busiest inland waterway in the United States. The waterway is linked to 10 deep-draught ports and 26 shallow-draught channels, serving as a connection between the coastal area and the interior part of the United States. During World War II, the canal served as a route transporting goods and military personnel. And now its major function is the

墨西哥湾沿海航道

美国墨西哥湾沿海航道。作为美国南部沿海航道的一部分,墨西哥湾沿海航道全长1 770千米,自佛罗里达州的卡拉贝尔一直延伸至得克萨斯州的布朗斯维尔。该航道为人工开凿的浅水航道,深3.7米,宽38米,可通行驳船和轻量级运载船只。为满足内陆运输的迫切需求,1808年,时任美国财政部部长艾伯特·加勒廷就曾提议修建海湾沿海航道,但由于种种原因,直到1949年才完工。如今,墨西哥湾沿海航道是美国第三大繁忙的内陆运输航道。该航道与10个深水港和26个浅水河道连通,将美国沿海地区与内陆地区相连。第二次世界大战期间,墨西哥湾沿海航道用以运输货物和军事人员,现主要用于货物运输。美国墨西哥湾沿岸地区盛产石油、天然气,该航

transportation of goods, especially oil- or gas-related products, as the Gulf area is the major producer of petroleum and natural gas. Therefore, the canal is of great economic significance. It plays a recreational function as well. Residents and visitors go fishing, sightseeing, and travelling on the waterway. The Gulf Intracoastal Waterway also provides some environmental benefits. Most parts of the waterway are designed to allow barge transportation, which is more environmentally friendly as it produces less air pollution than road or rail transportation and reduces congestion caused by these two systems.

道运输的货物多为油气产品, 经济价值突出。该航道还用于休闲娱乐, 当地居民和游客可在此垂钓、旅游和观光。墨西哥墨西哥湾沿海航道也发挥了一定的环保作用。航道的主要目的是方便驳船运输。相比于铁路运输和公路运输, 驳船运输造成的空气污染更少, 更有利于环保, 同时还能缓解铁路、公路运输系统的交通拥堵状况。

Haarlem Trek Canal

A canal located in the province of North Holland, the Netherlands. The Haarlem Trek Canal connects Amsterdam and Haarlem. It was constructed in 1631 and opened in 1632 as the first trek canal in the Holland Region. The Leiden Canal was an extension of this canal, which starts from the Haarlem Port to the Amsterdam Port and flows through Amsterdam, Halfweg and Haarlem. In the 17th and 18th centuries, barges were the primary and most comfortable means of transportation for the Dutch people. In the mid- to late 19th century, the canal's transportation function was gradually replaced by the faster railway system. Today it still retains its water management function.

哈勒姆拖船运河

荷兰北荷兰省运河。哈勒姆拖船运河连接阿姆斯特丹市与哈勒姆市。运河1631年开凿，1632年通航，为荷兰大区第一条拖船运河。莱顿运河为该运河的扩建河段，从哈勒姆港流至阿姆斯特丹港，中途流经阿姆斯特丹、哈尔夫韦赫和哈勒姆等城市。17—18世纪时，驳船是荷兰人主要且最适宜的交通工具。19世纪中后期，运河的交通运输功能逐渐为速度更快的铁路系统所取代。如今，哈勒姆拖船运河仍保留有水务管理功能。

Haccourt-Visé Canal

An inland canal located in the province of Liège, Belgium. The Haccourt-Visé Canal is 866 metres in length with one lock. It links the Albert Canal in Haccourt and the Meuse in Visé. The canal was constructed in 1863. It once served as a commercial waterway while its navigation function decreases over time. Now it is mainly used for recreation.

哈库特-维塞运河

比利时列日省内陆运河。哈库特—维塞运河全长866米，建有1座船闸，在哈库特市与阿尔贝特运河相通，在维塞市与默兹河相通。哈库特—维塞运河修建于1863年，曾是一条商业航道，后失去航运功能，目前主要用于休闲娱乐。

Hadeln Canal

A canal located in northern Germany. The Hadeln Canal is about 31.7 kilometres in length and has one lock in Otterndorf with dual functions of drainage and shipping. As a part of the Elbe-Weser

哈德尔恩运河

德国北部运河。哈德尔恩运河长约31.7千米，在奥滕多夫河段上建有1座船闸，兼具通航和排水功能。该运河是易北—威悉航道的一

Waterway, it links the Elbe near Otterndorf and the lake near Bad Bederkesa. The canal is designed for ships with a length of up to 33.5 metres and a width of up to 5 metres. With the purpose of controlling the floods in Sietland, the construction of the canal began in 1852 and was completed in 1854. The canal helped put an end to the frequent floods and boosted the economic development of the previously backward Hadler Sietland. Between 1957 and 1965 the Hadeln Canal was deepened and expanded with the bottom width reaching 14 metres. At present, the canal serves as both a drainage canal and a navigable shortcut between the Weser and the Elbe for small coasters and pleasure boats.

部分, 在奥滕多夫附近连通易北河, 也连通巴特贝德凯萨附近的湖泊, 按设计可通航船只的最大尺寸为长33.5米, 宽5米。为防治锡特兰地区的洪水, 1852年哈德尔恩运河开凿, 历时2年竣工。运河修建后, 锡特兰地区的洪涝灾害频次大幅降低, 哈德勒锡特兰地区原本落后的经济也得到快速发展。1957—1965年间, 运河得以加深和拓宽, 运河底部的宽度达到14米。如今, 哈德尔恩运河不仅作为排水运河, 还是小型贸易船和游船往返于易北河和威悉河之间的一条航行捷径。

Halden Canal

A canal located near Halden, Norway. The Halden Canal has a length of 80 kilometres, running from Skulerud in the north to Tistedal in the south. It was constructed between 1852 and 1860 for the purpose of transporting timber. The canal has 4 locks to control the water, which can allow the passage of boats within 24 metres in length, 6 metres in width and 1.6 metres in draught. The Strømsfoss and Ørje locks were constructed between 1857 and 1860. Today, the Halden Canal is mainly used for recreation. As a cultural heritage, the canal is under proper protection, attracting many people to swim, fish, cycle and walk along the route.

哈尔登运河

挪威近哈尔登市运河。哈尔登运河全长约80千米, 从斯屈勒吕自北向南流向蒂斯特达尔。运河于1852—1860年间开凿, 旨在运输木材。哈尔登运河上建有4座船闸, 用以调控水位, 可容最长24米、最宽6米、吃水深度1.6米以内的船舶通航。运河上的斯特姆弗斯船闸和厄里耶船闸建于1857—1860年间。如今, 哈尔登运河主要用于休闲娱乐。运河作为一处文化遗迹受到了良好保护, 吸引众多游客在沿线游泳、垂钓、骑行和散步。

Hang-Yong Canal

A canal located in the province of Zhejiang, China. See Eastern Zhejiang Canal.

杭甬运河

中国浙江省运河。见浙东运河。

Haren-Ruitenbrock Canal

A cross-border canal located in Europe. Also known as Ruitenbrock Canal. The Haren-Ruitenbrock Canal is about 13 kilometres in length, connecting the Ter Apel Canal in Groningen with the Ems River at the Lower Saxon Haren. The canal is the only navigable connection between Germany and the Netherlands on the north of the Rhine. It was constructed between 1870 and 1878 with a water depth of 1.8 metres and a bed width of 8.5 metres, allowing ships with a capacity of 200 tonnes to pass through. The Haren-Ruitenbrock Canal also serves to drain the surrounding bogs.

哈伦－吕滕布罗克运河

欧洲跨国运河。亦称吕滕布罗克运河。哈伦—吕滕布罗克运河全长13千米，连通荷兰格罗宁根省的泰尔阿珀尔运河和德国下萨克森州的埃姆斯河，是德国和荷兰两国在莱茵河北部的唯一航道。该运河于1870—1878年间开凿完成，当时水深1.8米，河床宽8.5米，可容载重量达200吨的船只通航。哈伦—吕滕布罗克运河还是周边沼泽地的排水通道。

Harlem River Ship Canal

A canal located in New York, the United States. The Harlem River Ship Canal is 13 kilometres in length, separating the northern end of Manhattan Island from the Bronx. The Spuyten Duyvil Creek, Harlem River Ship Canal, and Harlem River form a continuous channel. With the advent of large steamships in the second half of the 19th century, the plan of constructing a canal between the Harlem River and Hudson River for large ships was put on the agenda. However, the construction of this canal was not put into practice until the New York

哈勒姆河通海运河

美国东北部纽约州运河。哈勒姆河通海运河全长13千米，将曼哈顿岛北端与布朗克斯区隔开。斯派腾戴维尔河、哈勒姆河通海运河和哈勒姆河共同构成一条连续航道。随着19世纪下半叶大型汽船的出现，在哈勒姆河与哈德孙河之间修建能通航大型船只运河的计划被提上议程。但直到1888年纽约州议会颁布修建法令后，哈勒姆河通海运河工程才正式启

State Legislature passed a decree for construction in 1888. The canal was completed in 1895. Across the canal there are 3 lift bridges, 4 arch bridges, and 7 swing bridges. Some areas along the canal are designed for recreation.

动。1895年，哈勒姆河通海运河竣工，其上建有3座升降桥、4座拱桥和7座平旋桥，沿岸部分区域被规划为休闲区。

Harlingen Canal

哈灵根运河

A canal located in the province of Friesland, the Netherlands. Also called Bols Canal. Running from Bolsward to Harlingen, the Harlingen Canal is 14.5 kilometres in length. It was initially constructed to facilitate the shipping between Bolsward and Harlingen, but nowadays it is only used for recreational boating.

荷兰弗里斯兰省运河。亦称博尔斯运河。哈灵根运河从博尔斯瓦德流向哈灵根，全长14.5千米。该运河最初用来服务于博尔斯瓦德与哈灵根之间的水上运输，如今仅供娱乐观光船只通行。

Havel Canal

哈弗尔运河

A canal located in the state of Brandenburg, Germany. The Havel Canal is 34.2 kilometres in length. It was constructed in 1951 and completed in 1952. The only lock of the canal is at Schönwalde.

德国勃兰登堡州运河。哈弗尔运河全长34.2千米，1951年开凿，次年竣工。该运河仅在申瓦尔德建有1座船闸。

Havel-Oder Waterway

哈弗尔-奥得河航道

A canal located in Germany. Connecting Berlin and the German-Polish border, the Havel-Oder Waterway is approximately 135 kilometres in length. As a Class IV channel, the waterway consists of four sections, namely Havel, Scheitel, Oder and the Hohensaaten-Friedrichsthaler Waterway, which are connected by the Lehnitz Lock, the Niederfinow ship lift and the Hohensaaten West Lock. A part

德国运河。哈弗尔-奥得河航道连接柏林和德国与波兰边界地区，全长约135千米。该航道为四级航道，由4个河段组成，即哈弗尔河段、希特尔河段、奥得河段和霍恩萨滕-弗里德里希沙尔河段。4个河段由莱尼茨船闸、尼德菲诺升船机和霍恩萨滕西船闸连通。

of the Havel-Oder Waterway is also called the Oder-Havel Canal, which specifically refers to the section between the Havel and the Lehnitz Lock (6 kilometres in length), and Scheitel (48 kilometres). During the Middle Ages, Berlin businessmen began to look for a navigable route across the Oder to the Baltic Sea. But the development of hydraulic engineering at that time did not allow them to cross the 80-kilometre-long distance. Not until the invention of the lock chamber in the 16th century were people able to construct a canal. The Finow Canal, the oldest German shipping canal, was constructed shortly before the Thirty Years War, which later turned into a part of the Havel-Oder Waterway. In the 19th century, the Havel below Liebenwalde became navigable, bringing the Havel-Oder Waterway into being. In the 20th century, different parts of the Havel-Oder Waterway were constructed and named.

哈弗尔—奥得河航道的一部分也称作奥得—哈弗尔运河，特指6千米长的哈弗尔至莱尼茨船闸的河段和48千米长的希特尔河段。中世纪时期，柏林商人已开始寻找穿过奥得河通向波罗的海的航道，但受限于当时的水利技术，无法开凿长达80千米的运河。直至16世纪，得益于船闸闸室的发明，运河修建才有了技术保障。菲诺运河是德国最古老的通航运河，在三十年战争爆发不久前修建完成，后成为哈弗尔—奥得河航道的一部分。19世纪时，利本瓦尔德镇的哈弗尔河通航，哈弗尔—奥得河航道开始成形。至20世纪，哈弗尔—奥得河航道的不同部分得以修建和命名，形成了当今航道的全貌。

Havre-Tancarville Canal

阿弗尔-唐卡维尔运河

A canal located in the region of Normandy in France. Also known as Tancarville Canal. The Havre-Tancarville Canal connects the Havre to the Seine. The 25-kilometre-long canal, fed by the Seine and the Lézarde River, has 3 locks. It was completed and opened in 1887. There was once a canal constructed in the 17th century, linking the Harfleur to the Havre. The shipment of the canal, however, was restricted considering its carrying capacity, and failed to meet the need of transportation by the 19th century. The Seine had performed ship-

法国诺曼底大区运河。亦称唐卡维尔运河。阿弗尔—唐卡维尔运河连通阿弗尔河和塞纳河，全长25千米，河上共建有3座船闸，河水引自塞纳河和莱扎德河。1887年，阿弗尔—唐卡维尔运河竣工通航。19世纪时，由于不能通行大吨位船只，17世纪以来连通阿夫勒河与阿弗尔河的运河已不能满足当时的运输需求，航运船只只能转向塞纳河。塞纳河有通过船闸来控

ping tasks through lock-controlled mobile dams, which offered access for larger ships to Paris and elsewhere. The Seine estuary was a key area along which a maritime canal needed to be constructed. The design and construction work were entrusted to engineers Alfred-Henri Soclet, Ernest Bellot and Pierre-François Frissard. They reached the consensus to connect the Harfleur directly with the Havre-Tancarville Canal.

制的活动水坝，这样大吨位船舶可抵达巴黎等地区。塞纳河河口地理位置很重要，有必要开凿一条通海运河。运河的设计和修建工作由工程师阿尔弗雷德—亨利·索克莱、埃内斯特·贝洛和皮埃尔—弗朗索瓦·弗里萨尔共同负责。三位工程师达成共识，决定将阿夫勒尔港与阿弗尔—唐卡维尔运河直接相连通。

Hawthorne Canal

霍桑运河

A canal located in Australia. Also called Long Cove Creek. The Hawthorne Canal was originally a natural waterway, and is now an artificial one, situated on a southern tributary of the Parramatta River, west of the Sydney Harbour. Together with the Iron Cove Creek, this canal is among the most significant tributaries that flow into the Iron Cove. Constructed from January 1890, it was intended for drainage improvement and to provide a convenient ferry access for the Drummoyne-Leichhardt Ferry Company. The canal was named after John Stuart Hawthorne, who first made a proposal for its construction in the Parliament in 1890.

澳大利亚运河。亦称长湾溪。霍桑运河曾为澳大利亚天然航道，现为悉尼港西部帕拉玛塔河南部支流上的一条人工运河，与艾恩湾溪同为艾恩湾最重要的支流。该运河1890年1月起开凿，旨在改善排水条件，同时也为德拉莫因—莱卡特渡轮公司旗下的渡轮提供便捷通道。1890年，约翰·斯图尔特·霍桑首次在议会提出运河修建事宜，霍桑运河因此得名。

Hayy River

海伊河

An ancient canal located in Iraq. See Al-Gharraf River.

伊拉克古运河。见阿尔—盖拉夫河。

Heimanswetering

A canal located in the province of South Holland, the Netherlands. The Heimanswetering is 2.2 kilometres in length, linking the Old Rhine to the Woudwetering. The canal was excavated around 1200 with the aim of removing peat and soil from swamps along both sides of the canal as well as connecting the Old Rhine and the Leiden Lake. Around 1660, the New Canal was constructed, and the navigational function of the Heimanswetering began to decline. In 1825, as the Aar Canal was opened, the canal was further diminished. In around 1920, the overall transport in the Netherlands grew, making the Heimanswetering important again. From 1952 to 1953, the canal was deepened and became an essential waterway to transport kerosene to the Schiphol Airport. In the 1970s, pipelines were constructed and replaced the kerosene transport. Nowadays, the Heimanswetering is only available for recreational ships and functions as one of the most popular pleasure boat routes in the Netherlands.

海曼斯维特林运河

荷兰南荷兰省运河。海曼斯维特林运河全长2.2千米，连通旧莱茵河与瓦德维特林运河。运河于公元1200年前后开凿，旨在运送当时运河两侧沼泽地挖出的泥煤和废土，同时连通旧莱茵河与莱顿湖。1660年前后，新运河修建后，海曼斯维特林运河的航运功能日渐衰退。1825年，阿尔运河的开通进一步削弱了海曼斯维特林运河的重要性。1920年前后，荷兰全国整体运输量有所增长，海曼斯维特林运河的重要性再次得以体现。1952—1953年间，该运河得以加深，成为向斯希普霍尔机场运输煤油的重要航道。20世纪70年代，地下输油管道建成，取代了煤油的航运。如今，海曼斯维特林运河仅供游船通行，是荷兰最受欢迎的游船路线之一。

Heinooms Canal

A canal located in the province of Utrecht, the Netherlands. The Heinooms Canal is 6 kilometres in length and has one lock, connecting Wilnis with Woerden Verlaat. At the end of the bend where the canal widens, there is a recreational area with parking spaces, where people can go fishing and enjoy a wonderful view of reed and lily fields.

海诺姆斯运河

荷兰乌特勒支省运河。海诺姆斯运河全长6千米，建有1座船闸，连接维尔尼斯和沃尔登弗拉特。在该运河河道变宽的弯道末端，设有一个带停车场的娱乐休闲场所，可供人们垂钓、欣赏芦苇荡和百合田美景。

Heloma Canal

A canal located in the province of Friesland, the Netherlands. Also called Jonkers Canal. The Heloma Canal is 6.5 kilometres in length with one lock, running from the Tjonger River to the Linde River. Excavated in 1774, the canal is a part of the Overijssel-Prinses Margriet Canal route. The Heloma Canal was commissioned by the Heloma family and named after it as well. The canal has the functions of transportation, drainage and recreation.

Hennepin Canal

An abandoned canal located in northwest Illinois, the United States. The original Hennepin Canal was 121 kilometres in length. It was named as Illinois and Mississippi Canal for connecting the Mississippi River and the Illinois River. The project of the Hennepin Canal was conceived in 1834, but the idea was not put into practice due to financial problems. In 1890, this project received federal funds from the Congress and was completed in 1907. The Hennepin Canal was of great significance in terms of commerce and industry in the United States. With the railway transportation becoming more competitive, the canal was officially closed in 1951. Despite its limited use in navigation, the canal witnessed many innovations and had many fun facts during the construction. For example, it was the first canal in history in the United States to apply Portland cement, the same material used later in the construction of the Panama Canal. Another case in

黑洛玛运河

荷兰弗里斯兰省运河。亦称约恩克斯运河。黑洛玛运河全长6.5千米，建有1座船闸，自勇尔河流至林德河。运河开凿于1774年，是上艾瑟尔河—玛格丽特公主运河路线的一部分。黑洛玛运河受黑洛玛家族委托而建，故此得名。该运河具有航运、排水、娱乐观光等功能。

亨内平运河

美国伊利诺伊州西北部废弃运河。亨内平运河最初全长121千米，因连通密西西比河与伊利诺伊河，曾被称为伊利诺伊—密西西比运河。亨内平运河修建计划始于1834年，后因资金问题被搁置。1890年，该计划获得国会批准的联邦资金支持，1907年运河竣工。亨内平运河对美国工商业发展起到了重要推动作用。由于不敌铁路运输，该运河于1951年正式停航。尽管运河在航运方面作用有限，但其修建有不少创新之举及趣事为人津津乐道。例如，该运河是美国历史上第一条采用硅酸盐水泥修建的运河，这种材料后来也用于巴拿马运河的修建。再如，运河的部分船闸采用列奥纳多·达·芬奇发明的人字门技术。1978年，亨内平运河被列入

point is that some of its locks applied a technology called mitre gates, which was invented by Leonardo Da Vinci. In 1978, the Hennepin Canal was listed in the National Register of Historic Places. Since the 1970s the canal has become the Hennepin Canal Parkway State Park, which is now mainly a site for outdoor enjoyment.

美国国家历史遗迹名录。20世纪70年代后，亨内平运河被改建为亨内平运河步道州立公园，现主要作为户外娱乐活动场所。

Hennepin Feeder Canal

A canal located in northwest Illinois, the United States. The Hennepin Feeder Canal is situated at nearly the mid-point of the Hennepin Canal. It is 47.2 kilometres in length, running north from Rock Falls to Sheffield. The feeder canal was aimed at introducing the water from the Rock River into the main canal. The Hennepin Feeder Canal only had one guard lock, which was mainly used to protect the canal from the impact of water dropping from a higher elevation. This canal is now obsolete and mainly used for outdoor activities.

亨内平引水运河

美国伊利诺伊州西北部运河。亨内平引水运河邻近亨内平运河中段，全长47.2千米，从罗克福尔斯向北延伸至谢菲尔德。该引水运河的作用是将罗克河的水引入主运河。亨内平引水运河只建有1座保护闸，防止高处水流对运河造成破坏。如今，运河的引水功能已被废弃，主要用于户外娱乐活动。

Henri IV Canal

A canal located in France. The Henri IV Canal is a branch of the Briare Canal, linking the Loire with the Briare Canal. It is 1.5 kilometres in length and has 3 locks. The canal joins the Briare Canal and the Loire Lateral Canal at Briare-Henri IV Junction. It is a waterway for boats up to 30.4 metres in length and 5.2 metres in width. Its maximum headroom and draught are 3.5 metres and 1.2 metres respectively.

亨利四世运河

法国运河。亨利四世运河是布里亚尔运河的一条支线，连通卢瓦尔河与布里亚尔运河，全长1.5千米，河上建有3座船闸。该运河与卢瓦尔旁侧运河和布里亚尔运河在布里亚尔—亨利四世运河枢纽处交汇。亨利四世运河最大可容长30.4米、宽5.2米的船只通航，其最大净空高度及吃水深度分别为3.5米和1.2米。

Hereford and Gloucester Canal

赫里福德-格洛斯特运河

A canal located in the west of England, the United Kingdom. See Herefordshire and Gloucestershire Canal.

英国英格兰西部运河。见赫里福德郡—格洛斯特郡运河。

Herefordshire and Gloucestershire Canal

赫里福德郡-格洛斯特郡运河

A canal located in the west of England, the United Kingdom. Also called Hereford and Gloucester Canal. The Herefordshire and Gloucestershire Canal runs for 55 kilometres from Hereford to Gloucester, where it connects the Severn River. First opened in 1798 and then in 1845, the canal was closed in 1881 when its southern sections were changed to be a part of the Ledbury and Gloucester Railway. Although the route from Hereford to Ledbury continued to be open, the canal still fell into disuse gradually. In 1992, the Herefordshire and Gloucestershire Canal Trust was formed, aiming at the canal preservation and full restoration of the canal. With its efforts, the canal was officially reopened in 2012.

英国英格兰西部运河。亦称赫里福德—格洛斯特运河。赫里福德郡—格洛斯特郡运河全长55千米，由赫里福德流至格洛斯特后，与塞文河连通。该运河曾于1798年和1845年两度通航，后因其南部航道被改造成为莱德伯里—格洛斯特铁路的一段，最终于1881年停航。尽管赫里福德至莱德伯里的河段继续保持通航状态，但运河仍渐遭废弃。1992年，为保护和全面修缮该运河，赫里福德郡—格洛斯特郡运河信托基金会成立。在该组织努力下，2012年运河重新通航。

Heusden Canal

赫斯登运河

A canal located in the Netherlands. The Heusden Canal has a total length of about 2.3 kilometres, connecting the Bergen Maas and the Afgedamde Maas. The Maas splits near Huesden. The main stream, known as Bergen Maas, stretches from North Brabant to Gelderland, while the other

荷兰运河。赫斯登运河全长约2.3千米，连通贝亨马斯河与阿夫赫丹德马斯河。马斯河流经赫斯登并在此处分成两条主要支流，其中一条是贝赫马斯河，从荷兰的北布拉班特省流至海尔德兰省；另一

stream called the Afgedamde Maas heads north to join the Waal River, the main branch of the Rhine River. The original canal was excavated in the middle of the Middle Ages to guarantee the accessibility of Heusden. The Afgedamde Maas came into being in the late Middle Ages when a flood connected the Merwede and the Maas. Since the completion of the dam at its southern inlet in 1904, the Afgedamde Maas has no longer received water from the Maas. The current Heusden Canal was excavated under the Maasmond Act released in 1883. Some parts of the old canal are still kept.

条是阿夫赫丹德马斯河,向北汇入莱茵河的主要支流瓦尔河。中世纪中期,为确保到赫斯登的交通便捷,人们开凿了赫斯登运河。中世纪后期,一场洪水使得梅尔韦德河和马斯河连通,形成了阿夫赫丹德马斯河。1904年,阿夫赫丹德马斯河南部河口大坝建成,阻断马斯河河水流入阿夫赫丹德马斯河。现今的赫斯登运河于1883年由马斯蒙德法案批准开凿而成,部分河段保留至今。

Hilversum Canal

希弗萨姆运河

A canal located in the province of North Holland, the Netherlands. The Hilversum Canal is 7.8 kilometres in length and has one lock. It is navigable for 50-metre-long ships with a draught of less than 2.4 metres. In the 20th century, due to the poor navigational conditions on the Gooi Canal and the 's-Graveland Canal in Hilversum, the locals wished to construct a new canal for the transport of building materials to reduce costs. In 1933, the canal was excavated. The western part of the canal was opened in 1936 and the canal became fully navigable in 1937. The construction of the 't Hemeltje Sluice on the Hilversum Canal began in 1931. Equipped with roller doors, it is situated at the confluence of the Hilversum Canal and the Vecht. In 1980, the 't Hemeltje Sluice was only navigable for ships with a maximum capacity of 600 tonnes, thus not profitable. Due to its small size, the lock was damaged by ships travelling from

荷兰北荷兰省运河。希弗萨姆运河全长7.8千米,建有1座船闸,可容长达50米、吃水深度不超过2.4米的船只通航。20世纪时,由于霍伊运河和斯赫拉弗兰运河流经希弗萨姆市的河段航运条件不佳,当地人希望修建一条新运河来运输建筑材料,以降低运输成本。1933年,希弗萨姆运河开凿,1936年,该运河西段通航,1937年全线通航。希弗萨姆运河上的特海默尔彻船闸1931年修建,位于希佛萨姆运河与费赫特河的交汇处,配有卷闸门。1980年,特海默尔彻船闸最多只能通行载重量600吨的船舶,无法盈利。由于船闸过小,从布利克湖到费赫特河的船只通行时对船闸造成了损坏。1990年,

Lake Blik to the Vecht. In 1990, the lock was rarely used as it further deteriorated. In 1998, the lock was restored successfully. Since the Hilversum Canal was opened, it has played an important role in entertainment. Various recreational activities can be carried out on the canal, including cruising, paddling, fishing, and skating.

该船闸情况进一步恶化, 几乎无法使用。1998年船闸成功修复。希弗萨姆运河自开通以来就是娱乐休闲胜地, 可供人们进行各类娱乐活动, 如游船、划船、垂钓、滑冰等。

Hiwassee River ≈

A canalized river located in northern Georgia, the United States. The Hiwassee River is approximately 237 kilometres in length. The river flows northward into North Carolina and then turns westward into Tennessee. The 37-kilometre-long section of the Hiwassee River flowing from the North Carolina-Tennessee state line to U.S. Highway 411 near Delano is designated as a state scenic site, regulated by the Resource Management, and it is used primarily for recreational purposes. Through a gorge, the Hiawassee River flows along the U.S. Highway 11 in Calhoun and Charleston, Tennessee, where it is used primarily for industrial purposes. There are many marshes and wetlands over the river's junction with Chickamauga Dam in Chattanooga, Tennessee, offering places for hunting and fishing. Thus, the river is very popular with boaters, fishermen, and water skiers.

海沃西河

美国佐治亚州北部运河化河流。海沃西河全长约237千米, 河水向北流入北卡罗来纳州后, 向西流经田纳西州, 之后从两州的州界流向德拉诺附近的美国411号公路, 这段长37千米的河段被定为州级景区河, 由资源管理部门管理, 主要用于休闲娱乐。海沃西河穿过峡谷后, 沿美国11号公路流动, 在田纳西州的卡尔洪和查尔斯顿一带主要用作工业水源。海沃西河与田纳西州查塔努加的奇克莫加大坝交界处有多处沼泽和湿地, 为狩猎和捕鱼提供了场所, 该河因此深受划船爱好者、钓鱼者和滑水爱好者的喜爱。

Hjälmare Canal

A canal located in Sweden. The Hjälmare Canal is totally 13.7 kilometres in length, of which 5 kilo-

耶尔马运河

瑞典运河。耶尔马运河全长13.7千米, 其中5千米为人工开凿河道,

metres are man-made. It connects Lake Hjälmaren with Lake Mälaren. The canal was constructed between 1623 and 1639 to facilitate the transport of iron, grain, and timber from Bergslagen to Stockholm or Baltic Sea and further abroad. Because of high maintenance fees, the Hjälmare Canal was not used frequently, which led to the relocation of the canal in 1830. This considerably reduced the maintenance costs and the navigating conditions were improved. It was still in operation for commercial traffic in the 1970s. However, as railway transportation developed and metallurgic and timber industry moved further north in Sweden in the late 19th century, the significance of the canal declined. The Hjälmare Canal is now for recreational purposes only. The boats that are allowed to pass are up to 30 metres in length and 1.95 metres in draught. It has an estimated 22-metre elevation difference, which is overcome by 9 locks.

连通耶尔马伦湖和梅拉伦湖。该运河修建于1623—1639年，便于人们将铁、谷物和木材由贝格斯拉根运往斯德哥尔摩或波罗的海，继而转运至国外。由于耶尔马运河维护费用高昂，其使用率不高。1830年，该运河改道并修整，维护费用大幅降低，通航条件得到改善，至19世纪70年代，耶尔马运河主要用于商业运输。19世纪末，由于铁路运输业的发展，瑞典的冶金业和木材工业重心北移，耶尔马运河的重要性下降。如今，该运河仅有休闲功能，可容长达30米、吃水深1.95米的船只通行。河上建有9座船闸，以便调节约22米的水位落差。

Hlaing River

A canal located in the south of Yangon, Myanmar. See Yangon Canal.

莱恩河

缅甸仰光市南部运河。见仰光运河。

Hocking Canal

A canal located in southern Ohio, the United States. The Hocking Canal was initially a 14.5-kilometre-long canal that connected Carroll and Lancaster. It was built by private investors in order to transport salt and other commodities to the market. The construction lasted from 1831 to 1838. The state took

霍金运河

美国俄亥俄州南部运河。霍金运河起初长14.5千米，连接卡罗尔和兰卡斯特，由私人投资修建，旨在将盐及其他商品运往市场。运河1831年开凿，1838年竣工。此后，俄亥俄州政府接管运河，将运河

over the canal and extended it to Athens. In 1843, the rebuilt Hocking Canal was about 90 kilometres in length with 26 locks, 7 culverts, and 1 aqueduct. The canal connected Athens to Lancaster and the Ohio and Erie Canal. Through the canal, salt, coal, pork products, wool, lumber were transported to the markets, while furniture, and iron products were shipped into Athens and Hocking counties. However, the canal made little profit because of the slowness of the vessels on the canal and the fact that the river was often frozen in winter. In 1857, the canal faced fierce competition from the Columbus-Hocking Valley Railway. In the late 19th century, a few major floods destroyed the Hocking Canal and it was never rebuilt. In 1890, the canal was closed. In the mid-1930s, much of the bed of the Hocking Canal was filled in to build State Route 33.

延伸至阿森斯。1843年，扩建后的霍金运河长约90千米，建有26座船闸、7座涵洞和1座渡槽，连接阿森斯、兰卡斯特以及俄亥俄—伊利运河。盐、煤、猪肉制品、羊毛和木材经由该运河运往市场，家具和铁制品等则通过该运河运达阿森斯县和霍金县。霍金运河盈利微薄，主要由于船只在河段内航速较低，且冬季则经常结冰而无法通航。1857年起，该运河面临哥伦布—霍金谷铁路的激烈竞争。19世纪末，霍金运河被几次大洪水损毁，后未能重建。1890年，霍金运河停航。20世纪30年代，为修建美国33号公路，该运河多处河段被回填。

Hoen Canal

霍恩运河

A canal located in the province of Groningen, the Netherlands. The Hoen Canal is 15 kilometres in length and has one lock, running through the city of Groningen to Zuidhorn. The Hoen Canal was commissioned in 1616. It was extended to north from 1654 to 1657, flowing to Noordhorn, then running along the Van Starkenborgh Canal and joining the Colonels Canal. In 1863, a waterway linking the Hoen Canal to Westerheaven Harbour was constructed. In order to further shorten the shipping time between the two waterways, the Eendrachts Canal was constructed in 1909 and greatly improved the winding water route.

荷兰格罗宁根省运河。霍恩运河全长15千米，建有1座船闸，由格罗宁根市流至泽伊德霍伦。1616年，该运河获准开凿。1654—1657年间，霍恩运河向北延伸至诺德霍伦，再转向西沿范斯塔肯博赫运河流动，与科洛奈尔运河交汇。1863年，人们新修了连接霍恩运河和韦斯特黑文港的航道。1909年，为进一步缩短霍恩运河和韦斯特黑文港之间的航运时间，人们将河道裁弯取直，修建了团结运河。

Hoge Canal

A canal located in Flevoland, the Netherlands. The Hoge Canal is 30.6 kilometres in length and has 2 locks. The canal starts from Almere and travels across the whole Flevopolder. Its branch, the Hoge Dwars Canal, ends in the Veluwe Lake. The Larser Canal connects the Hoge Canal with the Lage Canal.

霍赫运河

荷兰弗莱福兰省运河。霍赫运河全长30.6千米，建有2座船闸。运河始于阿尔默勒，横穿弗莱福兰圩田。霍赫运河的支线是霍赫杜瓦希运河，注入费吕沃湖。该运河经由拉瑟运河连通拉赫运河。

Hohenzollern Canal

A cross-border canal located in Europe. See Oder-Havel Canal.

霍亨索伦运河

欧洲跨国运河。见奥得—哈弗尔运河。

Holland IJssel≈

A canalized river located in Utrecht Province and South Holland Province, the Netherlands. Flowing from Gouda City to Krimpen City, the Holland IJssel connects Nieuwegein and New Maas to the east of Rotterdam. This 20-kilometre-long river was originally a branch of the Lek River until the creation of a dam in 1295. Since then, the Holland IJssel has been fed exclusively by canal waters, especially the Doorslag Canal. After the 1953 North Sea flood, a storm surge barrier was constructed at the Krimpen-on-the-IJssel Town as a part of the Delta Works to protect a large area of land around the Rhine-Meuse-Schelde Delta from the flood.

荷兰艾瑟尔河

荷兰运河化河流。荷兰艾瑟尔河流经乌特勒支省和南荷兰省，全长20千米，由豪达市流向克林彭市，连通尼沃海恩河和鹿特丹以东的新马斯河。荷兰艾瑟尔河起初是莱克河的支流。1295年，自河上建起水坝后，荷兰艾瑟尔河水源主要来自运河，特别是多斯拉赫运河。1953年北海洪灾后，在艾瑟尔河畔克林彭镇修建了移动挡潮闸。这一项目属于荷兰三角洲工程，可使莱茵—默兹—斯海尔德三角洲周边地区免遭洪灾。

Holland River Division

An unfinished canal located in Ontario, Canada.

霍兰河段

加拿大安大略省未完工运河。见

See Newmarket Canal.

纽马基特运河。

Honggou Canal

鸿沟

An ancient canal located in Henan Province, China. Also called Langdang Ditch in ancient China. Connecting the Yellow River with the Huaihe River, the Honggou (or literally Wide Gap) Canal drew water from the Yellow River at Xingyang, and ran southwards to empty into the Yingshui River, a tributary of the Huaihe River. It connected with the Ziji Canal in the east. The water system of the Honggou Canal was formed by linking multiple waterways between the Yellow River and the Huaihe River. This made Henan Province a key hub of national water transportation. In 361 BC, King Hui of the State of Wei ordered to construct the Honggou Canal in order to satisfy the needs of agricultural and commercial development as well as military transportation. This project was completed after two rounds of large-scale construction. The completion of the Honggou Canal successfully connected the Jihe River, the Huaihe River as well as the Yellow River. It became a must-win battleground for military strategists throughout history. After the State of Qin unified China, the Honggou Canal became the strategic passage between the waterways in the north and those in the south. Qin Shi Huang, the First Emperor of the Qin Dynasty (221 BC—206 BC), made full use of the Honggou water system to transport large quantities of grain collected in the south to the northern areas. At the end of the Qin Dynasty, the States of Chu and Han were divided

中国河南省古运河。古时亦称蒗荡渠。鸿沟连通黄河与淮河两大水系，从荥阳引黄河水，向南汇入淮河的支流颍水，在东部连通淄济运河。鸿沟连通黄河与淮河之间的多条航道，构成鸿沟水系，河南省因此成为全国水路运输枢纽之一。公元前361年，为了发展农业和商业，运送军队，魏惠王下令开凿鸿沟，鸿沟历经两次大规模修建而成。鸿沟连通济河、淮河和黄河，成为历代兵家必争之地。秦朝统一中国后，鸿沟成为南北水路交通的咽喉之地。秦始皇利用鸿沟水系将在南方征集的大批粮食运往北方。秦朝末年，楚汉以鸿沟为界，中分天下。自战国至南北朝，鸿沟是黄河和淮河之间中原地区的主要水运交通线路之一，为大运河的开凿奠定了基础。然而，连绵不断的战争损毁了鸿沟水系。汉代以后，黄河不断泛滥改道，导致鸿沟河道阻塞淤积，最终成为平地。

with the Honggou Canal as the boundary. During the period from the Warring States (475 BC—221 BC) to the Northern and Southern Dynasties (420—589 AD), the Honggou Canal had always been one of the main water transport lines in the Central Plains between the Yellow River and the Huaihe River. The excavation of the Honggou Canal also laid a foundation for the later construction of the Grand Canal. However, continuous wars led to the disruption of the Honggou water system. After the Han Dynasty (206 BC—220 AD), since the Yellow River went through floods and diversions, the Honggou Canal eventually turned into a flat land due to blockage and siltation.

Hoofdwijk

A canal located in the province of Drenthe, the Netherlands. See Scholtens Canal.

霍夫维克运河

荷兰德伦特省运河。见舒尔腾斯运河。

Hoogeveen Canal

A canal located in the province of Drenthe, the Netherlands. Running from the Meppel Canal near Meppel to Hoogeveen, the Hoogeveen Canal is 25 kilometres in length, consisting of 4 locks. The canal has an extension called the Hoogeveen Extension Canal, a small part of which is located in Germany, where the waterway is called the Schalinghsdorf-Hoogeveen Canal. This part of channel is no longer navigable and only used for drainage. The excavation of the canal was started as early as 1627. More than two centuries later, the canal was

霍赫芬运河

荷兰德伦特省运河。霍赫芬运河全长25千米，河上共建有4座船闸，从梅珀尔附近的梅珀尔运河流向霍赫芬市。霍赫芬扩建运河为该运河的延伸河段，有一小部分位于德国境内，这一部分被称为舍宁斯多夫—霍赫芬运河，现仅用于排水，已不适合航运。1627年，霍赫芬运河开凿。200多年后，运河由德伦特·卡纳尔·马特沙皮公司接管。1964—1988年间，该运河成

taken over by N.V. Drentse Canal Maatschappij (DKM). From 1964 to 1988, the channel served as a modern shipping waterway. The Hoogeveen Canal is a CEMT (Classification of European Inland Waterways) Class II canal, and allows ships with a maximum length of 65 metres, a width of 7.3 metres, and a draught of 2.2 metres to pass.

为现代水运航道。根据欧洲内陆航道分级标准，霍赫芬运河属于二级运河，能容最长65米、最宽7.3米、最大吃水深度2.2米的船只通航。

Hoorn Canal

A canal located in the province of Groningen, the Netherlands. Also known as Hulp Canal over Den Hoorn. The Hoorn Canal is about 6.7 kilometres in length. It runs from the Mensingeweer Canal and flows into the Hunsingo Canal together with the Warfhuister Canal near 't Stort. It was constructed in the 19th century.

霍伦运河

荷兰格罗宁根省运河。亦称登霍伦辅助运河。霍伦运河全长约6.7千米，始于门辛赫韦尔运河，在缇斯托特地区附近与瓦尔夫赫伊斯特运河一起汇入亨辛豪运河。霍伦运河开凿于19世纪。

Horncastle Canal

A canal located in England, the United Kingdom. The Horncastle Canal runs for 17.7 kilometres with 12 locks largely along the course of the Bain River. It starts from the Witham River, and ends with Horncastle in Lincolnshire. The canal was opened on 17 September 1802, and the day was later declared a public holiday in Horncastle for celebration. After being officially abandoned in 1889, the main line was still used to transport sand and gravel from Kirkby for a decade. The lower reaches continued to be used as well to transport coal from Goole to the Coningsby wharf until 1910. Since 1975, the voices of restoring the canal had been heard con-

霍恩卡斯尔运河

英国英格兰运河。霍恩卡斯尔运河全长17.7千米，自威瑟姆河流至林肯郡的霍恩卡斯尔镇，河上共建有12座船闸，船闸主要位于贝恩河一段。1802年9月17日，霍恩卡斯尔运河通航，这一天后来被定为霍恩卡斯尔镇公共假日。1889年，该运河正式被废弃，在之后的10年间，霍恩卡斯尔运河主河道仍然用于从基尔比镇运输沙子与砾石。另外，其下游支线也一直沿用到1910年，主要用于将煤炭从古尔运送到科宁斯比码头。1975年以来，修

stantly. In 2003, a restoration scheme was proposed by the Horncastle and Tattershall Coningsby Canal Heritage Group at a public meeting, which agreed to raise funds in support of the feasibility research of the reconstruction. Now some restoration plans are financially supported by the Lincolnshire County Council.

复重建霍恩卡斯尔运河的呼声不断。2003年，霍恩卡斯尔—塔特歇尔·孔斯比运河遗产集团在一次公开大会上提出重建霍恩卡斯尔运河的计划，同意为开展运河重建的可行性研究筹集资金。目前，林肯郡议会已经为部分运河修复计划提供资金支持。

Houston Ship Channel

A waterway located in Houston, Texas, the United States. The Houston Ship Channel is 80 kilometres in length, 160 metres in width, and 14 metres in depth. It was dredged from the Buffalo Bayou and Galveston Bay, and it connects with the Port of Houston, one of the world's busiest seaports, with a number of piers and berths along the watercourse. The upstream tip of the channel begins at the Turning Basin, approximately 6.4 kilometres east of downtown Houston, and its downstream tip at an entrance to the Gulf of Mexico between the Galveston Island and the Bolivar Peninsula. The Houston Ship Channel provides transportation access for ocean-going vessels that navigate between Houston-area terminals and the Gulf of Mexico, and for more and more inland barges, transporting important supplies such as petrochemicals and the Midwestern grain. It was continuously widened and deepened to accommodate a growing number of larger ships, with projects commenced in 1910, 1922 and 1933. The history of the channel dates back to 1826, when residents began interfering

休斯敦通海航道

美国得克萨斯州休斯敦市航道。休斯敦通海航道全长80千米，宽160米，深14米。该航道是在布法罗河口和加尔维斯顿湾的基础上挖掘修建而成，是休斯敦港的一部分，休斯敦港是世界上最繁忙的海港之一，沿线有很多码头和泊位。航道上游始于休斯敦市中心以东约6.4千米的回船池，下游端位于加尔维斯顿岛和玻利瓦尔半岛之间通往墨西哥湾的入口处。休斯敦通海航道为往返于休斯敦地区码头和墨西哥湾之间的远洋船舶以及越来越多的内陆驳船提供运输通道，运输石油化工产品和中西部地区生产的粮食等重要物资。为了容纳更多更大吨位的船只，休斯敦通海航道先后于1910年、1922年以及1933年拓宽加深。休斯敦通海航道的历史可以追溯至1826年，那时当地居民为方便货物运输，曾对河流进行过改造。自

with the river to facilitate the transport of goods. The Houston Ship Channel has been used for the maritime transport of goods since 1836, and was officially opened by President Woodrow Wilson in November 1914. Due to its geographical proximity to the Texas oil fields, a number of petrochemical refineries were built along the waterway. In 1987, the channel was designated as a National Civil Engineering Landmark by the American Society of Civil Engineers (ASCE). Today, the Houston Ship Channel and the surrounding area are the great supporters of the second-largest petrochemical complex in the world.

1836年起，休斯敦通海航道开始用来运输海上货物。1914年11月，伍德罗·威尔逊总统宣布休斯敦通海航道正式通航。因邻近得克萨斯油田，休斯敦通海航道沿岸建立了许多石化炼油厂。1987年，该航道被美国土木工程师协会列为国家土木工程地标。如今，休斯敦通海航道及其周边地区支撑着世界第二大石化产业综合体。

Huigen Canal

惠根运河

A canal located in the province of North Holland, the Netherlands. The Huigen Canal is a part of the Alkmaar-Huigendijk-Ursum-Avenhorn Waterway. In November 2020, North Holland Province carried out maintenance work on the bank of the Huigen Canal in the hope that it would last another 30 years.

荷兰北荷兰省运河。惠根运河是阿尔克马尔—惠根迪克—乌尔瑟姆—阿文霍伦航道的一段。2020年11月，北荷兰省对惠根运河河岸进行维护，以期该运河能够再使用30年。

Hulp Canal over Den Hoorn

登霍伦辅助运河

A canal located in the province of Groningen, the Netherlands. See Hoorn Canal.

荷兰格罗宁根省运河。见霍伦运河。

Huningue Canal

于南格运河

A canal located in eastern France. The Huningue Canal links the Rhine with Niffer. The construction work began in 1801 and was completed in 1828. It

法国东部运河。于南格运河连接莱茵河与尼费尔。运河1801年开凿，1828年建成，1831年正式通航。

was put into use in 1831. In 1961, this canal was enlarged, with an additional section constructed between Mulhouse and the Grand Alsace Canal, which runs parallel to the Rhine. At the same time, the section between Mulhouse and Friesenheim was closed. Nowadays, the locks are no longer operational, but a small section of the canal from Niffer to Kembs has remained navigable, which allows boats to reach the marina of Kembs. Originally constructed only for the purpose of supplying water, the Huningue Canal is now also used to irrigate neighbouring crops.

1961年，于南格运河得到扩建，位于米卢斯与阿尔萨斯大运河之间的新增河段与莱茵河并行。与此同时，米卢斯至弗里森海姆之间的河段停航。目前，于南格运河上的船闸已被废弃，仅有位于尼费尔和康斯之间的一小段河道可通航，船只可经此驶往康斯的停泊港。于南格运河最初为供水而建，如今也用以灌溉沿岸作物。

Hunsingo Canal

亨辛豪运河

A canal located in the northwest of the province of Groningen, the Netherlands. Also known as Hunsingo Drainage Canal. The Hunsingo Canal is about 6.6 kilometres in length and 7.9 metres in width, and has one lock. It runs from 't Stort to Zoutkamp, connecting the Hoorn Canal to the Reit Canal. The canal is formed at the confluence of the Hoorn Canal and the Warfhuister Canal, and was named after the Hunsingo Water Board established in 1852. The Hunsingo Canal was constructed in the mid-19th century to improve the drainage of the Marne area. During the construction, existing watercourses were canalized. The Zoutkamp Channel, the connection between Zoutkamp and Ulrum, was made into a canal, and the barge canal from Ulrum to 't Stort was widened. In addition, a drainage sluice was constructed in the sea dyke near Zoutkamp. With the completion of the canal, the drainage of the Marne was significantly improved.

荷兰格罗宁根省西北部运河。亦称亨辛豪排水运河。亨辛豪运河全长约6.6千米，宽7.9米，河上建有1座船闸。该运河从缇斯托特流向佐特坎普，连通霍伦运河和哈伊特运河。亨辛豪运河位于霍伦运河与瓦尔夫赫伊斯特运河交汇处，以1852年成立的亨辛豪水务局的名称命名。19世纪中叶修建亨辛豪运河是为了改善马恩地区的排水状况。在此期间，已有的水道被改造成运河。例如连接佐特坎普和于尔勒姆的佐特坎普航道被开凿成运河，连接于尔勒姆和缇斯托特的接驳运河也被拓宽。此外，人们在佐特坎普附近的海堤上修建了一座排水闸。亨辛豪运河的修建极大地改善了马恩地区的排水状况。

Hunsingo Drainage Canal

A canal located in the northwest of the province of Groningen, the Netherlands. See Hunsingo Canal.

Hunte-Ems Canal

A canal located in Germany. The Hunte-Ems Canal is 69.6 kilometres in length and has 2 locks, connecting the Ems River with the Hunte River. Johann Georg Amann published an anonymous proposal for the Hunte-Ems Canal in 1826. Considering the improvement of the infrastructure and the benefits of the canal to the agricultural development in Oldenburg, the government finally approved the proposal. The actual construction began in 1855 and took about 38 years. The canal was opened in 1935. Later, because of the large shipping demands and the inefficiency of the canal, a new 29-kilometre-long route was constructed, which now serves as a coastal canal.

Huntsville Canal

A canal located in Alabama, the United States. See Fearn Canal.

Hunze River≈

A canalized river located near the border between Drenthe and Groningen in the Netherlands. Also called Oostermoerse Canal. The Hunze River has a

亨辛豪排水运河

荷兰格罗宁根省西北部运河。见亨辛豪运河。

洪特－埃姆斯运河

德国运河。洪特－埃姆斯运河全长69.6千米，连通埃姆斯河与洪特河，运河上建有2座船闸。1826年，约翰·格奥尔格·阿曼匿名发表修建洪特－埃姆斯运河的提案。考虑到修建运河可改善基础设施条件，促进奥尔登堡地区农业发展，当地政府最终批准该提案。运河工程于1855年动工，历时约38年完工。1935年，洪特－埃姆斯运河开通。后来，由于大规模货运需求与洪特－埃姆斯运河低效航运之间的矛盾愈发凸显，人们修建了一条长29千米的新航线，新航线如今发挥着沿海运河的作用。

亨茨维尔运河

美国亚拉巴马州运河。见弗恩运河。

浑泽河

荷兰德伦特省与格罗宁根省边界运河化河流。亦称奥斯特莫尔斯运河。浑泽河可通航河段长约9千

navigation length of about 9 kilometres. The name Hunze probably comes from German, meaning yellow or mud. Before the end of the 18th century, the Hunze River was mainly used to transport peat. However, this function was later taken over by the Stads Canal, and the Hunze River started to serve as a drainage river. In the 1960s, many meanders of the river were straightened to facilitate the drainage system and to facilitate agriculture. Channels were excavated and dams as well as pumping stations were constructed to keep the water under control. Since most of the water that fed the Hunze River was seepage water which made water level hard to control, the river was seen as more of a display of natural landscape after the 1990s. Now, some parts of the Hunze River have been transformed into nature reserves.

米。"浑泽"一词可能源于德语，意为"黄色"或"泥沙"。18世纪末之前，浑泽河主要用以运输泥煤，后被斯塔茨运河取代，而浑泽河则开始用作排水渠。20世纪60年代，为了方便排水和改善农业生产，浑泽河很多弯曲的河段被改直，同时人们为控制水位而开挖河道并修建大坝和泵站。由于浑泽河的水源大多是渗透水，其安全水位难以控制，航运受到一定影响。20世纪90年代以后，浑泽河被视为欣赏自然风光的好去处。现在该河部分河段已被改造成自然保护区。

Hurden Ship Canal

A canal located in central Switzerland. The Hurden Ship Canal is 500 metres in length, linking the upper section of Lake Zürich with its lower section. Shipping services between the two halves of the lake can bypass shallow waters. Its construction was completed in 1943. Due to the limitation of the width, the canal allows the passage of one ship only at a time and therefore, ships going upstream must give way to ships going downstream. The Hurden Ship Canal is spanned by a bridge which carries both road and railway. To the west of the bridge, the canal runs through a nature reserve with a significant bog landscape.

赫登通海运河

瑞士中部运河。赫登通海运河全长500米，连接苏黎世湖上游和下游两片水域，通航船只经此可避开浅滩。该运河1943年竣工，由于宽度受限，每次只能容纳1艘船只通过，故而上行船只需要给下行船只让路。赫登通海运河上建有1座大桥，桥上同时架设公路和铁路。在大桥西面，赫登通海运河流经一个有沼泽景观的自然保护区。

Ibrahimiya Canal

A canal located in Egypt. As one of the largest artificial canals in the world, the Ibrahimiya Canal is 350 kilometres in length. It runs northwards from the left bank of the Nile in Assiut, and flows a distance of 60 kilometres before dividing into two branches, one called the Bahr Yussef and the other called the Ibrahimiyah Canal. The canal was built in 1873 for irrigation under the Egypt Ministry of Public Works during the reign of Ismail Pasha, the Khedive of Egypt then. It provided perennial irrigation for a land of 2,300 square kilometres and flood irrigation for another 1,700 square kilometres. The Ibrahimya Canal is not navigable after Dairut, as it was designed only for irrigation.

伊布拉希米亚运河

埃及运河。伊布拉希米亚运河全长350千米，是世界上最大的人工运河之一。运河始于尼罗河左岸的艾斯尤特市，北行60千米后，分为两支，一条名为尤瑟夫运河，另一条则仍命名为伊布拉希米亚运河。1873年，伊斯梅尔·帕夏出任埃及总督期间，该运河在埃及公共工程部监管下修建而成，主要用于灌溉。运河常年可灌溉土地面积逾2 300平方千米，涨洪期可增加灌溉面积1 700平方千米。伊布拉希米亚运河在代鲁特之后的河段不可通航，仅作灌溉之用。

Ieper-IJzer Canal

A canal located in the province of West Flanders, Belgium. Also called Ieper River. Built between 1636 and 1641, the Ieper-IJzer Canal is 17 kilometres long, with a maximum width of 30 metres and an average depth of 2.3 metres. It starts from Heuvell and flows via the city of Ieper into the IJzer River at Fort Knokke. There are two locks on the canal. During the French-Spanish War in the 17th century and World War I in the 20th century, fortifications were built along the canal, which played an important military role. After World War I, roads, landscapes and farms near the canal were rebuilt. The canal was reopened in 1933 when 2 locks were added. The Ieper-IJzer Canal forms a beautiful

伊珀尔-艾泽尔运河

比利时西佛兰德省运河。亦称伊珀尔河。伊珀尔－艾泽尔运河于1636－1641年间开凿，全长17千米，最宽处30米，平均深度2.3米。运河始于赫弗尔市，流经伊珀尔城后在克诺克城堡汇入艾泽尔河。运河上建有2座船闸。17世纪法西战争以及20世纪第一次世界大战期间，运河沿岸建了防御工事，这些工事发挥了重要的军事作用。战后，运河附近的道路、景观和农场得到重建。1933年，伊珀尔－艾泽尔运河重新通航，并新修了2座船闸。运河堤岸与周边绿树和城墙

landscape with the embankments and surrounding trees and city walls.

共同形成了一道美丽的景观。

Ieper River

伊珀尔河

A canal located in the province of West Flanders, Belgium. See Ieper-IJzer Canal.

比利时西佛兰德省运河。见伊珀尔—艾泽尔运河。

Illinois and Michigan Canal

伊利诺伊-密歇根运河

A canal located in the midwestern United States. The Illinois and Michigan Canal is 154 kilometres in length, 18 metres in width and 1.8 metres in depth, linking the Great Lakes to the Mississippi River and the Gulf of Mexico. The canal drops 42 metres and comprises 15 locks. The construction of the canal was approved by Representative Abraham Lincoln and his House colleagues in the Illinois General Assembly in February 1835. The construction was started in 1836 but suspended for several years owing to a financial crisis in the State of Illinois. The canal was finished and opened in 1848. Its passenger service was popular until 1853, when a parallel railroad was put into use. The freight traffic was on the increase in the 1880s. It was replaced by the Sanitary and Ship Canal and the Illinois Waterway and was out of use in 1933. The canal links the scattered waters of the Illinois River and Lake Michigan, forming an all-water route from New York to St. Louis, by which it only took 12 days while 30—40 days were needed taking the Ohio River Route. The canal, with less time and freight costs, served as a reliable link for travelers, com-

美国中西部运河。伊利诺伊—密歇根运河全长154千米，宽18米，深1.8米，连通五大湖、密西西比河和墨西哥湾，全程水位落差为42米，建有15座船闸。1835年2月，时任伊利诺伊州议会议员的亚伯拉罕·林肯及其同仁投票批准了该运河修建工程。1836年，运河工程正式启动，后受伊利诺伊州金融危机影响，工程停滞数年。1848年，伊利诺伊—密歇根运河通航。该运河航运一直很繁忙，但到1853年，一条与河道平行的铁路投入运营后，运河航运量逐渐减少。19世纪80年代起，运河的航运量又开始日益增加。1933年，环境卫生和通海运河及伊利诺伊航道建成后，该运河正式关闭。伊利诺伊—密歇根运河将伊利诺伊河和密歇根湖分散的水域贯通，共同组成从纽约市至圣路易斯的全程水上通道。沿这条水路从纽约到圣路易斯只需12天，省时又省钱，而如

modities and ideas to circulate in the vast North American continent. The canal enabled the produce of farmers in northern Illinois to be shipped to eastern markets, making Illinois the grain basket of the country. It also benefited the mining, industry and manufacture as well as strengthening the cultural bonds to the Northeast, which were the prerequisites for Illinois to become the most populous inland state of the United Sates. The canal was also essential for the rapid development of Chicago since it drew trade from St. Louis and facilitated its industrialization, allowing Chicago to become the fastest growing city of the country in the 19th century. In 1964, the Illinois and Michigan Canal was designated a National Historic Landmark. It was listed in the National Register of Historic Places since 1966. The canal with its banks, also designated by the U.S. Congress in 1984 the country's first National Heritage Corridor, is now for historical, natural, economic and recreational uses.

果选择俄亥俄河一线，则需30—40天。该运河成为广袤北美大陆上的重要航线，方便了人员往来、商品流通以及思想的传播。运河开通后，伊利诺伊州北部的农民能够把农产品运送到东部市场，伊利诺伊州逐渐成为全国的粮食基地，采矿业、工业和手工业也随之发展起来，该州和美国东北部的文化联系也得到加强，这些都为伊利诺伊州成为美国人口最多的州创造了条件。同时，伊利诺伊—密歇根运河通航后，圣路易斯的大量贸易业务被吸引到芝加哥，促进了芝加哥的工业化进程。芝加哥之所以能够成为19世纪美国发展最快的城市，该运河功不可没。伊利诺伊—密歇根运河于1964年被列为美国国家历史名胜，1966年被收录于美国国家历史遗迹名录，1984年被国会设立为美国首条国家遗产廊道。如今，伊利诺伊—密歇根运河已经成为一个历史悠久、风光宜人、为人们提供休闲娱乐的景点，同时带动了当地的经济发展。

Illinois Waterway

A waterway located in the north of Illinois, the United States. The Illinois Waterway is 541 kilometres long, running from Lake Michigan and the Calumet Harbour at Chicago to the Illinois River

伊利诺伊航道

美国伊利诺伊州北部航道。伊利诺伊航道全长541千米，始于芝加哥的密歇根湖和卡柳梅特港区，在伊利诺伊州的格拉夫顿汇入伊

at Grafton, Illinois. It is a water system consisting of rivers, lakes, and canals to connect the Great Lakes and the Gulf of Mexico via the Illinois and Mississippi rivers. In 1848, the Illinois and Michigan Canal was finished, and became an important part of the Illinois Waterway. The waterway is not only significant for its role in transportation and industry in the Midwest but also for the function of its 8 extant locks that are managed by the United States Army Corps of Engineers. The Illinois waterways usually carry more than 29 million tonnes of cargo each year, including approximately 10 million tonnes of agricultural products and 4 million tonnes of fertilizers. There are two basic advantages concerning the transportation of bulk commodities, i.e., low cost and reliability.

利诺伊河。它是由河流、湖泊和运河组成的航道系统，通过伊利诺伊河和密西西比河将五大湖区和墨西哥湾贯通。1848年，伊利诺伊—密歇根运河竣工，成为伊利诺伊航道的重要组成部分。该航道对中西部交通和工业的发展起到重要作用，其现存的8座船闸依然发挥重要作用，这些船闸现由美国陆军工程兵团负责管理。伊利诺伊航道每年可运载2 900多万吨货物，其中包括大约1 000万吨农产品和400万吨肥料。通过该航道运输大宗商品，成本低廉且安全可靠。

Indiana Harbour and Ship Canal

印第安纳港口与通航运河

A canal located in Indiana, the United States. Linking the Grand Calumet River with Lake Michigan, the Indiana Harbour and Ship Canal consists of two branch canals and a harbour, including the 2-kilometre-long Lake George Branch, and the 3-kilometre-long Grand Calumet River Branch. The canal and the harbour were built in 1901 by Inland Steel Company. With the industrial development, the canal was filled with waste. Without any alternative to disposing wastes, the harbour and the canal have gradually accumulated approximately 760,000 cubic metres of sediment, thus hindering deep draught commercial navigation, reducing shipping capacity and meanwhile increasing ship-

美国印第安纳州运河。印第安纳港口与通航运河连通大卡柳梅特河与密歇根湖，由两条支流和一个港口组成，包括全长2千米的乔治湖支流和全长3千米的大卡柳梅特河支流。该运河和港口于1901年由内陆钢铁公司修建。随着工业的发展，大量工业垃圾排入运河中。由于没有采取垃圾处理措施，港口及运河中逐渐堆积了约76万立方米淤塞物，严重影响了运河的商用通航能力，并增加了运输成本。自20世纪90年代起，美国陆军工程兵团与东芝加哥河道管理局共同

ping costs. In the 1990s, the United States Army Corps of Engineers and the East Chicago Waterway Management District came up with plans for dredging this canal. The dredging was planned to be implemented over a period of 10 years to finally return the harbour to its authorized depths, with an additional 20 years of maintenance to remove future accumulated sediments.

推出一系列措施来疏通运河。疏通工作计划将耗时10年，最终港口恢复至政府要求的疏浚深度，再用20年进行维护，移除不断增多的淤积物。

Indragiri River≈

A canalized river located in the east of Sumatra, Indonesia. Originating in the Barisan Mountains, the Indragiri River is formed by the confluence of the Ombilin River and the Sinamar River, and finally flows eastwards into the South China Sea. It has a total length of 420 kilometres, with 150 kilometres navigable. The average water flow of the river is about 1,100 cubic metres per second. About 800 kilometres southeast of the river is Jakarta, Indonesia's capital. The areas the river travels through are dominated by the tropical rainforest climate, with an average annual temperature of 23 degrees Celsius and an average annual rainfall of 2,757 millimetres. The rain also provides a significant part of water for the river. The river boasts a variety of aquatic life and is suitable for recreation and fishing.

英德拉吉里河

印度尼西亚苏门答腊岛东部运河化河流。英德拉吉里河发源于巴里桑山脉，由翁比林河以及锡那玛河交汇形成，最终向东注入中国南海。该河平均流速为每秒1 100立方米，全长420千米，其中约150千米的河段可通航。其东南方向800千米处为印度尼西亚首都雅加达。英德拉吉里河所流经区域主要为热带雨林气候，年平均温度为23摄氏度，年平均降水量为2 757毫米，丰沛的降水也为该河提供了部分水源补给。该河水产丰富，适宜休闲和垂钓。

Industrial Canal

A canal located in Louisiana, the United States. Also called Inner Harbour Navigation Canal. The Industrial Canal is a 9-kilometre-long waterway

工业运河

美国路易斯安那州运河。亦称内港通航运河。工业运河全长9千米，连通密西西比河与庞恰特雷

which connects the Mississippi River to Lake Pontchartrain. As early as 1718, the French authorities planned to excavate a river-to-lake waterway between the Mississippi River and Lake Pontchartrain. But the plan never got off the ground. In the Spanish colonial times (1763—1803), Governor Hector Carondelet resumed the river-lake access plan. He had excavated the Carondelet Canal, linking the rear of New Orleans and Bayou St. John. However, the project of connecting the Carondelet Canal with the Mississippi failed due to the lack of technology and financing. Nearly 200 years after its original conception, the river-lake connection project finally moved forward. Under the authorization of the Louisiana State Government in July 1914, a deepwater shipping canal was built between the river and the lake. In June 1918, the canal was dredged. The waterway's official name used by the United States Army Corps of Engineers is Inner Harbour Navigation Canal, and the canal is called the Industrial Canal by commercial mariners and local residents.

恩湖。早在1718年，法国当局就计划在密西西比河和庞恰特雷恩湖之间开凿一条航道，但该计划未能实施。在西班牙殖民时期（1763—1803），总督赫克托—卡龙德莱特重新启动了河湖连通计划。他负责开凿卡龙德莱特运河，连接了新奥尔良北部与圣约翰河河口。然而，这一早先将河湖连通的计划终因技术落后和资金短缺而搁置。河湖连通的宏愿近200年后最终迎来实质性进展。1914年7月，路易斯安那州政府授权在密西西比河和庞恰特雷恩湖之间修建一条深水通航运河。1918年6月，该运河疏浚通航。美国陆军工程兵团将这条运河正式命名为内港通航运河，当地水手与居民则称其为"工业运河"。

Interlaken Ship Canal

A canal located in midwestern Switzerland. The Interlaken Ship Canal is 2.75 kilometres in length, linking Lake Thun with the town of Interlaken. The canal runs parallel to the Aare River and has the same water level as Lake Thun. It was built around 1890 to provide shipping services and respond to the expanding railway transportation.

因特拉肯大船运河

瑞士中西部运河。因特拉肯大船运河全长2.75千米，连接图恩湖和因特拉肯镇。该运河流向与阿勒河平行，水位与图恩湖持平。因特拉肯大船运河修建于1890年前后，主要为了提供船运服务，并应对铁路运输不断扩张的局面。

Irtysh-Karamay-Ürümqi Canal

A system of water transfer canals located in north-western China. The main trunk of the Irtysh-Karamay-Ürümqi Canal, with a span of 134 kilometres, starts from the 635 hydro-power project on the upper Irtysh, and splits into the west and the east trunk canals that run south and northwest respectively towards the Ulungur River, Xinjiang. The west branch flows towards Karamay while the east branch towards Ürümqi. There are several tunnels excavated along the course, of which the most famous is the Dingshan Tunnel with a length of 7,415 metres. The plan to construct the canal is also known as Irtysh River Diversion to Karamay (Ürümqi) Project or Project 635. In April 1997, the project was officially approved, and three months later the construction was started. In August 2000, it was completed and the water from the Irtysh was introduced to the torrid and arid Karamay. The canals irrigate 140,000 hectares of land along the waterways and provide water for the petroleum industry around Karamay, and thus considerably contribute to improving the living standard and boosting the economic development in the areas.

额尔齐斯－克拉玛依－乌鲁木齐运河

中国西北部调水运河系统。额尔齐斯－克拉玛依－乌鲁木齐运河总干渠全长134千米，始于新疆额尔齐斯河上游的635水利枢纽工程。该运河西干渠和东干渠分别向南和西北延伸至新疆乌伦古尔河，前者流向克拉玛依，后者流向乌鲁木齐。沿运河凿有许多隧道，其中最负盛名的是顶山隧道，全长7 415米。修建额尔齐斯－克拉玛依－乌鲁木齐运河的计划又称作"引额济克（乌）工程"或"635工程"。该运河项目于1997年4月正式获批，同年7月开始动工，2000年8月正式完工。建成后，运河顺利将额尔齐斯河河水调入炎热干旱的克拉玛依市。额尔齐斯－克拉玛依－乌鲁木齐运河为沿岸14万公顷的土地提供灌溉用水，同时也为克拉玛依市周边的石油工业提供用水，在很大程度上改善了当地人民的生活水平，促进了区域经济发展。

Isabella Canal

A cross-border canal located in Europe. Straddling Belgium and the Netherlands, the Isabella Canal is 5.5 kilometres long. It mainly flows in the Netherlands, starting from the Leopold Canal in Belgium

伊莎贝拉运河

欧洲跨国运河。伊莎贝拉运河流经比利时与荷兰两国，全长5.5千米，主体在荷兰境内，始于比利时利奥波德运河，注入布拉克曼湾。

and emptying into the Braakman. With an agreement reached between the Netherlands and Belgium, the Isabella Canal was excavated in 1920 as a way to improve the drainage system of the Braakman area, the Netherlands.

1920年，荷兰和比利时两国签署协议开凿伊莎贝拉运河，用以改善荷兰布拉克曼地区排水系统。

Isle≈

伊勒河

A canalized river located in southwestern France. The Isle is 255 kilometres in length and covers 7,700 square kilometres in drainage basin area. A part of this river once served as a canal. According to historical records, the navigation to the town of Périgueux was greatly obstructed before it was officially canalized. The project was launched in 1768 and completed by a private company in 1820, but it was not until 1837 that the upstream navigation was inaugurated from Dordogne to Périgueux. This section was 144 kilometres long, and yet it has now been abandoned due to the declining commercial navigation.

法国西南部运河化河流。伊勒河全长255千米，流域面积达7 700平方千米。该河流的部分河段曾具有运河功能。据历史记载，通往佩里格市的航道一度严重淤塞，直到正式运河化改造后才可顺利通行。1768年，该运河疏浚项目正式启动，由一家私人企业负责施工，1820年竣工。但从多尔多涅河到佩里格逆流而上的航线直到1837年才正式通航，这一段运河全长144千米，现已随着商业航运的衰落而被弃用。

Istanbul Canal

伊斯坦布尔运河

A canal under construction located in Turkey. The Istanbul Canal is a project designed for the Turkish Republic's centennial in 2023, which is excavated on the European side of Turkey. It is planned to connect the Black Sea to the Marmara Sea, and hence to the Aegean and the Mediterranean. The new canal will bypass the current Bosphorus and divide the European side of Istanbul into two parts, forming an island between the continents of Asia

土耳其在建运河。伊斯坦布尔运河项目是土耳其共和国为庆祝2023年建国100周年而设计，拟在土耳其的欧洲境内修建，连通黑海和马尔马拉海，进而通往爱琴海和地中海。新运河将绕开博斯普鲁斯海峡，将伊斯坦布尔目前在欧洲的部分一分为二，从而在欧洲大陆和亚洲大陆之间形成一座

and Europe, and the island would be surrounded by the Black Sea, the Marmara Sea, the new canal and the Bosphorus. The construction of the canal began in April 2013, and it will come into use in 2023. The planned length of the waterway will be 45 to 50 kilometres and its designed depth is 25 metres. It will be 150 metres wide on the surface and 120 metres at the bed. These dimensions will enable the canal to be navigable for large vessels and even submarines. The Istanbul Canal is built with the attempts to reduce the marine traffic through the Bosphorus and to minimize the risks and dangers caused by tankers. It will also preclude the pollution caused by cargo vessels passing through or berthed in the Marmara Sea before entering the southern entrance of the Bosphorus.

新的岛屿，这座岛屿四面环绕黑海、马尔马拉海、伊斯坦布尔运河和博斯普鲁斯海峡。2013年4月，运河工程开工，预计将于2023年正式通航。建成之后，该运河全长将达45—50千米，深25米，河面宽度达150米，河床宽度达120米，可供大型船舶甚至潜水艇通行。修建伊斯坦布尔运河旨在分担博斯普鲁斯海峡的通航量，降低油轮通行可能带来的风险，也可以防止货轮通过博斯普鲁斯海峡南入口前停经马尔马拉海时造成污染。

Jakarta Flood Canal

A canal system located in Jakarta, Indonesia. Also called Banjir Canal. As Jakarta has long suffered from floods, the main function of the Jakarta Flood Canal is to regulate the surface run-off of rivers in Jakarta, divert the flows northward to the sea, and minimize their detrimental impact on human activities. It flows northward from the south to make a circuit surrounding the inner city. The Jakarta Flood Canal consists of the West Flood Canal and the East Flood Canal. The West Flood Canal was first built in 1913, flowing from Matraman to Karet. It connects the Ciliwung River, the Krukut River and the Cideng River. The canal constructed in the first phase is 4.5 kilometres long, all excavated manually, with a width ranging from 13.5 to 16 metres. The second phase of the construction was carried out from 1915 to 1919. The canal was then extended northward from Karet into the sea at Muara Angke, a small fishing port in the north of Jakarta. In 1918, when Jakarta experienced its fourth catastrophic flood in history, the Dutch colonial government appointed Hendrik van Breen as the engineer in charge to build the Jakarta Flood Canal. In 1973, the Indonesian government, with the assistance of Netherland Engineering Consultancy, formulated the Master Plan for Drainage and Flood Control of Jakarta. As a part of the plan, the East Flood Canal was excavated on 22 June 2002, the 475th anniversary of Jakarta. The accelerated urbanization in Jakarta has not been effectively integrated and balanced with the natural river system, resulting in

雅加达泄洪运河

印度尼西亚雅加达运河系统。亦称班吉尔运河。由于雅加达长期遭受洪水侵袭，雅加达泄洪运河的主要功能是调节雅加达市内各河流的径流量，引流北上入海，减少对人类活动的影响和危害。该运河整体从南向北环绕城区，由西泄洪运河和东泄洪运河组成。西泄洪运河1913年开凿，从马特拉曼流至卡雷特，连通芝利翁河、克鲁库特河和西登河。该运河一期工程全长4.5千米，全靠人工挖掘而成，宽度13.5—16米。二期工程（1915—1919）从卡雷特继续向北开凿，于雅加达北部小渔港麻拉红溪注入大海。1918年，雅加达经历有史以来第四次灾难性的大洪灾后，当时的荷兰殖民政府决定委派工程师亨德里克·范布林负责修建雅加达泄洪运河。1973年，印度尼西亚政府在荷兰工程咨询公司的协助下制定了《雅加达排水与防洪总体规划》。作为规划项目之一，东泄洪运河于2002年6月22日雅加达建城475周年纪念日开工修建。雅加达快速发展的城市化进程未能与自然河流系统有效融合和保持平衡，导致地面沉降严重，在雨季难以应对暴雨与洪水侵袭。雅加达城区目前占地约650平方千米，而

serious land subsidence and insufficient capacity to accommodate rainstorms and floods in rainy seasons. Jakarta now encompasses about 650 square kilometres, while the Jakarta Flood Canal is only able to protect less than 5 percent of the area from flooding.

雅加达泄洪运河只能保护不到5%的地区免受洪涝灾害。

James River and Kanawha Canal

A canal located in southern Virginia, the United States. The James River and Kanawha Canal is about 317 kilometres long, connecting the Piedmont and Tidewater regions with 90 locks along the route. It was built to create a route to transport people and goods inland from Richmond. The project was proposed by George Washington when he was young. He advocated that a water route to the West would play a pivotal role in stimulating Virginia's economy. The construction of the canal was passed by the Virginia General Assembly and started in 1785. In 1790, the James River Company was established with Washington as the honorary head. In the following years, the Civil War, the shortage of funds and severe floods took a heavy toll on the construction progress. By 1851, the canal reached its furthest point, Buchanan. The canal not only saved time and costs of travelling but also significantly prompted the shipment of agricultural produce, leading to the trade boom in Virginia. Yet its importance declined greatly with the development of the railroad transportation. In 1971, the James River and Kanawha Canal Historic District was listed on the National Register of Historic Places. Now the

詹姆斯河－卡诺瓦运河

美国弗吉尼亚州南部运河。詹姆斯河—卡诺瓦运河全长约317千米，连接皮埃蒙特与泰德沃特地区，沿线共建有90座船闸。修建该运河旨在为弗吉尼亚州首府里士满提供航运服务。乔治·华盛顿年轻时就提出了该运河修建计划。他认为，修建一条通往西部的航道对于促进弗吉尼亚州经济发展至关重要。1785年，弗吉尼亚州议会批准了詹姆斯河—卡诺瓦运河修建计划并开始实施。1790年，詹姆斯河公司成立，由华盛顿担任名誉负责人。但此后因受美国南北战争、资金短缺以及大洪水的影响，运河修建进程缓慢。1851年，运河最远修至布坎南。得益于詹姆斯河—卡诺瓦运河，弗吉尼亚州居民出行时间大大缩短，交通成本也大幅降低，农产品运输更加便利，该州的贸易也随之蓬勃发展起来。随着铁路运输的发展，该运河的重要性日益降低。1971年，詹姆斯河—卡诺瓦运河历史街区被列入

district boasts boat rides and historic exhibits along the route.

美国国家历史遗迹名录。如今，游客可乘坐小船在运河沿岸观赏历史遗迹。

Jamestown Canal

An inland canal located in Ireland. The Jamestown Canal is 2.7 kilometres long. It was originally constructed by the Commissioners of Inland Navigation in 1775 to bypass a non-navigable section of the Shannon River between Jamestown and Drumsna to upgrade the Shannon Navigation. Initially it was very narrow with two S-bends, shallow and dangerous. Repairs were recommended after an inspection of the canal in 1794, but progress in the necessary modifications to the canal was slow. It was not until the 1840s that the Jamestown Canal was made satisfactorily navigable. There is a lock named Albert Lock built on the canal in 1848. Today, the Jamestown Canal and the Albert Lock are still in use though sometimes the lock will be closed for high flood levels.

詹姆斯敦运河

爱尔兰内陆运河。詹姆斯敦运河全长2.7千米，1775年由爱尔兰内陆航运部负责修建，旨在开凿一段新航道，绕过香农河詹姆斯敦至德拉姆斯纳之间不可通航的河段，从而提高香农河的航运能力。起初，该运河非常狭窄，全线有2个S型弯道，且河道浅，航行危险。1794年，在对运河进行勘察之后，有人提出了重修建议，但随后的工程进展十分缓慢。直到19世纪40年代，詹姆斯敦运河才变得真正适于通航。1848年，阿尔伯特船闸建成。如今，詹姆斯敦运河与阿尔伯特船闸仍在使用，但洪水水位较高时，船闸会关闭。

Jianghan Canal

A canal located in Hubei Province, China. The Jianghan Canal is 67 kilometres long, 3.2 metres deep and 60 metres wide. The canal ranks Class III with the navigation capacity of 1,000 tonnes. It is the longest man-made canal built after the founding of the People's Republic of China. The canal links the Yangtze River with the Hanjiang River. It is a part of the Middle Route Project for South-to-North

江汉运河

中国湖北省运河。江汉运河全长67千米，水深3.2米，宽60米，为三级航道，可容最大载重量达1 000吨的船舶通行。该运河是中华人民共和国成立后开凿的最长的人工运河。江汉运河连通长江和汉江，是南水北调中线工程和引江济汉工程的一部分。江汉运河2009年动

Water Transfer as well as the Project for Water Diversion from the Yangtze River to the Hanjiang River. The construction was started in 2009 and completed in 2013. Then the canal was opened in 2014. Along the canal, there are 2 ship locks, 3 turning basins, 54 road bridges and 2 railway bridges. The construction of the canal improves the ecological and irrigation conditions and enhances the capability of water supply. It also plays an important role in flood control, protecting local people's lives and property. Moreover, the canal bypassing Wuhan shortens the route from the Yangtze River to the Hanjiang River by 680 kilometres and significantly saves the time and cost of navigation. It helps to form a golden circle of canals with a total length of 810 kilometres, boosting the local economic development. Currently, the local government is making efforts to create a zone of ecotourism in this region, and a series of international marathons and road cycling races have been held.

工修建, 2013年竣工, 次年通航。河上建有2座船闸, 3处回船池, 54座跨河公路桥梁和2座铁路桥梁。江汉运河改善了沿线的生态、灌溉和供水条件, 同时也兼具防洪功能, 在保护沿岸人民群众生命与财产安全方面发挥着重要作用。此外, 江汉运河的修建提升了长江至汉江河段的航运能力, 使原先绕道武汉的航程缩短了680千米, 极大地节省了通航时间和成本。该运河形成了一个长达810千米的黄金航道圈, 促进了当地经济发展。目前, 当地政府正着力打造一个环江汉运河生态旅游带, 已有多场国际马拉松比赛和公路自行车赛在运河沿岸举办。

Jianghuai Canal

A canal under construction located in Anhui Province in eastern China. The Jianghuai Canal will link the Huaihe River, the Chaohu Lake and the Yangtze River, with an estimated total length of 700 kilometres after its completion. On the canal will be built 3 aqueducts and 7 locks which can lift ships of a tonnage over 1,000. More than 70 bridges will be rebuilt too. The canal stands as the kernel part of the project to divert water from the Yangtze River to the Huaihe River. The construction of this canal was

江淮运河

中国东部安徽省在建运河。江淮运河建成后将连通淮河、巢湖和长江, 全长约700千米。运河上预计建造7座可提升逾1 000吨级船舶的船闸, 改建70多座桥梁, 并修筑3座渡槽。该运河是引江济淮工程的核心部分, 2016年12月正式动工修建, 目前已完成70%, 预计2023年通航。江淮运河的功能以调水为主, 兼顾航运, 同时可改善

officially started in December 2016. At present, 70% of the project has been completed, and it is expected to be opened in 2023. The canal mainly serves for the purpose of water transfer, and at the same time it will promote navigation and improve the water quality of the Huaihe River and the Chaohu Lake. When the project is finished, it will improve the transportation between the Yangtze River and the Huaihe River and stands as a second estuary of the Huaihe River. The canal, together with the Shaying River, the Heyu Line and the Wushen Canal under construction, will form an important modern waterway parallel to the Beijing-Hangzhou Grand Canal, and it bears great significance to improve the waterway transportation network in Anhui Province and even in China.

淮河和巢湖的水质。运河竣工后，将缓解安徽省境内淮河与长江两大水系航运不畅的情况，同时为淮河增加第二个入海口。该运河与正在修建的沙颍河、合裕线与芜申运河航道连通，将共同形成一条与京杭大运河平行的现代化重要航道，对完善安徽乃至中国的水路交通网络意义重大。

Jiaolai Canal

胶莱运河

A canal located in Shandong Province, China. Formerly called Yunlianghe River. The Jiaolai Canal has a length of 130 kilometres and a total drainage area of 5,479 square kilometres. It runs through the Shandong Peninsula, connecting the Yellow Sea with the Dagu River, thus serving as a part of the link between the Yellow Sea and the Bohai Gulf. From the watershed in the east of Yaojia Village in Pingdu City, it branches into two river courses that extend respectively to the south and the north. The South Jiaolai River, also known as South Canal, is 30 kilometres in length and covers an area of 1,505 square kilometres. It flows into the Jiaozhou Bay of the Yellow Sea. The North Jiaolai River, also known

中国山东省运河。旧称运粮河。胶莱运河全长130千米，流域总面积5 479平方千米，贯穿山东半岛，连通黄海和大沽河，是黄海与渤海湾之间航道的一部分。该运河以平度市姚家村东的分水岭为界分为南北两条河道：南胶莱河，又称南运河，长30千米，流域面积1 505平方千米，注入黄海胶州湾；北胶莱河，又称北运河，长100千米，流域面积3 974平方千米，注入渤海湾。古时江南地区的粮米经由此河运往京师，故胶莱运河也以运粮河著称。胶莱运河修建于元朝。元世

as North Canal, is 100 kilometres in length and has a drainage area of 3,974 square kilometres, flowing into the Bohai Gulf. In the past, the Jiaolai Canal was known as Yunlianghe River because the grain and rice from the area south of the Yangtze River were shipped to the capital via this waterway. It was first built in the Yuan Dynasty (1206—1368). After occupying the area south of the Yangtze River, Kublai Khan, Emperor Shizu of the Yuan Dynasty planned to transport grain from the south to the capital by sea. In order to shorten the voyage and avoid the wind and waves at the Chengshan Cape, he decided to excavate the Jiaolai Canal. The excavation of the canal began in 1280, but was abolished in the middle of the project because of its huge amount of work and high cost. In the Ming Dynasty (1368—1644), the imperial court decided to continue the excavation of the canal. Since 1538, the Jiaolai Canal between the Haicang County and the Jiaozhou Bay was dredged. The canal was soon suspended due to the weak navigable capacity of some reaches caused by the immature canal construction technology at that time and the unstable water source. From the mid-Ming Dynasty to the end of the Qing Dynasty (1616—1911), the government implemented the policy of banning the shipping by sea due to the rampant pirates along the coast. The Grand Canal became the main channel for transporting grain and goods between the north and the south of China. The Jiaolai Canal therefore gradually lost its shipping value, and the dredging work of the canal was shelved since then. After the founding of the People's Republic of China, the Jiaolai Canal

祖忽必烈占领江南地区以后,欲将南方的粮食通过海运送至京师,为了缩短航程以及避开成山角处的风浪,决定开凿胶莱运河。运河开凿工程始于1280年,后因工程量大、耗资多,工程中途废止。明朝时期,政府决定继续开凿胶莱运河,自1538年起,海沧县至胶州湾之间的胶莱运河全部疏通。但因当时运河修建技术不成熟,部分河段通航能力较弱,加之水源不稳定,运河不久后停航。明代中期至清末,由于沿海倭寇猖獗,政府实行海禁政策,京杭大运河成为南北地区运输粮食和货物的主航道,胶莱运河逐渐失去航运价值,对该运河的疏浚工作也自此中断。中华人民共和国成立后,胶莱运河主要发挥泄洪和灌溉功能,未用于航运。

mainly acted as a water course for flood discharging and irrigation, but it remains unnavigable.

Johan Friso Canal

A canal located in the province of Friesland, the Netherlands. The Johan Friso Canal is 26 kilometres in length, connecting the city of Stavoren with the Prinses-Margriet Canal, which it meets at the east of Hommerts and north of the Koevord Lake. The canal runs over 4 lakes, namely the Heeger Lake, the Fluessen, the De Holken and the Morra. Currently, the Johan Friso Canal is mainly used for inland commercial navigation and leisure boating.

John Bennett Johnston Waterway

A canal located in southern Louisiana, the United States. See Red River Navigation.

Jonglei Canal

A cross-border canal in planning located in Africa. The Jonglei Canal crosses between Sudan and Egypt. The original aim of constructing this canal is to deflect the waterway from the Sudd wetlands of South Sudan to keep more water downstream for the use of agriculture in Sudan and Egypt, because it is estimated that 50% of the White Nile's water evaporates in the massive Sudd swamp. In 1978, the excavation of the Jonglei Canal was commenced. The project was brought to a halt in 1984 under the influence of the civil war between northern

约翰－费里索运河

荷兰弗里斯兰省运河。约翰－费里索运河全长26千米，连接斯塔福伦市与玛格丽特公主运河。该运河在霍默茨村以东、库福德湖以北与玛格丽特公主运河连通。该运河流经四个湖泊，分别是海赫湖、弗卢埃森湖、德霍尔肯湖和莫拉湖。目前，约翰－费里索运河主要用于内陆商业航运和休闲游船通行。

约翰·班尼特·约翰斯顿航道

美国路易斯安那州南部运河。见雷德河航道。

琼莱运河

非洲规划中的跨国运河。琼莱运河流经埃及和苏丹两国。因白尼罗河流经苏德沼泽时会蒸发损耗约50%的水量，开凿琼莱运河的水利项目旨在使白尼罗河绕开苏德沼泽，确保更多水流到下游，为苏丹和埃及的农业生产提供保障。运河1978年正式开凿。1984年，由于苏丹南北内战，项目停工，当时这条计划360千米长的运河已完成约三分之二。2005年《全面和平协

and southern Sudan. At the time, about two thirds of the 360-kilometre-long canal had already been finished. With the signature of the Comprehensive Peace Agreement in 2005, there arose voices suggesting resuming the excavation of the Jonglei Canal. The government of South Sudan hesitated to continue the project. The Jonglei Canal is projected to generate an additional 4.5 cubic kilometres of the White Nile water available annually, which is to be equally shared by Sudan and Egypt. The hard-to-predict ecological risks of the canal may fall on South Sudan. The potentially catastrophic environmental and social issues may include the collapse of fisheries, shortage of grazing areas, disruption of vital wildlife migration routes, and reduction of rainfall in the region. With the ongoing dialogues among nations and the arguments over the pros and cons of building the Jonglei Canal, an agreement has not been reached yet.

议》签订后，不断有提议希望重启该运河项目，南苏丹政府则持观望态度。修建琼莱运河可使尼罗河每年增加4.5立方千米的可利用水资源，供苏丹和埃及共享。但该项目也有可能给南苏丹的生态环境带来风险，引发环境和社会问题，例如渔业萧条、放牧区短缺、珍稀动物迁移路线被干扰及降水减少等问题。目前，苏丹和埃及两国仍在就该项目进行磋商，围绕琼莱运河项目的利弊展开讨论，但尚未达成一致意见。

Jonkers Canal

约恩克斯运河

A canal located in the province of Friesland, the Netherlands. See Heloma Canal.

荷兰弗里斯兰省运河。见黑洛玛运河。

Jouy-Metz Canal

茹伊—梅斯运河

A canal located in the province of Moselle, France. The Jouy-Metz Canal is 8.5 kilometres long. The construction of the canal began in 1867. It served as a part of the modernization of river infrastructure in northeast France.

法国摩泽尔省运河。茹伊—梅斯运河全长8.5千米，1867年开凿。该运河当时是法国东北部河流基础设施现代化建设工程的一部分。

Juliana Canal

A canal located in the province of Limburg, the Netherlands. The Juliana Canal, named after Juliana, Queen of the Netherlands (1948—1980), is 36 kilometres long and 60 metres wide, which offers an alternative to the unnavigable section of River Meuse from Maastricht to Maasbracht. The construction of the canal was started in 1925 and completed in 1934 while the official opening was in 1935. It was renovated and enlarged during 2016 and 2018. The canal was of vital significance for the development of coal mining in southern Limburg since its creation, but this function was terminated in the 1970s as alternative options of energy emerged. It also played an important role in World War II. In 1940, the canal stopped the German troops invading Flanders, which gave the Belgians more time to mobilize their army and strengthen their defence lines. In 1944, when the allied forces were chasing after the retreating Germans, they were also stopped by the canal, as the Germans blew up all the bridges. On 27 January 2004, the canal drew international attention as part of the town of Stein was in danger of being flooded after a dyke subsided. The cause appeared to be a leak from an old water pipe from the time when the canal was built.

Junction Canal (France)

A canal located in southern France. The Junction Canal is about 5 kilometres in length with an eleva-

朱丽安娜运河

荷兰林堡省运河。朱丽安娜运河因荷兰女王朱丽安娜（1948—1980年在位）而得名，全长36千米，宽60米。由于默兹河从马斯特里赫特到马斯布拉赫特段不能通航，这条运河便成为了一条理想的替代航道。朱丽安娜运河1925年开凿，1934年竣工，次年正式通航。运河于2016—2018年间得以翻新和扩建。朱丽安娜运河在竣工后相当长的一段时间里，对促进林堡南部煤矿业的发展发挥了重要作用。随着替代能源的出现，20世纪70年代后，该运河对于煤矿业的航运价值趋于消失。朱丽安娜运河在第二次世界大战中发挥了重要作用。1940年，运河阻止了德军入侵佛兰德，为比利时人调动军队和加强防线争取了更多时间。1944年，因所有桥梁被德军炸毁，盟军在追击撤退的德军时，也被该运河阻挡。2004年1月27日，该运河上的一个堤坝坍塌，斯泰因镇部分地区有被淹没的危险，引发了国际社会关注。事故原因与运河修建时安装的一根旧输水管道泄漏有关。

交界运河（法国）

法国南部运河。交界运河全长约5千米，水位落差23米，建有7座船

tion of 23 metres and 7 locks. It is exclusively located in the town of Sallèles, linking the Midi Canal to the Robine Canal via the Aude River. The canal's water supply is provided by the Midi Canal. The construction began in 1690 and finished in 1780 due to multiple obstacles. It was opened in 1787. Currently, the Junction Canal, boasting breathtaking landscapes, is a perfect place for walking, cycling, and fishing.

闸。整条运河全部位于萨莱莱镇，通过奥得河连通米迪运河和罗比纳运河。运河1690年开凿，经历各种困难后，1780年最终竣工。1787年正式通航。如今，交界运河两岸风光旖旎，是散步、骑行与垂钓的理想去处。

Junction Canal (the United States)

交界运河（美国）

An abandoned canal located in New York and Pennsylvania, the United States. Also called Arnot Canal. The Junction Canal was 29 kilometres in length and had 11 locks. In 1853, the canal was built to lengthen the reach of the Chemung Canal to join the canal systems in Pennsylvania. The Junction Canal was partly opened in 1854 and completely finished in 1858. With the increasing number of railroads and severe damage caused by a flood in 1865, the canal began to fall into decline. Later, it was closed in 1871 and then abandoned.

美国纽约州和宾夕法尼亚州废弃运河。亦称阿诺特运河。交界运河全长29千米，建有11座船闸。该运河开凿于1853年，旨在延长希芒运河的航程，使其与宾夕法尼亚州运河网相连通。1854年，交界运河部分河段通航，1858年全线竣工。后因铁路数量增加，加之受到1865年洪水造成的严重损坏，交界运河逐渐减少了使用。1871年运河关闭后便遭废弃。

Juniata Division

朱尼亚塔运河段

A canal located in Pennsylvania, the United States. The Juniata Division is one of the five sections of the Pennsylvania Main Line of Public Works. It is 64 kilometres long, connecting the Duncan's Island and Hollidaysburg. The construction began in 1827 and was completed and opened in 1832. There were 86 locks and 25 aqueducts along the

美国宾夕法尼亚州运河。朱尼亚塔运河段是宾夕法尼亚公共交通干线5个组成部分之一，全长64千米，连接邓肯岛和霍利迪斯堡。运河1827年开凿，1832年竣工通航，共建有86座船闸和25座渡槽，另有3座水库为运河上游提供水源。

canal. In addition, 3 reservoirs were constructed on Juniata tributaries to keep the upper parts of the canal full of water. In 1857, the entire Main Line was sold to the Pennsylvania Railroad. The Juniata Division played a decisive role in the economic development of central Pennsylvania. The canal was especially important in boosting the growth of the region's early charcoal iron industry. Like the rest of the Pennsylvania Canal system, the canal also gains technological importance as an exceptional case of incipient civil engineering. The Juniata Division was listed on the National Register of Historic Places in 2002.

1857年，整条运河主航道出售给宾夕法尼亚铁路公司。朱尼亚塔运河段对宾夕法尼亚州中部地区的经济发展至关重要，极大促进了该地区早期炭铁工业的发展。与宾夕法尼亚运河系统内的其他运河一样，朱尼亚塔运河段也是早期土木工程技术的卓越范例。2002年，朱尼亚塔运河段被列入美国国家历史遗迹名录。

Kaiser Wilhelm Canal

A canal located in Schleswig-Holstein, Germany. See Kiel Canal (Germany).

Kaiser Willem-Alexander Canal

A canal located in the Netherlands. The Kaiser Willem-Alexander Canal is 6 kilometres in length and connects the Scholten Channel and the Bladder Canal. It is the first infrastructural project named after Willem-Alexander (1967—), the King of the Netherlands. With its presence since 2013, it is possible to sail from Erica to Ter Apel. It is also a part of the larger Veen Canal Project, which is aimed at drawing more pleasure boats to the Peat District in the provinces of Drenthe and Groningen. To this end, dozens of locks and bridges have been built on this canal.

Kakatiya Canal

A canal located in Telangana State, India. Also known as Sri Ram Sagar Canal. The Kakatiya Canal is about 284 kilometres in length. The canal links the Sri Ram Sagar Reservoir with the Lower Manair Dam and provides irrigation as well as potable water for the major cities of North Telangana, making a great contribution to the agricultural development in this region. Serving as an instrumental inter-river basin transfer link, it feeds the water from the Godavari River into the Krishna River basin. The Kakatiya Canal is also of great importance in

皇帝威廉运河

德国石勒苏益格—荷尔斯泰因州运河。见基尔运河（德国）。

国王威廉·亚历山大运河

荷兰运河。国王威廉·亚历山大运河全长6千米，连通斯霍尔滕航道和布莱德运河。该运河是荷兰第一个以国王威廉·亚历山大（1967— ）之名命名的基础建设项目。2013年以来，人们可以经由该运河从埃里卡航行至泰尔阿珀尔村。国王威廉·亚历山大运河是更大的芬运河工程的一部分，其上建有多座船闸和桥梁，目的在于吸引更多的游客到德伦特省和格罗宁根省的泥炭产区观光旅行。

卡卡提亚运河

印度特伦甘纳邦运河。亦称斯里拉姆萨加尔运河。卡卡提亚运河全长约284千米，连接斯里拉姆萨加尔水库和马乃尔下游大坝，满足了特伦甘纳邦北部主要城市的灌溉和生活用水需求，为当地农业发展做出了巨大贡献。卡卡提亚运河把戈达瓦里河水引入克里希纳河流域，是跨流域水量调节的重要渠道。此外，该运河上还修建了发电厂，利用水位落差进行水力发电。

hydropower generation, equipped with power plants to harness the power of the moving water.

Kammer Canal

卡默运河

An inland canal located in the state of Mecklenburg-Vorpommern in Germany. The Kammer Canal is a part of the Upper Havel Waterway. The 5.25-kilometre-long canal runs from the Zierke Lake to the Woblitz Lake. It was built around 1790 and expanded between 1840 and 1843 to connect Neustrelitz with the Upper Havel Waterway. The canal is now under the administration of the Eberswalde Water and Shipping Office.

德国梅克伦堡—前波美拉尼亚州内陆运河。卡默运河为哈弗尔河上游航道的一部分，全长5.25千米，连通齐尔克湖与沃布利茨湖。运河1790年前后开凿，1840—1843年间进行了扩建，旨在连接新施特雷利茨与哈弗尔河上游航道。卡默运河现由埃伯斯瓦尔德水务船务局负责管理。

Karakum Canal

卡拉库姆运河

A canal located in Turkmenistan. The Karakum Canal is 1,375 kilometres long, spanning the southern border of the country. As one of the largest irrigation and water supply canals in the world, it diverts water from the Amu Darya River in the Central Asia to the Karakum Desert, transferring 13 cubic kilometres per year. The construction began in 1954, and was completed in 1988. Upon completion, the canal supplies water for cotton cultivation and daily use in Ashgabat, the capital of Turkmenistan. About 50% of the water would not make its way to the final destination but loses along the canal, forming a series of lakes. This also makes the ground water rise and hence cause soil salinization.

土库曼斯坦运河。卡拉库姆运河全长1 375千米，流经土库曼斯坦南部边境。该运河是世界上最大的灌溉兼供水运河之一，将位于中亚的阿姆河水引至卡拉库姆沙漠，每年输水量为13立方千米。卡拉库姆运河1954年开凿，1988年竣工，建成后，还为土库曼斯坦首都阿什哈巴德的棉花种植提供水源，并满足该市日常供水需求。在供水过程中，50%的水量损耗于运河沿线，由此形成了一系列湖泊，并提升了地下水水位，也带来土壤盐碱化的问题。

Karlberg Canal

A canal located in western and central Stockholm, Sweden. The Karlberg Canal disconnects the King's Islet from the northern municipality Solna. The canal was designed primarily for timber transport. It was originally excavated between 1832 and 1833. Upon completion, it was about 685.8 metres long and 1.8 metres deep. During the 1840s, the canal was dredged and further extended in the 1860s. The entire waterway was deepened to between 3 and 5.9 metres. Two bridges stretch over the canal, one of which is the Ekelund Bridge built in 1956, a fixed concrete one that replaced the former steel swing bridge, and the other is the Essingeleden Karlberg Bridge near the place where the Karlberg Canal flows into the Ulvsundas Lake. The traffic on the Karlberg Canal has been very lively. For many years, it has been used to ship passengers between Old Town (Knights' Islet) and Sundbyberg.

卡尔伯格运河

瑞典斯德哥尔摩中西部运河。卡尔伯格运河将国王岛和北部城市索尔纳隔开。运河旨在运输木材，1832—1833年间修建，建成后长约685.8米，深约1.8米。19世纪40年代，人们对该运河进行了疏浚扩建，并于19世纪60年代进一步加深了整条航道，深度达3—5.9米。卡尔伯格运河上建有2座大桥。其中，建于1956年的伊克隆德桥是一座固定的混凝土桥，取代了之前的钢制平旋桥；另一座为爱森格兰登·卡尔伯格桥，位于卡尔伯格运河与乌尔夫逊达湖的交汇处。长期以来，卡尔伯格运河交通繁忙，人们通过运河穿梭于老城（骑士岛）和松德比伯格两地。

Karl Heine Canal

A canal located in the west of Leipzig, Germany. The Karl Heine Canal is 3.3 kilometres long, linking the port of Linden to the White Elster. There are 15 bridges stretching over the canal and only small boats can pass through. The canal was named after Karl Heine, a lawyer in Leipzig, who first put forward the proposal of excavating a navigable canal as a connection between River Weisse Elster and River Saale. In 1898, all sections of the canal were completed and opened. The canal was renovated in

卡尔海涅运河

德国莱比锡西部运河。卡尔海涅运河全长3.3千米，连通林登港和白鹊河，河上共建有15座桥梁，仅供小型船只通行。运河得名于莱比锡律师卡尔·海涅，他最早提出修建该运河以连通维瑟埃尔斯特河和萨勒河。1898年，卡尔海涅运河所有河段竣工并通航。20世纪90年代，人们对卡尔海涅运河进行了翻修重建，并在沿岸筑起步道。2012

the 1990s, with a foot path paved along it. In 2012, the city council decided to extend the canal to the port of Lindenau and 18 million euros had been invested on the project by 2015. The Karl Heine Canal is now well preserved, standing as a historical monument of the waterborne navigation development in Germany.

年,市议会决定将该运河与林德诺港口连通,至2015年竣工时共投入了1 800万欧元。卡尔海涅运河迄今保存完好,在德国运河史上具有重要纪念意义。

Kaskaskia River

A canalized river located in southern and central Illinois, the United States. As a branch of the Mississippi River, the Kaskaskia River extends about 523 kilometres, the longest in Illinois, with its drainage area covering about 10.2% of Illinois. The confluence of the river with the Mississippi River is 16 kilometres northwest of Chester. The lower reach of the river has been canalized to allow the navigation of ships. The river travels through Shelby and Clinton, forming Lake Shelbyville and Lake Carlyle respectively. The Kaskaskia River boasts a variety of aquatic species and picturesque scenery along its bank. The Illinois Department of Natural Resources now assumes responsibility for the river.

卡斯卡斯基亚河

美国伊利诺伊州中南部运河化河流。卡斯卡斯基亚河全长约523千米,是伊利诺伊州内最长的河流,流域面积约占伊利诺伊州面积的10.2%。该河是密西西比河支流,与密西西比河交汇于切斯特市西北方向16千米处。卡斯卡斯基亚河下游经改造后已能容纳船只航行。该河流经谢尔比和克林顿,在两地分别形成了谢尔比维尔湖和卡莱尔湖。卡斯卡斯基亚河水产丰富,两岸风景优美。目前,该河由伊利诺伊州自然资源部管辖。

Katten Canal

A canal located in Overijssel, the Netherlands. The Katten Canal is 700 metres in length. Constructed in 1826, the canal was opened in 1940 as an outlet for the Ijssel River to flow into the Ketel Lake. It was built to reduce the volume of water the Ketel Canal carried. The Ketel Island was formed between

卡腾运河

荷兰上艾瑟尔省运河。卡腾运河全长700米。该运河1826年开凿,1940年通航,是艾瑟尔河流入凯特尔湖的一条航道。卡腾运河为减少凯特尔运河的水流量而建,建成后,凯特尔运河与卡腾运河之

these two canals after the completion of the Katten Canal.

间形成了凯特尔岛。

Käyhkää Canal

凯卡运河

A canal located in Ruokolahti, Finland. The Käyhkää Canal is one of the Suvorov Military Canals. It is 350 metres long in total including the canal entrances, while its actual length is only 80 metres. The construction of the canal began in the fall of 1791 and was finished in 1798. The predecessor of the existing bridge built over the canal can be traced back to the time of Alexander Suvorov. The post building alongside the canal has also been preserved and nowadays stands as a resort.

芬兰鲁奥科拉赫蒂市运河。凯卡运河是苏沃洛夫军事运河网的一部分，运河本身长度仅为80米，加上引河部分，总长为350米。运河于1791年秋开始动工修建，1798年竣工。在苏沃洛夫时代，运河上曾建有一座桥，如今人们又在其原址上重修了一座。凯卡运河附近的一处邮政大楼也保留了下来，现已成为旅游景点。

Keitele Canal

凯泰莱运河

A canal located in central Finland. The Keitele Canal is about 45 kilometres long with an elevation difference of 21 metres. It links the two biggest lakes in central Finland, namely, Lake Päijänne and Lake Keitele. The canal connects 6 lakes in total and creates a 400-kilometre-long water route. On the canal there are 5 self-service locks that are open from May to September. The idea of constructing the canal was first proposed in the late 19th century, with a concrete plan made in 1962 and another in 1981. The project began in 1990 and was completed in 1993 at a cost of 245 million Finnish marks. Originally the Keitele Canal was built for serving as a route for log floating and boosting the development of the wood industry in this region. Since the

芬兰中部运河。凯泰莱运河全长约45千米，全程水位落差21米，连通该地区最大的两个湖：派延奈湖和凯泰莱湖。运河共连通了6个湖泊，形成了总长度达400千米的水上航线。运河上建有5座自助船闸，每年5月至9月开放。开凿运河的想法最早于19世纪末提出，1962年和1981年人们又分别制订了具体计划。凯泰莱运河1990年开始修建，1993年竣工，总计花费2.45亿芬兰马克。运河修建的初衷是为了运输木材，发展当地木材产业。2002年当地禁止伐木后，这条运河改为专供私人船只

practice of timber rafting was put to an end in 2002, the canal has been exclusively used by private and cruise boats. Several companies are now offering canal and lake cruise service for tourists in the area.

和游船使用。如今这里坐落着数家公司，为游客提供运河和湖泊观光游览服务。

Kembs Niffer Branch Canal

An inland canal located in France. The Kembs Niffer Branch Canal is 13 kilometres long. It links the Grand Alsace Canal at Kembs in northeastern France with the Rhône-Rhine Canal.

康斯−尼费尔支线运河

法国内陆运河。康斯−尼费尔支线运河全长13千米，在法国东北部康斯连接阿尔萨斯大运河与罗讷−莱茵运河。

Kennet and Avon Canal

An inland canal located in southern England, the United Kingdom. The Kennet and Avon Canal is 140 kilometres long with 107 locks in total. It is composed of three waterways: a canalized section of the Avon River, a canalized section of the Kennet River, and an entirely artificial waterway linking Newbury and Bath. The first two became navigable in the early 18th century while the last section of 92 kilometres was excavated between 1794 and 1810. When the train service from London to Bristol was made available by the Great Western Railway in 1841, the prosperous railway transport industry began to exert an impact on the canal trade. As a result, the Kennet and Avon Canal gradually fell into disuse. The restoration did not start until the latter half of the 20th century, largely conducted by volunteers. Renovations of the canal lasted for decades and it was officially reopened in 1990. Today, it has turned into a popular tourist attraction for boating,

肯尼特−埃文运河

英国英格兰南部运河。肯尼特−埃文运河全长140千米，共建有107座船闸。该运河由3段河道构成，即埃文河运河化河段、肯尼特河运河化河段以及连接纽伯里与巴斯的人工航道。前两个河段于18世纪早期通航，长92千米的人工航道修建于1794—1810年间。1841年，英国大西部铁路公司开通了伦敦至布里斯托尔的铁路，蓬勃发展的铁路运输业给运河航运带来了冲击，最终导致肯尼特−埃文运河逐渐被废弃。20世纪下半叶，在志愿者努力下，肯尼特−埃文运河逐步修复，经数年修缮后终于在1990年正式重新通航。如今，肯尼特−埃文运河成为野生动物的重要栖息地，同时也是一处热门景点，游客可以在此划船、泛舟、垂钓、散步

canoeing, fishing, walking and cycling. It also plays a vital role in wildlife conservation.

和骑行。

Kensington Canal

A canal located in London, the United Kingdom. The Kensington Canal is about 3.2 kilometres long. It runs from River Thames between the parish of Chelsea and Fulham up to Kensington, where a canal basin is located near the Warwick Road. Under the proposal and support of Lord Kensington, William Edwardes, the construction plan was put on the agenda in 1822 and the canal was opened on 12 August 1828 despite a series of crises caused by the insufficient budget. It was built on the previously existing route of the Counter's Creek, a minor tributary of the Thames, aiming at shipping goods and minerals from the London docks to the Kensington area. Throughout the history when it was operational, the Kensington Canal was faced with the problem of siltation, which degraded its navigation conditions, especially at low tide. In 1836, the Kensington Canal was sold to the Bristol, Birmingham and Thames Junction Railway, which is now renamed as the West London Railway. The canal continued to be operational until 1967. Later, it became completely obliterated in the competition with the railway transportation. Now on the former route of the Kensington Canal runs the West London Line from the Willesden Junction Station to the Clapham Junction Station.

肯辛顿运河

英国伦敦运河。肯辛顿运河全长约3.2千米，始于切尔西与富勒姆教区之间的泰晤士河河段，最终流入肯辛顿地区沃里克路附近的运河内湾。在肯辛顿勋爵威廉·埃德华兹的提议与资助下，1822年，运河修建计划被提上日程。虽然遇到一系列资金短缺的困难，肯辛顿运河最终于1828年8月12日通航。该运河沿泰晤士河小支流康特河的原有河道重修，可将货物与矿产从伦敦的码头运往肯辛顿地区。运河运营期间遭遇了泥沙淤积等问题，给航运造成了困难（尤其在枯水期）。1836年，肯辛顿运河被出售给布里斯托尔、伯明翰和泰晤士枢纽铁路公司。该公司现已更名为西伦敦铁路公司。肯辛顿运河一直运营至1967年，后因铁路运输业崛起而完全被弃用。如今，人们在肯辛顿运河旧河道上修建了西伦敦铁路线，连通威尔斯登铁路枢纽和克拉珀姆铁路枢纽。

Kerk Canal

A canal located in the province of Utrecht, the Netherlands. The Kerk Canal is 3.1 kilometres in length. It is a part of the De Ronde Venen water system, connecting the Ring Canal and the Kromme Mijdrecht. The construction of the canal began in the 14th century while the early proposal of constructing it was made in the 12th century. It was built mainly for the purpose of transportation and drainage. It also contributed to the agricultural and industrial development in Mijdrecht and its surrounding areas. At present, the canal is only used for recreational purposes.

Ketel Canal

A canal located in the province of Overijssel, the Netherlands. The Ketel Canal is 3.4 kilometres in length, through which the IJssel flows into the Ketel Lake. At the beginning of the 16th century, it was one of the seven major IJssel estuaries, many of which later became silted up and were filled in. The Ketel Canal therefore became the main estuary. The canal is now located in the National Landscape IJssel Delta, with a breakwater built on each side, which improves the navigability of the IJssel estuary.

Ket-Kas Canal

An inland canal located in Russia. See Ob-Yenisei Canal.

凯尔克运河

荷兰乌特勒支省运河。凯尔克运河全长3.1千米，连接环形运河和克罗默迈德雷赫特河，是德龙德维纳水系的组成部分。早在12世纪，人们便提出开凿该运河，但直到14世纪才开始动工。凯尔克运河当时主要用于航运和排水，也促进了迈德雷赫特市及周边地区工农业的发展。目前，该运河仅用于休闲娱乐。

凯特尔运河

荷兰上艾瑟尔省运河。凯特尔运河全长3.4千米，是艾瑟尔河注入凯特尔湖的通道。16世纪初，包括凯特尔运河在内，艾瑟尔河约有7个河口，后多数河口因河道淤塞问题而被回填，凯特尔运河便成为艾瑟尔河的主要河口。凯特尔运河现位于艾瑟尔三角洲国家风景区内，河道两侧各筑有一道防波堤，这使艾瑟尔河的河口更适于航行。

克季-卡斯运河

俄罗斯内陆运河。见鄂毕—叶尼塞运河。

Keulse Canal

A cross-border canal located in the provinces of North Holland, Utrecht and South Holland, the Netherlands. The construction of the Keulse Canal was authorized by King William I in 1821. It was intended to improve the water connection of some major cities to the Rhine, including the capital city of Amsterdam. The canal was finished in 1825 and used mainly as a trade route. Later, it was widened and deepened as a part of the Merwede Canal in the 1880s.

科尔瑟运河

荷兰北荷兰省、乌特勒支省和南荷兰省跨境运河。1821年，威廉一世批准开凿科尔瑟运河，意在改善荷兰阿姆斯特丹等主要城市与莱茵河之间的水运条件。科尔瑟运河1825年竣工，开通后主要作为商业航线使用。19世纪80年代，科尔瑟运河又经过进一步拓宽和加深，成为梅尔韦德运河的一部分。

Keweenaw Waterway

A waterway located in Michigan, the United States. The Keweenaw Waterway has a length of 40 kilometres, which cuts through the Keweenaw Peninsula located on Lake Superior in the northern region of Michigan. As a tributary of the Torch Lake, the Keweenaw Waterway was once a natural river course before the 1850s. The waterway was further expanded in order to accommodate freight-carrying boats and allow them access to inland cities. In this sense, it is partially natural and partially artificial. The construction and operation of the Keweenaw Waterway were originally funded by private ventures and were later taken over by the government in 1891. Under the partnership between the private sector and the government, the waterway boosted commercial activities.

基威诺航道

美国密歇根州航道。基威诺航道全长约40千米，在密歇根州北部穿过苏必利尔湖中的基威诺半岛。19世纪50年代以前，基威诺航道为托奇湖支流，属于天然河道。为使货船通行驶往内陆城市，人们对河道进行了扩建。基威诺航道部分是天然形成，部分为人工开凿。其修建和运营最初由私人企业提供资金，1891年后运河由政府接管。在私人企业和政府的共同管理下，该航道促进了沿岸商业的发展。

Kidwelly and Llanelly Canal

A canal located in Carmarthenshire, Wales, the United Kingdom. The Kidwelly and Llanelly Canal was 4.8 kilometres long. It was constructed by the Kidwelly and Llanelly Canal and Tramroad Company with the authorization of an act of Parliament in June 1812 with the purpose to facilitate the transportation of anthracite coal. The construction progressed at a slow pace and ended in 1837. The canal could be divided into 2 distinct sections. The first section incorporated the previous course of the Kymer's Canal. It featured 3 inclined planes used to raise the water level of the canal. The second section ran southeastwards to the Burry Port. Currently, some sections of the canal survive alongside the mineral railway line in this region.

基德韦利－兰内利运河

英国威尔士卡马森郡运河。基德韦利－兰内利运河全长4.8千米，1812年6月由英国议会授权开凿，由基德韦利－兰内利运河和轨道运输公司负责相关修建事宜，主要是为了满足无烟煤的运输需求。运河修建工程进展缓慢，持续至1837年方才竣工。基德韦利－兰内利运河由两部分河段构成。第一段河段保留了原先的凯摩运河河道，并修建了3座用以提升运河水面的斜面升船机；第二段河段为东南流向，终于巴里港。如今，在曾用来运输矿物的铁路沿线仍能见到基德韦利－兰内利运河的遗迹。

Kiel Canal (Germany)

A canal located in the state of Schleswig-Holstein in northern Germany. Also known as Kaiser Wilhelm Canal. The Kiel Canal is 98 kilometres in length. It starts from Brunsbüttel at the mouth of the Elbe on the North Sea in the west, crosses the Jutland Peninsula, and ends at Holtenau, the Kiel Bay of the Baltic Sea in the east. With the presence of this canal, ships can bypass the Jutland Peninsula and a 460-kilometre-long journey can be saved. The initiative to construct this canal can be traced back to the end of the 19th century when the German Navy was in need of a shortcut to connect the naval bases in the Baltic and the North Sea, and bypass

基尔运河 (德国)

德国北部石勒苏益格－荷尔斯泰因运河。亦称皇帝威廉运河。基尔运河全长98千米，西起北海易北河口的布伦斯比特尔镇，穿过德兰半岛，向东注入波罗的海基尔湾的霍尔特瑙港。往来于北海和波罗的海的船只不必再绕行至日德兰半岛，可缩短460千米的航程。该运河的历史可追溯至19世纪末，当时德国海军希望修建一条运河连接波罗的海和北海的海军基地，同时避开丹麦海域。基尔运河1887年6月开凿，由9 000名工人施

the waters near Denmark. The project was started in June 1887, and the canal was officially opened on 20 June 1895 after 9,000 workers worked for 8 years. In order to meet the increasing demand of transportation for trade and for a better service for the Imperial German Navy, the canal was widened and deepened from 1907 to 1914, and 2 larger ship locks were built at the two ends of the canal. Being of great importance in both military and commercial affairs, the Kiel Canal was internationalized by the Treaty of Versailles (1919) with its jurisdiction kept by the Germans. Today, the canal remains the safest, cheapest, and the most convenient shipping route between the two seas and constitutes a major passage for shipping in the Baltic region.

工8年之后顺利竣工, 1895年6月20日正式通航。为支持日益增长的水路商运活动并进一步满足德意志帝国海军航运需求, 1907—1914年间人们拓宽了基尔运河的河床, 加深了河道, 并在运河两端的港口各修建了1座大型船闸。基尔运河具有重要的军事意义和商运价值。1919年《凡尔赛条约》签订后, 基尔运河成为一条国际航道, 管理权仍归属德国。目前, 基尔运河是波罗的海地区的主要航道, 也是北海与波罗的海之间最经济便捷且安全可靠的线路。

Kiel Canal (the Netherlands)

A canal located in the province of Groningen, the Netherlands. As a branch of the Winschoten Canal, the Kiel Canal connects Hoogezand to the Annerveen Canal. With an elevation difference of 1 metre, it was excavated in 1647 and extended to a length of 8.4 kilometres. This canal had been mainly used for the transport of agricultural products before the shipping stopped in 1973. In 2005, the canal was made navigable again. New bridges and locks were built and the existing bridges were restored. Nowadays, as a part of the shipping route from the Zuidlaard Lake to East Groningen, the Kiel Canal is mainly used for recreational instead of commercial purpose.

基尔运河（荷兰）

荷兰格罗宁根省运河。基尔运河是温斯霍滕运河的分支之一, 连接霍赫赞德和安纳芬运河。运河1647年开凿, 后延长至8.4千米, 全程水位落差1米, 主要用于运输农产品。1973年, 基尔运河停航, 2005年又恢复通航, 河上新建多座桥梁和船闸, 原有桥梁也得以修复。如今, 基尔运河已成为从泽伊德拉尔德湖通往格罗宁根省东部航线的一部分, 但不再用于商业运输, 而以休闲娱乐为主。

Kissimmee River≈

A canalized river located in the southeastern United States. Prior to the 1960s, the Kissimmee River was a 160-kilometre-long natural river, flowing southwards from Lake Kissimmee to Lake Okeechobee and meandering through central Florida. It caused floods persistently. The canalization project was carried out for the public interest under the approval of the government. The canalized section runs 90 kilometres, with the channel widened, deepened and straightened. Though the man-made section had fulfilled its function of flood control, disastrous consequences ensued. The canal destroyed much of a floodplain-dependent ecosystem that was home to endangered species and wetland-dependent animals. In order to address this problem, efforts have been made since 1999 with the Kissimmee River Restoration Project to restore about 104 square kilometres of floodplain ecosystem.

基西米河

美国东南部运河化河流。20世纪60年代之前，基西米河是一条蜿蜒流经佛罗里达州中部的自然河流，由基西米湖向南汇入奥基乔比湖，全长160千米。由于该河流域洪涝灾害持续不断，政府为保障民众利益同意将其改造为运河。人们拓宽、加深和拉直了部分河道，经运河化改造后的河段长约90千米。这一改造工程起到了防洪作用，但同时也带来了一些严重的环境问题，破坏了漫滩生态系统。这里原先栖息着许多濒危物种以及依赖湿地生存的各种动物。为解决这一问题，1999年人们启动了基西米河修复工程，旨在修复约104平方千米的漫滩生态系统。

Klodnica Canal

A canal located in Upper Silesia, southwest Poland. Formerly known as Klodnitz Canal. The Klodnica Canal is 46 kilometres in length, with an elevation difference of 49 metres. The canal connects the Oder River to the city of Gliwice. It was built between 1792 and 1812 when the Upper Silesia region was still owned by Prussia. John Baildon, a Scottish engineer, and Friedrich Wilhelm von Reden, the Director of the Silesian mining authority, designed the canal to serve for the local transportation of coal and ore. It had been expanded from

克罗迪尼卡运河

波兰西南部上西里西亚地区运河。旧称克罗迪尼兹运河。克罗迪尼卡运河全长46千米，连接奥得河和格利维采市，上下游水位落差49米。该运河修建于1792—1812年间，由苏格兰工程师约翰·贝尔登和西里西亚采矿管理局局长弗里德里希·威廉·冯雷登共同设计，当时上西里西亚地区尚属普鲁士管辖。克罗迪尼卡运河主要用于运输当地的煤和铁矿石，1888—

1888 to 1893, allowing the passage of vessels with a maximal capacity of up to 100 tons and a draught of 1.2 metres. However, the Klodnica Canal was less used after the railways connecting coalfields in Upper Silesia were constructed. The freight volume of the waterway fell from 70,000 tons in 1847 to 4,400 in 1865. The canal then became obsolete and was replaced by the Gliwice Canal, which was built from 1935 to 1939. After World War II, the territory of Upper Silesia was transferred to the Polish jurisdiction by the Potsdam Agreement (1945) and became a part of Poland.

1893年间扩建后，可通行最大载重量为100吨、吃水深度达1.2米的船只。上西里西亚煤田开通铁路后，克罗迪尼卡运河使用率随之降低，其货运量由1847年的7万吨降至1865年的4 400吨。后克罗迪卡运河被弃用，修建于1935—1939年间的格利维采运河取而代之。第二次世界大战后，根据《波茨坦协定》（1945），上西里西亚地区的管辖权移交给波兰，成为波兰的一部分。

Klodnitz Canal

克罗迪尼兹运河

A canal located in Upper Silesia, southwest Poland. See Klodnica Canal.

波兰西南部上西里西亚地区运河。见克罗迪尼卡运河。

Knollendam Canal

克诺兰达默运河

A canal located in the province of North Holland, the Netherlands. The Knollendam Canal is 3.7 kilometres long. As a part of the canal surrounding Starnmeerpolder, it connects the Oost-Knollendam Village to the Spijkerboor Village through the Alkmaar Canal. In 1636, the ring ditch and the eastern ring road were built in North Holland. The ditch was later renamed Knollendam Canal. In 1637, the canal was largely completed. The canal plays a primary role in water management. The canal offers a quiet and attractive option for leisure sailing. There is a lane on each side of the canal for cycling or walking. Structures along the banks, such as flood-

荷兰北荷兰省运河。克诺兰达默运河全长3.7千米，部分河道环绕施塔恩湖圩田，通过阿尔克马尔运河将奥斯特达默村和斯派克博尔村连接。1636年，北荷兰省修建环形渠和东环形路，环形渠后改名克诺兰达默运河。运河于次年基本完工，主要用以水调节。静谧的运河吸引了人们乘坐休闲游船游憩其上。游客还可沿着河岸两边的道路散步和骑行。河上的防洪工程、船闸和信号杆等建筑设施为运河增添了历史感。

ing control works, locks and signal poles, bring a sense of history.

Kollam Canal

A canal located in the state of Kerala, India. Also called Quilon Canal. The Kollam Canal is 7.7 kilometres long, passing through the capital city of Kollam. As a part of the 205-kilometre-long National Waterway No.3 and the 78-kilometre-long Kollam-Trivandrum State waterway project, it connects the Ashtamudi Lake in the north and the Paravur Lake in the south. The Kollam Canal was constructed in 1880 and served as an arterial inland waterway of the old Kollam city. Giant cargo ships with different types of goods were often seen on this canal those days. The canal was also used for leisure activities, irrigation and drinking water supply. The canal was later blocked and contaminated by industrial waste, plastics and poultry waste. Local people and government are now taking the initiative to renovate and revive the canal.

科拉姆运河

印度喀拉拉邦运河。亦称奎隆运河。科拉姆运河流经喀拉拉邦首府科拉姆市，全长7.7千米。科拉姆运河北连阿什塔穆迪湖，南接帕拉武尔湖，是205千米的印度3号国家航道和78千米的科拉姆—特里凡得琅航道工程的组成部分。该运河1880年开凿，曾是科拉姆城的内陆水运干线。当年运河上常通行装载各种货物的大型货船。科拉姆运河还兼有休闲娱乐、灌溉和供水功能。后因人们往运河中倾倒工业废料、塑料品、家禽粪便等，科拉姆运河出现淤积堵塞，水质被污染。如今，当地政府和居民正提议整修科拉姆运河，使其重焕生机。

Kolme

A cross-border canal located in Belgium and France. See Bergen Canal.

柯尔梅运河

欧洲比利时和法国跨国运河。见贝亨运河。

Kolonels Canal

A cross-border canal located in the provinces of Friesland and Groningen, the Netherlands. It was constructed between 1573 and 1576 by Caspar de

科洛奈尔运河

荷兰跨境运河。科洛奈尔运河流经弗里斯兰和格罗宁根两省。运河由弗里斯兰和格罗宁根时任执

Robles, the Stadholder of Friesland and Groningen, hence the canal is also called Caspar de Robles Canal. The canal was built to bypass the pirate-threatened shipping route between Dutch cities (still in Spanish hands) and cities in northern Germany. In the mid-17th century, the Hoen Canal extended to Stroobos and Friesland. The connection made the Kolonels Canal redundant, leading to the decline of the canal. In 1955, it became a part of the Prinses Margriet Canal, which runs from Stroobos to Lemmer, and it is the oldest stretch of the canal.

政长官卡斯帕尔·德·罗伯勒斯1573—1576年间开凿，因而运河也称作卡斯帕尔·德·罗伯勒斯运河。当时西班牙治下的荷兰城市和德国北部城市之间的海上运输通道常受海盗威胁，修建科洛奈尔运河以绕开那段航线。17世纪中期，霍恩运河延伸到了斯特罗博斯和弗里斯兰，科洛奈尔运河因而变得多余而逐渐衰败。1955年，科洛奈尔运河成为玛格丽特公主运河的一部分。玛格丽特公主运河从斯特罗博斯流至莱默，科洛奈尔运河是其最早修成的河段。

Korte Canal

科特运河

A canal located in the province of South Holland, the Netherlands. The Korte Canal is 2.1 kilometres long with 3 bridges, connecting the Old Rhine and the Rhine-Schie Canal. It was excavated in the 1960s as a replacement of the Korte River and the Trek River with the aim to shorten the shipping voyage so that it was no longer necessary to pass through Leiden.

荷兰南荷兰省运河。科特运河全长2.1千米，连通旧莱茵河与莱茵—斯希运河，运河上建有3座桥梁。科特运河20世纪60年代开凿，旨在取代科特河与特雷克河的运输功能，不必再绕道经过莱顿，缩短了过往船只的航程。

Kra Canal

克拉运河

A canal under planning located in Thailand. Also called Kra Istthmus Canal. See Thai Canal.

泰国拟建运河。亦称克拉地峡运河。见泰运河。

Kra Isthmus Canal

克拉地峡运河

A canal under planning located in Thailand. Also called Kra Canal. See Thai Canal.

泰国拟建运河。亦称克拉运河。见泰运河。

Kromme Raken Canal

克罗梅拉肯运河

An inland canal located in Groningen Province, the Netherlands. The Kromme Raken Canal is 2.4 kilometres long and has one lock and one bridge. As one of the tributaries of the Reit Canal, the canal mainly flows through the city of Groningen and into the Zuidwending Canal.

荷兰格罗宁根省内陆运河。克罗梅拉肯运河全长2.4千米，其上建有1座船闸和1座桥梁。该运河为哈伊特运河的支线之一，主要流经格罗宁根市，汇入南文丁运河。

Kubaard Canal

库巴德运河

A canal located in Friesland Province, the Netherlands. The Kubaard Canal is 1.8 kilometres in length with no lock built on it. It connects the Lathum Canal with the Bolsward Trek Canal near Wommels. The canal flows past Kubaard (from which it derives its name), De Grits and Swarte Beien. The Kubaard Canal is narrow and there is a lot of yellow waterlily.

荷兰弗里斯兰省运河。库巴德运河于沃默尔斯连通拉土姆运河与博尔斯瓦德拖船运河，全长1.8千米，河上无船闸。运河流经库巴德（运河因此得名）、德格里茨和斯沃特贝恩。库巴德运河很窄，河里长有很多萍蓬草。

Kuikhorne Canal

库伊霍恩运河

A canal located in Friesland Province, the Netherlands. The Kuikhorne Canal has a length of 5 kilometres, running from the New Canal to the Bergum Lake. The canal stands as a part of the connection between the Dokkum Grand Canal and the Bergum Lake, along with the New Zwem, the Petsloot

荷兰弗里斯兰省运河。库伊霍恩运河全长5千米，始于新运河，终于贝赫姆湖。该运河同新兹维默河、佩茨洛特河与新运河组成的航道连通了多克默大运河与贝赫姆湖。

and the New Canal.

Kukonharju Canal

A canal located on the border of Ruokolahti and Puumala, Finland. Built in the late 18th century, the Kukonharju Canal has a length of 800 metres. It is one of the four canals of the Suvorov Military Canals. The Kukonharju Canal played a vital role in transportation in the 18th century, allowing Russia's Saimaa navy to pass safely between the Lappeenranta, Kärnäkoski and Olavin Castle fortifications near the border. In 2003, the Finnish National Board of Antiquities began to carry out restoration work on the canal.

库康纳鸠运河

芬兰鲁奥科拉赫蒂市和普马拉市交界处运河。库康纳鸠运河长800米，开凿于18世纪晚期，是芬兰苏沃洛夫军事运河网四大运河之一。18世纪，库康纳鸠运河在交通运输中发挥了重要作用，保障俄国塞马海军安全通过位于拉彭兰塔、卡内科斯基和奥拉维城堡三地的边境防御工事。2003年起，芬兰国家文物局开始实施运河修复工作。

Kuloy-Pinega Canal

A canal located in northern Russia. The Kuloy-Pinega Canal is 8 kilometres in length, equipped with one lock. At its narrowest point, it is 20 metres wide. The canal was built between 1926 and 1928 to link the Kuloy River with the Pinega River. Back to 1840, it was proposed to construct a more convenient waterway to transport the timber from the Kuloy River basin to the Pinega River basin and downstream to Northern Dvina. However, it was seen as an unprofitable project then. Until 1925, with the growth of timber business in the Kuloy River basin, the decision to build the canal was finally made. Currently, though too shallow for large boats, the Kuloy-Pinega Canal remains navigable.

库洛伊－皮涅加运河

俄罗斯北部运河。库洛伊—皮涅加运河全长8千米，连通库洛伊河和皮涅加河，河面最窄处为20米，河上建有1座船闸。运河1926年开凿，1928年竣工。早在1840年，为了方便将库洛伊流域内的木材运到皮涅加河地区，再沿下游运送到北德维纳河地区，就有人提出过修建运河的想法，但当时人们认为这不会带来经济效益。直到1925年，随着库洛伊流域伐木业日趋兴盛，人们才最终决定开凿这条运河。如今，库洛伊—皮涅加运河仍可通航，但水位太浅，不能容纳大型船只。

Kuma-Manych Canal

A canal located in Stavropol Krai, Russia. The Kuma-Manych Canal links the Kuma River with the East Manych River. Completed in 1965, it was built mainly for irrigation. The canal starts at a small reservoir on the Kuma River, runs first towards the northeast, then the northwest, and ends at the southern shore of the East Manych River.

Küsten Canal

A summit-level canal located in Lower Saxony, Germany. Also called Coastal Canal. The Küsten Canal is 70 kilometres long with 10 bridges. It starts from Oldenburg, linking the Dortmund Ems Canal with the Weser River. Its predecessor was a drainage channel, which was widened from 1922 to 1935 and transformed into the existing canal. The canal has two tributaries, i.e., the Börgerwald Canal and the Ohe-Ableiter, is navigable for ships with a draught of 3.5 metres. The Küsten Canal is at present serving for the local peat industry and is used to transport coal from the Ruhr Area to Bremen.

Kutvele Canal

A canal located in Finland. The Kutvele Canal is on the border of Ruokolahti and Taipalsaari with a total length of 250 metres, a width of 90 to 100 metres, a depth of 2.4 metres and a maximum elevation difference of 12.5 metres. It has no lock. As a part of the Suvorov Military Canals, it was excavat-

库马-马内奇运河

俄罗斯斯塔夫罗波尔边疆区运河。库马—马内奇运河1965 年建成，连通库马河和东马内奇河，主要用于农业灌溉。运河始于库马河的一个小型水库，先流向东北方向，继而转向西北，最后流向东马内奇河南岸。

屈斯滕运河

德国下萨克森州越岭运河。亦称沿海运河。屈斯滕运河全长70千米，始于奥尔登堡，连通多特蒙德—埃姆斯运河和威悉河。运河1922—1935年间开凿，由一条旧排水通道拓宽而成。屈斯滕运河包括布尔格瓦尔德运河和奥厄—阿布莱塔两条支线，可通行吃水深度3.5米的船只。如今，屈斯滕运河主要用以将煤炭从鲁尔工业区运到不来梅港市，服务于当地的泥煤产业。

库特瓦勒运河

芬兰运河。库特瓦勒运河位于鲁奥科拉赫蒂和泰帕尔萨里交界处，长250米，宽90—100米，深2.4米，最大水位落差达12.5米，河上未建船闸。该运河是苏沃洛夫军事运河网的一部分，1791年开凿于塞马湖

ed in 1791 at Kyläniemi, an island on the south of Lake Saima, in order to help the Russians in terms of trade and military defence. The construction was finished in 1793. It was renovated then in 1949 and 1950, and was expanded in 1977. Its original structure is not preserved today.

南部的克拉涅米岛上，旨在方便俄国人开展贸易以及军事防御活动，1793年运河竣工。运河于1949—1950年间修复，并于1977年进行了扩建。但如今库特瓦勒运河原貌已不复存在。

Lachine Canal

An inland canal located in Quebec, Canada. The Lachine Canal is a 14-kilometre-long waterway punctuated by 5 locks. It runs between the Old Port and Lake Saint-Louis. It is said that its name was given by those European explorers, who were eager to find a shipping route from New France (Quebec now) to China, in the hope of good luck. As early as the founding of Montreal, the necessity had already been recognized of excavating a canal between Montreal and Lachine to ease the threats of the Lachine Rapids. The plan was suspended twice for multiple reasons, such as racial tension, inadequate financial supports and technological problems. In the second half of the 18th century, the importance of building a canal to facilitate the commercial transportation along the St. Lawrence was again highlighted. Excavated in 1821, the canal was completed in 1824, and officially put into use one year later. Due to its geographic location, the Lachine Canal dramatically boosted the economic growth in its surrounding region and made it the largest industrial area in Canada. The expansion of the Lachine Canal was carried out in 3 phases from 1843 to 1885. However, factories became less dependent on the canal with the improvement of the railway system in Montreal's industrial zone. It was gradually replaced by the St. Lawrence Seaway and closed to commercial navigation in 1970, which led to the depression of the surrounding communities. In 1974, the government decided to redevelop the Lachine Canal site, given the significant roles the canal had played in shipping and industrializa-

拉欣运河

加拿大魁北克省内陆运河。拉欣运河全长14千米，建有5座船闸。运河东起旧港，西至圣路易斯湖。据说，当时的欧洲探险家渴望找到一条从新法兰西（今魁北克）到中国的海运航线，因而将此运河命名为拉欣（意为"中国"），以祈求好运。早在蒙特利尔建城之初，当地居民就已经认识到有必要在蒙特利尔市和拉欣镇之间修建一条运河，以减少拉欣急流带来的威胁。后因种族冲突、资金短缺和技术落后等原因，运河修建计划两度搁置。18世纪下半叶，修建拉欣运河促进圣劳伦斯河上航运贸易的需求再次凸显。1821年，运河终于开凿，1824年修建完工，一年后正式通航。得益于区位优势，拉欣运河极大地促进了当地的经济发展，使之成为加拿大最大的工业区。1843—1885年间，运河历经3次扩建。然而，随着蒙特利尔工业区铁路系统的不断完善，附近工厂对拉欣运河的依赖程度逐渐减弱。圣劳伦斯海道开通后，拉欣运河的商业航运地位被逐渐取代。1970年，运河正式停航，周边地区经济也随之衰落。1974年，为纪念其在加拿大航运发展及工业化进程中的重要作用，加拿大政府决定重新修建拉欣运河。1996年，拉

tion. In 1996, the Lachine Canal was inscribed as a National Historic Site of Canada, serving as an impressive reminder of the history of the country's development. Today, under the administration of Parks Canada, the Lachine Canal has become a place of leisure and pleasure.

欣运河被确立为加拿大国家历史遗址。如今，在加拿大公园管理局运营下，拉欣运河旧址已经开发成为休闲度假胜地。

Ladoga Canal

拉多加运河

A canal located in Leningrad Oblast, Russia. The Ladoga Canal is about 117 kilometres in length, connecting the Neva River with the Svir River. In 1718, Emperor Peter I ordered the construction as the rapid economic development entailed a growing need for waterway routes. The construction of the Old Ladoga Canal, which was formerly called Peter the First Canal, was started in 1719 and completed in 1730. When finished, the canal was only less than 1 metre deep, which was far from the expectation. Then Empress Catherine II decided to extend the canal by constructing another section between the Volkhov River and the Syas River. The project was carried out between 1765 and 1802. Then the third part of the Ladoga Canal connecting the Syas River with the Svir River was constructed between 1802 and 1810. In the 19th century, the Ladoga Canal carried a considerable volume of traffic. It silted up so heavily that Emperor Alexander II decided to construct a new canal instead of repairing the old one. During 1866 and 1883, the New Ladoga Canal was built on the southern shore of Lake Ladoga. It is now navigable for small boats, and the Old Ladoga Canal has been abandoned since 1940.

俄罗斯列宁格勒州运河。拉多加运河全长约117千米，连通涅瓦河和斯维里河。由于经济快速发展，水路交通需求日益增长，1718年彼得一世下令修建运河。旧拉多加运河（旧称彼得一世运河）1719年开凿，1730年完工。竣工后，运河深度不足1米，远未达到预期。叶卡捷琳娜二世决定扩建拉多加运河。1765—1802年修建了连通沃尔霍夫河和夏西河的河段。1802—1810年又增修了连通夏西河和斯维里河的第三河段。19世纪，拉多加运河上航运业务繁忙，但河道淤塞问题非常严重。亚历山大二世决定放弃整修旧河段，另建新运河。新拉多加运河位于拉多加湖南岸，修建于1866—1883年间，如今仍可供小型船只通航。旧拉多加运河自1940年起被弃用。

Lage Canal

An inland canal located in Flevoland Province, the Netherlands. The Lage Canal flows from the Ketel Lake to the Marker Lake near Almere City with an average depth of 3 metres and a width of 35 to 50 metres. Its main branch is the Lage Dwars Canal. Together with the Hoge Canal, the Lage Canal forms the main drainage system of Flevoland Province. The canal is also used for transportation. Now the banks of the Lage Canal, originally made of wooden and concrete sheet piles, are being gradually changed into eco-friendly banks.

拉赫运河

荷兰弗莱福兰省内陆运河。拉赫运河平均深3米，宽35—50米，自凯特尔湖流向阿尔默勒市附近，注入马克尔湖，主要支线为拉赫—杜瓦希运河。拉赫运河除具航运功能，还与霍赫运河构成弗莱福兰省的主要排水系统。拉赫运河的河岸原本由木板桩和混凝土板桩修成，现正逐步改造成环保型河岸。

Lage Dwars Canal

An inland canal located in Flevoland Province, the Netherlands. The Lage Dwars Canal has a navigable length of about 5.5 kilometres. It starts as a branch of the Lage Canal, flows near Lelystad-Haven City and finally empties into the Marker Lake. There is a lock built next to the Wortman pumping station at the entrance of the Marker Lake. In 2018 and 2019, the banks of the Lage Dwars Canal were renovated for the purpose of sustainable development.

拉赫－杜瓦希运河

荷兰弗莱福兰省内陆运河。拉赫—杜瓦希运河可通航长度约5.5千米，为拉赫运河的支线运河，流经莱利斯塔德—哈文市附近，最后注入马克尔湖。运河在沃特曼泵站附近建有1座船闸，与马克尔湖相通。2018—2019年间，人们对拉赫—杜瓦希运河的堤岸进行了翻修改造，以促进其可持续性发展。

Lahn≈

A canalized river located in Germany. As a tributary of the Rhine, the Lahn is 245 kilometres in length and navigable over a distance of 137.4 kilometres with 22 locks. It originates in the Rothaar Hills, flows eastwards in the state of Hessen to Marburg

兰河

德国运河化河流。兰河为莱茵河支流，全长245千米，可通航河段长137.4千米，共建有22座船闸。该河源于罗塔尔山，先向东流经黑森州的马堡市，后向南流经吉森市，

and then turns southwards to Giessen, before it winds its way southwestwards to join the Rhine at Lahnstein in the state of Rhineland-Palatinate. The canalization of the Lahn can be traced back to 1808, after the establishment of Duchy of Nassau. The original plan was to make the Lahn navigable from its mouth to Marburg where another canal could be excavated to connect the Lahn with the Weser. In 1816, the Duchy of Nassau and the Kingdom of Prussia reached an agreement to extend the navigable section to Giessen. In 1847, 8 locks were built. The year 1863 witnessed a gradual decline in the shipping on the Lahn, with the operation of the Lahn Valley Railway, which became the major means of commercial transportation. In 1964, another round of expansion was executed to allow ships of 300 tonnes to pass through the waterway. The section stretching from the mouth to the Dehrn, with a minimum depth of 1.6 metres, is now still navigable, but not for freight transport. The section from Lahnau to its confluence with the Rhine is designated as a federal waterway and managed by the Federal Waterways and Shipping Administration. At present, the middle and lower parts of the Lahn are almost exclusively used for recreational purposes.

再蜿蜒转向西南方向，最终于莱茵兰－普法尔茨州的兰施泰因市注入莱茵河。兰河的运河化改造可追溯至1808年，即拿骚公国成立之后。最初计划是将兰河河口至马堡市之间的河段改造成为通航河段，并在马堡市另开一条运河将兰河与威悉河连通。1816年，拿骚公国和普鲁士王国达成协议，将兰河的通航河段延伸至吉森市。至1847年时，兰河上已建成8座船闸。1863年，兰河河谷铁路建成并成为主要货运方式，兰河航运随之逐渐衰落。1964年，兰河航道再次扩建，可容纳最大排水量为300吨的船只。从兰河河口到黑森州德赫恩市的河段水深至少有1.6米，船舶至今仍可通行，但不适合货物运输。从黑森州拉瑙市到与莱茵河汇合处的河段为联邦航道，由德国联邦水路与航运管理局负责管理。如今，兰河的中下游河段仅用于休闲娱乐活动。

Lahore Canal

拉合尔运河

A canal located in Punjab, Pakistan. Originally called Royal Canal. As an extended part of the Bambawali-Ravi-Bedian Canal, the Lahore Canal covers a distance of 60 kilometres towards the western part of Lahore. In 1861, the Lahore Canal was

巴基斯坦旁遮普省运河。旧称皇家运河。拉合尔运河全长60千米，为班巴瓦利－拉维－白地安运河的延伸段，流向拉合尔市西部地区。1861年，该运河由英国人主导

constructed by the British for the purpose of opening up fertile lands in Punjab to ensure that famines could be avoided. The Lahore Canal has been used both for irrigation and ground water recharge. As an important part of Lahore's cultural heritage, the Lahore Canal is the city's most beautiful linear park. The major problem that the Lahore Canal faces today is the pollution caused by the dumping of waste water from factories along the canal.

开凿，旨在服务于旁遮普省的土地开垦，以避免饥荒。拉合尔运河不仅可用于灌溉，还可补充地下水。如今，运河已成为拉合尔文化遗产的重要组成部分，是当地最美的带状公园。目前，由于两岸工厂排放废水，拉合尔运河面临着严重的水污染问题。

Lake Biwa Canal

A canal located in Japan. Also known as Canal of Hope. The Lake Biwa Canal runs from Otsu, Shiga to its end near Nanzen-ji Temple in Kyoto, with several tunnels through the mountains. The canal has three parts, with a total length of approximately 31 kilometres. The First Canal (20 kilometres long) was constructed between 1885 and 1890. The Second Canal (7.4 kilometres long) was excavated between 1908 and 1912, whose junction lies between Otsu and the Kamo River. The Third Canal (3.3 kilometres long) branched off from Keage to Kita-Shirakawa. Excavated in the Meiji Period (1868—1912), the Lake Biwa Canal served for water transfer, freight and passenger transportation from Lake Biwa to its neighbouring city of Kyoto. What is worth noting is that the canal also supplied water for Japan's earliest public hydroelectric power generation, which had provided electricity for Kyoto's trams since 1895. As the first modern civil engineering project completed by Japanese workers alone, the Lake Biwa Canal is famous for various

琵琶湖运河

日本运河。亦称希望运河。琵琶湖运河从滋贺县的大津市流向京都南禅寺附近，途中穿越多条山间隧道。该运河由三部分组成，全长大约31千米。其中1号运河（20千米）开凿于1885—1890年间，2号运河（7.4千米）开凿于1908—1912年间，与1号运河在大津市与鸭川之间交汇。3号运河（3.3千米）是一条从蹴上到北白川的支流。琵琶湖运河开凿于明治时期（1868—1912），满足了从琵琶湖到其相邻的京都市的调水、货运和客运等多种需求。值得一提的是，琵琶湖运河还为日本最早的公共水力发电设施提供水源，1895年以来是京都电车的电力来源。琵琶湖运河是日本工人独自完成的第一个现代土木工程项目，其开凿过程中所采用的各种技术方法享有盛誉，包括日本首次采用的竖井开挖法。如

technical methods used, including the excavation method utilizing shafts, a technique employed for the first time in Japan. The Lake Biwa Canal is still in use today.

今, 该运河仍在使用。

Lake Washington Ship Canal

华盛顿湖通海运河

A canal located in the Salmon Bay, Seattle, northwestern United States. Also called Salmon Bay Waterway. The Lake Washington Ship Canal is 13 kilometres long with a minimum depth of 8.7 metres, connecting Lake Washington with the Puget Sound. The intention of building a navigable waterway between Lake Washington and the Puget Sound can be traced back to 1854, with a view to the transportation of logs and timbers. In 1867, the United States Navy authorized the canal project. The specific plan had not been laid out until 1891 by the United States Army Corps of Engineers. The construction of the canal was started in 1911 and completed in 1934. After the construction, Lake Washington has been transformed successfully from a tidal inlet into a freshwater reservoir with its water level being lowered by 2.7 metres. The Lake Washington Ship Canal was inscribed on the list of the National Register of Historic Places in December 1978.

美国西北部西雅图市萨蒙湾运河。亦称萨蒙湾航道。华盛顿湖通海运河全长13千米, 水深8.7米以上, 连通华盛顿湖与皮吉特湾。早在1854年, 为方便运输原木和木材, 人们便有意在此处修建运河。1867年, 美国海军授权在华盛顿湖与皮吉特湾之间修建运河。但直至1891年, 美国陆军工程兵团才做出运河修建的具体规划。该运河1911年开凿, 1934年竣工。运河建成后, 华盛顿湖的水位降低了约2.7米, 由潮汐通道转变为淡水水库。1978年12月, 华盛顿湖通海运河被列入美国国家历史遗迹名录。

Lalinde Canal

拉兰德运河

A canal located in southwestern France. The Lalinde Canal runs near the Dordogne River and links the Mauzac-et-Grand-Castang with Tuiliéres. It is 15 kilometres in length with 9 locks. The first lock is

法国西南部运河。拉兰德运河位于多尔多涅河附近, 连接莫扎克—大卡斯唐与图利埃市, 全长15千米, 建有9座船闸。其中, 第1座船

situated at the village of Mauzac, and 2 more locks are found where the canal passes through Lalinde and Borie-Basse. Then it rejoins the Dordogne River with 2 sets of 3 locks in Tuilières. The canal was originally built for the purpose to bypass the rapids of the river. The construction began in 1838 and was completed in 1843. One year later, the Lalinde Canal was opened to meet the real need of shipping. On this busy route, 29,750 tons of goods were estimated to have passed through it in 1852, and 46,000 tons in 1858. In 1854, the Salvette Dam was built downstream to regulate the mooring of ships at the port of Bergerac, and further increase the flow of traffic on the canal to nearly 200,000 tons in 1860. With the development of both the railway and road transportation, the canal became disused, for the demand for waterway freight transportation gradually decreased. In 1926, the port was deserted and the boatmen unemployed, the Lalinde Canal was finally decommissioned. In September 1996, the Lalinde Canal was listed in the inventory of historical monuments. Most of the buildings along the canal have been or will be restored. It is now a popular place for fishing and walking.

闸位于莫扎克村，另外2座分别位于拉兰德市和博里—巴斯市。拉兰德运河在图利埃市再次汇入多尔多涅河，此处建有2组船闸，每组3座。最初修建该运河是为避开多尔多涅河的急流。拉兰德运河1838年开凿，1843年完工，1844年通航，极大地满足了当时的通航需求。该运河十分繁忙，据统计，其运货量1852年为29 750吨，1858年为46 000吨。1854年，为调节水位便于贝尔热拉克港的船只停泊，运河下游河段修建了萨尔维特大坝。此后，拉兰德运河的货运量进一步提升，1860年接近20万吨。但随着铁路运输和公路运输的发展，航道货运需求逐渐减少，拉兰德运河的航运业务量随之衰退。1926年港口被弃用，船工失业，拉兰德运河最终停航。1996年9月，该运河被列入法国历史古迹名录，运河沿线大部分建筑物此后陆续得以修复。如今，拉兰德运河已成为人们喜爱的垂钓和散步佳处。

Lanaye Canal

拉奈运河

A cross-border canal located in Europe. The Lanaye Canal is 1,934 metres long with 4 locks. The canal runs from Lanaye, Belgium, where it meets the Albert Canal, to Maastricht, the Netherlands. It plays a significant role in the regional waterway transport.

欧洲跨国运河。拉奈运河全长1 934米，建有4座船闸。该运河始于比利时拉奈市，并在此处与阿尔贝特运河相通，之后流向荷兰的马斯特里赫特市。拉奈运河在流经地区的水路运输中占有重要地位。

Landes Canal

A canal located in the southwest of France. The Landes Canal originates from the Arcachon Bay and flows mainly through the Aquitaine Region (now a part of Nouvelle-Aquitaine) before joining the Pond of Biscarrosse and Parentis. Initially, the canal was 20 kilometres long, 13 metres to 24 metres wide, with 8 locks to connect Lake Cazaux, Lake Parentis and the Arcachon Bay. The construction plan was put forward since 1681, but it was not until the 1830s that the construction of the canal was carried out with the support of the Landes Exploitation and Colonization Company. The construction was divided into two phases. The first phase was to connect Lake Cazaux to the Aureilhan area while the second was to construct the left 14-kilometre-long section. In 1840, the canal was put into service to transport raw iron. A bridge toll of 3.2 francs was paid for every 1,000 kilogrammes of iron transported in vessels with a deadweight of 12 to 13 tons. The annual traffic volume of the Landes Canal had reached an average of 7,000 tons and the annual revenue was from 18,000 to 20,000 francs, which was still not enough to cover the company's operation and maintenance costs. In 1845, to increase the revenue, the company started the tourism business on the canal, which, however, turned out a failure partly because of the siltation. The company declared bankruptcy in 1857 and the Landes Canal was closed in 1860. Today, only a short section of the Landes Canal remains operational, with self-service locks to maintain the navigation

朗德运河

法国西南部运河。朗德运河始于阿卡雄湾，流经法国阿基坦大区（今新阿基坦大区的一部分），注入比斯卡罗斯—帕朗蒂湖。该运河建成初期全长20千米，宽13—24米，建有8座船闸，连通卡佐湖、帕朗蒂湖和阿卡雄湾。1681年起该运河工程开始筹划，不过直至19世纪30年代，在朗德开发与拓殖公司的支持下，计划才得以实施。运河分两段建设，第一阶段旨在连接卡佐湖与奥雷汉地区，第二阶段修建余下的14千米。1840年，朗德运河开始通航，主要用于运输生铁。自重12—13吨的船只，每运输1000千克生铁需支付3.2法郎的通行费。当时朗德运河年均货运量7 000吨，年收入1.8万—2万法郎，但仍不足以支付公司运营和维护成本。为增加收入，朗德开发与拓殖公司1845年开发了运河旅游项目，但因泥沙淤积等问题而中止。1857年，该公司宣布破产。1860年左右，朗德运河关闭。如今，为保证卡佐湖与阿卡雄湾之间通航，朗德运河仍保留一条较短的可通航河段，配备了自助通行船闸。

between Lake Cazaux and the Arcachon Bay.

Landsford Canal

兰斯福德运河

A canal located in South Carolina, the United States. The Landsford Canal is 3.2 kilometres long, 3.7 metres wide and 3 metres deep with 5 locks. Designed by Robert Mills, its construction was started in 1820 in order to facilitate goods transportation and travel in the valley of the Catawba River. It was opened in 1823. Currently, remains of the canal are in today's Landsford Canal State Park, where visitors could walk on its 2.4-kilometre-long Canal Trail to enjoy historic heritages and Rocky Shoals Spider Lily, which is endemic to southeastern America. The Landsford Canal was listed in the National Register of Historic Places in 1969.

美国南卡罗来纳州运河。兰斯福德运河长3.2千米，宽3.7米，深3米，建有5座船闸。运河由罗伯特·米尔斯设计，修建初衷是为卡托巴河谷地区的货物运输和人员往来提供便利。1820年运河开凿，1823年建成通航。目前，该运河遗址位于兰斯福德运河国家公园内，游客可以沿2.4千米长的运河步道参观历史遗迹，观赏美国东南部特有的落基山浅滩蜘蛛百合。1969年，兰斯福德运河入选美国国家历史遗迹名录。

Landwehr Canal

兰韦尔运河

A canal located in Berlin, Germany. The Landwehr Canal is about 10 kilometres long, running westwards parallel to the Spree River. It links the upper part of the Spree River at the Osthafen in Friedrichshain and winds its way to Charlottenburg in the west. The canal was built between 1845 and 1850 according to the plan made by Peter Joseph Lenné. After experiencing two rounds of expansion respectively during 1883—1890 and 1936—1941, the canal had reached a breadth of 22 metres and a depth of 2 metres. Today the Landwehr Canal is mainly used by tourist boats and pleasure craft.

德国柏林运河。兰韦尔运河与施普雷河平行，全长约10千米，在腓特烈斯海恩的奥斯特霍芬连通施普雷河上游，之后向西蜿蜒穿行，流至夏洛滕堡地区。运河由彼得·约瑟夫·伦内设计，1845年开凿，1850年建成通航。1883—1890年和1936—1941年间运河先后两次扩建，河道加宽为22米，水深至2米。如今，兰韦尔运河主要通行观光游览船只。

Langdang Ditch

An ancient canal located in Henan Province, China. See Honggou Canal.

Langerhans Canal

A canal located in the state of Brandenburg, Germany. The Langerhans Canal is 1.3 kilometres long, serving as a part of the lower reaches of the Rüdesdorf Waterway.

Languedoc Canal

A canal located in southern France. See Midi Canal.

Larsen Canal

A canal located in the province of Flevoland, the Netherlands. The Larsen Canal is 11 kilometres long, connecting several waterways, including the Gelderse Canal, the Lage Canal and the Hoge Canal. It was named after Larsen, a village planned but not established in eastern Flevoland due to the change of plan. Along the canal, the wildlife habitat is now well conserved under the efforts of local water management authorities.

Lathum Canal

An inland canal located in Friesland, the Netherlands. With an estimated terrain elevation of 255

漮荡渠

中国河南省古运河。见鸿沟。

朗格汉斯运河

德国勃兰登堡州运河。朗格汉斯运河全长1.3千米，是吕德斯多夫航道下游的一部分。

朗格多克运河

法国南部运河。见米迪运河。

拉森运河

荷兰弗莱福兰省运河。拉森运河全长11千米，连通多条航道，包括海尔德瑟运河、拉赫运河和霍赫运河。该运河名称源自拉森村，这是原计划在弗莱福兰省东部建的一个村庄，后来由于规划有变，终未建成。如今，当地水务管理部门十分重视拉森运河沿岸的生态环境，附近动植物栖息地得到了很好的保护。

拉土姆运河

荷兰弗里斯兰省内陆运河。拉土姆运河海拔约255米，始于洛勒姆

metres, the Lathum Canal starts where the Lollum Canal and the Tzum Canal meet, then flows past Waaxens, and finally ends at Gemert to join the Harlingen Canal.

运河和曲姆运河交汇处，流经瓦克森斯，最终在海默特汇入哈灵根运河。

Lecarrow Canal

A canal located in Ireland. The Lecarrow Canal is 1.5 kilometres long, connecting the village of Lecarrow to Lough Ree. It was constructed in the 1840s to carry from a quarry to Athlone the limestone needed in construction projects by the Shannon Commissioners. Fewer than 20 years after the canal was constructed, it fell into disuse, but was cleaned up later in 1889 and further dredged in the 1960s by the Office of Public Works. Currently, the Lecarrow Canal is a frequented stopping-off point in Shannon and a popular destination for fishing excursions and boating trips in Lough Ree.

勒卡罗运河

爱尔兰运河。勒卡罗运河全长1.5千米，连接勒卡罗村和里湖。运河修建于19世纪40年代，当时，香农镇地方官员计划利用该运河把采石场的石灰石运到阿斯隆镇，用于建筑工程。运河建成不到20年便停用。1889年，人们对勒卡罗运河进行了疏浚。到了20世纪60年代，爱尔兰公共设施办公室再次对该运河进行清淤。如今，到香农镇的人们会经常光顾勒卡罗运河，这里也成为里湖地区备受欢迎的乘船游览和垂钓之地。

Leeds and Liverpool Canal

A canal located in northern England, the United Kingdom. The Leeds and Liverpool Canal has a full length of 204 kilometres with 91 locks on the main line, crossing the Pennines and connecting the cities of Leeds and Liverpool. The construction of the canal lasted 46 years, dating from 1770 to 1816. It was initially used to transport limestone and then coal, which remained as the main cargo until the 1970s. In the early 21st century, a new canal was excavated as a link in the Liverpool docks system at

利兹－利物浦运河

英国英格兰北部运河。利兹－利物浦运河全长204千米，主航道上共建有91座船闸。运河流经奔宁山脉，连接利兹和利物浦两座城市。利兹－利物浦运河1770年开凿，1816年竣工，历时46年。最初修建该运河的目的是运输石灰石，随后煤炭成为最主要的运输物资，这种情况一直持续到20世纪70年代。21世纪初修建了一条新运河，

a cost of £20 million. Opened in 2009, it reconnects the Leeds and Liverpool Canal to Liverpool's South Docks. Now, as a link between the textile towns of Blackburn, Burnley, and Bradford, the Leeds and Liverpool Canal also facilitates the import of wool and cotton from the docks at Liverpool.

耗资2 000万英镑，2009年竣工后开放通航。这条新运河将利兹—利物浦运河与利物浦的南码头相连。如今，利兹—利物浦运河成为布莱克本、伯恩利和布拉德福德等纺织品生产城镇的连接枢纽，为利物浦码头羊毛和棉花进口业务提供了极大便利。

Leem Canal

莱姆运河

A canal located in Flevoland, the Netherlands. Lying 80 kilometres east of Amsterdam, the Leem Canal is about 2.1 kilometres long with a terrain elevation of 1 metre above sea level. It flows north-eastward through the village Kraggenburg, Flevoland. The canal splits into two waterways at the end and intersects with Paardentocht and Hertentocht.

荷兰弗莱福兰省运河。莱姆运河位于阿姆斯特丹市以东80千米处，全长2.1千米，海拔约1米，向东北流经弗莱福兰省的克拉亨堡村。该运河在其末端分成两条航道，分别同帕登托赫特河与赫滕托赫特河交汇。

Leermens Canal

利尔曼斯运河

A canal located in the province of Groningen, the Netherlands. The Leermens Canal is a branch of the Eastern Wijtwerd Canal and has an elevation of —2 metres.

荷兰格罗宁根省运河。利尔曼斯运河为东维特维德运河的支线运河，水位低于海平面2米。

Lehigh Canal

利哈伊运河

A canal located in Pennsylvania, the United States. The Lehigh Canal is 116 kilometres long, which consists of upper and lower sections. The project to construct this canal was started in 1818, with the initial aim to improve the navigability of the Lehigh

美国宾夕法尼亚州运河。利哈伊运河全长116千米，包括上游和下游两个河段。运河1818年开始修建，最初是为了改善利哈伊河的航运条件。利哈伊运河上游河段

River. The Upper Lehigh Canal, built from 1837 to 1843, was steeper compared with the lower part. In 1862, a dam on the waterway collapsed resulting in a severe flood and the upper section was wiped out. The Lower Lehigh Canal, also known as Stone Coal Turnpike, runs to Jim Thorpe from Easton, where it meets the Delaware River and the Morris Canal. In history, the Lehigh Canal offered the transportation of a wide variety of goods including anthracite coal and pig iron, thus boosting the economic development of the towns along its route and fuelling the Industrial Revolution in the United States. The canal was used until the 1940s when the Great Depression halted its operation. In 1962, most parts of this channel were sold for recreational purposes. In 1978, parts of the Lehigh Canal were inscribed on the list of the National Register of Historic Places.

建于1837—1843年间，与下游河段相比，该段水流落差更大。1862年，利哈伊运河上一座水坝坍塌，引发洪水，摧毁了上游河段。利哈伊运河下游段又称石煤收费路段，从伊斯顿市流至吉姆索普市，在起始处与特拉华河和莫里斯运河连通。历史上，利哈伊运河曾是无烟煤、生铁等多种货物的运输通道，带动了运河沿线城镇经济的发展，对美国工业革命具有重要的推动作用。利哈伊运河运营至20世纪40年代，因经济大萧条而被迫关闭。1962年，利哈伊运河的多数河段已被出售，用于开发休闲娱乐项目。1978年，利哈伊运河的部分河段被列入美国国家历史遗迹名录。

Leicestershire and Northamptonshire Union Canal

莱斯特郡－北安普敦郡联合运河

A canal located in England, the United Kingdom. The Leicestershire and Northamptonshire Union Canal, as a part of the Grand Union Canal, is 77 kilometres long with 22 locks, 1 aqueduct and an 800-metre-long tunnel called the Saddington. It was excavated under the acts passed in 1793 and 1805. This channel winds its way to Foxton and Gumley, from where it runs along a 27-kilometre course to flow into the Grand Union Canal. Then it extends onwards to Northamptonshire, where it joins the Grand Junction Canal.

英国英格兰运河。莱斯特郡－北安普敦郡联合运河是大联盟运河的一部分，全长77千米，建有22座船闸、1座渡槽和1条800米长的隧道（即萨丁顿隧道）。经1793年和1805年的法案批准，运河得以修建。莱斯特郡－北安普敦郡联合运河蜿蜒流至福克斯顿和古穆利，又流过27千米后汇入大联盟运河。之后，运河继续延伸至北安普敦郡，与大连通运河交汇。

Leiden Trek Canal

A canal located in the Netherlands. The Leiden Trek Canal, one of the oldest canals in the Netherlands, connects Haarlem and Leiden. With a total length of 30 kilometres, the canal is 15—30 metres wide and 1.5 metres deep. It was excavated in 1657 as an extension of the Haarlem Trek Canal that connected Haarlem with Amsterdam. For almost two centuries, the Leiden Trek Canal was the major means of passenger transportation between Leiden and Haarlem until the railway system was established in the 19th century. People used to travel on the canal by trekschuit. With many low bridges on it, the Leiden Trek Canal is no longer suitable for recreational boating and mostly falls into disuse.

Leie River

A canalized cross-border river located in Europe. Also called Lys River. The Leie River originates at an altitude of 116 metres in Lisbourg in the north of France and flows into the Schelde in Ghent, Belgium. The river is 202 kilometres long, of which 109 kilometres is in Belgium and 24 kilometres forms a part of the Belgian-French border. The total basin area of the Leie River is 4,725 square kilometres, about 1,825 square kilometres in Belgium and 2,900 square kilometres in France. The Ring Canal, the actual estuary of the Leie River, was excavated in the 1960s for the purpose of flood control and the shipping traffic. Since 1997, the section of the Leie River in and around the Belgic city of Kortrijk was

莱顿拖船运河

荷兰运河。莱顿拖船运河连接哈勒姆市和莱顿市，是荷兰最古老的运河之一。运河全长30千米，宽15—30米，深1.5米。莱顿拖船运河1657年开凿，是连接哈勒姆和阿姆斯特丹的哈勒姆拖船运河的延伸段。19世纪铁路系统开通前，在几乎长达两个世纪的时间里，莱顿拖船运河一直是莱顿和哈勒姆两市之间的主要客运航道。过去人们通常乘坐拖船往返于两地。如今，因河上桥梁高度所限，莱顿拖船运河不再适合休闲观光船只通行，几乎被弃用。

莱厄河

欧洲运河化跨国河流。亦称利斯河。莱厄河始于法国北部海拔116米的里斯堡，在比利时根特市流入斯海尔德河。该运河全长202千米，其中109千米位于比利时境内，24千米的河段构成部分比法边界。莱厄河流域总面积达4 725平方千米，其中比利时境内流域面积约为1 825平方千米，法国境内约为2 900平方千米。为防止莱厄河发生洪涝灾害，同时方便航运交通，20世纪60年代，当地政府开凿了环形运河，目前该运河已成为莱厄河的实际河口所在地。自1997年

extensively expanded, which was officially opened in May 2015. As planned, the course of the Leie River will be further widened in the future, and 7 bridges will be renovated between the French border and Waregem, a Belgian city.

以来, 位于比利时科特赖克市及其周边地区的莱厄河河段进行了扩建, 2015年5月正式通航。莱厄河河道预计将会进一步拓宽, 位于法国边境和比利时瓦勒海姆市之间的7座桥梁也将整修。

Leine River

A canalized river located in Germany. The Leine River is 281 kilometres long, serving as a left tributary of the Aller and Weser. The river originates near the town of Leinefelde in Thuringia and reaches Lower Saxony after a course of 40 kilometres. It continues to flow north before reaching its confluence with Aller and finally empties into the North Sea via the Weser. Some parts of the river were changed into canals, and a few branches were added that went parallel with it. The Leine River was once one of the most important routes for barge transportation. With the development of railways, the navigation on the canal gradually decreased and now only some of its northern reaches are navigable for small-sized commercial carriers. Before the 1960s, the river was severely polluted by industrial activities, and its water could not be used for drinking. Now with the environment being noticeably improved, sport fishing has become quite popular along the riverside.

莱纳河

德国运河化河流。莱纳河全长281千米, 是阿勒尔—威悉河左岸支流。该河源于图林根州莱讷费尔德镇附近, 流过40千米后至下萨克森州, 之后向北与阿勒尔河交汇, 最后经威悉河注入北海。该河的部分河段已被改造为运河, 人们又新修了多条与其平行的支流。莱纳河曾是欧洲驳船运输的重要航线之一, 但通航量在铁路运输出现后逐年减少, 现仅北部部分河段可供小型商船通行。20世纪60年代前, 因工业污染, 莱纳河河水已不适合饮用。目前, 莱纳河河畔生态环境明显改善, 沿河垂钓已成为深受大众喜爱的活动。

Leinewijk

A canal located in the province of Groningen, the Netherlands. The Leinewijk is a draiage canal, with

莱讷韦克运河

荷兰格罗宁根省运河。莱讷韦克运河为排水运河, 全长2.99千米, 最

2.99 kilometres in length and a maximum draught of 1.5 metres. The canal is also a watercourse for sailing and it connects the Lake of Zuidlaren with the Stads Canal near Bareveld.

大吃水深度为1.5米。该运河也是帆船航道，在巴雷费尔德附近连通泽伊德拉伦湖和斯塔茨运河。

Leizhou Youth Canal

A canal located in the southwest of Guangdong Province, China. Also called Youth Canal, as the canal was excavated mainly by young workers under 35 years old. The Leizhou Youth Canal starts from the Hedi Reservoir and stretches across the Leizhou Peninsula. With a 74-kilometre-long main course, the canal has 5 large branches, namely, the Silian River, the Donghai River, the Xihai River, the Eastern Canal, and the Western Canal. There are altogether 4,039 distributaries and channels with a total length of more than 5,000 kilometres. As a subsidiary project for the Hedi Reservoir, the Leizhou Youth Canal was started on 1 September 1959, and completed in 1960. The canal is mainly used for irrigation, and also for water supply, flood control, hydroelectricity, aquaculture, navigation, and tourism. It not only provides nearby areas with water for industrial and daily use, but also supplies water for nearly 1,300 square kilometres of farmlands in the Leizhou Peninsula, solving the long-standing problem of drought. After over 50 years, the canal was severely eroded and damaged, so the Leizhou Youth Canal Authority implemented a water-saving and renovation project in 2010. After the project was completed, the irrigation area was expanded by nearly 310 square kilometres and 180 million cubic

雷州青年运河

中国广东省西南部运河。因该运河开凿者以35岁以下的青年人为主，亦称青年运河。雷州青年运河始于鹤地水库，纵贯大半个雷州半岛。运河主航道长74千米，另有四联河、东海河、西海河、东运河与西运河5条主要分支，共分出水渠4 039条，总长5 000千米有余。1959年9月1日，作为鹤地水库配套工程，雷州青年运河开始施工并于1960年竣工。雷州青年运河主要用于农业灌溉，兼有供水、防洪、发电、水产养殖、航运和旅游等综合功能。该运河为附近城镇提供工业和生活用水，也满足了雷州半岛近1 300平方千米农田的灌溉需求，解决了半岛常年的干旱问题。50多年后，雷州青年运河已严重老化受损。运河管理局于2010年专门实施了节水改造工程。工程竣工后，新增灌溉面积310平方千米左右，每年节水1.8亿立方米，实现了水资源的优化配置，解决了当地经济发展中的水资源短缺问题。

metres of water can be saved per year, which has solved the problem of water shortage and achieved the optimal allocation of water resources.

Lek Canal

An inland canal located in the province of Utrecht, the Netherlands. The Lek Canal, a branch of the Amsterdam-Rhine Canal, is a 4-kilometre-long shortcut, connecting the Lek River with the Amsterdam-Rhine Canal. It was officially opened in August 1938 and has been the most important inland route in the Netherlands. In the middle of the canal is located the Princess Beatrix Lock, the country's largest monumental inland navigation lock allowing ships to cross the country from north to south. In recent years, an increasing number of large ships are passing through this lock. To address the growing need of navigation, the Directorate-General for Public Works and Water Management of the Netherlands decided to build a new lock chamber in the Beatrix Lock and widen the Lek Canal. It was expected to improve the shipping conditions near the city of Nieuwegein and reduce waiting time for ships. The project was started in 2016 and the new section was officially put into service upon completion in 2019.

Lemster Canal

A canal located in the province of Flevoland, the Netherlands. The Lemster Canal runs for 16 kilometres from Emmeloord to Lemmer and empties

莱克运河

荷兰乌特勒支省内陆运河。莱克运河全长4千米，是阿姆斯特丹—莱茵运河支线运河，同时也是连通莱克河和阿姆斯特丹—莱茵运河的捷径。莱克运河自1938年8月正式通航以来，一直是荷兰最重要的内陆航线。运河段中建有荷兰最大的内河船闸贝娅特丽克丝公主船闸。通过该船闸，船只能够自北向南畅行荷兰。近年来，通行的大型船只数量不断增加，为满足不断增加的通航需求，荷兰公共工程与水务管理局决定新建1座闸室，并拓宽莱克运河，从而改善尼沃海恩市附近的运河航运条件，缩短过往船只的等待时间。该水利工程2016年动工，2019年完工，并正式投入使用。

莱姆斯特运河

荷兰弗莱福兰省运河。莱姆斯特运河全长16千米，自埃默洛尔德市流向莱默市，最终注入艾瑟尔

into the Ijssel Lake. It is connected to the Urker Canal and the Zwolse Canal at Emmeloord. In 2018, an emergency bridge across the canal was planned for the convenience of pedestrians, cyclists and moped riders. As a result, the shipping on the canal was halted.

湖。该运河同厄尔卡运河、兹沃尔瑟运河在埃默洛尔德市交汇。2018年，为方便行人、自行车和摩托车通行，政府计划在莱姆斯特运河上修建一座应急桥梁，运河因此停航。

Lens Canal

朗斯运河

A canal located in northern France. The Lens Canal links Lens with the Deûle Canal in the west of Oignies. The canal is 8 kilometres in length and has no lock. It is actually a branch of the Souchez Canal, heading towards the outskirts of Lens and ending near the Noyelles rolling mill. Nowadays it remains operational.

法国北部运河。朗斯运河连接朗斯和瓦涅西部的德勒运河，全长8千米，未建船闸。该运河实际上是苏谢运河支线之一，流向朗斯郊区，止于努瓦耶勒轧钢厂附近，现仍可通航。

Leopold Canal

利奥波德运河

A canal located in northern Belgium. The Leopold Canal is 46 kilometres in length and 1.2 to 2.3 metres in depth. It starts from Zelzate and joins the North Sea in Zeebrugge. Its name originated from Leopold I (1790—1865), the first king of Belgium. From 1843 to 1854, it was excavated under the proposal of Joseph Andries, a member of the National Congress. The original purpose of constructing this canal was for the drainage after Belgium proclaimed independence from the Netherlands. In 1920, after these two countries reached an agreement, the canal was connected via the Isabella Canal with the Schelde. In addition to the drainage function, it also served a military role in World War I and World

比利时北部运河。利奥波德运河全长46千米，河水深1.2—2.3米，始于泽尔扎特市，在泽布吕赫市注入北海。运河得名于比利时第一位国王利奥波德一世（1790—1865）。比利时宣布从荷兰独立后，为了保证正常排水，在当时国会议员约瑟夫·安德里斯的提议下，比利时于1843—1854年间修建了该运河。1920年，比利时与荷兰达成和解协议，运河通过伊莎贝拉运河与斯海尔德河相通。该运河具有排水功能，在第一次和第二次世界大战中也曾服务于军事。如

War II. It is now a tourist attraction for walking and fishing.

今，利奥波德运河是游客散步和垂钓胜地。

Let Wah Canal

A canal located in Pakistan. The Let Wah Canal starts from the Hyderabad District to Mirwah, a small town around 24 kilometres from Mirpurkhas.

让华运河

巴基斯坦运河。让华运河从海得拉巴德区流向距米尔布尔哈斯约24千米的米尔瓦小镇。

Leuven-Dyle Canal

An inland canal located in Flemish Brabant, Belgium. The Leuven-Dyle Canal has a length of 30 kilometres and a depth of 3.3 metres, functioning as the lateral canal of the Dyle. It starts at the Vaartkomin Leuven and has its end at the junction of the Senne and the Dyle. Initially, this canal was called Leuven Canal. Its current name came into use in 1994 when it was allocated to the Flemish region. The navigable part of the Dyle was built as early as 1327, equipped with weirs and locks. This initial canalization was proved to be insufficient when trade increased. In 1686, early plans of excavating a lateral canal of the river was put forward, but it was not until 1749 that the plan was finalized. The canal originally had 2 single locks and 1 double lock. The great differences in height, however, put a lot of pressure on the locks and dykes. After several cases of damage, followed by floods, the locks were caught in a dire need of repairing. In 1760, the lock at the Brussel Port disappeared, and 3 new locks were built in its place. In 1836, the canal was deepened, and the lock in Kampenhout was rebuilt.

鲁汶–迪乐运河

比利时佛兰芒布拉邦特省内陆运河。鲁汶–迪乐运河全长30千米，深3.3米，为迪乐河旁侧运河。运河始于鲁汶市法特康姆区，终于塞讷河与迪乐河交界处。鲁汶–迪乐运河最初被称为鲁汶运河，1994年划归佛兰芒地区后更为现名。迪乐河部分河段早在1327年就已通航，通航河段上建有拦河坝和船闸。随着贸易量增加，早期改造过的河段已不能满足通航需求。1686年，有人提出了为鲁汶河新修一条旁侧运河的计划，但直到1749年才确定。鲁汶–迪乐运河上原有2座单式船闸和1座复式船闸。然而，巨大的水位落差给船闸和水坝的正常运转带来了较大压力。遭遇多次洪水破坏后，船闸被迫重修。1760年，位于布鲁塞尔港的1座船闸被移除，取而代之的是3座新船闸。1836年，运河河道加深，人们重修了坎彭豪特市船闸，加固了其余船

The rest of the locks were also reinforced and the bascule bridges were renewed. The bridges can now be operated from a tower in Kampenhout. The infrastructure on the canal has been protected as an industrial heritage under a ministerial decree since 1997.

闸，并翻新了运河上的竖旋桥。如今，从坎彭豪特市的一座塔楼上可以操控这些桥梁。1997年，比利时政府颁布部长法令，鲁汶—迪乐运河上的基础设施此后被列为工业遗产保护对象。

Levee Canal

莱维运河

A canal located in the northern Columbia. See Dique Canal.

哥伦比亚北部运河。见狄克运河。

Licking River～

利金河

A canalized river located in northeastern Kentucky in the United States. The Licking River is believed to be named for the many prehistoric salt licks in the region. As a partly navigable tributary of the Ohio River, the Licking River is about 488 kilometres long. It originates from a hill in in southeastern Magoffin County and meanders northwest till its confluence with the Ohio River. In Rowan County, the Cave Run Lake Dam separating the Licking River into upper and lower sections. Encouraged by the construction of the Erie Canal in 1825, the Commonwealth of Kentucky proposed the Licking River navigation project. Unfortunately, in 1842, this plan failed due to lack of funding. Later, several efforts were made to revive the project, but to no avail. With no operating locks and dams, the Licking River was only navigable during freshets and floods, usually occurring in the Spring and Fall. Nowadays, the river mainly serves as a recreational

美国肯塔基州东北部运河化河流。利金河因沿岸地区丰富的舐盐资源而得名。利金河是俄亥俄河支流，全长约488千米，可部分通航。该河始于马戈芬县东南部的一座小山，向西北方向蜿蜒流淌，汇入俄亥俄河。在罗恩县，该河被洞润湖大坝分隔为两段。1825年伊利运河建成，肯塔基州受到鼓舞，提出利金河通航工程。不幸的是，该计划于1842年因资金短缺被搁置。后来，虽然仍有多次意在恢复此工程的努力，但均告失败。因缺乏可操控的船闸和大坝，利金河仅能在春秋季靠洪水实现通航。如今，该河已成为休闲胜地和野生动物天堂。

spot and a heaven for biodiversity.

Ligovsky Canal

An abandoned canal located in Saint Petersburg, Russia. The Ligovsky Canal was 23 kilometres long and 1 to 2 metres deep, with a bottom width of 2 to 4 metres. It was once one of the longest canals in the capital city. The construction of the canal was started in 1718, with the initial aim to connect the Liga River with the pools feeding water to the fountains in the Summer Garden. After it was completed in 1720s, the canal also supplied drinking water to Saint Petersburg and served as a defensive boundary. In 1777, the fountains in the Summer Garden were destroyed by a flood. The banks of the Ligovsky Canal were also severely damaged. By the end of the 19th century, the Ligovsky Canal had been left in a state of desolation. Its previous functions ceased to exist. Gradually, some sections of the canal became filled up. In its place now lies the Ligovsky Avenue.

利戈夫斯基运河

俄罗斯圣彼得堡废弃运河。利戈夫斯基运河全长23千米,水深1—2米,底宽2—4米,曾是圣彼得堡最长运河之一。运河1718年开凿,最初是为了连通里加河,为圣彼得堡夏宫喷泉供水。18世纪20年代建成后,利戈夫斯基运河还为圣彼得堡提供饮用水,同时具有城防功能。1777年,一场洪水摧毁了夏宫喷泉,利戈夫斯基运河河岸也严重受损。到了19世纪末,该运河已经变为荒芜之地,运河曾经的功能丧失殆尽。之后,利戈夫斯基运河的部分河段被陆续回填,如今的利戈夫斯基大道在原河道上修建而成。

Lingqu Canal

An inland canal located in Guangxi Zhuang Autonomous Region, China. Also called Xing'an Canal. The Lingqu Canal is about 30 kilometres in length and 5 metres in width. With a history of more than 2,000 years, it is recognized as one of the world's oldest canals and hailed as the Pearl of World's Ancient Water Conservancy Construction. Its construction could date back to the reign of

灵渠

中国广西壮族自治区内陆运河。亦称兴安运河。灵渠全长约30千米,宽5米。灵渠开凿至今已逾2 000年,是世界上最古老的运河之一,被誉为世界古代水利工程的明珠。秦始皇统一六国后,命史禄开凿一条运送粮草的运河,以助其征服南部的百越部,这便是灵渠的前身。

Emperor Qin Shi Huang (259—210 BC), who, after conquering all the other states, ordered Shi Lu to excavate a canal for grain transport to back up his aggression against the Baiyue tribes in the south. The project known as the Lingqu Canal today was completed in 214 BC. The canal boasted a location of strategic importance. For over 2,000 years, it has been in service as the major water transport route between the Lingnan region and Central China. The canal has played a crucial role in the national unification and facilitated the political, economic, and cultural exchanges between the south and the north. Under constant renovations in the course of history, it still functions at present day as a navigable waterway and comes into play in various economic activities. In 2008, the Lingqu Canal was placed on the UNESCO World Heritage Sites Tentative List.

灵渠于公元前214年修建而成，战略位置显要，在过去的2 000多年里，它一直是连接岭南和中原地区的水上通道，对巩固国家统一，加强南北政治、经济和文化交流均发挥着重要作用。经历代重修，灵渠至今依然保持通航，在诸多经济活动中发挥着重要作用。2008年，灵渠入选联合国教科文组织世界遗产预备名录。

Lion Canal

A canal located in California, the United States. The Lion Canal was one of the series of the Venice Canals. In the early 1900s, in order to build a Venice of America in South California, the Venice Canals were excavated under the direction of Abbot Kinney, a tobacco millionaire and real estate developer. During 1926 and 1927, some of them were filled in to provide roads for traffic. The Lion Canal was transformed into the Windward Avenue.

莱昂运河

美国加利福尼亚州运河。莱昂运河是威尼斯运河网中的一条。20世纪初，为打造美国南加州版"威尼斯"，烟草富豪和房地产开发商阿博特·金尼出资修建了威尼斯运河网。1926—1927年间，为修建公路，该运河网中多条运河被回填。莱昂运河也被填平，修建成温沃德大道。

Lishui River⁼

A canalized river located in Guangxi Zhuang Au-

漓水

中国广西壮族自治区运河化河流。

tonomous Region, China. See Guijiang River.

见桂江。

Litoranea Veneta

利多拉奈阿－威尼托运河网

A network of navigable waterways located in the Veneto region of northeastern Italy. The Litoranea Veneta, as a widespread system of canals and navigable tribunaries of river, stretches 600 kilometres, flowing parallel to the Adriatic coast and linking the Venetian Lagoon with the Gulf of Trieste. It came into being in the Middle Ages and had been instrumental to the transportation between the Adriatic coast and the Po Plain. During World War I, military pontoons and shipping were found on the waterways. In the 1950s, it also contributed much to the local economic development. Now the water network is under further rounds of planning and developing to attract tourists from around the world.

意大利东北部威尼托地区航运网。利多拉奈阿－威尼托运河网由众多运河及河流支流航道组成，长达600千米，流向与亚得里亚海海岸平行，连通威尼斯潟湖与特里雅斯特湾。利多拉奈阿－威尼托运河网的形成可追溯至中世纪，在亚得里亚海沿岸和波河平原地区之间一直发挥着重要的运输功能。第一次世界大战期间，该航运系统还曾服务于军用趸船和运输。到了20世纪50年代，当地经济亦因这一航运网而得以迅速发展。如今，为吸引世界各地游客，利多拉奈阿－威尼托运河网正处于规划开发的新阶段。

Little Bačka Canal

小巴奇卡运河

A canal located in northern Serbia. The Little Bačka Canal is 66 kilometres in length, equipped with 4 locks. It is a part of the larger Danube-Tisa-Danube Canal system, running from Mali Stapar on the Great Bačka Canal to Novi Sad on the Danube River. In history, the Little Bačka Canal was once named after the emperor Franz Josef during the Austrian rule and the king Alexander during the rule of the Kingdom of Yugoslavia. The passage from Bezdan to Novi Sad is shortened by 75 kilo-

塞尔维亚北部运河。小巴奇卡运河全长66千米，建有4座船闸。该运河是多瑙－蒂萨－多瑙运河网的一部分，从大巴奇卡运河上的马里斯塔帕流向多瑙河上的诺维萨德。历史上，小巴奇卡运河曾分别以弗朗茨·约瑟夫皇帝（奥匈帝国统治时期）和亚历山大国王（南斯拉夫王国统治时期）的名字命名。经由这条运河，从贝兹丹到诺维

metres via this canal.

萨德的航程可缩短75千米。

Liugongzhen Canal

瑠公圳

A canal located in Taiwan, China. The Liugongzhen Canal once ran from the Keelung River in the north to the Wenshan District in the south of Taipei City. The wide and navigable sections were used for transportation while the narrow ones for irrigation and drainage. During the reign of Emperor Qianlong (1736—1795), Guo Xiliu presided over the construction of this canal, which lasted 21 years. He was honoured by posterity as Liugong, hence the name of the canal. In the 1970s, most parts of the canal were replaced by roads and streets due to the increasing volume of traffic and decreasing need of water transportation and irrigation. Today, only a few sections remain in downtown Taipei and the Xindian District of New Taipei City.

中国台湾地区运河。瑠公圳原河道由台北市北部的基隆河延伸至城南的文山区。宽阔且可通航的河道用于交通运输,狭窄的沟渠则用于灌溉与排水。清朝乾隆年间,瑠公圳由垦户郭锡瑠监管修建,历时21年才完工。后人尊称郭锡瑠为瑠公,瑠公圳因此得名。到了20世纪70年代,由于陆路交通量不断增长,同时人们对水运与灌溉的需求逐步减少,瑠公圳大多数河道被回填,建成公路与街道。如今,仅在台北市区和新北市新店区保留有几小段河道。

Llangollen Canal

兰戈伦运河

A cross-border canal located in the United Kingdom. Crossing the border between England and Wales, the Llangollen Canal is 73.5 kilometres long and has 21 locks, 3 tunnels, 49 bridges and 2 large aqueducts. Extending from east to west, it starts at the Hurleston Junction, flows across the Shropshire and Cheshire plains and finally reaches near Llangollen. The canal was designed by William Jessop and Thomas Telford, who were known for their ingenious and bold solutions to successfully overcome the geographical difficulties and create such a re-

英国跨境运河。兰戈伦运河流经英格兰与威尔士,全长73.5千米,沿线建有21座船闸、3条隧道、49座桥梁以及2座大型渡槽。运河东起赫尔斯通交界处,途经什罗普郡和柴郡平原,向西流至兰戈伦镇附近。兰戈伦运河由威廉·杰索普和托马斯·特尔福德设计。为克服地理条件方面的困难,他们另辟蹊径,大胆设计,创造了这一引人注目的水利工程奇迹。兰戈伦

markable engineering masterpiece. The construction work was commissioned in 1793 and completed in 1805. It is worth noting that it has taken more than 10 years to construct the renowned Pontcysyllte Aqueduct that carries the Llangollen Canal over River Dee. After the opening of the canal, limestone was transported to limekilns along its course and to the ironworks in Shropshire. In 1845, the Llangollen Canal joined the Shropshire Union canal system. The traffic volume on the canal reached its peak in the 1860s and gradually declined afterwards, coming to an end in the 1930s. In 1944, the canal was closed following an act of the Parliament. Two decades later, the Transport Act passed in 1968 reclaimed its function of navigation officially. In 2009, the section with a length of 18 kilometres from the Gledrid Bridge to the Horseshow Falls was listed as a World Heritage Site by UNESCO. The Llangollen Canal has always attracted visitors worldwide for its picturesque views of countryside and breathtaking engineering.

运河1793年开凿，1805年竣工。著名的旁特塞斯特渡槽耗时10年之久建成，连接了兰戈伦运河，横跨运河之上。运河通航后，人们可将石灰岩运往沿线的石灰窑和什罗普郡的钢铁厂。1845年，兰戈伦运河成为什罗普郡联合运河网的一部分。19世纪60年代，兰戈伦运河上的运输量达到顶峰，此后开始不断下降，20世纪30年代停航。1944年，议会通过了关闭兰戈伦运河的议案。1968年，议会又通过了一项旨在恢复该运河航运功能的交通议案。2009年，从格勒德里德大桥至霍斯肖瀑布长约18千米的河段被联合国教科文组织列为世界文化遗产。长期以来，兰戈伦运河因其令人惊叹的水利工程技术及周边美丽如画的乡村风光吸引了世界各地的游客。

Lo Canal

罗运河

A canal located in the province of West Flanders, Belgium. The Lo Canal is 14 kilometres long, linking the Newport-Dunkirk Canal and the Yser River. It was originally constructed in 12th century for navigation. It was also used as a buffer to regulate the water level of the Yser River. For this purpose, a dam was built in the hamlet of Fintele, situated at the junction of the Lo Canal and the Yser River. In time of flooding, it could offer a channel for exces-

比利时西佛兰德省运河。罗运河全长14千米，连通新港—敦刻尔克运河与伊瑟河。该运河开凿于12世纪，最初用于航运。同时，它还曾作为河水缓冲区调节伊瑟河的水位。为此，人们在伊瑟河同罗运河交界处的芬特勒村修建了一座大坝，伊瑟河泛滥时可打开坝闸以疏导水流。13世纪时，罗运河宽度达

sive water in the Yser River. In the 13th century, the canal had a width of 7.6 metres. It was enlarged in 1622. Now the Lo Canal is a Class I waterway with 1 ship lock and 12 bridges, and is mainly utilized for transport and drainage.

到7.6米。1622年，人们对该运河进行了扩建。如今，罗运河建有1座船闸与12座桥梁，为一级航道，主要用于航运与排水。

Lockhart Canal

A canal located in South Carolina of the United States. As a part of the early Broad River navigation system, the Lockhart Canal is about 3.2 kilometres long, 24 metres wide and 3 metres deep. It draws water from the Broad River and flows upstream through the Lockhart Town. Designed by Robert Mills, the canal was originally constructed to allow ships to bypass the rocky parts of the Broad River. It was built between 1820 and 1823 and closed in 1849. The canal consisted of 7 locks which were made of local blue granite, including 6 lift locks and 1 guard lock. The Lockhart Canal served as a navigable route that would enable most cities of the state to be accessible by water. Due to the presence of the textile boom in South Carolina in the late 19th century, the canal was enlarged thereafter, and a dam was built to provide power for the cotton mills between the canal and the Broad River. Later, the rise of the railway system had drawn the business away from the canal. Currently, any form of traffic on the canal is not allowed, and it is in operation only as a source of hydroelectric power.

洛克哈特运河

美国南卡罗来纳州运河。洛克哈特运河约长3.2千米，宽24米，深3米，是早期布罗德河航道网的一部分。该运河始于布罗德河，上游流经洛克哈特镇，由罗伯特·米尔斯设计，最初修建目的是便于船只避开布罗德河多礁石河段。洛克哈特运河1820—1823年间开凿，1849年关闭，沿线共建有7座船闸，包括6座提升式船闸和1座防护闸，船闸建筑材质均为当地的蓝色花岗岩。经由洛克哈特运河，船只可抵达南卡罗来纳州内的大多数城市。19世纪末，随着南卡罗来纳州纺织业的兴起，人们对洛克哈特运河进行了扩建，并新建1座水坝，为该运河和布罗德河之间的棉纺厂提供电力。后来，铁路运输系统的兴起抢占了运河的运输业务。目前，洛克哈特运河已停航，仅用于水力发电。

Loing Canal

A canal located in France. The Loing Canal links the Seine with the Briare Canal, with a total length of 49.4 kilometres and 19 locks. It constitutes a section of the Bourbonnais Route between Saint-Mammès on the Seine and Chalon-sur-Saône on the Saône River. At the beginning of the 18th century, Philippe II, the Duke of Orleans, demanded a survey and sought authorization to build a canal along the river Loing. The construction was started in 1719 and completed in 1723. The Loing Canal improved the navigability of the river Loing. In 1809, the canal came under the management of the Orleans and Loing Canals Company. In 1861, the local government became the owner of the canal, which was then enlarged at the end of the 19th century. Today, the Loing Canal still carries freight boats and remains open all year long.

Loire Lateral Canal

A canal located in the region of Bourgogne-Franche-Comté in eastern France. The Loire Lateral Canal flows through 6 rivers, including the Loire, the Besbre and the Acolin, and is connected with 4 other canals such as the Central France Canal and the Briare Canal. The canal is 196 kilometres long, with 37 locks, 3 bridges and 26 ports. Proposed by the engineer Louis Didier Jousselin, the Loire Lateral Canal was originally constructed to meet the need of industrialization along the Loire in the early 19th century. The construction of the canal was

卢万运河

法国运河。卢万运河连通塞纳河与布里亚尔运河，全长49.4千米，建有19座船闸。该运河是波旁航道的一段，始于塞纳河畔的圣马梅市，止于索恩河畔的沙隆区。18世纪初，奥尔良公爵菲利普二世提议沿卢万河开凿卢万运河，命人对其进行勘察，申请工程许可。运河1719年开凿，1723年竣工。卢万运河修建后，卢万河的航运能力得到有效提升。1809年，奥尔良和卢万河运河公司成立，专门负责卢万运河的管理工作。1861年，运河收归当地政府所有，并于19世纪末扩建。如今，卢万运河仍可通行货船，常年保持通航状态。

卢瓦尔旁侧运河

法国东部勃艮第—弗朗什—孔泰大区运河。卢瓦尔旁侧运河流经卢瓦尔河、贝布尔河、阿科兰河等6条河流，与中部运河、布里亚尔运河等4条运河相通。运河全长约196千米，沿线建有37座船闸、3座桥梁、26个港口。修建卢瓦尔旁侧运河是为了满足19世纪早期卢瓦尔河沿岸地区工业化发展的需求，修建计划最早由工程师路易·迪迪埃·茹瑟兰提出。运河

carried out in 1822 and it was officially opened in 1838. After 1860, the canal was bought by the state. In the 1990s, a large-scale maintenance project was implemented to improve the canal's navigability and reinforce its banks. The canal remains navigable nowadays.

1822年开凿，1838年正式通航。1860年后，其所有权被法国政府收购。20世纪90年代，为恢复原有通航条件，政府对卢瓦尔旁侧运河大规模修缮，两岸河堤也得以加固。如今，运河仍保持通航状态。

Loire Maritime Canal

卢瓦尔通海运河

A canal located in eastern France. The Loire Maritime Canal is 52.5 kilometres in length and has no lock. The canal connects Nantes to Saint-Nazaire and it is linked with the Atlantic Ocean.

法国东部运河。卢瓦尔通海运河全长52.5千米，未建船闸，从南特市流向圣纳泽尔市，最后注入大西洋。

London-Portsmouth Canal

伦敦－朴次茅斯运河

A proposed inland canal located in England, the United Kingdom. The London-Portsmouth Canal, as its name would tell, was supposed to run from London to the headquarters of the Royal Navy at Portsmouth. The conception of the project could date back to the year of 1641 when it was proposed that the river Wey and the river Arun should be connected to each other. Several other schemes ensued. The proposal for constructing the London-Portsmouth Canal was to save those British vessels sailing between London and Portsmouth from venturing into the English Channel, which may possibly lead to the unexpected encounter of enemy ships.

英国英格兰拟建内陆运河。伦敦－朴次茅斯运河计划连接伦敦和朴次茅斯的皇家海军总部。修建该运河的想法可追溯至1641年，当时人们提出连通韦河与阿伦河。后又出现多套设计方案。当时计划修建该运河的目的是让往返于伦敦与朴次茅斯之间的船只不必涉险驶入英吉利海峡，从而减少遭遇敌舰的风险。

Lorraines Branch

A canal located in central France. The Lorraines Branch is 3 kilometres in length and has no lock, linking the Allier River with the Loire Lateral Canal. As a disused branch of the Loire Lateral Canal, it was used to carry traffic via a circular lock. It now functions as a feeder drawing water from the Allier River.

洛林支线运河

法国中部运河。洛林支线运河全长3千米，连通阿列河与卢瓦尔旁侧运河，未建船闸。该运河是卢瓦尔旁侧运河的一个废弃分支，曾通过圆形闸门发挥航运功能。如今，洛林支线运河是一条从阿列河引水的引水运河。

Lot≈

A canalized river located in southwestern France. The Lot has a total length of 485 kilometres, which is the longest tributary river in France. It rises in the Cévennes mountains and meanders westward till its confluence with the Garonne River. The navigation on the river is faced with some challenges, including the drop of elevation in the upper section and the zigzag course in the lower section, which entails the need of improvement. The first round of improvement took place in the late 17th century. From the 1830s onwards, a series of weirs and locks were built near Decazeville to facilitate the transportation of the coal from Decazeville to southwestern France. At the same time, canals were also built to bypass the meanders at Luzech, Cajarc, Montbrun and Capdenac, reducing the passage by 13 kilometres. The navigation of the Lot gradually came to an end with the rise of the railway transportation in the late 19th century. In 1926, the river was abandoned as a navigable waterway. Today, after restoration, the Lot is revived and serves as a cruising waterway

洛特河

法国西南部运河化河流。洛特河全长485千米，是法国境内最长的一条支线河流。该河源于塞文山脉，一路蜿蜒西流，最后汇入加龙河。因上游河段水位落差大，加之下游河段蜿蜒曲折，其航运功能较差，后经多次改造。17世纪末，洛特河进行了第一次改造。19世纪30年代后，为了将德卡兹维尔煤炭资源运往法国西南地区，人们在洛特河德卡兹维尔河段附近修建了一批船闸和大坝。同一时期，为了绕开吕泽什、卡雅克、蒙布兰和卡普德纳克等地的蜿蜒河段，新修建了多条运河，使航程比原来缩短了13千米。19世纪末以来，洛特河的航运业务逐渐被铁路取代。1926年，洛特河停航。如今，洛特河经重修已恢复航运功能，主要用作旅游观光航道。

open to tourists.

Louisville and Portland Canal

A canal located in Kentucky, the United States. The Louisville and Portland Canal has a total length of 3.2 kilometres. The falls of the Ohio River in Kentucky used to stand as a barrier to the navigation between the headstream of Ohio at Pittsburgh and the Port of New Orleans on the Gulf of Mexico. The Louisville and Portland Canal was constructed to bypass them. The canal was constructed in 1826 and completed in 1833. It was initially held privately by the Louisville and Portland Canal Company. The high tolls as well as the company's refusal to enlarge the canal aroused discontent among its customers. During the 19th century, the federal government, which had made great investments in the canal's construction and maintenance, finally claimed the ownership of the canal. The Louisville and Portland Canal, also known as the first major engineering project on the Ohio River, finally became a part of the McAlpine Locks and Dam system after extensive modernization.

Lower Chenab Canal

A canal located in Punjab, Pakistan. The Lower Chenab Canal is about 300 kilometres in length and 60 metres in width. It starts from River Chenab in the Gujrat District and is composed of the Upper Gogera Branch Canal, the Lower Gogera Branch, the Burala Branch and the Upper Rakh Branch. The

路易斯维尔—波特兰运河

美国肯塔基州运河。路易斯维尔—波特兰运河全长3.2千米。俄亥俄河上的几条瀑布曾给该河上游匹兹堡地区与墨西哥湾新奥尔良港之间的通航造成障碍，为帮助船只避开这些瀑布，实现两地通航，人们从1826年开始修建路易斯维尔—波特兰运河，1833年运河竣工。起初，该运河为路易斯维尔—波特兰运河公司私有，但由于该公司收取高额通行费，且拒绝扩建运河，引起人们不满。19世纪时，联邦政府投入大量资金来扩建和维护该运河，并最终获得其所有权。路易斯维尔—波特兰运河是俄亥俄河上第一个大型水利工程，经全面现代化扩建后，目前已成为麦卡尔平船闸和大坝系统的一部分。

奇纳布下游运河

巴基斯坦旁遮普省运河。奇纳布下游运河全长约300千米，宽60米，始于古吉拉特县的奇纳布河。该运河1892年开凿，由果格拉上支线运河、果格拉河下游支流、布拉拉河支流和勒克河上游支流组

canal was constructed in 1892. To address issues such as insufficient maintenance of water transport channels and related water power facilities, unauthorized utilization of water resources, and unequal allocation of water, a pilot project has been initiated by the Irrigation and Power Department of Punjab Government to hand over the Lower Chenab Canal to Farmers Organizations.

成。为解决输水渠道及相关水力设备疏于维护、水资源非法使用及分配不均等问题，旁遮普省水利部门将奇纳布下游运河作为试点工程移交给农民组织实行自治管理。

Lower Colme Canal

A cross-border canal located in Europe. The Lower Colme Canal extends from Bergues in France to Hondschoote on the border of Belgium. Running as the eastern part of the Colme Canal, it is 13 kilometres in length and has one lock. Built in 1293, the canal served as a trade route of great significance during the Middle Ages. In 1622, the Spanish built a lock to prevent flooding from Bergues. Its French section has been deepened and now serves an industrial purpose while in Belgium it has retained its medieval characters.

科尔莫下游运河

欧洲跨国运河。科尔莫下游运河从法国贝尔格市流至比利时边境的翁斯科特镇，构成了科尔莫运河的东段，全长13千米，河上建有1座船闸。该运河于1293年开凿，是中世纪时期非常重要的贸易航线之一。1622年，为阻隔来自贝尔格市的洪水，西班牙人在该运河上修建了1座船闸。科尔莫下游运河位于法国的河段已被加深，现主要用于工业运输，而位于比利时的河段则仍保持着中世纪时期的特点。

Ludwig Canal

An abandoned canal located in southern Germany. The Ludwig Canal is named after King Ludwig I of Bavaria. Running from Kelheim to Bamberg, the 172-kilometre-long canal linked the Danube River with the Main River. The plan to connect the two rivers with a canal can be traced back to the reign of Napoleon I, which however turned out to be abor-

路德维希运河

德国南部废弃运河。路德维希运河因巴伐利亚国王路德维希一世而得名，全长172千米，在凯尔海姆市和班贝格镇之间连通多瑙河与美因河。拿破仑一世曾计划修建一条连通这两条河流的运河，但这一计划因其1815年兵败滑铁卢

tive due to his defeat at Waterloo in 1815. Later, the canal was commissioned by King Ludwig and was opened in July 1846 after 10 years of construction. The shortage of water in the summit section posed a financial challenge to the operation of the waterway. In 1950, the abandonment of the canal followed the construction of the railway network. An approximately 60-kilometre-long section of the canal is still in good condition between Nuremberg and Berching. This section has currently become a nature reserve for bike excursions and other recreational activities.

而夭折。随后，该运河由路德维希国王下令修建，耗时10年，最终于1846年7月竣工通航。然而，因其高峰航段缺水，造成运河运营成本过高。同时因铁路网的修建，路德维希运河于1950年被弃用。但纽伦堡和贝兴之间仍有约60千米长的运河河段保存完好。目前，这一河段已划为自然保护区，供人们骑行及开展其他休闲娱乐活动。

Luts

卢茨河

A canalized river located in the province of Friesland, the Netherlands. The Luts is 5.1 kilometres long and runs through the town of Balk.

荷兰弗里斯兰省运河化河流。卢茨河全长5.1千米，流经巴尔克镇。

Luttelgeest Canal

吕特尔海斯特运河

A canal located in the province of Flevoland, the Netherlands. The Luttelgeest Canal is 5 kilometres long. The canal splits from the Zwolse Canal about halfway between Emmeloord and Marknesse. Then it heads north and soon bends northeast towards Luttelgeest.

荷兰弗莱福兰省运河。吕特尔海斯特运河全长5千米，由在埃默洛尔德与马克尼斯中间的兹沃尔瑟运河分流而成。之后，该运河先向北流，不久转至东北方向，流向吕特尔海斯特。

Maas≈

A canalized cross-border river located in Europe. Also called Meuse. Flowing through France, Belgium and the Netherlands, the Maas is 925 kilometres long, serving as the longest lateral canal of the Rhine. As a part of the river system of the Rhine, it rises on the Langres Plateau in France, flows through Belgium and the Netherlands, and finally empties into the North Sea through the Rhine-Meuse-Schelde Delta. After flowing through Masseik in the Belgian province of Limburg, the Maas then turns westward and forms the border between the Dutch provinces of Gelderland and North Brabant. The water volume had been stable for almost 1,000 years, but a major flood later in the Middle Ages forced it to shift its main course northwards. With a series of floods, it splits near Heusden into two main lateral canals, one to join the Merwede, and the other to go directly into the sea. The Maas is an important part of the inland navigation infrastructure. The river was an important shipping route historically, and many stretches were canalized. In the Belgian and Dutch sections, the Maas is developed for the navigation of large ships, connecting the Rotterdam-Amsterdam-Antwerp port areas to the industrial areas upstream. There is an unnavigable part between Borgharen and Maaseik.

马斯河

欧洲跨国运河化河流。亦称默兹河。马斯河流经法国、比利时和荷兰，全长925千米，是莱茵河最长的旁侧运河。该河发源于法国的朗格勒高原，流经比利时和荷兰，最终经莱茵—默兹—谢尔特三角洲注入北海，属莱茵河水系。流经比利时林堡省的马塞克之后，马斯河向西转弯，形成荷兰海尔德兰省和北布拉班特省的边界。起初近1 000年的时间里，马斯河的水流量一直保持稳定，但中世纪时一场大洪水使其主要河道向北偏移。随后的多次洪水使马斯河在赫斯登镇附近分成两条主要旁侧运河：一条汇入梅尔韦德河，另一条直接注入大海。马斯河是内陆航道的重要组成部分，历史上是重要的航运路线，许多河段已运河化。比利时和荷兰境内河段主要用于大型船舶航运，连接鹿特丹—阿姆斯特丹—安特卫普港区和上游工业区。但荷兰博格哈伦镇和比利时马塞克镇之间的河段仍不可通航。

Maas-Moezel Canal

A cross-border canal located in Belgium and Luxemburg, Europe. See Ourthe Canal.

马斯－摩泽尔运河

欧洲跨国运河，流经比利时与卢森堡。见乌尔特运河。

Maas-Schelde Canal

A canal located in the provinces of Limburg and Antwerp, Belgium. See Bocholt-Herentals Canal.

Maas-Waal Canal

A canal located in the province of Gelderland, the Netherlands. The Maas-Waal Canal is about 13 kilometres long and 82 metres to 145 metres wide, connecting the Maas River to the Waal River. The canal runs from Weurt (west of Nijmegen) to the south and ends at Heumen, which is the tripoint among the provinces of Gelderland, Limburg and North Brabant. The construction began in 1920 and the canal was officially opened by Queen Wilhelmina in 1927. In the late 1960s, the canal was further widened as it was one of the busiest waterways in the Netherlands. There were several consequences for constructing the canal. Some villages were isolated or partly torn down while some new districts were established in the following years. Since the canal was excavated, ships navigating from Heumen to Nijmegen to reach the German hinterland did not have to make a detour and the trip was shortened by approximately 100 kilometres. There is a waterlock at the Heumen Town to handle abnormal tides, and another one at Weurt City. The construction of the canal contributed greatly to the industrialization of Nijmegen. Businesses established themselves along the canal and at the Weurt lock, and activities on the Weurt side focused on shipping fuel oil and life necessities. In 2007 and 2008, some

马斯－斯海尔德运河

比利时林堡省和安特卫普省运河。见博霍尔特－海伦塔尔斯运河。

马斯－瓦尔运河

荷兰海尔德兰省运河。马斯－瓦尔运河全长约13千米，宽82—145米。该运河连通马斯河和瓦尔河，从奈梅亨以西的韦特向南流向赫门，后者成为海尔德兰、林堡和北布拉班特三省的交汇点。1920年，运河工程动工，1927年威廉敏娜女王宣布运河正式通航。马斯－瓦尔运河曾是荷兰最繁忙的航道之一。20世纪60年代末，运河被进一步拓宽。为开凿运河，当地一些村庄被隔开或部分拆除，也有部分新区在随后几年里建立起来。运河建成后，从赫门经奈梅亨进入德国腹地的船只不必再绕道远行，航程缩短了约100千米。赫门村建有1座可应对异常潮汐的船闸，韦特市也有1座同类型船闸。运河开凿后极大地促进了奈梅亨的工业化发展。运河沿线和韦特船闸附近建有多个公司。韦特市则重点发展燃料油和生活必需品运输业务。2007年和2008年，为了增加运河沿线的通航净高，几座桥梁被抬高了0.25—0.35米，运河可容装有四层集装箱的货船通行。

bridges were jacked up by 25 to 35 centimetres in order to increase the headroom along the canal. This allows ships with four layers of containers to pass the canal.

Macclesfield Canal

A canal located in Cheshire in northwestern England, the United Kingdom. The Macclesfield Canal has a total length of about 42 kilometres with 13 locks, and many stone bridges were built on it. It runs from Marple in Cheshire to Hall Green in Birmingham, and links the section of the Trent and the Mersey Canal in the Midlands and the section in Manchester. The canal was put into use in 1831. It was once used for saving travel time between Manchester, the Potteries and the Midlands. It also served the mills, quarries and mines in surrounding areas. Nowadays, the Macclesfield Canal is often used for cruising.

Mae Kha Canal

An inland canal located in Chiang Mai, Thailand. The Mae Kha Canal starts from the mountainous areas to the west of the city and flows southward over 20 kilometres to the Mae Ping River. It was canalized in 1296 as a major part of the Chiang Mai river system, and played an important role in local irrigation, flood prevention, ecological balance preservation and public recreation. Since 1985, due to the rapid pace of urbanization, the canal has been seriously contaminated by industrial and urban

麦克尔斯菲尔德运河

英国英格兰西北部柴郡运河。麦克尔斯菲尔德运河全长约42千米，河上建有13座船闸及多座石桥，自柴郡的马普尔镇流至伯明翰的霍尔格林区，连通英格兰中部地区的特伦特—默西运河和曼彻斯特河段，1831年通航。麦克尔斯菲尔德运河缩短了曼彻斯特、波特里斯区和中部地区之间的航程，也为周边地区的工坊、采石场和矿场提供航运服务。如今，麦克尔斯菲尔德运河常供游船通行。

湄卡运河

泰国清迈市内陆运河。湄卡运河始于清迈市西部山区，向南流动逾20千米汇入湄平河。运河1296年开凿，是清迈河道网的重要组成部分，为当地的灌溉与防汛做出了重要贡献，此外也兼具生态保护和休闲娱乐功能。1985年以来，由于城市化进程过快，湄卡运河受到工业和城市废水的严重污染。因沿岸居民区不断扩张，运河逐渐变

wastewater, and it is becoming narrower with the expansion of coastal communities. As a result, its ecological function has been reduced.

窄，其生态功能遭到严重破坏。

Mae Klong River (Thailand)≈

A canalized river located in western Thailand. The Mae Klong River (Thailand) is 132 kilometres long. It starts from Kanchaburi, where the Khwae Noi and the Khwae Yai River converge, and flows through Rachaburi and Samut Songkram, and finally empties into the Gulf of Thailand. The construction of the Mae Klong Dam was started in 1964. Once called the Vajiralongkorn Dam, the dam was renamed Mae Klong in 2001. Built to block the currents of the Mae Klong River, it was reinforced to reach a length of 117.5 metres with a drainage channel of 12.5 metres. The catchment area at the mouth of the Mae Klong River is 30,106 square kilometres, which can be used to provide water for agricultural and domestic use, and divert water to the Tha Chin River. The surrounding area boasts beautiful sceneries.

湄公河泰国段

泰国西部运河化河流。湄公河泰国段全长132千米，始于北碧府奎内河和奎艾河的交汇处，流经叻武里府和夜功府，注入泰国湾。这一河段上的湄公大坝建于1964年，曾被称为哇集拉隆功大坝，2001年更为现名。这座大坝用于拦截湄公河水流，大坝加固后，长度达117.5米，排水渠长12.5米。此河段的河口集水面积为30 106平方千米，可为周边地区提供农业灌溉用水和生活用水，也为他钦河补充水源。大坝周边地区景色优美。

Mahakam≈

A canalized river located in Kalimantan, Indonesia. The Mahakam is 980 kilometres long, and is the largest river in East Kalimantan and the second largest in Indonesia. It starts in the Cemaru Mountain and flows southeast from the Long Apari District of the Borneo Highland to the Strait of Makassar, with a basin area of approximately 77,100 square kilometres. The mouth of the Mahakam

马哈坎河

印度尼西亚加里曼丹省运河化河流。马哈坎河全长980千米，是东加里曼丹省最大的河流，也是印度尼西亚第二大河流。这条河源于泽马鲁山，从婆罗洲高地的朗阿帕里区向东南注入望加锡海峡，流域面积约为77 100平方千米。马哈坎河河口距东加里曼丹省省会

River is 48 kilometres away from Samarinda, the capital of East Kalimantan Province. There are two bridges over the river. One is the 400-metre-long Mahakam Bridge, and the other is the 710-metre-long Kutai Kartanegara Bridge. In November 2011, the Kutai Kartanegara Bridge collapsed. It took three years of planning and one year and a half to rebuild the bridge in the same place. The new Kutai Kartanegara Bridge was opened in December 2015. The Mahakam is mainly used for transportation, fishing, and farming, as well as providing fresh water for nearby residents. The river is also an important ecological zone, containing 147 species of local freshwater fish and some critically endangered species.

三马林达市48千米。马哈坎河上建有两座桥：一座是长400米的马哈坎桥，另一座是长710米的库泰－卡塔尼亚拉大桥。2011年11月，库泰－卡塔尼亚拉大桥倒塌。经过三年规划和一年半施工，大桥在原址上重建，并于2015年12月开通。马哈坎河主要用于航运、捕鱼和农业灌溉，也为附近居民提供淡水资源。此外，马哈坎河是重要的生态保护区，有147种本地淡水鱼类以及诸多濒危物种栖息于此。

Mahmoudiyah Canal

马赫穆迪亚运河

A canal located in Al Buhayrah, Egypt. Also called Canal of Alexandria. The Mahmoudiyah Canal, about 72 kilometres in length, is a branch of the Nile River. It originates from the Nile Port, runs through Alexandria and flows into the Mediterranean Sea. In 1817, Viceroy Mohamed Ali ordered to build a canal near the Alatf Village in order to channel the water of the Nile River to Alexandria as well as provide a waterway for ships. The canal was also built to supply Alexandria with food and fresh water from the Nile River. In April 1819, the construction stopped due to the outbreak of a plague. In January 1820, the project was completed and the canal was named after Sultan Mahmud II of Istanbul. Within twenty years, the sediment

埃及布海拉省运河。亦称亚历山大运河。马赫穆迪亚运河全长约72千米，是尼罗河的一条支流，始于尼罗河港口，流经亚历山大港，注入地中海。1817年，总督穆罕默德·阿里下令在阿拉特夫村附近开凿一条运河，旨在将尼罗河河水引入亚历山大港，并开辟一条航道。此外，运河还可向亚历山大港运送尼罗河地区的食物和淡水。1819年4月，因瘟疫爆发，运河工程暂停。1820年1月，工程竣工，运河以伊斯坦布尔苏丹马哈茂德二世的名字命名。通航20年后，河道上泥沙淤积日趋严重，运河几乎无法再

accumulation in the course became so serious that the canal became almost unnavigable. Muhammad Sa'id Pasha ordered to dredge the Mahmoudiyah Canal after his coming to power. The Mahmoudiyah Canal provides people in the area with water for irrigation and living, and the water has not been polluted so far. The Egyptian government and the province of Al Buhayrah attach great importance to the development along the canal, aiming at coordinating the economic and industrial development with the protection and utilization of the canal and achieving green development.

通航。穆罕默德·赛义德·帕夏执政后，下令疏浚河道，运河得以恢复通航。马赫穆迪亚运河为沿河地区居民提供灌溉和生活水源，河水至今未受到污染。埃及政府和布海拉省十分重视马赫穆迪亚运河沿线的经济开发，在保护和利用运河的基础上推动运河沿线地区经济和产业的绿色发展。

Mahoning Canal

马霍宁运河

A canal located in the United States. See Ohio and Pennsylvania Canal.

美国运河。见俄亥俄—宾夕法尼亚运河。

Maidenhead Waterways

梅登黑德航道网

A system of waterways under construction located in England, the United Kingdom. The Maidenhead Waterways rise from the Thames near Cliveden Reach. They are divided into two main streams, i.e., the York Stream and the Moor Cut, which meet at Green Lane and flow back to the Thames at Bray Marina. The system was previously abandoned due to problems such as narrow channels and silt blockage. In 2011, the British government announced that it would restore and upgrade the system. According to the plan, the waterways will be navigable firstly for small-sized craft, and eventually for narrow boats. On 14 March 2020, Theresa May, then

英国英格兰在建航道网。梅登黑德航道网始于泰晤士河克利夫登河段附近，分为两大干流：约克河段和穆尔航道，二者交汇于格林莱恩，在布雷马里纳回流至泰晤士河。梅登黑德航道网曾因河道狭窄、淤泥堵塞等问题遭弃用。2011年，英国政府宣布对航道网进行修复与扩建，计划先实现小型船只通航，最终可容纳常规运河船只。2020年3月14日，时任英国首相的特雷莎·梅宣布，航道网改造项目的第一期工程顺利完

British Prime Minister, announced the completion of the first phase of the renovation project of the waterways. So far, the total cost of the project has reached £8 million, which is provided by Windsor and the Maidenhead Council. The follow-up renovation projects are still in progress.

Main

A canalized river located in Germany. The Main, about 524 kilometres in length, is the longest tributary of the Rhine. It has two headstreams, the White Main and the Red Main. The river runs west through Bavaria, Baden-Württemberg and Hessen in central Germany, meets with the Rhine near Mainz in Rhineland-Palatinate. The total fall distance of the river is 895 metres, and its basin size is 27,208 square kilometres. The Main is navigable from the mouth of the Rhine to Bamberg in Upper Franconia, Bavaria with a length of 396 kilometres, and is connected to the Danube via the Rhine-Main-Danube Canal. Shipping on the Main could date back to the reign of the first Roman emperor Caesar Augustus. The river was of great importance to the expansion of the Roman Empire with its strategic position, and cities sprung up along the shores. In the Middle Ages, the Main was already a critical trade route. Ships with a cargo carrying capacity of 10 to 20 tonnes could travel about 100 kilometres per day downstream, while the ships upstream had to be towed. The advent of the railways in the 1850s marked a sharp decline in shipping on the Main. Nowadays, over the navigable section of

成。到目前为止，该项目已耗资800万英镑（由温莎和梅登黑德委员会提供），后续改造项目仍在进行中。

美因河

德国运河化河流。美因河全长约524千米，是莱茵河最长支流，由白美因河和红美因河汇聚而成。美因河向西流经德国中部的巴伐利亚州、巴登—符腾堡州和黑森州，在莱茵兰—普法尔茨州的美因茨附近汇入莱茵河。美因河总落差达895米，流域面积为27 208平方千米，可通航长度约396千米，从莱茵河河口延伸至巴伐利亚州上弗兰肯尼亚行政区的班贝格市，通过莱茵—美因—多瑙运河与多瑙河相通。早在罗马帝国开国皇帝奥古斯都统治时期，美因河就已用于航运。因其独特的战略位置，美因河在罗马帝国的扩张中发挥过重要作用，沿河两岸兴建了多座城市。中世纪时期，该河是重要的贸易航线。最大运载量为10—20吨的船舶每日可顺流下行约100千米，而前往上游的船舶则必须借助牵引船拖行。19世纪50年代铁路出现后，美因河的航运量大幅缩减。如今，美因河通航河道上有34

the river are 34 weirs built between the 1880s and the 1980s, most of which can generate electricity.

座堰坝，修建于19世纪80年代至20世纪80年代，大多数可用于水力发电。

Main-Danube Canal

美因－多瑙运河

A canal located in Germany. Also known as Europe Canal. The Main-Danube Canal, mostly in Franconia and partly in Bavaria, is approximately 171 kilometres long. The origin of the canal can be traced back to 793 AD. To open a route through the centre of Europe for his battle fleet, Charlemagne the Great attempted to excavate a canal between Rezat and Altmühl so as to cross the watershed between the North Sea and the Black Sea. The project was halted due to the collapse of the banks caused by heavy rains. In 1825, Ludwig I, King of Bavaria, resumed the ambitious plan. The Ludwig Canal between Bamberg and Kelheim was built from 1836 to 1845. The route was very similar to today's Main-Danube Canal. The canal remained in use until World War II. In 1921, the German government and the state of Bavaria co-funded the expansion of the canal. Before World War II, locks on the Main River were broadened and hydroelectric power stations were installed to many locks. The locks are among the largest and most modern structures of their kind in Europe. The construction of the Main-Danube Canal officially began in June 1960. The canal was finally opened on 25 September 1992. During its construction, the equivalent of almost 460 million euros went into ecological measures. As one of the world's largest civil engineering

德国运河。亦称欧洲运河。美因—多瑙运河主要河段位于德国弗兰肯尼亚地区，部分河段位于巴伐利亚州，全长约171千米。这条运河的历史可追溯至公元793年，当时查理曼大帝在雷察特河与阿尔特米尔河流域之间开凿运河，旨在为其舰队开辟一条穿越欧洲中部的航线，打通北海与黑海之间的水上交通。后因暴雨冲垮河岸，工程被迫中止。1825年，巴伐利亚国王路德维希一世下令重启这个宏大的运河项目，1836—1845年间在班贝格与凯尔海姆之间修建了路德维希运河。该运河与今天的美因—多瑙运河航线相似，第二次世界大战爆发前一直在使用。1921年，德国政府与巴伐利亚州共同资助了路德维希运河的扩建工程。第二次世界大战以前，美因河上的船闸得以扩建，多座船闸配建了水力发电站，这些船闸在欧洲同类船闸中规模最大且现代化程度最高。1960年6月，美因—多瑙运河工程开工，施工期间投入约4.6亿欧元用于生态保护。1992年9月25日该运河正式通航。美因—多瑙运河是

projects, the Main-Danube Canal greatly facilitates water traffic between the North Sea and the Black Sea. It takes on economic importance in connecting many trade routes and ports in inland Europe. Besides, the canal and its environs are increasingly used for recreation, making tourism along the canal one of the most important economic factors in the region.

世界上最大的土木工程项目之一，极大地促进了北海与黑海之间的航运交通。该运河连通欧洲内陆多条贸易航线和多个港口，具有重要的经济价值。运河周边地区的休闲娱乐产业得到开发，沿线的旅游业也成为这一地区最重要的经济支柱之一。

Main Turkmen Canal

土库曼主运河

A canal located in Turkmenistan. The Main Turkmen Canal is about 1,300 kilometres long, along which a series of water conservancy facilities, such as sluices, reservoirs, weirs and hydropower stations, are constructed. As a large-scale irrigation project, it was built to draw water from the Amu Darya River to Krasnovodsk (now Türkmenbaşy), facilitate cotton cultivation, make good use of the earth of the Karakum Desert, and connect the Volga River to the Amu Darya. The excavation began in 1950 and it was estimated that 10,000 workers were involved in the construction of the canal. In 1957, the canal was completed. The construction of the canal has caused serious ecological losses, leading to the drying up of the Amu Darya River, the severe reduction of the inflow of water to the Aral Sea, and the destruction of the native riparian forest.

土库曼斯坦运河。土库曼主运河全长约1 300千米，沿线建有水闸、水库、堰坝、水电站等一系列水利设施。开凿这条运河旨在将阿姆河河水引至克拉斯诺沃斯克(现称土库曼巴希)，以保障棉花种植灌溉用水，充分利用卡拉库姆沙漠的土地，并连通伏尔加河与阿姆河。该运河是一项大型灌溉工程，1950年开凿，约1万名工人参与了修建工程。1957年，运河竣工。土库曼主运河的修建引发了一系列严重的生态问题，使阿姆河干涸，咸海的入水量因而大幅降低，原生河岸林也遭到了破坏。

Makkum Ship Canal

马库默通海运河

A canal located in the northern Netherlands. The Makkum Ship Canal flows in the province of

荷兰北部运河。马库默通海运河流经弗里斯兰省，连通威特马索

Friesland, connecting the Witmarsum Canal with the Van Panhuys Canal.

姆运河和范班豪斯运河。

Manchester Ship Canal

曼彻斯特通海运河

An inland canal located in the northwest of England, the United Kingdom. The Manchester Ship Canal runs for 58 kilometres with 5 locks. It starts from the Mersey Estuary near Liverpool, flows to Manchester via Cheshire and Lancashire, and connects to the Irish Sea. The canal, dotted with weirs and bridges, was built with the Barton Swing Aqueduct (the only swing aqueduct in the world) and the Trafford Park (the largest industrial estate in Europe at present). The construction of the Manchester Ship Canal lasted from 1887 to 1893. It was the largest river navigation canal in the world when opened in January 1894, which turned the port of Manchester into the third busiest port in the United Kingdom. By the 1970s and 1980s, the size of freight ships increased, exceeding the capacity of the canal, and the transportation volume of the canal gradually declined. As large vessels and small vessels cannot navigate together, hired vessels were normally not permitted to use the canal. Boat owners had to ask for permission from the Manchester Ship Canal Company by offering evidence that their boats, with required safety equipment on board, were both seaworthy and insured. In 1993, the canal was acquired by Peel Holdings. In 2011, the company announced the implementation of the £50 billion Atlantic Gateway Project, aiming to redevelop the Liverpool Port and the Manchester

英国英格兰西北部内陆运河。曼彻斯特通海运河全长58千米，建有5座船闸。运河始于利物浦附近的默西河口，经柴郡和兰开夏郡流至曼彻斯特，注入爱尔兰海。运河上建有多座堰坝与桥梁，沿线有世界上唯一的巴顿下旋渡槽，还有欧洲最大的工业园区特拉福德园区。曼彻斯特通海运河1887年开凿，1893年竣工。运河1894年1月通航，是当时世界上最大的航运运河，曼彻斯特港也因此成为英国第三大繁忙港口。20世纪70—80年代，由于货运船只体积增大，超出了曼彻斯特通海运河的承载能力，河上的运输量逐渐下滑。又由于大、小型船只无法同时在运河上航行，通常不允许租用船只通行。船主必须向曼彻斯特通海运河公司申请，提供船只的适航证明、保险缴纳证明以及安全设施证明后方可通行。1993年，曼彻斯特通海运河被皮尔控股公司收购。2011年，该公司宣布实施总投资量达500亿英镑的"大西洋门户计划"，旨在重新开发利物浦港和曼彻斯特通海运河。运河水质欠佳，但两岸仍有几个对公众开放的自然保

Ship Canal. Despite poor water quality, there are still several nature reserves open to the public along the canal. The reserves are rich in wildlife and flora, acting as the habitat for diverse birds.

护区，区内野生动植物资源丰富，是多种鸟类的栖息地。

Manila Canal

A canal located in the northwestern part of the Philippines. The Manila Canal has an estimated elevation of 12 metres. The surrounding area of the canal is almost completely covered by houses, with a population density of 10,000 people per square kilometre.

马尼拉运河

菲律宾西北部运河。马尼拉运河海拔约12米，沿线区域基本为住宅区，人口密度大约为每平方千米10 000人。

Manych Ship Canal

A canal located in Russia. The Manych Ship Canal is 700 kilometres in length, connecting the basins of the Sea of Azov, the Black Sea, and the Caspian Sea. It runs through Lake Manych-Gudilo and the Veselovskoe and Proletarskoe reservoirs and extends to the Caspian Sea. The construction of the canal began in 1932 but was suspended through World War II. In order to promote the economic development in southern Russia, the project was resumed later. In the 21st century, the Volga-Don Shipping Canal can no longer meet the present navigation needs of the countries of the Caspian region. The completion of the construction of the Manych Ship Canal can help ease the problem and bring many benefits. First, it can provide a considerable number of job opportunities in oil refining chemical industry and other export-oriented productions. Second,

马内奇通海运河

俄罗斯运河。马内奇通海运河全长700千米，连通亚速海、黑海和里海流域。运河流经马内奇古季洛湖、韦谢洛夫斯科耶水库和普罗列塔尔斯卡亚水库，延伸至里海。马内奇通海运河1932年开凿。第二次世界大战中，工程被迫中断，后为振兴俄罗斯南部经济重启该运河项目。进入21世纪后，伏尔加—顿河航道无法满足里海地区国家的航运需求，而马内奇通海运河修建后有助于缓解这一问题，并可为当地经济发展带来诸多益处：一方面可创造大量就业机会，促进炼油化工企业及其他以出口为导向的生产行业的发展；另一方面可向干旱地区供水，以促进农业及畜

fresh water from the canal can increase yields of agriculture and husbandry in arid areas. Meanwhile, it will also cause environmental concerns. Transporting oil and oil products along the canal could lead to potentially large petroleum spills. Currently, there are plans to expand the Manych Ship Canal into a larger Eurasia Canal, with the course deepened to 6.5 metres and widened to 80 metres, which will greatly enhance the shipping capacity of the canal and will be of great significance in tapping the full economic potential of the adjacent region.

牧业发展。但同时，运河也有可能引发环境问题。例如，石油以及石油产品运输过程中可能会发生大规模泄漏事故，造成环境污染。目前已有人计划将马内奇通海运河扩建为更大的欧亚运河，预计河道将加深至6.5米，河面将拓宽至80米，这样可大幅提升运河航运能力，有力推动周边地区的经济发展。

Marala-Ravi Link Canal

A canal located in Punjab, Pakistan. The Marala-Ravi Link Canal is 100 kilometres in length, flowing from the Marala Headworks on River Chenab to the Ravi River. It is of great importance to irrigation. Built in 1954, the canal is designed to carry 623 cubic metres of irrigation water per second, and the canal irrigates the agriculture land of Sialkot and Narowal. It also feeds River Chenab's water into River Ravi. The banks of the canal are in collapsed condition because they have no fencing and have never been repaired since their construction. The canal is occasionally closed because of the water shortage in the Marala Headworks on River Chenab.

马拉拉-拉维连接运河

巴基斯坦旁遮普省运河。马拉拉-拉维连接运河全长100千米，从奇纳布河的马拉拉渠首流向拉维河，是重要的灌溉渠道。这条运河1954年修建，流速为每秒623立方米，为锡亚尔科特和拿热瓦尔两座城市提供农业灌溉水源。运河亦将奇纳布河河水引入拉维河。运河两岸未筑围栏，自建成后也未进行修缮，河岸处于坍塌失修状态。由于奇纳布河在马拉拉渠首的水量减少，马拉拉-拉维连接运河不时处于关闭状态。

Marans Canal

A canal located in Charente-Maritime, France. See Marans-Rochelle Canal.

马朗运河

法国滨海夏朗德省运河。见马朗-罗谢尔运河。

Marans-Rochelle Canal

A canal located in Charente-Maritime, France. Also called Marans Canal, Rompsay Canal or Rochelle Canal. The Marans-Rochelle Canal links the Sèvre Niortaise with the harbour at Rochelle and runs to Marans. It is 24.6 kilometres in length and has 4 locks. The canal was originally built for developing trade in this area and was a part of the great canal project connecting the Loire River with the Adour River. In 1806, the construction work was carried out under the order of Napoleon I and in 1875 the canal was opened. The advent of trains, especially the construction of a track between Nantes and La Rochelle, led to the disuse of the canal. After World War II, the canal was completely closed. Today, the Marans-Rochelle Canal is a nice place for walkers because of its picturesque scenery.

马朗－罗谢尔运河

法国滨海夏朗德省运河。亦称马朗运河、罗姆赛运河或罗谢尔运河。马朗－罗谢尔运河在罗谢尔连接塞夫尔－尼奥尔河和罗谢尔港口，之后流至马朗，全长24.6千米，建有4座船闸。这条运河最初为发展当地贸易而开凿，是连通卢瓦尔河与阿杜尔河的大型运河工程的组成部分。1806年，拿破仑一世下令开凿该运河。1875年，运河通航。随着铁路运输出现，特别是南特与罗谢尔之间建成了铁路，马朗－罗谢尔运河被弃用。第二次世界大战后，马朗－罗谢尔运河彻底关闭。如今，该运河因风景秀丽而成为徒步休闲胜地。

Marans Ship Canal

A canal located in the province of Charente-Maritime, France. Also called Brault Maritime Canal. The Marans Ship Canal links Marans on the Sèvre Niortaise to the sea. It is 5 kilometres in length and has 1 lock. The construction began in 1891 and the canal was put into use around 1900. This canal was constructed to facilitate the transport from the Sèvre Niortaise to the sea, but it has become a marina for pleasure boats after the cessation of maritime navigation.

马朗通海运河

法国滨海夏朗德省运河。亦称布劳特通海运河。马朗通海运河连接塞夫尔－尼奥尔河河畔的马朗至海滨，全长5千米，建有1座船闸。运河1891年开凿，1900年左右通航，旨在使塞夫尔－尼奥尔河至海滨的交通更为便利。如今，因海上航运业衰落，马朗通海运河主要用作游船航道。

Maribyrnong Explosives Magazine Canal

马瑞巴农-军火库运河

A canal located in Victoria, Australia. The Maribyrnong Explosives Magazine Canal has a length of 400 metres, connecting Jack's Magazine to the Maribyrnong River. It was constructed between 1875 and 1876 and opened in 1878. As a part of the large Victorian government explosives reserve, known as Jack's Magazine, the canal enables the barges to transfer explosives offload at its dock just outside the magazine walls.

澳大利亚维多利亚州运河。马瑞巴农—军火库运河全长400米，连接杰克军火库与马瑞巴农河。该运河1875—1876年间开凿，1878年通航。马瑞巴农—军火库运河是维多利亚州政府杰克军火库的一部分，运河码头可供运输弹药的驳船在军火库墙外卸货。

Mariinsky Canal

马林斯基运河

A canal located in Russia. See Belozersky Canal.

俄罗斯运河。见别洛焦尔斯克运河。

Mariinsky Canal System

马林斯基运河网

A canal system located in Russia. See Volga-Baltic Waterway.

俄罗斯运河网。见伏尔加—波罗的海航道。

Marjorie Harris Carr Cross Florida Greenway

马乔里·哈里斯·卡尔跨佛罗里达绿道

A canal located in the United States. See Cross Florida Barge Canal.

美国运河。见跨佛罗里达驳船运河。

Mark Canal

马克运河

A canal located in North Brabant, the Netherlands. The Mark Canal is 6 kilometres long, connecting the Mark River with the Welhelmina Canal. It runs

荷兰北布拉班特省运河。马克运河全长6千米，连通马克河和威廉敏娜运河，流经东豪特和泰海登。

across Oosterhout and Terheijden. The canal was constructed from 1913 to 1915. Then it underwent expansion in width in 1976. A total of three bridges and one lock were built across the canal.

运河1913—1915年间开凿，1976年河面拓宽，河上共建有3座桥梁和1座船闸。

Marknesse Canal

马克内瑟运河

A canal located in the province of Flevoland, the Netherlands. The Marknesse Canal has a length of 3.2 kilometres.

荷兰弗莱福兰省运河。马克内瑟运河全长3.2千米。

Mark-Vliet Canal

马克-弗利特运河

A canal located in the province of North Brabant, the Netherlands. The Mark-Vliet Canal, 9.5 kilometres long, connects the two branches of the Mark-Vliet River, the Mark River and the Vliet River. The canal project was approved in 1968, and officially put into use in 1983. It is at the current crossroads with the Steenbergen River and the Roosendaal River, and the latter is opened up to the industrial zones of the north and west of Roosendaal City. It now allows ships to transport from Roosendaal to Volkerak and Breda.

荷兰北布拉班特省运河。马克—弗利特运河全长9.5千米，连通马克—弗利特河的两条支流，即马克河和弗利特河。运河项目1968年获批，1983年运河正式通航。马克—弗利特运河现处于斯滕贝亨河和罗森达尔河交汇处。沿罗森达尔河可航行至罗森达尔市北部和西部的工业区。船舶可通过马克—弗利特运河从罗森达尔航行至沃尔克拉克和布雷达。

Marne ≈

马恩河

A canalized river located in Paris, France. The Marne is the eastern tributary of the Seine, and has a length of 514 kilometres. It was canalized from 1837 to 1867. Several canals were built to bypass the turning points of the river in order to promote the navigation. It was once an arterial waterway

法国巴黎运河化河流。马恩河是塞纳河东线支流，全长514千米，1837—1867年间进行了运河化改造。为使过往船只能够避开水流转弯的湍急之处，人们开凿了多条运河，以提升马恩河的航运功能。

that linked Paris and the Seine with other important channels to the east, including the Aisne-Marne Canal, the Marne-Rhine Canal, and the Champagne-Burgundy Canal. Many lateral canals were constructed alongside, among which the most extensive one was the Marne Lateral Canal. In the downstream of the Marne, there were three canals: the Meaux-Chalifert Canal, the Chelles Canal, and the Saint-Maurice Canal. The 290-metre-long Meaux-Chalifert Canal was constructed in 1837 and was out of use in 1846. The Chelles Canal was parallel to the Marne River. Its construction began in 1848 but was deserted shortly due to funding issues. The Saint-Maurice Canal was a 3.9-kilometre-long channel with two locks, connecting with the Marne. It was opened in 1864 but was filled in to construct a section of motorway in the 1950s.

马恩河曾是连接巴黎、塞纳河及法国东部河道（包括埃纳—马恩运河、马恩—莱茵运河和香槟—勃艮第运河）的主航道。马恩河沿线的多条旁侧运河中最大的一条是马恩河旁侧运河。马恩河下游有三条运河：莫—查理菲尔运河，全长290米，1837年开凿，1846年被废弃；谢勒运河，与马恩河平行，1848年开凿，但很快即因资金问题停工；圣—莫里斯运河，长3.9千米，建有2座船闸，与马恩河相通，1864年通航，但20世纪50年代因修建一段高速公路被回填。

Marne Lateral Canal

A canal located in the department of Marne in northeastern France. The Marne Lateral Canal links Vitry-le-François with Dizy. It has a total length of 67 kilometres and 15 locks. Starting from the junction with the Marne-Rhine Canal, the canal runs to the canalized river Marne and links with the Aisne-Marne Canal. Before the canal was excavated, it was difficult to travel to the upstream Epernay. This entailed the need for a canal to bypass the Marne River. The construction project was started in 1836 and completed in 1846. In the 1960s, a 2-kilometre-long section of the canal was constructed in an effort to bypass the town of Vitry-le-François. Although the

马恩河旁侧运河

法国东北部马恩省运河。马恩河旁侧运河连接维特里—勒弗朗索瓦和迪济，全长67千米，建有15座船闸。该运河始自与马恩—莱茵运河的交汇处，流至马恩河运河化河段，与埃纳—马恩运河相连。马恩河旁侧运河开挖前，航行至马恩河上游的埃佩尔奈很困难，需要修建一条运河绕开马恩河。运河1836年开凿，1846年完工。20世纪60年代，为绕过维特里—勒弗朗索瓦镇，新建了2千米长的航道。如今，马恩河旁侧运河依旧通航，但不再

canal remains open, it is no longer a wise option for pleasure cruising.

是乘船观光的理想线路。

Marne-Rhine Canal

A canal located in northeastern France. The Marne-Rhine Canal links the Marne River and the Champagne-Burgundy Canal. It was originally designed to connect Paris, Alsace, and Germany. The plan to build the canal was initiated in 1780. Barnabé Brisson, a bridge and road engineer, was responsible for the preliminary study and investigation in 1826, and then the work began in 1838 under the command of Charles-Étienne Collignon. The 313-kilometre-long canal was the longest canal in France when it was opened in 1853. The modernization of the Marne-Rhine Canal lasted for more than 150 years. One important move was the construction of Saint-Louis-Arzviller inclined plane in 1969, which successfully overcame an elevation difference of about 44.5 metres. From 2004 to 2008, 4 locks were reconstructed to become a part of automation system. The Marne-Rhine Canal was deepened first to 2.2 metres (for a 1.8-metre draught) at the end of the 19th century, and then to 2.5 metres (for a 2.2-metre draught) in the 1960s. The canal is suited for small ships with a maximum size of 38.5 metres in length and 5.05 metres in width. The route now consists of three parts: the Western section, the Eastern section, and the 25-kilometre-long canalized Moselle River. The Western section is about 130 kilometres long with 97 locks. It connects with the Meuse Canal.

马恩-莱茵运河

法国东北部运河。马恩－莱茵运河连通马恩河与香槟－勃艮第运河，最初的修建目的是连接巴黎、阿尔萨斯大区和德国。开凿马恩－莱茵运河的计划始于1780年。1826年，桥梁道路工程师巴纳贝·布里松负责开展运河项目前期调研工作。1838年，运河工程开始实施，由夏尔·埃蒂安·科利尼翁负责。马恩－莱茵运河1853年开通，全长313千米，是法国当时最长的运河。马恩－莱茵运河的现代化改造持续了150多年。1969年修建圣－路易－阿尔兹维莱斜面升船机是其中一项重要工程，解决了44.5米的运河水位落差难题。2004—2008年间，作为运河自动化系统工程的一部分，运河上的4座船闸得到改造。马恩－莱茵运河曾两次加深，19世纪末第一次加深后，水深为2.2米，船舶吃水深度可达1.8米；20世纪60年代第二次加深后，水深达到2.5米，船舶吃水深度可达2.2米。改造后的河道适合小型船只行驶，可通航最长38.5米、最宽5.05米的船只。目前，马恩－莱茵运河由西段、东段和长25千米的摩泽尔运河化河段三部分组成。西

This section is still used for commercial purposes. The 159-kilometre-long Eastern Section runs from Frouard to Strasbourg. This section is connected with the Nancy branch of the Vosges Canal and the Sarre Canal. It has 56 locks, and the maximum authorized draught is 2.2 metres. The Eastern section, as a commercial waterway, is mainly used for transporting iron ore, coal and building materials. The Moselle River runs from Toul to Frouard, and can be entered through a new lock. The landscapes presented by the Marne-Rhine Canal are diverse but all delightful along its full length.

段长130千米，建有97座船闸，与默兹运河相通，如今仍用于商业运输。东段长约159千米，自弗鲁瓦尔流至斯特拉斯堡，与孚日运河的南锡支流和萨尔运河交汇。东段共建有56座船闸，核定最大吃水深度为2.2米。该河段是商业航道，主要用于运输铁矿石、煤炭和建筑材料等。摩泽尔运河化河段是图勒和弗鲁瓦尔之间的河段，可由新船闸进入。马恩—莱茵运河沿岸风貌富于变化，一路美景令人心旷神怡。

Marseille-Rhône Canal

A canal located in northwestern France. The Marseille-Rhône Canal connects the Mediterranean Sea at Marseille to the Rhône at Arles with a total length of 81 kilometres. It is made up of several sections, including the Rove Tunnel from the harbour on the Mediterranean, the channel leading to the Étang de Berre, the Bouc-Martigues Canal, the Rhône-Fos Canal and the Saint-Louis Canal. The part between Marignane and Marseille was closed after the Rove Tunnel fell down in 1963. The channel leading to the Étang de Berre split into two ways at Martigues, namely, the Gallifet Canal and the Baussengue Canal, both of which are used only for recreational purposes. The Martigues Island is located between the two canals and is divided by the small Saint-Sébastien Canal. Martigues is given the name Venice of Provence for its complex waterways.

马赛－罗讷运河

法国西北部运河。马赛—罗讷运河自马赛流至阿尔勒，连通地中海和罗讷河，全长81千米。该运河由地中海港口处的罗夫隧道、通往贝尔潟湖的航道、布克—马蒂格运河、罗讷—福斯运河以及圣路易斯运河等多段水路组成。1963年，罗夫隧道坍塌，马里尼亚讷至马赛的河段随后关闭。通往贝尔潟湖的航道在马蒂格地区分出两条航线，分别是加利费运河和布桑格运河，仅供观光船只通行。马蒂格岛位于这两条运河之间，被圣塞巴斯蒂安运河一分为二。马蒂格地区航道密布，被誉为"普罗旺斯的威尼斯"。

Martesana Canal

A canal located in Lombardy, northern Italy. Also called Piccolo Canal. The Martesana Canal is approximately 38 kilometres in length, 9 to 18 metres in width, and 1 to 3 metres in depth. As a part of the Navigli system, it goes from the Adda River near Trezzo-on-Adda to Milan. The history of the canal began in June 1443, when Filippo Maria Visconti, Duke of Milan, approved the project of excavating a canal for irrigation and feeding up to 16 mill wheels. The plan was suspended due to political reasons until the year 1457, when Francesco Sforza's edict marked the commencement. The Martesana Canal was inaugurated in 1465.

马尔特萨纳运河

意大利北部伦巴第大区运河。亦称皮科洛运河。马尔特萨纳运河全长约38千米，宽9—18米，深1—3米。运河自阿达河畔特雷佐附近的阿达河流至米兰，是米兰纳维利运河网的一部分。马尔特萨纳运河的历史可追溯至1443年6月。当时米兰公爵菲利波·玛丽亚·维斯孔蒂批准了修建计划，旨在开凿一条用于农业灌溉的运河，同时为16架工坊水轮提供动力水源。然而，由于政治原因，直到1457年弗朗切斯科·斯福尔扎一世发布文书，运河才正式宣告动工。1465年，马尔特萨纳运河举行了开通典礼。

Masurian Canal

A cross-border canal located in Europe. The Masurian Canal is 50.4 kilometres long, with about 20 kilometres in Poland and the rest in Russia. It has 10 locks, 5 in Poland and 5 in Russia. It links the Lava River in Kaliningrad Oblast of Russia with the Mamry Lake in northeast Poland. The canal was built to boost the economic development in East Prussia. The construction began in 1911, and was suspended in 1914 at the outbreak of World War I. The project resumed in 1918 and again in 1934. By 1942, 5 locks, 3 railway bridges, 8 road bridges, and several dams had been built along the canal. Today the Masurian Canal is closed.

马祖里运河

欧洲跨国运河。马祖里运河全长50.4千米，约20千米在波兰境内，其余河段位于俄罗斯境内。运河连通俄罗斯加里宁格勒州的拉瓦河和波兰东北部的马姆雷湖，运河上建有10座船闸，波兰和俄罗斯境内各有5座。运河开凿于1911年，修建初衷是促进东普鲁士地区的经济发展。1914年第一次世界大战爆发，运河工程被中断，其后分别于1918年和1934年再次重启。截至1942年，运河沿线已建成5座船闸、3座铁路桥、8座公路桥

和若干座水坝。目前，马祖里运河
已关闭。

Mayenne-Maine River

A canalized river located in western France. The Mayenne-Maine River is 122.5 kilometres in length. It runs from the department of Orne southward to its junction with the Sarthe River. The combined river is named as the Maine River (Maine is the local pronunciation of Mayenne). Early in the 1550s, flash locks were constructed in the Mayenne. Later in the 17th and 18th centuries, they were supplanted by 45 dams and locks. The canalized length reached 117.5 kilometres.

马耶讷－曼恩河

法国西部运河化河流。马耶讷—曼恩河全长122.5千米，从奥恩省向南流动，与萨尔特河交汇形成曼恩河（曼恩是马耶讷的当地方言读音）。早在16世纪中期，马耶讷河上已建有多座单门船闸。到了17和18世纪，河上陆续建了45座大坝和船闸，取代了原来的单门船闸。马耶讷—曼恩河运河化的河段长达117.5千米。

Meaux-Chalifert Canal

A canal located in Seine-et-Marne, northern France. The Meaux-Chalifert Canal links Meaux with Chalifert along the Marne. It has a length of 12 kilometres and 3 locks respectively at Meaux, Lesches and Chalifert. The construction of the canal began in 1837 and was finished in 1846.

莫－查理菲尔运河

法国北部塞纳—马恩省运河。莫—查理菲尔运河连通马恩河沿岸的莫城和查理菲尔。运河全长12千米，分别在莫城、莱希和查理菲尔建有3座船闸。莫—查理菲尔运河1837年开凿，1846年竣工。

Melvidi Canal

A canal located in the provinces of Utrecht and South Holland, the Netherlands. See Merwede Canal.

梅尔韦迪运河

荷兰乌特勒支省和南荷兰省运河。见梅尔韦德运河。

Mensingeweer Canal

A canal located in the province of Groningen, the

门辛赫韦尔运河

荷兰格罗宁根省运河。门辛赫韦尔

Netherlands. The Mensingeweer Canal, 4.1 kilometres long, links the Hoorn Canal with the Winsum Canal, which mainly runs across Groningen City. Constructed in around 1660, the canal was built to create a navigable waterway between the De Marne area and the city of Groningen. A total of 7 bridges were built over the watercourse.

运河全长4.1千米，连通霍伦运河和温瑟姆运河，后者主要流经格罗宁根市。门辛赫韦尔运河1660年前后开凿，旨在开辟一条连接德马尔讷区域和格罗宁根市的航道。运河上共建有7座桥梁。

Meppel Canal

梅珀尔运河

A canal located in the province of Overijssel, the Netherlands. The Meppel Canal is 11 kilometres long and 110 metres wide, mainly flowing across Meppel. The construction of the canal was started from 1859. It connects the Drenthe Grand Canal and the Hoogeveen Canal with the IJssel Lake, and is important for the water management in Drenthe. There are 3 locks on the canal. As a part of the national main waterway network, the canal is suitable for ships up to 3,000 tons. The Meppel Canal was originally a natural waterway called Sethe. Later, in 1859, the Empire took over the canal from its private owners, after which it was further deepened, widened and straightened for peat extraction and water drainage. The canal is an important waterway for peat transportation. Because of the peat extraction, the Meppel Canal must carry more water, which used to lead to flooding. In 1974, the Zedemuden pumping station was built near the canal and put into use to increase its drainage capacity.

荷兰上艾瑟尔省运河。梅珀尔运河全长11千米，宽110米，主要流经梅珀尔市。运河1859年开凿，将德伦特大运河和霍赫芬运河与艾瑟尔湖连通，对于德伦特省的水资源管理有重要意义。河上建有3座船闸，是荷兰主航道网的一部分，最大可通航3 000吨级的船舶。梅珀尔运河最初为一条天然航道，人称"泽特"。1859年，荷兰帝国从私人手中接管该运河，并因泥煤开采和排水需要，对其进行加深、拓宽和改直。梅珀尔运河是泥煤运输的重要航线。因泥煤开采，梅珀尔运河需要处理的水量过多，常引发洪水。为解决这一问题，1974年，人们在梅珀尔运河旁建造了泽德牧登泵站来提高运河的排水能力。

Merwede Canal

A canal located in the Netherlands. Also called Melvidi Canal. The Merwede Canal flows in the provinces of Utrecht and South Holland, and it is 35 kilometres long and 40 metres wide. The canal connects the Amsterdam-Rhine Canal with the Upper Merwede. From north to south, the canal mainly passes through Utrecht, Nieuwegein, Vianen, Meerkerk and Gorinchem. It was constructed in 1880 and was opened in 1892. The Merwede Canal originally started in the eastern part of the port of Amsterdam. In part, the canal was constructed by widening and deepening the existing canals, including the Keulse Canal, which was excavated in 1825. The route from Amsterdam to Utrecht was new. In the 1920s, the project of the Amsterdam-Rhine Canal was born when the Merwede Canal no longer met the requirements of the time.

梅尔韦德运河

荷兰运河。亦称梅尔韦迪运河。梅尔韦德运河流经荷兰乌特勒支省和南荷兰省，全长35千米，宽40米。该运河连通阿姆斯特丹—莱茵运河和梅尔韦德河上游，自北向南依次流经乌特勒支、尼沃海恩、菲亚嫩、梅尔凯克和霍林赫姆等省市。梅尔韦德运河1880年开凿，1892年通航。运河始于阿姆斯特丹港口东部，部分河段在已有运河基础上拓宽、加深而成，其中有1825年开凿的科尔瑟运河。从阿姆斯特丹到乌特勒支的河段为新建河段。20世纪20年代，梅尔韦德运河已无法满足时代发展需求，阿姆斯特丹—莱茵运河项目应运而生。

Meuse≈

A canalized cross-border river located in Europe. The Meuse flows through France, Belgium and the Netherlands. See Maas.

默兹河

欧洲跨国运河化河流。默兹河流经法国、比利时和荷兰。见马斯河。

Meuse Canal

A canal located in France. Also known as Northern Branch of the East Canal. The Meuse Canal runs 272.4 kilometres from the middle of Ardennes to the confluence with the Marne-Rhine Canal. The Meuse Canal was constructed after the Fran-

默兹运河

法国运河。亦称东方运河北支线。默兹运河始于阿登高原中部，全长272.4千米，与马恩—莱茵运河交汇。默兹运河修建于19世纪70年代普法战争后，旨在为今法国东北

co-Prussian War in the 1870s, which was aimed to open up the Vosges for water transport in the northeastern part of today's France. The canal was officially named in March 2003. Nowadays, the Meuse Canal is an important navigable river in the continental Europe.

部的孚日山脉开辟航道，2003年3月被正式命名为默兹运河。如今，默兹运河是欧洲大陆重要的通航河道之一。

Midden Canal

A canal located in the province of Drenthe, the Netherlands. See Oranje Canal.

米登运河

荷兰德伦特省运河。见奥拉涅运河。

Middlesex Canal

An abandoned canal located in Massachusetts, the United States. The Middlesex Canal was an approximately 44-kilometre-long barge canal, connecting Chelmsford (today's Lowell) and Charlestown (today's Boston), as well as the Charles River, the Mystic River and the Merrimack River. The Middlesex Canal Company was formed in 1793 to build the canal from Boston to Middlesex. The canal was built in the hope of boosting Boston's trade and later it became an examplar for canal construction in America, for at that time relevant engineering knowledge barely existed. The construction began in 1795, with 8 aqueducts and 20 locks built. The canal was in use from 31 December, 1803, to about 1845. Throughout the 1830s, it carried large quantities of raw cotton and other materials to the mills, and end products back to Boston, consolidating Boston's position as the commercial centre of New England. It was later superseded by the emerging railway trans-

米德尔塞克斯运河

美国马萨诸塞州废弃运河。米德尔塞克斯运河曾是驳船运河，长约44千米，连接切姆斯福德（今洛厄尔）与查尔斯敦（今波士顿），也连通查尔斯河、米斯蒂克河和梅里马克河。1793年，为开凿从波士顿到米德尔塞克斯的运河，米德尔塞克斯运河公司成立。修建这条运河旨在促进波士顿贸易发展。运河工程于1795年开工，建成8座渡槽和20座船闸。由于当时人们对运河工程知之甚少，该运河完工后成为美国修建运河参照的模板。米德尔塞克斯运河1803年12月31日通航，1845年前后停航。19世纪30年代，人们通过该运河将大量原棉和其他原料运到工厂，也将成品运回波士顿，巩固了波士顿作为新英格兰地区商业中心的地

portation. Remnants of the canal still exist. In 1967, the canal was designated a National Historic Civil Engineering Landmark by the American Society of Civil Engineers. In 1972, it was listed on the National Register of Historic Places.

位。后该运河被新兴的铁路所替代，但仍留有遗迹。1967年，米德尔塞克斯运河被美国土木工程师协会列为美国国家历史土木工程地标，1972年，又被列入美国国家历史遗迹名录。

Midi Canal

A canal located in southern France. Also called Languedoc Canal. The Midi Canal is 240 kilometres long, and it was the first long-distance canal in the history of Europe. It runs from the Étang de Thau, a lagoon behind the Mediterranean port of Sète to Toulouse, where it connects with the Garonne Canal. The Midi Canal, as one of the most technologically significant canals in the world, features lock staircases, reservoirs, aqueducts, dams, bridges, and tunnels. The largest structure on the canal is the dam of Saint-Ferréol, which was the largest dam of its time. In 1667, during the reign of Louis XIV, the construction of the Midi Canal began, and it was completed and opened in 1681. Pierre-Paul Ricquet, a French engineer, was responsible for the design. The original purpose of the Midi Canal was to be a shortcut between the Atlantic and the Mediterranean, bypassing the Straits of Gibraltar and avoiding the long sea voyage. The Midi Canal has been called the greatest civil engineering project in Europe from Roman times to the 19th century. It is now one of the most popular cruising waterways in France. The Midi Canal was designated a UNESCO World Heritage Site in 1996.

米迪运河

法国南部运河。亦称朗格多克运河。米迪运河全长240千米，是欧洲历史上第一条长运河。米迪运河始于地中海港口城市塞特港的托泻湖，流至图卢兹附近与加龙运河相通。运河采用了梯级船闸、水库、渡槽、大坝、桥梁和隧道等设施，体现了当时最先进的工程技术。运河最大的工程圣—费雷奥勒大坝是当时最大的大坝。1667年，路易十四执政时期开始修建米迪运河，1681年竣工通航。法国工程师皮埃尔—保罗·里凯负责设计工作。修建米迪运河的初衷是连通大西洋和地中海，绕开直布罗陀海峡，避免了漫长的海上航行。米迪运河被誉为古罗马时代至19世纪欧洲最伟大的土木工程奇迹。该运河现在是法国最热门的旅游航线之一。1996年米迪运河被联合国教科文组织收入世界遗产名录。

Migliarino Porto Garibaldi Canal

米利亚里诺-波尔托-加里波第运河

A canal located in Emilia-Romagna, Italy. The Migliarino Porto Garibaldi Canal is 30 kilometres long. As a part of the Waterway of Ferrara, it flows from Migliarino to the Adriatic Sea. The canal is navigable by motor boats.

意大利艾米利亚—罗马涅大区运河。米利亚里诺—波尔托—加里波第运河全长30千米，是费拉拉航道的一部分，从米利亚里诺流向亚得里亚海，可供摩托艇航行。

Mignon Canal

米尼翁运河

A canal located in eastern France. The Mignon Canal connects the Sèvre-Nantaise with Mauzé-sur-le-Mignon. It is 11 kilometres in length and has 2 locks. The construction began in 1843 and the canal was opened in 1883.

法国东部运河。米尼翁运河连接塞夫尔—南特河和米尼翁河畔莫泽，全长11千米，建有2座船闸。运河1843年开凿，1883年通航。

Milan Canal

米兰运河

A canal located in Ohio, the United States. The Milan Canal is 8 kilometres in length, 4 metres in depth and 12 metres in width. It was excavated in 1831 to provide a waterway for transporting wheat from the city Milan to Lake Erie, and connected the city with the eastern market of America. Supported by the State's authorities, local people completed the construction of this canal in 1839. When the Milan Canal was operational, shipbuilding boomed in this area, with 75 schooners being built from 1841 to 1867. Due to the flood of 1868, a feeder dam at Milan was destroyed and the operation of the Milan Canal was ended. The canal and its towpath were transformed as a Wheeling and

美国俄亥俄州运河。米兰运河全长8千米，深4米，宽12米。运河修建的目的是开辟从米兰市至伊利湖的航道，便于运输小麦，使米兰市与美国东部市场相连接。1831—1839年间，在俄亥俄州政府的支持下，当地人修建了米兰运河。在该运河通航期间，当地造船业获得蓬勃发展，1841—1867年间共建造75艘中型帆船。1868年的洪水冲毁了米兰市的一座支线大坝，米兰运河就此停航。该运河及其纤道已被改造为惠灵和伊利湖铁路轨线。目前，米兰运河原路线成

Lake Erie Railroad track. Now, this route is a rail trail called the Huron River Greenway.

为铁路遗址步道，被称为休伦河绿道。

Mississippi River-Gulf Outlet Canal

密西西比河－海湾出口运河

A canal located in Louisiana, the United States. The Mississippi River-Gulf Outlet Canal is 122 kilometres long, linking the Gulf of Mexico with the Industrial Canal through the Intracoastal Waterway. The canal was constructed by the United States Army Corps of Engineers under the authorization of Congress in 1956, and was finished in 1968. Because of the rapid erosion of its surrounding marsh, the canal was three times wider by 1989 than it originally was. In 2005, the canal channeled Hurricane Katrina's storm surge into the heart of Greater New Orleans, leading to the subsequent multiple engineering failures in the region's hurricane protection network. In 2009, a permanent storm surge barrier was constructed in the canal, and the canal has been closed to maritime shipping since then.

美国路易斯安那州运河。密西西比河－海湾出口运河全长122千米，通过沿海航道连通墨西哥湾与工业运河。1956年，经国会授权，美国陆军工程兵团开始修建该运河，1968年建成。由于运河两岸湿地侵蚀速度加剧，到1989年时，运河宽度已是初建时的3倍。2005年，密西西比河－海湾出口运河把卡特里娜飓风的风暴潮引向大新奥尔良地区中心，导致该地区飓风保护网工程多处受损。2009年，运河上修建了用以抵挡风暴潮的永久性保护屏障，运河不再向海运船只开放。

Mittelland Canal (Osnabrück Branch)

中部运河（奥斯纳布吕克支线）

An inland canal located in Germany. The Mittelland Canal (Osnabrück Branch) is 14.5 kilometres in length and is equipped with 2 locks. As a branch of the Mittelland Canal, this canal starts at the junction of the Mittelland Canal (Main Line) with the Osnabrück Canal. The nearest mooring place in the direction of the Mittelland Canal (Osnabrück Branch) is Lock Hollager, which is 30 metres away.

德国内陆运河。中部运河（奥斯纳布吕克支线）全长14.5千米，建有2座船闸。该运河为中部运河支线，起点位于中部运河主航道与奥斯纳布吕克运河的交汇处。距离该运河最近的泊船点位于30米外的霍拉格船闸。

Moer Canal

An inland canal located in the province of East Flanders, Belgium. Formerly called Moer River. The Moer Canal is 22.4 kilometres long. It runs from Ghent to Lokeren and connects Stekene via the Stekense Canal. The canal was originally excavated around 1300 to improve the drainage of the alluvial Moer Canal depression and thus reclaim pasture and agricultural land. The Moer Canal became navigable in the 15th century as people tried to avoid the Zuidlede, the navigation of which was inconvenient. In the northern Moer Canal, there is a sandy patch. Until the beginning of the 20th century and the construction of drainage channels, the region remained swampy. In Wachtebeke there are two iron drawbridges over the Moer Canal, the Overlede Bridge and the Kalve Bridge, which are protected as monuments. Currently, the Moer Canal depression is mainly an agricultural area. The canal has little economic significance and is only used by pleasure craft. The Moer Canal valley is protected in Europe as a part of the Natura 2000 project.

莫尔运河

比利时东佛兰德省内陆运河。旧称莫尔河。莫尔运河全长22.4千米，自根特流至洛克伦，在斯泰克讷与斯泰克讷运河相通。莫尔运河开凿于公元1300年前后，旨在改善冲积洼地的排水状况，便于开垦牧场和农田。为了尽量绕开航行不便的祖得勒德河，15世纪时，当地人将莫尔运河改造成一条可通航运河。运河北部曾是沼泽地，20世纪初修建了排水渠之后成为沙地。瓦赫特贝克地区的河段上建有两座开合铁吊桥，即欧弗莱德桥和卡尔夫桥，现这两座桥均作为历史建筑受到保护。如今，莫尔运河洼地主要是农业区，运河经济价值不大，仅供游船通行。莫尔运河河谷已被纳入欧盟珍稀及濒危物种保护项目"自然2000"。

Moer River

An inland canal located in the province of East Flanders, Belgium. See Moer Canal.

莫尔河

比利时东佛兰德省内陆运河。见莫尔运河。

Mon≈

A canalized river located in Pennsylvania and West Virginia in the United States. See Monongahela

芒河

美国运河化河流。芒河流经宾夕法尼亚州和西弗吉尼亚州。见莫农格

River.

希拉河。

Monkland Canal

A canal located in Scotland, the United Kingdom. The Monkland Canal is 19.7 kilometres long with 4 branches, punctuated by a set of locks. It runs from Calderbank to the Townhead Basin. The canal was constructed to bring coal from the mining areas of Monkland to Glasgow. In 1770 the Monkland Canal Company was established and the construction began. With a long process of construction due to many difficulties, the Monkland Canal was opened from 1771 progressively upon the completion of some short sessions, and it reached its end in 1794 as planned. The canal comprised two sections at the beginning as well as a 29-metre-long vertical interval between the two at Blackhill, which were later connected by locks, hence linking the canal to the Forth and Clyde Canal. This brought great potential for the business on the canal. The rapid advancement of railways in the 1920s and 1930s posed a direct threat to the development of the Monkland Canal, which was closed in 1952. In the 1960s, the canal was partially filled in to build the M8 highway. Today, the Monkland Canal offers water supply for the Forth and Clyde Canal. Two sections of the canal still remain abundant in fish. The Drumpelier Park and the Calderbank near the waterway are natural habitats for many wild animals and also popular tourist attractions.

芒克兰运河

英国苏格兰运河。芒克兰运河全长19.7千米，有4条支线，建有多座船闸，自科尔德班克流向汤黑德内湾。开凿该运河旨在把芒克兰矿区的煤炭运往格拉斯哥。1770年，芒克兰运河公司成立，运河工程动工。由于修建过程漫长且困难重重，自1771年起，部分较短河段建成后，芒克兰运河实行逐段通航，至1794年才修至预定终点。芒克兰运河起初分为两条河段。在布莱克希尔，两条河段有29米的垂直落差，后由船闸转承，并将之与福斯—克莱德运河相通，这一设计为芒克兰运河带来了巨大商机。20世纪20—30年代，铁路迅猛发展，对运河航运业造成冲击。1952年，芒克兰运河停航。20世纪60年代，为建设M8高速公路，运河部分河段被回填。目前，芒克兰运河仍为福斯—克莱德运河补给水源。该运河的两条河段被保留，河内渔产丰富。运河航道附近的德拉姆彼利埃公园和科尔德浅滩是野生动物栖息地，吸引了众多游客前来参观。

Monmouthshire and Brecon Canal

A small network of canals located in Wales, the United Kingdom. The Monmouthshire and Brecon Canal has a total length of 56 kilometres, running through the Brecon Beacons National Park. It was built to transport coal, iron, lime, limestone, and timber for industrial purposes, and had its heyday in the early 19th century. By 1810, the canal transported 150,000 tons of coal annually. Later the coming of steam railways resulted in a sharp decline in the importance of the canals. At first, the Monmouthshire Canal and the Brecknock and Abergavenny Canal were two separate canals, which were abandoned in 1962. To restore their commercial traffic, the Monmouthshire and Brecon Canals Regeneration Partnership was founded. The restored canal was officially reopened in 2009. Currently, there are several bicycle lanes along the canal, which are very popular with cyclists. A section of the canal lies within the Blaenavon Industrial Landscape, a UNESCO World Heritage Site.

蒙茅斯郡-布雷肯运河

英国威尔士小型运河网。蒙茅斯郡-布雷肯运河全长56千米，流经布雷肯比肯斯国家公园，为运输工业所需的煤、铁、石灰、石灰岩和木材资源而修建。19世纪初是该运河航运的全盛时期，截至1810年，每年可运输15万吨煤。后来，蒸汽火车和铁路的问世使运河网络的航运价值锐减。蒙茅斯郡运河和布雷克诺克—阿伯加文尼运河原本是两条独立的运河，1962年被废弃。为恢复运河的商业航运功能，英国成立了蒙茅斯郡—布雷肯运河重建合作组织。修缮后的运河于2009年恢复通航。目前，蒙茅斯郡—布雷肯运河沿线建有多条自行车道，广受骑行爱好者欢迎。该运河有一处河段位于联合国教科文组织世界遗产布莱纳文工业景区内。

Monmouthshire Canal

A canal located in Wales, the United Kingdom. The Monmouthshire Canal is 18 kilometres in length with 32 locks, and has a difference in elevation of 109 metres. As a part of the Monmouthshire and Brecon Canal network, it connects Crumlin and its tramways to the Docks at Newport. The canal was completed in April 1799, now flowing along the M4 into the urban Newport at Barrack Hill Tunnel.

蒙茅斯郡运河

英国威尔士运河。蒙茅斯郡运河全长18千米，河上建有32座船闸，水位落差109米。该运河属于蒙茅斯郡—布雷肯运河网，连接克拉姆林及其通往纽波特码头的电车轨道。运河于1799年4月竣工，现沿M4公路流向巴克拉希尔暗河的纽波特市区。蒙茅斯郡运河在市

The section of the canal located in the city has already been replaced by modern roads and buildings. Today most sections of the canal have fallen into disuse. Only a section of about 12.8 kilometres is still navigable, but troubled with silt blockage. The restoration project of the original Monmouthshire Canal has been carried out since 1994 and some repaired parts have been reopened.

区的河段已被现代化的道路与建筑所替代。如今，运河大部分河段已废弃，仅有约12.8千米的河段仍可通航，但受淤泥滞塞困扰。蒙茅斯郡运河的修复工程自1994年起实施，已修缮的部分河段已恢复通航。

Monongahela River

莫农格希拉河

A canalized river located in Pennsylvania and West Virginia, the United States. Locally known as Mon. The Monongahela River is 210 kilometres long, 2.7 metres deep, and is wholly navigable due to the construction of dams and locks, and it mainly carries coal, iron ore, steel, etc. The river travels through the Allegheny Plateau from the confluence of the Tygart Valley River and the West Fork River to the Ohio River with a watershed of 19,000 square kilometres. In 1817, a private company undertook the canalization project to erect dams and lock chambers to make the river navigable, which is believed to be the earliest project of its kind in the United States.

美国宾夕法尼亚州和西弗吉尼亚州运河化河流。俗称芒河。莫农格希拉河全长210千米，深2.7米，河上建有多座大坝和船闸，全线可通航，主要用于煤炭、铁矿石、钢铁等货物运输。该河始于泰格特河和西福克斯河的交汇处，流经阿勒格尼高原，汇入俄亥俄河，流域面积1.9万平方千米。1817年，一家私人公司承包了莫农格希拉河运河化改造工程，兴修大坝、船闸，将该河流改造为可通航河道，这是美国历史上最早的运河化改造工程。

Monsin Canal

蒙辛运河

A canal located in the province of Liège, Belgium. The Monsin Canal was named after the Monsin Island. The canal has a length of about 750 metres and 1 lock. It originates from the Albert Canal and runs parallel to the Albert Canal and connects the

比利时列日省运河。蒙辛运河得名于蒙辛岛，全长750米，河上建有1座船闸。运河始于阿尔贝特运河，与阿尔贝特运河流向平行，连通阿尔贝特运河和马斯河，是比利时最

Albert Canal with the Maas River. It is one of the shortest shipping routes in Belgium.

短的航道之一。

Montauban Branch

蒙托邦支线运河

A canal located in southwestern France. See Montech Canal.

法国西南部运河。见蒙泰什运河。

Montech Canal

蒙泰什运河

A canal located in southwestern France. Also called Montauban Branch. The Montech Canal links the Garonne Canal with the Tarn River. It is an important branch of the Garonne Canal with a length of 10.9 kilometres and 9 locks. The canal was put into service in 1843. As a result of the leakage through its embankments, it was closed in 1996 for safety concerns. In 2006, the canal was restored and reopened. Now it boasts a well-facilitated boat harbour at Montauban. Since 2016, the harbour has been installed with 32 moorings and a 90-metre-long wooden pontoon, with an impressive mooring capacity for 25-metre-long ships.

法国西南部运河。亦称蒙托邦支线运河。蒙泰什运河全长10.9千米，河上建有9座船闸，连通加龙运河和塔恩河，是加龙运河的重要支流。运河1843年通航，但由于河堤渗漏，出于安全方面的考虑，1996年被迫关停。2006年，经修缮后，蒙泰什运河恢复通航。如今，蒙泰什运河在蒙托邦市建有一个设施完善的船港。自2016年以来，该港口配备了32个系泊装置和一道90米长的木制浮桥，可供25米长的船只泊船。

Montgomery Canal

蒙哥马利运河

A canal located in western England, the United Kingdom. Originally called Montgomeryshire Canal, now commonly known as Monty. The Montgomery Canal is 53 kilometres in length with 27 locks. Constructed to serve rural areas, it was once mainly used to transport lime for agricultural purposes, and make the land in the Upper Severn

英国英格兰西部运河。旧称蒙哥马利郡运河，现俗称蒙蒂运河。蒙哥马利运河全长53千米，河上建有27座船闸。运河主要用于为乡村地区运输农业所需的石灰，增强塞文河上游河谷的土地肥力。运河于1936年因决堤而被弃用，1944年正

Valley more fertile. Owing to a breach in 1936, the canal fell into disuse, and became officially abandoned in 1944. The canal was restored in 1987 and reopened at the end of the 20th century. Wildlife thrives along the canal and several nature reserves have been established along the canal. The Montgomery Canal has only an 11-kilometre-long navigable section left, running from the Frankton Junction to the Gronwyn Wharf. Restoration of other sections of the canal is still in progress.

式停航，后于1987年得到修缮，20世纪末恢复通航。蒙哥马利运河周边地区是野生动物的栖息地，设有几个自然保护区。如今，仅弗兰克顿枢纽与格罗文码头之间11千米长的河段可通航，其余河段仍在修复中。

Montgomeryshire Canal

蒙哥马利郡运河

A canal located in western England, the United Kingdom. See Montgomery Canal.

英国英格兰西部运河。见蒙哥马利运河。

Monty

蒙蒂运河

A canal located in western England, the United Kingdom. See Montgomery Canal.

英国英格兰西部运河。见蒙哥马利运河。

Morilor Canal

莫瑞勒运河

A canal located in western Romania. The Morilor Canal is 92 kilometres in length. It is in the lowland area of the south of the Crișul Alb River, and partly parallel to the river. Starting from the Crișul Alb River near Buteni, the canal runs westwards, crossing towns like Ineu and Chișineu-Criș, and joins again with the Crișul Alb River at Vărșand Town on the border with Hungary. The Morilor Canal was originally constructed in the 19th century to drive watermills. Currently, it is used for irrigation.

罗马尼亚西部运河。莫瑞勒运河全长92千米，地处白克里什河以南低地，部分河段流向与白克里什河平行。运河始于布泰尼附近的白克里什河，向西流经伊内乌和基希内乌克里什等城镇，在靠近匈牙利边境的沃尔尚镇再度汇入白克里什河。莫瑞勒运河修建于19世纪，最初用于驱动水磨，如今用于灌溉。

Morris Canal

A canal located in the northeast of the United States. The Morris Canal was about 172 kilometres in length, 12.2 metres in width and 1.5 metres in depth, flowing through northern New Jersey with a maximum height of about 279 metres above sea level near Lake Hopatcong. It was navigable from 1831 to 1924. Due to a whole elevation difference of over 270 metres, the canal was equipped with 23 lift locks and 23 inclined planes to ensure unobstructed movement of ship traffic. The maximum length of the navigable ship is 26.7 metres and the maximum beam of the ship is 3.2 metres. The idea of building such a canal was first put forward by a Morristown businessman. In 1824, the construction of the canal began and was administered by the Morris Canal and Banking Company. The canal was officially opened in 1832 and was extended to New York Harbour in 1836, which mainly transported coal, ironstone and pig iron of the time. Constant enlargement later boosted the canal traffic to the apex in 1866, and since then it gradually became obsolete and was closed in 1924. Nowadays, the Canal Society of New Jersey and local communities are making efforts to preserve the remaining parts of the canal and its historic and recreational value.

Moscow Canal

A canal located in Russia. Also called Moscow-Volga Canal. The Moscow Canal is 128 kilometres in length, linking the Moscow River with the Volga

莫里斯运河

美国东北部运河。莫里斯运河全长约172千米，宽12.2米，深1.5米，流经新泽西州北部，其海拔最高点在莱克霍帕孔附近，高约279米。运河曾于1831—1924年间通航。因水位落差超过270米，运河上建有23座单级船闸及23台斜面升船机以保证船只顺利通行，最大可容长26.7米、船幅为3.2米的船只通行。莫里斯顿的商人最早提出了修建该运河的构想。1824年，运河工程启动，由莫里斯运河和银行公司管理。1832年，运河正式通航。1836年，运河航线延长至纽约港，运输煤炭、铁矿石及生铁。运河经多次扩建，1866年通航量达到峰值。后莫里斯运河逐渐被废弃，1924年停航。目前，新泽西运河协会及当地市民致力于保存运河遗址，保留其历史和娱乐价值。

莫斯科运河

俄罗斯运河。亦称莫斯科—伏尔加运河。莫斯科运河全长128千米，连通莫斯科河和伏尔加河。

River. The canal was constructed between 1932 and 1937. It connects the capital city of Moscow with five seas, i.e., the White Sea, the Baltic Sea, the Caspian Sea, the Sea of Azov, and the Black Sea, which earns Moscow the name "the Port of the Five Seas". Besides the function of transportation, the Moscow Canal also provides about half of Moscow's water supply, and there are many recreational facilities along the canal.

运河1932年开凿，1937年完工，将首都莫斯科与白海、波罗的海、里海、亚速海和黑海五片海域相连，莫斯科因而得名"五海之港"。除了交通运输功能之外，莫斯科运河还为莫斯科市提供了约一半的用水量。该运河沿岸还建有多处休闲娱乐设施。

Moscow-Volga Canal

莫斯科－伏尔加运河

A canal located in Russia. See Moscow Canal.

俄罗斯运河。见莫斯科运河。

Moselle≈

摩泽尔河

A canalized cross-border river located in Europe. From its source in the Vosges mountains, the Moselle runs 544 kilometres through northeastern France, Luxembourg and western Germany with an average flow rate at its mouth of 328 cubic metres per second. The main body of the river has 314 kilometres in France, and 208 kilometres in Germany, with a 39-kilometre-long section serving as the border between Germany and Luxembourg. The three largest tributaries of the Moselle are the Saar, the Sauer and the Meurthe. The Moselle in France was canalized in as early as 1830, when the Becquey plan was put forward. According to the plan, the Nancy-Metz part of the river was remodeled to meet the Jouy-Metz Canal. The project was stopped as the Franco-Prussian War broke out in 1871. After the return of Lorraine to France, the Moselle Iron Mines Canal was con-

欧洲跨国运河化河流。摩泽尔河发源于孚日山脉，全长544千米，流经法国东北部、卢森堡和德国西部，河口平均流速为每秒328立方米。摩泽尔河有314千米位于法国境内，208千米位于德国境内，一段长39千米的河段是德国和卢森堡的边界。摩泽尔河有三大支流，分别是萨尔河、绍尔河和默尔特河。早在1830年，随着贝奎伊计划的提出，摩泽尔河法国段已经开始运河化。根据计划，南锡到梅斯的河段改造后将与茹伊—梅斯运河相通。1871年，普法战争爆发，工程被迫停止。洛林回归法国后，人们开凿了摩泽尔铁矿运河，该运河1932年完工，但在德国和卢森堡境内的摩泽

structed and completed in 1932 while the river was still not navigable in Germany and Luxembourg. As France was eager to improve the capacity of the Moselle for larger and heavier ships to cross the Lorraine industrial regions after World War II, the river ushered in its full canalization in the mid-20th century after the Moselle Treaty was concluded by France, Germany and Luxembourg on 27 October 1956. The project was started in 1958 and after six years of construction, the course from Metz to Koblenz was officially opened on 26 May 1964. The canalized Moselle had 14 locks at the beginning, and the number of locks doubled into 28 by 1979 as France kept extending it to as far as Neuves-Maisons. This waterway was later further deepened from 1992 to 1999 to allow 1,500-tonne vessels to pass through, and locks were upgraded to hold two 1,350-tonne barges at a time. Today, the Moselle owns the capacity for carrying large cargo ships 110 metres long between Koblenz and Neuves-Maisons. It also allows ships to travel to other parts of France through the East Canal and the Marne-Rhine Canal. The goods shipped upstream are mainly fuel and ores, while cargo ships heading downstream mainly carry steel products, gravel and rocks. Except for shipping, the Moselle, on which are some yachting marinas, is also open to tourists who come to visit the wine villages along the river.

Moselle Iron Mines Canal

A canal located in northeastern France. As a canalized section of the Moselle River, the Moselle Iron

尔河河段仍无法通航。第二次世界大战后，法国政府迫切希望提高摩泽尔河的运载能力，以便更大吨位的船只驶往洛林工业区。1956年10月27日，法国、德国和卢森堡三国达成《摩泽尔协议》。此后，摩泽尔河于20世纪50年代中期全线进行运河化改造。运河化工程始于1958年，历时6年。1964年5月26日，从法国梅斯到德国科布伦茨的河段正式通航。运河化改造后的摩泽尔河上最初建有14座船闸。随着运河河段不断延长，到1979年航线延长至讷沃迈松时，河上的船闸数翻了一倍，增加到28座。1992—1999年间，运河河道进一步加深，可容1 500吨级的船舶通行，升级后的船闸可同时容两艘1 350吨级的驳船过闸。如今，科布伦茨至讷沃迈松的河段上可容纳110米长的大型货船。船只也可以通过与摩泽尔河相交的东方运河和马恩—莱茵运河驶往法国其他地区。向上游运输的货物主要是燃料和矿石，往下游运输的主要是钢铁产品、砾石和岩石。除航运外，摩泽尔河还设有开放的游艇码头，供游客游览河流两岸的葡萄酒酒庄。

摩泽尔铁矿运河

法国东北部运河。摩泽尔铁矿运河是摩泽尔河的一段运河化河道，

Mines Canal connects Metz with Thionville and it has a length of 30 kilometres and 4 locks. The canal was constructed in 1867, and opened in 1932.

连接梅斯和蒂永维尔，全长30千米，河上建有4座船闸。运河1867年开凿，1932年通航。

Mosiński Canal

莫辛斯基运河

A canal located in the midwestern Poland. The Mosiński Canal is 26 kilometres long. As a branch of the Oder River, it crosses the Warta River, then runs roughly eastwards to a point north of Kościan, and intersects with other canals in the Oder watershed. The Mosiński Canal was opened in 1859. In the 1990s, it was interrupted by a small hydroelectric plant built in Borkowice.

波兰中西部运河。莫辛斯基运河全长26千米，是奥得河支流之一，与瓦尔塔河连通，大致向东流至科什恰镇以北地区，再与奥得河流域的其他运河交汇。莫辛斯基运河1859年通航，20世纪90年代被在博尔克维采新建的一座小型水电站截流。

Mozambique-Malawi Canal

莫桑比克-马拉维运河

A cross-border canal located in southeastern Africa. Also known as Shire-Zambezi Canal. The Mozambique-Malawi Canal is 238 kilometres in length, connecting the Shire River and the Zambezi River. The special geography of Malawi raises the cost of international trade, hindering investment in Malawi from other countries. The Government of Malawi had been trying to build a canal to improve the situation. The Mozambique-Malawi Canal project was initiated by the third President of Malawi, Bingu Wa Mutharika. The Government of Malawi had been promoting this project for several years in a row. The project was regarded as the priority regional infrastructure project by the Southern African Development Community. The Mozambique-Malawi Canal becomes a modern canal linking the

非洲东南部跨国运河。亦称夏尔—赞比西运河。莫桑比克—马拉维运河全长238千米，连通夏尔河与赞比西河。马拉维地理环境特殊，开展国际贸易的成本较高，不利于吸引外资。马拉维政府计划开凿一条运河来改善现状。莫桑比克—马拉维运河项目最初由马拉维第三任总统宾古·瓦·穆塔里卡提出，之后各届马拉维政府不断推动该项目的实施。南部非洲发展共同体把该项目视为区域优先基础设施项目。该运河现已成为一条现代化运河，为马拉维航运开辟了新航道，连接恩桑杰港与欣代港。浅吃水货船、自推式驳船

port in Nsanje and the port of Chinde. It opens a new waterway for Malawi. The shallow-draught, self-propelled barges and push tugs with interlocking barges can transport goods through the canal, which reduces the transport costs. The people of Nsanje enjoy better infrastructures and social benefits and have more job opportunities because of the construction of the canal. The canal, which provides alternative routes for transit traffic, eases the pressure on the region's dilapidated road, and rail network and reduces Malawi's costs of exporting through the ports of Mozambique. The Mozambique-Malawi Canal also offers Malawi a new mode of transportation with other landlocked countries such as Zimbabwe and Zambia.

和带互锁的顶推拖船都可通过该运河进行货物运输，降低了运输成本。恩桑杰港附近居民也享受到了更好的基础设施带来的社会福利，同时获得了更多工作机会。莫桑比克—马拉维运河为过境货船提供了新航线，为该地区落后的公路、铁路系统减轻了运输压力，降低了马拉维通过莫桑比克港口进行出口贸易的成本。此外，该运河还为马拉维与津巴布韦、赞比亚等内陆国家之间提供了新的交通方式。

Mulwala Canal

A canal located in New South Wales, Australia. The Mulwala Canal has a length of 156 kilometres, flowing from Lake Mulwala to Deniliquin. It is the largest irrigation canal in the Southern Hemisphere. Constructed between 1935 and 1942, the canal was intended to divert water from the Murray River to the Edward River. With an offtake capacity of 10,000 megalitres per day, it offers a water supply of over 1,000,000 megalitres annually for the 7,000 square kilometres of Murray Irrigation Area. Apart from providing water for agricultural purposes, it also serves the southern Riverina towns of Berrigan, Finley, Bunnaloo and Wakool. On the canal lies the Drop Hydro hydroelectric power station, the first hydroelectric power station on an irrigation canal in

穆尔瓦拉运河

澳大利亚新南威尔士州运河。穆尔瓦拉运河全长156千米，自穆尔瓦拉湖流向德尼利昆镇，旨在将默里河水引入爱德华河，是南半球最大的灌溉运河。穆尔瓦拉运河开凿于1935年，1942年完工。运河日流水量超过100亿升，每年为7 000平方千米的默里灌溉区提供约1万亿升的农业用水。该运河还为南方滨海沿岸城镇贝里根、芬利、班纳卢以及沃库尔提供生活用水。穆尔瓦拉运河上建有澳大利亚第一座位于灌溉运河之上的水力发电站，即水滴水力发电站，该发电

Australia, which is operated by the Pacific Hydro.

站由太平洋水电公司运营。

Munak Canal

穆纳克运河

A canal located in India. The Munak Canal is an aqueduct between Haryana and Delhi, with 102 kilometres in length. It is one of the main sources of drinking water for Delhi. As a section of the Western Yamuna Canal, it runs southward from the Yamuna River to Delhi. In 1996, the Haryana and Delhi governments signed a memorandum of understanding stating that the construction of the canal would be carried out by Haryana and funded by Delhi. The canal was excavated from 2003 to 2012. It was originally a porous ditch, and was thoroughly reinforced due to serious leakage. After its consolidation, the Munak Canal can save 80 million gallons of water every day.

印度运河。穆纳克运河是位于哈里亚纳邦和德里之间的一座渡槽，全长102千米，为德里地区饮用水的主要来源之一。该运河从亚穆纳河向南流往德里地区，是西亚穆纳运河的一部分。1996年，哈里亚纳邦和德里政府签署谅解备忘录，商定由哈里亚纳邦负责修建运河，德里承担费用。运河2003年开凿，2012年完工。运河最初为多孔渠，后因渗漏严重而进行了加固。重修后，穆纳克运河水流失量每天减少8 000万加仑。

Munnekezijl Canal

穆纳科宰尔运河

A canal located in the provinces of Friesland and Groningen, the Netherlands. Parallel to the small Reit Canal, the Munnekezijl Canal is 5.4 kilometres long with 1 lock, flowing from the Lauwers to the Friesche Sluis. It starts at Munnekezijl, and connects with the Zoutkamperril Canal. The Munnekezijl Canal was made to create a separate waterway from the Reit Canal.

荷兰弗里斯兰和格罗宁根省运河。穆纳科宰尔运河全长5.4千米，建有1座船闸，流向与哈伊特运河平行，自劳沃斯河流向弗里舍斯勒斯。运河始于穆纳科宰尔，与佐特坎佩里尔运河相通。修建穆纳科宰尔运河是为了从哈伊特运河分离出一条独立航道。

Müritz-Elde Waterway

米里茨－埃尔德航道

A waterway located in Mecklenburg-Western

德国梅克伦堡－前波美拉尼亚州

Pomerania, Germany. As a navigable section of the Elde, the Müritz-Elde Waterway is 180 kilometres in length with 17 locks, running from the southern edge of the Müritz to the Elbe near Dömitz. It is a Class I federal waterway. The Waterways and Shipping Office Lauenburg is in charge of the waterway. This section traverses several natural parks and is now mainly used for recreation and sightseeing. It has lost its economic value because it is narrow and not suitable for navigation.

航道。米里茨—埃尔德航道全长180千米，共建有17座船闸，是埃尔德河的通航河段。该航道始于米里兹湖南沿，在德米茨镇附近汇入易北河，为联邦一级航道，由劳恩堡航道和航运局负责管理。米里茨—埃尔德航道流经多个天然公园。因水路狭窄，不适合航行，航道已失去其商业价值，如今主要供人们休闲观光。

Murray Canal

A canal located in Ontario, Canada. The Murray Canal is around 8 kilometres long and has a maximum depth of 2.7 metres, with two swing bridges on it. Connecting the Bay of Quinte and Lake Ontario, it provides a shortcut for boats and ships so that they no longer have to go around the isthmus of the Prince Edward County. The construction of the canal was proposed in 1796 but was suspended to 1882 as the Welland Canal and the Rideau Canal were considered more important. It took 7 years to complete the Murray Canal, which was finally opened in 1889. The canal carried commercial boats for many years until the Saint Lawrence Seaway took most of its responsibility in the 1950s. Since then its recreational function has gradually overtaken its traffic function.

默里运河

加拿大安大略省运河。默里运河全长约8千米，最深处为2.7米，建有2座平旋桥。运河连通昆蒂湾和安大略湖，为往来两地的船只提供捷径，使其不必再绕行爱德华王子县的地峡。开凿默里运河的提议1796年就已提出，但因当时韦兰运河与里多运河更受重视，直到1882年，人们才动工修建默里运河，历时7年完工，1889年通航。默里运河运营多年，主要供商船通行。20世纪50年代，默里运河的商运功能逐渐被圣劳伦斯海道取代，后逐渐用于休闲观光。

Mussel-Aa Canal

A canal located in the southeast of the province of

米瑟尔–阿河运河

荷兰格罗宁根省东南部运河。米瑟

Groningen, the Netherlands. The Mussel-Aa Canal runs from the Mussel Canal to the Veelerveen, where it joins the Ruiten-Aa Canal to form the B. L. Tijdens Canal. The canal initially had 7 locks. The construction was started in 1911 and finished in 1916. The Mussel-Aa Canal played a vital role in clearing the moors and peat bogs in the region. The canal also served as a transport route. After the end of World War II, the canal was closed to navigation and its 7 locks were destroyed. Nowadays, the Mussel-Aa Canal is only open to canoes.

尔—阿河运河始于米瑟尔运河, 至费勒尔芬村与吕滕—阿河运河交汇, 形成蒂登运河, 最初建有7座船闸。运河1911年开凿, 1916年竣工, 在当地湿地和泥炭沼泽清理工作中发挥了重要作用。同时, 它也是一条运输通道。第二次世界大战结束后, 米瑟尔—阿河运河关闭, 其7座船闸也被损毁。如今, 米瑟尔—阿河运河仅供小型划艇通行。

Mussel Canal

A canal located in the province of Groningen, the Netherlands. The Mussel Canal is 61 kilometres long, 2 metres deep, allowing vessels up to 5.7 metres wide to go through. It forms a part of the Veendam-Stadskanaal-Ter Apel Waterway. In 1765, a decision was made to build a canal from Bareveld to Ter Apel, which was eventually completed in 1856. In the 19th century, it was one of the busiest shipping lines in the Netherlands due to the peat trade. After the peat became exhausted, many agricultural products such as potatoes were transported on the canal. Due to the competition from road transportation, the canal gradually lost its importance as a waterway from the 1930s onwards. In the 1970s, there were plans to fill up the canal, but an action among the local people prevented this. Nowadays, only recreational shipping can be found on the canal.

米瑟尔运河

荷兰格罗宁根省运河。米瑟尔运河长61千米, 深2米, 可容5.7米宽的船只通行, 是芬丹—斯塔茨卡纳尔—泰尔阿珀尔航道的组成部分。1765年, 人们决定在贝尔费尔德和泰尔阿珀尔之间开凿一条运河, 1856年运河修建完工。19世纪时, 米瑟尔运河因泥煤贸易成为荷兰最繁忙的航线之一。泥煤挖掘殆尽后, 人们又利用该运河运输土豆等各类农产品。自20世纪30年代起, 米瑟尔运河面临来自陆路运输的竞争, 逐渐失去了其水运交通的重要地位。20世纪70年代, 政府曾计划回填运河, 但因当地居民的反对并未实施。目前, 该运河仅供游船通行。

Muzza Canal

A canal located in Lombardy, northern Italy. The Muzza Canal is 39 kilometres in length and is dotted with villages. As the oldest irrigation canal in Europe, it starts near the castle of Cassano d'Adda, flows through the plains and flat rural areas in the province of Lodi, and empties into the Adda River. In accordance with the order of the emperor, the Lodi residents excavated the canal between 1220 and 1230. The canal transfers the Adda River water to a vaster irrigation area. It is one of the most important European water conservancy projects, providing support for agricultural development over the past few centuries.

穆扎运河

意大利北部伦巴第大区运河。穆扎运河全长39千米，是欧洲最古老的灌溉运河，沿线村庄密布。运河始于阿达河畔的卡萨诺城堡附近，穿过洛迪省平原，流经地势平坦的农村地区，最终汇入阿达河。1220年，在罗马帝国皇帝命令下，洛迪省居民开凿该运河，1230年工程竣工。穆扎运河将阿达河的河水引入广袤的灌溉区，是欧洲最重要的水利工程之一，在过去几个世纪里，为推动农业发展做出了重要贡献。

Naarden Trek Canal

A canal located in the province of North Holland, the Netherlands. The Naarden Trek Canal is 7 kilometres in length, flowing from Muiden to Naarden. Back to the 15th century, the city of Naarden was caught in the predicament of inaccessibility as a result of the siltation of the seaport built on the Zuiderzee. To address the problem, on 10 March 1640, the councils of Naarden and Muiden took the decision to excavate a canal between the two cities. The construction was completed in 6 weeks in 1641 and cost approximately 240,000 guilders. In 1859, there was a regular service between Naarden and Amsterdam: 4 ships sailed back and forth every day. There was also a steamboat service in the mid-19th century. Along with the construction of a railway line in 1874 and a tramway in 1881, the canal lost its business and the services ceased then. Nowadays, only pleasure craft and rowing boats owned by a club can be found on the Naarden Trek Canal.

Nagele Canal

A canal located in the province of Flevoland, the Netherlands. The Nagele Canal is 190 metres long, flowing from Nagele to the Urker Canal. About 60 kilometres southwest is located Amsterdam, the capital of the Netherlands.

Nanmao Canal

An inland canal located in the province of Hunan,

纳尔登拖船运河

荷兰北荷兰省运河。纳尔登拖船运河全长7千米，始于莫伊登市，终点在纳尔登市。15世纪时，由于须德海海港泥沙淤积严重，通往纳尔登市的交通渠道受阻。为解决这一问题，1640年3月10日，纳尔登市和莫伊登市市议会决定在两市之间开凿一条运河。1641年，纳尔登拖船运河开建，共耗时6周，耗资约24万荷兰盾。1859年，纳尔登市与阿姆斯特丹市之间有4艘轮船每日在运河上定时往返。19世纪中期运河还提供蒸汽船航运业务。然而，当地铁路和电车轨道1874年和1881年分别修建后，运河失去商业价值，航运业务因此终止。如今，仅有游船和体育俱乐部的划艇在纳尔登拖船运河上航行。

纳赫勒运河

荷兰弗莱福兰省运河。纳赫勒运河全长190米，始于纳赫勒镇，汇入厄尔卡运河。该运河西南方向约60千米处即荷兰首都阿姆斯特丹。

南茅运河

中国湖南省内陆运河。南茅运河全

China. The Nanmao Canal stretches about 54.9 kilometres, traversing the Nanxian County from the Nanzhou Town at the north to the Maocao Street Town at the south. The main channel is 43.9 kilometres long and 78 metres wide at the surface. In the 1970s, the canal was excavated manually against the technical and financial shortage. Nearly 80,000 people were involved in the construction work from the winter of 1975 to the spring of 1976. The Nanmao Canal flows through 5 villages, benefiting more than 187 square kilometres of arable land, which accounts for about 40% of the total in the county. The canal was extended by 2,620 metres in the autumn of 1994. There are 6 bridges along the canal in order to connect the towns on both sides of the channel. Assuming functions of flood control and irrigation, the Nanmao Canal is also an important transportation channel. With a steady 28-metre water level, it is navigable all year round, making great contributions to the development of local economy and society. The Nanmao Canal is honoured as the Mother River of the Nanxian County. Along the canal are now important areas for ecological protection and cultural tourism, with a 30-kilometre-long green belt on either side.

长约54.9千米, 北起南州镇, 南止茅草街镇, 贯穿南县南北。运河主河道长43.9千米, 河面宽78米。20世纪70年代, 在设备落后和资金不足的不利条件下, 南茅运河开始修建, 从1975年冬到1976年春, 有近8万人参与其中。建成后的南茅运河流经5个村庄, 可灌溉耕地面积超过187平方千米, 约占南县总耕地面积的40%。1994年秋, 南茅运河又进行扩建, 总扩建长度为2 620米。运河沿岸建有6座桥梁, 将两岸的城镇连接在一起。除了泄洪和灌溉功能外, 该运河还是重要的运输通道, 水位常年保持在28米, 四季均可通航, 为促进当地经济和社会发展做出了重要贡献。因此南茅运河被誉为南县的母亲河。如今, 南茅运河沿岸是重要的生态保护区和文化旅游区。两岸各有一条30千米长的绿化带, 当地的生态环境明显得到改善。

Nantes-Brest Canal

南特-布雷斯特运河

A canal located in northern France. Also called Brittany's Siberia. The Nantes-Brest Canal is 360 kilometres in length and has 236 locks, linking the cities of Nantes and Brest. It starts from the Loire River in Nantes, traverses the middle of Brittany,

法国北部运河。亦称布列塔尼的西伯利亚。南特-布雷斯特运河全长360千米, 河上建有236座船闸, 连接南特和布雷斯特两座城市。该运河始于卢瓦尔河畔的南特市, 穿过

and finally joins the Port of Brest. It was originally designed for military ends, with the purpose of securing an inland route between the 2 largest military seaports along the French Atlantic coast in case of a blockade of Brittany's ports by the British. This strategic link was built between 1804 and 1836. Besides the military significance, the canal is also of some commercial importance. For instance, in the 19th century, with the transport of slates facilitated by this canal, the slate industry developed well along its channel. From the 1850s, with the development of railways and highways, land transportation rose as a major means of freight transport. The traffic volume on the Nantes-Brest Canal began to show signs of faltering. The commercial navigation of the canal declined visibly in the 1970s. Today, the Nantes-Brest Canal has become a tourist hub and is open only to kayaks, sailboats and other motorized boats.

布列塔尼大区中部，最终注入布雷斯特港。开凿该运河最初是为了满足军事需要，目的是在英国海军封锁布列塔尼大区港口时确保法国大西洋沿岸的南特与布雷斯特这两座最大的军事海港之间往来畅通。这一战略要道于1804—1836年间修建。建成后的南特—布雷斯特运河除用于军事活动外，还具有一定的商用价值。例如，借助该运河，板岩运输愈加便利，运河沿岸的板岩业在19世纪呈现出良好的发展态势。19世纪50年代开始，随着铁路、公路交通的发展，陆路交通逐渐成为重要的货运方式，南特—布雷斯特运河上的货运量开始下降。到了20世纪70年代，该运河上商业运输业已明显衰落。如今，南特—布雷斯特运河已发展成为一个旅游中心，仅供皮划艇、帆船和其他机动船只通行。

Napoleon Canal

A canal located in Belgium. See Damme Canal.

拿破仑运河

比利时运河。见达默运河。

Nāra Canal

A canal located in the province of Sindh, Pakistan. The Nāra Canal is the longest canal in Pakistan, about 825 kilometres in length. With its source above Rohri, the canal flows southwards and then joins the Puran River, an old branch of the Indus

纳拉运河

巴基斯坦信德省运河。纳拉运河全长约825千米，是巴基斯坦境内最长的运河。该运河始于罗赫里市北部，向南汇入印度河的一条古老支流布兰河。运河实际流速高

River. Its actual flow velocity reaches 400 cubic metres per second, and its irrigation area is about 8,100 square kilometres. Around 1858, it was linked to the Indus River at Rohri by a 19-kilometre-long channel to guarantee the stable and perennial water supply for its branch canals. Along the Nāra Canal is located the Nāra Game Reserve, a complex of more than 200 wetlands of various sizes. It was established in 1972 with the purpose of preserving the local biodiversity.

达每秒400立方米,灌溉土地面积约为8 100平方千米。1858年前后,罗赫里镇开凿了一条长19千米的航道,将纳拉运河与印度河连通,以保证纳拉运河有充足的水量,能够为其分支运河持续稳定地供水。1972年,纳拉野生动物保护区成立,运河沿岸200余处大大小小的湿地被划入保护区,以维护当地的生物多样性。

Narmada Canal

A contour canal located in northwestern India. The Narmada Canal is 534 kilometres in length, with a 460-kilometre-long section lying in Gujarat and the rest in Rajasthan. It runs from the Sardar Sarovar Dam northwards into Gujarat and then to Rajasthan. Upon completion, the canal was inaugurated on 24 April 2008. As the world's longest and largest irrigation canal, it is the main channel of an irrigation system with a length of 750 kilometres and a coverage of 2,129,000 hectares, crossing many waterways and water bodies on the way. The flow velocity changes from about 1,133 cubic metres per second at its head in Kevadia to around 74 cubic metres per second at the Gujarat-Rajasthan border. The Narmada Canal is honoured as an engineering marvel, since it carries low-lying river water to high-altitude areas with many pumping stations.

讷尔默达运河

印度西北部等高运河。讷尔默达运河全长534千米,从沙达沙洛瓦大坝向北流至古吉拉特邦和拉贾斯坦邦。位于古吉拉特邦和拉贾斯坦邦的河段长度分别为460千米和74千米。2008年4月24日,讷尔默达运河举行了竣工仪式。这条运河是印度农田灌溉水系(总长750千米,灌溉区达212.9万公顷)中的干渠,沿途连通许多航道和水域,灌溉长度和面积为世界之最。讷尔默达运河的起始河段位于凯瓦迪耶镇附近,河水流速约为每秒1 133立方米,至古吉拉特邦和拉贾斯坦邦的边界处,流速降至约每秒74立方米。讷尔默达运河沿线修建了多个供水泵站,将河水输送至高海拔地区,因而被誉为水利工程上的一个奇迹。

Naru Kabari

A canal located in the south of Iraq. See Shatt-en-Nil.

纳鲁卡巴里运河

伊拉克南部运河。见沙特恩—尼尔运河。

National Waterway No. 3

A canal located in the state of Kerala, India. See West Coast Canal.

国家三号航道

印度喀拉拉邦运河。见西海岸运河。

Nauernasche Canal

A canal located in the province of North Holland, the Netherlands. The Nauernasche Canal is 8.5 kilometres in length, linking the IJ in Zaanstad and the Starnmeer in Alkmaar. It was built between 1633 and 1634 to help empty the drainage water in the Schimel area after the land reclamation. Besides this original purpose, the canal also plays an important role in navigation.

瑙尔纳什运河

荷兰北荷兰省运河。瑙尔纳什运河全长8.5千米，在赞斯塔德市与艾湾连通，在阿尔克马尔市连通斯塔恩湖。围海造陆后，斯希梅尔地区不能及时排出积水，为此，1633至1634年间修建了瑙尔纳什运河。该运河除了排水功能外，在航运方面也发挥着重要作用。

Nauru Canals

A canal network located in Naura. The Nauru Canals consist of 16 waterways, and they are constructed in the surrounding reefs which encircle the whole island. They provide not only the access to Naura by sailing, but also the convenience of docking boats and yachts.

瑙鲁运河网

瑙鲁共和国运河网。瑙鲁运河网由16条航道组成，在环绕瑙鲁全岛的暗礁上开凿而成。该运河网不仅为船只驶向瑙鲁提供了通道，还能缓解各类船舶停泊时的拥挤状况。

Navigli

A group of waterways located in the city of Milan,

纳维利运河网

意大利米兰市运河网。纳维利运

Italy. Dating back as far as the Middle Ages, the Navigli system includes 5 canals, namely the Grand Canal, the Pavese Canal, the Martesana Canal, the Paderno Canal and the Bereguardo Canal. Among them, the first 3 canals were once connected to each other via the Fossa Interna, also known as Inner Ring. Of the 5 canals, the Grand Canal was the most important one. It dates back to the 12th century, acclaimed as one of the largest medieval engineering projects. In the early 1930s, it was filled in along with a substantial section of the Martesana Canal. At present, navigation could be scarcely found on Navigli. Its original purpose of irrigation is foregrounded.

河网的历史可追溯至中世纪，由5条运河组成，分别是米兰大运河、帕维亚运河、马尔特萨纳运河、帕代诺运河和贝雷瓜尔多运河。前3条运河先前通过内河（也称内环）相互连通并贯穿米兰市。其中，米兰大运河最为知名，12世纪开凿，被称为中世纪时期最大的水利工程之一。20世纪30年代初，整个内环河段以及马尔特萨纳运河的大部分河段被回填。如今，整个纳维利运河网基本上不再通航，主要用于农业灌溉。

Neath and Tennant Canal

尼思－坦南特运河

A canal located in south Wales, the United Kingdom. The Neath and Tennant Canal is 28.9 kilometres long with 19 locks. It runs from Glynneath to Swansea Docks and consists of 2 separate but interconnected waterways. One is the Neath Canal, which was opened in 1795 for better transportation by shipping. The other is the Tennant Canal, which stemmed from the Glan-y-wern Canal, and was expanded by George Tennant in 1818 in order to connect the Neath River with the Tawe River. Once successful in serving the early manufacturing industries of brickmaking and shipbuilding for many years, the canal was closed in the 1930s, but still provided water for local industries and Swansea Docks. In 1974, the Neath and Tennant Canal Preservation Society was founded with a view to its

英国南威尔士运河。尼思－坦南特运河全长28.9千米，沿线建有19座船闸。运河从格林尼斯流至斯旺西码头，由两条独立但相连的航道组成。一条是尼思运河，于1795年通航，旨在改善船舶运输条件；另一条是坦南特运河，1818年由乔治·坦南特在格兰叶韦恩运河的基础上拓宽而成，旨在连通尼思河与塔乌河。尼思－坦南特运河曾长期为当地制砖、造船等早期制造业发展提供便利。20世纪30年代运河停航后，仍为当地工业和斯旺西码头供水。1974年，尼思－坦南特运河保护协会成立，旨在恢复该运河的航运功能。2003年，一项可

restoration. A feasibility study published in 2003 showed that the Neath and Tennant Canal can become a part of the small waterway network by being connected to the restored Swansea Canal via the Swansea Wharf.

行性研究认为，尼思—坦南特运河可通过斯旺西码头与修复后的斯旺西运河连通，形成一个小型航道体系。

Neath Canal

A canal located in South Wales, the United Kingdom. The 20.9-kilometre-long Neath Canal starts at Glynneath and runs southwest through Neath to Briton Ferry on the coast, flowing through 19 locks. The construction of the canal began in 1791 and was completed in 1795. The Neath Canal played an important role in the transportation of coal and iron ore, and it served as the second largest canal in South Wales, only next to the Glamorganshire Canal. It operated well until the railway in the Vale of Neath was opened in 1851. In 1934, the navigation ceased and the Neath Canal was closed. Since 1990, great efforts have been made to restore the Neath Canal. Now it is partially open.

尼思运河

英国南威尔士运河。尼思运河始于格林尼斯，向西南流经尼思，最终抵达位于海岸的布里顿费里，全长20.9千米，沿线建有19座船闸。运河1791年正式开凿，1795年竣工，建成后成为运输煤炭和铁矿石的重要通道，在当时是仅次于格拉摩根郡运河的南威尔士第二大运河。1851年尼思谷铁路开通之前，尼思运河的航运业务一直十分繁忙。1934年，尼思运河停航并被关闭。自1990年以来，人们为恢复尼思运河通航做出了巨大努力。如今，尼思运河部分河段已恢复通航。

Neckar≈

A canalized river located in Germany. The Neckar lies in southwestern Baden-Württemberg and Hessen. It has a total length of 367 kilometres. The navigable part, from Mannheim to the port of Plochingen, is 201.5 kilometres in length. With an offtake of 145 cubic metres per second, the Neckar is the 4th largest tributary of the Rhine, and the 10th longest river in Germany. It has been naviga-

内卡河

德国运河化河流。内卡河位于巴登—符腾堡州和黑森州西南部，全长367千米。其中从曼海姆市到普洛兴根港的河段可通航，长度为201.5千米。内卡河的排水量为每秒145立方米，是莱茵河第4大支流，也是德国第10大河流，自1968年起一直供货船通行。据统计，

ble for cargo ships since 1968. It has been estimated that 7,332 river boats have transited the river with a capacity of 7.5 million tons in 2012. With many harbours constructed for trade and transport along the Neckar, the industrialization in the Neckarian area was greatly facilitated, along with the growth in population. Nowadays, the Neckar also carries leisure ships for tourists and various kinds of sport boats.

2012年，共有7 332艘内河船只在此航行，货运总量达750万吨。河流沿岸有诸多贸易和运输港口，工业发达，人口稠密。如今，内卡河上还通行游船和各类运动艇。

Nete Canal

An inland canal located in the province of Antwerp, Belgium. The Nete Canal has a length of 15.1 kilometres, connecting the Albert Canal with the Nete River. It enables ships from the south or west to directly reach the Albert Canal without passing through Antwerp. The section between the Rupel and Duffel was made navigable in 1839, and the part to Viersel along Lier was opened in 1952. Since 1955, via the Antwerp Waterworks, the Nete Canal has been the main route for the drinking water supply from the Albert Canal to Antwerp. The canal used to serve transportation and drainage purposes, and now several marinas and water sports clubs can be found along the canal.

内特运河

比利时安特卫普省内陆运河。内特运河全长15.1千米，连通阿尔贝特运河与内特河。来自南部或西部的船只通过这条运河，无须穿过安特卫普省就能直接驶抵阿尔贝特运河。1839年，内特运河位于鲁佩尔河和迪弗尔市之间的河段实现通航。1952年，利尔市通往维尔塞尔镇的河段开始通航。自1955年起，通过自来水厂，内特运河成为阿尔贝特运河向安特卫普省供应饮用水的主要渠道。过去内特运河常用于航运和排水。如今，该运河成为游艇停靠区和水上运动俱乐部所在地。

Neufossé Canal

A canal located in France. The Neufossé Canal links the Aa River in Arques to the Aire Canal in Aire-sur-la-Lys. It is an 18-kilometre-long section

诺福塞运河

法国运河。诺福塞运河全长18千米，在阿尔克连通阿河，在利斯河畔艾尔连通艾尔河运河，为敦刻尔

of the Dunkirk-Escaut Canal. Its construction was started in 1753 and completed in 1774. The Neufossé Canal was initially used for the purpose of military defence. Later, it was used to connect the Lys River to the Aa River, making Lille accessible to the sea, along with other inland cities of France in this region.

克—埃斯科运河的一部分。诺福塞运河于1753年开凿，1774年竣工。修建该运河的初衷是用于军事防御。之后，诺福塞运河还将阿河与利斯河连通起来，同时使里尔和相邻的法国其他内陆城市得以与大海连通。

Neukölln Canal

新克尔恩运河

An inland canal located in Berlin, Germany. Also known as Neukölln Ship Canal. The Neukölln Canal is 4.1 kilometres long, linking the Teltow Canal and the Britz Canal at the Britz-Ost Port in the upper southern section, with the Landwehr Canal in the northern downstream. The Neukölln Ship Canal was constructed between 1902 and 1903, and was extended to the Teltow Canal 10 years later. The construction of the Neukölln Lock was carried out almost the same time. It has experienced its prime in terms of commercial navigation at the beginning of the 20th century.

德国柏林市内陆运河。亦称新克尔恩通海运河。新克尔恩运河长4.1千米，南北流向，在上游布里茨东港处连通泰尔托运河与布里茨运河，下游连通兰韦尔运河。该运河修建于1902—1903年间，10年后扩建至泰尔托运河，大致同期还修建了新克尔恩船闸。新克尔恩运河的辉煌期在20世纪初，当时运河上航运繁忙。

Neukölln Ship Canal

新克尔恩通海运河

An inland canal located in Berlin, Germany. See Neukölln Canal.

德国柏林市内陆运河。见新克尔恩运河。

Nevinnomyssk Canal

涅温诺梅斯克运河

An irrigation canal located in Russia. The Nevinnomyssk Canal lies in Stavropol Krai, which is 49.2 kilometres in length and its maximum flow velocity

俄罗斯灌溉运河。涅温诺梅斯克运河位于俄罗斯斯塔夫罗波尔边疆区，全长49.2千米，最大流速为

is 75 cubic metres per second. It links the Kuban River with the Yegorlyk River. The construction of the canal began in 1936 and was suspended due to the outbreak of World War II. The project resumed in 1944, and was finished in 1948, with 2 hydro-electric power stations built along the canal.

每秒75立方米。运河连通库班河和叶戈尔雷克河, 1936年开凿, 后因第二次世界大战爆发而中断。运河修建工程于1944年复工, 1948年竣工, 运河上建有2座水电站。

New Branch

A canal located in southern France. Running from the Midi Canal to the Mediterranean, the New Branch is a branch of the Midi. It is about 37 kilometres in length and consists of 3 waterways, namely, the 5.1-kilometre-long Junction Canal with 7 locks running from the Midi Canal to the Aude, the 0.8-kilometre-long section of the Aude and the 31.6-kilometre-long Robine Canal with 6 locks. The Junction Canal is a waterway located in Sallèles-d'Aude. It functions as a linkage between the Midi Canal and the Robine Canal via the river Aude. The Robine Canal was initially a feeder canal constructed about a century earlier than the Junction Canal. It brought drinking water to Narbonne after the Aude changed its course and went around Narbonne to the north. After the Midi Canal started to operate in 1681, this feeder was expanded for the purpose of navigation. The Junction Canal was not opened as a link between them until 1787. The entire branch was renovated to meet the 250-tonne-barge standard in the 1980s to maintain its competitiveness of water transport. There is no longer any commercial transport on this waterway. The New Branch is now inscribed on the UNESCO World

新运河支线

法国南部运河。新运河支线是法国南部米迪运河的一条支线, 从米迪运河流向地中海, 全长37千米, 共由3段航道组成。第一段是交界运河, 河上建有7座船闸, 长5.1千米, 从米迪运河流向奥得河; 第二段是奥得河的一小段, 长800米; 第三段是罗比纳运河, 河上建有6座船闸, 长31.6千米。交界运河位于萨莱莱多德, 通过奥得河河段连通米迪运河与罗比纳运河。罗比纳运河的开凿时间要比交界运河早100年左右, 最初是奥得河的引水运河。奥得河经纳博讷市向北流, 罗比纳运河的用途是向纳博讷市提供饮用水, 在1681年米迪运河开通后, 还被拓宽用作航道。交界运河直至1787年才开通, 连通了罗比纳运河与米迪运河。20世纪80年代, 为了保持航运竞争力, 新运河支线被重修扩建, 航运标准得以提高, 可供载重量达250吨的驳船通行。如今, 新运河支线被列入联合国教科文组织的世界遗

Heritage List.

产名录, 已不再用于商业运输。

New Canal

新运河

An inland canal located in the province of Friesland, the Netherlands. The New Canal is a part of the waterway extending northeast from the Bergum Lake to the Dokkum New Locks. Connected with the Kuikhorne Canal upstream and Nije Feart downstream, it forms one of the main watercourses that drain inner waters of Friesland to the Dokkum New Locks. The Dokkum New Locks plays an important role in the water management of this area, especially in the discharge of water in the province of Friesland. After the Dokkum Grand Canal was closed from the sea in 1729, a lock complex was constructed, which included 1 lock for the passage of cargo ships and another two for discharging excess water. The construction of the lock complex was carried out by the architect Claas Bockes Balck, and the famous hydraulic engineer William Loré was responsible for the construction of the dam in this area.

荷兰弗里斯兰省内陆运河。新运河是从贝赫姆湖向东北延伸至多克默新闸村的一段航道。该运河上连库伊霍恩运河,下通奈厄费特运河,是将弗里斯兰省内陆水源引至多克默新闸村的主要通道之一。多克默新闸村在该地区的水资源管理体系中,尤其是在弗里斯兰省的排水作业方面,发挥着至关重要的作用。该闸区的建设始于1729年,当时,多克默大运河通海航运业务关停,人们在建筑师克拉斯·鲍克斯·巴尔克的指导下修建了闸区,其中包括1座船闸供货船通行,以及2座水闸用于排水。著名工程师威廉·洛雷还负责修建了闸区的大坝。

New Grand Canal

新大运河

A canal under construction located in China. The New Grand Canal is designed to be an improvement and renovation of the existing Beijing-Hangzhou Grand Canal. The canal will be 1,794 kilometres in length. The main goal of the project is to restore navigation in the section north of the Yellow River and to deepen and dredge the section south

中国在建运河。作为京杭大运河的扩建改造工程,新大运河规划长度为1 794千米,重点是恢复大运河黄河以北河段的通航功能,并对其黄河以南河段进行加深与疏浚。该工程不会改变京杭大运河的整体原貌,对于无法改造的

of the Yellow River. The overall appearance of the Grand Canal will not be altered. New sections will be excavated in parallel to those that cannot be transformed. The renovation of the section south of the Yellow River is now mostly completed, while that of the section north of the Yellow River is still under planning and is expected to begin before 2022. The New Grand Canal project will facilitate the north-south and cross-basin waterborne transportation and improve the inland shipping network. When the project is completed, the Zhe-Gan Canal and the Gan-Yue Canal will be connected to the Grand Canal, enabling people to take a direct ship ride from Beijing to Guangzhou.

河段, 将会采取开凿平行新河段的方式。目前, 黄河以南河段大部分已修凿完工, 黄河以北河段的改造正在规划中, 预计2022年前动工。新大运河工程可打通中国南北跨流域水运通道, 完善内陆航运网络。整个修建项目完工后, 大运河将连通浙赣运河和赣粤运河, 届时人们可从北京乘船直达广州。

New Haven and Northampton Canal

A canal located in northeastern United States. Also known as Farmington Canal. The New Haven and Northampton Canal was about 128 kilometres long, 6 metres wide and 1.2 metres deep, linking the seaport of New Haven in Connecticut and Northampton in Massachusetts. Preceded by the success of the Erie Canal, it was built in 1822 to bypass the falls and rapids of the Connecticut River. The construction of the canal required the removal of 3 million cubic metres of earth and rocks and hundreds of mobile workers and farmers living along the planned route were involved in it. A total of 60 locks, 22 metres long and 3.6 metres wide, were built to overcome the elevation difference of 152 metres between New Haven and Northampton. Suffering from a financial shortage from the very

纽黑文-北安普敦运河

美国东北部运河。亦称法明顿运河。纽黑文—北安普敦运河全长约128千米, 宽6米, 深1.2米, 连接康涅狄格州的纽黑文港和马萨诸塞州的北安普敦市。因有伊利运河成功开凿的先例, 人们在1822年开始修建纽黑文—北安普敦运河, 旨在避开康涅狄格河上的瀑布与急流。数百名临时工和居住在运河沿线的农民参与了运河开凿工作, 挖出的泥石总量达300万立方米。纽黑文—北安普敦运河的水位落差超过152米, 为调节水位, 运河沿线共建有60座长宽分别为22米和3.6米的船闸。运河动工伊始便面临资金不足的问题, 直到1835年才

beginning, the construction of the whole section was not completed until 1835. As it turned out, the canal was not a commercial success. It only experienced a short prime during the first years of full operation as towns and business flourished along the channel. Apples, butter and wood were carried south to New Haven and imports such as coffee, flour, hides, syrup, salt and sugar flowed to towns upstream. Later, damaged by heavy rains and overflowing water, the canal went obsolete in 1847, 2 years after the train service became available in Northampton. The channel was filled in and converted into a railroad in the mid-19th century. At present, the section in Northampton has turned into a 6.4-kilometre-long multi-use rail trail.

全线完工。在运河全线通航的最初几年里,沿线城镇与商业兴起,运河航运经历了短暂的繁荣。通过该条运河,苹果、黄油和木材等物资可以向南运往纽黑文,同时,咖啡、面粉、毛皮、糖浆、盐和糖等进口商品可以运至上游城镇。后因暴雨和内涝对运河航道造成破坏,纽黑文—北安普敦运河1847年被弃用。此前2年,开往北安普敦市的火车线路开通。19世纪中期后,废弃的纽黑文—北安普敦运河回填后铺上了铁轨,北安普敦附近的一段现已辟为6.4千米长的多功能铁路轨道。

New Ladoga Canal

A canal located in Leningrad Oblast, Russia. The New Ladoga Canal was constructed in the 1860s as a replacement of the Old Ladoga Canal. As one of the largest hydroengineering projects throughout 18th century Europe, the Old Ladoga Canal was constructed between 1719 and 1810 during the reign of Peter the First to connect the Volkhov River and the Neva River so as to bypass the stormy waters of Lake Ladoga. This canal functions to carry small boats while the Old Ladoga Canal fell into complete disuse as a result of siltation by 1940.

新拉多加运河

俄罗斯列宁格勒州运河。新拉多加运河19世纪60年代开凿,旨在取代早先彼得大帝时期修建的旧拉多加运河。拉多加运河连通沃尔霍夫河和涅瓦河,船只从此运河航行可避开拉多加湖的汹涌急流。早期的拉多加运河是18世纪欧洲最大的水利工程之一,1719—1810年间开凿,至1940年因航道淤塞而停航。新拉多加运河现仍可供小型船只通行。

Newmarket Canal

An unfinished canal located in Ontario, Canada.

纽马基特运河

加拿大安大略省未完工运河。官

Officially known as Holland River Division. The Newmarket Canal was planned to be a southern branch of the Trent-Severn Canal, with a length of 16 kilometres. The construction of the canal began in 1906, planned to be divided into 3 stages. The first stage required the dredging of the section between Lake Simcoe and the Holland Landing Village, which would be followed by the construction of 3 locks between Holland Landing and Newmarket, and finally there would be 5 or 6 more locks built between Newmarket and Aurora. In 1912 when about 80 percent of the construction work was completed, the project was put on hold for political reasons and the pressure of the rising cost as well. At the time of abandonment, there were 4 swing bridges, 2 locks, and 1 overpass. Nowadays, along the east branch of the Holland River can still be found a swing bridge, a turning basin and some remains of the locks.

方名称为霍兰河段。纽马基特运河全长约16千米，原计划作为特伦特—塞文运河的南部支线。该运河1906年开凿，计划分三个阶段进行：第一阶段是对锡姆科湖到霍兰兰丁村之间的河段进行疏浚；第二阶段是在霍兰兰丁村和纽马基特镇之间的河段上修建3座船闸；第三阶段要在纽马基特和奥罗拉之间修建5—6座船闸。至1912年，运河开凿工作已完成80%左右，但因政治因素和成本增加被叫停。项目中止时，4座平旋桥、2座船闸和1座跨线桥已建好。如今，霍兰河东支流上仍可见1座平旋桥、1处回船池和一些船闸遗址。

New Meadows Canal

新梅多斯运河

An inland canal located in Maine, the United States. Also called Peterson Canal. The New Meadows Canal was 4 kilometres long, about 1 metre deep, 9 metres wide in most parts but narrowed down to 6 metres at some points. On 1 January 1786, 98 citizens from Brunswick and Bath signed a petition to excavate the New Meadows Canal, which was aimed to achieve direct transportation into the Casco Bay and to Falmouth without detouring to the sea or running the risk of navigating the rapid Kennebec River. The canal would also

美国缅因州内陆运河。亦称彼得森运河。新梅多斯运河全长4千米，深约1米，大部分河段宽9米，部分河段收窄至6米。1786年1月1日，为了直通卡斯科湾和法尔茅斯镇，避免绕行出海的麻烦和在湍急的肯纳贝克河上航行的危险，来自不伦瑞克和巴斯的98位民众联名签署了开凿新梅多斯运河的请愿书。他们指望运河开通后，还可将外地木材运进新梅多斯河沿岸

serve as a channel for the logs transported to the mills along the New Meadows River to solve the problem of timber scarcity. On 5 March 1790, the General Court of the Commonwealth of Massachusetts passed an act to establish a company to construct the canal, and specified that no tolls would be collected. Due to various obstructions, the canal failed to reach the Merrymeeting Bay, and it ended up connecting the New Meadows River and the Kennebec River. On 22 March 1793, the court passed another act that recognized the opening of the canal, and authorized the proprietors to maintain the operation of the canal while enjoying the right of navigation. After the canal was opened for about 120 years, causeways were built at the Kennebec end of the canal, disrupting the water flow of the canal. At present, almost all traces of the canal have gone.

的工坊，以缓解当地木材资源短缺问题。1790年3月5日，马萨诸塞州议会通过了成立公司开凿运河的决议，同时声明运河建成后不收取通行费。因重重障碍，新梅多斯运河最终没有按照计划直接通往梅里米廷湾，而是改道连通了新梅多斯河和肯纳贝克河。1793年3月22日，州议会通过法案宣布运河正式通航，同时确认运河公司全体投资人享有通航权利并负责运河运营。新梅多斯运河通航约120年后，邻近肯纳贝克河的一端修筑了堤道，这一工程导致运河河水流动不畅。如今，新梅多斯运河大部分遗迹已无处可寻。

New Merwede

新梅尔韦德运河

A canal located in the province of South Holland, the Netherlands. The New Merwede is 21 kilometres in length and 325 metres to 695 metres in width, connecting the Upper Merwede and the Holland Canal. Excavated between 1861 and 1874 and mainly fed by the Rhine River, the New Merwede forms a branch in the Rhine-Meuse Delta. It is conducive to the removal of silt in the delta, thus facilitating navigation and improving water transport conditions. The New Merwede merges with River Bergen Maas, forming the estuary of the Holland Canal and separating the Island of Dordrecht

荷兰南荷兰省运河。新梅尔韦德运河全长21千米，最窄处325米，最宽处695米，连通梅尔韦德河上游和荷兰运河。该运河开凿于1861—1874年间，主要由莱茵河提供水源，是其在莱茵—默兹河三角洲地区的一条支流。新梅尔韦德运河将促进莱茵—默兹河三角洲地区河道的疏浚排淤，便于船只航行，改善水运条件。新梅尔韦德运河与贝亨马斯河交汇，形成荷兰运河的河口，并将莎草森林国家公

from the Biesbosch National Park. With a stretch excavated along the track of some creeks of the Biesbosch National Park, the New Merwede diverts the water away from the Lower Merwede so as to reduce flood risks. There are 3 narrow navigable channels connected with the New Merwede, and 3 locks have been built to facilitate the navigation between these channels and the New Merwede, namely, the Biesbosch Lock, the Spiering Lock and the Otter Lock. There is no bridge or tunnel crossing the New Merwede, with a ferry boat line in service instead. Currently, the New Merwede also functions as a recreational destination as it is located next to the Biesbosch nature reserve.

园和多德雷赫特岛分开。新梅尔韦德运河沿莎草森林国家公园内一些小河道开凿，将梅尔韦德河下游的河水分流，从而降低了发生洪涝灾害的风险。新梅尔韦德运河河道分出了3条小型航道，为保障通航条件，人们在这3条航道与新梅尔韦德运河的交汇处分别修建了比斯博斯、斯皮灵和奥特这3座船闸。新梅尔韦德运河上未修建桥梁或隧道，仅有一条往返于两岸之间的轮渡专线。如今，新梅尔韦德运河紧靠森林自然保护区，也兼具休闲娱乐功能。

Newport-Dunkirk Canal

新港－敦刻尔克运河

A cross-border canal located in Europe. Also called Dunkirk-Newport Canal or Veurne Canal. The Newport-Dunkirk Canal lies between West Flanders Province, Belgium and the Nord and Pas-de-Calais departments, France. Built in 1630, it is 32 kilometres long, 18 metres wide on average and 2 to 3.5 metres deep. The canal connects the Belgian coastal town, Newport to the French port city, Dunkirk. As an extension of the Plassendale-Newport Canal, the Newport-Dunkirk Canal starts from the Veurne Sluis in Newport and runs parallel to the coastline, 2 to 4 kilometres away from the sea. After running almost 19 kilometres on the Belgian territory, the canal crosses the Franco-Belgian border in Adinkerke and flows further into France.

欧洲跨国运河。亦称敦刻尔克—新港运河或弗尔讷运河。新港—敦刻尔克运河位于比利时西佛兰德省和法国诺尔省和加莱海峡省之间，全长32千米，平均宽度18米，深度2—3.5米。该运河1630年开凿，始于新港的弗尔讷船闸，连接比利时沿海城镇新港和法国港口城市敦刻尔克，是普拉森达勒—新港运河的延伸河段，与海岸线平行，距离海边2—4千米。新港—敦刻尔克运河在比利时境内流经19千米后，于阿丁凯尔克小镇穿过法国和比利时边境流入法国。

Newport Pagnell Canal

A canal located in England, the United Kingdom. The Newport Pagnell Canal is 2 kilometres long and has 7 locks, running from the Grand Junction Canal at Great Linford to Newport Pagnell. It was constructed with the authorization of an act of Parliament in June 1814 and was opened in 1817. With coal as the major cargo, the canal also carried other goods such as lime and manure. In 1845, it reached its peak capacity of 14,887 tons of cargos. In the same year, the London and North Western Railway offered to purchase the canal. Although their offer was declined, the canal was finally sold to the Newport Pagnell Railway at £9,000 in 1862. In August 1864, the Newport Pagnell Canal was closed with a part of its route transformed into a railway line.

New Qinhuai River

A canal located in the city of Nanjing, Jiangsu Province, China. The New Qinhuai River has a total length of 16.9 kilometres and its width varies from 130 to 200 metres. The river flows through 2 districts of Nanjing, the Jiangning District and the Yuhuatai District. The watercourse was excavated in 1975 and put into use in 1980. The New Qinhuai River is the latest downstream flood diversion channel in the entire Qinhuai River system, and integrates the functions of flood discharge, irrigation and navigation. When the New Qinhuai River was first completed, there were 11 bridges in total on it. In addition to 1 railway bridge, the other 10 bridges

纽波特巴格内尔运河

英国英格兰运河。纽波特巴格内尔运河全长2千米，河上共建有7座船闸，从大林福德的大连通运河流至纽波特巴格内尔。1814年6月，英国议会通过了开凿该运河的授权法案，1817年运河开通。纽波特巴格内尔运河主要用来运输煤炭，也运输石灰和肥料等其他货物。1845年，运河的货运量为14 887吨，达到了顶峰。同年，伦敦西北铁路公司提议收购该运河，但未能成功。1862年，运河以9 000英镑的价格出售给了纽波特巴格内尔铁路公司。1864年8月，纽波特巴格内尔运河停航，部分河道被改建为铁路。

秦淮新河

中国江苏省南京市运河。秦淮新河全长16.9千米，河面宽130—200米不等，流经江宁和雨花台两个区。该运河1975年动工开凿，1980年开通，是整个秦淮河水系中最晚修建的一条运河，这是一条下游入江分洪道，集泄洪、灌溉和航运功能于一体。秦淮新河建成之初有11座桥梁，除1座铁路桥外，其余10座桥梁设计特色各异，被称为"十姊妹桥"。秦淮新河河道宽阔，坡岸平整，水势平稳。枯水期航道宽40—63米，深2.5—4米，符合国

adopted different designs and were called the Ten Sister Bridges. The New Qinhuai River has a wide channel, flat slopes and stable water conditions. During the dry season, the channel is 40 to 63 metres wide and 2.5 to 4 metres deep, which complies with the level V of the National Waterway Standard, and is navigable for ships of 100 to 300 tonnes all the year round. Nowadays, with the Nanjing South Railway Station as the hub of rail transport in Nanjing, both the Beijing-Shanghai high-speed railway and the Shanghai-Hankou-Chengdu high-speed railway cross the New Qinhuai River, which is a distinctively beautiful scene.

家五级航道标准,可常年通航100—300吨级船舶。如今,以南京南站为枢纽的京沪高铁、沪汉蓉高铁这两条铁路线都横跨秦淮新河,成为秦淮新河上一道亮丽的风景线。

New River Navigation

新河航道

An abandoned canal located in Virginia and West Virginia, the United States. The New River Navigation was 89 kilometres long and linked Carroll with Hinton. A part of the canal lay in the flood inundated area. Before the railway transportation took the place of the waterway entirely, the United States Army Corps of Engineers had undertaken several projects to improve the navigation of the New River from 1873 to 1892.

美国弗吉尼亚州和西弗吉尼亚州废弃运河。新河航道全长89千米,连接卡罗尔和欣顿,部分河段位于洪泛区。在铁路运输完全替代内河航运之前,为改善新河运河的航运条件,美国陆军工程兵团曾于1873—1892年间多次对其进行改造。

New Suez Canal

新苏伊士运河

A canal located in Egypt. The New Suez Canal, running parallel to parts of the Suez Canal, is 35 kilometres long, 24 metres deep and more than 300 metres wide. The canal is aimed to enhance the navigation conditions of the Suez Canal. The con-

埃及运河。新苏伊士运河与苏伊士运河部分河段平行,全长35千米,水深24米,河道宽度超过300米。开凿新苏伊士运河旨在改善苏伊士运河的现有通航条件。2014

struction was started in August 2014, with 40,000 workers involved and about $8 billion invested into the construction project. In August 2015, the construction was completed, allowing ships to travel in both directions at the same time. It has improved the daily capacity of the Suez Canal from 49 to 97 ships, generally shortening the waiting time from 11 hours to 3 hours, and decreasing the transit time from 18 hours to 11 hours. The New Suez Canal will continue to provide investment and employment opportunities for Egypt in the next few years.

年8月，新苏伊士运河项目正式开工，逾4万名工人参与该运河的修建工程，投入资金约80亿美元。2015年8月，运河项目完工，过往船只在此可双向通行。新苏伊士运河通航后，日通航量由原先的49艘货船增至97艘，平均等待时间从11小时缩短至3小时，通行时间也由18小时减至11小时。未来几年，新苏伊士运河工程将持续为埃及提供投资和就业机会。

New Vecht

新费赫特运河

An inland canal located in Zwolle, the Netherlands. The New Vecht is about 10 kilometres long, of which only a 3.8-kilometre-long course is navigable. It has an average width of no more than 20 metres. The canal was excavated in 1600 or so in order to shorten the shipping distance between the Overijssel Vecht and the centre of Zwolle. Ships on the New Vecht were mostly freighters carrying sandstone. There were also numerous windmills built along the waterway for irrigation, but only one of them, De Passiebloem, has been kept now. A lock was constructed immediately after the excavation of the canal and it was remodeled in 1914. From the beginning of the 20th century, the shipping volume on the New Vecht began to drop drastically. The lock was also gradually abandoned and was restored in 1987.

荷兰兹沃勒市内陆运河。新费赫特运河全长约10千米，通航长度仅为3.8千米，平均宽度不超过20米。该运河1600年左右开凿，旨在缩短上艾瑟尔—费赫特河与兹沃勒市中心之间的航行距离，主要通行运输砂石的货船。运河两岸还曾建有诸多用于灌溉的风车，其中仅有一个名为"西番莲"的风车保存至今。新费赫特运河开凿后随即修建了1座船闸，这座船闸于1914年经过改造。20世纪伊始，随着新费赫特运河上通行船只数量锐减，船闸也逐渐被废弃。1987年，船闸得到修复。

New York State Barge Canal

A canal located in the state of New York, the United States. See Erie Canal.

纽约州驳船运河

美国纽约州运河。见伊利运河。

Nicaragua Canal

A suspended canal located in Nicaragua. As planned, the Nicaragua Canal would run 278 kilometres and flow across Nicaragua and connect the Pacific with the Atlantic. It would start from the Punta Gorda River on the Caribbean, traverse Lake Nicaragua, and end in the mouth of the Brito River on the Pacific side. The canal would be 230—520 metres wide and 26.9—29 metres deep, with a projected navigation capacity of about 9,100 ships per year and a maximum ship tonnage of 400,000. In June 2013, Nicaragua's National Assembly passed a bill to authorize the Hong Kong Nicaragua Canal Development Investment Company a 50-year concession to fund and manage the project. Commenced in December 2014, it was supposed to be completed in 2019 with a budget of $50 billion. Currently, the canal project has not made any substantial progress yet.

尼加拉瓜运河

尼加拉瓜停建运河。按原计划，尼加拉瓜运河将始于加勒比海的蓬塔戈尔达河，流经尼加拉瓜湖，横穿尼加拉瓜，最后汇入太平洋海岸的布里托河口，从而连通太平洋与大西洋。该运河的规划长度为278千米，宽度为230—520米，水深为26.9—29米，年通航量约为9 100艘船只，可通行船舶最大吨位达40万吨。2013年6月，尼加拉瓜国民大会通过一项议案，授予来自中国香港的尼加拉瓜运河开发投资有限公司50年特许权以投资并管理这项工程。2014年12月，运河开凿，原定2019年竣工，总预算500亿美元。如今，该项目尚未取得任何实质性进展。

Nidau-Büren Canal

A canal located in the canton of Bern, Switzerland. The Nidau-Büren Canal stretches 12 kilometres, channeling the water of the Aare River from Lake Biel to Solothurn. On the canal stands a regulating dam which was completed in 1939 and has been in

尼道－比伦运河

瑞士伯尔尼州运河。尼道－比伦运河全长12千米，将阿勒河水由比尔湖引向索洛图恩市。运河上有一座建于1939年的水位调节坝，至今仍在使用。这座水坝上建有1座

regular use since then. The dam contains a 12-metre-wide and 25-metre-high lock on which a hydro-electric plant was built in 1995.

宽12米、高25米的水闸，1995年，水闸上修建了一座水力发电站。

Nieppe Canal

涅普运河

A canal located in northern France. The Nieppe Canal is 23 kilometres in length and has 4 locks. The canal is connected to River Lys at Thiennes. It then flows northeast to meet the Hazebrouck Canal. The Nieppe Canal was closed in 1970.

法国北部运河。涅普运河全长23千米，河上建有4座船闸。涅普运河在蒂耶讷与利斯河相通。后河道沿东北方向延伸，最终与阿兹布鲁克运河交汇。涅普运河1970年被关闭。

Nije Feart

奈厄费特运河

A canal located in the province of Friesland, the Netherlands. The Nije Feart is connected to the downstream of the New Canal.

荷兰弗里斯兰省运河。奈厄费特运河与新运河下游相连通。

Nimy-Blaton-Péronnes Canal

尼米－布拉通－佩罗讷运河

A canal located in the province of Hainaut, Belgium. The Nimy-Blaton-Péronnes Canal is 38.9 kilometres in length and has 2 locks. It runs from the Le Grand Large Lake to the Schelde River and connects the Central Canal to Peronnes. The canal was constructed to replace the Pommeroeul-Antoing Canal, with the purpose of transporting efficiently the coal harvested in Borinage, a Belgian region in Hainaut, which was home to former mining communities. Benefiting from the low slope of the valley of Haine, the canal only needs 2 locks at its junction with the Schelde River to overcome a

比利时埃诺省运河。尼米－布拉通－佩罗讷运河全长38.9千米，河上建有2座船闸，从大拉尔热湖流向斯海尔德河，连接比利时中部运河和佩罗讷。该运河旨在替代波默勒尔－昂图万运河，以便高效地运输采自埃诺省博里纳日地区（从前的矿业区）的煤炭。尼米－布拉通－佩罗讷运河修建时充分利用了艾讷河谷的低坡，只在该运河与斯海尔德河的交汇处修建2座船闸便解决了18米的水位落差问题。为

total difference of 18 metres in elevation. In Blaton, a sluice was also built to prevent the water from deluging in case of the breach of the dyke.

防止堤坝决口引发洪涝灾害，布拉通地区还修建了1座水闸。

Nivernais Canal

A canal located in France. The Nivernais Canal is 174 kilometres long and has 112 locks, linking the Yonne River to the Loire River. The canal starts in the village of Saint-Léger-des-Vignes and then flows across the department of the Nièvre. It reaches its halfway point in Clamecy and gets to its terminus in Auxerre on the river Yonne. The canal was constructed in 1784 and was opened in 1841. Originally, it served to float timber from the forests of the Morvan National Park to Paris by way of Clamecy and Auxerre. Besides timber transportation, the canal was soon used as a significant route for exporting stones, grains and wine, and bringing in coal. The Nivernais Canal made great contributions to the economic growth of the Nièvre and the development of quarries at Chevroches and Dornecy. With the construction of the railway in the 19th century, the canal's commercial service was in decline. Exclusively reserved for pleasure cruising, the Nivernais Canal now offers a way for tourists to appreciate the wide variety of landscapes and numerous places of interest.

尼韦内运河

法国运河。尼韦内运河全长174千米，沿线建有112座船闸，连接约讷河和卢瓦尔河。该运河始于圣莱热德维涅村，流经涅夫勒省，中段在克拉姆西区，最后在欧塞尔市到达其终点约讷河。运河1784年开凿，1841年通航。开凿尼韦内运河最初目的是将莫尔旺山国家公园森林的木材经由克拉梅西和欧塞尔漂流运往巴黎。事实上，通航后尼韦内运河不仅用于运输木材，很快也成为出口石材、粮食和红酒及进口煤炭的重要航道。尼韦内运河极大地促进了涅夫勒省的经济发展，谢夫罗谢市和多尔内西镇采石业也从中受益良多。随着19世纪铁路的修建，该运河的商业航运价值逐渐消失。目前，尼韦内运河仅供游船通行，游客泛舟运河之上，可遍览沿途各色美景和多处名胜。

Nœux Coalmine Canal

A canal located in northern France. See Beuvry Canal.

讷克斯煤矿运河

法国北部运河。见伯夫里运河。

Noord Canal (the Netherlands)

A canal located in the province of Limburg, the Netherlands. The Noord Canal is 15 kilometres long and 22 metres wide. The canal was originally constructed in 1808 as a part of the Napoleonic project called the Grand North Canal, but currently serves as a branch of the South Willems Canal. The Noord Canal branches off from the South Willems Canal at Nederweert in a north-easterly direction and runs straightly to Beringe. In 1853, a renovation work was carried out to deepen the channel. The Noord Canal remained navigable until November 2017. All public shipping traffic has been banned on the canal since then.

诺德运河（荷兰）

荷兰林堡省运河。诺德运河全长15千米，宽22米。该运河1808年开凿，本是拿破仑时期北方大运河工程的一部分。诺德运河在下韦尔特从南威廉斯运河分出一条支线，朝东北方向径直流向贝灵恩。1853年，运河河道进一步加深。2017年11月以前，诺德运河一直可通航。后运河上禁止一切公共航运。

Nordgeorgsfehn Canal

A canal located in the state of Lower Saxony, Germany. The Nordgeorgsfehn Canal is 31.8 kilometres long and 13 metres wide, linking the Jümme with the Ems-Jade Canal. It consists of 8 locks, 10 moveable bridges and 15 fixed bridges. The maximum draught and height of ships allowed to navigate on the canal are 1.4 metres and 2.2 metres respectively. The canal is owned by the state of Lower Saxony, and managed by the State Agency for Water Management, Coastal and Nature Conservation. The construction of the southern part of the canal was started in the 1820s and completed in 1829. The other parts of the canal were constructed section by section of short distances and the canal was finally completed in 1916.

诺德乔治斯芬运河

德国下萨克森州运河。诺德乔治斯芬运河全长31.8千米，宽13米，与于默河和埃姆斯—亚德运河相通。运河沿线建有8座船闸、10座可移动桥梁和15座固定桥梁，可供吃水深度小于1.4米、高度低于2.2米的船只通行。诺德乔治斯芬运河归下萨克森州所有，由本州的水务、海岸和自然保护局负责管理。运河南段19世纪20年代开凿，1829年完工，其他部分则采用分小段陆续修建的方式，直至1916年才全部竣工。

North Branch Division of the Pennsylvania Canal

A cross-border canal located in the United States. See North Branch Division.

North Branch Division (Pennsylvania)

A cross-border canal located in the United States. Also called North Branch Division of the Pennsylvania Canal. The North Branch Division lies between southern New York and north-central Pennsylvania with a total length of 272 kilometres. As a part of the Susquehanna network of the Pennsylvania Canal system, it began at Northumberland and extended to the New York state line, there connecting the Junction Canal and the New York canal system. It was a major avenue to the seaboard in the mid-to-late 19th century. The North Branch Division was built between 1828 and 1856. The first segment of 89 kilometres was constructed in 1828 and was opened in September 1831. The Wyoming extension to Pittston, measuring around 27.4 kilometres, was completed in 1834. The Tioga branch connected with the New York Canal system became under construction in 1836. In 1853, the entire section along with all the branches was finally finished, but the canal was not fully opened until 1856 when the Tonawanda passed up from Pittston to Elmira with a barge of coal. The complete canal had 43 well-constructed locks in total that overcame 100 metres of elevation between its end points, the southern end being 130 metres above the sea level, and the northern end 230 metres. In 1880, the traf-

宾夕法尼亚州北支运河

美国跨境运河。见北支运河。

北支运河（宾夕法尼亚）

美国跨境运河。亦称宾夕法尼亚州北支运河。北支运河流经纽约州南部和宾夕法尼亚州中北部,全长272千米。该运河为宾夕法尼亚运河系统中萨斯奎汉纳运河网的一部分,始于诺森伯兰,延伸至与纽约州交界处,连通交界运河和纽约运河网,是19世纪中后期通往沿海地区的一条重要航道。北支运河1828—1856年间开凿,第一河段长89千米,1828年开凿,1831年9月通航。怀俄明支线流至皮茨顿,总长约27.4千米,1834年竣工。连通纽约运河网的泰奥加支线运河1836年动工开凿。1853年,整条运河及其支线全部竣工,但当时并未全线通航。直到1856年,托纳旺达号货船将一船煤从皮茨顿运送至埃尔迈拉,该运河才全线开通。运河全线共建有43座精良的船闸,南端海拔130米,北端海拔230米,水位落差达100米。1880年,北支运河的通航量开始下降。1889年,洪水冲毁了朱尼亚塔运河段(牛顿汉密尔顿区到绳索渡口的河段),损

fic volume on the canal began to decline. The 1889 flood destroyed the Juniata Division from Newton Hamilton to Rope Ferry and damaged the West Branch Division, leaving the North Branch Division unconnected below Northumberland. The canal became almost useless and was abandoned in 1891.

毁了西支运河，导致北支运河在流经诺森伯兰市后无法通航。后该运河的航运价值几乎丧失，最终于1891年被废弃。

North Canal (China)

A canal located in Shandong Province, China. See North Jiaolai River.

北运河（中国）

中国山东省运河。见北胶莱河。

North Canal (France)

A canal located in northern France. The North Canal links the Sensée Canal (now a part of the Dunkirk-Escaut Canal) with the Oise Lateral Canal. It is 95 kilometres in length and has 19 locks. The canal was constructed to give an advantageous edge to the French coal-mining business in the competition with foreign companies. The construction began in 1908, supported by the French government along with the coal-mining companies in the Nord and Pas-de-Calais departments. Before the work was suspended in 1914 due to World War I, many locks and bridges had been built and three quarters of the excavation had been completed. The war caused great damage to this canal. A few attempts were made to resume its construction, but little had been achieved until the early 1960s, when the transport demand increased between northern France and the Seine Basin. The construction work was restarted in 1960 and the canal was finally

北方运河（法国）

法国北部运河。北方运河连通桑塞运河（现为敦刻尔克—埃斯科运河的一部分）和瓦兹河旁侧运河，全长95千米，沿线建有19座船闸。1908年，在法国政府以及诺尔省和加莱海峡省各煤矿公司的支持下，运河开始修建，旨在借此优先发展法国煤矿业，与国外煤矿公司展开竞争。1914年，第一次世界大战爆发，运河修建工程被迫中止。此时运河开凿工程已完成四分之三，多座桥梁和船闸已建成。战争对运河造成了巨大破坏，虽然法国政府多次尝试重启运河修建工程，但收效甚微。直到20世纪60年代初，因法国北部和塞纳河流域之间的交通运输需求增大，运河重修工程才得以实施。1960年，北方运河重修工程正式启动，最终于1965

open to shipping in 1965. As currently planned, over the years from 2018 to 2024, the North Canal is expected to be abandoned and replaced by the high-capacity Seine-North Europe Canal.

年实现通航。当地政府还计划在2018—2024年修建通航能力更强的塞纳—北欧运河，建成后将有望替代北方运河。

Northern Catherine Canal

北叶卡捷琳娜运河

An abandoned inland canal located in Perm Krai, Russia. The Northern Catherine Canal is 17.6 kilometres in length, linking the river basins of the Northern Dvina and the Kama. Named after Empress Catherine II, the canal was built between 1785 and 1822. In 1822, gates were built on the canal, but they only made the canal accessible to shipping in spring with higher water levels. In 1838, it was officially abandoned for economic reasons. Till the early 20th century, the canal was occasionally used by local merchants.

俄罗斯彼尔姆边疆区废弃内陆运河。北叶卡捷琳娜运河全长17.6千米，连通北德维纳河和卡马河流域。该运河于1785—1822年间开凿，因女皇叶卡捷琳娜二世而得名。1822年，运河上修建了闸门，但仍只能在春季水位较高时才可通航。1838年，由于经济原因，北叶卡捷琳娜运河被正式弃用。20世纪初之前，当地商人有时会利用该运河进行航运。

Northern Dvina Canal

北德维纳河运河

A canal located in Vologda Oblast, Russia. Previously called Alexander of the Württemberg Canal. The Northern Dvina Canal is 64 kilometres in length with 6 wooden locks, linking the Volga Baltic Waterway and the Northern Dvina River through the tributary of the Northern Dvina River, the Sukhona River. The canal is one of the two channels that connects the river basins of the Volga with the Northern Dvina. The Northern Dvina Canal was constructed during 1824 and 1828 and named after Duke Alexander Friedrich of Württemberg, the then Minister of Transportation in Russia. In 1834,

俄罗斯沃洛格达州运河。旧称符腾堡亚历山大公爵运河。北德维纳河运河全长64千米，河上建有6座木制船闸，通过北德维纳河的支流苏霍纳河与伏尔加—波罗的海航道相通。该运河是连接伏尔加河流域与北德维纳河流域的两条航道之一。北德维纳河运河于1824年开凿，1828年竣工通航，以时任俄国交通部长符腾堡公爵亚历山大·弗雷德里希的名字命名。1834年，该运河的支流苏霍纳河上修建了一座

a dam was built on the Sukhona River. In 1884, four locks were demolished and renovation was undertaken to increase the carrying capacity of the canal. Another round of renovation was undertaken from 1916 to 1921. After the renovation, the name of the canal was changed in order to rid it of the association with the royal family. Currently, the Northern Dvina Canal is still in use.

North Holland Canal

A canal located in the province of North Holland, the Netherlands. The North Holland Canal is about 75 kilometres long, runs from the IJ River at Amsterdam to Den Helder in the north, and flows into the North Sea. This canal has been used specifically as a waterway for ocean-going ships since its construction was commissioned by Dutch King Willem I in 1819. The North Holland Canal was opened in 1824 and had 4 locks, with the Willem I Lock at the southern end of the canal and a Buiksloot Flood Gate to its north which used to be kept open. To the north of Buiksloot Flood Gate was the Purmerend Lock. There was the Zijpersluis Flood Gate to the north of Alkmaar, and to the north of this floodgate there was the Zijpe Lock. The last lock was located in the New Canal. The 4 locks divided the canal into 3 sections. The first section, also called the southern section, stretches from the Willem Lock at Amsterdam to the lock near Purmerend, covering a distance of 16 kilometres. The second section, also known as the central section, goes from Purmerend to the Zijpesluis at the 't Zand Town. It

水坝。1884年，为提高航运能力，运河上的4座船闸被拆除，运河进行了一次修缮。1916—1921年间，运河进行了二次修缮。改造完成后，为切断运河与俄国皇室的联系，运河更名为北德维纳河运河。如今，该运河仍在通航。

北荷兰运河

荷兰北荷兰省运河。北荷兰运河全长约75千米，始于阿姆斯特丹，从艾河向北流向登海尔德市，最终注入北海。1819年经荷兰国王威廉一世（1772—1843）批准修建起，该运河就被专门用作供远洋船只通行的航道。北荷兰运河1824年通航，建有4座船闸。威廉一世船闸位于运河南端，运河北部有一座名为伯伊克斯洛特的防洪闸，通常处于开闸状态。该防洪闸北部建有皮尔默伦德船闸。阿尔克马尔北部有一座宰珀斯勒伊斯防洪闸，该防洪闸北部建有一座名为宰佩的船闸。最后一座船闸位于新运河。这4座船闸将北荷兰运河分为3段：第一河段，又称南部航道，从阿姆斯特丹的威廉船闸一直延伸到皮尔默伦德附近的船闸，全长16千米；第二河段，又称中部航道，从皮尔默伦德到特赞德的宰珀宰珀斯勒伊斯，全长约52千米，是三个

is about 52 kilometres in length, the longest among these three sections. The third section, namely the northern section, is 12 kilometres in length and ends at the Koopvaarders Lock at Den Helder. The North Holland Canal had been very important in the Dutch history, but the North Sea Canal, completed in 1876, shared its tasks. Today the North Holland Canal is still used for commercial transport, but its main function includes recreation and water management.

河段中最长的一段；第三河段，即北部航道，从特赞德到登海尔德的库普瓦尔德船闸，全长12千米。北荷兰运河在荷兰历史上举足轻重，1876年竣工的北海运河分担了该运河的航运功能。如今，北荷兰运河仍用于商业运输，但其主要功能是休闲娱乐和水资源调节。

North Jiaolai River

A canal located in Shandong Province, China. Also known as North Canal. The North Jiaolai River is 100 kilometres in length and has a drainage area of over 3,970 square kilometres. As a branch of the Jiaolai Canal, it flows into the Laizhou Bay of the Bohai Gulf at the town of Haicangkou in Yexian County.

北胶莱河

中国山东省运河。亦称北运河。北胶莱河全长100千米，流域面积超过3 970平方千米。该运河是胶莱运河的支流之一，于掖县海仓口镇注入渤海莱州湾。

North Michigan Waterway

An inland waterway located in the state of Michigan, the United States. The North Michigan Waterway is a 61-kilometre-long historic waterway located in Emmet and Cheboygan County. It is a chain of rivers and lakes including the Crooked Lake and the Cheboygan River. As a part of the Huron Blueways, it is also a coastal route that connects the Cheboygan City to Mackinaw City and the Straits of Mackinac. The waterway was originally used to avoid strong waves on Lake Michigan

北密歇根航道

美国密歇根州内陆航道。北密歇根航道位于埃米特县和希博伊根县之间，全长61千米。该航道历史悠久，由一系列湖泊和河流组成，其中包括克鲁克德湖和希博伊根河。作为休伦蓝道航道的一部分，北密歇根航道也是一条沿海交通线路，连通希博伊根河与麦基诺市和麦基诺航道。最初，美国土著居民借该航道避开密歇根湖上的巨

by Native Americans. In 1873, its surrounding areas were open to tourists and settlers when a railway reached Petoskey. Later, the waterway was reconstructed for transportation purposes. The railway, as a more cost-effective means of transportation, eventually devalued the waterway which ended up being abandoned. Today, the surrounding areas of the waterway have become a tourist attraction, notably a popular motor boat destination. There are also several state or private campgrounds along the route and hotels for accommodation.

North Sea Canal

A canal located in the province of North Holland, the Netherlands. The North Sea Canal is 24 kilometres long, 235 metres wide and 15 metres deep, with a capacity of 90,000-tonne oceangoing vessels. It flows in an east-west direction, connecting Amsterdam and IJmuiden on the North Sea coast. Constructed between 1865 and 1876, the canal has been enlarged several times with the last time in 2019. There are 5 locks on the canal, among which, the north canal lock was opened in 1929 and served as the largest canal lock in the world, with a dimension of 400 metres long by 50 metres wide. A lock established near the Spaarne Dam separates the North Sea Canal from the Spaarne. For the North Sea Canal, the Alkmaar Lake plays a vital role in transportation, drainage and water resources management. The North Sea Canal gives Amsterdam access to the sea and makes it a major port.

浪。1873年，铁路修建到皮托斯基市，航道周边地区向旅游业和定居者开放。之后，北密歇根航道经人工改造被用于货物运输。但铁路运输性价比更高，北密歇根航道逐渐失去了竞争力，最终被废弃。如今，该航道周边地区已成为旅游景点，吸引了大量的摩托艇爱好者。北密歇根航道沿途还设有公立或私人经营的露营地和住宿酒店。

北海运河

荷兰北荷兰省运河。北海运河长24千米，宽235米，深15米，可通行9万吨级远洋船只。该运河为东西流向，连接阿姆斯特丹和北海海岸的港口城市艾默伊登。北海运河开凿于1865—1876年间，经过数次扩建，最近一次是在2019年。运河上建有5座船闸，其中建于1929年的北运河船闸长400米，宽50米，是当时世界上最大的运河船闸。斯帕恩大坝附近建有一座船闸，将北海运河与斯帕恩河分隔开。阿尔克马尔湖在北海运河的运输、排水和水资源管理方面发挥着至关重要的作用。北海运河连接阿姆斯特丹与出海口，使其成为一个主要港口。

North Walsham and Dilham Canal

A canal located in England, the United Kingdom. The North Walsham and Dilham Canal has a total length of 8.7 kilometres with 6 locks. It runs from 2 mills at Antingham to the junction with River Ant at Smallburgh. Authorized by the Parliament in 1812, this canal started to be constructed after 1825, and was officially opened in August 1826. It was mainly used to carry goods and agricultural products. Being financially unsuccessful, it was first sold to the Edward Press at a price of £600 in 1886, and then at auction for £2,550 in 1906. It was sold for the third time in 1921 to the North Walsham Canal Co. Ltd, and the ownership remains today. The last ship known to use the canal was the Wherry Ella in 1934. Owing to silt, the Walsham and Dilham Canal fell into disuse afterwards.

North Willems Canal

A canal located in the north of the Netherlands. The North Willems Canal is 38 kilometres in length and 2 metres in depth, with 3 locks and 23 bridges, flowing north from the Drenthe Grand Canal in Drenthe to Groningen City. In Groningen, the canal becomes a part of a waterway network. It is linked with several waterways, among which are the Eendrachts Canal, the Ems Canal and the Verbindings Canal. The North Willems Canal was origi-

北沃尔沙姆-迪尔翰运河

英国英格兰运河。北沃尔沙姆—迪尔翰运河全长8.7千米，河上建有6座船闸。该运河始于安廷厄姆的两家工坊，最终与安特河在斯莫尔堡交汇。早在1812年英国议会即批准开凿该运河，但1825年后才动工，1826年8月北沃尔沙姆—迪尔翰运河正式通航，主要用于运送货物和农产品。由于经济收益低，该运河1886年以600英镑的价格首次出售给爱德华出版社。后在1906年又以2 550英镑的价格拍卖成交。1921年，该运河第三次被出售，售给了北沃尔沙姆运河有限公司，至今仍为该公司所有。已知最后一艘在北沃尔沙姆—迪尔翰运河上航行的船是1934年的"威丽艾拉号"平底货船。运河后因泥沙淤积问题而被弃用。

北威廉斯运河

荷兰北部运河。北威廉斯运河全长38千米，水深2米，河上建有3座船闸和23座桥梁，始于德伦特省，从德伦特大运河向北流至格罗宁根市，在格罗宁根市与团结运河、韦尔宾丁斯运河及埃姆斯运河等航道连通，形成了一个航道网。运河最初以尼德兰王国国王威廉三世的名字命名，但因荷兰南部地区

nally named after William III, King of the Netherlands, yet it had to be renamed later as the North Willems Canal because there were already 3 canals bearing the same name in southern Netherlands. Unlike most canals that were built by governments in the Netherlands, the North Willems Canal was constructed by a commercial company and was put into use in 1861. Currently, the canal is jointly managed by the provinces of Drenthe and Groningen. The whole canal belongs to CEMT (Classification of European Inland Waterways) Class II. The section from its confluence with the Drenthe Grand Canal to that with the Haven Canal is navigable for ships of up to 65 metres long, 6.6 metres wide and with a draught of 1.9 metres, while the other section from its confluence with the Haven Canal to Groningen City allows ships of up to 65 metres long, 7.3 metres wide and with a draught of 2.5 metres to pass. A bit north of its junction with the Meerweg lies a stretch of the Hoorne Dike, a winding dyke running parallel to the canal in this section, which is a popular route for cycling.

已有3条同名运河，故改名为北威廉斯运河。北威廉斯运河不像荷兰大多数运河那样由政府修建，而是由一商业公司负责开凿，1861年通航。目前，该运河由德伦特省和格罗宁根省共同负责管理。根据欧洲内陆航道分级标准，北威廉斯运河全河段属于二级航道，从该运河与德伦特大运河的交汇处至其与哈芬运河交汇处的河段可供长65米、宽6.6米、吃水深度达1.9米的船舶通行；由此北上至格罗宁根市的河段，可通行长65米、宽7.3米、吃水深度达2.5米的船舶。北威廉斯运河与环湖路交汇处的偏北部，沿河可以看到霍恩渠的一段。霍恩渠蜿蜒曲折，深受骑行爱好者欢迎，此段正好同北威廉斯运河平行。

North Wilts Canal

A canal located in England, the United Kingdom. The North Wilts Canal is 12.9 kilometres long. It splits from the Wilts-Berks Canal in the centre of Swindon. After flowing through 12 locks, the canal falls 18.3 metres before connecting with the Thames and Severn Canal at Latton Basin. It connects 4 rivers in total, including the Kennet River, the Avon River, the Thames River and the Severn River. The

北威尔茨运河

英国英格兰运河。北威尔茨运河全长12.9千米，在斯温登中部与威尔茨—博克斯运河分流，流经12座船闸，水位下降18.3米后与拉顿内湾的泰晤士—塞文运河相通。该运河与4条河流相连，分别是肯尼特河、埃文河、泰晤士河和塞文河。北威尔茨运河1814年开凿，

North Wilts Canal was built in 1814 and was officially opened on 2 April 1819. There are many aqueducts on the canal, which cross the Ray River north of Swindon, the Key River in Cricklade, the Thames River at the upper end of North Meadow and the Chuen River next to the Latton Basin, etc. At the same time, bridges on the canal allow roads and farm paths along the canal to cross it. The canal was originally used for coal trade, and was later widely used to transport grain supplies, as well as the transportation of bricks, slate, salt, flour, malt, iron and timber from Lechlade, Cricklade, Cirencester and Bristol. In 1820, the Wilts & Berks Canal Company purchased the North Wilts Canal just one year after the canal was completed. By the time the Great Western Railway was completed in the 1840s, most of the trade of the canal was occupied by this faster transportation system, and the canal began to decline in use. Due to the sluggish canal trade, there was not enough funding to carry out necessary maintenance and repair work, which led to its abandonment later. In December 2000, the North Wilts Canal was rebuilt, and the Moredon Lock on it was repaired to a great extent. A new investment in the construction of Hayes Knoll Lock began in 2005. Today, the North Wilts Canal is under the management of the Wilts and Berks Canal Trust Fund, which was established to maintain the canal line between Swindon and Cricklade and promote its use.

1819年4月2日正式通航。运河上建有多座渡槽，可以跨越斯温登以北的雷河、克里克莱德的基河、北梅多上端的泰晤士河和拉顿内湾旁边的丘恩河等。同时，运河上架有多座桥梁，方便行人从沿线道路和农场小路穿过运河。北威尔茨运河最初用于煤炭贸易，后被广泛用于运送莱奇莱德、克里克莱德、赛伦塞斯特和布里斯托尔等地的粮食、砖、板岩、盐、面粉、麦芽、铁和木材。1820年，北威尔茨运河竣工仅一年后被威尔茨与伯克斯运河公司收购。19世纪40年代大西部铁路建成后，北威尔茨运河上的多数商业航运业务被速度更快的铁路运输所替代，运河航运开始走向衰落。运河贸易业务低迷，管理方缺乏资金进行必要的维护和修整，导致运河被弃用。2000年12月，北威尔茨运河得到重建，运河上的莫顿船闸也基本修复。2005年起海斯诺尔船闸开始投资兴建。如今，北威尔茨运河由威尔茨和伯克斯运河信托基金会管理，该基金会旨在维护斯温登和克里克莱德之间的运河航线，促进其合理使用。

Notte Canal

诺特运河

An inland canal located in the state of Branden-

德国勃兰登堡州内陆运河。诺特

burg, Germany. The Notte Canal is 18 metres wide and 1.3 metres deep, consisting of 3 locks as well as a number of inland ditches, culverts and bridges. It flows northwards from the Mellen Lake to the Dahme. The canal is the canalized Notte River, a man-made left tributary of the Dahme. The construction of the canal was started in 1856. Then new locks in Königs Wusterhausen, Mittenwalde and Mellen were put into construction one after another. The entire project was completed in 1864. The canal, along with the Dahme River and the Spree River, served as an artery waterway to ship agricultural products and industrial materials, especially bricks, towards Berlin. The shipping traffic on the Notte Canal decreased sharply after the rise of the railroads in the following decades. Today, the canal is no longer used for freight shipping.

运河宽18米，深1.3米，河上建有3座船闸、多条内陆沟渠、涵洞及桥梁。该运河由诺特河（达默河左岸的一条人工支流）改造而来，从南部的梅伦湖向北流至达默河。诺特运河1856年开凿；随后，依次在柯尼希武斯特豪森、米滕瓦尔德和梅伦修建了船闸。整个项目1864年竣工。运河建成后，与达默河、施普雷河共同构成了一条水运干线，将农产品和工业原料（特别是砖块）运往柏林。但在随后的几十年中，随着铁路兴起，诺特运河的航运量大幅减少。如今，诺特运河已不再用于运输货物。

Nottingham Canal

A canal located in England, the United Kingdom. The Nottingham Canal, situated between the Langley Mill in Derbyshire and Nottingham, was 23.9 kilometres in length with 18 locks originally. It ran from its junction with the Cromford Canal to River Trent. The canal was completed in 1796 and closed in 1937. The canal facilitated the shipments of building materials, coal, and agricultural tools that came into Nottingham. Due to the development of railways in the 19th century, the Nottingham Canal was gradually disused. Nowadays, its southern section is a part of River Trent Navigation, while the northern section is a part of the local nature reserve.

诺丁汉运河

英国英格兰运河。诺丁汉运河位于英格兰诺丁汉和德比郡的兰利米尔之间，从与克罗姆福德运河的交汇处流向特伦特河。运河初建成时全长23.9千米，河上建有18座船闸。该运河1796年竣工，1937年停用。诺丁汉运河的开通使得建筑材料、煤炭和农具等更加便捷地运送至诺丁汉。后因19世纪铁路运输业的发展，该运河逐渐被弃用。如今，诺丁汉运河的南段是特伦特河航道的一部分，北段是当地自然保护区的一部分。

Nutbrook Canal

A canal located in England, the United Kingdom. The Nutbrook Canal is 7.2 kilometres long and has 13 locks in total. It starts from Shipley in Derbyshire and joins the Erewash Canal near Trowell. Excavated from 1793 to 1796, the canal was intended for the collieries at Shipley and West Hallam. Although the cost of £22,801 was beyond the budget, the over-expenditure problem was eventually resolved by calls on the shareholders. The traffic on the canal was never quite heavy. Even at its peak in October 1821, it was used only by about 9 vessels per day. The canal was very profitable at first. Since 1846, it had been suffering great pressure in competition with railways. The maintenance costs of this canal were high and the coal mines could not afford the tolls of the cargos via the canal. Under such circumstances, a large section of the Nutbrook Canal was closed in 1895, leaving the final 2.4-kilometre-long section still in use until 1949. Nowadays, a part of the abandoned canal is used for fishing.

Nyhavn

A canal located in the city of Copenhagen, Denmark. The Nyhavn is 450 metres long. The construction of the Nyhavn began in 1670 under the order of King Christian V of Denmark and was completed in 1673. It served as the link between the sea and the old inner city at Kongens Nytorv where cargos and fishes were transported. Later the canal was

纳特布鲁克运河

英国英格兰运河。纳特布鲁克运河全长7.2千米,河上建有13座船闸,始于德比郡的希普利村,在特罗维尔村附近汇入埃里沃什运河。运河1793年开凿,1796年竣工,旨在为希普利和西哈勒姆的煤矿提供运输便利。运河修建费用共计22 801英镑,超过预算,超支问题最终通过股东筹款的方式得以解决。纳特布鲁克运河上的交通并不繁忙,即便在1821年10月的鼎盛时期,每天也仅有约9艘货船通过。但运河开通之初还是盈利颇丰。自1846年起,纳特布鲁克运河开始面临来自铁路竞争的压力。因运河维护成本高昂,煤矿厂商逐渐无法负担起高价通行费。纳特布鲁克运河的大部分河段于1895年被迫停航,仅保留最后2.4千米长的河段继续通航至1949年。如今,部分废弃河段仍可用于垂钓。

新港运河

丹麦哥本哈根市运河。新港运河全长450米,经丹麦国王克里斯蒂安五世批准,于1670年开凿,1673年竣工。该运河使老城中心国王新广场与海洋相通,主要供货船和渔船通行。后因无法承载体积更大的远洋货轮,新港运河主要承

crammed with internal Danish small cargo boats as it failed to accommodate the oceangoing freighters of a growing larger size. After World War II, the channel was substituted by ways of land transportation, leaving only a few ships sailing on it. Today, this canal is a scenic waterway along which stand several tourist attractions, including brightly coloured townhouses, the Danish National Museum, and the Memorial Anchor.

运内河行驶的小型货船。第二次世界大战后，陆路运输方式逐渐取代了内河运输方式，新港运河的承运量大不如前。如今，新港运河成为观光水道，沿岸分布着多个旅游景点，包括色彩鲜艳的排屋、丹麦国家博物馆和新港纪念船锚等。

Nymphenburg Canal

A canal located in the city of Munich, Germany. The Nymphenburg Canal consists of two sections, namely the Pasing-Nympenburg Canal and the Palace Canal. The former conveys water from the Würm River in the west to the Nymphenburg Palace and the Palace Garden; while the latter, as the eastern part, was built for decorative purposes. In the district of Pasing, the Nymphenburg Canal is under the name of the Pasing-Nymphenburg Canal, a 2.8-kilometre-long branch of the Würm River. The Pasing-Nymphenburg Canal was built between 1701 and 1703, under the charge of Elector Maximilian II Emanuel, and later became one of the most prominent visible axes in the city of Munich. Due to the expansion of Nymphenburg Palace, the canal was constructed to supply water to the Palace Park, and its water flowing from the Würm River is regulated by a weir. After entering the park, the canal continues its straight course and splits into two 750-metre-long arms which reunite in front of the palace to form a pond with a fountain. This branch

宁芬堡运河

德国慕尼黑市运河。宁芬堡运河包括两个河段，分别是帕辛—宁芬堡运河和宫殿运河。帕辛—宁芬堡运河从西面的维尔姆河引水，流向宁芬堡宫及其花园；宫殿运河则在东部，为美化景观而修建。宁芬堡运河在帕辛区被称为帕辛—宁芬堡运河，长2.8千米，是维尔姆河支流。帕辛—宁芬堡运河开凿于1701—1703年间，修建工程由巴伐利亚选帝侯马克西米利安二世埃马努埃尔（1662—1726）主持，竣工后成为慕尼黑最重要的中轴线地标之一。该段运河的建造与宁芬堡宫扩建有关，主要为了给宁芬堡及其花园供水，其水量由一座拦河坝控制。河水被引入宫殿花园后，河道先是呈直线状态，后分为两路，长度各约750米，后在宫殿前合流，形成一个带有喷泉的池塘。宁芬堡运河在宫殿内的一段便是作

that runs in the palace is the Palace Canal, and it ends in the Hubertus Fountain. The canal feeds the cascade as well as the entire water system of the park, and also drives the pumping stations of the Nymphenburg Palace, pressurizing the water for the fountains in the Palace Park. Today, the Nymphenburg Canal is an ideal place for recreation. During the summer, tourists can take a gondola ride along the canal. In winter, people come here for various winter sports such as ice skating, ice hockey games and curling.

为支流的宫殿运河，终点位于胡贝图斯喷泉。该运河为位于其西端的园内瀑布以及整个公园的水系供水，同时还是宁芬堡宫驱动泵站的动力来源，为宫殿公园的喷泉加压。如今，宁芬堡运河已成为休闲娱乐的好去处。夏季，游客可以乘贡多拉小船欣赏运河沿线美丽的风景。冬季，人们经常在冰封的宁芬堡运河上开展各类冬季运动，如溜冰、冰球和冰壶运动。

Oakham Canal

A canal located in England, the United Kingdom. The Oakham Canal had a length of 24.9 kilometres and 19 locks in total, running from Oakham, Rutland, to Melton Mowbray, Leicestershire. It raised 38 metres in height from the start to the end of the whole course. Excavated in 1793 and opened in 1802, the canal was never successful financially. It suffered a shortage of water supply. After being closed in 1847, the Oakham Canal was bought by the Midland Railway with a view to building the Syston and Peterborough Railway partly along its original route. Although most of the course has been disused or infilled, traces can still be found, with some short sections even holding water today. The Melton and Oakham Waterways Society (MOWS), a local organization formed in 1997, is working on the preservation of the Oakham Canal.

Oberrhein~

A canalized cross-border river located in Europe. The Oberrhein is 360 kilometres long, which is the section of the Rhine in the Upper Rhine Plain. As one of the four sections of the Rhine, the river runs through Switzerland, France (Alsace) and the German states of Baden-Württemberg, Rhineland-Palatinate and Hessen. Between 1817 and 1876, the Upper Rhine was straightened and navigable between 1928 and 1977. The section from Basel to Iffezheim is virtually all canalized. Along the 180-kilometre-long stretch of the river, 10 dams,

奥克姆运河

英国英格兰运河。奥克姆运河全长24.9千米，河上共建有19座船闸。运河从拉特兰郡的奥克姆流向莱斯特郡的梅尔顿莫布雷，起点至终点的水位升高了38米。奥克姆运河1793年开凿，1802年通航，但其经济效益一直不佳，同时还面临供水不足的问题，最终于1847年被关闭。奥克姆运河后来由米德兰铁路公司收购，旨在沿部分旧河道修建西斯滕—彼得伯勒铁路。运河的大部分河道已被弃用或回填，但许多遗迹仍依稀可见，一些较短的河段现在仍有储水。1997年成立的梅尔顿和奥克姆航道协会正致力于奥克姆运河的保护工作。

莱茵河上游段

欧洲跨国运河化河流。莱茵河上游段全长360千米，是莱茵河在莱茵河上游平原的河段。作为莱茵河的四条河段之一，该河段流经瑞士、法国阿尔萨斯区以及德国的巴登—符腾堡州、莱茵兰—普法尔茨州和黑森州。1817—1876年间，莱茵河上游段河道被改直，1928年开始通航，1977年停航。通航期间，从瑞士巴塞尔到德国伊弗茨海姆的航道全部经运河化改造。180千

several hydropower stations and locks were built. The construction of the dams has resulted in a lack of sand and gravel, thus causing the erosion of the bottom of the dam. To solve this problem, sand and gravel has been dumped into the river every year since 1978. The Upper Rhine has great influence on flood control on the Middle and Lower Rhine. France, according to the Treaty of Versailles, is allowed to use this section for hydroelectricity.

米长的航道上建有10座大坝、数座水电站和船闸。大坝修建后, 河中沙石减少, 坝底受到侵蚀。为解决这一问题, 从1978年起, 人们每年都向河中倾倒沙石。莱茵河上游段对中游和下游的防洪有重要影响。根据《凡尔赛条约》, 法国可以利用莱茵河上游段进行水力发电。

Obvodny Canal

侧路渠运河

An inland canal located in Saint Petersburg, Russia. The Obvodny Canal, 8 kilometres in length, is the longest canal in Saint Petersburg. Its construction was started in 1769 and completed in 1835. The Obvodny Canal became the southern limit of Saint Petersburg in the 19th century. In the second half of the 19th century, it was turned into a sewer collecting industrial effluents discharged by the surrounding industrial companies, which eventually made the canal unnavigable. Although it is no longer a major waterway nowadays, its embankments remain an important part of the city routes of Saint Petersburg.

俄罗斯圣彼得堡市内陆运河。侧路渠运河全长8千米, 是圣彼得堡境内最长的一条运河。运河开凿于1769年, 1835年竣工。19世纪时, 侧路渠运河是圣彼得堡的南部边界。19世纪下半叶, 运河因周围工厂排放工业废水, 最终无法通航。如今, 侧路渠运河不再是主要航道, 但其堤岸仍然是圣彼得堡市道路的重要组成部分。

Ob-Yenisei Canal

鄂毕—叶尼塞运河

An inland waterway located in Russia. Also called Ket-Kas Canal. The Ob-Yenisei Canal is 7.8 kilometres in length and 2 metres in depth, linking the river basins of the Ob and the Yenisei. The canal was constructed between 1882 and 1891. Around 1911, some plans were put forward to renovate the

俄罗斯内陆运河。亦称克季—卡斯运河。鄂毕—叶尼塞运河全长7.8千米, 深2米, 连接鄂毕河和叶尼塞河流域。该运河修建于1882—1891年间。1911年前后, 有人提出重修鄂毕—叶尼塞运河的计划, 但

canal, but were interrupted with the outbreak of World War I. The Ob-Yenisei Canal was shallow in depth and narrow in surface width. The canal was severely damaged during the Civil War, and was shut down in 1921. Currently, the Ob-Yenisei Canal is fully abandoned.

因第一次世界大战爆发未能施行。鄂毕—叶尼塞运河水位浅且河道窄。该运河在内战期间遭受严重破坏，最终于1921年被迫停航。如今，鄂毕—叶尼塞运河已完全被弃用。

Oder

奥得河

A canalized cross-border river located in central Europe. The Oder is 840 kilometres in length. Originating in the Czech Republic, it flows through Poland and forms the northern border between Poland and Germany before entering the Baltic Sea. Most parts of the river are navigable. The upstream connects the Gliwice Canal and is also canalized in some parts for the navigation of larger barges. Frederick the Great was the first to initiate a project to divert the river from its course into a new straight waterway. A large swampland was developed in this project to cut off detour and confine the water into the new canal during 1746 and 1753. At the end of the 19th century, the waterway underwent three more alterations: the Oder-Spree Canal was constructed from 1887 to 1891 to connect the two rivers; the mainstream at Breslau, as well as the part from Eastern Neisse to the mouth of the Klodnitz Canal was canalized in 1896; and the waterways at the mouth and the lower reaches were deepened and regulated.

欧洲中部跨国运河化河流。奥得河全长840千米，始于捷克共和国，流经波兰，构成波兰和德国两国的北部分界线，最后注入波罗的海。该河的大部分河段都可通航，上游与格利维采运河相通，部分河段进行了运河化改造，较大的驳船也可通行。腓特烈大帝发起了改直奥得河航道的工程。1746—1753年间奥得河改造，为改直弯曲河段，同时将河水导入新运河，形成了大片沼泽地。19世纪末，该河流又经历了三次改造：第一次是1887—1891年间修建了奥得—施普雷运河，将奥得河和施普雷运河连通起来；第二次是在1896年，布雷斯劳的主河道以及从东尼斯河到克罗迪尼兹运河河口的河段都进行了运河化改造；第三次是加深和治理河口和下游航道。

Oder-Havel Canal

A cross-border canal located in Europe. Also called Hohenzollern Canal. The Oder-Havel Canal is 82.8 kilometres in length, 33 metres in width and almost 2 metres in depth, running from the town of Cedynia near the city of Szczecin, Poland, to the Havel near Berlin. The canal was excavated between 1908 and 1914. In 1934, a ship lift was built on the canal, whose vertical lift was 36 metres. The vessels it could lift amounted to 1,000 tons. As a waterway, its importance had been declining until 1945. The traffic of the canal became busy again after the chemical industry at Schwedt prospered.

奥得－哈弗尔运河

欧洲跨国运河。亦称霍亨索伦运河。奥得—哈弗尔运河全长82.8千米，宽33米，深近2米，从波兰什切青市附近的采迪尼亚镇汇入柏林附近的哈弗尔河。运河开凿于1908年，1914年竣工。1934年，运河上修建了1座升船机，可垂直提升高度为36米，可抬升总重达1 000吨的船只。1945年之前，该运河的重要性逐渐减弱。施韦特化工产业兴起后，运河上的交通再次繁忙起来。

Oder-Spree Canal

A canal located in the east of Germany. The Oder-Spree Canal is 20 kilometres long, connecting the Dahme River with the Oder River. Completed in 1891, it provides an important commercial navigable connection between Berlin and Oder. The canal has several connections to the Spree River, and it is now generally used by pleasure craft.

奥得－施普雷运河

德国东部运河。奥得—施普雷运河全长20千米，连通达默河和奥得河。运河1891年完工，是柏林与奥得之间的重要商业航道。奥得—施普雷运河与施普雷河之间有多处航道连通，目前主要供游船通行。

Oegstgeest Canal

A canal located in the province of South Holland, the Netherlands. The Oegstgeest Canal originates from the confluence of the Haarlem-Leiden Trek Canal and the Warmonderleede River, and discharges into the Old Rhine after flowing through Oegstgeest. It was excavated in 1840 to improve the

乌赫斯特海斯特运河

荷兰南荷兰省运河。乌赫斯特海斯特运河始于哈勒姆—莱顿拖船运河与瓦尔蒙德利德河交汇处，流经乌赫斯特海斯特，最后汇入旧莱茵河。该运河1840年开凿，旨在改善莱茵兰地区的排水状况，重

drainage of the Rhineland and reclaim the flooded Haarlem Lake. The water of this canal ends in the King Williem-Alexander Pumping Station. The canal is managed by the Rhineland Water Board, which plans to widen it in 2025 to further improve its capacity for water drainage. Currently, the canal is mainly used for drainage, transportation, and recreation. In 2019, a footpath was constructed by the municipality along the canal for recreation and natural experience.

新开发利用被洪水淹没的哈勒姆湖地区。乌赫斯特海斯特运河最终流至国王威廉—亚历山大水泵站。莱茵兰水务局负责管理这条运河，计划于2025年拓宽运河，以进一步提升其排水能力。目前，该运河主要用于排水、运输和观光旅游。2019年，当地政府沿运河修建了步道，用于休闲观光。

Oginski Canal

A canal located in Belarus. The Oginski Canal is 54 kilometres long, linking the Yaselda River and the Shchara River. It was excavated in 1765 and named after Count Michał Kazimierz Ogiński, who was the initiator of the canal construction.

奥金斯基运河

白俄罗斯运河。奥金斯基运河全长54千米，连通雅瑟达河和夏拉河。该运河于1765年开凿，由米哈尔·卡齐米日·奥金斯基伯爵倡议，故运河以其姓氏命名。

Ohio and Erie Canal

A canal located in Ohio, the United States. Also known as Grand Canal. The Ohio and Erie Canal is 496 kilometres in length. It starts from Lake Erie in Cleveland and ends in Portsmouth, connecting some canals in Pennsylvania. The canal was excavated in sections from 1825 to 1832, with 146 locks in total. It flourished from the 1830s to the early 1860s, generating the highest revenue between 1852 and 1855. The Ohio and Erie Canal went into recession after the Civil War, when maintenance costs exceeded the canal's revenues, and was gradually replaced by railway transportation. From 1862

俄亥俄－伊利运河

美国俄亥俄州运河。亦称格兰德运河。俄亥俄—伊利运河全长496千米，始于伊利湖畔的克利夫兰，流至朴次茅斯市，与宾夕法尼亚州的一些运河相连通。俄亥俄—伊利运河修建于1825—1832年间，采取分段开凿的方式，沿线共建有146座船闸。19世纪30年代至60年代初，运河航运业务十分繁忙，1852—1855年间收益达到顶峰。美国南北战争结束后，因维护费超过收益，该运河逐渐被铁路运输所

to 1913, it functioned as a source of water for towns and industries along the waterway. In 1913, due to a severe flood, many facilities of the canal were destroyed and it was gradually abandoned after that. Today, most remains of the canal are managed by the National Park Service or Ohio Department of Natural Resources for public activities. The Ohio and Erie Canal Historic District was listed as a National Historic Landmark in 1966. Currently, some sections are still used to supply water for industries.

取代。1862—1913年间，运河主要用来为沿岸城镇和工厂供水。1913年，洪水严重泛滥，运河上许多重要设施被毁，运河逐渐遭废弃。如今，俄亥俄—伊利运河大部分遗迹由国家公园管理局或俄亥俄州自然资源部管理，用于公共活动。1966年，俄亥俄—伊利运河历史保护区被列为美国国家历史地标。运河部分河段现仍用于提供工业用水。

Ohio and Pennsylvania Canal

俄亥俄−宾夕法尼亚运河

A canal located in the United States. Also called Mahoning Canal. The Ohio and Pennsylvania Canal has a length of 133.6 kilometres and 54 locks, connecting Akron, Ohio with New Castle, Pennsylvania. The canal was constructed from 1835 to 1840, and operated from 1840 to 1877. It was funded by private commercial interests to get more trade to compete with the New York City. The construction of this canal met many challenges such as the Panic of 1837, and deaths of numerous workers caused by cholera epidemic. The Ohio and Pennsylvania Canal was completed in 1840. Through this canal, passengers and freight could be transported from Pittsburgh to Cleveland, which contributed to the expansion and prosperity of the villages and towns along the canal. Some people also attributed the development of the iron ore industry in Ohio's Mahoning Valley to the canal. With the expansion of railway transportation, the traffic on the canal

美国运河。亦称马霍宁运河。俄亥俄—宾夕法尼亚运河全长133.6千米，沿线共建有54座船闸，连接俄亥俄州的阿克伦市与宾夕法尼亚州的纽卡斯尔市。该运河修建于1835—1840年间，1840—1877年间通航。运河由私人商业公司出资修建，旨在扩大贸易市场，与纽约市展开商业竞争。运河修建过程中曾遭遇许多挑战，包括1837年大恐慌以及霍乱疫情造成大量工人死亡等，最终于1840年竣工。乘客和货物可以通过该运河从匹兹堡市到达克利夫兰市。运河促进了沿岸村镇的发展和繁荣，有人将俄亥俄州马霍宁河谷地区铁矿石工业的发展归功于这条运河。后随着铁路运输的快速发展，运河航运量逐渐减小，1872年终被弃用。1877

gradually diminished and consequently it was abandoned in 1872. In 1877, the canal was officially closed and all relevant property was sold off. Today, some canal remains can be found in Kent.

年,运河被正式关闭,所有相关财产被抛售。如今,在肯特市,部分运河遗迹仍可见。

Oise[≈]

A cross-border inland canalized shipping waterway located in Europe. With a total length of 341 kilometres, the Oise flows in France and Belgium, linking the Seine with the coastal regions of northern France, Belgium, and the Netherlands through the Oise Lateral Canal. It extends from Hainaut Province in Belgium to the Seine at Conflans-Sainte-Honorine in northwestern Paris, France. Although it has long been used for navigation since the Middle Ages, the river was not canalized until 1835 when the locks were built. The size of the locks was 41 by 6 metres or 46 by 8 metres. Currently the size is 185 by 12 metres. The building of these locks was started in the 1960s with the purpose of accommodating them to the deepened North Canal. New locks are now under construction to prepare for the Seine-North Europe Canal, a projected high-capacity waterway that aims to connect the Oise with the Dunkirk-Escaut Canal.

瓦兹河

欧洲跨国运河化内陆航道。瓦兹河全长341千米,流经法国和比利时,通过瓦兹旁侧运河将塞纳河与法国北部、比利时和荷兰的沿海地区连接在一起。该河发源于比利时埃诺省,在法国巴黎西北部的孔夫朗—圣奥诺里讷地区汇入塞纳河。瓦兹河自中世纪起就已通航,但直到1835年才进行运河化改造,河上建起了数座船闸,其规格为41×6米(或46×8米)。现在该河中使用的船闸规格为185×12米,修建于20世纪60年代。当时修建船闸主要是应对因北方运河加深带来的河水流量变化。目前,新的船闸正在修建中,旨在为拟建中的塞纳—北欧运河的通航做准备。该运河通航能力定位很高,建成后将连通瓦兹河和敦刻尔克—埃斯科运河。

Oise-Aisne Canal

A summit-level canal located in northern France. The Oise-Aisne Canal links the Oise Lateral Canal at Abbécourt with the Aisne Lateral Canal at

瓦兹—埃纳运河

法国北部越岭运河。瓦兹—埃纳运河在阿贝库尔连通瓦兹河旁侧运河,在布尔—科曼连通埃纳旁侧

Bourg-et-Comin. It is 48 kilometres in length and has 13 locks. Between the two valleys, the summit level of the canal is 66 metres in height. Short aqueducts were built at each end of the canal over the river Oise and the river Aisne. The canal ascends slowly to a plateau, runs through the 2,365-metre Braye-en-Laonnois Tunnel and then descends fairly fast to Bourg-et-Comin. The canal is one of the last canals that were built in France. In 1890, it was opened and now it still carries commercial transport. It is one of the main routes for vessels heading southward from Belgium or from Calais and Dunkirk in France. There are up to 20 barges navigating on it every day.

运河，全长48千米，河上共建有13座船闸。该运河穿行于两个河谷之间，最高处达66米，其两端在瓦兹河与埃纳河上均建有短渡槽。该运河缓慢上升至高原，穿过2 365米长的布赖昂洛努瓦隧道，后急速下降至布尔—科曼。瓦兹—埃纳运河是法国最晚开凿的运河之一，1890年通航，现仍用于商业运输。瓦兹—埃纳运河是船舶从比利时或法国的加莱和敦刻尔克出发、驶往南方地区的主要航道之一，运河上每天有多达20只驳船航行。

Oise Lateral Canal

瓦兹河旁侧运河

A canal located in northern France. The Oise Lateral Canal links the Saint-Quentin Canal at Chauny with the Seine at Conflans-Sainte-Honorine. It is 34 kilometres in length and has 4 electrically operated locks. Along with the river Oise, it forms a part of the important waterway from the Seine to northern France, Belgium and the Rhine. The canal was excavated in 1831, offering a complete waterway between the Seine and the Saint-Quentin Canal, and thus avoiding the winding course of the river Oise in this part. After the North Canal was officially opened in 1965, the junction of the two canals was further ameliorated. Around the year of 1970, the Oise Lateral Canal was widened and deepened, with 2 more locks built on it. At present, the river Oise and its lateral canal are still busy with com-

法国北部运河。瓦兹河旁侧运河在绍尼连通圣康坦运河，在孔夫朗—圣奥诺里讷连通塞纳河，全长34千米，河上建有4座电动船闸。该运河与瓦兹河将塞纳河与法国北部、比利时和莱茵河地区连接起来，形成了一条重要的航道。运河1831年开凿，在塞纳河与圣康坦运河之间搭建起完整的航运线路，使船只避开了瓦兹河的迂回河道。1965年，北方运河正式开通后，瓦兹河旁侧运河与其交汇处得到修缮。1970年前后，该运河拓宽加深，并新建了2座船闸。目前，瓦兹河及其旁侧运河上的商业运输依旧繁忙，但旁侧运河的

mercial traffic, but a part of the lateral canal from Pont-l'Évêque to Janville is planned to be replaced by the high-capacity Seine-North Europe Canal.

蓬莱韦克至让维尔河段预计将被拟建中承载量高的塞纳—北欧运河所替代。

Okavango River

A canalized cross-border inland river located in southern Africa. The Okavango River is 1,600 kilometres in length and covers an area of 800,000 square kilometres, ranking the fourth among the rivers in Africa. Its name originates from the Okavango people of northern Namibia. The river forms a part of the border between Angola and Namibia. It rises from the Bié Plateau of middle Angola, and then flows southeastward to Botswana, forming the Okavango Swamp. With an area of 16,835 square kilometres, it is one of the world's largest deltas. After running eastward through the seasonal Boteti River, it disappears in the Kalahari Desert without flowing into the ocean. The average discharge of the river is 475 cubic metres per second, but in wet season, it can increase to 1, 000 cubic metres per second. Although Angola receives the highest rainfall in January, it takes nearly 5 months for the water to travel through the Okavango River and the delta. In June and July, the river extends to 3 times as large as usual, forming one of Africa's largest wildlife concentrations. Established in the northeastern corner of the Okavango Swamp, the Moremi Wildlife Reserve, with an area of 3,788 square kilometres, is home to a wide variety of wildlife. Except for small craft, the Okavango is virtually unnavigable. Due to the drought, there is conflict over the use of the wa-

奥卡万戈河

非洲南部运河化内陆河流。奥卡万戈河全长1 600千米，流域面积80万平方千米，在非洲所有河流中排名第四。奥卡万戈河得名于纳米比亚北部的奥卡万戈人。该河是安哥拉和纳米比亚边界线的一部分，发源于安哥拉中部的比耶高原，向东南流至博茨瓦纳，形成了奥卡万戈沼泽，面积达16 835平方千米，是世界最大的三角洲之一。奥卡万戈河向东穿过季节性的博泰蒂河，流至卡拉哈里沙漠后消失，并未注入海洋。该河流的常年平均流速为每秒475立方米，但是在雨季，流速可增至每秒1 000立方米。尽管安哥拉的降水主要集中在1月份，但雨水流过奥卡万戈河和三角洲却要花近5个月的时间。这条河6、7月份的流域面积比平时大两倍，是非洲野生动植物最集中的地区之一。在奥卡万戈沼泽的东北角建有莫雷米野生动物保护区，面积达3 788平方千米，是众多野生动植物的栖息地。航运方面，除了小型船只，奥卡万戈河几乎无法通行。由于干旱，安哥拉、纳米比亚和博茨瓦纳三国之间常因奥卡万

ter resources of the Okavango River among Angola, Namibia and Botswana. Namibia and Angola have built a 300-kilometre-long canal and a 250-kilometre-long pipeline to divert water from the river to relieve the drought. Botswana takes advantage of tourism income and the water from the Okavango Delta. In September 1994, an agreement to establish the Permanent Okavango River Basin Water Commission was signed by the three countries to deal with the use of the river's resources.

戈河水资源使用问题发生冲突。为便于从河流引水,缓解旱情,纳米比亚和安哥拉分别修建了300千米长的运河和250千米长的管道。博茨瓦纳则利用奥卡万戈三角洲的水源,通过旅游业获取收益。1994年9月,为妥善解决奥卡万戈河水资源使用问题,这三个国家签署协议,成立了奥卡万戈河流域常设水务委员会。

Okeechobee Waterway

A canal located in central and southern Florida, the United States. The Okeechobee Waterway is 248 kilometres long with 5 locks managed by the United States Army Corps of Engineers. It runs from the Atlantic Ocean at Stuart to the Gulf of Mexico at Fort Meyers. This relatively shallow waterway was built in 1937 in order to provide a water route across Florida, making it convenient for ships to pass Florida on an east-west route instead of detouring around its southern end. The Okeechobee Waterway has been constructed as a part of the Central and Southern Florida Flood Control Project. As a water-management system, this project covers 1,825 square kilometres.

奥基乔比航道

美国佛罗里达州中南部运河。奥基乔比航道全长248千米,河上建有5座船闸,船闸由美国陆军工程兵团管辖。运河在图尔特市与大西洋连通,流至迈耶斯堡市注入墨西哥湾。运河较浅,1937年修建,旨在方便过往船只自东向西横穿佛罗里达州,而无须从该州南端绕行。奥基乔比航道是佛罗里达州中南部防洪工程的一部分,这项工程是一个水务管理系统,覆盖面积达1 825平方千米。

Old Autize Canal

A canal located in western France. The Old Autize Canal is 10 kilometres long with 1 lock. It links the city of Courdault, which is in the east of

旧欧蒂兹河运河

法国西部运河。旧欧蒂兹河运河全长10千米,建有1座船闸。运河连接布伊勒—库尔多尔东部的库尔多尔

Bouillé-Courdault, to the Sèvre-Niortaise River. Courdault and Saint-Sigismond are the main cities along its route. The canal is one of the two principal arms of the Autize River, the other being the Young Autize Canal. The Old Autize Canal is supposed to be navigable to the port of Courdault. It is often in water shortage and encumbered with grasses.

市和塞夫尔—尼奥尔河，流经的主要城市有库尔多尔市和圣西吉斯蒙市。旧欧蒂兹河运河和新欧蒂兹河运河是欧蒂兹河的两条主要支流。船只应可经由旧欧蒂兹河运河直抵库尔多尔港，但该运河常常缺水，杂草蔓生，航运情况欠佳。

Old Basin Canal

旧内湾运河

A canal located in New Orleans, Louisiana, the United States. See Carondelet Canal.

美国路易斯安那州新奥尔良市运河。见卡龙德莱特运河。

Old Canal

旧运河

An inland canal located in the province of Friesland, the Netherlands. Also called Sneek Old Canal named after the former Sneek Old Canal Water Board. The Old Canal is 11 kilometres long with one lock, running from the village of Rauwerd to the Zomerrak Canal in Sneek City. There were once several water mills and oil mills along the route, which were later demolished.

荷兰弗里斯兰省内陆运河。亦称斯内克旧运河，得名于早先的斯内克旧运河水务局。旧运河全长11千米，河上建有1座船闸，自劳沃德村流至斯内克市后，汇入佐默拉克运河。运河沿线曾建有几座水磨坊和油坊，后被拆除。

Oldehove Canal

奥尔德霍弗运河

A canal located in the province of Groningen, the Netherlands. The Oldehove Canal starts from the Oldehove, runs through Saaksum and Ezinge, and flows into the Aduard Canal. The construction of the canal, ordered by the Saaksum Water Board, began in 1825 and was completed in 1827. The canal was designed to serve as a new drainage and to

荷兰格罗宁根省运河。奥尔德霍弗运河始于奥尔德霍弗，流经萨克瑟姆和埃津厄，汇入爱德华德运河。运河由当时的萨克瑟姆水务局下令修建，1825年开凿，1827年竣工。奥尔德霍弗运河设计为新的排水系统，同时用于货物运输。

facilitate the transport of freight.

Old Ems Canal

A canal located in the province of Groningen, the Netherlands. The Old Ems Canal is 26.5 kilometres long and 60 metres wide with 15 bridges. It is linked to Delfzijl, and is mainly used for drainage and transportation. The canal was constructed between 1866 and 1876. In 1953, measures have been taken to ameliorate its condition and in 1967 the renovated canal was officially put into use.

旧埃姆斯运河

荷兰格罗宁根省运河。旧埃姆斯运河全长26.5千米，宽60米，河上建有15座桥。运河与代尔夫宰尔市相连，主要用于排水和航运。旧埃姆斯运河于1866—1876年间开凿，1953年进行了修缮，1967年改建完成后正式通航。

Old Ladoga Canal

A canal located in Leningrad Oblast, Russia. Originally known as Peter the First Canal. The Old Ladoga Canal is a part of the Ladoga Canal, constructed between 1719 and 1810. The Old Ladoga Canal has been abandoned since 1940 and is now covered with grass.

旧拉多加运河

俄罗斯列宁格勒州运河。旧称彼得一世运河。旧拉多加运河是拉多加运河的一部分，1719—1810年间开凿。运河自1940年起被废弃，现已荒草蔓生。

Old Palace Canal

A canal located in Saint Petersburg, Russia. See Winter Canal.

旧宫殿运河

俄罗斯圣彼得堡运河。见冬运河。

Old Rhine

A canalized river located in the provinces of Utrecht and South Holland, the Netherlands. The Old Rhine has a length of about 52 kilometres. It starts from the town of Harmelen in Woerden, Utrecht,

旧莱茵河

荷兰运河化河流。旧莱茵河流经乌特勒支省和南荷兰省，全长约52千米，始于乌特勒支省武尔登市的哈默伦镇，流经莱茵河畔的阿尔

flows through Alphen-on-the-Rhine and Leiden, and finally empties into the North Sea. The section from Katwijk to the North Sea has been canalized. In ancient Rome, the river was a main branch of the Rhine. In the Middle Ages, the Old Rhine was an important route for cargo transport, and a towpath was constructed along nearly the whole course of the river. In the 17th century, the river silted up, leading to a sharp slump in navigation. Nowadays, people can sail on the Old Rhine to enjoy the beautiful scenery along its banks. Sailing bans were imposed in winter to prevent damage to lake ice, but sports fans are allowed to go ice-skating.

芬市和莱顿市，最终注入北海。卡特韦克至北海的河段进行了运河化改造。在古罗马时期，旧莱茵河曾是莱茵河的一条主要支流。中世纪时，旧莱茵河是重要的货物运输通道，沿河建有一条几乎覆盖整个河段的纤道。17世纪时，因淤塞严重，该河的航运量大幅减少。如今，人们可以沿着旧莱茵河航行，欣赏两岸美丽的风景。为避免破坏湖冰，冬季河上禁止航行，但体育爱好者可以在此滑冰。

Omval-Kolhorn Canal

奥姆瓦尔-科尔霍恩运河

An inland canal located in the province of North Holland, the Netherlands. See Alkmaar-Kolhorn Canal.

荷兰北荷兰省内陆运河。见阿尔克马尔—科尔霍恩运河。

Onega Canal

奥涅加运河

An inland canal located in northwest Russia. The Onega Canal is 69 kilometres in length and 50 metres in width, running along the southern bank of Lake Onega in Vologda Oblast and Leningrad Oblast. The construction of the canal was started in 1818, but was later interrupted, and was not fully completed until 1852. It allows small riverboats to bypass Lake Onega where shipwrecks often happen because of storms. Currently, the Onega Canal is still in use.

俄罗斯西北部内陆运河。奥涅加运河全长69千米，宽50米，流经沃洛格达州和列宁格勒州境内的奥涅加湖南岸。运河1818年开凿，工程曾一度中断，直到1852年才竣工。小型内河船只可经这条运河绕过奥涅加湖，那里常因风暴而发生沉船事故。目前，奥涅加运河仍保持通航状态。

Oneida Lake Canal

A canal located in the northeast of the United States. The Oneida Lake Canal was completed in 1835, 10 years after the completion of the Erie Canal. The canal connected the Sylvan Beach to the old Erie Canal. It was also linked to the Erie Canal in Higginsville at the present location of the Side-cut Road, and thus called Side Cut Canal. The canal continued until it joined the Wood Creek and then it turned westward to the opening of the Oneida Lake. The locks suffered severe leakage; the junction between the canal and the lake silted up with sand and mud. In 1863, the navigation on this route ceased officially. The newly enlarged canal, completed in 1877, was southwest of the former Oneida Lake Canal. It ran nearly straight to the Oneida Lake, thus shortening the voyage by about 3.2 kilometres. This waterway was plagued with quick sand which created many breaches in the walls. The route was closed on and off between 1877 and 1878, and was never opened again after 1878.

奥奈达湖运河

美国东北部运河。奥奈达湖运河连接西尔万比奇和旧伊利运河，1835年竣工，比伊利运河晚10年。运河与伊利运河在希金斯维尔，即现今的塞德卡路相通，因而也被称作塞德卡运河。该运河与伍德溪汇合，之后向西流至奥奈达湖入口处。运河船闸漏水严重，运河和湖泊交界处泥沙淤积。这条航道于1863年正式停用。新扩建的运河于1877年完工，位于原运河的西南面。新运河几乎直达奥奈达湖，航程缩短约3.2千米。但流沙在运河壁上造成许多裂缝。该航道在1877—1878年间历经多次停航、复航，1878年后被彻底关闭。

Ooster Canal

A canal located in the province of Groningen, the Netherlands. The Ooster Canal is 38 kilometres long, 2 metres deep, and allows the passage of ships up to 5.8 metres wide. The fairway belongs to CEMT Class I and has 3 locks. As a part of the Veendam-Stadskanaal-Ter Apel Waterway, it flows from Emmer Compascuum to the Zwarte Lake, connecting Emmer Compascuum to the Upper

奥斯特运河

荷兰格罗宁根省运河。奥斯特运河全长38千米，深2米，可通行宽度小于5.8米的船只。根据欧洲内陆航道等级标准，这条运河属于一级航道，沿线建有3座船闸。该运河始于埃默—孔帕斯屈姆，流入兹瓦特湖。运河连接埃默—孔帕斯屈姆和多瑙河上游，是芬丹—

Danube. In order to promote the peat exploitation of the Bourtange Swamp, the municipality of Groningen decided to excavate the Ooster Canal, which was completed in 1856. In the 19th century, the canal was one of the busiest shipping lanes for peat transportation in the Netherlands. After the peat exploitation was exhausted, it served as a transport route for agricultural products. Due to the competition from lorries and the increasing scale of inland shipping, the canal lost its importance as a waterway from the 1930s onwards. In the 1970s there were plans to fill in the canal, but they were rejected after meeting the opposition from the locals. Nowadays only recreational boats can be found on the canal.

斯塔茨卡纳尔—泰尔阿珀尔航道的一部分。为了方便开发布尔坦赫沼泽的泥炭资源，格罗宁根市政府决定开凿奥斯特运河。运河1856年完工。19世纪，奥斯特运河是荷兰泥炭运输最繁忙的线路之一。在泥炭资源枯竭后，该运河又成了运输农产品的主要通道。由于内陆航运规模不断扩大，加之卡车运输的竞争，20世纪30年代后，奥斯特运河逐渐失去其航运价值。20世纪70年代，政府曾计划回填奥斯特运河，因遭到当地居民反对而放弃。如今，奥斯特运河上只有游船通行。

Oostermoerse Canal

奥斯特莫尔斯运河

A canal located near the border between Drenthe and Groningen, the Netherlands. See Hunze River.

荷兰德伦特省与格罗宁根省边界运河。见浑泽河。

Opeinde Canal

奥潘德运河

A canal located in the province of Friesland, the Netherlands. The Opeinde Canal is 1.7 kilometres long, running from Opeinde where it connects the New Canal to De Leijen, a lake in Friesland. Since 12 March 2007, its official name has been changed to the Peinde Canal.

荷兰弗里斯兰省运河。奥潘德运河全长1.7千米，始于奥潘德，在此与新运河连通，最后注入弗里斯兰省的德莱恩湖。自2007年3月12日起，这条运河正式更名为潘德运河。

Oporelu Canal

奥波罗运河

A canal located in southern Romania. The Oporelu

罗马尼亚南部运河。奥波罗运河

Canal is 25 kilometres in length. It is a canalized section of the Olt River on the right bank of the Arceşti Lake, intercepting the Olt River's right tributaries and diverting them downstream of the Arceşti Dam.

全长25千米，为奥尔特河的运河化改造河段。该运河地处阿塞斯蒂湖右岸，阻断了奥尔特河右岸多条支流，使其改道流向阿塞斯蒂坝下游。

Opsterland Compagnons Canal

奥普斯特朗－康帕尼翁运河

A canal located in the province of Friesland, the Netherlands. The Opsterland Compagnons Canal is 35 kilometres long with 9 manually-operated locks. It runs from the New Canal near Gorredijk to the Drenthe Grand Canal near Smilde. The construction of the canal began in 1630 for the exploitation and transport of peat. By the early 18th century, the first part had been completed. Later, the project was taken over by Opsterland, a family company and one of the biggest peat companies at the time. In 1780, an agreement to connect the canal to the Smilde Canal was reached but was then objected out of the fear of water loss and flow of acidic water. In 1810, King Louis Bonaparte annulled the agreement. In 1894, the connection was finally established. The villages and hamlets along the Opsterland Compagnons Canal thrived economically because of the peat industry. Now, the commercial shipping has been replaced by pleasure boating.

荷兰弗里斯兰省运河。奥普斯特朗－康帕尼翁运河全长35千米，沿河建有9座手动船闸。该运河始于霍勒代克镇附近的新运河，流至斯米尔德镇附近汇入德伦特大运河。为便于泥炭开采及运输，1630年开始修建该运河。18世纪初，第一部分河段的挖掘工作已完成。运河工程后由当时最大的泥炭公司之一的奥普斯特朗家族公司接手。1780年，连通奥普斯特朗－康帕尼翁运河与斯米尔德河的协议达成，但因有人担心水量流失和酸性河水流入，该协议遭到反对而被搁置，1810年又被路易·波拿巴国王否决。直到1894年，连通计划才最终得以实现。泥炭产业推动了奥普斯特朗－康帕尼翁运河沿岸村庄的经济发展。如今，运河已无商业航运业务，只有游船观光。

Oranienburg-Havel Waterway

奥拉宁堡－哈弗尔航道

A waterway located in the state of Brandenburg, north of Berlin, Germany. The Oranienburg-Havel

德国柏林市以北勃兰登堡州航道。奥拉宁堡－哈弗尔航道全长

Waterway has a total length of 2.7 kilometres, crossing the Ruppin Canal, which was constructed in the late 18th century. The Sachsenhausen Lock was destroyed by the war in 1945 and the Friedenthal Lock was closed before 1960. Now, only the southwestern and the northwestern sections are accessible for navigation.

2.7千米，横穿18世纪末修建的鲁平运河。1945年，萨克森豪森船闸在战争中遭破坏，弗里丹塔尔船闸也于1960年前被关闭。如今，该航道仅西南段和西北段可通航。

Oranje Canal

奥拉涅运河

A canal located in the province of Drenthe, the Netherlands. Originally called Midden Canal. The Oranje Canal has a total length of about 48 kilometres and an elevation of about 7 metres. There are 4 locks on the canal, of which one is now abandoned. It flows from the Drenthe Grand Canal at Hoogersmilde to the Hoogeveen Canal in Klazienaveen, running mainly through the city of Rotterdam. The Oranje Canal was constructed between 1853 and 1861 to exploit the peat resources nearby and to trade the boulders found during excavation. But there was meagre success after the canal was completed. The canal was mainly used for drainage and transportation. In 1923, the canal was deepened and widened to create job opportunities. In 1976, the Oranje Canal was closed. Plans were made to reconstruct it as a route for pleasure craft but were abandoned for the high costs of renovating bridges and locks.

荷兰德伦特省运河。旧称米登运河。奥拉涅运河全长约48千米，海拔约为7米，河上建有4座船闸，其中1座已被废弃。该运河于霍赫斯米尔德镇连通德伦特大运河，至克拉济纳芬镇连通霍赫芬运河，沿途主要流经鹿特丹市。奥拉涅运河1853—1861年间开凿，旨在开发附近的泥炭资源并售卖在挖掘过程中发现的砾石，但收益甚微。该运河竣工后主要用于疏浚排水和交通运输。1923年，运河进一步拓宽加深，创造了就业机会。1976年，奥拉涅运河停航。后有人计划将该运河改造成供游艇行驶的航道，但因桥梁和船闸翻新成本过高而放弃。

Orleans Canal

奥尔良运河

A canal located in the department of Loiret, France. The Orleans Canal links the Loire River at Orle-

法国卢瓦雷省运河。奥尔良运河在奥尔良连通卢瓦尔河，在蒙塔日

ans and connects with the Loing Canal and the Briare Canal near Montargis. It is 78.5 kilometres in length and has 27 locks. The origin of this canal was traced back to 1676 when a timber merchant was authorized to construct a 28-kilometre-long canal to ship his timber to Montargis. The Duke of Orleans then extended it in order to connect the Loire at Combleux with the Loing. The canal was completed in 1692. At that time, it was 73 kilometres in length with 27 locks. In 1921, the canal was extended again to provide direct access to the centre of Orleans, which was unusual for a small-capacity canal. This extension increased the length by 5.5 kilometres. In 1954, the Orleans Canal was closed but 2 sections of it have been restored and are now used as a cycle trail. Some of the original locks can still be seen along the trail, as well as the pumping stations that were used to fill the canal with the water from the Loire.

附近连通卢万运河和布里亚尔运河。运河全长78.5千米,共建有27座船闸。奥尔良运河的历史可追溯至1676年。当时一位木材商为了将木材运送到蒙塔日镇,在得到官方授权后,开凿了一条长达28千米的运河。后奥尔良公爵延长该运河,在孔布勒连通卢万运河与卢瓦尔河。1692年,奥尔良运河扩建完工,全长73千米,建有27座船闸。1921年,奥尔良运河再次延长5.5千米,直通奥尔良市中心,这在小容量运河中实属罕见。1954年奥尔良运河停航,但其中两段河道后来得以修复,现用作自行车道。如今,沿着这条车道,依旧可见当时运河的船闸以及当年用来把卢瓦尔河的河水注入该运河的泵站。

Orne and Caen Maritime Canal

A canal located in the department of Calvados, northwestern France. The Orne and Caen Maritime Canal connects the Port of Caen to the English Channel with 2 locks, and the Orne River feeds the canal. It is about 14 kilometres in length, 10 metres in depth and its width reaches 200 metres. It is navigable directly from the Port of Caen to the Atlantic. Before the opening of the canal in 1857, the Orne River running parallel to the canal functioned as the only waterway from Caen to the sea. In 1837, for the benefits of commercial seaports, the local

奥恩-卡昂通海运河

法国西北部卡尔瓦多省运河。奥恩-卡昂通海运河连接卡昂港和英吉利海峡,河上建有2座船闸,奥恩河为该运河提供水源。运河全长约14千米,深10米,最大宽度达200米,可从卡昂港直通大西洋。在1857年该运河通航前,与其平行的奥恩河是卡昂港唯一的通海航道。1837年,为改善商业海港的运营情况,当地政府启动开凿了这条通海航道。运河1857年竣工

government initiated the construction of this maritime channel. It was opened in 1857 and deepened in 1920. The dock at the mouth of the canal near Ouistreham can accommodate large ships of more than 200 metres in length. The canal now chiefly serves for commercial navigation, the industrial activities at the port of Caen-Ouistreham and the yachting activities at the port of Caen. Meanwhile, it contributes to flood prevention.

通航, 1920年进一步加深。建于运河河口维斯特雷阿姆港附近的船闸可通行200多米长的大型船舶。如今, 该运河主要服务于商业航运、卡昂—维斯特雷阿姆港的工业活动以及卡昂港的游艇项目, 同时兼具防洪功能。

Oswego Canal

A canal located in the state of New York, the United States. The Oswego Canal is 38.1 kilometres long and 4.2 metres deep, punctuated by 7 locks. It links the Erie Canal at Three Rivers with Lake Ontario at Oswego. Excavated in 1825 and completed in 1828, the canal belongs to the New York State Canal System. It is the sole route from the Atlantic to Lake Ontario fully within the United States. The canal enabled trade of raw materials between the Atlantic Coast and Canada. In the early-to-mid 1900s, the Oswego Canal was renovated and was able to carry recreational cruisers to travel from the Atlantic to Lake Ontario. Today, there are some quaint towns, dams, and old locks on the canal to visit.

奥斯威戈运河

美国纽约州运河。奥斯威戈运河全长38.1千米, 深4.2米, 河上建有7座船闸, 在三河城连通伊利运河, 在奥斯威戈市连通安大略湖。运河1825年开凿, 1828年竣工, 为纽约州运河网的一部分, 也是唯一完全在美国境内连通大西洋与安大略湖的航道。该运河的开凿促进了大西洋沿岸和加拿大之间的原材料贸易。20世纪上半叶, 奥斯威戈运河修缮后, 游轮可经此从大西洋前往安大略湖。如今, 运河沿岸的一些古朴小镇及河上的水坝和旧船闸可供游客参观。

Ouachita-Black River Navigation

A waterway located in the southern United States. The Ouachita-Black River Navigation has a total length of 542.7 kilometres. The navigable area

沃希托—布莱克河航道

美国南部航道。沃希托—布莱克河航道全长542.7千米, 通航区域从阿肯色州的卡姆登市延伸至洛

stretches from Camden, Arkansas, to Jonesville, Los Angeles, where it joins the Tensas River and the Little River to form the Black River. The excavation project was authorized in 1871 and begun in 1902. The construction of a system of 6 locks and dams was completed in 1924. Each dam is 25.6 metres wide and 183 metres long with 3 to 5 tainter gates. By 1984, all of these dams had been replaced by 4 modern locks and dams which were spaced from Carlion to Jonesville. Currently, the Ouachita-Black River Navigation has an annual transportation volume of less than 1 million tons. The dam-and-lock system of the navigation promotes the recreational use of the river, and makes it more convenient for regional water supply.

杉矶的琼斯维尔市，并在此与滕萨斯河和利特尔河汇合形成布莱克河。该航道挖掘项目1871年获得批准，1902年开始实施。1924年，修建完成6座船闸和大坝，每座大坝宽25.6米，长183米，有3—5个弧形闸门。1984年，所有大坝被4座现代化船闸和水坝所替代，依次分布在卡利恩市到琼斯维尔市的河段上。目前，沃希托—布莱克河航道每年的运输量不到100万吨。该航道的水坝和船闸系统改善了河流的休闲娱乐功能，区域供水也更加便捷。

Oudon

A canalized river located in western France. The Oudon is 103 kilometres long and flows southeast from its source near La Gravelle to Angers and the Loire. It rus through the Mayenne and Maine-et-Loire departments as the right tributary of the Mayenne. The canalization of the Oudon was completed in the first half of the 19th century. In order to connect the small town of Segré to the Mayenne, an 18-kilometre-long course of the river was remodeled and 3 locks were built on the river. The waterway was mainly used to convey timber, granite and slate from the upper valley to Segré, but was out of use after World War II. It was restored to navigation in 1980 and now serves as a popular water course of the cruise ship.

乌东河

法国西部运河化河流。乌东河全长103千米，始于拉格拉韦勒附近，向东南流向昂热市，汇入卢瓦尔河。该河流为马耶讷河的右岸支流，流经马耶讷和曼恩—卢瓦尔两省。19世纪上半叶，该河流运河化改造完成。为了连接瑟格雷镇和马耶讷河，人们改造了长达18千米的河道，修建了3座船闸。该河流主要用来将木材、花岗岩和板岩从上游河谷地区运送至瑟格雷镇。第二次世界大战后，乌东河渐遭弃用。1980年，乌东河恢复航运，现已成为乘船观光的热门路线。

Ourcq Canal

A canal located in Paris, France. The Ourcq Canal extends from the hamlet on the edge of the Retz Forest to the Villette Basin in Paris, where it joins the Saint-Martin Canal. It is 108.1 kilometres in length and has 10 locks. The canal is a part of Paris municipal canals, along with the canalized river Ourcq, the Saint-Denis Canal, the Clignon Branch Canal, and the Saint-Martin Canal. In 1802, Napoleon Bonaparte gave the order to build the canal for the purposes of providing shipping channels and bringing water to Paris. Its width was originally 3.2 metres and was enlarged to 3.7 metres later. In the 1980s, the Paris City Council decided to open up the entire system for recreational business due to the declining commercial transport and the rising popularity of cruising throughout France. Since 1983, the waterway has been used only by pleasure boats, and its water has been undrinkable. Nowadays, the canal mainly provides water for street cleaning in Paris and feeding the Saint-Denis Canal and the Saint-Martin Canal. At the beginning of 2020, a 35-square-metre green island was constructed between the Marne Quay and the Oise Quay on the Ourcq Canal to promote biodiversity.

Ourthe Canal

A cross-border canal located in Europe. Also known as Maas-Moezel Canal. The Ourthe Canal

乌尔克河运河

法国巴黎运河。乌尔克河运河从雷斯森林附近小村庄流至巴黎的维莱特湖流域,并在此汇入圣马丁运河。乌尔克河运河全长108.1千米,河上建有10座船闸,与运河化的乌尔克河、圣但尼运河、克利尼翁支线运河和圣马丁运河共同构成巴黎市政运河网。1802年,拿破仑·波拿巴下令修建该运河,旨在将其用作航运通道,同时为巴黎供水。该运河初建成时宽3.2米,后又拓宽至3.7米。20世纪80年代,乌尔克河运河上的商业运输量日益减少,但乘船游览在法国境内日益流行。巴黎市议会遂决定开放整个运河河道,供游客休闲娱乐之用。从1983年开始,乌尔克河运河就专供游船航行,运河水无法作为饮用水源。如今,乌尔克河运河主要向巴黎提供街道清洁用水,并为圣但尼运河和圣马丁运河提供水源补给。2020年初,为保护该运河的生物多样性,乌尔克河运河在马恩码头与瓦兹码头之间的河段上建造了一个35平方米的绿岛。

乌尔特运河

欧洲跨国运河。亦称马斯—摩泽尔运河。乌尔特运河最初规划总长

was initially designed to connect the Maas River at Liège City and the Moezel River at Wasserbilig Town with a total length of 261 kilometres. Initiated by the Dutch King Willem I (1771—1843), the construction of the canal began in 1827. Designed for ships up to about 60 tons, the canal was assumed to connect the basins of the Maas and the Rhine. A tunnel was also built at the highest point of the canal. Following the Belgian Revolution of 1830, the project stagnated due to financial difficulties and political instability. The rise of railway transport was another factor that undermined the project. In 1839, the full independence of Luxembourg put an end to the construction. Today, only a part of the canal remains and the tunnel has silted up.

261千米，在列日市连通马斯河，在瓦瑟比利希镇连通摩泽尔河。在荷兰国王威廉一世（1771—1843）倡议下，1827年乌尔特运河开凿。按照最初的设计，这条运河可通航最大载重量约60吨的船只，建成后可以连通马斯河流域和莱茵河流域。人们在运河的最高处修建了一条隧道。1830年比利时革命爆发后，该运河项目因资金短缺和时局动荡而陷入停滞状态，铁路运输的兴起使运河项目进一步停滞。1839年，卢森堡宣布独立，该项目宣告终止。如今，该运河仅保存部分河段，隧道均已淤塞。

Overijssel's Vecht

A canalized cross-border river located in the Netherlands and Germany. The Overijssel's Vecht has a total length of 167 kilometres, of which 60 kilometres is located in the Netherlands and the section in Germany is called the Vechte. Its drainage area reaches 3,780 square kilometres. The river runs from the Münsterland, a region of Germany, to the Zwarte Water near Zwolle, the capital of the Dutch province of Overijssel. This river flows through some important regions and cities such as German municipalities of Nordhorn, Emlichheim and Hardenberg and Ommen in the Netherlands. During the first half of the 19th century, the river played an important role in shipping and navigation. As a natural rain river, it is characterized with

上艾瑟尔的费赫特河

欧洲跨国运河化河流。上艾瑟尔的费赫特河全长167千米，其中有60千米长的河段位于荷兰境内，位于德国境内的河段称为费赫特河，总流域面积达3 780平方千米。该河始于德国明斯特兰地区，在荷兰上艾瑟尔省省会兹沃勒市汇入兹瓦特河。上艾瑟尔的费赫特河流经德国的诺德霍恩市、埃姆利希海姆市以及荷兰的哈登贝赫市、奥门市等重要地区和城市。19世纪上半叶，该河发挥了重要的航运功能。作为天然雨水补给河，其水量波动大，夏季水位极低，只有在10月至来年4月前后的雨季期间适

Paderno Canal

A canal located in Lombardy, Italy. The Paderno Canal is approximately 3 kilometres in length and over 11 metres wide, with a depth of more than 1.2 metres. As a part of the Navigli system, it was built to bypass the rapids on the Paderno Dugnano section of the Adda River. As early as 1516, the idea of excavating a navigable canal between Milan and Lake Como was initiated under the aegis of Francis I, King of France. Leonardo da Vinci was appointed as the engineer who applied the contrivance of mitre gates on locks. The construction work began in 1520 but was soon interrupted in the next year by the war between Francis I and Charles V. Once completed, the canal prospered until the arrival of the railway.

Pagalayan Canal

A cross-border canal located in Asia. The Pagalayan Canal, running across Malaysia and Brunei, is an inland artificial watercourse on the Kalimantan Island, north of Rumah Imba and south of Lubok Pauh. It runs through the Malaysia-Brunei land border. The estimated terrain elevation above sea level is 6 metres.

Palace Canal

A canal located in Munich, Germany. The Palace Canal is a branch of the Nymphenburg Canal in

帕代诺运河

意大利伦巴第大区运河。帕代诺运河全长约3千米，宽逾11米，水深近1.2米以上。该运河是纳维利运河网的一部分，旨在绕开阿达河上帕代诺杜尼亚诺河段上的急流。早在1516年就有人提议在米兰市与科莫湖之间开凿运河，提议得到法国国王弗朗西斯一世的支持。列奥纳多·达·芬奇被任命为工程师，他首次将人字形闸门应用于船闸设计中。帕代诺运河工程始于1520年，但次年由于弗朗西斯一世和查理五世之间爆发战争，工程被迫中断。在铁路运输时代到来前，帕代诺运河的航运业一直很兴盛。

巴加拉延运河

亚洲跨国运河。巴加拉延运河流经马来西亚和文莱，为加里曼丹岛上一条内陆人工航道，位于马来西亚的鲁马印巴以北和鲁保坡以南，从马来西亚与文莱两国间的陆地边界穿过。巴加拉延运河海拔约6米。

宫殿运河

德国慕尼黑市运河。宫殿运河是宁芬堡运河东部的一条支流，始于

the east. It runs in the Nymphenburg Palace and ends after around 1.5 kilometres in the Hubertus Fountain. The canal was built to serve decorative purposes.

宁芬堡宫内，经大约1.5千米后流至胡贝图斯喷泉。该运河为美化景观而修建。

Pamunkey River

帕芒基河

A canalized river located in eastern Virginia, the United States. See York River.

美国弗吉尼亚州东部运河化河流。见约克河。

Panama Canal

巴拿马运河

A canal located in Panama. The Panama Canal runs across the Panamanian Isthmus, linking the Pacific with the Atlantic. The canal is 82 kilometres long, and is recognized as one of the seven wonders of the modern world. In 1534, the king of Spain, Charles V, ordered the first survey for the excavation of a canal through a section of the isthmus. In 1880, French companies under the direction of Ferdinand de Lesseps, the builder of the Suez Canal, started to excavate the Panama Canal. Due to the hardships brought by the epidemics, the jungle terrain and tropical rainforest climate, Ferdinand de Lesseps had to discontinue the project seven years later. In 1903, Panama declared its independence from Colombia and immediately signed the Hay-Bunau-Varilla Treaty, which authorized the United States to begin the construction of the canal in 1904. It was opened in 1914. In 1977, the Torrijos-Carter Treaties were signed between the United States and Panama, stipulating that the sovereignty of the Panama Canal should be handed over to

巴拿马运河。巴拿马运河穿过中美洲的巴拿马地峡，连通太平洋和大西洋。运河全长82千米，被誉为当今世界七大工程奇迹之一。1534年，为修建一条穿过巴拿马地峡的运河，西班牙国王查理五世下令对巴拿马地峡进行首次勘查。1880年，苏伊士运河项目工程师斐迪南·德雷赛布组织法国公司开始修建巴拿马运河。由于传染病肆虐、丛林地形复杂及热带雨林气候的不利影响，7年后斐迪南·德雷赛布被迫终止这一工程。1903年，巴拿马宣布脱离哥伦比亚统治而独立，随即与美国签订了《海—比诺—瓦里亚条约》，授权美国于1904年开始修建巴拿马运河。1914年，巴拿马运河通航。1977年，美国和巴拿马签订了《巴拿马运河条约》（又称《托里霍斯—卡特条约》），双方约定美国在1999年12

Panama before 31 December, 1999. An expansion project was launched in 2007. The expanded canal began commercial operation in 2016. Nowadays, it is beyond the builders' expectation that the canal is such a busy traffic route. In 1934, it was estimated that the maximum capacity of the canal would be around 80 million tons per year. By 2012, more than 815,000 vessels had traversed the canal. The canal traffic in 2015 reached 340 million tons of shipping.

月31日前将运河经营权归还巴拿马。2007年，巴拿马运河扩建工程正式启动。2016年，扩建后的巴拿马运河投入商业运营。如今，该运河通航量远远超出了初期规划。1934年，运河的年通航船运总量大约为8 000万吨。截至2012年，通航船只累计达815 000余艘。2015年，巴拿马运河通航船运总量约达3.4亿吨。

Pangalanes Canal

潘加兰运河

A canal located in Madagascar. The Pangalanes Canal is 600 kilometres long, consisting of several natural rivers and man-made lakes. It runs along the east coast of Madagascar, crossing Tamatave and Farafangana. The navigable part of the canal is to the north of the Mananjary River. The canal was constructed between 1896 and 1904. Now the canal also functions as a scenic spot. Apart from the charming scenery, various kinds of boats on the canal and the villages nearby are also quite attractive to tourists.

马达加斯加运河。潘加兰运河全长600千米，由一些天然河流和人工湖泊组成。运河沿马达加斯加东海岸流经塔马塔夫湾和法拉凡加纳港，其中马南扎里河以北的河段可通航。这条运河修建于1896—1904年间。如今，潘加兰运河也是一处旅游景点。除了怡人的自然风光，河上形态各异的大小船只以及岸边附近的村落对游客也颇具吸引力。

Pannerden Canal

潘讷登运河

A canal located in the province of Gelderland, the Netherlands. The Pannerden Canal is located between Doornenburg and Huissen, south of Arnhem. It is 6 kilometres long and 135 metres wide, connecting the Bijlands Canal and the Nederrijn, and flowing through the cities of Doornenburg and

荷兰海尔德兰省运河。潘讷登运河位于阿纳姆市南部的多恩堡市和赫伊森镇之间，全长6千米，宽135米，连通白兰茨运河与尼德兰河，流经多恩堡市和昂赫伦市。该运河于1701—1709年间开凿，是荷

Angeren. As one of the oldest canals in the Netherlands, it was excavated between 1701 and 1709, initially as a defence line without direct connection with the Rhine and the Waal. It was only a few years later that these connections were created in order to guarantee the water supply of the IJssel and the Lower Rhine. With a flow rate of around 700 cubic metres per second, the Pannerden Canal ensured the water supply of the new defence line of Holland. The canal also played an instrumental role in the establishment of the Public Works and Water Management in 1798 under the Dutch Ministry of Infrastructure and Water Management. In 2007, the Pannerden Canal celebrated its 300th anniversary.

兰历史最悠久的运河之一。运河最初作为一道军事防线，并未与莱茵河和瓦尔河直接相通，几年后为保证艾瑟尔河和莱茵河下游地区的供水才将其连通。潘讷登运河水流速度约为每秒700立方米，保证了荷兰新防线的供水。潘讷登运河对于1798年荷兰基础设施和水力资源管理部下属的公共工程水务管理局的建立也发挥了重要作用。2007年，潘讷登运河举行了通航300周年庆典活动。

Paravur Canal

帕拉乌尔运河

A canal located in the Varkala Region of India. The 2.45-kilometre-long Paravur Canal is a section of the Thiruvananthapuram-Shoranur Canal which links Thiruvananthapuram, the capital of the Indian state of Kerala, with its municipality Shoranur. The canal was built to connect the Paravur Lake and the Edava-Nadayara Lake.

印度瓦卡拉地区运河。帕拉乌尔运河全长2.45千米，是特里凡得琅—斯霍拉努尔运河的一部分。特里凡得琅—斯霍拉努尔运河连接喀拉拉邦首府蒂鲁文南特布勒姆与其自治市斯霍拉努尔。开凿帕拉乌尔运河旨在连通帕拉乌尔湖和埃德瓦—那达雅拉湖。

Paris Canals

巴黎运河网

A canal network located in Paris, France. The Paris Canals run over 100 kilometres, which are composed of several waterways flowing through the city, including the Ourcq Canal (completed in 1821), the Saint-Martin Canal (completed in 1825), and

法国巴黎运河网。巴黎运河网全长超过100千米，由贯穿巴黎市的数条航道组成，包括1821年竣工的乌尔克运河、1825年竣工的圣马丁运河和1895年竣工的圣但尼运

the Saint-Denis Canal (completed in 1895), etc.

河等。

Parvati Puthannar

帕尔瓦蒂新河

A canal located in India. The Parvati Puthannar is 31 kilometres long. It flows southeastward from the Kadinamkulam Lake in the north, through the western coast of the Trivandrum District, terminating in a little delta near Poonthura and at last feeding into the Indian Ocean. It was constructed in the 18th century as a part of the West Coast Canal Project. The Parvati Puthannar was named after Rani Gouri Parvati Bai, the regent Queen of Travancore during the time when it was built. Puthannar means new river in Malayalam. A delta called Poonthura Pozhi was formed by the canal. The canal was constructed to connect the Travancore capital with Kadinamkulam, then with the Vamanapuram River and finally with Kochi, and then it provided direct access to Vallakadavu, the landing place of the king. The water quality of the Parvati Puthannar was the best among all natural rivers and man-made canals in India. It is overgrown with weeds and heavily polluted, to the extent that some portions are even not navigable. Recently it has been declared a section of the West Coast Canal.

印度运河。帕尔瓦蒂新河长31千米，始于印度北部的卡丁南姆库拉姆湖，沿东南方向流经印度西海岸的特里凡得琅区，止于彭哈拉区附近的小三角洲，注入印度洋。帕尔瓦蒂新河修建于18世纪，是西海岸运河工程的一部分。该运河因其修建时期的特拉凡哥尔摄政女王拉尼·古里·帕尔瓦蒂·白的名字而得名，其中"帕特罕纳尔"在马拉雅拉姆语中意为"新河"，该运河所形成的三角洲名为彭哈拉珀智。修建运河的初衷是连接特拉凡哥尔首府与卡丁南姆库拉姆地区，并与瓦马纳帕勒姆河相通，最终连接科钦市，直接通往国王泊船处瓦拉卡达夫。帕尔瓦蒂新河的水当初是印度所有自然河流和人工运河中最干净的。如今，运河河道杂草丛生，污染严重，有些河段甚至无法通航。最近，帕尔瓦蒂新河已被划入印度西海岸运河。

Patowmack Canal

波托马克运河

A series of cross-border canals located in the United States. The Patowmack Canal, situated in Maryland and Virginia, consists of five canals. It was a life-long endeavour of George Washington, who

美国跨境运河网。波托马克运河流经马里兰州和弗吉尼亚州，由5条运河组成。修建波托马克运河是乔治·华盛顿的毕生心愿，他坚

believed that the construction of the canal would function as a trade link so as to unite the American people as a whole. According to the original plan, the canal was in a critical position since it had access to the East Coast and trans-Atlantic trade, as well as to the headwaters of the Ohio River and the western frontier. By George Washington's lobbying, the political, physical, and financial obstacles of building the canal were overcome. The construction was started in 1785 and completed in 1802. Five canals were built along the Potomac River, around Little Falls, Great Falls, Seneca Falls, Payne's Falls of the Shenandoah, and House Falls. Locks were needed in the sections of Little Falls and Great Falls. The canal was operational from February to May. Farmers transported raw goods such as flour and iron to Georgetown markets to do business. The Patowmack Company went bankrupt in 1828 and was sold to the Chesapeake and Ohio Canal Company, which abandoned the Patowmack Canal in 1830 and used some of its old canals for the construction of the Chesapeake and Ohio Canal. Although considered a financial failure, the Patowmack Canal was the first in the United States to have locks and it heralded a wave of canal construction in the country. Now the National Park Service is in charge of the management and preservation of the remains of the Patowmack Canal. The historical significance of the Patowmack Canal is recognized in that it is a National Historic Civil Engineering Landmark, and a Virginia Historic Landmark.

信这些运河作为商业纽带能将美国人民紧密团结起来。根据最初规划,该运河地理位置重要,船只既能驶达东海岸和跨大西洋贸易圈,也能通往俄亥俄河源头区域和美国西部地区。经华盛顿游说,关乎修建波托马克运河的政治、物力和财力方面的问题均得以解决。波托马克运河项目1785年开工,1802年竣工。人们在波托马克河沿线共开凿了5条运河,分别位于小瀑布、大瀑布、塞内卡瀑布、谢南多厄河上的佩恩瀑布、豪斯瀑布附近,其中小瀑布和大瀑布附近的河段需要修建船闸。每年2—5月为运河通航期。农民通过该运河将面粉和铁等原材料运往乔治敦市场售卖。波托马克运河公司1828年宣告破产,被出售给切萨皮克—俄亥俄运河公司,后者在1830年弃用了波托马克运河,将其中部分河段用于切萨皮克—俄亥俄运河的修建。尽管波托马克运河运营失败,但它对美国而言具有重要的历史意义。该运河首次运用了船闸技术,并引发了后续的运河修建热潮。如今,波托马克运河历史遗迹的管理和保护工作由美国国家公园管理局负责,该运河被列为美国国家土木工程历史地标及弗吉尼亚州历史地标。

Pavese Canal

A canal located in Lombardy, northern Italy. The Pavese Canal is 33 kilometres long, 10.8 metres wide and 11.8 metres deep, with 6 locks built on it. It is a part of the Navigli system, connecting the city of Milan to River Ticino. The construction work began in 1564, but was interrupted 20 years later because of some technical problems. The construction of the canal resumed at the beginning of the 19th century and was completed in 1819. Until about the middle of the 20th century, it was intensively used for commercial shipping. The Pavese Canal was closed in 1965. Recently some work has been done to fully restore its function of transporting.

帕维亚运河

意大利北部伦巴第大区运河。帕维亚运河全长33千米，宽10.8米，深11.8米，河上建有6座船闸。该运河连接米兰市与提契诺河，属纳维利运河网的一部分。帕维亚运河1564年开始修建，20年后因某些技术问题而被迫中断，19世纪初得以复工，1819年竣工。20世纪中叶前，帕维亚运河一直承担着商业运输的重任。1965年，运河被关闭。近年来，一些旨在恢复帕维亚运河通航功能的工作已陆续展开。

Peacock Canal

A canal located in the city of Ghent, Belgium. See De Pauw Canal.

孔雀运河

比利时根特市运河。见迪堡运河。

Peak Forest Canal

A canal located in northern England, the United Kingdom. The Peak Forest Canal is a part of the English and Welsh inland waterway network. With a length of 23.8 kilometres and a width of 2.1 metres, it is composed of two parts with different levels, known as the Upper Peak Forest Canal and the Lower Peak Forest Canal. The elevation difference of the two canals is 64 metres, which is overcome by the 16 locks on the Lower Peak Forest Canal. With the authorization of an act of Parliament in 1794,

皮克福里斯特运河

英国英格兰北部运河。皮克福里斯特运河是英格兰—威尔士内陆运河网的一部分，全长23.8千米，宽2.1米，由两段水位不同的运河组成，分别为皮克福里斯特运河上游河段和皮克福里斯特运河下游河段。这两段运河之间的水位落差有64米，经由皮克福里斯特运河下游河段上的16座船闸来调节落差。1794年英国议会通过法

the construction of the canal was started and completed in 1805. The aim of the canal was to improve the transportation of bulk manufactured goods and raw materials, particularly limestone from the quarries at Dove Holes in the Peak Forest. With the development of railway transportation in the 20th century, the importance of the canal began to decline. Since the late 1960s and early 1970s, much of the course has been restored with the joint efforts of the Peak Forest Canal Society and the Inland Waterways Association.

案批准开凿该运河，1805年竣工。修建运河的主要目的是便于运输大量的成品和原料，尤其是皮克福里斯特鸽子洞采石场丰富的石灰石。20世纪，随着铁路运输的发展，皮克福里斯特运河的运输功能不再重要。20世纪60年代末至70年代初以来，在皮克福里斯特运河协会与内陆运河协会的共同努力下，皮克福里斯特运河的多段航道得以重修。

Pechora-Kama Canal

伯朝拉－卡马运河

An inland canal located in western Russia. The Pechora-Kama Canal is 112 kilometres in length, linking the basin of the Pechora River and the basin of the Kama, a tributary of the Volga. In the 19th century, most transportation between the two basins was conducted through a 40-kilometre-long portage road because the water condition was far from ideal for shipping. The transportation into and out of the Pechora basin was costly at that time. In November 1933, the USSR Academy of Sciences approved the reconstruction of Volga and its basin which included the building of a canal between the Pechora and the Kama. The canal project had remained a blueprint with no actual construction work for decades that followed. In 1961, the canal project became a part of a bigger programme that involved water diversion projects of similar rivers in Siberia, but it was not until 1971 that the actual construction work was done. The excavation techniques of using

俄罗斯西部内陆运河。伯朝拉—卡马运河全长112千米，连接伯朝拉河流域和伏尔加河支流之一的卡马河流域。19世纪时，由于当地水运条件较差，两个流域之间的交通运输方式主要依赖40千米长的陆路，进出伯朝拉流域的交通费用非常昂贵。1933年11月，苏联科学院通过了改造伏尔加河及其流域的计划，其中包括在伯朝拉河流域与卡马河流域之间开凿运河。此后数十年，修建运河的计划一直处于规划阶段，并未付诸实施。1961年，苏联提出了一项更宏大的水利工程计划，该计划包括伯朝拉—卡马运河的修建项目，也包括西伯利亚地区一些类似河流的调水工程。但直到1971年，伯朝拉—卡马运河的修建工程才开始启动。

nuclear bombs were employed at the beginning of the construction, which later was called off for not being feasible. Before the railway was available, this canal project was of great importance. Later on, transferring the water of the Pechora to the Volga and further to the Caspian Sea became the major concern.

工程早期曾使用核弹爆破技术来开凿运河，后因可行性差而被叫停。在铁路时代之前，伯朝拉—卡马运河工程在交通运输方面发挥着重要作用。后该运河主要用于将伯朝拉河的河水引入伏尔加河以及更远的里海。

Pennsylvania State Canals

A canal system located in the state of Pennsylvania, the United States. The Pennsylvania State Canals, extending a length of over 1,168 kilometres, are a combined transportation infrastructure, comprising canals, locks, dams, towpaths, aqueducts, and via-ducts. The project of the system and the Main Line of Public Works lasted several decades after the ini-tiative of the first enabling act and budget items in 1824. The construction began in 1826 and was com-pleted in 1840. The canal system was constructed to achieve the transportation of heavy or bulk goods by ship and to connect Philadelphia to Pittsburgh, and more importantly, to connect Philadelphia through the Ohio River with the new growth markets in developing the Northwest Territory (now called the Midwest) and boost its development. The system, updated in 1837, was also applied to railways and new canals added to the state transportation system. Though most of the canals no longer have any func-tion, some segments retain their value as historic and recreational sites.

宾夕法尼亚州运河网

美国宾夕法尼亚州运河网。宾夕法尼亚州运河网总长度1 168多千米，是个错综复杂的交通运输网络，由运河、船闸、大坝、纤道、渡槽和高架桥等组成。1824年，有人提出修建该运河网的授权法案，并列举相关的预算项目。运河工程始于1826年，1840年竣工。修建宾夕法尼亚州运河网和公共工程主线项目耗时数十年，其目的是为了实现大宗货物水路运输以及打通费城和匹兹堡之间的水上航线。更重要的是，运河网建成以后，可以通过俄亥俄河实现费城和西北区域（今美国中西部地区）的通航，借助该区域新兴的市场促进其全面发展。1837年，宾夕法尼亚州运河网进一步升级，铁路和新开凿的运河也纳入其中。目前，尽管多数运河已停用，但仍有部分河段作为历史遗迹被保留下来，用作休闲场所。

Peterson Canal

An inland canal located in Maine, the United States. See New Meadows Canal.

Peter the First Canal

A canal located in Leningrad Oblast, Russia. See Old Ladoga Canal.

Petworth Canal

A canal located in England, the United Kingdom. The Petworth Canal, a relatively short-lasting canal, ran from the upstream of the Shopham Cut to Haslingbourne in West Sussex. The canal was 2 kilometres long together with 2 locks only, each of which was 2.6 metres in height. With the authorization of the Act of Parliament in 1791, the canal was constructed by 20 workers only, and was officially opened in October, 1795. The main cargoes on the canal included chalk, coal, and timber. Owing to its underuse and much dredging work, the canal was closed in 1826.

Piast Canal

A canal located in northwest Poland. Also called Emperor's Way. Linking the Oder Lagoon with the Świna River, the Piast Canal is about 12 kilometres long and 10 metres deep. The canal was built between 1874 and 1880 under the reign of the first Emperor Wilhelm I of the German Empire. It

彼得森运河

美国缅因州内陆运河。见新梅多斯运河。

彼得一世运河

俄罗斯列宁格勒州运河。见旧拉多加运河。

佩特沃思运河

英国英格兰运河。佩特沃思运河存在时间不长,由西萨塞克斯郡肖普翰河上游流至哈斯灵本。该运河全长2千米,仅设两座高2.6米的船闸。1791年,运河在英国议会法案授权下开始修建,当时只有20名工人参与开凿工程。1795年10月,运河正式通航,主要运输白垩、煤炭和木材等物资。由于使用率不高,且需要进行大量疏浚工作,运河1826年被关闭。

皮亚斯特运河

波兰西北部运河。亦称帝王之路。皮亚斯特运河连通奥得潟湖和希维纳河,全长12千米,深10米。该运河1874—1880年间开凿,正值德意志皇帝威廉一世统治时期。第二次世界大战后,根据波兰第一个王

adopted the current name from the Piast Dynasty, the first Polish royal dynasty after World War II. The canal bypassed the eastern branch of the Świna River, which was difficult to navigate, and provided a more convenient waterway to the seaport Szczecin for ships from the Baltic Sea. The canal greatly raised the status of Szczecin.

朝皮亚斯特王朝的名称改为现名。该运河避开了不易航行的希维纳河东部支流，为从波罗的海通往什切青港口的船只提供了一条更便捷的航道，极大地提升了什切青港口的地位。

Piccolo Canal

A canal located in Lombardy, northern Italy. See Martesana Canal.

皮科洛运河

意大利北部伦巴第大区运河。见马尔特萨纳运河。

Pinglu Canal

A proposed canal located in Guangxi Zhuang Autonomous Region, China. The Pinglu Canal is designed to be an ocean-bound canal 151 kilometres away from Nanning City in Guangxi, running from the Pingtang Estuary of the Xijin Reservoir in Hengxian County in the north to the Shajing Port of the Qinjiang River in the south. The canal will be a Class II channel with a total length of 133 kilometres and a depth of more than 4 metres. The canal drops 60 metres and will be punctuated by 4 to 6 staircase locks as planned. It will cross the tributaries of the Pingtang River and the Qinjiang River as well as the watershed of the Xiaoxijiang River, connecting to the Qinjiang River. Most of the reaches of the canal are to be reconstructed along the existing Shaping River and the Qinjiang River, with about a total length of 20 kilometres. The canal is meant to address the unbalanced transport in

平陆运河

中国广西壮族自治区拟建运河。平陆运河将是一条通海运河，距离广西南宁市151千米，北起横县西津水库平塘江口，南至钦江出海口沙井港。该运河规划等级为二级航道，全长预计133千米，水深超过4米，水位落差60米，计划建造4—6座梯级船闸。平陆运河跨平塘江与钦江支流、小西江分水岭，与钦江相通。平陆运河大部分河段将在现有的沙坪河和钦江上改建而成，实际开凿长度约为20千米。修建平陆运河旨在改善广西不平衡的运输结构，开辟西江至北部湾的水运通道。目前，平陆运河项目正处于筹备阶段，预计2022年底开工建设，2029年前完工通航。该运河工程投资约700亿元人民币，工程

Guangxi, and to open up a water transport channel from the Xijiang River to the Beibu Gulf. At present, the Pinglu Canal project is in its preliminary stage. It is expected that the excavation will begin at the end of 2022, and the canal will be opened in 2029. The investment of the project is estimated to be 70 billion *yuan*, which primarily covers the construction of the main body of the complex, channel dredging and excavation, flood control works, migrant resettlement, environment protection as well as water and soil conservation. The construction of the canal is of crucial significance in many aspects. First of all, the journey between inland rivers of Guangxi and the sea can be greatly shortened and the transportation cost can be reduced. After the completion of the canal, the journey to the sea will be cut by 563 kilometres as the route from Nanning to the sea will be only 291 kilometres by then. Secondly, the canal allows sea ships with a tonnage of 3,000 to navigate directly from coastal ports to Nanning. The canal can also provide irrigation water for farmland on both sides of the tributaries and the mainline of the Qinjiang River and supply Qinzhou City with freshwater. Finally, the project will exert a positive influence on regional tourism and economic development in southwest China.

项目具体包括中心枢纽、航道疏浚开挖、防洪工程、移民安置、环境保护及水土保持等方面。修建平陆运河具有重要意义。运河可以有效缩短广西内河出海里程，减少运输成本。运河完工后，广西内河通海里程将缩短563千米，自南宁出海里程缩减至291千米。平陆运河可容纳3 000吨位的出海船从沿海港口出发直达南宁，还可为钦江支流和干流两岸提供灌溉用水，并为钦州市提供淡水资源。运河项目对发展区域旅游、促进中国西南地区经济发展也将产生积极影响。

Plassendale Canal

普拉森达勒运河

An inland canal located in the province of West Flanders, Belgium. See Plassendale-Newport Canal.

比利时西佛兰德省内陆运河。见普拉森达勒—新港运河。

Plassendale-Newport Canal

An inland canal located in the province of West Flanders, Belgium. Also called Plassendale Canal. The Plassendale-Newport Canal connects the Bruges-Ostend Canal and the IJzer via the lock complex in Newport. It is about 21 kilometres long and 20 metres wide with 6 bridges and 2 locks. The canal was constructed between 1632 and 1640. The aim was to connect Ghent to the sea, because the access to the mouth of the Schelde was blocked during the Eighty Years' War (1568—1648). It was called "the New River" in the 17th century. Today, the canal has limited economic benefits. Along the northern bank, the asphalted and almost car-free towpath is recognized as an international cycling route. The lock complex in Plassendale has been protected and the first lock gate still has to be operated by hand.

Pogangdu Canal

A canal located in the north of the Maoshan Mountain in Jurong City of Jiangsu Province, China. With a length of more than 15 kilometres, the Pogangdu Canal runs eastward from the Xiaoxi Village in Chuncheng Town to the village of Nantang, through places including the Bixu Village and Tuolong Temple, and finally empties into the Tongji River of the Baoyan Town. The canal was excavated in 254 AD by Chen Xun, an army officer sent by Sun Quan, the King of the Wu State during the Three Kingdoms Period (220—280 AD).

普拉森达勒－新港运河

比利时西佛兰德省内陆运河。亦称普拉森达勒运河。普拉森达勒－新港运河通过新港船闸群连通布鲁日－奥斯坦德运河和艾泽尔河，全长约21千米，宽约20米，建有6座大桥和2座船闸。运河修建于1632—1640年间。八十年战争（1568—1648）期间，根特市通往斯海尔德河口的通道被封锁，修建运河是为了连通根特市与海洋。17世纪，普拉森达勒－新港运河被称为"新河"。如今，该运河带来的经济效益已十分有限。沿运河北岸铺设的柏油路和基本无车的纤道被开辟为国际自行车道。普拉森达勒市的船闸群已受到保护，最早的闸门仍需手动操作。

破岗渎

中国江苏句容市茅山以北运河。破岗渎全长15千米有余，从春城镇小溪村向东流经毕墟村和罩龙庙等地到达南塘庄，汇入宝堰镇通济河。公元254年，该运河由三国时期东吴统治者孙权派遣校尉陈勋开凿。破岗渎共分13段，筑有14道土埭，以保持各段水位。由于航道不够宽，每逢冬春两季，行船不便，破岗渎到梁代就被弃用，到陈代才得以修复。隋朝以后，建康

Pugangdu consisted of 13 sections, and 14 earth banks were built to maintain the water level of each section. Since its channels were not wide enough, it was inconvenient for sailing in winter and spring. Consequently, the Pogangdu Canal was abandoned once in the Liang Dynasty (502—557 AD) but was repaired later in the Chen Dynasty (557—589 AD). After the Sui Dynasty (581—618 AD) replaced the Chen Dynasty, Jiankang (now Nanjing) was no longer the capital city, and it lost its water transport function and was gradually abandoned. The complete silting-up of the canal probably took place in the middle and late Tang Dynasty (618—907 AD). The Pogangdu Canal has played a positive role in saving water sources, regulating water conservancy, and promoting the economic and cultural development of the central and eastern parts of Jurong City. Its significance also lies in opening up the shipping channels between the Qinhuai River system and the area south of the Yangtze River, and connecting Nanjing, Zhenjiang, and even the Taihu Lake Basin, standing as a key channel of water transportation for more than 300 years during the Six Dynasties Period (220—589 AD).

（今南京）不再作为都城，破岗渎的漕运作用也随之丧失，逐渐被废弃。在唐代中晚期，破岗渎完全淤塞。破岗渎对储蓄水源、调节水利以及促进句容中东部地区经济文化发展起到了积极作用。该运河的重要性还在于打通了秦淮河水系与江南地区水运之间的航运通道，连接南京、镇江等多个城市和太湖流域，是六朝300多年间的漕运要道。

Point Pleasant Canal

A canal located in New Jersey, the United States. The Point Pleasant Canal connects the Manasquan Inlet and the Manasquan River with the Bay Head Harbour on the northern end of the Barnegat Bay. The 3.2-kilometre-long canal is a part of the Intracoastal Waterway. The construction of this canal

波因特普莱森特运河

美国新泽西州运河。波因特普莱森特运河连接马纳斯宽湾、马纳斯宽河与巴尼加特湾最北端的贝黑德港。运河全长3.2千米，是沿海航道的一段，1916年修建工程启动，1925年年末竣工。后巴尼加特

was started in 1916 and completed in late 1925, after which the Barnegat Peninsula became an island, being connected to the mainland by two lift bridges that span the canal.

半岛成为独立岛屿，经由横跨运河的两座升降桥与内陆相连。

Polder Main Canal

A canal located in the province of Friesland, the Netherlands. The Polder Main Canal is 7.5 kilometres in length, flowing from the Grietmansrak Canal at De Veenhoop Village in Smallingerland to the Schipsloot at Nij Beets Village in Opsterland. Its construction dates from 1875, originally for transportation and drainage. Nowadays, the canal mainly serves for recreation. Because of the exceptional water quality, the canal boasts a variety of flora and fauna.

波尔德主运河

荷兰弗里斯兰省运河。波尔德主运河全长7.5千米，始于斯马灵厄兰市德维恩霍夫村，从赫里特曼斯拉克运河流至奥普斯特兰市尼伊贝兹村，与史基浦斯运河联通。运河修建工程最早可追溯至1875年，最初用于交通运输和排水，如今主要供休闲观光。由于水质优良，运河沿线动植物种类丰富。

Pommeroeul-Antoing Canal

A canal located in the province of Hainaut, Belgium. Connecting Pommeroeul Town and Antoing City, the Pommeroeul-Antoing Canal has a length of 26 kilometres and an elevation of 33 metres. After the Battle of Waterloo in 1815, the rivers and canals in Belgium were no longer controlled by France. France used to demand tolls for the passage through the French part of the canals, doubling the cost of transporting coal. In order to reduce the cost of coal transportation, Dutch King William I (1772–1843) ordered to construct the Pommeroeul-Antoing Canal. The canal was built between 1823 and 1826, and closed in August,

波默勒尔–昂图万运河

比利时埃诺省运河。波默勒尔–昂图万运河连接波默勒尔镇和昂图万市，全长26千米，海拔33米。自1815年滑铁卢战役之后，比利时境内的河流和运河不再受法国管辖。法国此前要求过往船只支付通行费，煤炭运输成本因此翻倍。为降低煤炭运输成本，荷兰国王威廉一世（1772—1843）下令开凿波默勒尔–昂图万运河。该运河1823—1826年间修建，1976年8月关闭，取而代之的是能承载更大吨位船只的尼米—布拉通—佩

1976, and replaced by the Nimy-Blaton-Péronnes Canal, which allows ships with larger tonnage. The canal is nicknamed by the locals "the old canal", and the Nimy-Blaton-Péronnes Canal is nicknamed "the new canal".

罗讷运河, 当地人称前者为"旧运河", 称后者为"新运河"。

Pommeroeul-Condé Canal

A cross-border canal located between Hainaut Province in Belgium and Valenciennes of the Nord Province in France. The Pommeroeul-Condé Canal is 5 kilometres long with a maximum depth of 3 metres with no lock. It connects the Escaut River at Condé-sur-l'Escaut Town in France and the Nimy-Blaton-Péronnes Canal at Pommeroeul Town in Belgium. The canal was excavated between 1968 and 1982 and became navigable in 1982. In 1992, it was closed due to heavy siltation. The desilting began in September 2020 and the canal was expected to be reopened at the end of 2022. The Pommeroeul-Condé Canal is no longer used for transportation, and only retains the function of recreation for fishermen and water skiers. The area is a habitat for many species of birds.

波默勒尔-孔代运河

欧洲跨国运河。波默勒尔—孔代运河位于比利时埃诺省和法国诺尔省瓦朗谢讷地区之间, 全长5千米, 最大水深3米, 未建船闸。该运河在法国孔代镇与埃斯科河连通, 在比利时的波默勒尔镇与尼米—布拉通—佩罗讷运河连通。波默勒尔—孔代运河1968年开凿, 1982年竣工, 同年实现首次通航。1992年, 运河因河道严重淤塞而停航。2020年9月, 运河清淤工作开始, 并有望于2022年末重新开放。波默勒尔—孔代运河现不再用于航运, 已成为旅游休闲地, 供渔民和滑水爱好者使用。运河周边地区还是许多鸟类的栖息地。

Pontcysyllte Aqueduct and Canal

A canal located in Wales and England, the United Kingdom. As a navigable aqueduct, the Pontcysyllte Aqueduct and Canal carries the Llangollen Canal across River Dee in northeastern Wales, sometimes considered a part of the Llangollen Canal. It is 18 kilometres in length, including 17 kilometres in

旁特塞斯特渡槽和运河

英国威尔士与英格兰运河。旁特塞斯特渡槽和运河为可通航渡槽运河, 它引导兰戈伦运河穿越威尔士东北部的迪河, 有时也被视作兰戈伦运河的一部分。该渡槽运河全长18千米, 其中17千米在威尔

Wales and 1 kilometre in England. Designed by Thomas Telford, the canal was built in 1795 by him and William Jessop, and was opened in 1805. The canal was built without using locks to overcome the water level difference in a difficult geographical environment. An aqueduct of cast iron was constructed instead, and it was supported by 18 tall and slender masonry piers. The design of the aqueduct was light and strong and the overall effect was both monumental and elegant. The Pontcysyllte Aqueduct is now the oldest and longest navigable aqueduct in the United Kingdom and the highest in the world. It is also recognized as an innovative ensemble that inspired many projects all over the world. In the latter half of the 20th century, leisure boating traffic began to rise. It has since become one of the most popular canals for holidaymakers in the United Kingdom because of its aqueducts and scenery. The canal was inscribed by UNESCO on the World Heritage List in 2009.

士境内，1千米在英格兰境内。运河由托马斯·泰尔福德设计，并由其与威廉·杰索普于1795年共同负责修建，1805年竣工。运河修建过程中，设计师并未通过建造船闸来解决恶劣地理环境下水位落差大的困难，而是修建了一座由18个细长砖石墩支撑的高架铸铁渡槽。渡槽的设计轻便牢固，且渡槽运河的整体效果壮观而典雅。旁特塞斯特渡槽是英国最古老、最长的通航运河，也是世界上最高的高架航道。工程富有创意，受人瞩目，为后世诸多工程所效仿。20世纪后半叶开始，游船娱乐业兴起，该河道因其独特的渡槽及景观成为英国最受度假者青睐的运河之一。旁特塞斯特渡槽和运河2009年被列入联合国教科文组织的世界遗产名录。

Pont-de-Vaux Canal

蓬德沃运河

A canal located in eastern France. The Pont-de-Vaux Canal links the Saône at Fleurville with Pont-de-Vaux and runs parallel to the Reyssouze River. It is 3.7 kilometres in length and has only one semi-automatic lock at its entrance to the Saône. The construction began in 1783, but was suspended due to the French Revolution. In 1810, Napoleon restarted the project, but the construction work could not be funded because of wars. In 1835, the canal was then transferred to the council of Pont-

法国东部运河。蓬德沃运河从弗勒维尔镇的索恩河流往蓬德沃市，流向与雷苏兹河平行，全长3.7千米，在索恩河入口处建有1座半自动船闸。运河1783年开凿，后因法国大革命爆发，修建工程中断。1810年，拿破仑重启运河修建工程，但因战争拖累而无力负担运河修建费用。蓬德沃运河1835年被移交给蓬德沃市，但其后修建费

de-Vaux. The financial need was still not well addressed. The canal was at last completed in 1843 by the state. It was closed in 1954 due to the cease of traffic. The restoration was carried out in 1994. Currently, the canal has turned into a popular destination for boating with the development of the marina close to the town centre.

用问题仍未解决。1843年，运河最终由国家修建完成。1954年，因航运停止，蓬德沃运河被关闭，直到1994年才得以恢复。如今，随着城镇中心附近船坞的修建，蓬德沃运河已成为人们划船或乘船游玩的热门去处。

Portage Canal

A canal located in Wisconsin, the United States. The Portage Canal is about 4 kilometres in length, connecting the Fox River with the Wisconsin River at the city of Portage. It is a significant part of the Fox-Wisconsin Navigation. The planning of the canal was started in the 1820s, but the project was forced to close because of the lack of funding. The construction was taken over by the US Government. In 1849, a new route was chosen for the canal, which is the present one. With some misunderstanding between the contractor and the state, the project was later abandoned. The Army Corps of Engineers revived the construction in 1874 and completed it in 1876. From 1878 to 1908, the canal was used heavily by large ships and pleasure craft. In 1951, the Portage Canal was closed due to its declining usage.

波蒂奇运河

美国威斯康星州运河。波蒂奇运河全长约4千米，在波蒂奇市连通福克斯河和威斯康星河，是福克斯—威斯康星航道的重要组成部分。波蒂奇运河的规划始于19世纪20年代，但由于资金短缺，该项目被迫终止。后波蒂奇运河工程项目由美国联邦政府接管。1849年，联邦政府为该运河规划了一条新线路，即现在的运河线路。但因承包商与政府之间沟通不畅，该项目又被搁置。后陆军工程兵团于1874年恢复运河修建项目，运河于1876年得以完工。1878—1908年间，运河上有很多大型船只和游船通行。1951年，因通航量大幅减少，波蒂奇运河被迫关闭。

Portage Lake Ship Canal

A canal located in Michigan, the United States. As a part of the Keweenaw Waterway, the Portage Lake Ship Canal connects Lake Superior with such

波蒂奇湖通海运河

美国密歇根州运河。波蒂奇湖通海运河为基威诺航道的一段，流经波蒂奇湖、托奇湖，最终注入

sections as the Portage Lake and the Torch Lake in between. The canal was 3.3 kilometres in length, 30.5 metres in width and 4.3 metres in depth. In 1935, it was widened to 152.4 metres. Before the dredging of this canal in the 1860s, it was a small river used only by the locals. In 1861, the Portage Lake & Lake Superior Ship Canal Co. was founded, and the construction of the canal was authorized. By 1874, the Portage Lake Ship Canal was finally completed by the Lake Superior Ship Canal, Railway and Iron Company. The canal allows the transportation of copper ores from the mines of the Keweenaw Peninsula out to larger cities, making great contributions to the local economy.

苏必利尔湖。该运河长3.3千米，宽30.5米，深4.3米，1935年拓宽至152.4米。19世纪60年代疏浚前，该运河是条小河流，仅供当地人使用。1861年，波蒂奇湖与苏必利尔湖通海运河公司成立，运河修建工程获批。1874年，苏必利尔湖通海运河、铁路及钢铁公司最终完成了该运河的修建。波蒂奇湖通海运河修建后，基威诺半岛上丰富的铜矿资源通过该运河运往大城市，极大促进了当地经济发展。

Port Jefferson Feeder Canal

An inland canal located in Ohio, the United States. See Sidney Feeder Canal.

杰斐逊港引水运河

美国俄亥俄州内陆运河。见锡德尼引水运河。

Port Sandfield Canal

A canal located in Ontario, Canada. The Port Sandfield Canal, with a length of around 182 metres, connects Lake Joseph and Lake Rosseau. The canal was named after John Sandfield MacDonald, the Premier of Ontario at that time. In 1865, Alexander Peter Cockburn, a member of the Ontario Provincial Parliament, played an essential role in facilitating the construction of the canal as well as ensuring enough funds to complete the project. In 1866, he built a steamer Wenonah which, in 1871, became the first ship to pass the newly-built canal.

桑菲尔德港运河

加拿大安大略省运河。桑菲尔德港运河连通约瑟夫湖和罗索湖，长约182米，运河名称源于当时的安大略省省长约翰·桑菲尔德·麦克唐纳。1865年，安大略省议会议员亚历山大·彼得·科伯恩有力推动了该运河的修建，同时保障了资金来源，从而确保工程顺利完成。他在1866年建造了汽船"威诺娜号"，1871年，"威诺娜号"成为第一艘通过该运河的船舶。该船航

As the Wenonah was stuck in the waterway, the canal was further dredged and reopened in 1872. The canal allowed steamers to carry freight and timber to navigate between Lake Rosseau and Lake Joseph. In 1924, over the canal was built a swing bridge which is now the oldest one in Ontario. Due to later economic downturn, the canal was not used and maintained for a time. In 1999, it was rehabilitated and is still open at present.

行时被卡在航道中，故运河得以进一步疏浚，并在1872年重新开通。运河开通后，汽船能装载货物和木材在罗索湖和约瑟夫湖之间来往航行。1924年，运河上方修建了平旋桥，这是安大略省最古老的平旋桥。后因经济低迷，该运河被废弃了一段时间，无人进行维护。1999年，桑菲尔德港运河得到修复，使用至今。

Portsmouth and Arundel Canal

朴次茅斯-阿伦德尔运河

A canal located in the south of England, the United Kingdom. The Portsmouth and Arundel Canal runs from Portsmouth to Arundel with a length of 20.4 kilometres. The canal has three major sections: the Ford to Hunston section, the Hunston to Birdham section, and the Portsea section. At a cost of £125,452, it was built in 1823 by the Portsmouth & Arundel Navigation Company. With the advent of railroads, the Ford to Hunston section started to decline since 1847. The traffic on the other two sections also dropped to about 4,000 tons in the 1880s. Never being financially successful, the canal was finally abandoned in 1928. Later the canal was sold to the West Sussex County Council at a price of £7,500 in 1957.

英国英格兰南部运河。朴次茅斯—阿伦德尔运河连接朴次茅斯市和阿伦德尔市，全长20.4千米。运河分福特至亨斯顿河段、亨斯顿至伯德姆河段以及波特西河段三个主要河段。1823年朴次茅斯运河由朴次茅斯—阿伦德尔航运公司花费125 452英镑开凿。随着铁路运输的出现，福特至亨斯顿河段自1847年以后逐渐衰落，至19世纪80年代，另两个河段的运载量也下降到4 000吨左右。由于经济效益一直欠佳，朴次茅斯—阿伦德尔运河最终于1928年被弃用。1957年，运河以7 500英镑的价格被西萨塞克斯郡议会收购。

Port Townsend Ship Canal

汤森港通海运河

A canal located in the northwest of the United

美国西北部运河。汤森港通海运

States. Sharing a boundary with Indian Island County Park, the Port Townsend Ship Canal connects the Port Townsend Bay and the Oak Bay in Jefferson County, Washington, the United States.

河与印第安岛县公园相邻，连通美国华盛顿州杰斐逊县的汤森港湾与橡树湾。

Potomac River

A canalized river located in the middle and the east of the United States. The Potomac River has two sources. The North Branch originates in the Fairfax Stone Historical Monument State Park, West Virginia, while the source of the South Branch is located near Hightown, Virginia. The north and south branches converge at Green Spring, West Virginia to form the Potomac River which flows southeastwards and empties into the Chesapeake Bay. The total length of this river amounts to 652 kilometres. The section between the confluence of the two branches and Point Lookout is 486 kilometres long. The Potomac River is also regarded as the Nation's River as many heritage sites are located along the river. The Potomac River has a 190-kilometre-long tidal navigation which extends from the connection between Washington D.C. and the Chesapeake & Ohio Canal to the Chesapeake Bay. During the 18th and 19th centuries, multiple canal projects were carried out along the Potomac Basin. The construction of the Patowmack Canal began in 1785 and was completed in 1802. The canal was disused in 1830. In 1831, the Chesapeake and Ohio Canal was excavated along the bank of the Potomac River to link Washington D.C. and Cumberland. In the early 1920s, the canal was ob-

波托马克河

美国中东部运河化河流。波托马克河有两个源头：北部支流始于西弗吉尼亚州的费尔法克斯石历史纪念碑州立公园，南部支流始于弗吉尼亚州的海敦镇附近。南、北部支流在西弗吉尼亚州的格林斯普林镇汇合形成波托马克河，之后继续流向东南方，最终注入切萨皮克湾，总长达652千米。波托马克河从南、北部支流汇合处至卢考特角的河段长486千米，沿岸有许多历史遗址，故该河也被称为"民族之河"。波托马克河有一段长约190千米的潮汐航道，从其在华盛顿哥伦比亚特区与切萨皮克—俄亥俄运河的交汇处流向切萨皮克湾。18世纪至19世纪时，波托马克河流域修曾建多条运河。波托马克运河1785年开凿，1802年竣工，1830年停用。1831年，波托马克河旁修建了切萨皮克—俄亥俄运河，用以连接华盛顿哥伦比亚特区和马里兰州的坎伯兰市，但运河在20世纪20年代初被弃用。波托马克运河和切萨皮克—俄亥俄运河现已成为旅游景点。1864年，波托

solete. The Patowmack Canal and the Chesapeake and Ohio Canal are now tourist spots. In 1864, the Washington Aqueduct of the Potomac River was opened to provide major source of drinking water for Washington D.C. by using a water intake constructed at Great Falls. After the big floods in 1936 and 1937, the United States Army Corps of Engineers proposed to build dams and reservoirs to stabilize the water supply. The proposal was rejected by the U.S. Supreme Court. Only the Jennings Randolph Lake on the North Branch was built. In 1959, an extra water intake was constructed at Little Falls for the Washington Aqueduct.

马克河的华盛顿渡槽启用后, 通过大瀑布城所建的取水口为华盛顿哥伦比亚特区提供主要饮用水源。1936—1937年大洪水后, 美国陆军工程兵团提议建造大坝和水库, 稳定水资源供应。该提议遭到美国高等法院反对, 最终只在北部支流开挖了詹宁斯·伦道夫湖, 并于1959年在小瀑布城为华盛顿渡槽另建取水口。

Potsdam Havel Canal

An inland canal located in the east of Germany. The Potsdam Havel Canal is a section of the Havel Canal in the State of Brandenburg. It starts from the Göttin Lake in the Lower Havel and flows into the Jungfern Lake. The canal is 28.8 kilometres long and consists of several large, shallow lakes and narrow rivers. There are 19 bridges on the main stream and tributaries of the Potsdam Havel. As a part of the main route of the Lower Havel Waterway, the canal connected the rivers of Spree and Elbe, and was responsible for the transport of bicycles, cars and personnel on that section. After the Sacrow-Paretz Canal was opened in 1876, the Potsdam Havel became a waterway of minor importance for cargo shipping. Since the German reunification, it was no longer used for cargo shipping for economic and environmental concerns. Today, the canal is man-

波茨坦哈弗尔运河

德国东部内陆运河。波茨坦哈弗尔运河为勃兰登堡州哈弗尔运河的一段, 从哈弗尔下游航道的格廷湖注入永弗恩湖, 全长28.8千米。运河由几个面积较大的浅湖与小河组成, 主河道和支流上共建有19座桥梁, 曾是哈弗尔下游航道的一段, 连通施普雷河与易北河, 用于自行车和汽车的运输或人员往来。1876年萨克罗—帕雷茨运河通航后, 该运河的交通运输价值下降, 仅用于货运。东西德国统一后, 出于对经济发展和环境保护问题的综合考量, 波茨坦哈弗尔运河不再用于货物运输。目前, 波茨坦哈弗尔运河由施普雷哈弗尔航道与航运局负责管理, 主要供客

aged by the Spree-Havel Waterways and Shipping Office, and is primarily open to passenger ships.

船航行。

Prince Friedrich Leopold Canal

弗里德里希·莱奥波德王子运河

A canal located in Berlin, Germany. See Griebnitz Canal.

德国柏林运河。见格里布尼茨运河。

Prinses Margriet Canal

玛格丽特公主运河

A canal located in the province of Friesland, the Netherlands. The Prinses Margriet Canal flows from Stroobos, runs through multiple lakes, and empties into the IJssel Lake in Lemmer. The canal is 65 kilometres long and 60 metres wide with 2 locks and 11 bridges. It is named after Prinses Margriet of the Netherlands. The section of the canal continuing in Groningen Province is called Van Starkenborgh Canal. The construction of the Prinses Margriet Canal began in the 1930s, but the last sections of the canal were only excavated after World War II. The canal was opened in 1951. The canal, together with the Van Starkenborgh Canal and the Ems Canal, constitutes the Lemmer-Delfzijl shipping route, which is one of the most important and busiest shipping routes in the Netherlands with the number of freighters and pleasure craft increasing. To meet the transport and safety needs, the route will be widened and deepened.

荷兰弗里斯兰省运河。玛格丽特公主运河始于弗里斯兰省的斯特罗博斯，流经多个湖泊，在莱默注入艾瑟尔湖，全长65千米，宽60米，沿线建有2座船闸和11座桥梁。运河因荷兰玛格丽特公主的名字而得名，流经格罗宁根省的河段名为范斯塔肯博赫运河。玛格丽特公主运河开凿于20世纪30年代，最后一段在第二次世界大战结束后才动工修建，1951年玛格丽特公主运河正式通航。该运河与范斯塔肯博赫运河、埃姆斯运河共同组成莱默—代尔夫宰尔航线，成为荷兰最重要、最繁忙的航线之一，航线上的货船和游船数量一直在不断增加。为满足运输和安全需求，航线上的3条运河即将拓宽加深。

Prorva Channel

普罗尔瓦运河

A canal located in the Danube Delta, Ukraine. The

乌克兰多瑙河三角洲地区运河。

Prorva Channel, flowing into the Black Sea, is 74 kilometres long, 61 metres wide and 4.8 metres deep, with a natural section and an artificial section built by the Soviet Union in 1957. The channel provided the major shipping service for the delta area between the late 1950s and the early 1990s. Its exploitation significantly declined after the Soviet Union disintegrated, and it was then gradually silted. At the turn of the 21st century, there were proposals to restore the channel along with other Ukrainian waterways. In 2013, the channel was made available to tourists.

普罗尔瓦运河注入黑海，全长74千米，宽61米，深4.8米。运河的一部分为天然河道，一部分是1957年苏联动员人工开凿而成。20世纪50年代末至90年代初，运河是多瑙河三角洲地区的主要船运通道。苏联解体后，该运河的使用率大幅降低，河道逐渐淤塞。21世纪伊始，有人提议恢复该运河和乌克兰境内其他航道的航运。2013年，普罗尔瓦运河对游客开放。

Prosperity Canal

繁荣运河

An inland canal located in Iraq. See Glory River.

伊拉克内陆运河。见荣耀河。

Pudong Canal

浦东运河

A canal located in Shanghai, China. Also called Yunyanhe Canal. The Pudong Canal is 43.5 kilometres long, starting from the Cangtou River in the north and ending at the Nanjie River in the south. The canal, with a long history of more than 800 years, was firstly excavated for salt transportation during the Southern Song Dynasty (1127–1279). After the founding of the People's Republic of China, the canal was dredged and expanded three times, in 1961, 1973 and 1977 respectively, and became a major waterway running north-south through Pudong District. Today, the Pudong Canal plays an important role in flood control and drainage, navigation, water storage and irrigation.

中国上海市运河。亦称运盐河。浦东运河全长43.5千米，北起仓头河，南至南界河。该运河历史可追溯至南宋年间（1127—1279）开凿的运盐河，距今已有800多年。新中国成立后，浦东运河分别于1961年、1973年和1977年历经3次疏浚和拓建，成为一条贯通浦东南北的骨干航道。如今，浦东运河在防汛排涝、航运、蓄水、灌溉等方面发挥着重要作用。

Punan Canal

A canal located in the city of Shanghai, China. With a total length of 39 kilometres, the Punan Canal starts from the Longquan Port, flows eastwards through Fengxian District, and empties into the Dale Port. The excavation work began in 1958 and was completed between 1975 and 1977. It is the longest canal in southeast Shanghai, consisting of two sections. In 1994, the south section of the Pudong Canal running in a west-to-east direction was renamed the Punan Canal. In early 2017, under a green landscape project the construction work commenced on the north bank of the Punan Canal. The project covered an area of about 740,000 square metres with a length of 1.75 kilometres along the canal. In early 2018, the construction work came to an end. The green landscape is a public space for relaxation and recreation where people can ramble and enjoy beautiful views. The Punan Canal is now navigable for ships with a gross tonnage of up to 60 to 100, providing irrigation water for about 54 square kilometres of farmland, and is capable of regulating all waters in Fengxian District.

Purmer Ring Canal

A canal located in North Holland Province, the Netherlands. The Purmer Ring Canal, connected with the North Holland Canal, runs through Purmerend City in the west, and is connected via a short canal to Edam Town in the east. This canal has an elevation of −2 metres, a length of 2.2 kilometres and covers an area of 1.3 square kilometres.

浦南运河

中国上海市运河。浦南运河全长39千米，西起龙泉港，主要流经奉贤区，向东注入大泐港。运河的开凿工作始于1958年，于1975—1977年间竣工。浦南运河分为南、北两个河段，是上海市东南部最长的运河。1994年，浦东运河的南部东西向河段更名为浦南运河。2017年初，浦南运河北岸开始建设绿化景观工程。该项目占地面积约为740 000平方米，覆盖河段长达1.75千米。2018年初，项目完工。这一绿色景观空间可供人们开展各类娱乐活动，当地人在放松身心的同时也能欣赏周边美丽的景色。目前，运河全程可通航60至100吨级船舶，为面积约54平方千米的农田提供灌溉用水，并能够调蓄奉贤区内所有水体。

皮尔默环形运河

荷兰北荷兰省运河。皮尔默环形运河连通北荷兰运河，流经西部的皮尔默伦德市，并通过一条短运河与东部的埃丹镇相连。皮尔默环形运河低于海平面2米，全长2.2千米，流域面积为1.3平方千米。

Quilon Canal

A canal located in the state of Kerala, India. See Kollam Canal.

奎隆运河

印度喀拉拉邦运河。见科拉姆运河。

Quogue Canal

A canal located in the state of New York, the United States. The Quogue Canal is about 4.8 kilometres long and 45.7 metres wide, connecting the Quantuck Bay and the Shinnecock Bay. It is a part of the Long Island Intracoastal Waterway. The canal is mainly for recreational purposes.

夸格运河

美国纽约州运河。夸格运河全长约4.8千米，宽约45.7米，连通匡图克湾和欣纳科克湾，是长岛沿海航道的一部分。夸格运河如今主要用于娱乐休闲。

Rance Maritime Canal

A canal located in northwestern France. The Rance Maritime Canal connects the Saint Malo Harbour and the Ille and Rance Canal in Dinan. The canal is 22.6 kilometres long with 2 locks. It is the first section of the series of waterways across Brittany that connects the English Channel to the Atlantic.

滨海朗斯运河

法国西北部运河。滨海朗斯运河连接圣马洛海港与迪南的伊勒—朗斯运河，全长22.6千米，沿线建有2座船闸。该运河为布列塔尼大区运河网一系列航道的第一段，与英吉利海峡相通，最终注入大西洋。

Rangsit Canal

A canal located in central Thailand. The Rangsit Canal is in the eastern part of the Chao Phraya valley, which starts at the east bank of the Chao Phraya River in the Mueang Pathum Thani District, Pathum Thani Province and flows eastward and ends at the Nakhon Nayok River in the Ongkharak District, Nakhon Nayok Province. By order of King Chulalongkorn (Rama V), the canal was constructed in 1890, and got its name from the King in honour of his son, Rangsit, who was the Prince of Chai Nat. It was the first irrigation project of Thailand in hope of facilitating rice cultivation in the fallow land of the outer Chao Phraya Basin. According to the plan, the Rangsit Canal Passenger Boat Service provides a water bus service operating on the canal in Pathum Thani Province. The Rangsit Canal Passenger Boat Service has been put into operation in March 2014. Although the amenities had been completed in June 2015, the service had not been put into use by 2019.

兰实运河

泰国中部运河。兰实运河位于湄南河河谷东侧，始于巴吞他尼府巴吞他尼直辖县湄南河东岸，东流汇入坤西育府翁卡叻县的坤西育河。1890年，泰王朱拉隆功（拉玛五世）下令开凿该运河。泰王为纪念其子猜纳王子兰实，以其名兰实为运河命名。兰实运河是泰国第一个灌溉工程，旨在利用湄南河流域外围的休耕地种植水稻。兰实运河客船服务部将按计划在运河巴吞他尼府段提供水上巴士服务。其客船服务部于2014年3月开始启用，配套设施已于2015年6月完工，但直到2019年，水上巴士服务仍未投入运营。

Rappahannock Navigation System

An abandoned canal system located in eastern Virginia, the United States. The Rappahannock Navigation System was 24 kilometres long. Started in 1829, the Rappahannock Navigation System was not completed until 1849. When the project was done, there were 80 locks, 25 of which were stone locks and the rest were wooden locks. The navigation system also had 20 dams. It was abandoned in 1855.

拉帕汉诺克航道网

美国弗吉尼亚州东部弃用运河网。拉帕汉诺克航道网全长24千米，1829年开凿，1849年竣工。建成时，该航道网总计有80座船闸，包括25座石制船闸和55座木制船闸，另外还有20个坝体。1855年起拉帕汉诺克航道网被弃用。

Rappahannock River~

A canalized river located in eastern Virginia, the United States. The Rappahannock River is about 316 kilometres long, rising from the Blue Ridge Mountains and flowing southeastward by Fredericksburg, where its main tributary the Rapidan joins the Rappahannock River a few kilometres upstream, and empties into the Chesapeake Bay. A part of the river is used for navigation, extending 180 kilometres from Fredericksburg to the Chesapeake Bay. The name Rappahannock comes from an Algonquian word, which means quick rising water. The river was seen as the boundary between the North and the South during the Civil War. In colonial times, the river served as a major route for transporting goods, including tobacco, salted fish, iron ore, and grains. Now the river is more of a source of recreation and beauty than a route of transport.

拉帕汉诺克河

美国弗吉尼亚州东部运河化河流。拉帕汉诺克河全长316千米，发源于蓝岭山脉，呈东南流向，经弗雷德里克斯堡市，最终注入切萨皮克湾，其主要支流拉皮丹河在弗雷德里克斯堡上游几千米处汇入拉帕汉诺克河。拉帕汉诺克河位于弗雷德里克斯堡和切萨皮克湾之间的河段可通航，通航距离为180千米。该河流名称源于阿尔贡金语，意为"迅速上涨的水"。拉帕汉诺克河在美国南北战争时期被视为南北方的分界线，在殖民时期成为运输烟草、腌鱼、铁矿石和粮食等货物的主要通道。如今的拉帕汉诺克河更多用于娱乐消遣和旅游观光。

Raritan River〰

A canalized river located in New Jersey, the United States. The Raritan River, 112 kilometres long, forms at the confluence of the North Branch Raritan and the South Branch Raritan rivers and ends its way at the Raritan Bay of the Atlantic Ocean. It was navigable over a distance of 22.2 kilometres from New Brunswick to the Raritan Bay. The Raritan River has been an important route of transport since pre-colonial times. It also plays a part in colonial times and modern times. The Delaware and Raritan Canal along the south bank of the river serves as a connection between New York City and Philadelphia. The trade and transport were more efficient between these two major cities via the lower 22.2-kilometre-long part of the river and the canal in terms of cost and time than the original route along the Atlantic Ocean Coast, the Delaware Bay, and the Delaware River. Now, the river is also used for recreational purposes and serves as an important source of drinking water for the nearby region.

拉里坦河

美国新泽西州运河化河流。拉里坦河全长112千米，源于拉里坦河南、北支流交汇处，注入大西洋的拉里坦湾。拉里坦河位于新不伦瑞克市和拉里坦湾之间的河段可通航，其间距离超过22.2千米。早在北美殖民时期以前拉里坦河就已是重要的运输通道，在殖民时期和近现代也发挥过重要作用。拉里坦河南岸的特拉华—拉里坦运河连接纽约市和费城。先前往返于纽约和费城之间的轮船需要绕行大西洋沿岸、特拉华湾以及特拉华河，得益于特拉华—拉里坦运河及拉里坦河下游22.2千米的可通航河道，两城之间的运输费用降低，时间缩短，运输更加高效。如今，拉里坦河既是周边地区重要的饮用水源，也用于休闲娱乐。

Rasquert Canal

A canal located in the province of Groningen, the Netherlands. The Rasquert Canal rises at the fixed bridge between Rasquert and Baflo, and flows eastward into the Andel Canal. The 4.3-kilometre-long canal, lying between the Baflo-Mensingeweer and the Warffum Canal, is connected to the Old Weer River. In 2017, an environmentally friendly embankment was built to the east of the canal, and land-

拉斯奎尔特运河

荷兰格罗宁根省运河。拉斯奎尔特运河始于拉斯奎尔特和巴夫洛之间的固定桥梁处，向东汇入安德尔运河。运河全长4.3千米，位于巴夫洛—门辛赫韦尔运河和瓦尔弗姆运河之间，与旧韦尔河相通。2017年，拉斯奎尔特运河东部修建了一条环保堤岸，景观拖车道被拓

scaped trailer lanes were expanded into bike lanes.

展为自行车道。

Rec Comtal

里克孔塔勒运河

A canal located in northeastern Spain. The Rec Comtal was constructed near Barcelona in the middle of the 10th century. In nearly a millennium that followed, the canal had been a vital waterway in Barcelona, and it had supported the local textile industries. It also delivered the water of the Besòs River to Barcelona until the mid-20th century. Lots of the remains of the canal were uncovered when the Glòries, a large square in Barcelona, was undergoing excavations in March 2016.

西班牙东北部运河。里克孔塔勒运河位于巴塞罗那附近，10世纪中叶开凿。在其后近1 000年内，该运河一直都是巴塞罗那的重要航道，促进了当地纺织业的发展。20世纪中叶以前，里克孔塔勒运河还将贝索斯河的河水输送至巴塞罗那城，为巴塞罗那市提供水源。2016年3月，在巴塞罗那荣耀广场的挖掘现场发现了大量与该运河相关的遗迹。

Red River Navigation

雷德河航道

A canal located in southern United States. Also called John Bennett Johnston Waterway. The Red River Navigation was a reach of the Red River. The channel has 5 locks and it is 2.7 metres in depth, 60 metres in width, and 380 kilometres in length. It is navigable from Shreveport, Louisiana to the Mississippi River. In the 20th century, the portion between Shreveport and the Mississippi River was impeded, leading to much inconvenience for local residents in such cases as flooding, blocked navigation, and erosion on the river banks. Later an interest group called the Red River Valley Association was formed, led by the Democratic senator from Louisiana John Bennett Johnston and others, to persuade the Congress into providing financial support in making

美国南部运河。亦称约翰·班尼特·约翰斯顿航道。雷德河航道为雷德河的一段，航道长380千米，水深2.7米，宽60米，共建有5座船闸，从路易斯安那州什里夫波特至密西西比河之间的河段可通航。到了20世纪，这一河段淤塞严重，引发了洪水、通航不便、河岸侵蚀等问题，给沿岸居民的生活带来极大不便。后来，路易斯安那州民主党参议员约翰·班尼特·约翰斯顿和其他参议员共同组建了雷德河谷协会，说服国会提供经济支持，使雷德河恢复通航。1994年运河维修项目竣工，雷德河航运交通更

this river navigable. After the project was completed in 1994, the watercourse has made navigation much more convenient and brought about more job opportunities. It is now used for both public ports and private terminals.

加便利, 同时还提供了更多就业机会。如今, 雷德河航道沿岸既有公共码头, 也有私人码头。

Regent's Canal

A canal located in England, the United Kingdom. The Regent's Canal is situated in the north of central London with a total length of 13.8 kilometres, connecting the Grand Union Canal at Little Venice and River Thames at Limehouse. The canal was named after the Prince Regent, later George IV. With the idea of "barges moving through an urban landscape", the designer John Nash played a part in the construction of the canal. The excavation began after the Regent's Canal Act was passed by the parliament in 1812. Nash's assistant, James Morgan, was appointed as the engineer. After lots of setbacks both legally and financially, the canal was completed in 1820. It was used as the industrial transport system of London until the 1840s. The rise of railway transportation posed a threat to the Regent's Canal afterwards. Attempts were made to turn the canal into a railway but were all in vain. When the canal was nationalized in 1948, its commercial transportation had begun to dwindle. In 1979, a new function was found for the canal. The British Waterways Board allowed the installment of underground cables below the towpath between St John's Wood and City Road, and the pumped canal water is circulated to cool the cables that form a part of

摄政运河

英国英格兰运河。摄政运河位于伦敦中北部, 全长13.8千米, 在小威尼斯连通大联盟运河, 在莱姆豪斯连通泰晤士河。运河以当时的摄政王(即后来的乔治四世)的名字命名。摄政运河设计师约翰·纳什的设计理念是"让驳船穿行于城市风景之中"。1812年, 《摄政运河法案》获议会批准, 开凿工作也随之启动, 纳什的助手詹姆斯·摩根被任命为工程师。在克服法律和财政方面的多种困难后, 运河于1820年竣工。在19世纪40年代之前, 摄政运河一直都是伦敦工业运输的重要通道。后铁路运输兴起, 对运河构成了威胁。有人曾试图把运河改建成铁路, 但均未果。1948年运河被收归国有时, 其商业运输已开始萎缩。1979年发掘了运河的一项新功能, 英国水务局批准在圣约翰伍德和城市大道之间的纤道下铺设电缆, 水泵抽取的运河水循环起来, 冷却国家电网的电缆, 为伦敦提供电力。如今, 摄政运河已成为一处贯穿伦敦

the National Grid and provide electricity for London. Today, the canal is a leisurely corridor through London. It is a place of tranquility for Londoners and visitors alike.

的休闲廊道, 是伦敦市民和游客钟爱的静谧之地。

Reit Canal

哈伊特运河

A canal located in the Netherlands. The Reit Canal is 30.6 kilometres long and flows through the northwest of the city of Groningen to the Lauwers Lake. The name is said to come from the reeds, the meaning of "reit" in Dutch. From Wierumerschouw, the Reit Canal is the canalized lower course of the Hunze. The course between Groningen and Dorkwerd was established in the first half of the 13th century to facilitate shipping. The Reit Canal includes the old Hunze, the starting point of the route from Groningen to the sea, which was later transformed into a canal and thus became a significant route between the city of Groningen and Garnwerd. It was directly connected with the sea before 1877, which caused ebbs and flows of the cities' canals. This problem was solved by the construction of locks and dams, turning the Lauwerszee into the Lauwers Lake by blocking the river inlet. Nowadays, the canal is mainly used by cruise ships. The Reit Canal area is one of the oldest cultural landscapes in Europe. In the current landscape, the old riverbeds are still clearly visible in many places. The Reit Canal and its immediate surroundings form an ecologically interesting area, a large part of which has been laid out as nature reserves.

荷兰运河。哈伊特运河长30.6千米, 流经格罗宁根市西北部, 注入劳沃斯湖。运河的名称据说来自荷兰语词汇reit, 意为"芦苇"。从维鲁默绍开始, 哈伊特运河其实是浑泽河下游的运河化河道。为方便航运, 格罗宁根和多克沃德之间的河段早在13世纪上半叶就已开凿。哈伊特运河包括旧浑泽河, 旧浑泽河连接格罗宁根市和海洋, 后被改造为运河, 成为连接格罗宁根市与哈伦韦德市之间的重要航道。1877年之前, 浑泽河直接与海洋相通, 使格罗宁根市内的运河水位随海潮涨退而起落。后来在运河上修建了船闸与水坝, 通过阻挡海水将劳沃斯湾改造为劳沃斯湖, 运河水位随海潮涨退起落的问题得以解决。如今, 哈伊特运河主要通行游船, 运河区是欧洲最古老的文化景观之一, 许多地方古老的河床仍清晰可见。哈伊特运河及其周边地区形成令人关注的生态区域, 其中大部分地区已经被建为自然保护区。

Rengers Canal

An inland canal located in the province of Groningen, the Netherlands. See Slochteren Canal.

Rhin Canal

A canal located in Germany. The Rhin Canal is a part of the Ruppin Waterway, which is a collective name given to a series of rivers and lakes connecting the Mecklenburg Lake Plateau with Berlin waterways.

Rhine-Herne Canal

A canal located in Germany. The Rhine-Herne Canal is 45.6 kilometres long and equipped with 5 locks. It is a federal waterway in the Ruhr area, linking the harbour in Duisburg on the Rhine with the Dortmund-Ems Canal near Henrichenburg. Its excavation was started in April 1906 and finished in July 1914. From 1958 to 1965, a chain of pumping stations were built on the canal to guarantee self-sufficient water supply. The route between Duisburg-Meiderich and Wanne-Eickel was later expanded between 1968 and 1995. The canal once served as the busiest inland shipping route in Europe, with multiple ports standing along its route, including the city ports of Essen, Gelsenkirchen, Grimberg, and Recklinghausen, etc. In April 2021, a new bridge with a steel lattice superstructure was built over the canal to carry part of the Betuwe rail line. Now the Rhine-Herne Canal has been trans-

伦格斯运河

荷兰格罗宁根省内陆运河。见斯洛赫特伦运河。

林河运河

德国运河。林河运河是鲁平航道的一部分，鲁平航道是连通梅克伦堡湖区和柏林航道一系列河流和湖泊的统称。

莱茵－黑尔讷运河

德国运河。莱茵－黑尔讷运河全长45.6千米，建有5座船闸，是德国鲁尔区的联邦航道，连通杜伊斯堡港口，并在亨利兴堡附近同多特蒙德－埃姆斯运河交汇。该运河开凿于1906年4月，1914年7月竣工。1958至1965年间，为在供水方面实现自给自足，人们在运河上修建了一系列泵站。随后，从1968年到1995年，人们又拓宽了从杜伊斯堡－梅德里希到万纳艾克尔的河段。莱茵－黑尔讷运河曾是欧洲最繁忙的内陆航线，途径多个港口，包括埃森港、盖尔森基兴港、格林贝格港和雷克灵豪森港等。2021年4月，运河上又新修了一座钢网架结构桥梁，从鹿特丹到德国铁路货运会途经此处。如

formed into a recreation centre for water sports.

今，莱茵－黑尔讷运河已被打造为一个休闲中心，可进行各项水上运动。

Rhine Lateral Canal

莱茵旁侧运河

A canal located in eastern France. See Grand Alsace Canal.

法国东部运河。见阿尔萨斯大运河。

Rhine-Main-Danube Canal

莱茵－美因－多瑙运河

A canal located in Bavaria, Germany. The Rhine-Main-Danube Canal, 171 kilometres in length, has 16 locks and runs from Bamberg to Kelheim. By connecting the North Sea and the Atlantic Ocean to the Black Sea, it provides a navigable artery. The largest authorized size of vessels is 190 metres long and 11.45 metres wide. The plan for the construction of the canal was first initiated in 1938 but was dropped after World War II broke out. Later in September 1966, a contract was signed to finance the project and the present canal was completed in September 1992. In total, the construction of the canal cost 2.3 billion euros. It is currently used for transportation of goods, especially food, iron, stones, soil and fertilizers.

德国巴伐利亚州运河。莱茵－美因－多瑙运河从班贝格流至凯尔海姆，全长171千米，河上建有16座船闸。该运河连通北海、大西洋与黑海，是一条主干航道，最大通航船只可达190米长、11.45米宽。1938年，运河开凿计划首次提出，第二次世界大战爆发使计划搁置。1966年9月，德国政府签署了资助运河开凿的合同。1992年9月，运河竣工，共耗资23亿欧元。目前，莱茵－美因－多瑙运河用于运输食物、钢铁、石头、泥土及化肥等货物。

Rhine-Schie Canal

莱茵－斯希运河

A canal located in the province of South Holland, the Netherlands. The Rhine-Schie Canal links the Schie and the Old Rhine, which is about 24 kilometres in length with one lock. The canal consists

荷兰南荷兰省运河。莱茵－斯希运河连通斯希河和旧莱茵河，全长约24千米，河上建有1座船闸。该运河包含多段航道，每段均有

of several sections of waterways, each with its own name and history, including the Delft Schie Canal, the Delft Vliet Canal, the Trek Canal, and the Vliet Canal. The Delft Schie Canal is 14.5 kilometres in length, connecting Delft with Overschie, and was built upon a marshy stream called Delft. The Delft Vliet Canal is 4.6 kilometres long, located between Delft and Rijswijk, connecting the Leiden River with Overschie. The Trek Canal was excavated in 1638 to link the city of Delft and the Hague. In 1891, it was widened and extended to the Rhine and the Galgewater River, allowing large cargo ships to reach the centre of Leiden. The Vliet Canal flows from Leiden and reaches Delft through the Delft Schie Canal with a lock in Leidschendam. Currently, the Rhine-Schie Canal is still of great importance to the freight transport between the Hague and Rotterdam, and is a vital route for leisure shipping as well.

各自的名称和历史，包括斯希运河代尔夫特段、代尔夫特—弗利特运河、特雷克运河和弗利特运河。斯希运河代尔夫特段全长14.5千米，连接代尔夫特与上斯希河，在代尔夫特沼泽溪流的基础上修建而成。代尔夫特—弗利特运河长4.6千米，位于代尔夫特和赖斯韦克市之间，连通莱顿河和上斯希河。特雷克弗利特运河开凿于1638年，连接代尔夫特和海牙。1891年，该运河得以拓宽，并延伸至莱茵河和豪赫沃特河，使得大型货船可以驶往莱顿市中心。弗利特运河始于莱顿市，在代尔夫特市与斯希运河代尔夫特段汇合，在莱岑丹市的河段上建有1座船闸。目前，莱茵—斯希运河在海牙和鹿特丹两市之间的货运中仍发挥着重要作用，同时也是一条重要的观光旅游路线。

Rhône

A canalized cross-border river located in Switzerland and France. The Rhône originates from the Rhône Glacier in the Swiss Alps, and mainly flows through Geneva, Lyon and Vienne, and finally runs into the Mediterranean Sea. It is 813 kilometres in length with a drainage basin of around 97,775 square kilometres. The navigable sector is 310 kilometres in length with twelve locks. The main canals include the Rhône-Sète Canal and the Rhône-Rhine Canal. Featuring fierce currents, shallows,

罗讷河

欧洲跨国运河化河流，流经瑞士和法国。罗讷河发源于瑞士阿尔卑斯山脉的罗讷冰川，主要流经日内瓦、里昂和维埃纳，最后注入地中海，全长813千米，流域面积97 775平方千米。该河通航长度为310千米，共建有12座船闸，主要运河有罗讷—塞特运河和罗讷—莱茵运河。春夏时节，河流时涝时旱，不宜航行。1933年，为治理罗

floods and droughts in springs and summers, the river was difficult to navigate. In 1933, the French government established the National Company of the Rhône to renovate the river, thus deepening the navigation channels. In 1948, the government started to build a set of locked barrages and canals, which improved the navigation. The most extensive transformation was between Lyon and the Mediterranean, where shoals had been submerged by dams and canals, and original gradients were alleviated by locks. In France, the river has been an essential hinge linking the north and the south. In Switzerland, with the construction of rails and tunnels under some mountain barriers, the river valley in Valais has been playing a similar role.

讷河, 法国政府成立国立罗讷河公司, 对航道进行了加深改造。1948年, 政府修建堰坝, 开凿运河, 进一步改善航运条件。其中规模最大的改造工程位于里昂和地中海之间的河段, 修建水坝和运河减少了浅滩, 新增船闸也解决了原有的坡度问题。在法国, 罗讷河是连通南北的水路枢纽。在瑞士, 一些山体下修建了铁路和公路隧道, 位于瓦莱州的罗讷河谷因此也是重要的交通枢纽。

Rhône-Fos-Bouc-Marseille Liaison

罗讷-福斯-布克-马赛运河网

A waterway located near the Mediterranean coast in France. The Rhône-Fos-Bouc-Marseille Liaison is 47 kilometres long. It is a series of the canal sections connecting the Rhône all the way to Marseille. The waterway is composed of several sections, i.e. the Rhône-Fos Junction Canal, the basins of the port of Fos, the Fos-Bouc Junction Canal and the Marseille-Rhône Canal. Due to the collapse of the Rove Tunnel, the Marseille-Rhône Canal was closed in 1963, which meant the waterway from the port of Bouc to Marseille was not navigable any more. Now the canal only extends to the port of Bouc, with a dead end in Marseille. This waterway still plays a prominent role today in helping large push-tows of international dimensions bypass the

法国近地中海海岸航道。罗讷-福斯-布克-马赛运河网全长47千米, 是罗讷河到马赛的水上通道。该航道由多个河段组成, 其中包括罗讷-福斯港交界运河河段、福斯港内湾河段、福斯港-布克港交界运河河段和马赛-罗讷运河河段。1963年, 由于罗夫隧道坍塌, 马赛-罗讷运河关闭, 这意味着从布克港到马赛的航道再也无法通航。如今, 罗讷-福斯-布克-马赛运河网只通航到布克港而无法与马赛连通。尽管如此, 该航道仍发挥着重要作用, 为大型国际顶推驳船绕过福斯湾提供相对

Gulf of Fos and providing a relatively safe inland course for them.

安全的内陆航道。

Rhône-Fos Junction Canal

A canal located in the south of France. The Rhône-Fos Junction Canal connects the canalized Rhône with the city of Fos-sur-Mer. It is one of several canals comprising the Rhône-Fos-Bouc-Marseille Liaison. The canal, built in 1980, is about 16 kilometres long and flows through Darse 1 Port in the Fos-sur-Mer before joining the Mediterranean Sea via the Gulf of Fos. Today, the canal only carries cargos between the Rhône and the Gulf of Fos.

罗讷－福斯港交界运河

法国南部运河。罗讷－福斯港交界运河连接经运河化改造的罗讷河与滨海福斯市，是构成罗讷－福斯－布克－马赛运河网的数条运河之一。该运河开凿于1980年，全长约16千米，流经滨海福斯市的达斯1号港口后，经由福斯湾注入地中海。目前，罗讷－福斯港交界运河仅有罗讷河与福斯湾之间的航道能运输货物。

Rhône-Rhine Canal

A canal located in eastern France. The Rhône-Rhine Canal, linking the Saône at Saint-Symphorien to the Upper Rhine at Niffer, is about 237 kilometres in length. Built in 1784 and completed in 1833, this canal is a part of the French inland water network, and links the Nordic and Mediterranean seaports, including those of the Rhône, the Saône, the Rhône-Rhine Canal, the Rhine Lateral Canal and the Rhine. The canal originally had 112 locks, 72 of which were on the Saône including 2 double-staircase locks, and the remaining 40 were on the Rhine. Since its construction, the canal has undergone many changes and currently has 84 locks. It consists of two parts: the 224-kilometre-long canal linking the Saône near Saint Jean de Losne with Mulhouse,

罗讷－莱茵运河

法国东部运河。罗讷－莱茵运河在圣桑福里安连通索恩河，在尼弗连通莱茵河上游，全长约237千米。运河1784年开凿，1833年完工，属于法国内陆航道网，将北欧海港和地中海的海港连在一起，包括罗讷河、索恩河、罗讷－莱茵运河、莱茵旁侧运河以及莱茵河沿岸的港口。罗讷－莱茵运河最初建有112座船闸，其中72座位于索恩河段，包括两个双层梯级船闸，而其余40座则位于莱茵河上。运河自修建以来历经多次改建，目前留有84座船闸。罗讷－莱茵运河由两段运河组成：其中一段运河长224千

and the 13-kilometre-long embranchment Kembs-Niffer running from Mulhouse to the Grand Alsace Canal at Niffer. There are two tunnels across it respectively at Thoraise and under the citadel at Besançon, both of which are about 6 metres and only wide enough for one-way traffic. There are also many 5.18-metre-wide bridgeholes, aqueducts and one-way cuttings. The first section of the canal from the Saône to the Dôle was authorized by the Burgundy Council in 1783 and was completed 19 years later. In 1834, the whole canal was finally completed and opened. Upgrading works was started in 1882 and were completed in 1904. At present, the canal is difficult to play its role economically because of its low carrying capacity. Its importance as a professional shipping channel is diminishing visibly. Because of the beautiful scenery on both sides of the canal, it is now mainly used for river tourism. The sporting boats and yachting projects established in the Franche-Comté region are popular among people. From Saône to Basel, both sides of the canal have also been transformed into bike lanes. Since the spring of 2011, people can travel along the bike lanes from Horbourg-Wihr to Strasbourg.

米，在圣让—德洛讷附近连接索恩河与米卢斯；另一段为康斯—尼弗支流，长13千米，始于米卢斯，在尼弗连通阿尔萨斯大运河。运河沿线的托赖斯和贝桑松城堡下方各建有一条隧道，宽约6米，只能容船只单向通行。运河上还有多个宽约5.18米的桥孔，以及渡槽和单向路堑。索恩至多勒的第一段运河1783年由勃艮第地方议会批准修建，历时19年竣工。1834年，运河全段竣工后通航。1882年，运河升级改造工程启动，1904年竣工。由于承运能力弱，罗讷—莱茵运河如今已难作为专用航道产生经济效益。运河两岸风景优美，目前主要用于河流旅游项目。在弗朗什—孔泰大区，运动气艇和游艇项目深受游客喜爱。从法国索恩到瑞士巴塞尔的运河两岸已被改造为自行车道。自2011年春季起，沿自行车道可从法国奥尔堡维尔市骑行至斯特拉斯堡市。

Rhône-Sète Canal

A canal located in southern France. The Rhône-Sète Canal has a length of 98 kilometres with 1 lock on it, and consists of two canals, the Étangs Canal and the Beaucaire Canal. It connects the Thau Lake in Sète to the Rhône River in Beaucaire, Gard. At the entrance to the Thau Lake, the canal connects with

罗讷-塞特运河

法国南部运河。罗讷—塞特运河全长98千米，建有1座船闸，由埃唐运河与博凯尔运河组成。这条运河在塞特连通拓潟湖，在加尔省博凯尔镇连通罗讷河，在拓潟湖入口处与米迪运河相通。由于罗讷河

the Midi Canal. Because of canalization, the Rhône cannot be accessed through the entrance lock at Beaucaire. The navigation instead uses the lock located to the west of Saint-Gilles, which connects the canal with the Small Rhône and a short length of canal at Saint-Gilles. The Rhône-Sète Canal is almost totally situated at sea level and the western part from the Vidourle River to the Thau Lake is a sea water canal. Major work has been started to upgrade the canal in recent years, so that it can be used by 1,200-tonne convoys instead of the previous 350-tonne barges. Recreational boats such as hotel barge cruises and self-drive canal boats are popular on the canal.

进行了运河化改造, 船只无法通过博凯尔运河入口处的船闸进入罗讷河, 仅能通过圣吉勒市以西的船闸, 经由与运河相连的小罗讷河以及圣吉勒市附近的一小段运河驶入罗讷河。罗讷—塞特运河水位与海平面几乎持平, 从维杜勒河到拓潟湖的运河西段为海水运河。近年来, 为提升运河运载能力, 相关升级改造工程已经启动。以往罗讷—塞特运河只能承载350吨重的驳船, 改造后, 其最大承载力可提升至1 200吨。如今, 由驳船改造的酒店游船和自驾运河船之类的休闲船在运河上很受欢迎。

Rideau Canal

里多运河

A canal located in Canada. The Rideau Canal is 202 kilometres in length, starting from the city of Ottawa, Ontario and ending at the city of Kingston, Ontario. The canal connects the Ottawa River and Lake Ontario. The original name for the Rideau River is Algonquian, meaning the river passes between the rocks. Its present name "Rideau" comes from the French expression for "curtain", since the waterfall on this canal hangs like a curtain. Reportedly, after the War of 1812, the construction of the canal was proposed as a preventive military measure in the early 19th century. It was used to connect Montreal and Kingston, where the British naval base was located. After its opening in 1832, this canal served as a commercial waterway, for travelling

加拿大运河。里多运河始于安大略省渥太华市, 流向金斯顿市, 连通渥太华河与安大略湖, 全长202千米。运河最早的名称源于阿尔贡金语, 意思是 "穿流于岩石间的河流", 现名 "里多" 在法语中意为 "窗帘", 因运河上有好似窗帘的瀑布而得名。里多运河据说是19世纪早期, 1812年美英战争后, 出于军事防御目的而提议开凿的, 旨在连通蒙特利尔市与当时英国海军驻地金斯顿市。1832年里多运河通航后被用作商业航道, 因为该航道比圣劳伦斯海道航行更为便捷。在加拿大公园管理局管理下,

on the canal was more convenient than that on the Saint Lawrence Seaway. It is currently used as a leisure resort for boaters under the operation of Parks Canada. As the oldest continuously operating canal in North America, the canal has been registered as a UNESCO World Heritage Site in 2007.

里多运河如今已成为划船爱好者的休闲胜地。里多运河是北美洲目前仍在使用的最古老的运河，2007年被联合国教科文组织列为世界遗产。

Rijs Canal

A canal located in the province of Friesland, the Netherlands. Also called Schwartzenberg Trench. The Rijs Canal, 4 kilometres long, rises from Rijs and flows north into the Fluessen, bounding the former municipal territories Gaasterland-Sleat and Nijefurd. The canal was excavated in the 17th century at the suggestion of the Thoe Schwartzenberg and the Hohenlansberg families. Since 15 March 2007, Ryster Feart has become the official name of the canal.

赖斯运河

荷兰弗里斯兰省运河。亦称施瓦岑贝格沟渠。赖斯运河全长4千米，始于赖斯，向北注入弗卢埃森湖，为旧时市镇哈斯特兰—斯利特与奈厄福特之间的边界。在图·施瓦岑贝格和霍恩兰斯贝格家族的提议下，运河于17世纪开凿。2007年3月15日起，运河正式更名为赖斯特费尔特运河。

Ring Canal (Bruges)

A canal located in Belgium. The Ring Canal of Bruges rings around a roughly circular centre of the city of Bruges, connecting with the Zwin River to the northeast at Damme. It was built by reshaping the Reie River.

环形运河（布鲁日）

比利时运河。环形运河环绕近乎圆形的布鲁日市中心地带，在达默市东北地区与茨温河汇合。该运河由莱伊河改造而成。

Ring Canal (Ghent)

A canal located in the province of East Flanders,

环形运河（根特）

比利时东佛兰德省运河。环形运

Belgium. The Ring Canal of Ghent connects the Ghent-Terneuzen Canal and the Schelde River. Built with a lock near Evergem and a tide lock of Merelbeke, the 21.6-kilometre-long canal connects all the watercourses that flow through Ghent. The canal is divided into 3 components: the southern section, the western section and the northern section from east to west. The construction of the canal was started in 1950 and was completed on 18 November 1969. The canal plays an important role in flood prevention in the city centre of Ghent, and makes the transportation around Ghent more convenient, allowing ships to avoid the locks in the city centre. Nowadays, the canal is navigable for inland ships up to 2,000 tons, and it will be further widened and deepened as a part of the Seine-Schelde Network. The Ring Canal greatly boosted the city's economic development, forming a new industrial zone along the bank with a series of steel plants, lorry plants, power stations and chemical plants.

河连通根特—特尔纽曾运河和斯海尔德河，全长21.6千米，连通流经根特市的所有河道。运河上建有两座船闸，一座位于埃弗海姆附近，另一座潮汐闸位于梅勒尔贝克。环形运河从东到西分成南、西和北三段。运河于1950年开凿，1969年11月18日竣工，对根特市中心的防洪防汛起着重要作用，也使根特市周围的交通更加便捷，使船只可以绕开市中心的船闸。如今，环形运河可供排水量在2 000吨以下的内河船舶通行，还将进一步扩建，成为塞纳—斯海尔德运河网的一部分。环形运河极大地促进了根特市的经济发展，运河沿岸形成了新的工业区，建有多家钢铁厂、货车生产厂、发电站和化工厂。

River Don Navigation

唐河航道

A canal located in Lincolnshire, England, the United Kingdom. The River Don Navigation is connected with River Trent at Keadby by the Stainforth and the Keadby Canal.

英国英格兰林肯郡运河。唐河航道在基德比村经由斯坦福斯—基德比运河与特伦特河相通。

Roanne-Digoin Canal

罗阿讷－迪关运河

A canal located in France. The Roanne-Digoin Canal

法国运河。罗阿讷—迪关运河全

starts at Roanne, connecting with a short naviga-ble length of the river Loire and joining the Loire Lateral Canal near the town of Digoin. It is 55.6 kilometres in length. The canal was excavated in 1827, designed by engineer De Varaigne and opened in 1838. It was built to offer adequate navigation conditions for the industrial era, and meanwhile to serve as a feeder to the Loire Lateral Canal. After the decline in commercial traffic, the three depar-tements, Loire, Saône-et-Loire and Allier, formed an association to promote its use for tourism. The canal, passing through the unspoilt countryside of the upper Loire valley, is an ideal place for pleasure cruising.

长55.6千米，始于罗阿讷，与卢瓦尔河一小段航道相通，在迪关镇附近汇入卢瓦尔旁侧运河。该运河由工程师德瓦雷涅设计，1827年开凿，1838年通航。修建罗阿讷—迪关运河旨在满足工业化时代的航运需求，同时为卢瓦尔旁侧运河提供水源。后该运河的商业航运业务逐渐萧条，卢瓦尔省、索恩—卢瓦尔省和阿列省联合成立协会以开发运河旅游业。罗阿讷—迪关运河流经卢瓦尔河上游河谷保持原有风貌的乡村，是游船观光的理想去处。

Roanoke Canal

A canal located in North Carolina, the United States. The Roanoke Canal is near Roanoke Rapids, the Halifax County and is approximately 4.6 metres deep and 12.2 metres wide, bordered by a 3-metre-wide towpath. The canal extends from the Roanoke Rapids Lake into the Roanoke River at Weldon, North Carolina. It was constructed in 1823 as a part of the Roanoke Navigation System, which was built to connect the Blue Ridge Mountains with the Atlantic Ocean. In 1885, the Roanoke Navigation and Waterpower Company commenced using the water from the canal for manufacturing, milling and foundry operations. Five years later, the company's directors announced plans to use the canal to gen-erate electricity. In 1892, the canal provided Weldon and the surrounding area with electricity for the

罗阿诺克运河

美国北卡罗来纳州运河。罗阿诺克运河邻近哈利法克斯县的罗阿诺克拉皮兹，深约4.6米，宽约12.2米，毗邻一条3米宽的纤道。运河始于罗阿诺克拉皮兹湖，在北卡罗来纳州韦尔登汇入罗阿诺克河。罗阿诺克运河是罗阿诺克航道系统的一部分，于1823年开凿，旨在连接蓝岭山脉和大西洋。1885年，罗阿诺克航运和水务公司开始利用运河发展制造业、铣削和铸造业务。5年后，公司董事会宣布计划利用该运河发电。1892年，该运河首次为韦尔登市及其周边地区供电。1900年，两座发电站全面投入使用。位于罗斯马里和罗阿诺克

first time. By 1900, two power stations were fully operational. As a result, the small village on the border between Rosemary and Roanoke flourished and became the present city of Roanoke Rapids. With the competition against a newly developed canal near the Roanoke Canal used also for generating electricity, the high cost of maintaining the canal and the need for larger hydroelectric facilities led to the closure of the navigable canal in 1912. For decades afterwards, facilities of the Roanoke Canal power station were used to build and maintain civic infrastructure. The canal was also used for commercial and tourist purposes. In 1976, the remains of the canal were added to the National Register of Historic Places.

之间的小村庄蓬勃发展, 成为今天的罗阿诺克拉皮兹市。后在罗阿诺克运河附近又开凿出一条也用于水力发电的新运河, 两条运河之间形成一定的竞争。维护罗阿诺克运河成本高昂, 加之对更大型水电厂的现实需求, 罗阿诺克运河于1912年被弃用。此后数十年, 该运河上的发电站一直用于建设和维护公共基础设施, 运河也一直用于商业发展和旅游开发。1976年, 罗阿诺克运河遗迹被列入美国国家历史遗迹名录。

Robine Canal

A canal located in southern France. The Robine Canal is a feeder canal of the New Branch.

罗比纳运河

法国南部运河。罗比纳运河是新运河支线的一条引水运河。

Rochdale Canal

A canal located in Northern England, the United Kingdom. The Rochdale Canal lies between Manchester and the Sowerby Bridge. Its name refers to the town of Rochdale through which it passes. The canal flows for 51 kilometres with 92 locks. Its construction was conceived in 1776. After two denials, on 4 April 1794 an act was finally obtained which created the Rochdale Canal Company and authorized the construction. The Rochdale is a broad canal because its locks are wide enough to allow

罗奇代尔运河

英国英格兰北部运河。罗奇代尔运河位于曼彻斯特市和索厄比布里奇市之间。运河名称来源于其流经的罗奇代尔镇。运河全长51千米, 共有92座船闸。罗奇代尔运河的修建计划始于1776年, 议会在两次否决该计划之后, 最终于1794年4月4日通过法案, 成立了罗奇代尔运河公司, 批准开凿运河。罗奇代尔运河河道宽阔, 其船闸可容4.3

vessels of 4.3 metres in width, which made the canal the main highway of commerce between Lancashire and Yorkshire. Cotton, wool, coal, limestone, timber, salt and general merchandise were transported. The volume of traffic peaked in 1845, when 979,443 tons were carried. After years, most of the length was closed in 1952 apart from a short profitable section in Manchester linking the Bridgewater and Ashton Canals. The construction of the M62 motorway in the late 1960s cut the canal in two. The canal was restored several times from 1971 and on 1 July 2002 the canal was reopened for navigation along its entire length. The Rochdale Canal, as one of the three canals which cross the Pennines, is significant for leisure boating. The Rochdale Canal has had many problems since reopening, including a shortage of water because of its reservoirs having been sold off in 1923 and the high frequency of navigation restrictions.

米宽的船只通过，因此成为兰开夏郡和约克郡之间主要的商业航道，运输棉花、羊毛、煤炭、石灰石、木材、盐和日用商品，1845年运输量达到顶峰，达979 443吨。罗奇代尔运河使用多年后，大部分河段于1952年关闭，只有曼彻斯特境内连接布里奇沃特和阿什顿运河的一小段因仍能盈利而继续通航。20世纪60年代末，因建设M62高速公路，运河被一分为二。自1971年起，人们多次对罗奇代尔运河进行修复，2002年7月1日运河全线恢复通航。如今，罗奇代尔运河作为流经奔宁山脉的三条运河之一，是休闲划船的好去处。但自重新通航以来，罗奇代尔运河问题不断，如因1923年出售水库导致的缺水问题及频繁的航行限制等。

Rochelle Canal

罗谢尔运河

A canal located in the province of Charente-Maritime, France. See Marans-Rochelle Canal.

法国滨海夏朗德省运河。见马朗—罗谢尔运河。

Roeselare-Leie Canal

鲁瑟拉勒－莱厄运河

A canal located in the province of West Flanders, Belgium. The Roeselare-Leie Canal is a 16.5-kilometre-long Class IV waterway with 1 lock, 13 bridges and 2 pipelines. It flows from Roeselare City to the Leie River at Ooigem Town. The canal was built between 1862 and 1872. Ships with a capacity up

比利时西佛兰德省运河。鲁瑟拉勒—莱厄运河全长16.5千米，为四级航道，河上建有1座船闸、13座桥梁和2条管道。运河始于鲁瑟拉勒市，在奥伊海姆镇汇入莱厄河。运河1862年开凿，1872年竣工。鲁

to 600 tons could bring sand, grain and other basic products to factories along the canal. Now the local government is trying to develop its recreational function.

瑟拉勒—莱厄运河通航后，600吨级的船只可把沙子、谷物和其他产品运送到河流沿岸的工厂。如今，当地政府正在开发鲁瑟拉勒—莱厄运河的娱乐休闲功能。

Romanian Sulina Canal

A canal located in Romania. The Romanian Sulina Canal is actually 84 kilometres long, with a width of 120—150 metres and a depth of 7—7.5 metres as a result of the straightening and deepening of the channel. It is the main navigation route for passenger and commercial traffic. Between 1880 and 1902, the canal was excavated to facilitate the river traffic, shortening the natural course of the Sulina Arm and allowing for easier access to villages in the Delta.

罗马尼亚苏利纳运河

罗马尼亚运河。罗马尼亚苏利纳运河经改直和加深后，实际全长84千米，宽120—150米，深7—7.5米，是客运和商运的主要航道。1880—1902年间，为改善航运条件而开凿了该运河，从而缩短了苏利纳河湾的天然航道，前往多瑙河三角洲上的村庄更为便捷。

Rompsay Canal

A canal located in the province of Charente-Maritime, France. See Marans-Rochelle Canal.

罗姆赛运河

法国滨海夏朗德省运河。见马朗—罗谢尔运河。

Roosendaal Canal

A cross-border canal located in Europe. The Roosendaal Canal starts from Kalmthout, Belgium, where it is called the Kleine, and flows through Roosendaal, North Brabant, Netherlands, where it is renamed the Roosendaal Canal. It links Roosendaal to the Volkerak, with a length of 11.5 kilometres. The construction of this canal was started as early as 1451, and it was further canalized and silted

罗森达尔运河

欧洲跨国运河。罗森达尔运河始于比利时卡尔姆豪特市（此段称为克莱因河），流经荷兰北布拉班特省罗森达尔市（当地人称之为罗森达尔运河），全长11.5千米，连接罗森达尔市与比利时的沃尔克拉克河。运河1451年开凿，后来又进行了运河化改造，但1792—1823

up from 1792 to 1823. The canal area was usually flooded at high tide by seawater, and the situation was not improved until 1824 when the locks of Benedensas were built. As a major waterway in this area, the canal allowed raw materials and products including sugar, sand, gravel, concrete mortar and oil to be shipped to and from local factories, hence boosting the local economy. The navigation of this canal reached its zenith during the years of 1967 and 1968. In 1983, its freight traffic was reduced along with the completion of the Mark-Vliet Canal. Alternative road freight transport also accelerated the closure of this canal by the end of the 20th century. Recently, this canal has boomed in tourism and has become a place of leisure with an increasing recreational function.

年间运河淤塞。涨潮时,运河周边地区常被海水淹没,这种情况直到1824年贝内登萨斯船闸建成后才得以改善。罗森达尔运河是当地主要航道,为当地工厂运输糖、沙子、砾石、混凝土砂浆和石油等原材料和产品,促进了当地经济发展。1967—1968年间是该运河航运业务的鼎盛时期。自1983年马克—弗利特运河建成后,罗森达尔运河的货运量逐渐减少。20世纪末,公路货运兴起加速了运河的关闭。但近来,罗森达尔运河旅游业蓬勃发展,娱乐功能日益突出,已成为一处休闲胜地。

Roubaix Canal

鲁贝运河

A cross-border canal located in Europe. Running 28.7 kilometres and equipped with 10 locks, the Roubaix Canal connects the Deûle Canal at the north of Lille in France with the Espierres Canal in Belgium and leads to the Escaut. It has two branches, the Tourcoing Branch and the Croix Branch. The construction of the canal was started in 1823, and the canal was not opened until the year 1877. The canal was closed in 1985 because of the structural degradation and restored in 2009. Today, the Roubaix Canal is well known for the varying and delightful landscape, threading from the bustling urban area in France towards the rural Belgian border.

欧洲跨国运河。鲁贝运河全长28.7千米,河上建有10座船闸,连通法国里尔北部的德勒运河与比利时的埃斯皮埃尔运河,最终汇入埃斯科河。该运河共有两条支线,即图尔宽支线运河和克鲁瓦支线运河。鲁贝运河开凿于1823年,直至1877年才通航。1985年,鲁贝运河因结构性损坏而被迫关闭,于2009年修复。如今,运河沿线风光多姿多彩,从法国的繁华都市到比利时的边境乡村,景色宜人,享有盛誉。

Rouge River

A canal located in the province of Jiangsu, China.
The Rouge River lies in the west of Lishui District,
Nanjing. Originating from the estuary of the Yigan
River, the river empties into the Shijiu Lake after
connecting the Qinhuai River, with a total length of
7.5 kilometres and a maximum depth of 35 metres.
The canal construction can be traced back to more
than 600 years ago. The name "Rouge (Yanzhi in
Chinese) River" comes from the "rouge-dyed" cliffs
on both banks, the colour of which was formed with
the oxidation of iron in sedimentary rocks for tens
of millions of years. The excavation of the river was
a large-scale water conservancy project after Zhu
Yuanzhang, the first emperor of the Ming Dynasty
(1368—1644), chose Nanjing as the capital in 1368.
The canal enabled goods around the region of Taihu
Lake to reach Nanjing through the Taihu Lake-
Xuhe River-Rouge River-Qinhuai River route, thus
meeting the demands of various consumer groups
in the capital. The canal construction was presided
over by Li Xin, and it was started in 1393 and completed in 1395, all carried out manually. After the
capital was moved to Beijing in 1421, the Rouge
River continued to play its role as a regional water
conservancy project. Several dredging projects were
carried out in the following centuries. In 1966, the
authorities of Zhenjiang, a city beside Nanjing,
presided over the re-planning of the Rouge River,
including the construction of sluices, bridges and
dredging. The river was officially named Tiansheng
(the Chinese for "natural") Bridge River in 1966,

胭脂河

中国江苏省运河。胭脂河位于南京
市溧水区西部，北起一干河的河
口，连接秦淮河，注入石臼湖，全
长7.5千米，最深处35米，距今已有
600余年的历史。运河由于河道两
岸几千万年的沉积岩石中铁成分
被氧化，如胭脂点染于两岸崖壁，
故而得名胭脂河。明朝开国皇帝朱
元璋1368年定都南京后，开始开凿
胭脂河。这在当时是一项大型水
利工程，可使太湖物资通过太湖—
胥河—胭脂河—秦淮河的漕运水
路直抵南京，满足都城各类消费
群体的需求。运河工程由李新负
责，1393年开凿，1395年竣工，全
部为人工作业。1421年明朝迁都北
京后，该运河作为区域水利工程继
续发挥作用，随后几百年内经历了
多次疏浚。1966年，镇江市政府主
持了胭脂河的重新规划工作，包括
建设套闸、架设桥梁和疏浚河道。
同年，胭脂河正式定名为"天生桥
河"，1978年改称"洪昌河"，后又
恢复原名。1988年，"胭脂河—天
生桥"被列为江苏省文物保护单
位。该地区如今除了发挥基础水
利功能外，也是游客青睐的自然风
景区。

then renamed Hongchang (the Chinese for "prosperous") River in 1978, and later restored to the former one. In 1988, the "Rouge River-Tiansheng Bridge" site was listed as a cultural heritage under the protection of Jiangsu Province. Now, in addition to its basic functions, this place has also become a natural scenic spot favoured by tourists.

Rüdesdorf Waterway

A waterway located in the state of Brandenburg, Germany. The Rüdesdorf Waterway is 11.3 kilometres long with one lock built on it. It runs from the southern end of the Dämeritz Lake to the Stienitz Lake, consisting of several river stretches and lakes in its lower reaches, such as the 10.6-kilometre-long Löcknitz River and the 1.3-kilometre-long Langerhans Canal. The river is designated a Class III waterway. In the reconstruction period after World War II, Rüdersdorf gradually became the largest producer of building materials in East Germany. The Rüdersdorf Waterway was thus designated as the main waterway. With the unification of Germany, it became a federal waterway. The Berlin Waterways and Shipping Office is now responsible for the Rüdesdorf Waterway.

Ruiten-Aa Canal

A canal located in the province of Groningen, the Netherlands. The Ruiten-Aa Canal lies in the east of Groningen, close to the German border. The canal takes its name from the Ruiten-Aa, a local river.

吕德斯多夫航道

德国勃兰登堡州航道。吕德斯多夫航道全长11.3千米，始于代梅里茨湖南端，注入施蒂尼茨湖，航道上建有1座船闸。下游的支流及湖泊也属于该航道，包括10.6千米的勒克尼茨河及1.3千米的朗格汉斯运河。该航道被认定为三级航道。第二次世界大战后的重建期间，吕德斯多夫逐渐成为东德最大的建材生产地，吕德斯多夫航道因而被视为当地主要的航道。德国统一后，吕德斯多夫航道成为联邦航道，现由柏林航道和航运办公室负责管理。

吕滕－阿河运河

荷兰格罗宁根省运河。吕滕－阿河运河位于格罗宁根东部，毗邻德国边境，得名于当地的吕滕－阿河。该运河连接泰尔阿珀尔和费勒

It connects Ter Apel and Veelerveen, where it joins with the B.L. Tijdens Canal and the Mussel-Aa Canal. The exploitation of the marshes and peat bogs brought economic benefits as well as flooding problems to this region. Led by Boelo Luitjen Tijdens, a Dutch politician, the excavation of the canal was started in 1911 to drain flood water out of Westerwolde. When finished in 1920, it was a 51.5-kilometre-long canal punctuated by 8 locks, with a branch to Bourtange. The canal played an important role in the clearing of moors and peat bogs and in the development of the cleared lands. Boats shipped silt and fertilizers from the Dollard Bay to this region, and then sent agricultural products such as potatoes to local factories for further process. Due to World War II, the navigation function of the canal gradually declined and the branch to Bourtange was abandoned. In the 1990s, the main stream and branch of the canal became navigable again as they were rebuilt to boost local tourism. Currently, some parts of the canal are still interrupted, and the local government is considering removing some interruptions to restore its currents. Now its main functions are drainage, recreation, and transportation.

尔芬，在费勒尔芬与蒂登运河和米瑟尔—阿河运河交汇。沼泽和泥炭资源的开发曾为运河区带来经济效益，也使这一区域易受洪水侵袭。为帮助韦斯特沃尔德市排洪泄涝，1911年，在荷兰政治家伯尔罗·路易登·蒂登的带领下，人们开始挖掘吕滕—阿河运河，1920年竣工。运河全长51.5千米，河上建有8座船闸，还有一条通往布尔坦赫城的支线。该运河在清理荒地与泥炭沼泽以及土地开发方面起到了重要作用。通过吕滕—阿河运河，船只将淤泥和肥料从多拉德湾运到该地区，再把土豆等农产品送到当地工厂进行深加工。受第二次世界大战影响，该运河的航运功能逐渐衰退，通往布尔坦赫城的支线也被废弃。20世纪90年代，为促进当地旅游业的发展，政府重修了吕滕—阿河运河的干流和支线，使其恢复通航。目前，该运河的部分河段仍然无法通航，当地政府正在考虑清除障碍以实现全面通航。运河如今主要用于排水引流、休闲娱乐和航运。

Ruitenbrock Canal

吕滕布罗克运河

A canal located between Germany and the Netherlands. See Haren-Ruitenbrock Canal.

欧洲跨国运河，流经德国和荷兰。见哈伦—吕滕布罗克运河。

Ruppin Canal

A canal located in Germany. The Ruppin Canal was constructed in the late 18th century and is still in use today. As a part of the Ruppin Waters, the canal connects the city of Neuruppin with the Havel Canal.

Rutten Canal

A canal located in the province of Flevoland, the Netherlands. The Rutten Canal is 6.3 kilometres long and has a navigable distance of about 5.7 kilometres, passing through Ruteng, Lemer and other towns. There is no lock built on it. In 2017, the canal was dredged, with the removal of 36,500 cubic metres of sediment during two weeks.

鲁平运河

德国运河。鲁平运河修建于18世纪晚期，目前仍可通航。鲁平运河属于鲁平水域，连接新鲁平市和哈弗尔运河。

吕滕运河

荷兰弗莱福兰省运河。吕滕运河全长6.3千米，通航河段长约5.7千米。该运河流经吕滕、莱默等市镇，河上未建船闸。2017年，该运河得到疏浚，两周内共清理出大约36 500立方米的淤积泥沙。

Saar ≈

A canalized cross-border river located in Europe. Formerly known as Saar-Coal Canal. The Saar flows through northeastern France and western Germany. As the longest tributary of the Moselle, it originates from the Vosges on the border of Alsace and Lorraine, and then flows into the Moselle at Konz between Trier and the Luxembourg border. The total length of the Saar is 246 kilometres, with 129 kilometres in France and on the French-German border, and 117 kilometres in Germany, covering a basin area of 7,431 square kilometres. The river has a 71.6-kilometre-long navigable part punctuated by 5 locks. The Saar became more important from the 17th century when a large amount of timber was transported down to the North Sea via the Moselle and the Rhine. Since 1866, it has been linked to the Marne-Rhine Canal via the Saar Canal. The Saar was very important for the coal, iron and steel industries of Saarland. Raw materials and finished products were shipped on it via the Saar-Coal Canal, the Marne-Rhine Canal and the Rhine, to the Ruhr area or the port of Rotterdam. In 1974, the lower course of the river, starting from its mouth, was upgraded for larger ships and the upgradation was completed in 2001. Regular ships transiting the river are the European vessels (length: 85 metres, width: 9.5 metres, draught: 2.5 metres) with a deadweight tonnage of 1,350. The expansion to upper Saarbrücken had been planned before, but it was postponed for political reasons. On the banks of the Saar could be found the Völklingen Iron-

萨尔河

欧洲跨国运河化河流。旧称萨尔—科尔运河。萨尔河流经法国东北部和德国西部,是摩泽尔河最长的支流。萨尔河源于阿尔萨斯大区和洛林大区交界处的孚日山脉,在德国特里尔市和卢森堡边境之间的孔茨市汇入摩泽尔河。萨尔河全长246千米,其中法国境内129千米,德国境内117千米,流域面积7 431平方千米,可通航距离71.6千米,沿线建有5座船闸。17世纪时,大量木材通过摩泽尔河和莱茵河运往北海地区,萨尔河的重要性日渐突显。1866年起,萨尔河经萨尔运河与马恩—莱茵运河相通。萨尔河促进了萨尔兰州的煤炭与钢铁工业发展。原材料和成品先经萨尔河运输至萨尔—科尔运河、马恩—莱茵运河和莱茵河,再运送到德国鲁尔区或鹿特丹港。1974年,为容纳大型船只通行,人们开始扩建始于河口处的下游河段,2001年完工。河上的常见船舶为载重量达1 350吨的欧洲船舶(长85米,宽9.5米,吃水2.5米)。萨尔河至上萨尔布吕肯市的扩建计划因政治原因搁置。河流两岸建有弗尔克林根钢铁厂。该厂1994年被联合国教科文组织列为世界文化遗产,其所在地至今仍是欧洲最重要的工业和文化区之

works, and it was declared by UNESCO as a World Heritage Site in 1994. By now the place is still one of the most important industrial and cultural areas in Europe. The lower Saar crosses through the Rhineland-Palatinate, which is Germany's leading producer of wine in terms of grape cultivation and wine export.

一。萨尔河下游穿过莱茵兰–普法尔茨州，该州是葡萄酒产地，其葡萄种植产业和葡萄酒出口业务在德国一直处于领先地位。

Saar-Coal Canal

A cross-border canal located in Europe. See Saar.

萨尔–科尔运河

欧洲跨国运河。见萨尔河。

Sabine-Neches Waterway≈

A canalized cross-border waterway located in the United States. The Sabine-Neches Waterway flows in the states of Louisiana and Texas and it is about 127 kilometres long. It is a water system consisting of parts of the Sabine River, the Sabine Lake, the Neches River, and the Taylor Bayou. The canal is the third busiest waterway in terms of cargo tonnage in the United States. According to the American Association of Port Authorities, it is the largest waterway for the transportation of bulk liquid cargo, ranking as the top U.S. crude-oil importer, and projected to be the top U.S. liquified natural gas exporter. The Port of Beaumont, located at the northern end of the waterway, and the Port Arthur, at the southern end, are among the top 20 ports in the United States, according to the 2013 U.S. Port Ranking. A deepening project costing $1.1 billion has been implemented since 2019 to improve the navigability of the waterway.

萨宾–内奇斯航道

美国跨境运河化航道。萨宾—内奇斯航道流经路易斯安那州和得克萨斯州，全长127千米，由萨宾河、萨宾湖、内奇斯河和泰勒湖组成。就货运吨位而言，萨宾—内奇斯航道是美国最繁忙的第三大航道。根据美国港口管理局协会的统计数据，该航道是保障美国散装液体货物运输的最大航道，其进口原油的总运载量位居全美第一；出口液化天然气的运载量预计也将成为全美第一。根据2013年美国港口排行数据，萨宾—内奇斯航道北端的博蒙特港和南端的亚瑟港均在美国20个主要港口之列。为了提升其航运能力，2019年起人们开始实施航道加深工程，总投入11亿美元。

Sacramento River Deep Water Ship Channel⁼

A canalized waterway located in the state of California, the United States. The Sacramento River Deep Water Ship Channel connects the Port of Sacramento and the Sacramento River, and flows into the San Francisco Bay. It is 69 kilometres long, 9 metres deep and 61 metres wide. The channel consists of a section of the Sacramento River and a 52-kilometre-long navigation channel, of which 45 kilometres is man-made. The construction of the waterway began in 1949 by the United States Army Corps of Engineers and was completed in 1963. The Sacramento River Deep Water Ship Channel was mainly used for the transport of agricultural products, including grain, rice and lumber. Restricted by the configuration of the channel, the cargo ships could not be fully loaded for safety's sake in the first years. Then the canal went through a round of enlargement in width and depth to reduce the cost of transportation. The economic benefits were increased as well, with an enhanced navigation safety. The Sacramento River Deep Water Ship Channel needs regular dredging to ensure adequate depth for navigation. The dredging leads to the increase in salinity, which not only affects the quality of drinking water, but also does harm to local fisheries. This also poses a threat to the habitats of some rare and endangered species.

萨克拉门托河深水航道

美国加利福尼亚州运河化航道。萨克拉门托河深水航道连接萨克拉门托港口和萨克拉门托河，最终汇入旧金山湾。该航道全长69千米，深9米，宽61米，由两部分组成：一是萨克拉门托河部分河段，二是长52千米的航道，其中包含45千米长的人工航道。萨克拉门托河深水航道由美国陆军工程兵团负责修建，1949年开凿，1963年完工。该航道主要用于运输谷物、稻米等农产品和木材。运营初期，受制于航道构造，同时出于安全考虑，船只不能满载。之后，人们对航道进行了拓宽和加深改造，增强了通航安全性，降低了货运成本，经济效益也随之提高。为保证航道深度，人们必须定期疏浚航道，但疏浚工程也会增加河水含盐量，这不仅影响饮用水质量，还会危害当地渔业发展，对一些稀有和濒危物种的栖息环境也会构成威胁。

Sacrow-Paretz Canal

An inland canal located in the state of Brandenburg, northeastern Germany. The Sacrow-Paretz Canal is 12.5 kilometres long, of which 7.5 kilometres is an artificial channel, while the rest comprises several natural lakes. Four bridges are built across the canal. It provides a shortcut for ships navigating River Havel, and links the Jungfern Lake with Paretz. The Sacrow-Paretz Canal was built in 1874 and opened in 1876. The main reasons of the construction of the canal were threefold: to bypass some bridges in Potsdam and Havel that are difficult for navigation, to shorten the route on the waterway by 13.5 kilometres, and to avoid travelling through the then hazardous areas of the Schwielow Lake. Since it was completed, the canal has undergone two rounds of expansion: from 1888 and 1890, and in the 1920s. In 2008, a new expansion plan was put forward but was severely protested against by the local government due to unforeseeable ecological consequences. It was in 2010 that a settlement was reached, stating that the canal can be deepened, the canal bottom smoothed, but not widened. Now protection zones for beavers and sand lizards have been established.

Saimaa Canal

A cross-border canal located in Europe. The Saimaa Canal crosses Finland and Russia, linking Lake Saimaa with the Vyborg Bay near the Gulf of Finland. Running from Lappeenranta of Finland to

萨克罗－帕雷茨运河

德国东北部勃兰登堡州内陆运河。萨克罗—帕雷茨运河长12.5千米，其中7.5千米为人工运河，其余5千米由几个自然湖泊组成。运河沿线建有4座桥梁，连接永芬湖和帕雷茨区，为哈弗尔河上的航船提供了捷径。萨克罗—帕雷茨运河于1874年开凿，1876年通航。其修建目的主要有三个：其一，绕过波茨坦市与哈弗尔河上妨碍航运的桥梁；其二，缩短航程13.5千米；其三，避开施维洛湖上的危险航段。运河建成后先后经历两次大规模扩建，一次是在1888—1890年间，另一次是在20世纪20年代。2008年，新的运河扩建项目遭到当地政府反对，人们认为运河扩建将对生态环境造成无法预估的不利影响。2010年最终达成的扩建协议规定，仅能加深运河，也可改造运河底部，使之平整，但不允许拓宽。如今，萨克罗—帕雷茨运河流经区域设有河狸栖息地和沙蜥蜴保护区。

塞马运河

欧洲跨国运河。塞马运河流经芬兰和俄罗斯两个国家，从芬兰拉彭兰塔市流向俄罗斯维堡市，连接塞马湖和芬兰湾附近的维堡

Vyborg of Russia, the Saimaa Canal is 42.9 kilometres in length, with 23.3 kilometres in Finland and the other 19.6 kilometres in Russia. The canal measures 34 metres wide in minimum and 55 metres in maximum. Equipped with 8 locks, it connects 4 lakes and crosses 14 bridges along the way. The construction of the Saimaa Canal spanned 11 years from 1845 to 1856, and it was officially put into use in September 1856. In 1940, the city of Vyborg and the Karelian Isthmus were ceded to the Soviet Union according to the Moscow Peace Treaty. The Saimaa Canal was split in half, and all traffic was forced to halt. From 1963 to 1968, the canal went through an overhaul and was widened. According to an agreement made in 1963, the Soviet Union would lease the Soviet section of the canal area and the Maly Vysotsky Island to Finland for 50 years. In 2010, in replacement of the former treaty, Finland and Russia signed a new Saimaa Canal lease treaty, which renewed the lease of the Russian section of the canal for another 50 years starting from 2013.

湾。塞马运河全长42.9千米，其中23.3千米在芬兰境内，其余19.6千米在俄罗斯境内，最窄处34米，最宽处55米。该运河连通4个湖泊，建有8座船闸和14座桥梁。运河于1845年开凿，历时11年，1856年9月正式通航。1940年，芬兰和苏联签订了《莫斯科和平协定》，将维堡市以及卡累利阿地峡割让给苏联，塞马运河被分割成两部分，交通往来被迫中断。1963—1968年间，人们对塞马运河进行全面改造，河道被拓宽。1963年，苏联同意将小维索茨基岛及塞马运河的苏联河段使用权租借给芬兰，为期50年。2010年，俄罗斯与芬兰重新签订塞马运河租借协议，使之取代1963年的旧协议。根据新协议，俄罗斯将其所有的塞马运河河段使用权续租给芬兰，自2013年开始，为期50年。

Saint Lawrence Seaway

圣劳伦斯海道

A cross-border waterway located in North America. The Saint Lawrence Seaway is comprised of a series of canals, channels and locks of Canada and the United States. It links the Great Lakes to the Atlantic Ocean, Lake Superior lying at its west end. The seaway is named after the Saint Lawrence River, which runs from Lake Ontario to the Atlantic Ocean. It is 3,700 kilometres in length, including the whole Welland Canal. The upstream stretch of

北美洲跨国航道。圣劳伦斯海道流经加拿大和美国，由一系列运河、航道和船闸构成，贯通大西洋和北美五大湖，其最西端延伸至苏必利尔湖。包括韦兰运河在内，圣劳伦斯海道全长3 700千米，因连通安大略湖和大西洋的圣劳伦斯河而得名。该海道上游部分包括多条航道，建有数座船闸，避开了

the seaway includes several channels, a number of locks along the Saint Lawrence River to avoid the rapids and dams along the way. Among the 7 locks, five are located on the Welland Canal in Canada and the other two in the United States. Though the plan was put forward in the 1890s, the construction of the cross-national waterway along the Saint Lawrence River was started and finished several decades later due to the disagreement of both sides on how to connect the canals. In 1959, large ocean vessels began to steam to the centre of North America through this seaway. It is also important for the international trade in the United States and Canada, handling 40 to 50 million tonnes of cargo annually, and offering outdoor recreational activites such as scuba diving, fishing, and boating.

沿途多处急流与堤坝。河上的7座船闸中，有5座建在加拿大境内的韦兰运河上，2座在美国境内。早在19世纪90年代，就有人提出在圣劳伦斯河沿岸修建跨国航道，但因美国和加拿大无法就如何连通两国运河这一问题达成共识，航道直至几十年后才得以建成开通。1959年起，大型海运船只可通过该海道驶向北美洲中心地区。圣劳伦斯海道对美国和加拿大的国际贸易起到重要保障作用，每年运送4 000万—5 000万吨货物。海道上的休闲娱乐活动丰富，包括潜水、钓鱼和划船等。

Saint-Pierre Canal

圣皮埃尔运河

A canal located in the centre of Toulouse, Haute-Garonne, France. See Brienne Canal.

法国上加龙省图卢兹市中心运河。见布里耶纳运河。

Saint Roque's Canal

圣罗克运河

A canal located in Portugal. As a route of the Aveiro Canals, the Saint Roque's Canal is located at the northern limit of the city of Aveiro, Portugal. It runs from the Pyramid Canal to the northeast limit of the parish of Glória and Vera Cruz. With a completely rectilinear course, it has 4 bridges. Along its southern bank there used to be several salt warehouses, many of which have now been converted into restaurants, shops and housing. The northern

葡萄牙运河。圣罗克运河位于葡萄牙阿威罗市北部边界，属于阿威罗运河网。该运河始于金字塔运河，流至格罗利亚和韦拉克鲁斯教区的东北边界。圣罗克运河的河道呈直线型，河上建有4座桥。运河南岸曾有几座盐仓，大多已被改造成餐馆、商店和住房，北岸近期也进行了改造，奥运赛艇公园就建在北岸。

bank has also been recently revamped and the Olympic Rowers' Park is built along this route.

Salmon Bay Waterway

A canal located in the Salmon Bay, Seattle, the United States. See Lake Washington Ship Canal.

Sambre≈

A canalized cross-border river located in Europe. As a left tributary of the Meuse, the Sambre extends 193 kilometres with a drainage area of around 2,740 square kilometres. Originating from the Aisne department in France, the river runs through an industrial district of historical importance, the Franco-Belgian coal basin, and flows into the Meuse at Namur in Belgium. Its division in Belgium is located at the western end of the industrial valley. A part of the river has been canalized, with a navigable length of 54.2 kilometres and 9 locks. It is connected with the Oise by the Sambre-Oise Canal.

Sambre-Oise Canal

A canal located in northern France. The Sambre-Oise Canal connects the river Sambre (Meuse basin) and the Oise (Seine basin). Built with 38 locks, it is 71 kilometres long. It is only accessible to small vessels with a maximum length of 38.5 metres. The canalized river Sambre, together with the Sambre-Oise Canal, forms what used to be one

萨蒙湾航道

美国西雅图萨蒙湾运河。见华盛顿湖通海运河。

桑布尔河

欧洲跨国运河化河流。桑布尔河是默兹河左岸支流，全长193千米，流域面积2 740平方千米。桑布尔河始于法国埃纳省，流经昔日重要的工业区弗朗科—比利时煤田，在比利时的那慕尔市汇入默兹河。在比利时境内的河段位于河谷工业带的西端。桑布尔河部分河段现已经过运河化改造，可通航长度为54.2千米，沿线建有9座船闸。桑布尔河通过桑布尔—瓦兹运河与瓦兹河相通。

桑布尔-瓦兹运河

法国北部运河。桑布尔—瓦兹运河连通默兹河流域的桑布尔河与塞纳河流域的瓦兹河，全长71千米，河上建有38座船闸。该运河仅容纳小型船只通行，船只长度不超过38.5米。运河化的桑布尔河与桑布尔—瓦兹运河一度成为由

of the most popular routes entering France from Belgium and the Netherlands. It had to be closed in 2006 when two aqueducts were found to be in danger of failing. Currently, the canal is not navigable. It is expected to be reopened in 2021. By then, people can navigate their way along this canal into France, starting from Charleroi in the southern part of Belgium, and enjoy attractive views alongside.

比利时和荷兰进入法国的热门线路之一。2006年，因发现两座渡槽有损毁迹象，运河被迫关闭。目前，桑布尔—瓦兹运河已停航，计划在2021年复航。届时，人们可以通过此运河从比利时南部城市沙勒罗瓦进入法国，并可欣赏沿途美景。

San Antonio Canal

圣安东尼奥运河

A canal located in Texas, the United States. The San Antonio Canal was initially opened for drainage and flood control in the 1930s. In recent years the rapid development of the lands along the canal has made the city of San Antonio one of the top tourist destinations in the country.

美国得克萨斯州运河。圣安东尼奥运河于20世纪30年代开通，起初用于排水和防洪。近年来，运河沿线区域发展迅速，圣安东尼奥市已成为全美最热门的旅游目的地之一。

Sandy and Beaver Canal

桑迪—比弗运河

A canal located in the northeastern United States. Stretching from Ohio to Pennsylvania, the Sandy and Beaver Canal is 117 kilometres long with 90 locks. In 1828, the project of constructing the canal was proposed to facilitate the commerce between the Ohio and Erie Canal and the Ohio River. In 1834, the construction began. Due to the hilly terrain, the cost was significant. In 1837, the project faced a financial shortage, and the construction was suspended for nearly 7 years. In 1848, the construction was finally completed. Persistent problems emerged around the middle section of the canal during and after the construction. The middle sec-

美国东北部运河。桑迪—比弗运河连接俄亥俄州与宾夕法尼亚州，全长117千米，沿线建有90座船闸。1828年，有人提出运河修建计划，旨在促进俄亥俄—伊利运河与俄亥俄河之间的贸易运输。1834年，运河开凿。由于地处丘陵，工程成本巨大。1837年，因项目资金短缺，工程搁置近7年，最终于1848年完工。桑迪—比弗运河中段自修建之初就存在许多问题，一直未得到妥善处理，最终失修。1852年，俄亥俄州冷流水库大坝溃决，

tion gradually fell into disrepair. In 1852, the failure of the Cold Run Reservoir Dam in Ohio caused damage to the struture of the canal. In the same year, the Cleveland and Pittsburgh Railroad was completed. The Sandy and Beaver Canal ceased to be important and was gradually abandoned.

运河多处设施遭到损毁。同年，克利夫兰-匹兹堡铁路建成，这条运河的航运价值大大削弱，后渐遭弃用。

San Joaquin River

A canalized river located in central California, the United States. Also known as Stockton Deep Water Ship Channel. With a length of 589 kilometres, the San Joaquin River starts from the Sierra Nevada and runs through the San Joaquin Valley, emptying into the Suisun Bay. In the 20th century, in order to meet the increasing demands for electricity and flood control, a great number of dams were built on the San Joaquin River. In 1926, a navigation project was proposed to start around Stockton, a seaport city, including cutting off meanders as well as widening and deepening the waterway. The project began in 1928, and the San Joaquin River was deepened to 11 metres and shortened by 6.4 kilometres. Today, the navigational waterway is capable of handling ships loaded with 54,000 tons of goods. However, the navigation project, as well as the pollution from the surrounding cities and harbours, has negative effects on the habitat of local fishes. Nowadays, a series of plans are underway to increase flows of the river, restore habitats of wildlife and improve the water quality.

圣华金河

美国加利福尼亚州中部运河化河流。亦称斯托克顿深水通海航道。圣华金河全长589千米，始于内华达山脉，流经圣华金谷，汇入休松湾。20世纪时，为满足不断增长的供电和防洪需求，人们在圣华金河上修筑了多座大坝。1926年，人们提出一项航运计划，在海港城市斯托克顿附近截断曲流、加深并拓宽河道。1928年项目开工，圣华金河河道加深至11米，长度缩短6.4千米。如今，这条航道可容载货量达5.4万吨的船只通行。但这一工程建设以及来自附近城市、港湾的污染物也给当地鱼群的栖息环境造成了破坏。为了增加河水流量、恢复野生动物栖息环境并改善水质，一系列整改计划正在稳步推进中。

Sankey Canal

A canal located in England, the United Kingdom. The Sankey Canal is originally entirely within Lancashire, and now in Cheshire and Merseyside, northwest of England. It links the St. Helens with River Mersey, stretching 27.4 kilometres in total, and is considered as the first modern English canal, or the first canal of the industrial age. The construction of the canal was authorized by the parliament in 1755 and it was opened for traffic in 1757. The canal soon became busy as it witnessed a massive coal traffic heading to Liverpool. In 1845 the Sankey Canal merged with the St. Helens Railway to form the St. Helens Canal and Railway Company. Although it gradually fell into disuse between 1931 and 1963, the restoration has been discussed frequently since the establishment of the Sankey Canal Restoration Society in 1985.

桑基运河

英国英格兰运河。桑基运河全段曾位于兰开夏郡境内，现流经英格兰西北部的柴郡和默西赛德郡。桑基运河连通圣海伦斯河与默西河，全长27.4千米，被视为英格兰第一条现代化运河或工业时代的第一条运河。1755年，议会授权开凿桑基运河，1757年，运河通航。运河业务繁忙，大量煤炭经此航道运往利物浦。1845年，桑基运河公司与圣海伦斯铁路公司合并，成立了圣海伦斯运河铁路公司。1931—1963年间，该运河渐遭废弃，但自1985年桑基运河修复协会成立以来，人们已就该运河的复建工作进行了多次商讨。

Santee Canal

An abandoned canal located in the southeastern United States. The Santee Canal is one of the earliest canals in the United States. It was constructed to provide a direct waterway to connect Charleston and Columbia. The construction began in 1793 and the canal was opened in 1800. It was 35 kilometres long and 11 metres wide at the water's surface and 6.1 metres wide at the bottom. Its depth was 1.2 metres. It was not used any longer after 1865 because of its poor construction and droughts.

桑蒂运河

美国东南部废弃运河。桑蒂运河是美国最早修建的运河之一。修建该运河是为了在南卡罗来纳州的查尔斯顿市和哥伦比亚市之间提供一条直通航道。运河于1793年开凿，1800年通航。运河当时全长35千米，河面宽11米，河底宽6.1米，深1.2米。因修建工程质量欠佳和受旱灾影响，1865年以后运河便被弃用。

Saône-Marne Canal

A canal located in northeastern France. See Champagne-Burgundy Canal.

索恩－马恩运河

法国东北部运河。见香槟－勃艮第运河。

Saône-Moselle Canal

A planned cross-border canal system located in Europe. The Saône-Moselle Canal, which is scheduled to be completed by 2050, is a key element of the European Multimodal Corridor that is intended to improve the accessibility to Mediterranean ports from the Grand East Region. Since the Rhine-Rhône Canal was abandoned in 1998, this project is of great importance to fill up the missing link between the basins of the Rhône, the Moselle and the Rhine. The Saône-Moselle Project would function as a link to make the river network in eastern France a complete one. Currently, this project is still under discussion and the feasibility study has been conducted.

索恩－摩泽尔运河

欧洲拟建跨国运河网。索恩－摩泽尔运河是欧洲多模式联运走廊项目的重点工程，计划于2050年建成。该运河网建成后，从法国东部大区前往地中海沿岸海港的交通将更加便利。莱茵－罗讷运河于1998年停航后，重建连接罗讷河流域、摩泽尔河流域和莱茵河流域之间的交通网络意义重大。索恩－摩泽尔运河网项目可将法国东部的内河运输线路串联为水运网。目前，该项目仍在探讨阶段，并已开展可行性论证。

Saône River ≈

A canalized river located in eastern France. The Saône River is a right tributary of the Rhône, running from Vioménil in the Vosges department to the Rhône in Lyon. It is 480 kilometres long with a drainage area of 29,950 square kilometres. Together with the Rhône, the Saône River forms the inland waterway that connects the north of France with the Mediterranean Sea. The navigable section starts from Corre to the Rhône. Stretching

索恩河

法国东部运河化河流。索恩河是罗讷河的右岸支流，始于孚日省的维奥默尼市，在里昂市汇入罗讷河。该运河全长480千米，流域面积共计29 950平方千米。索恩河和罗讷河共同构成连接法国北部和地中海的内陆航道。科尔至罗纳河的河段可通航，几乎完全运河化，长度超375千米，并建有30座

over 375 kilometres, this part is almost completely canalized, with 30 locks along its course. The river is linked with a number of canals, including the Central Canal, the Burgundy Canal, the East Canal and the Rhône-Rhine Canal. Its northern section, from Corre to St-Symphorien, is named the Small Saône, and the southern section, the Lower Saône. The Small Saône flows through the Franche-Comté region. The navigation of this section has been improved through the excavation of 20 canals and the construction of 2 tunnels. The Lower Saône is wide and slow, crossing flat plains of central France with little elevation change. The entire river retains its importance in the national waterway systems, and may be upgraded to form the high-capacity Saône-Moselle Waterway in the future.

船闸。索恩河与多条运河连通，如中部运河，勃艮第运河，东方运河与罗讷—莱茵运河等。索恩河北部从科尔市到圣桑福里安村的河段被称为小索恩河，南部河段被称为索恩河下游河段。小索恩河流经弗朗什—孔泰大区，人们在此处修建了20条运河和2条隧道，改善了这一河段的通航条件。索恩河下游河段水面宽阔，水流较缓，流经法国中部平原地带，无明显水位落差。如今，整个索恩河在法国航运系统中仍有重要影响，未来可能与摩泽尔河相通，升级为通航能力更强的航道。

Sarthe

萨尔特河

A canalized river located in western France. The Sarthe starts from the town Soligny-la-Trappe and ends at the Maine. The navigable part of the river is about 132 kilometres from a weir situated in the town Le Mans to its confluence with the Mayenne upstream. The first 113 kilometres of the river, down to the lock at Cheffes, has been canalized. The remaining section of the Sarthe is free-flowing, but during the dry summer periods, it can only offer limited water. A new weir and a lock on the Maine downstream in Angers were constructed to solve the problem. The Sarthe, Oudon and Mayenne form the Anjou River system, a cruising network. The town Le Mans actively promoted canalizing rivers in the

法国西部运河化河流。萨尔特河始于法国索利尼拉特拉普小镇，汇入曼恩河。该运河可通航河段长约132千米，始于勒芒镇的堰坝，止于该河与马耶讷河上游的交汇处。萨尔特河上游至谢弗市船闸的河段长113千米，已经过运河化改造。萨尔特河其余河段未建闸坝，但在夏季枯水期水量有限。为解决夏季枯水问题，人们在昂热市的曼恩河下游新建了堰坝和船闸。萨尔特河与乌东河、马耶讷河一同构成了安茹河游船航道网。18世纪初，勒芒镇积极推动河流运河

early 18th century and works were commissioned to a private company via contract in 1741. The project was shelved, and was revived in the mid-19th century. After World War II, the navigation of the Sarthe ceased for decades, and was revived from the 1970s.

化改造，1741年将工程承包给一家私人公司。项目随后被搁置，19世纪中叶重新启动。第二次世界大战后，萨尔特河停航数十年，20世纪70年代恢复通航。

Sault St. Marie Canal

苏圣玛丽运河

A canal located in Ontario, Canada. The Sault St. Marie Canal is about 1.6 kilometres long. It is a part of the shipping route from the Atlantic Ocean to Lake Superior. It has a lock to bypass the rapids on the St. Mary's River. The construction of the canal began in 1798. It suffered destruction during the War of 1812. As a part of the all-Canadian navigational chain, the reconstruction of the canal and its lock was completed in 1895. It was opened in the same year. The lock was 274 metres long and 18 metres wide. At that time its lock was the largest and the first electrically operated one in the world. Most of the original machines used to operate the lock remain in place. There are several heritage buildings on the site: the administration building, the superintendent's residence, the canal men's shelter, the powerhouse and the blacksmith shop, all of which were constructed from red sandstone dug up during the canal's construction. In 1987, the Sault St. Marie Canal was designated one of the National Historic Sites of Canada.

加拿大安大略省运河。苏圣玛丽运河长约1.6千米，是大西洋与苏必利尔湖之间航道的一段。运河之上建有1座船闸，以引导船只避开圣玛丽河的急流。苏圣玛丽运河于1798年开凿，1812年美英战争期间遭到破坏。1895年，苏圣玛丽运河及其船闸作为加拿大国家运河网的组成部分续建完成，同年通航。所建船闸长274米，宽18米，是当时世界上规模最大的首座电动船闸。用于操作船闸的大部分机器至今仍在。运河沿线有多处历史建筑遗迹，包括行政大楼、运河负责人住所、运河工人住所、发电厂和锻铁厂，这些建筑由开凿运河时挖出的红砂岩建成。1987年，苏圣玛丽运河被列为加拿大国家历史遗址。

Savannah-Ogeechee Barge Canal

萨凡纳－奥吉奇驳船运河

A canal located in Georgia, the United States. The

美国佐治亚州运河。萨凡纳－奥

Savannah-Ogeechee Barge Canal starts from the Savannah River to the Ogeechee River and has a length of 26.5 kilometres. The canal, comprised of 6 locks, begins from the tidal lock at the Savannah River, winds through 4 lift locks and ends at another tidal lock at the Ogeechee River. Three locks originally built with timber were later replaced by brick locks with stone. The Savannah-Ogeechee Barge Canal passes through Savannah's 19th Century industrial corridor, timber tracks, and a river swamp and sand hill environment where several unique species of flora and fauna inhabit. Commenced in 1824 and completed in 1830, the Savannah-Ogeechee Barge Canal is a part of the extensive network of former southern canals. During the first few years of operation, the canal suffered from diverse issues including the decay of wooden locks and repeated reinforcement of embankments. In 1836, a new company took over the construction of the Savannah-Ogeechee Barge Canal and widened and improved the structures within the canal. Between the 1840s and the 1860s, the canal was used for the transportation of cotton, rice, bricks, and natural fertilizer, as the canal began to prosper as a major part of the South Georgia economy. A confluence of several factors such as wars and diseases led to the decline of the canal. In the early 1890s, it was closed as the centre of Georgia Railroad served transportation needs. In 1997, the Savannah-Ogeechee Barge Canal was inscribed in the National Register of Historic Places. A century after the canal ceased commercial operations, the locals have started to restore the waterway as well as the surrounding natural environment.

吉奇驳船运河连通萨凡纳河与奥吉奇河,全长26.5千米,河上建有6座船闸。该运河始于萨凡纳河的潮汐船闸,流经4个提升式船闸,流至奥吉奇河的潮汐船闸。3个木制船闸后改为砖石结构。萨凡纳—奥吉奇驳船运河流经萨凡纳的19世纪工业走廊、木材运输线路以及作为几种特有动植物栖息的河流沼泽和沙丘地域。萨凡纳—奥吉奇驳船运河于1824年开凿,1830年完工,是早期南部运河网的一部分。该运河在运营初期遭遇了各种问题,包括木制船闸腐烂和堤坝的反复加固。1836年,一家新公司接管萨凡纳—奥吉奇运河修建项目,拓宽了运河,并改善运河的内部结构。19世纪40—60年代,该运河逐步成为推动佐治亚州南部经济发展的一个重要动力,是棉花、大米、砖块和天然肥料运输的主要通道。因受战争和疫情等因素的影响,萨凡纳—奥吉奇运河逐步走向衰落。19世纪90年代初,因佐治亚铁路中心满足了该地区的运输需求,该运河随之停航。1997年,萨凡纳—奥吉奇驳船运河被列入美国国家历史遗迹名录。在该运河停止商业航运一个世纪后,当地着手修复其航道及周围的自然环境。

Schagen-Kolhorn Canal

An inland canal located in the province of North Holland, the Netherlands. With a length of 7.1 kilometres, the Schagen-Kolhorn Canal connects Schagen and Kolhorn. Its construction began in 1933 and was finished in 1936. Along the route, there are 8 bridges and 1 lock, one of which is a railway bridge.

斯哈亨-科尔霍恩运河

荷兰北荷兰省内陆运河。斯哈亨—科尔霍恩运河全长7.1千米，连接斯哈亨和科尔霍恩。该运河于1933年开凿，1936年竣工，建有1座船闸和8座桥梁，其中1座为铁路桥。

Schelde≈

A canalized river located in Europe. See Escaut.

斯海尔德河

欧洲运河化河流。见埃斯科河。

Schelde-Rhine Canal

A cross-border canal located in Europe. The Schelde–Rhine Canal starts at Antwerp, Belgium and ends at Volkerak, the Netherlands, connecting the Schelde River and the Rhine River. The canal is about 35 kilometres long with 1 lock, 4 bridges and 2 dams. In the 1920s, the plan to construct this canal was proposed by the Belgian government in order to make Antwerp more easily accessible to the Rhine trade. The plan had undergone a few rounds of discussion and modification before being carried out in 1963. The canal was opened in 1975.

斯海尔德-莱茵运河

欧洲跨国运河。斯海尔德—莱茵运河始于比利时的安特卫普，止于荷兰的沃尔克拉克，连通斯海尔德河与莱茵河。该运河全长约35千米，建有1座船闸，4座桥梁以及2座大坝。20世纪20年代，为促进安特卫普与莱茵河流域的贸易往来，比利时政府提出运河修建计划，后几经讨论与调整，于1963年动工开凿。1975年，斯海尔德—莱茵运河正式通航。

Schermer Ring Canal

A canal located in the province of North Holland, the Netherlands. The Schermer Ring Canal has a length of 5.85 kilometres. It is near Schermerhorn, and has an elevation of —3 metres.

斯海默环形运河

荷兰北荷兰省运河。斯海默环形运河全长5.85千米，毗邻斯海默霍恩，水位低于海平面3米。

Schie Canal

A canal located in the province of South Holland, the Netherlands. The Schie Canal consists of 4 waterways, namely, the Delft Schie, the Delfshaven Schie, the Rotterdam Schie and the Schiedam Schie. The canal is 14 kilometres long from Delft to the mouth at Delfshaven. It used to be a swampy creek flowing into the former Merwede at the current town of Overschie. The cities of Delft, Rotterdam, and Schiedam rivaled for toll rights in medieval times, which led to the construction of the four streams. Currently, the Delfshaven Schie is the main shipping passage between the Delft Schie and New Maas, while the Rotterdam Schie and the Schiedam Schie are seldom used for navigating.

Schildgroeve and Damster

An inland canal located in the province of Groningen, the Netherlands. See Groeve Canal.

Schipdonk Canal

A canal located in the provinces of East Flanders and West Flanders, Belgium. With a length of 56 kilometres, the Schipdonk Canal runs northward from Deinze to meet the North Sea near Heist. The construction began in 1846 and was completed in 1860. The Schipdonk Canal, together with the Leopold Canal, is one of the first fundamental projects

斯希运河

荷兰南荷兰省运河。斯希运河由4条航道组成，即斯希运河代尔夫特段、斯希运河代尔夫哈芬段、斯希运河鹿特丹段以及斯希运河斯希丹段，全长14千米，始于代尔夫特市，止于代尔夫哈芬镇河口。斯希运河最初是一条沼泽溪流，在奥佛斯希小镇附近汇入旧梅尔韦德河。中世纪时，因代尔夫特市、鹿特丹港市和斯希丹市竞争通行费征收权，4条航道得以修建。如今，斯希运河的代尔夫哈芬段是连通斯希运河的代尔夫特段和新马斯河的主要航道，而斯希运河鹿特丹段和斯希运河斯希丹段这两段运河已基本停航。

斯希尔德赫鲁夫－达姆斯特运河

荷兰格罗宁根省内陆运河。见赫鲁夫运河。

斯希普顿克运河

比利时东佛兰德省和西佛兰德省跨境运河。斯希普顿克运河全长56千米，始于丹泽市，向北流至海斯特，在其附近注入北海。该运河于1846年开凿，1860年竣工，与利奥波德运河同属比利时独立后的首批重大基础设施工程。该运河

of the newly independent Belgium. The canal prevented Ghent from being attacked by the periodic flooding. The canal has another name, the Stinker, because of the pollution brought by the development of the textile industry in the mid-19th century. In contrast, the Leopold Canal is sometimes called the Blinker, for its clean water. At present, cycle paths have been built alongside the banks of the Schipdonk Canal. It has become a place for recreational boat trips.

保护根特免受周期性洪水侵扰。后因19世纪中叶纺织业发展造成污染，斯希普顿克运河也被称为"臭河"。相反，利奥波德运河则因其河水清澈干净有时被称为"净河"。如今，斯希普顿克运河沿岸建有自行车道，成为泛舟休闲胜地。

Schipsloot

史基浦斯运河

A canal located in the province of Friesland, the Netherlands. See Burum Canal.

荷兰弗里斯兰省运河。见布鲁默运河。

Scholtens Canal

舒尔腾斯运河

A canal located in the province of Drenthe, the Netherlands. Also called Hoofdwijk. The Scholtens Canal is named after Jan Evert Scholten, son of the founder of the Groningen Potato Flour Group. It is 6 kilometres long, connecting the Hoogeveen Extension Canal with the Stads Canal. It was first opened in 1907 and closed in 1969. Nowadays, the Scholtens Canal is used exclusively for drainage.

荷兰德伦特省运河。亦称霍夫维克运河。舒尔腾斯运河以格罗宁根马铃薯粉集团创始人之子扬·埃弗特·舒尔腾的姓氏命名。舒尔腾斯运河全长6千米，连通霍赫芬扩建运河与斯塔茨运河。运河1907年首次通航，1969年停航。如今，舒尔腾斯运河仅用于排水。

Scholtens Extension Canal

舒尔腾斯扩建运河

A canal located in southern Netherlands. The Scholtens Extension Canal, together with the Willems Canal, the Scholtens Canal and the Runde, connects the Hoogeveen Extension Canal with the Stads Canal.

荷兰南部运河。舒尔腾斯扩建运河与威廉斯运河、舒尔腾斯运河和伦德河形成一个运河网，将霍赫芬什运河与斯塔茨运河相连通。

Schöninghsdorf-Hoogeveen Canal

A cross-border canal located in Europe. The Schöninghsdorf-Hoogeveen Canal connects the province of Drenthe in the Netherlands with the state of Lower Saxony in Germany. The canal is around 50 kilometres in length. It runs from Schöninghsdorf and flows into the Meppel River at Meppel. Originally, the Schöninghsdorf-Hoogeveen Canal was suitable for ships with a load capacity of up to 200 tons. Today it is only used for drainage.

舍宁斯多夫-霍赫芬运河

欧洲跨国运河。舍宁斯多夫—霍赫芬运河连接荷兰德伦特省和德国下萨克森州。该运河全长约50千米，始于舍宁斯多夫，在梅珀尔市汇入梅珀尔河。舍宁斯多夫—霍赫芬运河最初可容负载能力达200吨的船只通行。如今，这条运河只用于排水。

Schulz Canal

A canal located in the state of Queensland, Australia. The Schulz Canal was named after William Schulz, an alderman on the Toombul Shire council. It runs from Kedron, a northern suburb of Brisbane, to Moreton Bay on the eastern coast of Australia. It was built in the early 20th century to mitigate floods.

舒尔茨运河

澳大利亚昆士兰州运河。舒尔茨运河因图姆布尔郡高级市政官威廉·舒尔茨而得名。运河始于布里斯班北郊的凯德伦，止于澳大利亚东海岸的莫顿湾。舒尔茨运河于20世纪初开凿，旨在减轻洪涝灾害。

Schuylkill Canal

A canal located in the state of Pennsylvania, the United States. Also called Schuylkill Navigation. The Schuylkill Canal is 140 kilometres in length with 44 locks. Originally, this canal was 174 kilometres in length with 72 locks. In the early 19th century, it was built as a commercial waterway for cheap and efficient transportation. In 1791, the Schuylkill and Susquehanna Navigation Company was founded to improve the waterway. The canal

斯库尔基尔运河

美国宾夕法尼亚州运河。亦称斯库尔基尔航道。斯库尔基尔运河现全长140千米，沿线建有44座船闸，运河最初全长174千米，建有72座船闸。这条运河是19世纪早期建成的商业航道，运费低而效率高。1791年，斯库尔基尔和萨斯奎汉纳航运公司于宾夕法尼亚州创立，以改善斯库尔基尔运河的通

made a substantial contribution to the industrial growth along the river. In the 1860s, the railroads dominated the transportation system in North America, hence the Schuylkill Canal was gradually abandoned. A flood damaged the navigation in 1869 but the operation continued until 1931. Later, most parts of the Schuylkill Canal were almost completely filled in for the purpose of the removal of coal silt during 1947 and 1979. Nowadays, some sections of the Schuylkill Canal have been restored for recreation and commemoration.

航能力，为推动运河沿岸地区的工业发展做出巨大贡献。19世纪60年代，铁路运输成为北美主要的运输方式，斯库尔基尔运河逐渐停止使用。尽管1869年的一场洪水损坏了航道，但直到1931年，斯库尔基尔运河才停止运营。1947—1979年间，为清除煤泥，斯库尔基尔运河几乎大部分河段都被完全回填。如今，该运河部分河段已重新修缮，供游客观光，同时具有历史纪念意义。

Schuylkill Navigation

斯库尔基尔航道

A canal located in Pennsylvania, the United States. See Schuylkill Canal.

美国宾夕法尼亚州运河。见斯库尔基尔运河。

Schwartzenberg Trench

施瓦岑贝格沟渠

A canal located in the province of Friesland, the Netherlands. See Rijs Canal.

荷兰弗里斯兰省运河。见赖斯运河。

Sea Canal

滨海运河

A cross-border canal located in Europe. See Ghent-Terneuzen Canal.

欧洲跨国运河。见根特—特尔纽曾运河。

Seddin Lake-Gosen Canal

塞丁湖－格森运河

A canal located in Berlin, Germany. The Seddin Lake-Gosen Canal is 4 kilometres long, legally a section of the Federal Waterway and a part of

德国柏林运河。塞丁湖—格森运河全长4千米，属于德国联邦航道的一部分，也是奥得—施普雷运河

the Oder-Spree Canal. As a Class III waterway, the canal holds little water level difference and has no lock. It connects the Seddin Lake and the Dämeritz Lake, functioning as a channel between the Oder-Spree Canal and the industrial area in Rüdersdorf. In 1872, a plan was proposed to establish a canal between the Seddin and Dämeritz lakes on the basis of the existing river Gosen Graben, but the plan was shelved for many years. In 1931, Germany was designated the hosting country of the 11th Olympic Games, and one section of the Oder-Spree Canal would be closed for the Olympic canoeing and rowing competitions. Then the Seddin Lake-Gosen Canal was excavated as an alternative to guarantee the water transportation. The canal experienced one-sided extension in 1933 and was deepened to 3 metres. At the end of January 1936, the Seddin Lake-Gosen Canal was officially opened. It shortened the distance between the two industrial zones upstream and downstream by 18 kilometres, and alleviated the transportation pressure of the Oder-Spree Canal.

的组成部分。该运河属于三级航道，水位几无落差，无须建造船闸，连通塞丁湖和代梅里茨湖两个湖泊，同时连接奥得—施普雷运河和吕德斯多夫工业区。1872年，有人提议在格森—格拉本河的基础上修建一条连通塞丁湖和代梅里茨湖的运河，但该计划搁置多年未果。1931年，德国获得第11届奥运会的举办权，奥得—施普雷运河部分河道因用于皮划艇比赛而封闭。为保证水路正常通航，德国政府开凿了塞丁湖—格森运河以替代封闭的河段。1933年，运河进行单侧拓宽，河道加深至3米。1936年1月运河正式通航。塞丁湖—格森运河使处于上下游的两个工业区之间的水路距离缩短18千米，同时也缓解了奥得—施普雷运河的运输压力。

Seeswood Canal

西斯伍德运河

A canal located in Warwickshire, England, the United Kingdom. The Seeswood Canal belongs to Arbury Canals, a system of private canals. When completed, the Seeswood Canal was 1,810 metres long. It linked the Seeswood Lake, the starting point of the system. The Seeswood Lake was enlarged to achieve navigability and in 1784 another lock was built to give access from the canal into the lake.

英国英格兰沃里克郡运河。西斯伍德运河属于私人运河网阿伯里运河网。运河全长1 810米，连接阿伯里运河网的起点西斯伍德湖。该湖后来被扩建用以通航，1784年人们建造了1座船闸，以便船只从运河进入西斯伍德湖。

Seille Canal

A canal located in France. The Seille Canal lies in the lower reach of the river Seille. It originates from Ladoyo-sur-la-Seille, flowing through a wine-producing area in Jura and finally joining the river Saône. It is navigable for 39 kilometres. The canalization largely owes to Émiland Gauthey, the engineer, at the end of the 18th century. There are 4 6-metre-high locks, among which the first lock was the only one that maintained a record of commercial navigation at the end of the 19th century, and then the Seille Canal was no longer known for any navigation use and became a boating channel. With wide water, slow currents and winding beds, the canal boasts gorgeous landscape along the banks, being a decent place of interest. It also irrigates Cuisery, the book town. The Seille Canal has also been a famous habitat of catfish since 1960s.

Seine-North Europe Canal

A canal under construction located in northern France. The Seine-North Europe Canal is expected to be 106 kilometres in length, and planned to link the Oise River at Janville, and the Dunkirk-Escaut Canal, east of Arleux. The 4.2 billion-budget canal project to include such large structures as 7 locks and 3 aqueducts is co-financed by the European Union, the French government, and local regional governments through public-private partnerships. The project has encountered twists and turns during the past few years. Due to the doubtful concerns

塞耶运河

法国运河。塞耶运河为塞耶河下游河段，始于塞耶河畔拉杜瓦约市镇，流经汝拉葡萄酒产区，最终汇入索恩河。运河通航里程为39千米，其开凿主要归功于18世纪末的工程师埃米朗·戈泰。运河之上建有4座6米高的船闸，其中，第一座船闸是19世纪末唯一有商业通航记录的船闸。后该运河停航，仅作为一条游船观光航道。塞耶运河河面宽阔，水流缓慢，河道蜿蜒曲折，两岸风景优美，是宜人的观光胜地。该运河也为"书镇"奎瑟里提供灌溉水源。自20世纪60年代以来，塞耶运河还是著名的鲶鱼产地。

塞纳-北欧运河

法国北部在建运河。塞纳—北欧运河工程预计全长106千米，计划在让维尔市连通瓦兹河，在阿尔勒镇以东连通敦刻尔克—埃斯科运河。运河上将建7座船闸和3座渡槽，工程总预算为42亿欧元，由欧盟、法国政府和地方政府通过公私联营方式共同出资。近几年来，运河修建事宜一波三折。2012年，该工程引起公众诸多质疑，故2014年做出大幅度降低成本的决

raised about it in 2012, a significant cost reduction was decided in 2014. In April 2016, the newly-formed Seine-North Europe Canal Company was commissioned by the president of France to take charge of the construction. When completed, it will connect the surrounding northern European countries such as Belgium, Germany and the Netherlands. The promising high-capacity of the canal is expected to considerably facilitate the transport of goods through inland waterways further into other regions or beyond.

Seine-Schelde Network

An ongoing cross-border canal system located in Europe. The Seine-Schelde Network is scheduled to be 1,100-kilometre-long and be completed by 2030. The decision of creating large-gauge inland waterways on the North Sea-Mediterranean Corridor was adopted by the European Commission in 2019. The complex project is a joint effort of France, the Belgian regions of Flanders and Wallonia and the European Commission. The canal is aimed at improving the economy of Europe and promoting the modal shift of transport from road freight transport to the waterways. Building the Seine-Schelde Network will link the Seine basin through continuous high-gauge inland waterway to the Schelde basin in the north of France, Belgium and the Netherlands, as well as to other important European waterway basins such as the Rhine and the Maas. Through the network, the maritime and inland ports in this wider European cross-border

定。2016年4月，法国总统授权新成立的塞纳—北欧运河公司来统筹塞纳—北欧运河的建设工作。工程竣工后，运河将连接比利时、德国和荷兰等邻近的北欧国家。塞纳—北欧运河将拥有强大的运输能力，有望通过内陆运河将货物运送到法国其他地区或欧洲其他国家，从而大大提升货物运输的便捷程度。

塞纳－斯海尔德运河网

欧洲在建跨国运河网。规划中的塞纳—斯海尔德运河网总长达1 100千米，预计于2030年建成。2019年，欧盟委员会将大规模内陆航运网的修建工程纳入"北海—地中海走廊"项目。该运河网修建工程复杂，由法国、比利时的佛兰德区和瓦隆尼亚区以及欧洲委员会合作共建。其修建目的是促进欧洲经济发展，推动运输模式由陆路货运向水路货运转变。塞纳—斯海尔德运河网建成后，塞纳河河谷地区的船只可经由畅通的高承载量内陆航道通往位于法国、比利时和荷兰三国以北的斯海尔德河流域地区，也可通往欧洲其他重要流域地区，如莱茵河流域或马斯河。该运河项目将串联起运河网覆盖区域的多个海

region will be connected. It is believed that the network will exert a large range of economic impacts.

港和内陆港口，从而带来巨大的经济效益。

Sekanak Canal

A canal located in the province of South Sumatra, Indonesia. The Sekanak Canal is a branch of the Musi River, winding through Palembang City. Previously, the canal was full of household waste, with the stench strong enough to drive the passing-by residents away. Later, the Palembang City government painted a variety of murals on the banks of the canal, whose images and their combination of paint colours make this location the main destination for instagramable photo hunters and known as "Sekanak Bersolek". In addition, many of the modern commercial centres of Palembang are located along the banks of the canal, making the Sekanak Canal one of the city's most popular tourist centres. The Sekanak Canal today signals the rise of "the Venice of the East". This nickname was once pinned to the Musi River for its beauty.

塞卡纳克运河

印度尼西亚南苏门答腊省运河。塞卡纳克运河是穆西河的一条支流，穿行巨港市。该河道曾经充斥着生活垃圾，臭气熏天，路人避之唯恐不及。后巨港市政府在运河两岸绘上图案各异的壁画，色彩丰富绚丽，引得许多摄影爱好者前来游玩和拍照，塞卡纳克运河获誉"盛装的塞卡纳克"。巨港市的许多现代商业中心也矗立于运河两岸，塞卡纳克运河由此成为该市最受欢迎的旅游景点之一。如今，塞卡纳克运河的发展被誉为"东方威尼斯"的崛起，这个称号曾属于风光旖旎的穆西河。

Sethusamudram Shipping Canal

A planned cross-border canal located in Asia. Flowing through India and Sri Lanka, and billed as India's Suez Canal, the Sethusamudram Shipping Canal was aimed at offering a channel navigated by ships sailing between the west and the east coasts of India by avoiding the circumnavigation of Sri Lanka. The voyage time between India's western and eastern coasts would be reduced by as much as 36

塞述沙姆德伦通海运河

亚洲拟建跨国运河。塞述沙姆德伦通海运河流经印度和斯里兰卡，被誉为印度的"苏伊士运河"，旨在于印度东、西海岸之间开通一条航运线路，使船只不必绕道至斯里兰卡。该运河开凿之后，印度东西海岸之间的航行时间将缩短36小时，航行里程将减少约772千

hours, and the voyage distance by up to 772 kilometres. As planned, two channels will be created: one across Adam's Bridge, southeast of Pamban Island, and the other through the shallows of the Palk Bay, deepening the Palk Straits. The total length of these two channels would be 89 kilometres. In 1860, the project was first proposed by the British commanders in the Indian Navy. But this idea has remained in hibernation for the last 144 years. There have been several versions of plans for the proposed channel, but no decision was ever made. The construction of the canal was started in 2005. In 2007, dredging in the Adam's Bridge region was stopped by the Supreme Court following petitions filed by individuals and groups. Since then the project has been opposed for multiple reasons. Economic, ecological, international relations and security concerns are the main factors impeding the advancement of the project. It appears that the Sethusamudram Shipping Canal is slowly dying due to continuous litigations.

米。按照计划人们将开辟两条航道：一条横穿班本岛东南的亚当桥，另一条穿过保克湾的浅滩，拓深保克海峡。这两条航道的总长度将达到89千米。1860年，该运河项目首次由印度海军中的英国指挥官提出。在其后的144年里，这一构想却一直悬而未决。其间出现过不同版本的开凿计划，但均未能付诸实施。2005年，运河修建工作终于启动，但两年后，因当地个人和团体请愿不断，印度最高法院下令中止了亚当桥区域的建设工作。此后，运河修建又遭多方面的反对，经济、生态、国际关系及安全方面的考虑都成为阻碍工程继续推进的主要因素。在持续不断的诉讼中，塞述沙姆德伦通海运河工程似乎渐遭废弃。

Seton Canal

西顿运河

A canal located in the province of British Columbia, Canada. The Seton Canal is 3.5 kilometres long, running from the Seton Dam to the Seton Powerhouse on the Fraser River. The end of the canal is below a bridge, which is a part of the Texas Creek Road. The canal can carry water from the Bridge River to the Seton Lake through the generating stations at Shalalth.

加拿大不列颠哥伦比亚省运河。西顿运河全长3.5千米，自西顿水坝流经弗雷泽河上的西顿发电站，止于得克萨斯溪路的一座桥下。该运河可通过位于沙拉尔斯镇的发电站将布里奇河的河水引入西顿湖。

Sèvre-Nantaise≈

A canalized river located in the Loire region, southern France. The Sèvre-Nantaise is a tributary on the left bank of the Loire, running from Deux-Sèvres to Nantes, where it joins the Loire. Its total length is 141.8 kilometres with 27.5 kilometres navigable for boats. The river contains two sections. The first section, 21.5 kilometres long, flows from Port Domino to its confluence with the river Loire. The maximum size of boats allowed is 5.5 metres by 31.5 metres. There are two facilities in the river, the Rousseau Bridge Dam and the Vertou Lock. The Rousseau Bridge Dam was built in 1995. It maintains a stable water level upstream and alleviates the impacts of tides, but high tides can still overflow it. The Vertou Lock was constructed in 1755 with the aim to make the river navigable at Causeway of Moines. The rebuilding project in the 19th century allowed boats to sail at the upstream stretch of the river Monier. The second section is its left tributary, the Small Maine. This section is navigable for 6 kilometres, flowing to the Caffino Bridge. There used to be 1 lock in the river to make the channel straightway to the south reach, which has been abandoned now. During the 18th and 19th centuries, it was proposed to construct a canal from Sèvre-Nantaise to Sèvre-Niortaise in order to connect Nantes and Niort. As a part of the plan, new locks should also be built to make the river navigable to Clisson or the further south. The plan failed because of the numerous mills and rock shoals along the banks, as well as the plan of building the faster railway.

塞夫尔-南特河

法国南部卢瓦尔河地区运河化河流。塞夫尔—南特河是卢瓦尔河的左岸支流，全长141.8千米，其中可通航部分长27.5千米，从德塞夫勒省流至南特市，与卢瓦尔河交汇。塞夫尔—南特河分为两段：第一段始于多米诺港至与卢瓦河交汇处，长21.5千米，可通行船只的最大规格为5.5×31.5米，河上建有卢梭桥大坝和韦尔图船闸。卢梭桥大坝于1995年建成，一定程度上能维持上游水位稳定，减少潮汐对水流的影响，但高潮水位仍能漫过大坝。为方便梅因坝地区的航运，1755年人们修建了韦尔图船闸，后于19世纪进行了一次修复，使得莫尼耶尔河上游可通航。第二段为左岸支流小曼恩河，可通航长度为6千米，流至卡菲诺桥。该河段上曾建有1座船闸，使得航船可继续向南航行至上游，现已废弃不用。18和19世纪，为连接南特市和尼奥尔市，当地计划在塞夫尔—南特河和塞夫尔—尼奥尔河之间开凿一条运河。根据该计划，还将新建船闸，使运河可通航至克利松市或更远的上游地区。但由于沿途有众多工厂和岩石浅滩，加上当时计划修建更加快速的铁路，该计划最终未能实施。通过塞夫尔河，人们将红酒、沙土运往下游，将谷

Through the river Sèvre, people transported wine and sand to the lower reach and cereals, lime, stones and wood to the upper reach. A passenger service line was open from 1899 to 1960. Now the river is a significant tourism resource for the region.

物、石灰、石材和木材运至上游。1899—1960年间，塞夫尔—南特河曾开辟客运航线。如今，该河已成为当地重要的旅游资源。

Sèvre-Niortaise≈

A canalized river located in western France. The Sèvre-Niortaise originates from Deux-Sèvres, flows through the city of Niort and pours into the Atlantic Ocean. It is 158.4 kilometres long, with 108.6 kilometres navigable and 15 locks on the river and its tributaries. The average flow is 44 cubic metres per second. There are canals running over 100 kilometres downstream and its tributaries, distributed to 9 parts from the lock in Niort to the lock of Brault. The Brault Sea Canal, built in the late 19th century, is a bypass of the complex network. Other channels were constructed to promote navigation in the early 19th century. Located in Clavé, the Touche Poupard Dam ensures a stable flow upstream and enough agricultural irrigation. The Sèvre-Niortaise has tens of tributaries. The branches on its left bank include the Lambon, the river Mignon (with the Mignon Canal), etc. On the right bank, there are the Old Autise (with the canal of the Old Autise), the Young Autise, the Vendee, etc.

塞夫尔-尼奥尔河

法国西部运河化河流。塞夫尔—尼奥尔河始于德塞夫勒省，经尼奥尔市向北注入大西洋。该河全长158.4千米，其中可通航长度为108.6千米，河道及其支流上共建有15座船闸，平均流速为每秒44立方米。该河下游及支流总长达100多千米，分为9个小河段，分布在尼奥尔闸至布劳特闸之间。其中，布劳特海运运河建于19世纪晚期，为塞夫尔—尼奥尔河航道网的支流。其他河道均建于19世纪初期，为改善航运条件而开凿。图什普帕尔大坝位于克拉维，能确保该河流上游水流稳定，保障农业灌溉用水。塞夫尔—尼奥尔河有数十条支流，左岸支流有兰邦河和米尼翁河（含米尼翁运河）等，右岸支流有旧欧蒂兹（含旧欧蒂兹运河）、新欧蒂兹河和旺代河等。

Shaal Gharraf

An ancient canal located in Iraq. See Al-Gharraf River.

夏尔盖拉夫河

伊拉克古运河。见阿尔—盖拉夫河。

Shangombo-Rivungo Canal

A cross-border canal located in southeastern Africa. The Shangombo-Rivungo Canal is 10 kilometres long, 34 metres wide and 3 metres deep, connecting the Rivungo Town in Angola and the Shangombo District in Zambia. The construction was completed by the contractor Clay Disposal Zambia Limited in 2017, with a total cost of $40 million. The canal could allow 2 passenger ships with a capacity of 25 people each and 2 cargo vessels with a capacity of 10 tonnes each to pass. Piers have been built on both sides of the canal for loading and unloading. The canal promotes mutual trade as well as communication between Angola and Zambia. Tourism and foreign exchange earnings have increased since it takes tourists from Shangombo only 15 minutes to reach Rivungo by waterway, along which there are beautiful sceneries. The opening of the canal provides more job opportunities and convenient trade and services, and thus improves the lives of people living along the canal.

尚贡博－里温戈运河

非洲东南部跨国运河。尚贡博－里温戈运河全长10千米，宽34米，深3米，连接安哥拉的里温戈镇和赞比亚的尚贡博区。该运河修建工程由赞比亚黏土处理有限公司承包，2017年项目完工，耗资总计4 000万美元。尚贡博－里温戈运河可同时供2艘载客量25人的客船和2艘载货量10吨的货船通行，两岸设有码头，供乘客上下船和装卸货物。尚贡博－里温戈运河促进了安哥拉和赞比亚两国之间的贸易往来和人文交流。游客乘船只需15分钟就可从尚贡博到达里温戈，沿途美景尽收眼底。旅游业的发展为两国带来了更多外汇收益。尚贡博－里温戈运河为两岸居民创造了更多就业机会，为贸易和服务业带来许多便利，提高了当地人民的生活水平。

Shangxin River

An abandoned canal located in the city of Nanjing, Jiangsu Province, China. The 9-kilometre-long Shangxin River was excavated in the early Ming Dynasty (1368—1644) to connect the Yangtze River with Nanjing for shipping. The Shangxin River ("shang" in Chinese means "up") had its name because it was located in the upper reaches of the Xinhe ("new river" in Chinese) River. The Shangxin

上新河

中国江苏省南京市废弃运河。上新河全长9千米，开凿于明朝初年，旨在连通长江至南京的航运。由于该河位于新河上游，故称上新河。上新河地理位置优越，便于木材等物资运输及船只停靠。因上新河取得了巨大的经济效益，为了满足运输需要，人们又在新河下

River had advantages of its location, which made it convenient for shipping and docking of materials such as timber. After huge economic benefits, the Zhongxin River and the Xiaxin River were excavated in the lower reaches of the Xinhe River in order to meet the needs of transportation. During the Ming and Qing Dynasties (1368—1911), the Shangxin River was a major waterway for transporting timber and other materials, and its dock was one of the most prosperous docks at that time. The rapid development and prosperity of this area attracted a large number of people to settle down, and thus a unique commercial centre was formed. Benefiting from their timber business, many Huizhou (the neighbouring province) merchants built guilds. Many scholars described the famous Shangxin River in their books during the Ming and Qing Dynasties. As Nanjing was opened as a commercial port in the late Qing Dynasty (1616—1911), coupled with the impact of a few wars, the Shangxin River area gradually declined. The river channel was also silted up with the change of the course of the Yangtze River and the expansion of Nanjing City, but the "Shangxin River" is still in use as a place name today.

游开凿了中新河和下新河。明清时期，上新河是运输木材和其他物资的主要航道，上新河码头是当时最繁华的码头之一。这一地区的发展繁荣吸引了大量人口前来定居，形成了独特的商业集市。许多徽商因在此经营木材生意而发家，在此兴建会馆。上新河在明清时期非常有名，许多文人都曾在书中描绘过上新河。由于清末南京开埠，加之战争影响，上新河逐渐衰落。因长江航道的变化以及南京城区的扩张，上新河河道日渐淤塞，但"上新河"作为一个地名沿用至今。

Shannon-Erne Waterway

香农－厄恩航道

A cross-border canal located in Europe. Originally called Ballinamore and Ballyconnell Canal. The Shannon-Erne Waterway lies on the Irish Island, connecting River Shannon in the Republic of Ireland with River Erne in Northern Ireland, the

欧洲跨国运河。旧称巴利纳莫尔－巴利康奈尔运河。香农－厄恩航道位于爱尔兰岛，连通爱尔兰共和国境内的香农河与英国北爱尔兰境内的厄恩河。该航道全长63千

United Kingdom. It has a length of 63 kilometres with 16 locks in total, flowing from the Leitrim Village in the Leitrim County to the Upper Lough Erne in the Fermanagh County. It was first built in 1846, and then opened in 1860. The canal remained inactive until the 1960s. With an increase of pleasure boating on the Shannon, its restoration began to be considered on the part of some enthusiasts. Renovation was undertaken from 1991 to 1994, utilising largely the riverbed of the deserted old waterway. The canal was renamed the Shannon-Erne Waterway, which reflected its purpose of linking the two river systems.

米，沿线共建有16座船闸，由利特里姆郡的利特里姆村流向弗马纳郡的上厄恩湖。香农—厄恩航道于1846年开凿，1860年建成通航。20 世纪60年代之前，航道处于闲置状态。随着香农河上游游船数量不断增加，热心人士考虑修复该运河。1991—1994年间，该运河得到修缮，原有的大部分河床得以改造。修复后的运河更名为香农—厄恩航道，体现这条运河连通两个河流系统的用意。

Shatt-en-Nil

A canal located in the south of Iraq. Also called Naru Kabari. The Shatt-en-Nil, a dry canal, was 60 kilometres long, and 4.6—6.1 metres deep. Starting from the north of Babylon, it ran through Nippur, and rejoined the Euphrates River in Larsa. The canal, known as Euphrates of Nippur, was an important means for irrigation and transportation for the city of Nippur in ancient times. It also served the city of Tel Abib and Uruk. The so-called Murashu documents which noted commercial trades around Nippur include reference to this waterway.

沙特恩—尼尔运河

伊拉克南部运河。亦称纳鲁卡巴里运河。沙特恩—尼尔运河全长60千米，深4.6—6.1米，已干涸。该运河始于巴比伦北部，途经尼普尔市，流向拉尔萨，与幼发拉底河交汇。沙特恩—尼尔运河古时曾是尼普尔市重要的灌溉水源和水上航道，也曾为提勒亚毕城和乌鲁克城发挥过类似作用，被称为尼普尔的幼发拉底河。在记录尼普尔商贸活动的穆拉希公文中有这条运河的相关记载。

Sheas Creek

A canal located in the United States. See Alexandria Canal.

谢伊斯河

美国运河。见亚历山大运河。

Shinnecock and Peconic Canal

A canal located in the state of New York, the United States. See Shinnecock Canal.

欣纳科克-佩克尼克运河

美国纽约州运河。见欣纳科克运河。

Shinnecock Canal

A canal located in the state of New York, the United States. Also called Shinnecock and Peconic Canal. The Shinnecock Canal is 1.4 kilometres long, running through the South Fork of Long Island at Hampton Bays and linking the Peconic Bay with the Shinnecock Bay. The construction of the canal was started in 1884 and completed in 1892. In 1919, in order to mitigate the difference in the elevation between the two bays, a canal lock system was built, and it is still the only navigation lock operating on Long Island.

欣纳科克运河

美国纽约州运河。亦称欣纳科克—佩克尼克运河。欣纳科克运河全长1.4千米，自汉普顿贝斯流经长岛的南福克，连接欣纳科克湾与佩克尼克湾。运河于1884年开凿，1892年完工。1919年，为解决两个海湾之间的水位落差问题，欣纳科克运河上修建了船闸控制系统，这也是长岛目前唯一在用的通航船闸。

Shire-Zambezi Canal

A cross-border canal located in southeastern Africa. See Mozambique-Malawi Canal.

夏尔-赞比西运河

非洲东南部跨国运河。见莫桑比克—马拉维运河。

Shropshire Union Canal

A canal located in the Midlands of England, the United Kingdom. The Shropshire Union Canal is 106 kilometres long, 2.13 metres wide, allowing the navigation of ships with up to 1.1 metres draught. The canal runs from Staffordshire to Cheshire through Shropshire, connecting the canal system of the West Midlands with River Mersey and the

什罗普郡联合运河

英国英格兰中部运河。什罗普郡联合运河全长106千米，宽2.13米，允许吃水深度1.1米以内的船只通行。运河从斯塔福德郡途经什罗普郡流向柴郡，连通西米德兰兹郡运河网与默西河以及曼彻斯特通海运河。运河于18世纪70年代开

Manchester Ship Canal. Its construction was started in the 1770s. The canal derives its name from the Shropshire Union Railways and Canal Company, which was founded in 1846 by amalgamating several companies. As the canal traffic started to decline following the breakout of World War I and the use of motor lorries, the company became a part of the London, Midland and Scottish Railway in 1921. Now the Shropshire Union Canal Society has been founded so as to maintain and restore the canal. Being one of the most beautiful canals in Britain, the Shropshire Union Canal is very popular with tourists in narrow boats every summer.

凿，因什罗普郡联合铁路与运河公司而得名。该公司成立于1846年，由多个公司合并而成。因第一次世界大战爆发及运货卡车的使用，运河航运量下滑。1921年，什罗普郡联合铁路与运河公司被并入伦敦—米德兰—苏格兰铁路公司。如今，为维护和修复这条运河，成立了什罗普郡联合运河协会。什罗普郡联合运河是英国风景最优美的运河之一，每年夏天都会吸引众多游客乘坐运河小船观光游览。

Shubenacadie Canal

舒贝纳卡迪运河

An inland canal located in central Nova Scotia, Canada. The Shubenacadie Canal is 114 kilometres in length with 9 locks. It runs from the Halifax Harbour in the south to the Bay of Fundy in the north, connecting the Shubenacadie River and the Shubenacadie Grand Lake. The construction of this canal began in 1826 and was completed in 1861. Nova Scotia planned and surveyed the canal as early as 1767, with the idea of using it for the transportation of agricultural products, timber, and coal between the Halifax Harbour, northern Nova Scotia and the Annapolis Valley. Since 1826, the Shubenacadie Canal Company had been responsible for the construction of the canal, bringing in Scottish and Irish craftsmen to work on the project. In 1831, the company went bankrupt and the project was put on hold. In 1854, the canal was rebuilt

加拿大新斯科舍省中部内陆运河。舒贝纳卡迪运河全长114千米，建有9座船闸，南起哈利法克斯港，北至芬迪湾，连通舒贝纳卡迪河与舒贝纳卡迪大湖。该运河于1826—1861年间开凿。早在1767年，新斯科舍省就计划修建运河，并实地考察，设想在新斯科舍省北部的哈利法克斯港与安纳波利斯谷之间修建一条航道，用以运输农产品、木材和煤炭。1826年起，舒贝纳卡迪运河公司一直负责运河的修建工作，来自苏格兰和爱尔兰的工匠们也参与其中。1831年，该公司破产，工程也随之被搁置。1854年，内河航运公司接管了运河修建项目，改变了原有的英国石质船闸设

by the Inland Navigation Company, while the original design of the British stone locks was changed to a more inexpensive North American stone and wood structure. In the years after the completion of the Shubenacadie Canal, especially during the Waverley Gold Rush of the 1860s, the traffic was great. Due to the cold winter, the lock that connected the freshwater lake was damaged, and the canal company was barely profitable and faced many problems. In 1870, the Waverley draw bridge over the Shubenacadie Canal was replaced by a fixed bridge, which obstructed steamships and severely restricted the canal traffic. The canal was taken over by the town of Dartmouth in 1871 for the city's water supply and has not been operated since. In 1983, a historic recreation park was first constructed on the section between Lake Charles and the Micmac. The Shubenacadie Canal is now a Canadian Society of Civil Engineering National Historic Site and has two interpretive centres. Three of the canal's 9 original locks, combining British and North American construction techniques, have been restored, and one is still in use. A plan for a larger restoration of the canal is underway.

计，采用造价更低的北美石材和木质结构。舒贝纳卡迪运河通航后的最初几年，尤其在19世纪60年代的韦弗利淘金热期间，航运量非常可观。后因冬季严寒天气破坏了连通淡水湖的船闸，运河公司几乎难有收益且面临许多问题。1870年，舒贝纳卡迪运河上的韦弗利吊桥被固定桥替代，蒸汽船只通航受阻，运河上的通航业务也受到严重制约。1871年，该运河由达特茅斯镇接管，主要用于城市供水，航运业务自此关停。1983年，运河的查尔斯湖至密克马克河段修建了一个历史休闲公园。如今，舒伯纳卡迪运河已由加拿大土木工程学会认定为国家历史遗址，并建有两处解说中心。运河9座船闸中有3座采用英国与北美建筑技术的船闸得到修复，其中1处船闸仍在使用。关于该运河更大规模的修复工作正在计划当中。

Sidney Feeder Canal

锡德尼引水运河

An inland canal located in the state of Ohio, the United States. Also known as Port Jefferson Feeder Canal. The Sidney Feeder Canal, as a 22.5-kilometre-long tributary of the Miami and Erie Canal, begins in the village of Lockington and runs from the south through Sidney, towards north along the

美国俄亥俄州内陆运河。亦称杰斐逊港引水运河。锡德尼引水运河是迈阿密—伊利运河的一条支流，长22.5千米，始于洛金顿村，自南向北流经锡德尼，沿迈阿密河谷流至达杰斐逊港上游水坝。运河

Miami Valley, and finally reaches the dam in the upstream of Port Jefferson. It was finished by 1841. The Logan County's Indian Lake was largely expanded to provide a steady supply of water for the canal. When it freezes in winter, the canal allows locals to skate from Sidney to Port Jefferson.

于1841年完工。为了给锡德尼引水运河持续供水，人们还曾大规模扩建过洛根县的印第安湖。冬季河面冰封以后，当地居民可在运河的锡德尼至杰斐逊港段溜冰。

Silo Canal

A canal located in the state of Brandenburg, Germany. The 5.26-kilometre-long Silo Canal was built between 1907 and 1910, mainly to offer a shortcut for vessels on River Havel. There is a lock at the end of the upstream of the Silo Canal, and that is where the canal descends into River Havel and flows into the Beetz Lake. Now the canal is used not only for commercial shipping but also for leisure boating.

西洛运河

德国勃兰登堡州运河。西洛运河于1907—1910年间开凿，全长5.26千米，旨在为哈弗尔河上通行的船只提供一条捷径。西洛运河上游最末端建有1座船闸，运河自此流至哈弗尔河，最终注入贝茨湖。如今，西洛运河不仅可供商业船只通行，还是划船休闲的好去处。

Slochteren Canal

An inland canal located in the province of Groningen, the Netherlands. Formerly known as Rengers Canal. The Slochteren Canal runs through Slochteren and Ruischerbrug, flowing into the Ems Canal. The canal is 15 kilometres in length with a navigable distance of 11 kilometres. There is 1 lock and 3 bridges along the route. In 1659, it was constructed under the order of Osebrandt Johan Rengers, who was then the richest and most powerful baron living near Slochteren, hence the former designation of the canal. Nowadays, the Slochteren Canal serves as a good place for pleasure boats which have a draught of 1.3 metres to 1.9 metres.

斯洛赫特伦运河

荷兰格罗宁根省内陆运河。旧称伦格斯运河。斯洛赫特伦运河流经斯洛赫特伦市和瑞斯赫尔布鲁赫市，最终汇入埃姆斯运河。该运河全长15千米，通航长度11千米，建有1座船闸和3座桥梁。1659年，奥斯布兰特·约翰·伦格斯下令开凿该运河，他是当时住在斯洛赫特伦市附近最富有和最有权势的男爵，该运河早前的称名也由此而来。如今，该运河主要供游船行驶，河上游船吃水深度为1.3—1.9米。

Sloot Canal

An inland canal located in the province of North Holland, the Netherlands. The Sloot Canal runs from the Wieringermeer Polder to the Amstel Lake. It is 9 kilometres in length, with 2 locks along the route. The canal is mainly used for transportation.

斯洛特运河

荷兰北荷兰省内陆运河。斯洛特运河自维灵厄梅尔圩田流至阿姆斯特尔湖，全长9千米，沿线建有2座船闸。该运河主要用于航运。

Small Rhône and Saint Gilles Canal

A canal located in the province of Gard, France. The Small Rhône and Saint Gilles Canal serves as a branch from the stream at Fourques. Originally, the Small Rhône River was a narrow shallow channel of the Rhône Delta along which only small boats could travel. Later, the channel was deepened over 20 kilometres from its entrance at Fourques to Saint Gilles for the passage of high-capacity barges. There are no locks on the Small Rhône Canal itself. The lock on the Saint Gilles Canal gives access to the Rhône-Sète Canal. Down to Saint Gilles, the canal forms the first section. The total distance from the Rhône at Fourques to the junction with the Rhône-Sète Canal is 22.5 kilometres.

小罗讷－圣吉勒运河

法国加尔省运河。小罗讷—圣吉勒运河是富尔克地区一条溪流的支流。最初，小罗讷河只是罗讷河三角洲地区狭窄的浅水航道，仅容小型船只通航。后为使大容量驳船能够通航，人们加深了从富尔克河口至圣吉勒之间长达20千米的河道。小罗讷运河上未建船闸，人们可通过圣吉勒运河上的船闸前往罗讷—塞特运河。从小罗讷河至圣吉勒构成此运河的第一段。从罗讷河的富尔克段到与罗讷—塞特运河交汇处的长度为22.5千米。

Small Saône$^{\approx}$

A canalized river located in eastern France. The Small Saône is 365 kilometres in length. It originates from the Vosges Canal in Corre and flows into the Rhône in Lyon. It also forms the backbone of the French waterway network, being joined by four major canals: the Champagne-Burgundy Ca-

小索恩河

法国东部运河化河流。小索恩河全长365千米，始于孚日运河科尔市河段，最终在里昂市汇入罗讷河。小索恩河是法国航道网的核心组成部分。四大主要运河，即香槟—勃艮第运河、罗讷—莱茵运河、勃

nal, the Rhône-Rhine Canal, the Burgundy Canal, and the Central France Canal. The Small Saône is divided into two sections: Corre to Auxonne (150 kilometres) and Auxonne to Lyon (215 kilometres). The entire waterway remains in the national priority network, and may one day be adapted to form the high-capacity Saône-Moselle Waterway. The river has always been the most navigable of French rivers, with a very gentle gradient and regular flow, albeit subject to floods which can make the broad valley look like an inland sea.

艮第运河和法国中部运河均汇集于此。小索恩河分为两个河段，一段从科尔市到欧索讷市，长150千米；另一段从欧索讷市到里昂市，长215千米。如今，该河的整条航道仍属于国家重点交通网的组成部分，未来有可能会改造为具有高承运量的索恩—摩泽尔航道。每遭遇洪水时，小索恩河宽阔的河谷看起来就像是一片内海。小索恩河具有斜坡缓、水流稳的特点，是法国通航能力最强的河流。

Sneek Old Canal

斯内克旧运河

An inland canal located in the province of Friesland, the Netherlands. See Old Canal.

荷兰弗里斯兰省内陆运河。见旧运河。

Södertälje Canal

南泰利耶运河

A canal located in Södertälje, eastern Sweden. The Södertälje Canal has a length of 5.2 kilometres, linking Lake Mälaren with the Baltic Sea. In the early 1900s, it was far too narrow and winding for modern ships. Between 1917 and 1924, the canal was largely widened, deepened and equipped with a new lock which is 135 metres in length, 17 metres in width and still in use. Södertälje has largely grown up as a society around the canal. Today, the Södertälje Canal is the main shipping route into Lake Mälaren, which allows the navigation of vessels with max width 19 metres and max draught of 7 metres. The traffic is busy on the canal.

瑞典东部南泰利耶市运河。南泰利耶运河全长5.2千米，连通梅拉伦湖和波罗的海。20世纪初，南泰利耶运河过于狭窄曲折，现代船只难以通行，故人们于1917—1924年间进行大范围拓宽和加深，并修建了一座长135米、宽17米的新船闸，该船闸至今仍在使用。南泰利耶市的发展很大程度上得益于这条运河。如今，南泰利耶运河是进入梅拉伦湖的主要航道，可通行最大宽度19米、最大吃水深度7米的船只，河上交通繁忙。

Somerset Canal

A canal located in the state of North Carolina, the United States. The Somerset Canal connects the Phelps Lake with the Scuppernong River. It is 6 kilometres in length, 6 metres in width, and 3.6 metres in depth. The canal was first constructed in 1786 and completed in 1788. In 1784, the North Carolina General Assembly authorized an organization from Halifax and Edenton to drain and farm the Phelps Lake. The organization also suggested that irrigation systems should be constructed to make the nearby marshland suitable for rice cultivation. After replacing the organization, the Lake Company quickly acquired the land near the Phelps Lake and constructed this canal with the goal of promoting the transport of goods and drainage of land in the area. Currently, the Somerset Canal has a variety of uses. First, it can be used for navigation, transporting timber, food crops and other materials, through which all the heavy cargo on the plantations in the area is transported. Second, it is utilized to drain water from the marshes near the north shore of the Phelps Lake, transforming them into productive land. The canal can also provide water to new fields to ensure the normal cultivation of rice and other staple crops. The waterway supplies electricity to sawmills, a gristmill and other machinery nearby.

Songliao Canal

A cross-border inland canal in planning located in northeastern China. The Songliao Canal is planned

萨默塞特运河

美国北卡罗来纳州运河。萨默塞特运河连通费尔普斯湖和斯卡珀农河,全长6千米,宽6米,深3.6米。运河于1786年开凿,1788年竣工。1784年,北卡罗来纳州议会授权一个来自哈利法克斯和伊登顿地区的组织,将费尔普斯湖排干并改造为耕地。该组织建议修建灌溉系统,将附近的沼泽地变为适合水稻种植的耕地。后为促进该地区货运业发展,改善土地排水,莱克公司取代了该组织,并迅速收购费尔普斯湖附近的土地,开凿了这条运河。如今,萨默塞特运河具有多种功能。首先是航运功能,该地区种植园里的大宗货物如木材、粮食作物以及其他材料都通过此运河运输。其次,运河有助于排干费尔普斯湖北岸附近沼泽地的积水,将其转化为耕地。萨默塞特运河还可为新田地供水,以保证水稻和其他主要作物的正常种植。运河还可为附近的锯木厂、磨粉厂和其他机械设施提供电力保障。

松辽运河

中国东北地区拟建跨境内陆运河。松辽运河计划开凿长度为1 000千

to have a total length of 1,000 kilometres, going from the Songhua River in the north to the West Liaohe River in the south. It runs through Heilongjiang Province, Jilin Province, Inner Mongolia Autonomous Region, and Liaoning Province. This canal is a Class III channel with a depth of at least 3.2 metres and a bottom width of 45 metres. As early as 1683, the Emperor Kangxi of the Qing Dynasty (1616—1911) began to carry out the plan of "Songliao Combined Transport" to deliver military supplies from the Liaohe River to the Songhua River. In the early 20th century, a plan to construct the Songliao Canal was put forward. From 1949 to 1959, the Chinese Academy of Sciences and the Chinese Ministry of Water Resources conducted field surveys and plans, and held symposiums on the construction of the canal. The project was suspended due to the ecological destruction of the Liaohe River basin. The Songliao Canal, connecting the Songhua River and the Liaohe River as planned, is aimed to relieve the flood hazard of the Songhua River and water shortage of the Liaohe River. It also aims to form the Northeast Asia International Shipping Channel from the Yingkou Port of the Bohai Sea in the south to the Russia Tatar Strait in the north. The transport of goods for foreign exchanges will promote the development of industrial and agricultural production, economy, and inland waterway transport in the provinces of northeast China. The planning for the route and design of the Songliao Canal has been completed, and the construction of the Nierji Reservoir, the Hadashan Reservoir, the Yilan Navigation-Power Junction,

米，北起松花江，向南汇入西辽河，流经黑龙江省、吉林省、内蒙古自治区和辽宁省。该运河计划为三级航道，水深在3.2米以上，河底宽45米。早在1683年，清朝康熙皇帝就开始推行"松辽联运"计划，从辽河向松花江运输军事物资。20世纪初有人提出开凿松辽运河的计划。1949—1959年，中国科学院和中国水利部进行了实地勘测和规划，并召开了运河修建座谈会。但这项计划因辽河流域生态环境恶化而中止。松辽运河计划连通松花江与辽河，从而减轻松花江的洪水危害并缓解辽河的水资源紧张问题，同时形成南起渤海营口、北至俄罗斯鞑靼海峡、贯穿南北的东北亚国际航道。对外货物运输将促进东北省份工农业生产、经济和内河航运发展。松辽运河的航道规划和设计工作已经完成，尼尔基水库、哈达山水库、宜兰航电枢纽工程等前期水利工程也已竣工。如今，松辽运河修建计划正在进行项目论证及环保评估，并已被纳入中国内河航运中长期规划，预计将于2030—2035年间修建。

among many other preparatory water conservancy projects, has been finished. Now, the assessment of the project feasibility and its environmental impact is underway. The construction of the canal has been included in China's medium-and-long-term inland navigation projects. It will be started around 2030—2035.

Soot Canal

苏特运河

A closed canal located in Norway. With a length of 1.5 kilometres, the Soot Canal lies at Eidskog in Innlandet, Norway. It spans from Lake Skjervangen at 185 metres above the sea level to Lake Mortsjølungen at 201 metres above sea level. It is equipped with the oldest sluice gates in Norway and punctuated by 16 locks. In 1849, Egbert Soot excavated the Soot Canal to transport timber to the Halden sawmills.

挪威停用运河。苏特运河位于挪威内陆郡的埃兹库格，全长1.5千米。该运河从海拔185米的谢尔旺恩湖延伸至海拔201米的莫兹朗恩湖，沿线共建有16座船闸，并配有挪威最古老的船闸门。苏特运河于1849年由恩格布雷特·苏特负责修建，旨在向哈尔登锯木厂运送木材。

Soulanges Canal

苏朗日运河

An abandoned inland canal located in the province of Quebec, Canada. The Soulanges Canal is 23 kilometres long and 4.6 metres deep. It serves as a waterway that bypasses the Cascades rapids, the Cedars rapids, and other rushing waters, connecting Lake Saint-Louis and Lake Saint-Francis. It functions with 5 lock chambers, each measuring 85.3 metres long and 14 metres wide, to reach a total lift of 25 metres with a maximum draught of 4.3 metres. A redbrick hydroelectric powerhouse is built to power locks, swing bridges and offer lighting for

加拿大魁北克省废弃内陆运河。苏朗日运河全长23千米，水深4.6米，绕过喀斯喀特湍流、锡达斯湍流等急流，连通圣路易湖与圣弗朗西斯湖。运河上建有5座85.3米长、14米宽的闸室，总提升水位高度为25米，最大吃水深度4.3米。运河上建有1座红砖水电站，为整个运河的船闸、平旋桥和夜间照明系统供电。苏朗日运河曾极大地促进了当地内河航运的发展。苏朗日运河的

the whole canal at night. The canal greatly facilitates the local inland navigation. The Soulanges Canal was first finished in 1899 after 8 years' excavation and operated for more than 50 years until it was replaced by the larger Beauharnois Canal. Now, there is a water trail beside the canal to retain its recreational value.

修建耗时8年,于1899年建成通航,在通航50余年后,被更大的博阿努瓦运河取代。如今,该运河旁的一条航道仍保有休闲娱乐功能。

Soundane Cut

桑丹运河

A deep canal located in the state of Maharashtra, India. The Soundane Cut is close to the village Soundane in Mohol Town, Solapur District and runs from the Ujani Dam located on the Bhima River, a major river in south India.

印度马哈拉施特拉邦深水运河。桑丹运河邻近索拉普尔县莫霍尔乡桑丹村,始于印度南部主要河流皮马河上的乌贾尼大坝。

South Beveland Canal

南贝弗兰运河

A canal located in Zeeland, the southwestern Netherlands. The South Beveland Canal is about 11 kilometres in length. It runs southwards from the Wemeldinge Village to the Hansweert Village, connecting the Eastern Schelde with the Westen Schelde. There are 3 bridges over the canal. The locks at Wemeldinge were no longer used for shipping, while a new lock complex with two lock chambers was built in the Hansweert. These east and west lock chambers are 280 metres in length and 24 metres in width. The canal was constructed from 1850 and put into use in 1866. In the 20th century, the canal had been one of the busiest waterways in Europe until the opening of the Rhine-Schelde Canal in 1976. In the late 20th century, the canal

荷兰西南部泽兰省运河。南贝弗兰运河全长约11千米,北起韦默尔丁厄村,南至汉斯韦尔特村,连通东斯海尔德河和西斯海尔德河。运河上建有3座桥。位于韦默尔丁厄的船闸已不再用于航运,在汉斯韦尔特的河段上新建了一座组合船闸,包含东西两个长280米、宽24米的闸室。南贝弗兰运河于1850年开凿,1866年通航。在1976年莱茵—斯海尔德运河开通之前,该运河一直是20世纪欧洲最繁忙的航道之一。20世纪末,人们又大幅度拓宽了南贝弗兰运河,并在运河上新建了铁路桥和公路桥。

was markedly widened, across which rail and road bridges were built.

South Canal

A canal located in the city of Shenyang, Liaoning Province, China. The South Canal is 14.5 kilometres in length, 15 to 22 metres in width, and 1.5 metres in depth, with an average flow of about 1.5 cubic metres per second. The canal starts at the lock near the East Pagoda, flows through the south of Shenyang's main urban area, and ends at the lock in the Longwangmiao Park. The canal was constructed upon the old course of the Wanquan River from 1952 to 1955. As one of the old watercourses of the Hun River, the city's "mother river", the South Canal is interconnected with the North Canal and the Weigong River by channels, forming a water system around the urban area north of the Hun River. The South Canal is a seasonal landscape river, which stops storing water in mid-to-late October every year and starts restoring water in April of the following year. The South Canal activates 800,000 square metres of water from other smaller rivers, and nourishes many parks and green fields along it, covering an area of approximately 2,000,000 square metres. These parks and green fields constitute the South Canal Strip Park, which was planned and constructed in 1984 by the Shenyang Municipal People's Government. The whole project lasted one year and four months and was completed in August, 1985. Built on both sides of the Canal, the South Canal Strip Park comprises 6 large parks

南运河

中国辽宁省沈阳市运河。南运河全长14.5千米，河宽15—22米，水深约1.5米，平均流量约为每秒1.5立方米。南运河始于靠近东塔的进船闸，流经沈阳市区南部，止于龙王庙公园的闸口。南运河于1952—1955年间修建，是在万泉河故道基础上修建的。南运河是沈阳市"母亲河"浑河的旧河道之一，与北运河、魏公河经河道相互连通，形成浑河以北的环城水系。南运河属季节性景观河道，每年10月中下旬停止蓄水，翌年4月开始重新蓄水。南运河调活了周围80万平方米的细流，滋养着近200万平方米的公园和绿地，这些公园和绿地共同构成了南运河带状公园。该公园于1984年由沈阳市市政府规划、建设，整个工程历时1年零4个月，于1985年8月竣工。带状公园沿南运河两岸而建，包含6个大型公园和18处河滨公园，绿树成荫，植被丰富。南运河及其周边已成为沈阳市的靓丽风景线。南运河在泄洪排涝、改善环境、净化空气和调节气候等方面也起着至关重要的作用。

and 18 riverside gardens with a variety of vegetation and extensive green spaces. The South Canal and its surroundings make the city more beautiful. It also plays a significant role in flood discharge, environmental improvement, air purification, and climate regulation.

South Hadley Falls Canal

A canal located in the state of Connecticut, the United States. The South Hadley Falls Canal is the earliest man-made canal operating in the United States, with a length of 3.6 kilometres. In 1795, the South Hadley Falls Canal, funded by the Connecticut government and Dutch investment companies, was finished under the guidance of Benjamin Prescott. With the presence of the canal, ships could directly pass through the Great Falls without unloading cargo to land transport. The South Hadley Falls Canal was also the first canal in the United States that harnessed inclined planes rather than lock chambers to enable canal boats to be lifted or lowered. Ships would be loaded onto a huge cart and be raised up a stone-made slope measuring 84 metres long and 9.1 metres wide. In 1805, a system of 5 locks replaced the inclined planes, further enhancing the traffic. The canal together with the Turners Falls Canal, which was opened in 1798, made the Connecticut River reach its peak in traffic volume. The local economy was significantly promoted and the population at the Connecticut River Valley witnessed a twofold growth. The canal officially ceased operations in 1862, and the remains of

南哈德利福尔斯运河

美国康涅狄格州运河。南哈德利福尔斯运河长3.6千米，是美国最早投入运营的人工运河。在康涅狄格州政府及荷兰投资公司资助下，南哈德利福尔斯运河于1795年完工并通航，总工程师是本杰明·普雷斯科特。运河建成后船只可以直接通过大瀑布，而无须卸货通过陆路转运。南哈德利福尔斯运河也是全美第一条运用斜面升船机而非闸阀升降船只的运河。船只被装进巨大的厢体大车中，沿着84米长、9.1米宽的石制斜坡升降。1805年，由5座船闸构成的闸区取代了斜面升船机，运河的航运能力进一步提升。借助该运河以及1798年开通的特纳斯福尔斯运河，康涅狄格河的航运量达到顶峰，当地经济也得到极大发展，河谷地区人口得以翻倍增长。南哈德利福尔斯运河于1862年正式停运，其遗迹被重新开发为二百周年运河公园，游客可以在此一览汤姆山山岭和康涅狄格河的景色。如

it were redeveloped as the Bicentennial Canal Park, from which tourists can enjoy a view of the Mount Tom Range and the Connecticut River. Now, the canal is recognized as the South Hadley Canal Historic District, and one of the National Register of Historic Places.

今，南哈德利福尔斯运河被认定为南哈德利运河历史遗迹，同时被列入美国国家历史遗迹名录。

South Jiaolai River

南胶莱河

A canalized river located in Shandong Province, China. The South Jiaolai River is 30 kilometres in length and covers an area of 1,505 square kilometres. The canalization began in 1280 and took 5 years. As a branch of the Jiaolai Canal, it flows into the Jiaozhou Bay of the Yellow Sea at the Jiaodong Town.

中国山东省运河化河流。南胶莱河全长30千米，流域面积为1 505平方千米。其运河化改造工程始于1280年，耗时5年完工。南胶莱河是胶莱运河的一条分支，于胶东镇注入黄海的胶州湾。

South-North Canal

南北运河

A canal located in the town of Schöninghsdorf, Germany. The South-North Canal is connected to the Hoogeveen Canal at Hoogeveen in the Netherlands by the Schöninghsdorf-Hoogeveen Canal.

德国舍宁斯多夫镇运河。南北运河经舍宁斯多夫—霍赫芬运河在荷兰霍赫芬市与霍赫芬运河交汇。

Southwick Canal

绍斯威克运河

A canal located in England, the United Kingdom. See Southwick Ship Canal.

英国英格兰运河。见绍斯威克通海运河。

Southwick Ship Canal

绍斯威克通海运河

A canal located in England, the United Kingdom. Also called Southwick Canal. The Southwick Ship Canal starts from Southwick of West Sussex, En-

英国英格兰运河。亦称绍斯威克运河。绍斯威克通海运河始于英格兰西萨塞克斯郡绍斯威克镇，

gland. It runs westwards for 2.8 kilometres and links River Adur near Hove. It can accommodate ships with a draught of 4.6 metres, a beam of 12 metres, and a length of 73 metres. The Southwick Ship Canal was opened in 1855, providing a docking area for craft. Two locks were built on the canal as improvements: one was the Prince George Lock in 1933, and the other was the Prince Philip Lock in 1958.

向西延伸2.8千米, 在霍夫附近与阿杜尔河连通, 可承载吃水4.6米深、73米长、12米宽的船只。该运河于1855年通航, 设有船只停泊区。后为改善通航条件, 人们修建了2座船闸, 即1933年建成的乔治王子船闸和1958年建成的菲利普王子船闸。

South Willems Canal

南威廉斯运河

A cross-border canal located in Europe. The South Willems Canal flows in the south of the Netherlands and the east of Belgium. It is 121.9 kilometres in length, running from Bassin, Maastricht to Dieze, 's-Hertogenbosch, connecting the Campine Canals and the Wilhelmina Canal. Before the construction of the South Willems Canal, there were many plans to build a canal from 's-Hertogenbosch to the Belgian border. Most of them were around the Aa (Meuse), the bed of which was the main route of South Willems Canal. In history, the business centre of the United Kingdom of the Netherlands was located around the west harbours and the industrial centre was near Liège, which contributed to the heavy traffic on the Meuse then. Against this background, the South Willems Canal was planned to serve as an alternative shortcut reducing the voyage distance from 233 kilometres to 122 kilometres. On 23 February, 1818, A. F. Goudriaan was ordered to design a canal from Maastricht to 's-Hertogenbosch. According his design, the canal would be 2.1

欧洲跨国运河。南威廉斯运河流经荷兰南部和比利时东部, 全长121.9千米, 自马斯特里赫特市的巴辛流向斯海尔托亨博斯市的迪策, 与康宾运河网和威廉敏娜运河相通。在修建南威廉斯运河之前, 关于在斯海尔托亨博斯与比利时边境之间开凿运河的线路问题, 就有许多不同规划。其中, 大部分规划都提议围绕阿河 (默兹河) 开凿运河, 南威廉斯运河的主要河段也正是沿着阿河的河床而建。那时, 尼德兰联合王国的商业中心在西部港口周围, 而工业中心则位于列日附近, 这也使得默兹河上的航运尤为繁忙。在此情况下, 人们提出修建南威廉斯运河的计划, 旨在将其作为交通捷径, 以便把两中心之间的航程从233千米缩短到122千米。1818年2月23日, 古德里安奉命设计一条从马斯特里

metres deep, 10 metres wide at the bottom and 18 metres wide at the water level. The canal would have 19 locks, each with a door that would be 7 metres wide and at least 50 metres long. On 11 November, 1822, the canal was named after King Willem I of the Netherlands. The canal was opened in Maastricht on 24 August 1826 with a great celebration. The South Willems Canal provided opportunities and promoted the development of the poor towns in North Brabant. In its early days, the canal was to provide regular transportation for passengers and cargos between 's-Hertogenbosch and Maastricht. In 1841, more than 4,000 ships and barges passed through the canal. Nowadays, the canal is being expanded to make more space for larger ships and thereby develop industries in a larger scale.

赫特到斯海尔托亨博斯的运河。根据他的设计，运河深2.1米，底部宽10米，水平面宽18米。运河将设有19座船闸，每座船闸都有一扇宽7米、长至少50米的闸门。1822年11月11日，这条运河以荷兰国王威廉一世的名字命名。运河于1826年8月24日在马斯特里赫特开通，当时举行了盛大庆典。南威廉斯运河给布拉班特北部的贫困城镇带来了发展机遇。运河早期用于斯海尔托亨博斯和马斯特里赫特之间的定期客运与货运。1841年，通过运河的船只和驳船数量超过4 000多艘。如今，运河正在扩建，以便更大型船舶通航，进一步促进工业发展。

Spaarne River≈

A canalized river located in the province of North Holland, the Netherlands. The Spaarne River is 10.5 kilometres long, running between the Ring Canal and a tributary of the North Sea Canal. The river winds its way through Haarlem, Heemstede, and Spaarndam. A lock established near Spaarndam separates Spaarne from the North Sea Canal. Over the Spaarne lie several traffic bridges and road bridges. On the riverbank lie the Cruquius Museum and the old Castle Heemstede. As the former economic lifeblood of Haarlem, the Spaarne River was deepened to benefit the industries on its riverbank. Today, no large-scale industry exists on either side

斯帕恩河

荷兰北荷兰省运河化河流。斯帕恩河全长10.5千米，连通环形运河和北海运河的一条支流。河流蜿蜒穿过哈勒姆、海姆斯泰德和斯帕伦丹。斯帕伦丹附近建有1座船闸，将斯帕恩河与北海运河隔开。斯帕恩河上建有多座行人桥和公路桥，河岸上坐落着克吕屈于斯博物馆和海姆斯泰德古堡。斯帕恩河曾经是哈勒姆的经济命脉，为促进两岸工业发展，人们加深了河道。如今，河岸两边工厂林立的景象已不复存在，该河流现主要用于

of the river. It is now mainly used for the transport of goods and provides boating and other water sports service.

运输货物，并提供游船及其他水上运动服务。

Spijk Canal

斯派克运河

A canal located in the province of Groningen, the Netherlands. The Spijk Canal is 170 kilometres northeast of Amsterdam. The canal is one branch of the Eastern Wijtwerd Canal and has an elevation of —2 metres.

荷兰格罗宁根省运河。斯派克运河位于荷兰首都阿姆斯特丹东北170千米处，是东维特维德运河的一条支线运河，水位低于海平面2米。

Spoy Canal

斯波伊运河

A canal located in the state of North Rhine-Westphalia, Germany. As a part of the Rhein-Kleve shipping route, the Spoy Canal is 10.2 kilometres long and has one lock. The history of the canal can be traced back to the beginning of the 15th century when it had dual roles: a shipping route and a drainage ditch. Its name also suggests the latter function. The word "spoy" is etymologically related to "spit", indicating its drainage function. In 1658, the canal was restored with the funding from the government and made accessible by a new lock at Brienen. In 1809, the canal and the lock were destroyed by a flood with ice. After a few makeshift measures from 1843 to 1846, Prussia took over the expansion of the canal and lock for the navigation of 300-tonne ships. From 1907 to 1910, the waterway was able to adapt to the increased size of ships, after an extension to a depth of 3 metres and a bottom width of 10.5 metres. A new lock and a new harbour was

德国北莱茵—威斯特法伦州运河。斯波伊运河是莱茵—克莱沃航线的一部分，通航距离为10.2千米，河上建有1座船闸。该运河的历史可追溯至15世纪初。当时，该运河不仅是航道，也是一条排水渠。其名称中spoy一词的词源义"吐出"表明其排水功能。1658年，政府出资重新修建这条运河，布里恩附近新建的船闸将其与其他河流连通起来。1809年，一场混有浮冰的洪水冲毁了运河和船闸。经1843—1846年间的几次简单整修后，普鲁士王国接手运河和船闸的扩建工程，以方便通行载重300吨的船只。1907—1910年间，斯波伊运河加深到了3米，河床拓宽至10.5米，已足够容纳载重量较大的船舶，还新建了1座船闸和1个港

built in the area, where today's Rhein-Waal University of Applied Sciences is situated. The canal and the port were vital to Kleve's large-scale industry at that time. Currently, the Spoy Canal is a favourite area for recreational athletes as well as a tourist attraction. It is the oldest German canal that is still used for shipping, although it is almost filled with exclusively pleasure craft. Pedal boats, barbecue boats and canoes can be hired nearby.

口,现在的莱茵—瓦尔应用科技大学就坐落于此。斯波伊运河和港口曾对克莱沃市的大型工业产生了重要影响。如今,斯波伊运河是一处旅游景点,也是休闲运动的理想场所。斯波伊运河是德国现存最古老的可通航运河,现主要用于游船航行,运河附近可以租赁脚踏船、水上烧烤船和独木舟。

Sri Ram Sagar Canal

A canal located in the state of Telangana, India. See Kakatiya Canal.

斯里拉姆萨加尔运河

印度特伦甘纳邦运河。见卡卡提亚运河。

Stads Canal

A cross-border inland canal located in the Netherlands. The Stads Canal flows in the provinces of Groningen and Drenthe, and it is 32 kilometres in length and 2 metres in depth. The canal was built under the support of the city of Groningen. It was excavated to connect the villages of Bareveld and Ter Apel so as to drain the bogs of Bourtange under the proposal of the Groningen city council on 11 February 1765. The canal was accomplished in 1856, and immediately became one of the busiest Dutch inland waterways in the 19th century with the popularization of peat as fuels. There were 3 locks on the canal in total, and sometimes the ships could wait in line for several hours to pass the lock. These locks were later surrounded by bistros and small shops that eventually developed into towns

斯塔茨运河

荷兰跨境内陆运河。斯塔茨运河流经格罗宁根省和德伦特省,全长32千米,深2米,由格罗宁根市出资修建。1765年2月11日,格罗宁根市议会提议修建该运河,旨在连接贝尔费尔德和泰尔阿珀尔两个村庄,从而排干布尔坦赫地区的沼泽。1856年,运河竣工通航。这一时期,泥炭被广泛用作燃料,斯塔茨运河通航后很快成为荷兰19世纪最繁忙的内陆航道之一。河上共建有3座船闸,来往船只有时甚至要排队等候数小时方可通行。船闸周围建起很多小酒馆和商店,最终发展成为城镇。泥炭业没落之后,以土豆和稻草为主的农产品

and cities. When the peat industry declined, agricultural products, mainly potatoes and straw, turned into the principal cargo on the Stads Canal. From the 1930s, the canal saw a sharp decrease in cargo ships. There were even plans to fill the canal in the 1970s, but the residents of the Stads Canal managed to save it. Nowadays, the canal is only used by pleasure craft.

成为斯塔茨运河上的主要运输货物。20世纪30年代起，斯塔茨运河上货船数量大幅度减少。到70年代，甚至有人提议将斯塔茨运河回填，但当地居民设法保住了运河。如今，斯塔茨运河仅供观光游船使用。

Stads-Compascuum Canal

斯塔茨－孔帕斯屈姆运河

A canal located near Emmer-Compascuum in Drenthe Province, the Netherlands. The Stads-Compascuum Canal is 3.9 kilometres long and has an elevation of 13 metres.

荷兰德伦特省埃默－孔帕斯屈姆附近运河。斯塔茨－孔帕斯屈姆运河长3.9千米，海拔13米。

Stadsgraven

斯塔茨赫拉芬运河

A canal located in the city of Copenhagen, Denmark. The Stadsgraven is connected to the principal harbour on both north and south sides of the Christian Port, hence separating the neighbourhood from other areas of Amager. It is crossed by 2 footbridges and 4 causeways. In the early 17th century when the Christian Port was under construction, the canal was built originally as a fosse running along the Christian Port Rampart and constituting a part of the city's Bastioned Ring Fortifications.

丹麦哥本哈根市运河。斯塔茨赫拉芬运河在克里斯钦港南北端均与主港口相连，将克里斯钦港街区与阿迈厄岛其他地区分隔开来。运河上建有2座步行桥和4条堤道。17世纪初期，克里斯钦港还在修建中，当时人们开凿斯塔茨赫拉芬运河，旨在将其用作克里斯钦港城的护城河，并构成城市环形堡垒防御工事的一部分。

Staffordshire and Worcestershire Canal

斯塔福德郡－伍斯特郡运河

A canal located in the Midlands of England, the United Kingdom. The Staffordshire and Worcester-

英国英格兰中部运河。斯塔福德郡－伍斯特郡运河航道较窄，全

shire Canal is narrow with a full length of 74 kilometres, connecting the Severn River with the Trent and Mersey Canal. The chief engineer James Brindley tried to link Hull, Liverpool, and Bristol via waterways. The construction of this canal was a part of his plan. It was completed in 1771, and became a commercial success afterwards. Its trade extended from the Staffordshire Potteries southwards to Gloucester and Bristol, and from the Black Country northwards to the Potteries. In 1790, a part of the Severn River was improved to allow ships to sail from and to the canal more conveniently. The Worcester and Birmingham Canal built in 1815 offered a more direct waterway from Birmingham to Bristol, the trade was affected on the Staffordshire and Worcestershire Canal. The situation became even worse when the Birmingham and Liverpool Junction Canal was built. In 1948, the canal was nationalized. Since it was declared a conservation area in 1969, many historical buildings and structures along the canal have been retained and protected.

长74千米，连通塞文河与特伦特—默西运河。该运河总工程师詹姆斯·布林德利试图通过水路连接赫尔、利物浦与布里斯托尔等城市，修建运河为此计划的一部分。1771年，运河竣工。运河开通后带来巨大的商业效益。大量商品从斯塔福德陶瓷工业区经运河向南运往格洛斯特和布里斯托尔，也从黑乡向北运往陶瓷工业区。1790年，为便利来往船只，塞文河部分河段被改造。1815年开凿的伍斯特—伯明翰运河使伯明翰至布里斯托尔更便捷，斯塔福德郡—伍斯特郡运河沿线贸易也随之受到冲击。而自伯明翰—利物浦交界运河建成后，这条运河沿线的贸易形势更是每况愈下。1948年，斯塔福德郡—伍斯特郡运河被收归国有。自1969年该运河被划为保护区以来，沿岸诸多历史建筑得以保存和维护。

Stainforth and Keadby Canal

斯坦福斯-基德比运河

A canal located in England, the United Kingdom. The Stainforth and Keadby Canal connects the Don River Navigation with the Trent River and runs from west to east with a length of 24 kilometres and 3 locks. The canal can accommodate ships with a length of 18.8 metres and a width of 15.8 metres. After the canal was opened in 1802, its improvements were discussed in 1828. A new deep-water jetty was constructed on the Trent River in 1933 as

英国英格兰运河。斯坦福斯—基德比运河为东西流向，全长24千米，共有3座船闸，连通唐河航道与特伦特河。运河最大可容纳长18.8米、宽15.8米的船只通行。1802年运河通航，1828年运河改建被提上议程。1933年，特伦特河上新建一个深水码头，以改善运河基德比端的通航条件。面对来

an improvement of the end of the canal at Keadby. In the face of competitions from other canals, its traffic remained stable. To compete with railways, more improvements on the canal were made subsequently. In the winter of 1947, the canal was temporarily closed because of ice. In 2012, the ownership of the Stainforth and Keadby Canal was transferred to the Canal & River Trust.

自其他运河的激烈竞争，斯坦福斯—基德比运河通航量一直保持稳定。铁路运输兴起后，为保持竞争力，运河进行了多次改造。1947年冬，运河因河面结冰暂时被关闭。2012年，该运河的所属权被转交给英国运河与河流基金会。

St. Andries Canal

A canal located in the province of Gelderland, the Netherlands. The St. Andries Canal is 2.1 kilometres in length and 45 metres in width, flowing from the Maas to the Waal. The water level difference of these two rivers is overcome by the canal's St. Andries Lock, where the NO. 322 provincial road crosses the canal. The original canal was excavated in 1599, which was then called the Schanse Gat. In 1859, it was closed because of the construction of a lock. After the mass canalization in the 1930s, the current St. Andries Canal was built. Now the canal mainly serves for transportation.

圣安德烈斯运河

荷兰海尔德兰省运河。圣安德烈斯运河长2.1千米，宽45米，从马斯河流至瓦尔河。为解决马斯河和瓦尔河之间的水位落差问题，人们修建了圣安德烈斯船闸，322号省道也由此横跨运河。运河最初开凿于1599年，当时被称作斯汉斯河。1859年，为了修建船闸，运河被关闭。在20世纪30年代经大规模运河化改造之后，有了如今的圣安德烈斯运河。如今，这条运河主要发挥航运作用。

St. Clair Flats Canal

A canal located in the state of Michigan, the United States. The St. Clair Flats Canal is 2.2 kilometres in length, constructed between 1866 and 1871. Originally 91.4 metres in width and 4 metres in depth, it was bounded on each side by a dyke. In 1873, the canal was deepened to 4.8 metres. In 1893, it was dredged to a depth of 6.1 metres.

圣克莱尔平原运河

美国密歇根州运河。圣克莱尔平原运河全长2.2千米，1866年开凿，1871年竣工。运河最初宽91.4米，深4米，两岸都筑有堤坝，1873年加深到4.8米，1893年疏浚至6.1米深。

Steenenhoek Canal

An inland canal located in the province of South Holland, the Netherlands. The Steenenhoek Canal originates from the northern part of Gorinchem City and extends westward from its connection with the Linge to join the Lower Merwede in the city of Hardinxveld-Giessendam. It is 8.7 kilometres in length, flowing along the railway and A15 (Rotterdam-Nijmegen) motorway. With 4 bridges and 2 locks, it was excavated around 1819 to act as drainage of the Linge. At its mouth, the municipality of Hardinxveld-Giessendam, a pumping station was constructed to maintain the water level.

Steenwijk Canal

A canal located in the province of Overijssel, the Netherlands. As the canalized part of the Steenwijk River, the Steenwijk Canal is 9.5 kilometres in length. It runs across the city of Steenwijk and connects the Steenwijk River to the Wetering Canal. The canal was excavated to improve the shipping capacity of the Steenwijk River. At the very beginning, ships used to sail from Steenwijk and follow the old course through the Steenwijk River, the Giethoorn Lake, and the Noord Canal to reach Blokzijl. The Steenwijk River being too narrow, shallow and winding for large vessels, goods are transshipped in Blokzijl before reaching their final destination. The river was sometimes only available in winter for the insufficient water volume in other seasons. All these made it a barrier for goods

斯蒂嫩胡克运河

荷兰南荷兰省内陆运河。斯蒂嫩胡克运河始于霍林赫姆市北部，与灵厄河交汇后向西流动，于哈丁克斯费尔德—希森丹市与梅尔韦德河下游连通。运河全长8.7千米，其流向同当地铁路及A15高速公路（鹿特丹—奈梅亨）走向一致。斯蒂嫩胡克运河约1819年开凿，河上建有4座桥梁与2座船闸，用于灵厄河排水。在该运河河口的哈丁克斯费尔德—希森丹市还建有一座用以控制水位的泵站。

斯滕韦克运河

荷兰上艾瑟尔省运河。斯滕韦克运河是斯滕韦克河的运河化河段，全长9.5千米，流经斯滕韦克市，连通斯滕韦克河与韦特林运河。开凿斯滕韦克运河旨在提高斯滕韦克河的航运能力。起初，船只通常从斯滕韦克市出发，沿斯滕韦克河、希特霍恩湖和诺德运河这一旧航线驶抵布洛克宰尔市。对大型货船而言，斯滕韦克河水面狭窄，水深不够且河道过于蜿蜒曲折，货物运抵目的地之前常需在布洛克宰尔市进行中转。由于其他季节水量不足，斯滕韦克河仅冬天才能通航。这些不利因素给斯滕韦克河的货物运输与交易活动带来

shipping and trading in this area, thus bringing complaints from residents. The excavation of the Steenwijk Canal between Steenwijk and Muggenbeet was started in 1626 and was finally completed in 1632, which enabled vessels to sail directly to the sea without goods transhipment. The newly built canal is connected to the Steenwijk River through the Paardenmarkt Lock constructed in 1865, now listed as a heritage object. Cargoes on the canal were mostly dried peat as fuels. In 1932, the ownership, management, and maintenance of the canal were passed from the municipality of Steenwijk to the province of Overijssel.

不便，饱受当地居民抱怨。连通斯滕韦克市与穆亨贝特村的斯滕韦克运河于1626年动工开凿，1632年竣工。运河通航后，船只可直接从斯滕韦克市驶向海洋，货运无须中转。新修的斯滕韦克运河通过1865年修建的帕登马克特船闸与斯滕韦克河相连通，该船闸目前已被荷兰政府列为文化遗产。斯滕韦克运河上运送的货物多是用作燃料的干泥炭。1932年，运河所有权、管理权和维护权均由斯滕韦克市移交至上艾瑟尔省。

Stieltjes Canal

斯蒂尔切斯运河

A canal located in the province of Drenthe, the Netherlands. The Stieltjes Canal is 13 kilometres long, running northeast from Coevorden to the Hoogeveen Extension Canal in New Amsterdam. The canal was constructed from 1880 to 1884 and opened in November 1884. The Stieltjes Canal was named after Thomas Joannes Stieltjes, who was then in charge of the construction work. Along the canal, there is also a hamlet named Stieltjes Canal.

荷兰德伦特省运河。斯蒂尔切斯运河全长13千米，从库福尔登市沿东北方向流至新阿姆斯特丹，与霍赫芬扩建运河交汇。运河于1880—1884年间开凿，1884年11月通航。斯蒂尔切斯运河得名于当时监管该运河修建的工程师托马斯·约翰内斯·斯蒂尔切斯。运河沿岸还有一个同名村庄。

Stockton Deep Water Ship Channel

斯托克顿深水通海航道

A canalized river located in central California, the United States. See San Joaquin River.

美国加利福尼亚州中部运河化河流。见圣华金河。

Stolpen-Kolhorn Canal

A canal located in the province of North Holland, the Netherlands. The Stolpen-Kolhorn Canal is 11.5 kilometres in length. It consists of two parts: the Stolpen-Schagen Canal with a length of 4.4 kilometres, and the Schagen-Kolhorn Canal with a length of 7.1 kilometres. The canal connects the North Holland Canal via the port of Schagen with the village of Kolhorn.

Storkow Canal

A canal located in the state of Brandenburg, Germany. The Storkow Canal is a part of the Dahme Waterways, originating in the north end of the Scharmützel Lake. The canal flows through the Wolzig Lake and the Langen Lake and empties into the Dahme River. In 1732, the Storkow Rafting Canal was excavated to facilitate timber transportation towards Berlin but only existed for a short time. In 1746, the Storkow Canal was built. Between 1825 and 1828, locks were built on the Storkow Canal. In 1862, the locks at Kummersdorf were rebuilt, and the canal was widened and deepened, while the other locks were also reconstructed from 1863 to 1865. Between 1892 and 1897, the canal was widened again. After World War II, the demand for cargo shipping was decreasing. Between 2001 and 2003, the old Storkow Lock built in 1863 was demolished and replaced by a new self-service lock 150 metres below the original site. At present, there are 3 locks on the waterway, with a navigable

斯托尔彭－科尔霍恩运河

荷兰北荷兰省运河。斯托尔彭－科尔霍恩运河全长11.5千米，由4.4千米长的斯托尔彭－斯哈亨运河和7.1千米长的斯哈亨－科尔霍恩运河组成。该运河在斯哈亨港连通北荷兰运河和科尔霍恩村。

施托尔科运河

德国勃兰登堡州运河。施托尔科运河是达默河航道网的一部分，始于沙米策尔湖北端，流经沃尔齐希湖和朗根湖，汇入达默河。1732年，为便于向柏林运输木材，人们开凿了施托尔科排筏运河，但该运河存在时间较短。1746年，施托尔科运河建成。1825—1828年间，运河上修建了多座船闸。1862年，库默斯多夫处的船闸重修，运河被拓宽和加深。1863—1865年间，其他船闸也陆续重修。1892—1897年间，河道再次拓宽。第二次世界大战后，运河上的货运量日渐减少。2001—2003年间，建于1863年的施托尔科旧船闸被拆除，在其原址下游150米处重建了1座新型自助通行船闸。如今，施托尔科运河共有3座船闸，可通航长度为33.4千米。

length of 33.4 kilometres.

Stör Waterway

A waterway located in the west of Mecklen-burg-Vorpommern, Germany. The Stör Waterway runs northwards from Elde Triangle to Hohen Viecheln. As a Class I federal waterway, the Stör Waterway is 44.7 kilometres long and comprises the Stör, the Stör Canal and the Schwerin Lake. It flows through Banzkow, Plate, Raben Steinfeld, etc. There is one lock built in Banzkow in order to regulate the water level of Lake Schwerin. As early as the 16th century, the river was used to transport wood from Lewitz for heating the Schwerin Castle. In 1830, the water depth was increased by the construction of dams on both sides. In the following centuries, the channel was further expanded and deepened with a view to obtaining more economic benefits. After 1990, the commercial value of the waterway declined, and the Stör Waterway was gradually transformed into a recreational waterway for boat trips and sightseeing.

施特尔航道

德国梅克伦堡—前波美拉尼亚州西部航道。施特尔航道全长44.7千米，为联邦一级航道，由施特尔河、施特尔运河和什未林湖组成。该航道始于埃尔德三角地区，向北流至霍亨菲歇尔恩，途经班茨科、普拉特、拉本斯泰因费尔德等城镇。班茨科境内的河段上建有1座船闸，用以调控什未林湖的水位。早在16世纪，人们就开始利用施特尔航道运送来自莱维茨的木材，以满足什未林城堡冬日取暖之需。1830年，两岸修建水坝后，河道进一步加深。之后的几个世纪里，为增加经济收益，人们对施特尔航道不断地进行拓宽和加深。1990年后，施特尔航道商业价值下降，被逐步改造为乘船观光的休闲航道。

Stourbridge Canal

A canal located in the West Midlands of England, the United Kingdom. The Stourbridge Canal connects Staffordshire with the Metropolitan Borough of Dudley. The construction of the canal began in 1776, and its main line is 9.3 kilometres in length with 20 locks. Originally meant to carry coal from Dudley to Stourbridge, the canal was put into use

斯陶尔布里奇运河

英国英格兰西米德兰兹郡运河。斯陶尔布里奇运河连接斯塔福德郡与达德利都市自治区，主航道全长9.3千米，河上建有20座船闸。该运河于1776年开凿，1779年通航，最初用于将达德利的煤炭运往斯陶尔布里奇。后运河货运种类不断

in 1779. The cargoes carried via the canal were later extended to a large variety, including ironstone, limestone, earthenware, glass, and so on. In the 19th century, the canal tolls kept increasing despite the influence of railways. Later, dredging programmes and other improvements promoted the local trade and profited the Stourbridge Canal Company. In fierce competition with road vehicles, the commercial traffic on the canal was reduced continually until it came to a full stop. The Stourbridge Canal started to be restored in 1964 and was reopened in 1967.

增加，包括铁矿石、石灰岩、陶器和玻璃等。19世纪，虽然受到铁路运输的影响，斯陶尔布里奇运河通行费一直呈上涨趋势。运河疏浚及其他修缮工程促进了当地贸易的持续发展，斯陶尔布里奇运河公司也从中获益。在与公路运输的激烈竞争中，斯陶尔布里奇运河的商业运输功能逐步衰落，直至运河彻底关停。1964年斯陶尔布里奇运河启动重修工程，并于1967年重新开通。

Stourbridge Extension Canal

斯陶尔布里奇扩建运河

An abandoned canal located in Staffordshire, England, the United Kingdom. The Stourbridge Extension Canal ran for 3.2 kilometres from the Stourbridge Extension Canal Stop Lock to the Stourbridge Canal. Opened in 1840, the canal was intended to serve coal mines in the Kingswinford area. In the early 1900s, trade on the canal began to decline. Later, in competition with railways, it was almost closed down. The canal was finally abandoned in 1935 with most of its channels filled in, and later, a trading estate and a housing complex were built on the original canal. Since 2004, a short section of the canal has been used as moorings for ships on the Stourbridge Canal.

英国英格兰斯塔福德郡废弃运河。斯陶尔布里奇扩建运河全长3.2千米，经斯陶尔布里奇扩建运河节制闸流向斯陶尔布里奇运河。该运河于1840年开通，旨在服务于金斯温福特地区的煤矿运输。20世纪早期，运河上的贸易量开始下滑。后在与铁路运输的竞争中，运河几近关停。1935年，斯陶尔布里奇扩建运河被废弃，大部分航道被回填，人们后来在运河原址上又修建了工商业区和住宅区。自2004年以来，该运河有一小段航道成为斯陶尔布里奇运河的泊船处。

St. Ours River

圣乌尔河

A canalized river located in southern Canada. The

加拿大南部运河化河流。圣乌尔河

St. Ours River lies on the eastern shore of the Darvard Island. It was opened in 1849, which enabled boats to bypass the obstacles on the waterway between Montreal and New York. It has been playing an important role in international, regional and local business. Today, the canal is a place of relaxation and fish observation. It is a National Historic Site in Canada.

位于达瓦尔特岛东岸，1849年开放通航，使往来船只可以避开蒙特利尔和美国纽约州之间航道上的障碍。自通航之日起，该河就一直在国际、区域和当地贸易活动中发挥着重要作用。如今，圣乌尔河已成为休闲胜地和鱼类观赏地，被列为加拿大国家历史遗址。

St. Peter's Canal

圣彼得运河

A canal located in Canada. The St. Peter's Canal lies on the Cape Breton Island with a length of 800 metres, connecting the Atlantic Ocean to the Bras d'Or Lake. It was constructed in 1854 and opened in 1869. The water flow direction of most canals never changes. The St. Peter's Canal is unusual in that the direction of its water flow changes regularly because of the tides. Unusual gates are applied on this canal. The usual canal lock has a gate on either end and each gate is made up of two doors which may form a shallow "V" shape when they are closed. The point of the "V" points upstream. At the locks of the St. Peter's Canal, each gate consists of 4 doors. They form a diamond when they are closed. Among the canals listed as national historic monuments in Atlantic Canada, the St. Peter's Canal is the only working one. It is also an important historic landmark of the Cape Breton Island.

加拿大运河。圣彼得运河位于布雷顿角岛，全长800米，连通大西洋与布里多尔湖。该运河1854年开凿，1869年通航。运河的水流方向大多不会改变，而圣彼得运河则较为特殊，受潮汐影响，其水流方向会定期改变。圣彼得运河上的船闸也有所不同。一般情况下，船闸两端分别设有闸门，每处闸门由两扇门组成。闸门关闭状态下，两扇门呈浅V形状，V字尖端指向上游。而圣彼得运河上的每处船闸闸门共由4扇门组成，闭合时呈一个菱形。圣彼得运河是加拿大大西洋沿海地区国家历史古迹运河中唯一一条仍在使用的运河，同时也是布雷顿角岛上重要的历史地标。

Strasbourg Canals

斯特拉斯堡运河网

A canal system located in Strasbourg, France. The

法国斯特拉斯堡运河网络。斯特

Strasbourg Canals include the Marne-Rhine Canal, the Rhône-Rhine Canal, and the Faux-Rempart Canal. In the 18th and 19th centuries, starting from Strasbourg, the Marne-Rhine Canal and the Rhône-Rhine Canal were excavated successively, making it easy to reach Paris and Lyon by water. Strasbourg thus became the hub for trade between France and central Europe, and wine-making and food industries developed along with it. The opening of these canals also established Strasbourg as a shipping hub and changed people's conception of urban rivers. The mayor thought that the city should be provided with spacious freight and navigation channels. In 1840, the Faust-Rempart Canal in the northern part of the Grand Island was opened. After World War II, with the Strasbourg Canals as the link, Strasbourg continued to extend to the northeast of the old city to develop new areas.

拉斯堡运河网包括马恩—莱茵运河、罗讷—莱茵运河和福—朗帕运河。18—19世纪时，以斯特拉斯堡为起点，马恩—莱茵运河和罗讷—莱茵运河先后开凿，通过水路到达巴黎和里昂因此更为便捷。斯特拉斯堡成为法国与中欧地区的贸易枢纽，周边地区的酿酒业和食品业也随之发展起来。马恩—莱茵运河和罗讷—莱茵运河的开凿和通航也奠定了斯特拉斯堡的航运枢纽地位，使人们对城市河流的观念发生转变。当时的斯特拉斯堡市市长认为应当在城内修建宽阔的货运和通航运河。1840年，格兰德岛区北部的福—朗帕运河开放通航。第二次世界大战后，斯特拉斯堡继续以该运河网为纽带，向老城东北方向延伸，拓展新的发展区域。

Stratford-upon-Avon Canal

埃文河畔斯特拉特福运河

A canal located in the south Midlands of England, the United Kingdom. The Stratford-upon-Avon Canal is near the birthplace of the Elizabethan playwright William Shakespeare. The canal is 41 kilometres in length with 56 locks, connecting the Worcester and Birmingham Canal to River Avon. Divided into two sections at the Kingswood Junction, the canal finally connects with the Grand Union Canal. The canal was constructed in 1793 and put into use in 1800, while the southern section

英国英格兰中南部运河。埃文河畔斯特拉特福运河毗邻伊丽莎白时代剧作家威廉·莎士比亚出生地。运河全长41千米，沿线共建有56座船闸，连通伍斯特—伯明翰运河与埃文河。该运河在金斯伍德交界处分为两段，并最终与大联盟运河连通。运河1793年开凿，1800年通航，但其南部河段直至1816年才完工。人们修建埃文河

was not completed until 1816. The Stratford-up-on-Avon Canal was intended to transport coal from the Dudley Canal and the Stourbridge Canal to Oxford and London. By the late 1930s, the southern section had fallen into disuse. Although the northern section was never officially closed, its traffic had practically come to an end by 1939. In 1964, the canal was made fully navigable after restoration. Since then, it has again become a part of the direct route to River Severn.

畔斯特拉特福运河最初是为了方便将煤炭从达德利运河和斯陶尔布里奇运河运往牛津与伦敦。20世纪30年代末，运河南部河段被废弃。运河北部河段虽未正式停用，但实际上，截至1939年已基本停航。1964年，埃文河畔斯特拉特福运河重修后再次全面开通。如今，该运河已再次成为直达塞文河航道的组成部分。

Strecknitz Canal

斯特雷克尼茨运河

An abandoned canal located in northern Germany. The Strecknitz Canal originates from Lauenburg, flows to Lübeck, and connects the Elbe River with the Trave River. As one of the first artificial waterways in Europe on the Old Salt Route, the canal was built in 1391 and completed in 1398, with a length of 97 kilometres and 17 locks. The Strecknitz Canal was mainly used for freight transportation, especially that of salt. In 1893, the canal was closed to barge traffic. In 1895, the construction of the Elbe–Lübeck Canal began, which replaced the Strecknitz Canal. Today the canal is no longer in use.

德国北部废弃运河。斯特雷克尼茨运河始于劳恩堡，流向吕贝克，连通易北河和特拉沃河，是欧洲运盐古道上最早的人工航道之一。运河1391年开凿，1398年竣工，全长97千米，建有17座船闸。斯特雷克尼茨运河主要用于货运，尤其是盐运。1893年，该运河停止驳船运输业务。1895年，易北—吕贝克运河开始修建，竣工后取代了斯特雷克尼茨运河。如今，斯特雷克尼茨运河已停用。

Strömma Canal (Finland)

斯特伦玛运河（芬兰）

A canal located in Finland. Lying on the border between the cities of Kimitoön and Salo, the Strömma Canal connects the two bays of Tykö and Finnar in the Gulf of Finland. The old Strömma Canal was constructed in the 1840s and enlarged in the 1890s.

芬兰运河。斯特伦玛运河流经芬兰的凯米托恩和瑟洛两市交界地区，连接芬兰湾的泰库和芬纳两个湾区。旧斯特伦玛运河19世纪40年代开凿，19世纪90年代进一步拓建。

To the west of the old canal, a new Strömma Canal was built in the 1960s with a lift bridge operated by electrically driven mechanical machinery. The new canal is 28 metres wide and 5.5 metres deep. It is said that the Strömma Canal is a unique location in Finland where the tide can be observed clearly.

新斯特伦玛运河位于旧运河以西，20世纪60年代开凿，河上建有1座机械电动控制的升降桥。新斯特伦玛运河宽28米，深5.5米。据说在芬兰，只有在斯特伦玛运河上才能清楚地观察到潮汐现象。

Strömma Canal (Sweden)

斯特伦玛运河（瑞典）

A canal located in Sweden. The Strömma Canal lies in the city of Värmdö, east of Stockholm, and it is 2 metres in depth and 7 metres in width. The sailing-free height below the bridge is 2.7 metres. The canal provides a short and safe route from Stockholm to the outer Stockholm islands. Today, the channel is used mainly by small pleasure boats.

瑞典运河。斯特伦玛运河位于斯德哥尔摩东部韦尔姆德市，运河深2米，宽7米，桥下通航船只限高2.7米。该运河是斯德哥尔摩前往城外诸岛的一条安全快捷的水上通道。如今，斯特伦玛运河主要供小型游船通行。

Strömsholm Canal

斯特伦斯霍尔姆运河

A canal located in Sweden. The Strömsholm Canal runs from Smedjebacken to Lake Mälaren near Strömsholm. As one of Sweden's longest channels, the canal is about 110 kilometres in length. It has 26 locks and comprises a series of small lakes joined by many short artificial cuts. The canal was constructed between 1777 and 1795, mainly for iron transportation. With the railways and road traffic increasing, the canal began to lose its significance. In 1990, the Strömsholm Canal was declared a memorial site. Today, the canal is only visited by pleasure boats.

瑞典运河。斯特伦斯霍尔姆运河从斯梅杰巴肯市流至斯特伦斯霍尔姆附近的梅拉伦湖，全长约110千米，是瑞典最长的航道之一，沿线建有26座船闸，流经许多由人工短程运河相连的小湖泊。该运河1777年开凿，1795年竣工，主要用于运输铁。随着铁路和公路交通运输的发展，运河航运的重要性逐渐降低。1990年，斯特伦斯霍尔姆运河被认定为一处具有纪念意义的历史遗址。如今，该运河仅供观光船只通行。

Stroobos Trek Canal

A canal located in the province of Friesland, the Netherlands. Also called Dokkum Trek Canal. The Stroobos Trek Canal runs from Dokkum to Gerkesklooster and Stroobos, where it joins the Prinses Margriet Canal and the Van Starkenborgh Canal. In the 16th century, the part of the trek between Kollum and Gerkesklooster was constructed and initially used as a hunting ground for many years, which was considered a bad connection between Dokkum and Gerkesklooster. Supervised by the city council of Dokkum, the construction of the canal was started in 1654 and finished in 1656. People of Dokkum believed that improving the connection between the water and Groningen could attract more shipping traffic. The city of Dokkum went bankrupt due to the high cost of the navigation project. Later, the ownership of the shipping company was transferred to a group of creditors. For years, they have set up a number of toll booths to ensure that the traffic pays off.

Sturgeon Bay and Lake Michigan Ship Canal

A canal located in the state of Wisconsin, the United States. The Sturgeon Bay and Lake Michigan Ship Canal connects the Green Bay with Lake Michigan. It is 13.6 kilometres in length, 38 metres in width, and 6.1 metres in depth. Joseph Harris planned to build this canal as a shorter and safer waterway to facilitate the selling of building lots

斯特罗博斯拖船运河

荷兰弗里斯兰省运河。亦称多克姆拖船运河。斯特罗博斯拖船运河始于多克姆，流向赫尔克罗斯特和斯特罗博斯，并在此与玛格丽特公主运河和范斯塔肯博赫运河交汇。科勒姆和赫尔克罗斯特之间的拖船河道修建于16世纪。该航道最初用作渔场，不能满足多克姆和赫尔克罗斯特之间的航运需求。在多克姆市议会监督下，斯特罗博斯拖船运河1654年动工开凿，1656年竣工。多克姆人认为，改善这条水路与格罗宁根省之间的通行状况能够提高航运流量，但因航运建设项目成本高昂，最终导致多克姆市破产。船运公司的所有权被转让给其债权人。多年来，债权人通过建立多座收费站来收回前期的投资成本。

斯特金湾-密歇根湖通海运河

美国威斯康星州运河。斯特金湾－密歇根湖通海运河连通格林湾和密歇根湖，全长13.6千米，宽38米，深6.1米。约瑟夫·哈里斯提出开凿这条运河的规划，旨在修建一条更快捷安全的水上航道，促进运河沿线建筑用地的出售，推

along this canal and boost the local economy. After much work, the canal was authorized in 1864, but the construction was not started until 1872. Constructed by a private group of Chicago and North Western Railway from 1872 to 1881, this canal was originally only accessible for smaller boats. Larger craft could not be seen on it until 1890. Since it was sold by the Ogden Private Investor Group, it has been managed by the United States Army Corps of Engineers. It serves as a crucial link in shipbuilding and transport industries, and is used as a shortcut for boats to transport directly between Lake Michigan and the Green Bay, bypassing the Door of Death, a strait known for shipwrecks. Several lighthouses along the canal attract many tourists. The most visited ones include the Sturgeon Bay Canal Lighthouse. Tourists can also go hiking and sightseeing along the northern side of this canal. Currently, the local government has considered building a coal-fueled power plant and an aquatic-based industrial centre to exploit this canal better.

动当地经济发展。经不懈努力，该修建计划于1864年获得批准，但直到1872年才动工实施。运河的修建工作由芝加哥和西北铁路公司某私人团队负责。1881年，斯特金湾—密歇根湖通海运河刚完工时仅能容纳小型船只，直到1890年才有大型船只通航。运河被奥格登私人投资集团出售后，一直由美国陆军工程兵团负责管理。该运河是联通造船业和运输业的重要纽带，它使船只能够绕过因沉船事故而著称的"死亡之门"海峡，直接从密歇根湖驶往格林湾。运河沿岸的几座灯塔吸引许多游客，其中最受欢迎的包括斯特金湾运河灯塔。游客还可沿运河北岸远足和观光。如今，为充分开发利用该运河，当地政府正在规划建设燃煤发电厂和水上工业中心。

Sturgeon Bay Ship Canal

斯特金湾通海运河

A canal located in the state of Wisconsin, the United States. The Sturgeon Bay Ship Canal stretches approximately 11 kilometres in length and links the Sturgeon Bay with Lake Michigan. The canal comprises two parts: a dredged portion of the Sturgeon Bay and an approximately 2-kilometre-long canal built through the eastern side of the Door Peninsula. Although smaller craft began using the canal in 1880, it was not open to large-scale watercraft

美国威斯康星州运河。斯特金湾通海运河全长约11千米，连通斯特金湾与密歇根湖。运河由两段构成，即斯特金湾经过人工疏浚的一段河道和多尔半岛东侧一段长约2千米的运河。1880年，该运河上已有小型船只通行，但直到1890年，运河才开始容纳大型船只通行。1893年，美国政府从奥格登

until 1890. In 1893, the United States government bought all interests in the canal from the Ogden Private Investors Group. The canal has been maintained by the United States Army Corps of Engineers. Several famous lighthouses mark the course of the canal, including the Sturgeon Bay Canal Lighthouse at the eastern entrance on the northern side of the canal, the Sturgeon Bay Canal North Pierhead Light on Lake Michigan coastline, and the Sherwood Point Lighthouse on the west side of the north entrance to the Sturgeon Bay.

私人投资者集团购买运河全部股份。后整条运河一直由美国陆军工程兵团负责管理。斯特金湾通海运河上矗立着数座知名灯塔，包括位于运河北侧东入河口处的斯特金湾灯塔、密歇根湖湖岸的斯特金湾北防波堤灯塔和斯特金湾北入河口西侧的舍伍德角灯塔。

Suez Canal

苏伊士运河

A canal located in Egypt. The Suez Canal is a sea-level waterway, and it starts from the south of Port Said and ends at the south of Suez City. It is 193 kilometres in length, about 313 metres in width and 24 metres in depth, linking Europe, Asia, and Africa. The concept of connecting the Red Sea with the Mediterranean Sea dates back to the period of the Pharaohs of Ancient Egypt. After conquering Egypt in 1798, Napoleon Bonaparte sent a team of surveyors to investigate the feasibility of building a canal from the Red Sea to the Mediterranean. The idea was later given up, for a mistake in measurement showed that any attempt to create a canal could result in catastrophic flooding across the Nile Delta. Plans for a canal stalled until 1847, when researchers finally proved no significant difference in altitude between the Red Sea and the Mediterranean. In 1854, the French ambassador Ferdinand Marie de Lesseps (1805—1894) was authorized by

埃及运河。苏伊士运河为海平式航道，始于塞得港南部，止于苏伊士城南，全长193千米，宽约313米，深约24米，连接欧洲、亚洲和非洲。最早在古埃及法老统治时期，人们就有连通红海与地中海的设想。1798年，拿破仑·波拿巴征服埃及后，曾派遣勘测队前往埃及考察在红海与地中海间开凿运河的可行性。勘测报告中出现一处失误，得出的结论是无论执行何种运河修建方案，均会导致整个尼罗河三角洲出现灾难性洪灾。正是这一勘测失误促使拿破仑放弃了开凿运河的想法。直到1847年，有研究者最终证实红海与地中海之间的海拔高度不存在显著性差异后，该运河的开凿计划才再次被提上议事日程。1854年，经奥

the Egyptian governor of the Ottoman Empire to set up a company to construct the Suez Canal. The construction began in 1859. After 10 years' labour, the canal was officially opened in November 1869. The canal provides an avenue for vessels to pass between Asia, especially the Middle East and Europe, and ships do not have to go around the Cape of Good Hope in Africa. In 2015, Egypt completed a major expansion of the Suez Canal that deepened the main waterway. The Suez Canal is an artery of world trade. Approximately 12 percent of global trade uses the canal, carrying close to $10 billion in goods per day. On 23 March 2021, Ever Given, a 20,000 TEU (Twenty-foot Equivalent Unit) container ship, became stuck across the canal in high winds. The ship remained grounded for six days, halting traffic in both directions and disrupting global trade.

斯曼帝国埃及总督授权，法国驻埃及大使斐迪南·玛利·德·雷赛布（1805—1894）获准成立公司，开凿运河。1859年，运河开凿，历经10年后于1869年11月正式通航。苏伊士运河为亚洲，尤其中东与欧洲之间的航行提供了一条通道，使船只无须绕道非洲好望角。2015年，埃及完成对苏伊士运河的扩建工作，加深了主航道。苏伊士运河是世界贸易大动脉之一，全球约12%的贸易均通过该运河完成，每天承载价值近100亿美元的航运货物。2021年3月23日，"长赐"号货轮（一艘载重2万标准箱的集装箱货轮）因突遭强风吹袭而搁浅，造成运河停航6天，严重影响了运河上的双向交通及全球贸易。

Susquehanna and Tidewater Canal

萨斯奎汉纳－泰德沃特运河

An abandoned canal located in the United States. The Susquehanna and Tidewater Canal runs between Wrightsville, Pennsylvania and Havre de Grace, Maryland. It is 69 kilometres in length, with 48 kilometres in Pennsylvania and 21 kilometres in Maryland. It has 29 locks along the course, each being 5.2 metres wide and 52 metres long. In 1835, the Susquehanna Canal Company was charted by Pennsylvania to build a canal from Columbia to the State line. The company later merged with the Tidewater Canal Company to form the Susquehanna and Tidewater Canal Company. The construction

美国废弃运河。萨斯奎汉纳－泰德沃特运河自宾夕法尼亚州的赖茨维尔流至马里兰州的哈弗尔德格雷斯港。运河全长69千米，其中48千米位于宾夕法尼亚州，21千米位于马里兰州。沿线共建有29座船闸，每座船闸宽5.2米，长52米。1835年，宾夕法尼亚州政府特许萨斯奎汉纳运河公司修建一条从哥伦比亚至该州边界的运河，该公司后来同泰德沃特运河公司合并为萨斯奎汉纳－泰德沃特运河公司。

began in 1838. The west bank of the Susquehanna was considered a more feasible route for the canal. The river was dammed, feeding water into the canal under construction. In 1840, the Susquehanna and Tidewater Canal was opened. Coal, lumber, grain and iron were shipped along the canal, mostly heading south to Baltimore and Philadelphia. Mainly due to the rise of the railway, the canal's significance gradually declined, and by 1894, the canal was abandoned. Today, people can still see remnants of the canal in Maryland, and locks No. 12 and 15 in Pennsylvania have been preserved.

Susquehanna Division

A canal located in the northeastern United States. The Susquehanna Division is a part of the Pennsylvania Canal system. The canal runs 66 kilometres along the west bank of the Susquehanna River, with 12 locks overcoming a water level difference of 26 metres. Beginning at Duncannon, it joins the west branch and north branch of the Susquehanna River at Northumberland. As an essential part of the water transportation system, it links the public and private canals upstream and the Main Line of Public Works. It also bridged the traffic between the Union Canal and the Allegheny Portage Railroad. The canal was excavated in 1827 and finished in 1831. To facilitate the navigation, a dam was built, which was 609 metres long and 2.6 metres high, with two locks controlling the water level. With the dam, a pool was formed between the lower end of Duncan's Island and the east bank of the Susque-

1838年运河开凿。当时人们认为萨斯奎汉纳河西岸更适合开凿运河，于是在河上筑坝，把水引入在建运河。1840年，运河通航，主要运输煤炭、木材、谷物和铁，这些货物大多向南运往巴尔的摩和费城。后因受铁路运输冲击，萨斯奎汉纳—泰德沃特运河逐渐失去航运价值。1894年，运河被弃用。如今，在马里兰州仍能看到该运河遗迹。在宾夕法尼亚州，运河上的12号和15号船闸得以保存。

萨斯奎汉纳河段

美国东北部运河。萨斯奎汉纳河段为宾夕法尼亚运河网的一部分，沿萨斯奎汉纳河西岸延伸，全长66千米，河上建有12座船闸，调节26米的水位落差。该运河始于邓肯嫩，在诺森伯兰市与萨斯奎汉纳河的西、北两条支流交汇。萨斯奎汉纳河段是宾夕法尼亚航运网的重要组成部分，连接公有和私有运河网上游与公共工程（商业交通）主线。它还连接联合运河和阿勒格尼波蒂奇铁路。萨斯奎汉纳河段1827年开凿，1831年竣工。为方便通航，人们在萨斯奎汉纳支线运河之上修建了1座长609米、高2.6米的大坝，利用2座船闸来控制水位。大坝建成后，邓肯岛南端和萨斯奎汉纳河东岸之间形成一个坝

hanna River. Boats and vessels can be lifted to a two-tier towpath bridge at the Clark's Ferry and then navigate between the dam pool and the canals.

池。来往船只首先被吊升至位于克拉克渡口的双层拖带桥，后可在坝池和运河之间航行。

Sutlej-Yamuna Link Canal

A canal under construction located in northern India. The Sutlej-Yamuna Link Canal connects the Sutlej and Yamuna rivers. The planned length of the canal is 214 kilometres. Up to now, 85 percent of the canal has been completed.

萨特莱杰－亚穆纳连接运河

印度北部在建运河。萨特莱杰—亚穆纳连接运河连通萨特莱杰河与亚穆纳河，计划开凿长度为214千米，目前运河85%的工程已完工。

Suvorov Military Canals

A canal system located in Finland. The Suvorov Military Canals are composed of four canals, namely, the Kutvele, Käyhkää, Kukonharju, and Telataipale canals. As the oldest canals in Finland, these canals were constructed between 1791 and 1798. All were open canals with no locks. After the Russo-Swedish War (1788—1790), Russia constructed a series of canals in southeastern Finland in order to bypass Puumala and improve the defence in Finland. The construction was completed in 1798. In 1816, civilian authorities took over the responsibility for the canals and dwindled the use of the canals to local inhabitants. Located on the border of Taipalsaari and Ruokolahti, the Kutvele Canal was enlarged twice during the 20th century, with nothing of the original construction left. The canal provided a shipping route with a depth of 2.4 metres and a maximum height of 12.5 metres. The Käyhkää Canal is located in Ruokolahti and is 350 metres

苏沃洛夫军事运河网

芬兰运河网络。苏沃洛夫军事运河网包括库特瓦勒运河、凯卡运河、库康纳鸠运河和泰勒泰佩尔运河。这4条运河于1791—1798年间开凿，构成芬兰最古老的运河网，均为不设船闸的开放式运河。俄瑞战争（1788—1790）后，俄国在芬兰东南部开凿多条运河，旨在绕过普马拉，提高俄军在芬兰的防御能力。1798年，4条运河全部竣工。1816年，苏沃洛夫军事运河网交由民事部门管理，仅供当地居民使用。库特瓦勒运河位于泰帕尔萨里和鲁奥科拉赫蒂交界处，20世纪时经历过两次扩建，最初的样貌已不复存在。库特瓦勒运河航道深2.4米，可容船只最大净空高度12.5米。凯卡运河位于鲁奥科拉赫蒂，加上入口处的河段，

in total length (including the canal entrances), but the length of the canal is only 80 metres. Being the longest of the canals, the Kukonharju Canal has a length of 800 metres. It is located on the border of Ruokolahti and Puumala. As the northernmost of the canals, the Telataipale Canal located in Sulkava is 300 metres in length. The last-mentioned three canals remained almost untouched from the early 19th century to 2003, when the Finnish National Board of Antiquities began to restore them. Now, the Suvorov Military Canals have become tourist attractions.

全长350米，但运河本身长度仅有80米。库康纳鸠运河是4条运河中最长的一条，全长800米，位于鲁奥科拉赫蒂和普马拉交界处。泰勒泰佩尔运河位于苏尔卡瓦，是4条运河中最靠北的一条，全长300米。从19世纪早期到2003年，除库特瓦勒运河外，另3条运河几乎未经任何修整。2003年，芬兰国家文物局开始对这3条运河进行修缮。如今，苏沃洛夫军事运河网已成为旅游景点。

Suwannee Canal

A canal located in southeast Georgia, the United States. The Suwannee Canal is 19 kilometres in length, running from north to south across Georgia. In 1889, the Georgia General Assembly authorized the Governor to sell a land of about 963.6 square kilometres containing the Okefenokee Swamp. In January 1891, the land was bought by the Suwannee Canal Company. In the same year, the Suwannee Canal was designed to drain large portions of the Okefenokee Swamp. The drainage work was started on 20 September 1891. The company spent three years building an 18.5-kilometre-long canal into the swamp. Work was abandoned in October 1894 due to various problems, like bad weather and financial difficulties. Now, the swamp is changed into the Okefenokee National Wildlife Refuge. And the Suwannee Canal serves as a major waterway into the swamp, attracting thousands of visitors each year.

萨旺尼运河

美国佐治亚州东南部运河。萨旺尼运河全长19千米，自北向南流经佐治亚州。1889年，佐治亚州议会授权州长出售约963.6平方千米土地，其中就包括奥克弗诺基沼泽。1891年1月，萨旺尼运河公司买下该块土地。同年，为疏浚奥克弗诺基沼泽地，修建萨旺尼运河的计划被提上日程。沼泽疏浚工程于1891年9月20日正式启动。萨旺尼运河公司花费3年时间开凿了一段长18.5千米、通向该沼泽地的运河。1894年10月，因天气恶劣和财政困难等，该运河项目被迫终止。如今，奥克弗诺基沼泽已被改建为奥克弗诺基国家野生动物保护区。萨旺尼运河是通向沼泽的主要航道，每年吸引成千上万游客来此观光。

Swansea Canal

A canal located in Wales, the United Kingdom. The Swansea Canal is 26.6 kilometres in length with 36 locks, connecting the Swansea Harbour with South Wales. Built by the Swansea Canal Navigation Company between 1794 and 1798, the canal was mainly used to export coal from the Upper Swansea Valley to other docks in Swansea, or serve the early metallurgical industries in the Lower Swansea Valley. The Swansea Canal was quite a commercial success until 1895, when it started to decline. The last commercial traffic was seen on the canal in 1931. In 1981, the Swansea Canal Society was established for its restoration.

Swifter Canal

A canal located in the province of Flevoland, the Netherlands. The Swifter Canal is a branch of the Lage Canal.

Szlak Batorego

A canal located in northeastern Poland. The Szlak Batorego starts from the Vistula in Warsaw, and leads through the Zegrze Reservoir, the Biebrza, the Augustów Canal and further to the Neman River. Along the canal, there are Ostrołęka, Łomża, and Augustów, etc. It was first developed in the 1600s under the reign of Stephen Báthory.

斯旺西运河

英国威尔士运河。斯旺西运河连接斯旺西港与南威尔士，全长26.6千米，建有36座船闸。运河由斯旺西运河航运公司于1794—1798年间开凿，主要用于将斯旺西上游河谷地区的煤炭运往斯旺西其他码头以供出口，或为斯旺西下游河谷地区的早期冶金业服务。斯旺西运河盈利颇丰，1895年后逐渐衰落。运河的最后一次商业通航是在1931年。1981年，致力于运河修复工作的斯旺西运河协会成立。

斯威夫特运河

荷兰弗莱福兰省运河。斯威夫特运河是拉赫运河的一条支线。

什拉克贝托瑞哥运河

波兰东北部运河。什拉克贝托瑞哥运河始于华沙的维斯图拉河，经兹格兹水库、别布扎河和奥古斯图夫运河，最终汇入尼曼河。运河沿线有奥斯特罗文卡、沃姆扎和奥古斯图夫等城镇。这条运河最初修建于17世纪斯特凡·巴托里统治时期。

Tainan Canal

A canal located in Tainan of Taiwan, China. The Tainan Canal connects the central area of Tainan City with Anping District, stretching 3.9 kilometres in length, with a 37-metre surface width and a 27.3-metre bottom width. The Anping District has been traditionally known as a hub of waterborne commercial activities. In August 1903, the previously existing channel in this area was damaged during a flash flood and later became silted up. This entailed the excavation of a new canal, which is now known as the Tainan Canal. The construction was started in April 1922 and completed in March 1926. On 25 April 1926, the Tainan Canal was opened. Encircling Anping District, this new channel enabled vessels transiting from open waters to reach the main districts of Tainan, making a noticeable contribution to its economic prosperity. In 1979, the Anping New Port was opened, about 2.6 kilometres away from the old port, which had to be closed temporarily for siltation and took fishery as the main business later. The new port, with a 7.4-metre depth of water, allows vessels up to a tonnage of 6 000. In 2001, the Tainan Canal experienced a thorough round of dredging, after which the water became crystal clear. The 3.6-kilometre-long walkway along its route becomes a popular public space. Nowadays, the significance of the canal lies more in its historical status than its function of commercial navigation. Standing as a piece of cultural heritage and known as the spring of vivacity for Tainan City, the Tainan Canal has turned into a tourist attraction

台南运河

中国台湾台南市运河。台南运河连接台南市区和安平区，全长3.9千米，河面宽37米，河底宽27.3米。历史上，安平区是台南地区的水路贸易中心。1903年8月，台南地区洪水暴发，先前的河道溃堤，泥土淤积，开凿一条新运河很有必要，新运河即如今的台南运河。台南运河1922年4月开凿，1926年3月竣工，同年4月25日通航。过往船只自此得以通过台南运河从开放水域抵达台南市主要区域，极大地促进了当地的经济发展。1979年，距离旧港2.6千米处的安平新港落成开放，水深达7.4米，可容纳排水量达6 000吨的船只。安平旧港则由于日渐淤塞而被关闭整治，重新开放后逐渐转型为渔港。2001年，人们对台南运河进行了全面疏浚，治理后的河水愈发清澈，沿线修建的3.6千米长景观步道成为公众运动休闲的绝佳去处。如今，这条运河的商业航运价值日渐式微，但其历史意义愈发突显，被称为台南市的"生命之河"。台南运河正逐渐成为一条观光运河，每逢端午佳节，人们都会在此举办活动。

and a venue for the Dragon Boat Festival every year.

Taivallahti Canal

A canal located in southern Savonia of Finland. The Taivallahti Canal is 800 metres long, and connects to the Varisvesi Lake via the Varistaipale Canal. It is equipped with 2 locks, overcoming an elevation difference of 4.95—5.45 metres and allowing a maximum draught of 1.8 metres. Built between 1911 and 1914, the Taivallahti Canal is a self-service channel. The locks can be operated remotely by the control tower located along the Varistaipale Canal.

Takase River

A canalized river located in Kyoto, Japan. The Takase River rises from Nijō-Kiyamachi, running along the Kiyamachi Street and roughly parallel to the Kamo River. It is 10 kilometres long and 7 metres wide, linking Kyoto with the Fushimi Port. This channel was named after the Takasebune boats used for water transportation. Its construction was started in the early 17th century. Suminokura Ryōi, a prominent and wealthy Kyoto-based merchant provided funding for the project at that time. With the excavation of the canal, goods could be transported from Osaka and elsewhere to Kyoto, the ancient capital and an inland city with no port of its own. The channel was also used for transporting rice and sake from Kyoto to the southern part of the country. At present, the Takase River is famous for

泰瓦拉蒂运河

芬兰南萨沃尼亚区运河。泰瓦拉蒂运河全长800米，通过瓦里斯泰佩勒运河连通瓦里斯韦西湖。运河上建有2座船闸，可调节4.95—5.45米的水位落差，容纳最大吃水深度为1.8米的船只。泰瓦拉蒂运河1911年开凿，1914年竣工，是一条自助通行航道。运河上的船闸可从瓦里斯泰佩勒运河上的主控塔远程遥控。

高瀬川

日本京都市运河化河流。高瀬川始于木屋町二条，沿木屋町街流动，与鸭川的流向大致平行。河道全长10千米，宽7米，连接京都和伏见港。高瀬川的名称源自用于水运的高瀬舟。高瀬川于17世纪初开凿，由当时京都著名富商角仓了资助。京都这座日本古都位于内陆，没有港口。高瀬川开凿后，货物可以从大阪和其他地区运往京都，同时还可将京都地区的大米和清酒运至南方地区。如今，高瀬川的樱花景观闻名遐迩，给木屋町通增添了特色，使该地区既具时尚气息，又有历史韵味。

its delightful view of cherry blossom, which brings character to Kiyamachi-dôri, making it quite classy and historic.

Tămaşda Collector Canal

A canal located in western Romania. The Tămaşda Collector Canal is the lower reach of the Criş Collector Canal.

Tancarville Canal

A canal located in the region of Normandy in France. See Havre-Tancarville Canal.

Tàu Hừ Canal

A canal located in southern Vietnam. The Tàu Hừ Canal stretches over 5 kilometres in the middle part of Hồ Chí Minh City. Its predecessor was a small and narrow channel. In 1819, under the order of King Gia Long, the silted channel was dredged up. As it flew across Cho Lon, it was also called Cho Lon Canal. Many documents suggest that the Tàu Hừ Canal further experienced two rounds of dredging respectively in 1887 and 1895, and was then expanded again in 1922 to its current dimensions of 37 metres in width and 17.8 metres in depth. During the rule the French, along the canal were located a series of wharves, a positive sign of the economic development around Cho Lon. Back then, the Tàu Hừ Canal was the artery for the trade and served for the transportation of fruit from

塔马斯达集流运河

罗马尼亚西部运河。塔马斯达集流运河是克里什集流运河的下游河段。

唐卡维尔运河

法国诺曼底大区运河。见阿弗尔—唐卡维尔运河。

头胡运河

越南南部运河。头胡运河长5千多米，流经胡志明市中部地区。该运河最初是一条狭小河道，因日渐淤塞，1819年，阮朝嘉隆皇帝下令开展疏浚工作。疏浚后的头胡运河流经堤岸区大市附近，也被称为大市运河。据记载，1887年和1895年，该运河又分别经历了2次疏浚，并于1922年再次拓建至37米宽，17.8米深。在法国统治越南期间，堤岸区经济发展良好，头胡运河两岸分布着多个码头，是一条通商要道。当时，人们通过该运河将越南西南地区的水果运至西贡。后随着胡志明市内东西向的武文杰路开建，这些码头渐遭弃用，头

southwestern Vietnam to Saigon. Along with the construction of Vo Van Kiet, an east-west boulevard, these wharves gradually disappeared and so did the traffic on the Tàu Hủ Canal.

胡运河上的航运也不复存在。

Tay Canal

泰河运河

A canal located in Ontario, Canada. As a part of the Tay River and also a branch of the Rideau Canal, the Tay Canal runs from the Beveridge Lock station on the Rideau Canal to the town of Perth. It is 9.8 kilometres in length, consisting of 2 locks, namely the Upper Beveridge Lock and the Lower Beveridge Lock, which overcome an elevation difference of 7.6 metres. Its predecessor is the First Tay Canal, built in 1831 by the Tay Navigation Company. Altogether 5 locks, 6 dams, 2 swing bridges and several embankments had been built by the end of 1834. The First Tay Canal did not achieve commercial success as there was no sufficient revenue for maintenance. In 1865, several locks on it were destroyed, and the canal was forced to be closed. In 1883, the Government of Canada authorized a contract with the A. H. Manning & Macdonald Company to build a new canal known as the Tay Canal. The entire previous section was deepened to 1.7 metres. Meanwhile, an additional 18-metre-wide and 2-kilometre-long section was excavated to connect the Beveridge Bay. Besides, 2 locks with the same size and design of those on the Rideau Canal were built near the southern end of the canal from 1885 to 1887. Vessels permitted for navigation are up to 27.4 metres in length, 7.9 metres in width, and 6.7

加拿大安大略省运河。泰河运河是泰河的一部分，也是里多运河的一条支线。该运河自里多运河上的贝弗里奇船闸流至珀斯镇，全长9.8千米，建有2座船闸，即贝弗里奇河上游船闸和贝弗里奇河下游船闸，可调节7.6米的水位落差。泰河运河的前身是第一泰河运河，1831年由泰河航运公司开凿。至1834年底，运河上共修建有5座船闸、6座水坝、2座平旋桥和多道河堤。但第一泰河运河运营不善，其收益无法满足运河维护与修缮的经费需求。1865年，运河上的船闸被毁，运河被迫关闭。1883年，加拿大政府授权A.H.曼宁—麦克唐纳公司开凿一条新运河，即如今的泰河运河。原先的运河河道深度整体加深至1.7米，同时还开凿了一条宽18米、长2千米的新河段，通往贝弗里奇湾。1885—1887年间泰河运河的南端附近又新修了2座船闸，其设计及规格与里多运河上的船闸相同，每年5月中旬到10月中旬，可容尺寸不超过27.4米长、7.9米宽、6.7米高的

metres in height. The locks on the canal are in operation from mid-May to mid-October. The canal is currently operated by Parks Canada.

船只通行。泰河运河目前由加拿大公园管理局运营。

Telataipale Canal

A canal located in Sulkava, Finland. The Telataipale Canal is 300 metres long. Excavated in the late 18th century, it was one of the four Suvorov military canals. The other three canals were the Kutvele Canal, the Käyhkää Canal and the Kukonharju Canal.

泰勒泰佩尔运河

芬兰苏尔卡瓦市运河。泰勒泰佩尔运河长300米，18世纪末开凿，是苏沃洛夫四大军事运河之一。其余三条分别为库特瓦勒运河、凯卡运河和库康纳鸠运河。

Telemark Canal

A canal located in southern Norway. The Telemark Canal links Skien to Dalen by connecting a number of long lakes in the Skien watershed. It is 105 kilometres long, with 8 locks and 18 chambers to cope with the difference in elevation of 72 metres. Hewn out of the rocks, the Telemark Canal was once regarded as "the eighth wonder" in Europe in the 19th century. The whole section comprises 2 parts, the Nordsjö-Skien Canal at the eastern side and the longer western section, the Bandak-Nordsjö Canal. The former was built from 1854 to 1861, connecting the Nordsjö to the sea with 2 locks respectively built in Skien and Løveid. The latter was built from 1887 to 1892 mainly for the purpose to facilitate the transportation of lumber. It is worth noting that the Bandak-Nordsjö section was also viewed as a technical and cultural heritage for the successful construction of 2 locks under harsh conditions. Today, the Telemark Canal is no longer a primary

泰勒马克运河

挪威南部运河。泰勒马克运河将希恩分水岭处的数条狭长湖泊相连，从而连通希恩与达伦。泰勒马克运河全长105千米，水位落差达72米，建有8座船闸，18个闸室。该运河于多岩石路段开凿，19世纪修建完成后，在欧洲曾被称为"第八大奇迹"。泰勒马克运河由东部的诺德斯约—希恩运河与西部较长的班达克—诺德斯约运河两部分构成。诺德斯约—希恩运河1854年开凿，1861年竣工，在希恩和鲁维德分别建有船闸，使诺德斯约得以通海。班达克—诺德斯约运河1887年开凿，1892年竣工，主要用于运输木材。值得一提的是，当时人们通过技术手段克服了艰苦的自然条件，在班达克—诺德斯约运河上成功修建2座船闸，该河段现为重

transport channel but more of a popular tourist attraction.

要的科技文化遗产。当今，泰勒马克运河不再作为重要航道，已成为热门旅游景点。

Teltow Canal

泰尔托运河

A canal located in Germany. With a length of 37.8 kilometres, the Teltow Canal flows from Berlin to Brandenburg, linking the Havel River with the Dahme River near Berlin. Built between 1900 and 1906, the canal has alleviated Berlin's heavy traffic. The Teltow Canal has only 1 lock and is navigable for vessels with a draught up to 1.75 metres. When the canal was completed, it was not wide enough. A towing railway was then constructed alongside the canal to pull the barges. Much of today's Teltow Canal Walk, which covers the canal's entire length, follows the route of the previous railway track.

德国运河。泰尔托运河全长37.8千米，位于柏林市和勃兰登堡州之间，连接哈弗尔河和柏林附近的达默河。泰尔托运河1900年开凿，1906年竣工，建成后缓解了柏林繁忙的交通状况。运河上仅有1座船闸，可通行吃水深度为1.75米的船只。泰尔托运河最初修建完工时，河道较窄，为方便拖曳驳船，人们还沿河修建了拖驳轨道。如今，泰尔托运河拖驳轨道变成了步道，覆盖运河全段。

Templin Waterways

滕普林航运系统

A navigation system located in the north of Brandenburg, Germany. The Templin Waterways are a Class I inland waterway and a left tributary of the Havel. The Templin Waterways have a total length of 30 kilometres, consisting of several lakes and the Templin Canal. The navigation system was built around 1744 and expanded between 1894 and 1896. The Templin Waterways were opened around 1745, and the Eberswalde Waterways and Shipping Office was responsible for its maintenance and management. In history, there have been 5 locks built on it. However, since 1812, with the traffic volume

德国勃兰登堡州北部航运系统。滕普林航运系统全长30千米，包括数个湖泊和滕普林运河，属于一级内河航道，也是哈弗尔河的左岸一条支线。滕普林航运系统约1744年开凿，1745年通航，由埃伯斯瓦尔德航道和航运局负责维护和管理，并于1894—1896年进行了拓宽。该航运系统历史上共建有5座船闸。1812年以后，随着该地区水运业务逐渐萧条，一些船闸渐遭弃用。使用至今的仅剩滕普林船

declining, some locks were abandoned subsequently. Still in use is the Templin Lock, built in 1894—1895 and modernized during 2004 and 2005. The Templin Waterways are now also a destination for recreation and leisure.

闸。该船闸建于1894—1895年间，并于2004—2005年间进行了现代化改造。如今，滕普林航运系统也是一处娱乐休闲景点。

Tennant Canal

A canal located in South Wales, the United Kingdom. The Tennant Canal is about 8 kilometres long. It runs from Port Tennant, Swansea to its junction with the Neath Canal at Aberdulais. The Tennant Canal was a development of its predecessor, the Glan-y-Wern Canal, which was built to transport coal from a colliery to a creek on River Neath. The construction of the Tennant Canal was started in 1821, aiming to link River Neath with River Tawe. In 1934, the commercial traffic on the Tennant Canal ceased. The canal was then used to supply water to local industries. In 1974, the Neath & Tennant Canals Preservation Society was founded to restore the navigability of the canal. Now the Tennant Canal is of noticeable importance for nature conservation. It provides a wetland habitat for a variety of species such as kingfishers, sedge warblers and otters.

坦南特运河

英国南威尔士运河。坦南特运河全长约8千米，始于斯旺西市的坦南特港，在阿博杜莱与尼思运河交汇。坦南特运河前身为格兰叶韦恩运河，主要用以将煤炭运往尼思河。运河于1821年开凿，旨在连通尼思河和塔威河。1934年，坦南特运河停止商业航运。随后，人们用该运河为当地工厂供水。1974年，尼思和坦南特运河保护协会成立，旨在恢复该运河的航运功能。坦南特运河在自然保护方面具有重要意义，为翠鸟、莎草莺等多种鸟类以及水獭等动物提供湿地栖息地。

Tennessee River ≈

A canalized river located in Tennessee, the United States. The Tennessee River is the largest tributary of the Ohio River in the Tennessee Valley. It is formed by the confluence of the Holston River

田纳西河

美国田纳西州运河化河流。田纳西河是田纳西河谷内俄亥俄河最大的支流，由霍尔斯顿河和弗伦奇布罗德河汇合而成。田纳西河自诺克

and the French Broad River. From its headwaters in Knoxville, the river flows southwest towards Chattanooga before turning westward through the Cumberland Plateau into northeastern Alabama. Then it heads north through Tennessee and toward Kentucky, where it joins the Ohio River at Paducah. The river is approximately 1,049 kilometres in length, with a drainage area of 105,960 square kilometres. It is equipped with a large number of locks, reservoirs and dams, performing multiple functions of navigation, hydropower production and flood control. With various natural obstructions on its upper and middle course, only its lower course is convenient for navigation. Initially, the Tennessee River only allowed the passage of flatboats. In 1933, with the founding of the Tennessee Valley Authority, importance began to be attached to the development of the river system and efforts have been made to improve its navigability since then. By 1945, the navigation channel was completed, anticipating the booming of traffic on the Tennessee River for the following decades. Today, it is estimated that over 28,000 barges transporting 45 to 50 million tons of goods transit the river every year. The active water transportation has greatly contributed to the economic and industrial development of the Tennessee Valley.

Tennessee-Tombigbee Waterway

A waterway located in the southeastern United States. The Tennessee-Tombigbee Waterway connects the Tennessee River in northeastern

斯维尔市流向西南方向的查塔努加市，流经坎伯兰高原后向西转入亚拉巴马州的东北部，再向北穿过田纳西州，最终到达肯塔基州，在帕迪尤卡与俄亥俄州河交汇。该河全长约1 049千米，流域面积达105 960平方千米。河上建有大量船闸、水库和大坝，发挥着航运、供电和泄洪等多种作用。该河上游和中游的自然条件不利于通航，仅有下游河段通航条件较佳。起初，田纳西河仅能通行平底船。1933年，田纳西河谷管理局成立后，田纳西的河流系统开发及其通航能力的提升备受重视。1945年，田纳西河河道改造工程完工，在这之后的数十年里，田纳西河的通航量激增。如今，每年约有28 000多艘驳船在田纳西河上通行，货运量达4 500万—5 000万吨。繁忙的航运业务也极大地促进了田纳西河河谷地区经济和工业的发展。

田纳西－汤比格比航道

美国东南部航道。田纳西－汤比格比航道全长377千米，连通位于密西西比州东北部的田纳西河和亚

Mississippi with the Tombigbee River in western Alabama. It is 377 kilometres in length and empties into the Gulf of Mexico. To provide a shortcut for commercial navigation from the midsection of the United States to the Gulf, the Tennessee-Tombigbee Waterway was constructed under the administration of the United States Army Corps of Engineers. In 1874, the federal government conducted a study proving the feasibility to connect the two rivers with a man-made channel. The construction was not approved by the Congress until 1946, and it was delayed, along with persistent objections, until 1972, due to financial shortages. The greatest challenge lies in the construction of the 47-kilometre-long Divide Cut, which required the excavation of more than 115 million cubic metres of sand and clay. The Tennessee-Tombigbee Waterway was finally completed in December 1984 at a cost of 2 billion dollars. It saved vessels heading toward the Gulf of Mexico from detouring to the Mississippi River. During the first few years, the volume of commercial traffic appeared to be much less than previously predicted. The turning point came in 1988 when the Mississippi River was closed as a result of a drought. As an alternative route, this waterway since then had witnessed a steady increase in trade for several years. Today, the Tennessee-Tombigbee Waterway mainly transports coal and timber, with an estimated accumulated profit of 43 billion dollars according to a cooperative study by Troy University and the University of Tennessee in 2009.

拉巴马州西部的汤比格比河,最终注入墨西哥湾。该航道由美国陆军工程兵团负责修建,旨在为美国中部和墨西哥湾之间的商业运输提供一条捷径。1874年,联邦政府调研后认为连通田纳西河和汤比格比河的航道修建计划可行。但直到1946年,国会才予以批准。之后,修建计划一度因资金短缺而搁置,同时因预估成本过高而不断引发争议。1972年,田纳西—汤比格比航道终于动工修建。施工期间,田纳西河与汤比格比河之间47千米长的迪韦德运河开凿工程最为艰巨,需要挖掘1.15亿立方米的泥沙。1984年12月,耗资20亿美元的田纳西—汤比格比航道工程竣工。田纳西河上驶往墨西哥湾的船只从此不必绕道至密西西比河。运河通航后的最初几年,田纳西—汤比格比航道的商业航运量远低于预期。1988年,密西西比河因干旱而停航,这给作为备选航道的田纳西—汤比格比航道的航运带来转机。此后,这条航道上的通航量稳步上升。如今,田纳西—汤比格比航道主要运输煤炭和木材。由田纳西大学和特洛伊大学于2009年联合发布的一项研究表明,田纳西—汤比格比航道运营以来已累计带来近430亿美元的经济利润。

Ter Apel Canal

A canal located in the province of Groningen, the Netherlands. The Ter Apel Canal is a part of the Veendam-Stadskanaal-Ter Apel Waterway, connecting Musselkanaal with Stads Compascuumkanaal. With a depth of 2 metres, the 38-kilometre-long canal allows vessels up to 5.8 metres wide. Its origin can be traced back to 1765. Back then, it was decided by the city of Groningen to construct a canal connecting Bareveld with Ter Apel in order to facilitate the mining industry around the Bourtange Swamp. The route of the canal ran parallel to the Semslinie, the previously established border between Groningen and Drenthe of a 150-year standing. The canal was completed in 1856, which was followed by the construction of the Stads Canal and the Mussel Canal. Since the 1930s, the importance of the Ter Apel Canal as a waterway had gradually decreased due to the competition of lorries as a means of transport and the increase in the scale of other inland waterways. In the 1970s, there were plans to abandon the canal, which was prevented by the local citizens. Nowadays, only recreational transport is permitted on the canal.

Termunterzijl Canal

A canal located in the province of Groningen, the Netherlands. The Termunterzijl Canal is connected to the Oosterhorn Port, rising from the confluence of the Meeden Canal and the Op Canal, flowing through the hamlet of Scheemda in the north and

泰尔阿珀尔运河

荷兰格罗宁根省运河。泰尔阿珀尔运河是芬丹—斯塔茨卡纳尔—泰尔阿珀尔航道的一部分，连接米瑟尔卡纳尔和斯塔茨—孔帕斯屈姆卡纳尔。该运河全长38千米，深2米，可容最大宽度为5.8米的船只通行。1765年，为了促进布尔坦赫沼泽地区采矿业的发展，格罗宁根市决定修建一条连接巴雷费尔德和泰尔阿珀尔的运河。运河线路同格罗宁根省与德伦特省之间的塞姆分界线平行，该分界线具有150年的历史。1856年，泰尔阿珀尔运河工程竣工，随后又陆续开凿斯塔茨运河和米瑟尔运河。20世纪30年代后，随着货车运输行业崛起，同时，其他内河航道规模也逐步扩张，泰尔阿珀尔运河的航运功能逐渐衰退。20世纪70年代，政府曾计划废弃该运河航运，但遭到当地居民反对。如今，泰尔阿珀尔运河仅供游船通行。

泰尔蒙特宰尔运河

荷兰格罗宁根省运河。泰尔蒙特宰尔运河与东霍恩港相连，始于梅登运河和奥普运河交汇处，流经北部的施海姆达村，与洪德沙尔斯特湖西部相通。河上建有1座船闸

is connected with the western Hondshalster Lake. On the canal was built 1 lock and 1 bridge. The Termunterzijl Canal was constructed in 1601 as a substitute for the former Munte River, which was once flooded in 1509. The canal was initially built as a drainage channel and later grew into an instrumental shipping connection. In the 1950s, commercial shipping eventually declined heavily on the canal, which was at a disadvantage in the competition with lorries as a means of transport. In 1986, the canal was reopened for shipping, and now it is used mainly for recreational purposes.

和1座桥梁。该运河1601年开凿，用以取代1509年暴发过洪灾的曼特河。泰尔蒙特宰尔运河最初用作排水渠，后发展为重要的航运通道。20世纪50年代，由于受到货车运输行业强有力的竞争，泰尔蒙特宰尔运河的航运业务最终走向衰落。1986年起，该运河重新通航，如今主要用于开展水上娱乐项目。

Ternaaien Canal

A cross-border canal located in Europe. The Ternaaien Canal is 1.9 kilometres in length, flowing from Liège Province, Belgium to Limburg Province, the Netherlands, and connecting the Albert Canal with the Meuse. It was constructed in 1836 and put into use in 1939. There are 4 locks along the canal, and the latest one has been opened in 2015, which allows ships up to 9,000 tons.

特尔奈恩运河

欧洲跨国运河。特尔奈恩运河全长1.9千米，流经比利时列日省和荷兰林堡省，连通阿尔贝特运河和默兹河。特尔奈恩运河1836年开凿，1939年通航，河上共建有4座船闸，其中最新的一座于2015年开通，可容纳9 000吨级的船舶。

Thai Canal

A proposed canal located in Thailand. Also called Kra Canal or Kra Isthmus Canal. The Thai Canal is proposed to link the Gulf of Thailand with the Andaman Sea across southern Thailand. With the South China Sea in the east and the Andaman Sea in the west, the canal is supposed to improve the transportation conditions around Asia. Many plans

泰运河

泰国拟建运河。亦称克拉运河或克拉地峡运河。泰运河计划穿过泰国南部，连接泰国湾和安达曼海，东临中国南海，西靠安达曼海，建成后将改善亚洲地区的通航状况。自1677年起，人们就曾提出并讨论过多个运河修建方案，

of canal construction have been initiated and discussed since 1677, none of which, however, has been implemented because of the high cost and potential impacts on the environment. Recently, there are two construction plans for the canal readily available, namely, the north route and the south route. In the proposal of the north route, a 90-kilometre-long canal will be constructed to connect Changwat Chumphon in the Gulf of Thailand with Ranong Province near the Andaman Sea across the narrow strip of the Kra Isthmus. The proposed south route is longer but smoother than the north route, running 102 kilometres between Songkhla and Satun. When the canal is fully operational, ships travelling between the Indian Ocean and the South China Sea will not have to travel through the Straits of Malacca. The voyage shortened by over 1,000 kilometres will significantly reduce the transit time and cut the transportation cost. In 2020, a committee has been formed by the House of Representatives of Thailand to conduct preliminary studies over this project.

但考虑到造价高昂而且可能会对环境造成影响，工程始终未能实施。当前，主要有北线和南线两个修建方案。据北线方案，泰运河将穿越克拉地峡的狭长地带，连接位于泰国湾的春蓬府和邻近安达曼海的拉廊府，全长90千米。南线方案则选择在宋卡府和沙敦府之间开凿一条全长102千米的运河，长度比北线长，但地势较为平坦。运河开通后，往来于印度洋和中国南海之间的船只将无须绕行马六甲海峡，航程可以缩短1 000千米以上，从而大幅减少航行时间并降低海运成本。2020年，泰国众议院专门成立了一个委员会来研究这一运河项目。

Thames and Severn Canal

泰晤士－塞文运河

A canal located in Gloucestershire of southern England, the United Kingdom. Running from east to west, the Thames and Severn Canal connects the Thames River to the Stroudwater Navigation and River Severn. Built between 1783 and 1789 with the chief engineer Josiah Clowes in charge, the canal is a little less than 46.7 kilometres and equipped with 44 locks. As a part of a route from Bristol to London, this canal has provided the first inland

英国英格兰南部格洛斯特郡运河。泰晤士－塞文运河东西流向，将泰晤士河与斯特劳德沃特航道和塞文河连通起来。运河1783年开凿，1789年竣工，由工程师乔赛亚·克洛斯主持修建。泰晤士－塞文运河全长近46.7千米，建有44座船闸。该运河构成布里斯托尔至伦敦的部分航道，也是往返于伦

waterway between London and the Midlands. The canal flows through the roughly 3.4-kilometre-long Sapperton Tunnel at 110.6 metres above sea level, the highest point of the canal. Back then, it was once the longest canal tunnel in Britain, and it is now the fourth longest. By the end of the 19th century, the Thames and Severn Canal had lost much commercial traffic in competition with railways. Most of its sections were abandoned in 1927, with its western stretches remaining in use until 1933. Since 1972, along with many other canals in Britain, the restoration of the Thames and Severn Canal has been put on the agenda. The canal is currently undergoing a three-phase restoration programme managed by the Stroudwater and Severn Canal Trust.

和英格兰中部地区之间的首条内陆航道。运河从萨珀顿隧道穿行而过,在此期间地势渐高,最高海拔达110.6米。3.4千米长的萨珀顿隧道曾是英国最长的运河隧道,至今仍是英国第四长运河隧道。19世纪末期,在与铁路运输的竞争中,运河上的航运业务大多流失,到了1927年,大部分河段已废弃不用,运河西侧部分河段则继续使用至1933年。自1972年起,英国境内许多运河得以修复,泰晤士—塞文运河修复计划也被提上日程。该运河的修复工作分为三个阶段,目前,该项工作由斯特劳德沃特与塞文运河信托机构负责。

Thiruvananthapuram-Shoranur Canal

特里凡得琅-斯霍拉努尔运河

A canal located in the Varkala Region of India. The Thiruvananthapuram-Shoranur Canal, 420 kilometres long, links Thiruvananthapuram, the capital of the Indian state of Kerala, with its municipality Shoranur. Commissioned by those three erstwhile states of Madras, Cochin and Travancore, the construction of this canal was carried out during the 18th and 19th centuries in stages and lasted until 1880. The first completed section was between Channankara and Thiruvananthapuram, which was followed by the Paravur Canal. It was built to connect the Paravur Lake with the Edava Lake. Then the Quilon Canal came next, linking the Paravur Lake and the Ashtamudi Lake. The connected

印度瓦卡拉地区运河。特里凡得琅—斯霍拉努尔运河全长420千米,连接喀拉拉邦首府特里凡得琅与斯霍拉努尔市。18—19世纪时,马德拉斯、科钦和特拉凡哥尔这三个印度旧邦先后授权,开始分段开凿运河。运河修建工作持续至1880年。其中,钱南卡拉和特里凡得琅之间的河段最先完工。随后,帕拉乌尔运河又修建完成,至此,帕拉乌尔湖和埃德瓦湖连通。最后通航的是连通帕拉乌尔湖和阿什塔穆迪湖的奎隆运河。这些分段修建的航道连通后,人

waterways in this region were used to transport goods and passengers among the southern parts of Travancore. At present, the canal is almost disused. Low bridges over it and the shallowness of its channel have rendered it unnavigable. Since 2005, the government has started the development and restoration of the Thiruvananthapuram-Shoranur Canal. Now parts of the Kollam-Ponnani section and the Parvathi Puthanaar reaches become navigable.

们可在喀拉拉邦的特拉凡哥尔南部地区进行货运和客运。由于桥梁低矮且航道变浅，如今，特里凡得琅—斯霍拉努尔运河基本被弃用。自2005年起，印度政府开始实施运河开发与整修工作。目前，科拉姆—波纳尼河部分河段及帕尔瓦蒂普塔那尔河段已可通航。

Thun Ship Canal

A canal located in Berne, Switzerland. The Thun Ship Canal stretches 500 metres and runs parallel to parts of the Aare River. The canal connects Lake Thun with Thun's railway station. It was constructed and completed in 1925 with the aim to connect the shipping services with railway services. Today it is regularly navigated by Lake Thun passenger ships.

图恩通海运河

瑞士伯尔尼州运河。图恩通海运河连接图恩湖和图恩镇的火车站，流向与阿勒河部分河段平行。图恩通海运河全长500米，1925年开凿，同年竣工，旨在打通当地的船舶运输和铁路运输。如今，该运河上时常有往来于图恩湖的客船通行。

Tjonger

A canalized river located in southeastern Friesland, the Netherlands. The Tjonger connects the Upper Tjonger River with the Tusschenlinde River. It is 41.7 kilometres in length, 1.8 metres in depth and 7.5 metres in width. Three large locks equipped with water pumps were built on the canal. From 1886 to 1888, the 35-kilometre-long river section was canalized to facilitate navigation and drainage. The nearby Tjonger Valley is renowned for its outstanding ecological environment and is home to unique flora and fauna. The Tjonger is included in the traditional

勇尔河

荷兰弗里斯兰省东南部运河化河流。勇尔河连通勇尔河上游和图岑林德河，全长41.7千米，1.8米深，7.5米宽。河上建有3座大型船闸，船闸处配有水泵。1886—1888年间，为方便航运和排水，勇尔河上长约35千米的河段进行了运河化改造。附近的勇尔河谷生态环境良好，动植物物种独特。勇尔河还是早前弗里斯兰泥炭运输路线的一部分，目前主要用于航运及排水。

Frisian Turf route and now is primarily utilized for shipping and drainage.

Tongnan Canal

A canal located in the district of Tongnan, Chongqing, China. The Tongnan Canal is a diversion channel connected with the Sankuaishi Hydropower Station. It is about 15 kilometres in length and 110 metres in width, with a water flow at 280 cubic metres per second. The canal was built in the 1970s with the initial purpose to solve the problem of electricity shortage and the irrigation inconvenience in the farmland of the Tongnan District. About 60,000 people are involved in this 3-year project. It has been in operation for over 30 years and assumes multiple functions such as hydroelectric power generation, flood control, irrigation and navigation. There are 13 footbridges across the canal. Along the canal are beautiful views of rustic scenery.

潼南运河

中国重庆市潼南区运河。潼南运河是三块石水电站的引水河。该运河长15千米，宽110米，每秒流量为280立方米。潼南运河修建于20世纪70年代末，最初是为了解决潼南地区的缺电问题，同时满足潼南区的农田灌溉需要。总计约6万人参与到这一运河修建工程当中，工程历时3年。潼南运河至今已运营30多年，具有发电、防洪、灌溉及航运等多项功能。运河上建有13座人行桥，运河沿岸乡村风光优美。

Torani Canal

A canal located in northeastern Guyana. The Torani Canal was constructed to transfer water from the Berbice River to the Canje River. The canal runs 19 kilometres in length. The inlet on the Berbice River is located some 80 kilometres from the sea. Despite the influence of the tide of the sea, its flow is fresh throughout the year. A five-door sluice controls the flow of water into the canal. Its outlet is on the Canje River in East Berbice-Corentyne. A three-door sluice is set up to control the flow out of the

托拉尼运河

圭亚那东北部运河。托拉尼运河全长19千米，其修建目的是将伯比斯河的水引入坎赫河。该运河的入口位于伯比斯河上，距大海约80千米，尽管受潮汐影响，流入运河的终年都是淡水。运河上建有1座有5道闸门的船闸，用来控制运河的进水流量。运河出口位于东伯比斯—科兰太因区的坎赫河，出水量由1座有3道闸门的船闸控制。农业

canal. During the practice of farm irrigation, the canal also functions to flush saltwater out of the Canje River. Due to the growing siltation, the channel at the head section of the canal has gradually become shallower, which increases the risk of flooding. There is currently an urgent need for the canal to be dredged.

灌溉时，还可通过托拉尼运河将坎赫河的咸水冲走。后因泥沙大量沉积，托拉尼运河源头段水流逐渐变浅，加剧了沿岸遭受洪涝灾害的风险。目前，托拉尼运河的疏浚工作已成为当务之急。

Tor Bay Canal

托尔湾运河

A canal located in eastern Nova Scotia, Canada. For the benefits of fisheries, the Tor Bay Canal was excavated by the residents in Nova Scotia in 1849 without the financial support from the government. Residents from Whitehead started the excavation on the eastern side and those from Port Felix on the western side. There was initially a drawbridge on the canal, which was later substituted by a fixed bridge, only allowing the passage of small rowboats and sailing boats that could lower their masts.

加拿大新斯科舍省东部运河。1849年，为满足渔场发展需求，当地居民开始修建托尔湾运河，当时并未得到政府的财政支持。怀特黑德和菲利克斯港的居民分别从东西两边开凿。运河上原有1座开合桥，后来被固定桥取代，只能容小型划艇及可调节桅杆高度的帆船通行。

Tralee Ship Canal

特拉利通海运河

A canal located in County Kerry, Ireland. The Tralee Ship Canal is 3.2 kilometres in length. It was initially constructed to transport freight and passengers between the Tralee Bay and the town of Tralee. Under the authorization of an act of Parliament by the House of Commons in June 1829, the construction was started in 1832. Due to the lack of funding, which influenced the progress of the construction, it was not completed and opened until 1846. The canal could then accommodate large ships of up

爱尔兰凯里郡运河。特拉利通海运河全长3.2千米，修建之初是为了方便特拉利湾与特拉利镇之间的客运与货运。1829年6月，爱尔兰议会下议院通过法案批准修建该运河。1832年，特拉利通海运河开始修建，但由于资金短缺，直到1846年才竣工通航。该运河当时可容纳载重量达300吨的大型船只，但不久之后就开始出现淤塞。

to 300 tons, but started to suffer from silting soon afterwards. By the 1880s when the Fenit Harbour, a deep-water harbour, was built, the silting problem became relieved but not solved yet. Later a railway was constructed between Fenit and Tralee, carrying cargo and freight from ships anchored there. As a result of silting, the Tralee Ship Canal was no longer used and finally closed in 1951. Not until 1999 was its restoration started by the Office of Public Works. Now it is mainly used for rowing and other recreational purposes.

直到19世纪80年代费尼特深水港建成后，运河的淤塞问题才有所缓解，但仍未得到根本解决。之后，费尼特与特拉利镇之间的铁路开通，为停靠在此的船舶运送货物。由于泥沙淤积，特拉利通海运河被弃用，并于1951年关闭。直至1999年，运河修复工程才由公共事务局启动。现在该运河主要用于赛艇运动及其他休闲娱乐活动。

Trek Canal

A canal located in Leiden, South Holland, the Netherlands. As a part of the Rhine-Schie Canal, the Trek Canal was excavated in 1638 to link Delft and the Hague. In 1891, it was widened and extended allowing large cargo ships to reach the centre of Leiden.

特雷克运河

荷兰南荷兰省莱顿市运河。特雷克运河是莱茵—斯希运河的一部分，于1638年开凿，旨在连接代尔夫特和海牙两座城市。1891年，人们拓宽并延伸了特雷克运河，大型货船得以通过运河驶往莱顿市中心。

Trent and Mersey Canal

A canal located in England, the United Kingdom. The Trent and Mersey Canal connects River Trent in Derbyshire to River Mersey. The canal has a length of 150.5 kilometres with more than 76 locks and 5 tunnels. It is narrow for most of its length but those sections grow quite wide in the east of Burton-on-Trent and the west of Middlewich. With the Harecastle Tunnel as the dividing line, the canal falls into northern and southern sections. Constructed in 1766, the canal was completed and put

特伦特－默西运河

英国英格兰运河。特伦特—默西运河连通德比郡的特伦特河与默西河，全长150.5千米，建有至少76座船闸和5条隧道。运河大部分河段狭窄，只在特伦特河畔伯顿镇以东以及米德尔威奇以西的河段较为宽阔。以海尔卡斯尔隧道为界，该运河被划分为南北两段。特伦特—默西运河1766年开凿，1777年完工并通航。1988年，运河所在

into use in 1777. In 1988, the canal was declared to be a Conservation Area. In the 1990s, the towpath on the canal was upgraded and improved as a part of the National Cycle Network. The Victorian Anderton Boat Lift on the canal, which was known as the model for other European boat lifts, was fully restored to operation in 2002 after 20 years of disuse, which enables vessels to lower about 15 metres from the Trent and Mersey Canal to the Weaver River. The canal is still open today.

区域被划为保护区。20世纪90年代，运河纤道得以升级改造，成为英国国家自行车道网的一部分。运河上曾风靡欧洲的维多利亚安德顿升船机在被弃用20年之后于2002年全面复建。借此升船机，经特伦特—默西运河通行的船只可下降约15米驶入威弗河。目前，特伦特—默西运河仍可通航。

Trent-Severn Waterway

A waterway located in Ontario, Canada. The Trent-Severn Waterway is 386 kilometres in length, linking Lake Ontario at Trenton with Lake Huron at Port Severn. In 1833, the first lock of the canal was built with the aim to facilitate the navigation between the Kawartha Lakes and also between stretches of the Trent River. In the 1880s, under the support of the Prime Minister John A. Macdonald, some new locks were added and the canal was extended westward. However, the progress slowed down noticeably before long, with the construction being carried out in sporadic bits and bursts. It was not until the turn of the century that the construction of the waterway was pushed back on track. After the delay caused by World War I, the canal was finally completed in July 1920, making it possible to travel from the Georgian Bay to Lake Ontario. Later, with the growing importance of the railway transportation, the commercial function of the waterway has been weakened. The waterway is

特伦特－塞文航道

加拿大安大略省航道。特伦特—塞文航道全长386千米，在特伦顿连通安大略湖，在塞文港连通休伦湖。特伦特—塞文航道上的第一座船闸修建于1833年，当时是为了连通卡沃萨湖泊群以及特伦特河各支流。19世纪80年代，在加拿大总理约翰·麦克唐纳的支持下，又新修一批船闸，并向西延伸航道。然而，该航道的修建工作不久就被搁置，之后几年进展缓慢，直到19至20世纪之交才得以重启，后又因第一次世界大战爆发而再次推延，最终于1920年7月竣工。航道建成后，船只可直接从乔治亚湾驶往安大略湖。后因铁路运输业的崛起，特伦特—塞文航道的商运价值日渐减弱。目前，该航道每年5月至10月间通航，已被列为加拿大国家历史遗址，成为安大

currently navigable between May and October. Now inscribed on the list of the National Historic Site of Canada, the Trent-Severn Waterway becomes an important tourist attraction of Ontario, appealing to thousands of visitors each year.

略省的重要旅游景点之一，每年吸引成千上万的游客。

Trinity River

A canalized river located in Texas, the United States. The 680-kilometre-long Trinity River has 4 branches, namely the West Fork, the Clear Fork, the Elm Fork, and the East Fork, flowing from the west of Dallas, Texas to the Gulf of Mexico. The river had been navigable to Dallas as early as 1836, and several attempts to launch commercial navigation on the river had been made by the 1850s. During the latter half of the 19th century, several surveys on the navigability of the Trinity River were conducted by the federal government. On 18 June, 1878, the River and Harbor Act appropriated $10,000 to deepen the channel from its mouth to the town of Liberty and to remove all obstructions in the river. This section covered about 66 kilometres and was considered most suitable for navigation on this river. In 1891, the Trinity River Navigation Company was founded to promote the construction of facilities on the Trinity to improve its navigability. A temporary dam was constructed 21 kilometres south of Dallas at McCommas Bluff. Later, the construction came into a standstill when World War I broke out and has never been resumed. After the war, millions have been spent on the river primarily for the purpose of flood control, while the navigation project

特里尼蒂河

美国得克萨斯州运河化河流。特里尼蒂河全长680千米，共有4条支流，分别为西支流、克利尔支流、埃尔姆支流和东支流，从得克萨斯州达拉斯西部流至墨西哥湾。早在1836年，就有船只从特里尼蒂河航行至达拉斯。19世纪50年代之前，人们已多次尝试在这条河上进行商业运输。到19世纪下半叶，美国联邦政府就特里尼蒂河的通航条件先后开展过几轮调研。1878年6月18日，《河流与港口法案》批准拨款1万美元用来加深从河口至利伯蒂小镇的河段，同时支持人们开展清淤工作，这一河段长约66千米，最适合通航。1891年，特里尼蒂河航运公司成立，旨在推进河上水利设施的建设，并在达拉斯以南21千米处的麦克科马斯布拉夫修建1座临时大坝。不久之后，第一次世界大战爆发，特里尼蒂河的运河化改造工作被迫终止。此后，人们在特里尼蒂河改造方面累计花费数百万美元，但多用于防洪防涝，通航改造工作并不受重视。如

assumes secondary importance. Nowadays, the Trinity River Corridor Project is aimed to transform the river's flood zone into an urban park.

今，在特里尼蒂河廊道工程的带动下，特里尼蒂河的洪泛区将被改造成城市公园。

Twante Canal

端迪运河

A canal located in Yangon, Myanmar. The Twante Canal covers a length of 35 kilometres, linking the Irrawaddy River and the Yangon River. The canal is named after the town of Twante located roughly midway along the route of the canal, with a bridge built on it bearing the same name. The construction of the canal was commenced in 1903 and completed in 1915. In 1935, the government widened and deepened the canal to pave the way for the large steamers from the Irrawaddy Flotilla Company sailing to Mandalay. For lack of regular maintenance, the canal has become gradually silted and its channel narrower. In 2010, the mouth of the canal was widened by 180 metres. The navigation problems remain due to the failure to implement the planned construction of the concrete embankment. Nowadays, the canal is still heavily used.

缅甸仰光运河。端迪运河全长35千米，连通伊洛瓦底江和仰光河，因该运河中段的端迪镇而得名。运河上还建有1座同名桥梁。端迪运河于1903年开凿，1915年竣工。1935年，为了让伊洛瓦底舰船公司的大型蒸汽机船顺利抵达曼德勒，缅甸政府拓宽并加深了该运河。由于缺乏定期维护，端迪运河日渐淤塞，河道也变窄。2010年，人们将端迪运河河口拓宽180米，但由于修建混凝土堤岸的计划未能实施，运河航道问题仍未解决。如今，端迪运河上的航运业务依然繁忙。

Twente Canal

特文特运河

A canal located in the northeast of the Netherlands. Also called Zutphen-Enschede Canal. The 63-kilometre-long Twente Canal flows through the provinces of Gelderland and Overijssel, running almost parallel to the Zutphen-Enschede Railway Line. It connects the largest cities of the Twente region, namely, Almelo, Hengelo and Enschede, with some

荷兰东北部运河。亦称聚特芬—恩斯赫德运河。特文特运河流经海尔德兰省和上艾瑟尔省，将特文特地区最大的3座城市即阿尔默洛市、亨厄洛市和恩斯赫德市同几条河流连接起来。该运河全长63千米，其主航道长47千米，建有

rivers. Its 47-kilometre-long main branch runs from the IJssel at Zutphen and ends in Enschede, equipped with 3 locks and joined by a 16-kilometre-long branch at Delden. The initiative to build the canal can be traced back to the 19th century. Nevertheless, due to the disagreement over the plan, it was not until 1930 that the construction of the canal was started and finally completed in 1938. Initially, the canal was built to facilitate the transport of raw cotton for the Twente textile industry and coal from the mines in Limburg. It was later widened and deepened between 2004 and 2007 to allow large Rhine ships to pass through. Currently, the Public Works and Water Management is working on reinforcing the bridges and the maintenance of the locks and pumping stations. Nowadays, the Twente Canal is used for the shipping of sand, gravel and salt. The canal also plays a role in recreational activities and the practice of drainage.

3座船闸。特文特运河始于聚特芬的伊瑟尔河，流向恩斯赫德市。此外，在代尔登还有一段长16千米的支线运河汇入。特文特运河整体流向几乎与聚特芬－恩斯赫德铁路线平行。早在19世纪，人们便有了修建该运河的计划，但由于对运河设计方案意见不一致，直到1930年才动工，8年后竣工。修建该运河最初是为了向特文特地区的纺织工业供应原棉，并从林堡的煤矿运输煤炭资源。2004—2007年间，为满足来自莱茵河大型船只的航行需求，特文特运河又经过拓宽和加深。目前，公共工程与水务管理局正在加固运河上的桥梁，同时整修维护船闸和泵站。如今，特文特运河多运输沙子、砾石和盐。此外，该运河还具有休闲娱乐和排水功能。

Ucker≈

A canalized river located in northwestern Germany. See Uecker.

乌克河

德国西北部运河化河流。见于克河。

Uecker≈

A canalized river located in northwestern Germany. Also known as Ucker. The name "Uecker" comes from the West Slavic language, meaning "fast". The Uecker starts from the Uckermark District, 1 kilometre north of Ringenwalde, runs through Brandenburg and Mecklenburg-Vorpommern, and joins the Szczecin Lagoon. Its total length is 102 kilometres, and its basin covers an area of 2,200 square kilometres, with an average flow velocity of 7.7 cubic metres per second. The navigable part of this river is 33 kilometres in length, connecting Oberuckersee and Unteruckersee. The lower reaches of the Uecker are almost unnavigable. In the 19th century, the Von Arnim family had attempted to canalize it for the passage of large vessels, but ceased the effort after a few decades.

于克河

德国西北部运河化河流。亦称乌克河。"于克"这一名称来自西斯拉夫语, 意为"快速"。于克河始于林根瓦尔德市以北1千米处的乌克马克区, 流经勃兰登堡州和梅克伦堡—前波美拉尼亚州, 最后注入什切青潟湖。于克河全长102千米, 流域面积为2 200平方千米, 平均流速为每秒7.7立方米。该河可通航部分长33千米, 连通上乌克湖和下乌克湖。其下游河段几乎无法通航。19世纪时, 为便于大型船只通行, 冯·阿尼姆家族曾尝试改造河道, 但数十年后无果而终。

Union Canal (the United Kingdom)

A canal located in Scotland, the United Kingdom. The Union Canal flows from Falkirk to Edinburgh with a length of 50 kilometres, following a contour line with an elevation of 73 metres. This contour canal saves freighters the time of passing through locks. The canal was originally built to transport coal to Edinburgh. Opened in 1822, it was a success

联盟运河 (英国)

英国苏格兰运河。联盟运河从福尔柯克流向爱丁堡, 全长50千米。联盟运河为等高运河, 沿海拔73米的等高线而建, 船只通行无须借助船闸, 从而节省了时间。修建该运河最初是为了将煤炭运往爱丁堡。1822年运河开通, 起初运营

at the beginning, but in the competition with railways, particularly with the Edinburgh and Glasgow Railway, which came into service in 1842, it was heavily affected as a transport medium. After a period of gradual commercial decline, the Union Canal was closed to commercial traffic for the first time in 1933. The official announcement of closure came in 1965. There are several navigable aqueducts on the canal, including the Slateford Aqueduct, which takes the Union Canal over the Water of Leith in Edinburgh, the Almond Aqueduct near Ratho, and the 250-metre-long Avon Aqueduct near Linlithgow. In 2001, the canal was reopened, and was relinked to the Forth and Clyde Canal by the Falkirk Wheel in 2002. Now it becomes a leisure place for the public.

良好。但在与铁路运输的竞争中，特别是1842年爱丁堡—格拉斯哥铁路开通后，联盟运河的运输要道地位受到严重影响。随着商业通航量逐渐减少，联盟运河先于1933年停航，后于1965年正式被关闭。联盟运河上有多座通航渡槽，包括使运河横跨爱丁堡利斯河的斯雷特福德渡槽、拉索附近的阿尔蒙德渡槽以及林利斯哥附近长达250米的埃文渡槽。2001年，联盟运河重新通航。次年通过"福尔柯克轮"这一旋转式船舶升降机，联盟运河与福斯—克莱德运河再次连通。如今，该运河已成为人们休闲观光的好去处。

Union Canal (the United States)

联合运河（美国）

An abandoned canal located in southeastern Pennsylvania, the United States. Also called Golden Link. With a total length of 132 kilometres, the Union Canal ran from Reading to Middletown, connecting the Schuylkill River to the Susquehanna River. The Union Canal travelled westward and rose 95 metres to the summit at Lebanon and fell 59 metres to the Susquehanna River at its end. The canal had 93 lift locks in total. The idea of building a canal connecting the Schuylkill River and the Susquehanna River was proposed by William Penn (the founder of the English North American colony in the Pennsylvania Colony) in 1690, as he wanted to establish a second settlement along the

美国宾夕法尼亚州东南部废弃运河。亦称黄金航道。联合运河全长132千米，从雷丁市流至米德尔敦市，连通斯库尔吉尔河与萨斯奎汉纳河。联合运河自东向西流至最高处莱巴嫩县时，海拔上升95米，最终汇入萨斯奎汉纳河时，海拔下降59米，沿线共建有93座升降式船闸。1690年，英属北美宾夕法尼亚殖民地创建者威廉·佩恩打算在萨斯奎汉纳河旁建立第二个殖民点，于是提议开凿一条运河以连通斯库尔吉尔河和萨斯奎汉纳河。1791年，斯库尔吉尔—萨斯奎

Susquehanna River. The Schuylkill and Susquehanna Navigation Company was formed in 1791 and was in charge of the construction of the navigable waterway between Reading and Middletown. The work began in 1792 but ceased due to financial shortage before long. The construction continued in 1821 and was not completed until 1828. The vessel "Fair Trader" travelling from Philadelphia to Middletown in 5 days was the first traveler on the canal. Back then, the Union Canal served as a vital route for transporting hard coal and lumber to Philadelphia. In the 1850s, a round of expansion was carried out to make the locks accessible to large vessels and heavy freighters. The canal was officially abandoned in 1885.

汉纳航运公司成立，负责雷丁市和米德尔敦市之间的航道建设。1792年，运河工程启动，但因财力不足，不久便停工。联合运河开凿工程于1821年重启，直至1828年才竣工。"费尔翠德号"是第一艘在这条运河上航行的船舶，该船从费城出发，历时5天抵达米德尔顿市。联合运河曾是向费城运输无烟煤和木材的交通要道，具有重大经济意义。运河上原先的船闸过小，大型船只以及重载货船无法通行，19世纪50年代运河进一步拓宽。1885年，联合运河正式被弃用。

United Canal (the Netherlands)

联合运河（荷兰）

A canal located in the east of Groningen, the Netherlands. See B. L. Tijdens Canal.

荷兰格罗宁根省东部运河。见蒂登运河。

Unstrut〜

温斯特鲁特河

A canalized river located in eastern Germany. The Unstrut is a tributary of the Saale. Originating near Dingelstädt in northern Thuringia, the Unstrut spans across the Thuringian Basin and Saxony-Anhalt and flows into the Saale near Naumburg. The river is 192 kilometres in length, and its major tributaries are Gera, Wipper and Helme. Towns along its course include Mühlhausen, Sömmerda and so forth. Initially, the Unstrut was not suitable for navigation. Between 1790 and 1794, the river was made

德国东部运河化河流。温斯特鲁特河是萨勒河支流之一，源于图林根州北部丁格尔施泰特市附近，流经图林根盆地和萨克森—安哈尔特州，最终在瑙姆堡附近汇入萨勒河。温斯特鲁特河全长192千米，主要支流包括格拉河、维珀河和赫尔姆河等，沿线城镇有米尔豪森和瑟默达等。起初，温斯特鲁特河并不具备通航条件。1790—

navigable. Cargos like sandstone and limestone were shipped along the river. In the following century, the Unstrut became an important waterway of Germany. In 1889, the Unstrut Railway was built along the river, reducing the importance of the Unstrut River in transportation. The Unstrut nowadays is an ideal destination for entertainment. Tourists can rent canoes and rowing boats to navigate the river.

1794年间，人们对温斯特鲁特河成功进行了运河化改造，用来运输砂岩和石灰岩等物资。此后百年间，温斯特鲁特河一直是德国重要的航运线路之一。1889年运河沿线修建了温斯特鲁特铁路，温斯特鲁特河的航运功能随之被削弱。如今，温斯特鲁特河已成为休闲娱乐的理想去处，游客可以租借独木舟和划艇游览沿途风光。

Unterweser

A canalized river located in Germany. The Unterweser is the lower reach of the canalized Weser River. Starting at the Weser Weir in Bremen, the river is 69.5 kilometres in length and finally reaches the North Sea. Its water flow is influenced by tides. After the artificial intervention in the structure of Weser, the tidal range in Bremen has risen from 1 metre to over 4 metres today. There are multiple bridges and ferries on the Unterweser.

下威悉河

德国运河化河流。下威悉河是威悉河的下游部分，始于不来梅市的威悉坝，最后注入北海，全长69.5千米。下威悉河水流受潮汐影响，经改造后，威悉河不来梅河段的潮差从原来的1米增加到了如今的4米以上。下威悉河上建有多处桥梁和渡口。

Upper Chenab Canal

A canal located in the province of Punjab, Pakistan. The Upper Chenab Canal has a total length of about 128 kilometres. It was constructed between 1905 and 1912 to meet irrigation requirements.

切纳布河上游运河

巴基斯坦旁遮普省运河。切纳布河上游运河全长约128千米，1905年开凿，1912年竣工，主要用于满足当地的灌溉需求。

Upper Colme Canal

A canal located in northern France. As the western

科尔莫上游运河

法国北部运河。科尔莫上游运河是

segment of the Colme Canal, the Upper Colme Canal is linked with the Aa River at Watten, and then flows northeast to meet the Bergues Canal and the Lower Colme Canal at Bergues. It is 25 kilometres in length and has 3 locks, one of which is now out of service. The canal was opened in 1753.

科尔莫运河的西段，全长25千米，在瓦唐市与阿河相通，之后沿东北方向流至贝尔格市，连通贝尔格运河和科尔莫河下游运河。科尔莫上游运河1753年通航，河上建有3座船闸，其中1座已被废弃。

Upper Escaut Canal

埃斯科上游运河

A canal located in northern France. See Escaut Canal.

法国北部运河。见埃斯科运河。

Upper Havel Waterway

哈弗尔河上游航道

An inland waterway located in Germany. The Upper Havel Waterway lies between the states of Brandenburg and Mecklenburg-VorPomerania, and it is 97.4 kilometres in length with 11 locks in total. It consists of a part of the upper reaches of the Havel as well as various canals and waterways connected with it. This waterway was built in the 17th century and was extended to Neustrelitz in the 19th century. Given that the locks are far too small for modern inland waterway vessels, the Upper Havel Waterway now only carries passenger ships and sports boats.

德国内陆航道。哈弗尔河上游航道位于德国东北部勃兰登堡州和梅克伦堡－前波美拉尼亚州之间，全长97.4千米，河上共建有11座船闸，由哈弗尔河部分上游河段及其他与之相通的多条运河和航道组成。该航道于17世纪修建，19世纪时延伸至新施特雷利茨市。但因河上船闸过小，现代内河船舶无法通行。如今，哈弗尔河上游航道仅供客船和运动艇通行。

Upper Jhelum Canal

杰赫勒姆河上游运河

A canal located in the north of Punjab Province, Pakistan. The Upper Jhelum Canal is an irrigation canal. The canal leaves the Jehlum River at Mangla Dam and runs eastward to the Chenab River. It was one of the three rivers in the project called the Triple Canal System (TCS) in Punjab. The Upper Jhelum

巴基斯坦旁遮普省北部运河。杰赫勒姆河上游运河是一条灌溉运河，始于杰赫勒姆河上的门格拉大坝，向东汇入切纳布河，是旁遮普省运河网工程中的三条运河之一。修建杰赫勒姆河上游运河旨在为

Canal provides water to the northwestern part of the district Gujrat and the whole Mandi Bahauddin. In the spring of 1916, the Upper Jhelum Canal was put into use, bringing fertility to great stretches of wheat and paddy fields, forests of acacia and shisham and lush vegetable patches. The outlook of the district Gujrat had been thoroughly changed since then. At present, the Upper Jhelum Canal still functions as an irrigation channel.

古吉拉特市西北部和整个门迪巴哈丁地区供水。1916年春, 杰赫勒姆河上游运河启用。河水滋润着大片麦田和稻田、金合欢树和阔叶黄檀林以及郁郁葱葱的菜地。古吉拉特市的面貌自此得以彻底改变。杰赫勒姆河上游运河至今仍具有灌溉功能。

Upper Rhône

罗讷河上游运河

A canal located in eastern France. The Upper Rhône has a navigable distance totaling 104 kilometres. It consists chiefly of two parts, namely, an 81-kilometre-long section from the dam at Sault-Brénaz to Seyssel, and a 23-kilometre-long section running through the Savière Canal into Lake Bourget, the biggest natural lake in France. Historically, the Upper Rhône was navigable up to Le Parc, where it ran into a narrow gorge with rapids. In the 1880s, in order to bypass the rapids, a large lock was built at Sault-Brénaz to facilitate the navigation for both passengers and freight from Lyon to Aix-les-Bains. In the 1980s, a series of hydropower projects launched by the CNR (Compagnie Nationale du Rhône) changed the waterway in important ways and several diversion canals excavated later rendered the Upper Rhône navigable for its most parts.

法国东部运河。罗讷河上游运河可通航距离总计104千米, 主要由两部分组成, 其中一段长81千米, 从索布雷纳的水坝延伸至塞塞勒; 另一段长23千米, 经萨维耶尔运河注入法国最大的天然湖泊布尔歌湖。历史上, 船只经由罗讷河上游运河可至勒帕尔克, 此处为峡谷入口, 河道狭窄, 水流湍急。19世纪80年代, 在索布雷纳修建了1座大型船闸, 以帮助船只绕开急流, 提升里昂与艾克斯莱班之间的客运和货运能力。20世纪80年代, 罗讷河国营公司启动一系列水力发电工程, 给罗讷河上游航道带来重大变化, 开凿的数条引水运河也使得罗讷河上游运河的大部分河段可通航。

Upper Schelde~

A canalized cross-border river located in France and Belgium. Running from south to north, the Upper Schelde is the upper part of the 350-kilometre-long Schelde, which rises from Gouy, a municipality in northern France, and flows through Belgium and the southwest of the Netherlands to the North Sea. The Upper Schelde stretches from Gouy to the tidal lock at Merelbeke, near Ghent, Belgium. In France, the Upper Schelde is linked to the Lys via the Bossuit-Courtrai Canal and to the Deûle via the Espierres Canal. In Belgium, its navigable section measures 91.9 kilometres with 6 locks. The draught permitted on the Upper Schelde varies, with the maximum of 3 metres at the section from the Asper Lock to the Ring Canal.

上斯海尔德河

欧洲跨国运河化河流。上斯海尔德河为斯海尔德河上游河段，流经法国和比利时。斯海尔德河全长350千米，源于法国北部的古伊市境内，流经比利时及荷兰西南部，最后注入北海。上斯海尔德河则从斯海尔德河源头自南向北流向位于比利时根特附近梅勒尔贝克的潮汐闸。在法国境内，博西特—库特雷运河将上斯海尔德河与利斯河连通起来，而埃斯皮埃尔运河又将上斯海尔德河与代勒河连通。在比利时境内，上斯海尔德河可通航河段长91.9千米，建有6座船闸。上斯海尔德河不同河段的吃水深度也有差异，其中，从阿斯珀船闸到根特环形运河之间的河段吃水深度最深达3米。

Upper Seine Canal

An abandoned canal located in central France. The Upper Seine Canal was 76 kilometres long, but only 44 kilometres were put into service. It connected the navigable Seine to Troyes. The canal was constructed between 1805 and 1846. It was equipped with 8 locks, each of which was 185 metres long and 12 metres wide, to overcome an elevation difference of 20 metres. The canal gradually became less used due to poor navigability and competition from the railway. In 1968, it was closed to navigation. Since

塞纳河上游运河

法国中部废弃运河。塞纳河上游运河全长76千米，但仅44千米可通航。该运河连接塞纳河可通航河段与特鲁瓦市。运河于1805—1846年间开凿，河上曾建有8座船闸，每座船闸长185米，宽12米，用以调节20米的水位落差。后因通航条件差以及来自铁路运输的竞争激烈，该运河逐渐被弃用。1968年，运河停航。自2000年起，人们付出了诸

2000, several efforts have been made to make the canal more touristic.

多努力来提升该运河的旅游观赏功能。

Upper Silesia Canal

上西里西亚运河

A canal located in Poland. See Gliwice Canal.

波兰运河。见格利维采运河。

Upper Spree Waterway

施普雷河上游航道

An inland waterway located in the state of Brandenburg, Germany. As a part of the Spree River, the Upper Spree Waterway runs from the Neuhaus Lock onwards, with a length of 57.7 kilometres and 4 locks in total. Currently, the waterway is mainly used as a route for sightseeing.

德国勃兰登堡州内陆航道。施普雷河上游航道是施普雷河的一部分，始于诺伊豪斯船闸，全长57.7千米，河上共建有4座船闸。如今，施普雷河上游航道主要用于旅游观光。

Urker Canal

厄尔卡运河

A canal located in the province of Flevoland, the Netherlands. The Urker Canal is 13 kilometres in length, running from Emmeloord, where it intersects with two other canals, namely, the Lemster Canal and the Zwolse Canal, and emptying into the IJssel Lake at the town of Urk. The canal was constructed before World War II and witnessed the transfer of the industrial area in Emmerloord to its south bank in 1943.

荷兰弗莱福兰省运河。厄尔卡运河全长13千米，始于埃默洛尔德市，在此处与另外两条运河，即莱姆斯特运河和兹沃尔瑟运河交汇，最终在于尔克镇注入艾瑟尔湖。该运河开凿于第二次世界大战爆发之前。1943年埃默洛尔德市工业区搬迁至其南岸。

Ursem Canal

乌尔塞姆运河

A canal located in the province of North Holland, the Netherlands. The Ursem Canal runs from Ursem to Avenhorn with a total length of 4 kilome-

荷兰北荷兰省运河。乌尔塞姆运河由乌尔塞姆村流至阿文霍伦镇，全长4千米。运河的名字来自

tres. The canal was named after Ursem, where it begins.

其起始地乌尔塞姆村。

Usquert Canal

A canal located in the province of Groningen, the Netherlands. The Usquert Canal has a length of 5.82 kilometres. It originates from Usquert with its name coming from the town. The canal emerged in a swamp area during the Middle Ages, with an initial purpose for drainage. Later, it was also used for transportation. Since the 1970s, the canal has been dammed. In Usquert town, there is a wooden drawbridge built in 1866 over the Usquert Canal, which now stands as a cultural heritance.

于斯奎特运河

荷兰格罗宁根省运河。于斯奎特运河全长5.82千米，始于于斯奎特镇，其名即源于此。中世纪时，这条运河开凿于沼泽地区，最初用来排水，后来也开始发挥航运功能。自20世纪70年代以来，于斯奎特运河上修建水坝。在于斯奎特镇，有一座建于1866年的木制吊桥，现已列为文化遗产。

Uttoxeter Canal

A canal located in Staffordshire, England, the United Kingdom. The Uttoxeter Canal, an extension of the Caldon Canal, runs from Froghall to its terminus at Uttoxeter. The canal is 21 kilometres in length with 19 locks in total. With the authorization in 1797 by the Parliament, the canal was constructed. It was completed and opened in 1811. It was not financially rewarding as the canal lies in rural areas, without any major industrial centres around. In January 1849, the canal was closed, except for the short section at Froghall, which remained open until 1930. On parts of the canal bed was paved the Churnet Valley Railway. The railway was dismantled later and plans have been made to restore the canal.

尤托克西特运河

英国英格兰斯塔福德郡运河。尤托克西特运河是卡尔顿运河的延伸河段，从弗洛格霍尔流至终点尤托克西特，全长21千米，河上建有19座船闸。1797年，英国议会授权开凿尤托克西特运河。1811年，运河建成并通航。尤托克西特运河地处乡村地带，远离工业中心，开通后经济收益不佳。1849年1月，尤托克西特运河的大部分河段被关闭，仅有弗洛格霍尔处的部分河段保持开放至1930年。尤托克西特运河的部分河床被改建成了楚奈特河谷铁路。后来铁路被拆除，人们又计划修复尤托克西特运河。

Vadu Crișului-Aștileu Canal

A canal located in northwestern Romania. The Vadu Crișului-Aștileu Canal is 14.5 kilometres in length. It originates from the vicinity of Vadu Crișului and ends near Chistag, and runs parallel to the Crișul Repede River. Built in 1954, the canal diverts the water of the Crișul Repede River and its tributaries to serve the Aștileu hydroelectric plant, which can generate nearly 2.8 megawatts of electricity.

克里什河畔瓦杜-阿什蒂莱乌运河

罗马尼亚西北部运河。克里什河畔瓦杜—阿什蒂莱乌运河全长14.5千米，从克里什河畔瓦杜村附近流向齐斯塔格村附近，流向与湍克里什河平行。该运河1954年修建，把湍克里什河及其支流的水引向阿什蒂莱乌水电站发电，水电站装机容量达2.8兆瓦。

Vaires Canal

A canal located in France. See Chelles Canal.

威尔运河

法国运河。见谢勒运河。

Vallei Canal

A canal located in the provinces of Utrecht and Gelderland, the Netherlands. The Vallei Canal is approximately 40 kilometres in length. Its name is derived from the Gelderse Vallei, through which the canal flows in a northerly direction. The canal is for the drainage of the Gelderse Vallei and thus preventing flooding. It joins several Veluwe creeks in Amersfoort to form the Eem. When water levels are low in summer, water is pumped from the Lower Rhine to the Eem through the Vallei Canal.

瓦莱运河

荷兰乌特勒支省和海尔德兰省运河。瓦莱运河长约40千米，向北流经海尔德瑟瓦莱河谷，其名称即源自该河谷。修建该运河是为便于海尔德瑟瓦莱河谷排水，防止洪水泛滥。瓦莱运河在阿默斯福特市与源于费吕沃地区的多条溪流交汇形成埃姆河。夏季水位较低时，人们会利用水泵从下莱茵河抽水，经瓦莱运河输送至埃姆河。

Van Harinxma Canal

A canal located in the province of Friesland, the Netherlands. Originally known as Harlingen Trek

范哈林克斯马运河

荷兰弗里斯兰省运河。旧称哈灵根拖船运河。范哈林克斯马运

Canal. The Van Harinxma Canal has a length of 37.5 kilometres, extending from Leeuwarden to Harlingen Harbour, where it connects with the Wadden Sea. It was named after Pieter Albert Vincent van Harinxma thoe Slooten in 1950 who was King's Commissioner to Friesland from 1909 to 1945. The Tsjerk Hiddessluizen Lock is located at the Harlingen Harbour to maintain the water level of the canal. There are 10 bridges over the canal and 4 aqueducts under it. The Van Harinxma Canal was excavated between 1935 and 1951, and was further widened and deepened. At Suawoude it joins the Prinses Margriet Canal. Now, the canal is navigable for CEMT (Classification of European Inland Waterways) Class IV ships.

河全长37.5千米，从吕伐登市延伸至哈灵根港口，注入瓦登海。1950年，运河以1909—1945年间荷兰国王派驻弗里斯兰省专员彼得·阿尔贝特·文森特·范哈林克斯马·图·斯洛滕的名字命名。哈灵根港口处建有切克希德斯路易岑船闸，以维持运河水位。运河上共建有10座桥梁，下方建有4座渡槽。运河修建于1935—1951年间，后又进一步拓宽与加深，在斯瓦沃德村汇入玛格丽特公主运河。如今，运河可供欧洲内陆航道标准四级船舶通行。

Van Panhuys Canal

A canal located in southeastern Friesland, the Netherlands. The Van Panhuys Canal is 5 kilometres in length. It starts from the Workum Trek Canal and empties into the Makkum Canal. The canal was built between 1876 and 1877, named after Johan Aemilius Abraham Van Panhuys (1836—1907), a local magistrate. In March 2007, Friesland Province began to widen and deepen the waterway for the passage of ships with larger capacity. After reconstruction, the Van Panhuys Canal is navigable for ships with a draught of 1.9 metres. The canal also plays a part in drainage and tourism.

范班豪斯运河

荷兰弗里斯兰省东南部运河。范班豪斯运河全长5千米，始于沃尔克姆拖船运河，汇入马库默运河。运河修建于1876—1877年间，因当地一名治安法官约翰·埃米利乌斯·亚伯拉罕·范班豪斯（1836—1907）而得名。为便于更大载重量的船只通行，2007年3月，弗里斯兰省开始对运河进行拓宽和加深。改造后的运河可供吃水深度达1.9米的船只通行。范班豪斯运河还具有排水和旅游观光功能。

Van Starkenborgh Canal

A canal located in the province of Groningen, the Netherlands. The Van Starkenborgh Canal is 27 kilometres in length and 50 metres in width, with 14 bridges and 2 locks. It connects the Prinses Margriet Canal and the Ems Canal, and can be used for transportation and recreation. First constructed in 1935, the canal, together with the Prinses Margriet Canal and the Ems Canal, formed the main shipping route from Lemmer to Delfzijl. In 1911, Groningen and Friesland set up a special committee to build a new passage from Lemmer to Groningen. In 1924, the Groningen government built a new lock in Gaarkeuken. In 1928, the Groningen government employed about 1,400 people to start the construction without an agreement with the Friesland government. In 1938, a part of the Groningen waterway was completed. Queen Wilhelmina (1880—1962) presided over the navigation ceremony, and the canal was officially opened for the first time. In 1966, the canal was widened to accommodate 1,350-DWT (Deadweight Ton) ships. In 1981, a larger lock was built in Gaarkeuken.

Varistaipale Canal

A canal located in Finland. The Varistaipale Canal is 1,100 metres in length with 4 locks, linking the lakes of Juojärvi and Varisvesi with the Taivallahti Canal. It allows vessels with a maximum length of 31.2 metres and a width of 7.1 metres to pass

范斯塔肯博赫运河

荷兰格罗宁根省运河。范斯塔肯博赫运河连通玛格丽特公主运河和埃姆斯运河，全长27千米，宽50米，沿线建有14座桥梁和2座船闸，兼具交通运输和休闲娱乐功能。运河开凿于1935年，与玛格丽特公主运河和埃姆斯运河共同构成从莱默到代尔夫宰尔的主要航运路线。1911年，格罗宁根省和弗里斯兰省成立专门委员会，负责修建一条从莱默到格罗宁根的新航道。1924年，格罗宁根当地政府在加尔库肯村修建了一座新船闸。1928年，在未能与弗里斯兰省达成协议的情况下，格罗宁根当地政府雇用了约1 400人修建格罗宁根航道。1938年，格罗宁根航道部分河段竣工，荷兰女王威廉敏娜（1880—1962）主持运河正式通航仪式。1966年，运河拓宽，可供载重1 350吨级的船只通行。1981年，在加尔库肯村建造了一座更大的船闸。

瓦里斯泰佩勒运河

芬兰运河。瓦里斯泰佩勒运河连通尤奥湖、瓦里斯韦西湖和泰瓦拉蒂运河，全长1 100米，河上建有4座船闸，可供最大规格为长31.2米、宽7.1米的船舶通行。该运河

through. The canal was built between 1911 and 1913 as a part of the Heinävesi Route. It has a drop height of 14.5 metres and is the deepest canal in Nordic countries. Nearby the canal sits the Varistaipale Canal Museum.

1911年开凿，1913年完工，是黑奈韦西航线的一部分。瓦里斯泰佩勒运河水位落差达14.5米，是北欧地区最深的运河。运河附近建有瓦里斯泰佩勒运河博物馆。

Veen Canal

芬运河

An inland canal located in the province of Groningen, the Netherlands. The Veen Canal has a navigable length of 4.9 kilometres with 1 lock. It starts from the Westerwolder Aa River and ends at the B. L. Tijdens Canal. The nearby lakes and forests together form a nature reserve that has been given the same name as the Veen Canal.

荷兰格罗宁根省内陆运河。芬运河通航长度为4.9千米，河上建有1座船闸，始于韦斯特沃尔德阿河，汇入蒂登运河。附近的湖泊和森林共同构成一个与该运河同名的自然保护区。

Veendam-Stadskanaal-Ter Apel Waterway

芬丹－斯塔茨卡纳尔－泰尔阿珀尔航道

A canal system located in the province of Groningen, the Netherlands. The Veendam-Stadskanaal-Ter Apel Waterway runs from Veendam to Ter Apel. It consists of 5 channels: the A.G. Wildervanck Canal, the Ooster Canal, the Stads Canal, the Mussel Canal and the Ter Apel Canal. The total length of the waterway is 45 kilometres, and 10 locks and 64 bridges were built along the route.

荷兰格罗宁根省运河系统。芬丹—斯塔茨卡纳尔—泰尔阿珀尔航道从芬丹流向泰尔阿珀尔，由5条运河组成，分别为维尔德万克运河、奥斯特运河、斯塔茨运河、米瑟尔运河和泰尔阿珀尔运河。该航道全长45千米，沿线建有10座船闸和64座桥梁。

Velten Stich Canal

费尔滕支渠

A canal located in the state of Brandenburg, Germany. The Velten Stich Canal is 3.2 kilometres long, which is a tributary of the Oder-Havel Waterway.

德国勃兰登堡州运河。费尔滕支渠全长3.2千米，是奥得—哈弗尔航道的一条支流。该运河属于四

The canal is a Class-IV waterway capable of accommodating ships up to 600 gross tons. It is under the administration of the Oder-Havel Waterways and Shipping Office.

级航道，可供最大载重量600吨级的船只通行，由奥得—哈弗尔航道和航运局负责管理。

Venice Canals (the United States)

威尼斯运河网（美国）

A canal system located in southern California, the United States. The Venice Canals are a series of wetland canals adjacent to the Venice Beach. In the early 1900s, the canals were excavated under the direction of Abbot Kinney, a tobacco millionaire and real estate developer, who financed to build a "Venice of America" in South California. The original canals were about 26 kilometres in length. Kinney named the 7 canals the Aldebaran Canal, the Altair Canal, the Cabrillo Canal, the Coral Canal, the Grand Canal, the Lion Canal and the Venus Canal. By the late 1920s, due to the rise of car culture in Los Angeles, many of the Venice Canals had been filled in and paved to create roads for driving. The remaining canals gradually fell into disrepair. After being widely renovated, the Venice Canals are now a quaint upscale neighbourhood in Venice. This neighbourhood has become one of Los Angeles' top attractions. Tourists greatly appreciate the postcard scenes and enjoy the serenity.

美国南加利福尼亚州运河网。威尼斯运河网毗邻威尼斯海滩，由一系列湿地运河构成。20世纪初，为打造美国南加州版威尼斯，烟草富豪兼房地产开发商阿博特·金尼出资修建了该运河网。威尼斯运河网总长度约26千米，金尼将各7个分段运河分别命名为阿尔德巴伦运河、阿尔泰运河、卡布里约运河、科勒尔运河、格兰德运河、莱昂运河和维纳斯运河。20世纪20年代末，洛杉矶汽车文化盛行一时，为修建公路，威尼斯运河网中多条运河被回填，留存下来的运河也日渐萧条。经过大规模翻修后，威尼斯运河网所在地区如今已成为高端住宅区，是洛杉矶最著名的景点之一，如画的风景和静谧的氛围令游客沉醉其中。

Venus Canal

维纳斯运河

A canal located in Los Angeles, California, the United States. The Venus Canal is a part of the series of the Venice Canals.

美国加利福尼亚州洛杉矶市运河。维纳斯运河是威尼斯运河网中的一条运河。

Verbindings Canal

A canal located in the province of East Flanders, Belgium. The Verbindings Canal is 2 kilometres in length with a draught of 2.5 metres and a width of 12 metres. It connects the Ghent-Bruges Canal in the west with the Ghent-Terneuzen Canal in the east. The canal was constructed in 1863 in the then rural area. This project boosted local development as many factories were set up near the canal, and many workers were attracted to settle there.

韦尔宾丁斯运河

比利时东佛兰德省运河。韦尔宾丁斯运河全长2千米，吃水深度2.5米，宽12米，西连根特—布鲁日运河，东接根特—特尔纽曾运河。1863年，运河从当时的乡村地区开挖，完工后，附近兴建了许多工厂，吸引众多工人来此定居，促进了当地经济的繁荣发展。

Veurne Canal

A cross-border canal located in Europe. See Newport-Dunkirk Canal.

弗尔讷运河

欧洲跨国运河。见新港—敦刻尔克运河。

Veurne-Dunkirk Canal

A cross-border canal located in Europe. The Veurne-Dunkirk Canal runs 32 kilometres and links Veurne in western Belgium and Dunkirk in northern French.

弗尔讷—敦刻尔克运河

欧洲跨国运河。弗尔讷—敦刻尔克运河长32千米，连接比利时西部城市弗尔讷和法国北部城市敦刻尔克。

Veurne-Saint-Winoxbergen Canal

A cross-border canal located in Europe. The Veurne-Saint-Winoxbergen Canal runs between Veurne, Belgium and Saint-Winoxbergen, France. It is 23.7 kilometres in length. Built in 1293, the canal served as an essential commercial waterway between Veurne and Saint-Winoxbergen in the Middle Ages. The Belgian part is not navigable now.

弗尔讷—圣温诺克斯贝亨运河

欧洲跨国运河。弗尔讷—圣温诺克斯贝亨运河全长23.7千米，连接比利时弗尔讷市和法国圣温诺克斯贝亨市。运河开凿于1293年，中世纪时是弗尔讷和圣温诺克斯贝亨两地之间一条重要的商业航道。如今，该运河位于比利时境内的河段已不通航。

Victoria Barge Canal

A canal located in Texas, the United States. The Victoria Barge Canal lies in the lower reaches of the Guadalupe River, and runs parallel to the Guadalupe River. It is 56 kilometres in length, connecting the Port of Victoria to the Gulf Intracoastal Waterway. Built in 1968, the canal had a depth of 2.7 metres and a width of 30.5 metres. Later on, it was widened and deepened to 3.7 metres and 38.1 metres in response to the parametre standard of the Gulf Intracoastal Waterway. The establishment of the canal marked the opening of the Port of Victoria. The port is connected to highways, railways and airports. Because of its convenient transportation and unique strategic position, the port became a portal to domestic and international markets. As the Gulf Intracoastal Waterway connects to other major coastal and inland ports, channels and cities, products and cargo can be hauled in and shipped out from and to every corner of the world via the canal, the Gulf Intracoastal Waterway system and other means of transportation.

维多利亚驳船运河

美国得克萨斯州运河。维多利亚驳船运河位于瓜达卢普河下游，流向与该河平行。运河全长56千米，连接维多利亚港与墨西哥湾沿海航道。维多利亚驳船运河1968年建成，深2.7米，宽30.5米，为达到海湾沿海航道标准，后又加深至3.7米，并拓宽至38.1米。运河开通后维多利亚港得以正式启用。维多利亚港还与高速公路、铁路和机场相连。由于交通便利，战略位置独特，维多利亚港成为通向国内外市场的门户。维多利亚驳船运河与墨西哥湾沿海航道相通，而后者又与其他主要海港、内陆港、航道以及城市相连。通过维多利亚驳船运河、墨西哥湾沿海航道及其他交通方式出入维多利亚港，大量商品和货物可运往世界各地。

Vilaine︦

A canalized river located in the west of France. The Vilaine has a navigable length of 137 kilometres and 12 locks. As a part of Brittany's Canal System, it links the Mayenne department to the Atlantic Ocean. Joined by the Ille and Rance Canal, the canalized river is navigable from Rennes to the Atlantic Ocean. The Vilaine was one of the first natural

维莱讷河

法国西部运河化河流。维莱讷河可通航长度为137千米，河上建有12座船闸，是布列塔尼运河网的一部分，与伊勒—朗斯运河相通，也是连接马耶讷省与大西洋的纽带，其中从雷恩市到大西洋的河段可以通航。维莱讷河是法国最早

rivers in France to be canalized. Some locks were built in 1540, while the complete canalization project was started after 1784. In 1834, the canal was completed. The Vilaine is now entirely under the responsibility of the Brittany region, which enjoys a significant boom in inland cruising and attracts many visitors worldwide.

进行运河化改造的自然河流之一。部分船闸建成于1540年，但整体的运河化工程在1784年后才开始，1834年竣工。如今，维莱讷河全线归布列塔尼大区管辖，其内陆水上观光业十分兴旺，吸引来自世界各地的游客。

Vĩnh Tế Canal

永济运河

A canal located in southern Vietnam. The Vĩnh Tế Canal runs along the Cambodia-Vietnam border, connecting the territory of Châu Đốc and the Hà Tiên sea gate, the Gulf of Siam. The 87-kilometre-long canal was built at the end of 1819. Emperor Gia Long ordered Nguyễn Văn Thoại to undertake the project. About 80,000 local people were involved in the project. The canal was completed in 1824. Today, the Vĩnh Tế Canal occupies a significant position in the communication and transportation of southern Vietnam, and plays a significant role in national security and defence.

越南南部运河。永济运河全长87千米，流经越南与柬埔寨边境地区，连接朱笃市和暹罗湾河先海口。1819年末，嘉隆皇帝命令阮文话沿越柬边境开凿一条新运河，约8万越南人参与了该运河的修建工作。1824年，永济运河竣工。如今，永济运河对越南南部的区域交流及运输意义重大，在越南国家安全中亦具有重要的战略意义。

Visvliet Canal

费斯夫利特运河

A canal located in the province of Groningen, the Netherlands. Formerly called Besheers Canal. The Visvliet Canal is 6 kilometres in length. It flows from Visvliet to the Van Starkenborgh Canal, crossed by a railway bridge of the Leeuwarden-Groningen line.

荷兰格罗宁根省运河。旧称贝希尔斯运河。费斯夫利特运河全长6千米，始于费斯夫利特镇，汇入范斯塔肯博赫运河。吕伐登—格罗宁根铁路线上的一座铁路桥横跨该运河。

Vliet Canal

A canal located in the province of South Holland, the Netherlands. The Vliet Canal flows from Leiden and reaches Delft through the Delft Schie Canal, and it has a lock in Leidschendam. It was excavated in 47 AD by order of Roman general Corbulo, whose intention was to connect the current Old Rhine stream, a main branch of the Rhine in Roman times, to the Meuse estuary. The canal functioned as an essential trade link in the Middle Ages, and a range of windmills were constructed along its banks. Now two popular annual events are celebrated alongside the canal: the Vliet Days every September and Saint Nicholas' Day every November. The Vliet Canal is also a well-liked boating route during the sailing season. Visitors may moor at the visitor harbour and stay there the whole night.

弗利特运河

荷兰南荷兰省运河。弗利特运河始于莱顿市，经斯希运河代尔夫特段流至代尔夫特，在莱岑丹市的河段上建有一座船闸。公元47年，罗马将军科布洛下令修建弗利特运河，旨在将古罗马时期莱茵河一条主要支流，即现今的旧莱茵河连通至默兹河口。中世纪时该运河是重要的贸易通道，河流两岸风车林立。如今，弗利特运河沿线地区每年举行两项重要活动：9月份的弗利特节和11月份的圣尼古拉节。在适宜划船的季节，弗利特运河也是深受人们欢迎的一条游览航线，游客可以在专用港口泊船、过夜。

Vodootvodny Canal

A canal located in downtown Moscow, Russia. The Vodootvodny Canal is 4 kilometres in length, and its width varies from 30 to 60 metres, with 11 bridges built on it. The southern part of the Moscow River was once a flat plain and inflicted by flood during spring. To control floods, residents dredged the river and built dams, but to no avail. To solve this problem, Russian Neoclassical architect Matvey Kazakov proposed a plan in 1775. Not until 1783, when a disastrous flood destroyed a stone bridge, did the plan come into practice. The river bed was cleared and widened and became the Vo-

维多陀夫德尼运河

俄罗斯莫斯科市运河。维多陀夫德尼运河全长4千米，最窄处30米，最宽处60米，河上建有11座桥梁。莫斯科河南段的河畔区昔日地势平坦，每到春季就会受到洪水侵袭，当地居民挖壕沟筑堤坝以治理水患，但成效甚微。为解决这一问题，俄国新古典主义建筑师马特维·卡扎科夫于1775年提出一个防洪计划。但直到1783年一场灾害性洪水冲毁一座石桥后，这套防洪计划才得以真正付诸实施。人们清

dootvodny Canal of today. The construction created the Balchug Island between the Moscow River and the canal.

理并拓宽莫斯科河原有的河床，在此基础上修建了现在的维多陀夫德尼运河。因开凿运河，莫斯科河与维多陀夫德尼运河之间形成了一座人工岛，即巴尔舒格岛。

Voedings Canal

沃丁斯运河

A canal located in the province of Limburg, the Netherlands. The Voedings Canal is a short feeder connecting the Meuse River and the South Willems Canal. It flows through the Boschpoort housing estate and empties into the Meuse River from the Sappi Paper Mill. The canal was built to provide enough water supply for the South Willems Canal. Several years ago, a local regulation said that the canal should be closed at high tide to protect parts of Boschpoort from the flood.

荷兰林堡省运河。沃丁斯运河是一条短的引水运河，连通默兹河和南威廉斯运河。运河流经博世波特住宅区，经沙皮造纸厂汇入默兹河。修建该运河旨在为南威廉斯运河提供足够的水源补给。几年前，当地出台一项规定，在涨潮时关闭运河，以防博世波特部分地区被洪水淹没。

Volga-Baltic Waterway

伏尔加－波罗的海航道

A canal located in Russia. Formerly called Mariinsky Canal System. The Volga-Baltic Waterway is 368 kilometres in length, running from Cherepovets at the north end of the Rybinsk Reservoir to the south end of Lake Onega, and linking the Volga with the Baltic Sea via the Neva River. It was a masterpiece of hydro technics in the early 19th century and an important propeller for developing the national economy. The waterway went through constant improvement during the Soviet times. New locks were built, 2 on the Svir River and 3 on the Sheksna River. Between 1960 and 1964, 39

俄罗斯运河。旧称马林斯基运河网。伏尔加－波罗的海航道全长368千米，由雷宾斯克水库北端的切列波韦茨市流至奥涅加湖南端，通过涅瓦河将伏尔加河与波罗的海连通。该航道是19世纪早期水利工程的杰作之一，极大地推动了俄国经济的发展。苏联时期该航道又经历了一系列改造。运河上新建了一批船闸，其中斯维里河上新建2座船闸，舍克斯纳河上新建3座船闸。1960－1964年间，航

old wooden locks were replaced by 7 new locks. On 5 June 1964, the new Volga-Baltic Waterway was opened after major improvements. The locks allow for ships of 210 metres in length, 17.6 metres in width, and 4.2 metres in depth at most. They allowed river-sea ships with 5,000 tons of displacement to sail directly across the three big lakes. The travel time from Cherepovets to Saint Petersburg were shortened from 15 days to about 3 days. At present, the Volga-Baltic Waterway plays an active role in the export of oil and lumber and becomes a popular tourist route.

Volga-Don Ship Canal

A canal located in Volgograd Oblast, western Russia. The Volga-Don Ship Canal links the lower courses of both the Volga River and the Don River at their closest points, thus providing the most direct passable way between the Caspian Sea and the Sea of Azov. Starting south of Volgograd, near the settlement of Krasnoarmeysk, the canal runs west, then northwest, and drains into the Tsimlyansk Reservoir near Volgodonskoy. It is 101 kilometres in length, 45 kilometres of which are rivers and reservoirs. The canal has 13 locks. The attempt to connect the two lower courses had a long history. The construction of today's Volga-Don Ship Canal was started in 1938 and completed in 1952. Although the general dimensions of the 13 canal locks are smaller than those on the Volga River,

道又进行了一些重要改造，7座新船闸替换了原有的39座木制船闸。1964年6月5日，新的伏尔加—波罗的海航道正式开通。新建船闸最大可允许长210米、宽17.6米、深4.2米的船只通行，可供排水量达5 000吨的通海船只通航。经由该运河，大型船只可以直接跨越三大湖，从切列波韦茨到圣彼得堡的航程由15天缩短至3天左右。如今，伏尔加—波罗的海航道为俄罗斯的石油和木材出口做出了重要贡献，同时也是一条颇受欢迎的旅游航线。

伏尔加－顿河通海运河

俄罗斯西部伏尔加格勒州运河。伏尔加—顿河通海运河连通伏尔加河下游与顿河下游之间距离最近的两处水域，是里海和亚速海之间最近的通航运河。伏尔加—顿河通海运河始于伏尔加格勒市南部的红军村附近，先向西延伸，而后转向西北，最终流入伏尔加顿斯克附近的齐姆良斯克水库。运河长101千米，其中45千米为自然河流和水库，建有13座船闸。把伏尔加河下游与顿河下游连通起来的设想由来已久，但伏尔加—顿河通海运河的修建工作直到1938年才正式开始，并于1952年竣工。运河上修建的13座船闸规模虽不

they can allow the passage of ships with a cargo capacity of 5,000 tons. Coal, minerals and grain were transported from the Don area to the Volga area, while lumber, pyrites, and petroleum products were transported in the opposite direction. According to a 2007 report, the Volga-Don Ship Canal had allowed the passage of 450,000 vessels, which had carried 336 million tons of cargo in its first 55 years of operations. In the 1980s, the construction of a second Volga-Don Canal was approved. However, the programme was abruptly cancelled in 1990 due to financial concerns.

如伏尔加河上的船闸大，但载重量5 000吨的货轮也可通航。从顿河向伏尔加河方向运输的货物主要是煤炭、矿产和粮食，而从伏尔加河向顿河方向运输的货物主要是木材、硫化铁矿石和石油产品。2007年的一份报告显示，在伏尔加—顿河通海运河通航的前55年里，共有45万艘船舶通过，货运总量达3.36亿吨。20世纪80年代，在两河之间修建伏尔加—顿河二号运河的计划得到批准，但因资金问题，该项目于1990年突然被取消。

Vollenhove Canal

福伦霍弗运河

A canal located in the province of Overijssel, the Netherlands. The Vollenhove Canal, 5 kilometres in length, starts from the Zwanen Canal, flows through the Vollenhove Lake and ends in the Blokzijl Village.

荷兰上艾瑟尔省运河。福伦霍弗运河长5千米，始于天鹅运河，流经福伦霍弗湖，终于布洛克宰尔村。

Vridi Canal

弗里迪运河

A canal located in Abidjan, Côte d'Ivoire. Taking its name from the village of Vridi, the Vridi Canal is 3.2 kilometres in length, 370 metres in width, and 15 metres in depth, and has an elevation of 77 metres. After the opening of the Vridi Canal, the city Abidjan soon became a major shipping and financial centre of French-speaking West Africa. The canal is navigable, and ships with large draughts can dock in the deep-water port Abidjan (the second larg-

科特迪瓦阿比让市运河。弗里迪运河得名于阿比让的弗里迪村。该运河长3.2千米，宽370米，深15米，海拔77米。弗里迪运河开通后，阿比让一跃成为西非法语区的主要航运和金融中心。该运河可通航，大吨位海船可停泊在阿比让深水港。阿比让港位于科特迪瓦东南海岸临大西洋的几内亚湾，是非洲

est in Africa), which lies on the southeast coast of the country, on the Gulf of Guinea of the Atlantic Ocean.

第二大深水港。

Vũng Gù Canal

万古运河

A canal located in the Mekong Delta, Vietnam. See Bảo Định Canal.

越南湄公河三角洲运河。见保定运河。

Waard Canal

A canal located in the province of North Holland, the Netherlands. The Waard Canal starts from the Kolhorn Canal and flows through Nieuwesluis before emptying into the Amstel Lake. It is 10 kilometres in length, 9 kilometres of which is navigable. Boasting a large fish stock, the canal is popular among anglers.

Wabash and Erie Canal

A canal located in the north of the United States. The Wabash and Erie Canal stretches up to 753.2 kilometres from Toledo to Evansville, connecting the Great Lakes and the Ohio River. It is composed of 4 sections: the Maumee River Section, the Wabash River Section, the Cross Cut Canal Section, and the Central Canal Section. The construction of the canal began in 1832 in Fort Wayne and extended to Lafayette by 1843, Terre Haute by 1848 and Evansville by 1853. Despite the short prosperity it brought to the nearby area, the Wabash and Erie Canal was gradually abandoned and was finally auctioned off in 1876 due to the lack of funds and the growing importance of railroads. Today, the Wabash and Erie Canal Interpretive Centre in Delphi, Indiana, offers insights into the canal's changes through history and values as a cultural heritage.

Walcheren Canal

A canal located in the province of Zeeland in the

瓦德运河

荷兰北荷兰省运河。瓦德运河始于科尔霍恩运河，流经新斯勒伊斯，最后注入阿姆斯特尔湖。运河全长10千米，可通航长度为9千米。运河中鱼类资源丰富，深受垂钓爱好者欢迎。

沃巴什－伊利运河

美国北部运河。沃巴什—伊利运河从托莱多流向埃文斯维尔，连通五大湖和俄亥俄河，全长753.2千米，由莫米河、沃巴什河、横断运河和中部运河4段组成。该运河1832年自韦恩堡开凿，1843年延伸至拉斐特，1848年至特雷霍特，1853年至埃文斯维尔。沃巴什—伊利运河曾给附近地区带来短暂的繁荣，后因缺乏资金，加之铁路运输崛起，逐渐被弃用，1876年被拍卖。如今，印第安纳州的德尔斐建有沃巴什—伊利运河展示中心，帮助人们了解该运河的历史变迁和作为文化遗产的价值。

瓦尔赫伦运河

荷兰西南部泽兰省运河。瓦尔赫

southwestern Netherlands. The Walcheren Canal is 14.5 kilometres long with 3 locks. It connects the Veerse Lake to the Western Schelde. In 1870, the construction of the canal commenced. On 8 September 1873, King William III announced the opening of the canal. The canal has contributed to the economic recovery of Middelburg, but compared to the role it plays in commercial shipping, the canal is much more important for pleasure and recreation. As the water in this canal is relatively salty and seldom freezes in winter, rowing clubs come here for training when other waterways in the country are frozen in winter. Along the canal a towpath was constructed, where men walk with horses to pull ships. The environment in the towpath is well protected, with sheep grazing and birds nesting in the meadow next to the canal.

伦运河全长14.5千米，沿线建有3座船闸，连通费尔瑟湖与西斯海尔德航道。1870年，瓦尔赫伦运河开凿。1873年9月8日，国王威廉三世宣布运河通航。运河促进了米德尔堡地区的经济复苏，但其休闲娱乐功能比商业运输功能更为重要。瓦尔赫伦运河含盐量较高，冬季几乎不结冰，当荷兰其他地区航道结冰时，划船俱乐部都会来此训练。瓦尔赫伦运河沿岸还建有一条纤道，以便马匹拖拉船只，附近生态环境保护良好，在运河旁边草地上常能见到绵羊觅食、禽鸟栖息。

Walhonding Canal

A canal located in the Coshocton County of Ohio, the United States. As a feeder canal for the Ohio and Erie Canal, the 40-kilometre-long Walhonding Canal starts from Cavallo and empties into the Ohio and Erie Canal. Its construction was started in 1836 and ended in 1842. Later, there were appeals to further extend the Walhonding Canal, but the construction did not begin due to the lack of authorization. In 1896, the canal was officially abandoned and a project of railroad construction took place, partly following the towpath of the abandoned canal.

沃尔洪丁运河

美国俄亥俄州科肖克顿县运河。沃尔洪丁运河是俄亥俄—伊利运河的引水运河，全长40千米，始于卡瓦洛，最后汇入俄亥俄—伊利运河。该运河于1836年开凿，1842年完工。后曾有人呼吁继续扩建沃尔洪丁运河，但未获批准。1896年，该运河被正式弃用，后沿废弃运河的部分纤道修建铁路。

Wantij and Otter Canal

A canal located in the province of South Holland, the Netherlands. The Wantij and Otter Canal consists of the Wantij River and the Otter Canal. The Wantij Rriver runs through the Dordrecht from the south to the north, with the Old Maas, the Noord and the Lower Merwede connected to it in the north and Kikvorschkil in the south. There are 3 bridges crossing the Wantij. A part of this river belongs to the Biesbosch National Park. Local authorities are planning to carry out a large-scale urban transformation project along the river, aiming to build it into a thriving industrial zone. By protecting its natural environment, the local government aims to make the Wantij an ideal zone for living, working and recreation. The Otter Canal is an inland canal, connecting the New Merwede on the south side and the Helsloot and Wantij on the north side. The Otter Lock is the only lock on this canal, lying between the New Merwede and the Wantij River. The navigation lock, 39 metres in length and 7 metres in width, was built in 1863, and was later equipped with an iron bridge for pedestrians. In 1933, it was overhauled. The lock was transformed mechanically in the late 1970s and was declared a national cultural relic in 2015. It remains an important lock that enables smooth recreational shipping.

万泰－奥特运河

荷兰南荷兰省运河。万泰－奥特运河由万泰河和奥特运河组成。万泰河由南向北穿过多德雷赫特市区，南连基克沃尔施基尔河，北通旧马斯河、诺德河和梅尔维德河下游。万泰河上建有3座桥梁。该河部分河段属于比斯博斯国家公园。地方政府计划沿河实施大规模的城市改造项目，将其打造成一个繁荣的工业区。政府也致力于保护河流自然环境，使万泰河地区成为人们理想的生活、工作和娱乐场所。奥特运河是一条内陆运河，南连新梅尔维德河，北通赫尔斯洛特河和万泰河。奥特船闸位于新梅尔维德河与万泰河之间，是该运河上唯一的船闸，长39米，宽7米，建于1863年，后河上又修建了一座人行铁桥。船闸于1933年进行重修，20世纪70年代末进行机械化改造，2015年被列为国家历史文物。如今，该船闸仍然发挥着重要作用，确保游船畅行。

Warffum Canal

A canal located in the province of Groningen, the

瓦尔弗姆运河

荷兰格罗宁根省运河。瓦尔弗姆运

Netherlands. The Warffum Canal runs from the Warffum Port to Onderdendam, where it joins the Winsum Canal. It is 7 kilometres in length with 7 bridges. The canal meanders into the Usquert Canal near Usquert.

河自瓦尔弗姆港流至翁德登丹，与温瑟姆运河交汇。该运河全长7千米，建有7座桥梁，在于斯奎特附近汇入于斯奎特运河。

Warfhuister Canal

瓦尔夫赫伊斯特运河

A canal located in the province of Groningen, the Netherlands. The Warfhuister Canal has a length of 3.3 kilometres. It was built in the mid-19th century, crossing the Hunsingo Canal to the west and flowing through Warfhuizen .

荷兰格罗宁根省运河。瓦尔夫赫伊斯特运河全长3.3千米，于19世纪中叶开凿，与西部的亨辛豪运河交汇，流经瓦尔夫赫伊曾市。

Warren County Canal

沃伦县运河

An abandoned canal located in southwestern Ohio, the United States. The Warren County Canal was 32 kilometres long and 12 metres wide with a 3-metre-wide towpath. It began at Middletown, confluenced with the Miami and Erie Canal, and ended at Lebanon, the Warren County seat. The construction was initially carried out in 1830 by a private company but was delayed and unfinished. Not until 1836, it was taken over by the Canal Commissioners after the order from the Ohio General Assembly. Since the ground at Lebanon was about 13 metres higher than that of Middletown, 6 locks were built on the canal to cope with the drop. Of all the locks, 4 were near Lebanon, allowing boats to be raised and lowered to a height of more than 8 metres, while the other two raised and lowered ships for 4 metres or so. The canal was fully navigable in 1840.

美国俄亥俄州西南部废弃运河。沃伦县运河全长32千米，宽12米，建有一条3米宽的纤道。该运河始于米德尔敦，与迈阿密—伊利运河交汇，流至沃伦县县治莱巴嫩市。1830年，沃伦县运河由一家私人公司负责开凿，但进展缓慢，迟迟无法完工。1836年，俄亥俄州议会下令运河专员接管该工程。莱巴嫩的地势比米德尔敦高出13米左右，故运河上修建了6座船闸解决这一落差问题，其中有4座位于莱巴嫩附近，可升降水位，调整幅度达8米多，另外2座船闸可升降调整水位4米左右。1840年，运河全线通航，但岸堤多次被谢克伦河河水淹没，泥沙淤积严重。1848年，谢克

The stream Shaker Run not only frequently flooded the banks of the canal but also caused serious sediment deposits. In 1848, the stream Shaker Run completely destroyed the embankment of the canal. By that time, the canal had operated for less than a decade. Due to the costly repairs, the State of Ohio abandoned it, and in 1854 sold its remnants to John Owen, the engineer of the Miami and Erie Canal. The boulders of the locks were later used for local buildings, and around 1970 the canal was converted into the Colonial Park by Lebanon City. Now only a few ditches of the canal remain.

Washington Canal

A canal located in Washington D.C., the United States. The Washington Canal began to be constructed in 1810. There was a 0.3-metre-deep and 0.5-metre-wide furrow initially. According to the canal's charters those days, the canal should be at least 24 metres wide and 1 metre deep for the passage of vessels. After years of further excavation, the canal was opened in 1815. Because of the siltation, the canal couldn't support water transportation at low tide. Its management also faced growing financial difficulties. Later in 1831, the city government took over the canal project from private owners for urban development. After the extension in 1832, the canal followed a route from the basin on Rock Creek, cut through Easby's Point to near the 22nd Street, and ran the shoreline to the wharf at the 17th Street. Two locks were built to allow for the drop in elevation below Georgetown. The first one

伦河河水彻底冲毁运河堤岸。此时沃伦县运河的通航时间还不足10年。由于维修费用高昂，俄亥俄州弃用了这条运河，1854年将其残存部分出售给迈阿密—伊利运河工程师约翰·欧文。建船闸的大石块后被用于当地建筑。1970年前后，莱巴嫩市将沃伦县运河改造为科勒尼尔公园。如今，该运河只有少数沟渠得以保留。

华盛顿运河

美国华盛顿特区运河。华盛顿运河开凿于1810年，当时只有一条0.3米深、0.5米宽的水沟。据当时的运河规章，运河应至少宽24米，深1米，以便船只通过。经过数年挖掘，华盛顿运河于1815年通航。由于泥沙淤积严重，运河在退潮时无法通行，同时还面临日益严重的财政困难。为推进城市发展，当地政府于1831年从私人企业手中接管该运河。1832年扩建后，运河从罗克里克河流域穿过伊斯比角，流经第22街附近，后沿海岸线到达第17街码头，同时还修建了2座船闸，解决乔治敦以下的运河水位落差问题。第一个船闸修建于华盛顿运河与波托马克河之间，另一个则位于第17街。美国南北战争时

was to link the canal to the Potomac River, and the other was at the 17th Street. During the Civil War, the Washington Canal served not only as an essential transportation link, but an open sewer to collect the waste of the downtown area. After the Civil War, the canal's utility in navigation was increasingly undermined. It became one of the main arteries of the sewerage of the city. In 1871, the Washington Canal was put under the charge of the Board of Public Works and was filled soon after. In the end, the canal was transformed into a sewer for the Constitution Avenue.

期，华盛顿运河不仅是交通要道，而且还用作排污渠，排放市中心地区的污水。南北战争结束之后，运河的通航功能日益削弱，沦为城市的主要排污渠道之一。1871年，华盛顿运河转由公共工程局负责，不久后被回填。华盛顿运河最终变成宪法大道的下水道。

Waterway of Ferrara

A canal located in the province of Ferrara, Italy. The Waterway of Ferrara is over 70 kilometres long, consisting of three parts, namely the Boicelli Canal from Pontelagoscuro to Ferrara (5.5 kilometres in length), the Volano branch of the river Po from Ferrara to Fiscaglia of Migliarino (34.5 kilometres in length), and the Migliarino-Port Garibaldi Canal from Migliarino to the sea (30 kilometres in length). The canal connects the river Po of Ferrara with the Adriatic at Port Garibaldi, flowing through the Po Delta Park. It is suitable for motorboat sailing.

费拉拉航道

意大利费拉拉省运河。费拉拉航道全长超过70千米，由3部分组成，即博采里运河、波河博拉诺支线运河和米利亚里诺—加里波第港运河。博采里运河全长5.5千米，自蓬泰戈斯库罗流向费拉拉；波河博拉诺支线运河全长34.5千米，自费拉拉流向米利亚里诺的菲斯卡利亚；米利亚里诺—加里波第港运河全长30千米，自米利亚里诺注入海洋。费拉拉航道在加里波第港连接波河费拉拉段和亚得里亚海，流经波河三角洲公园。费拉拉航道适合摩托艇航行。

Weesp Trek Canal

A canal located in the province of North Holland,

韦斯普拖船运河

荷兰北荷兰省运河。韦斯普拖船

the Netherlands. The Weesp Trek Canal connects the Amstel with the Vecht. It has 2 locks and the navigable length is 9.2 kilometres. Built in 1639, the canal made use of several existing waterways, including two ring canals, i.e. the Gaasp River, and the canalized Smal Weesp River.

运河连通阿姆斯特尔河和费赫特河，河上建有2座船闸，通航长度为9.2千米。该运河修建于1639年，在修建过程中利用几条现有航道，包括加斯普河及运河化改造的斯莫韦斯普河这两条环形运河。

Welland Ship Canal

A canal located in Ontario, Canada. The Welland Ship Canal is 43 kilometres in length, linking Lake Ontario with Lake Erie. As a part of the St. Lawrence Seaway, it allows transportation to bypass the Niagara Falls. In 1824, the Welland Canal Company was founded, and commenced the construction of the First Welland Canal in the same year. The canal was deepened and lengthened respectively in 1843, 1887 and 1913. The current name actually refers to the Fourth Welland Canal.

韦兰通海运河

加拿大安大略省运河。韦兰通海运河全长43千米，连通安大略湖与伊利湖。该运河是圣劳伦斯河海道的一部分，用以引导船只绕开尼亚加拉瀑布。1824年，韦兰运河公司成立，并于同年开启韦兰运河一期修建工程。后运河分别于1843年、1887年和1913年加深并延伸扩建。如今的韦兰运河实为其第四期工程。

Werbellin Canal

A canal located in the state of Brandenburg, Germany. The Werbellin Canal connects the lake Werbellin with the Oder-Havel Canal and the Finow Canal. It is 7 kilometres in length, including a 3.15-kilometre-long section lying southwest of the Oder-Havel Canal and a 2.7-kilometre-long section backfilled in the 1920s and 1930s for agricultural purposes. The canal, equipped with 2 automatic locks, is a part of the federal waterway Werbellin Waterbody and a branch of the Oder-Havel Canal. As early as 1609, the Werbellin Canal was con-

韦尔贝林运河

德国勃兰登堡州运河。韦尔贝林运河连通韦尔贝林湖和奥得—哈弗尔运河及菲诺运河，全长7千米，其中3.15千米位于奥得—哈弗尔运河的西南方向，有2.7千米在20世纪20和30年代被回填，用于农业种植。该运河隶属联邦航道韦尔贝林水域，也是奥得—哈弗尔运河的支线，运河沿线建有2座自动化船闸。早在1609年，韦尔贝林运河就已建成，最初是为了给菲诺运河供

structed to provide water resources for the Finow Canal. Later, it replaced the Finow Canal as a supplementary water supply for the Oder-Havel Canal in dry seasons. As a part of the Water Tourism Initiative North Brandenburg funded by the state of Brandenburg, the backfilled section was restored between September 2008 and June 2011 at a cost of 4.5 million euros to boost water tourism. In 2015, the section was prohibited from navigation due to the damage to the embankments and banks, and it was reopened in February 2019.

水。后每逢旱季，韦尔贝林运河就取代菲诺运河为奥得—哈弗尔运河补充水源。为促进当地水上旅游业的发展，勃兰登堡州拨款资助"北勃兰登堡水上旅游计划"。作为该计划的一部分，被回填的河道于2008年9月至2011年6月期间得到修复，工程共耗资450万欧元。2015年，因运河堤岸受损，韦尔贝林运河被迫停航，后于2019年2月复航。

Wesel-Datteln Canal

A canal located in the state of North Rhine-Westphalia, Germany. The Wesel-Datteln Canal runs from the Rhine near Wesel to the Dortmund-Ems Canal near Datteln. It is 60 kilometres in length with 6 locks, allowing large motor cargo ships to pass. Running parallel to the Rhine-Herne Canal and River Lippe, it connects the Lower Rhine and the northern and eastern Germany. The construction of the Wesel-Datteln Canal began in 1915, stopped in 1916, and resumed in 1924, and the trial navigation finally began on 2 June 1930. It has relieved the burden on the Rhine-Herne Canal to some extent. In 2003, 17.5 million tonnes of goods were transported on the canal while the transshipment in 2004 dropped to approximately 6.1 million tonnes. Managed by the Duisburg-Meiderich Waterways and Shipping Office, the canal now serves as a busy waterway in Germany.

韦瑟尔－达特尔恩运河

德国北莱茵—威斯特法伦州运河。韦瑟尔—达特尔恩运河始于韦瑟尔附近的莱茵河，最后在达特尔恩附近汇入多特蒙德—埃姆斯运河，全长60千米，河上建有6座船闸，可容大型货运汽船通行。该运河与莱茵—黑尔讷运河和利珀河流向平行，连接着莱茵河下游和德国北部及东部地区。韦瑟尔—达特尔恩运河1915年开凿，次年停工，1924年恢复修建，1930年6月2日试航。该运河建成后，在一定程度上减轻了莱茵—黑尔讷运河的航运负荷。2003年，韦瑟尔—达特尔恩运河的货物运输量为1 750万吨，2004年的货物转运量约降至610万吨。如今，韦瑟尔—达特尔恩运河仍是德国繁忙航道之一，由杜伊斯堡—梅德里希水运事务所负责管理。

Wessem-Nederweert Canal

An inland canal located in the province of Limburg, the Netherlands. The Wessem-Nederweert Canal is 17 kilometres in length, with only 1 lock and 9 bridges. It flows from Wessem to Nederweert, connecting the South Willems Canal and the Noord Canal with the Maas. The canal was opened on 22 October 1929.

West Coast Canal

A canal located in the state of Kerala, India. Also known as National Waterway No. 3. The West Coast Canal has a total length of 205 kilometres, running from Kollam in the south to Kottapuram in the state of Kerala. It forms a part of an intricate network of 44 rivers and their tributaries. To promote tourism as well as transportation, the Government of India approved and implemented inland waterways policy, in which the West Coast Canal is covered. The West Coast Canal has been developed into a navigable channel with full-fledged terminal facilities at 11 locations and 24-hour navigational aids. The canal runs almost parallel to the major State and National Roadways enabling yachters to visit the inland villages and cities while their yachts are safely anchored at any of the 11 terminals. Weirdly shaped ferries, canoes, and larger rural fishing boats can be seen everywhere. Some are loaded with cargo, and some are responsible for transporting children to school and people to work. The West Coast Canal covers 5 districts of Kerala,

威塞姆-下韦尔特运河

荷兰林堡省内陆运河。威塞姆-下韦尔特运河全长17千米，河上建有1座船闸和9座桥梁，自威塞姆流至下韦尔特，连通南威廉斯运河、诺德运河与马斯河。威塞姆-下韦尔特运河于1929年10月22日通航。

西海岸运河

印度喀拉拉邦运河。亦称国家三号航道。西海岸运河全长205千米，从喀拉拉邦南部的科拉姆流向北部的戈德布勒姆。该运河是复杂水路网的一部分，这个网络由44条河流及其支流组成。为了促进旅游业和交通运输业的发展，印度政府批准并实施内陆航道建设政策，西海岸运河的修建因此受惠。该运河已经成为一条拥有11个设施完备的航运码头并能提供24小时航运援助的航道。西海岸运河与主要的州级公路及国家公路流向大致平行，游客乘坐快艇可以在任何码头停靠，前往内陆的村落和城市游玩。外形独特的渡船、独木舟以及较大的乡村渔船随处可见，有些运载货物，有些则负责接送孩子上学和人们上班。西海岸运河流经喀拉拉邦5个区域，分别是特里胡尔、埃尔南

namely Trichur, Ernamkulam, Kottayam, Allepey and Quilon. It is lined with breath-taking beauty of water lilies, lush paddy fields, rustic homes, ancient temples, mosques and synagogues, Ayurveda treatment centres and coconut groves on both sides of the waterway.

库拉姆、科塔亚姆、阿勒佩和奎隆。运河两岸风景优美，游客可以欣赏美丽的睡莲、郁郁葱葱的稻田、斑驳的房舍、古老的寺庙、清真寺、犹太教堂和阿育吠陀治疗中心和椰子林。

Western Schelde

A canal located in the province of Zeeland, the Netherlands. As the only tributary of the Schelde River directly connected to the North Sea, the Western Schelde is an important waterway leading to the Port of Antwerp, Belgium. It is 50 kilometres in length and 2 to 8 kilometres in width. The waterway mainly passes through Walcheren, South Beveland and Zeelandic Flanders. The water to the sea could not be blocked by the dams, so the dykes along the banks were heightened and consolidated. In 1995, the Netherlands and Belgium reached an agreement to clear out the sunken ships to unchoke the canal, and totally 38 sunken ships were removed by 2003. Currently, the Western Schelde remains one of the most crowded waterways of the world today.

西斯海尔德航道

荷兰泽兰省航道。西斯海尔德航道是斯海尔德河唯一直接连通北海的支流，也是通向比利时安特卫普港的一条重要航道。该航道长50千米，宽2—8千米，主要流经瓦尔赫伦岛、南贝弗兰岛和泽兰省佛兰德地区。由于堤坝无法阻挡入海水流，周围岸堤已增高加固。1995年，荷兰和比利时政府签订一项协议清理河道沉船，疏通航道。至2003年，共有38艘沉船被打捞清理。如今，西斯海尔德航道仍为世界上航运最繁忙的航道之一。

West Flood Canal

A canal located in Jakarta, Indonesia. Formerly known as Banjir Kali Malang Canal. The West Flood Canal and the East Flood Canal form the Jakarta Flood Canal. The West Flood Canal is 17.3 kilometres in length, running from the Manggarai sluice gate to Muara Angke in the north of Ja-

西泄洪运河

印度尼西亚雅加达运河。旧称班吉尔卡利玛琅泄洪运河。西泄洪运河与东泄洪运河共同组成雅加达泄洪运河。西泄洪运河全长17.3千米，从芒加赖船闸流向雅加达北部的穆阿拉红溪渔港。该运河1913

karta. First built in 1913, the canal constructed in the first phase is 4.5 kilometres in length with the width ranging from 13.5 to 16 metres. This section flows from Matraman to Karet, which connects the Ciliwung River, the Krukut River and others. The second phase of the construction started from 1915 and ended in 1919. The canal was then extended northward from Karet into the sea at Muara Angke, a small fishing port in the north of Jakarta.

年开凿，一期工程全长4.5千米，宽度为13.5～16米，从马特拉曼区流向卡雷特，连通芝利翁河、克鲁库特河等河流。二期工程于1915开始，1919年结束，西泄洪运河从卡雷特向北延伸，于雅加达北部小渔港穆阿拉红溪注入大海。

Westhafen Canal

A canal located in Berlin, Germany. The Westhafen Canal is 3.1 kilometres in length and 3.75 metres in depth. It connects the Westhafen inland port and the Berlin-Spandau Ship Canal at its eastern end, with the river Spree in Charlottenburg at the western end. The construction of the Westhafen Canal was started in 1938 and did not resume until 1956, after being shelved since the outbreak of World War II. After its completion, the canal replaced the Charlottenburg Canal to some extent as an important transport connection between the Berlin-Spandau Ship Canal and the river Spree. As a part of the German Unity Transport Project No.17, the Westhafen Canal has been widened on its northern bank.

韦斯特哈芬运河

德国柏林市运河。韦斯特哈芬运河长3.1千米，深3.75米，东连韦斯特哈芬内陆港口和柏林—施潘道通海运河，西通夏洛滕堡的施普雷河。该运河于1938年开凿，第二次世界大战爆发后工程被搁置，直至1956年才重新开始。竣工后，韦斯特哈芬运河在一定程度上取代夏洛滕堡运河，成为柏林—施潘道通海运河和施普雷河之间的重要交通纽带。作为德国统一运输第17号项目的一部分，该运河北岸已拓宽。

Wetering Canal

A canal located in the Netherlands. The Wetering Canal is connected by the Steenwijk Canal to the Steenwijk-Aa River at Steenwijk.

韦特林运河

荷兰运河。韦特林运河在斯滕韦克通过斯滕韦克运河与斯滕韦克—阿河连通。

White Sea-Baltic Canal

A canal located in northwestern Russia. Also called White Sea Canal. Running from the Povenets Bay to the Soroka Bay, the White Sea-Baltic Canal links up the White Sea and Lake Onega, and leads to the Baltic Sea. The canal is 227 kilometres in length, including a man-made section of 48 kilometres. Its navigable section is 36 metres in width and 3.5 metres in depth. It has 19 locks, 7 on the southern part, forming the "Stairs of Povenets", and 12 on the northern part. The minimum lock dimensions are 14.3 metres in width and 135 metres in length. The construction was completed in 20 months almost entirely by manual labour. In August 1933, the canal was opened. In 1941, the canal became the front line, and all locks of the "Stairs of Povenets" were demolished by the Soviet for self-defence. The rebuilding of the canal was started in September 1944, and was completed by July 1946, with navigation restored on 28 July 1946. Later, it went through a few more overhauls and upgrades in the 1950s and the 1970s. The canal has made it possible to transport oil products from oil refineries on the Volga River to the Murmansk Oblast and overseas. It also enables vessels to transport heavy and bulky cargoes from Russia's industrial centres to the White Sea and further to Siberia's northern ports.

White Sea Canal

A canal located in northwestern Russia. See White Sea-Baltic Canal.

白海－波罗的海运河

俄罗斯西北部运河。亦称白海运河。白海－波罗的海运河从波韦涅茨湾向北流入索罗卡湾，连通白海和奥涅加湖，后注入波罗的海。该运河全长227千米，其中48千米为人工运河，可通航河段宽36米，深3.5米，共建有19座船闸，其中7座分布在南部河段，形成"波韦涅茨阶梯"，其余12座位于北部河段，最小的船闸宽14.3米，长135米。开凿白海－波罗的海运河耗时20个月，几乎完全依靠人力完成。运河于1933年8月通航。1941年，白海－波罗的海运河成为战争前线，为自卫，苏联炸毁了"波韦涅茨阶梯"的7座船闸。白海－波罗的海运河于1944年9月开始修复，1946年7月完工，7月28日恢复通航。后运河分别于20世纪50年代和70年代进行了几次大修和升级改造。通过白海－波罗的海运河，伏尔加河上炼油厂生产的石油产品可以远销到摩尔曼斯克州及海外，俄罗斯工业中心制造的大宗商品也可以运送到白海以及西伯利亚的北部港口。

白海运河

俄罗斯西北部运河。见白海—波罗的海运河。

Whitewater Canal

A canal located in the state of Indiana, the United States. The Whitewater Canal is 122.3 kilometres long, flowing from Lawrenceburg to Hagerstown. Because of the steep slope, there were 56 locks and 7 dams in the basin. To establish a rapid transit system connecting the Whitewater Valley and the Ohio River, the Indiana State legislature approved the Mammoth Internal Improvement Act in 1836, allowing the construction of the Whitewater Canal and other transportation improvement projects within the state. It was started in September 1836 and suspended when Indiana went bankrupt in the summer of 1839. The canal had not been resumed until 1842, when Indiana transferred the ownership of the canal to the Whitewater Valley Canal Company. The whole canal was finally completed in 1847. In November of the same year, the Whitewater Valley was flooded and a part of the canal was washed away. Ten months later, the section north of Harrison was reopened, while the section between Harrison and Lawrenceburg was never rebuilt. Few sections of the Whitewater Canal are navigable today, mainly in Metamora. Some remains of locks and the Laurel Feeder Dam in Indiana can still be seen. Rebuilt in the 1940s, the dam now provides water for Metamora and mills nearby. As the Whitewater Canal Historic District, the section from the Laurel Feeder Dam to Brookville was listed on the National Register of Historic Places in 1973. The place recreates the city in the canal era, where tourists enjoy a feeling of wandering in the

怀特沃特运河

美国印第安纳州运河。怀特沃特运河全长122.3千米，从劳伦斯堡流向黑格斯敦。因沿岸地势陡峭，运河流域内共建有56座船闸和7座大坝。为修建连接怀特沃特河谷和俄亥俄河的快速运输系统，印第安纳州州议会于1836年通过《曼莫斯内部经济改良法案》，批准开凿怀特沃特运河和州内其他交通改进工程。怀特沃特运河于1836年9月开凿。1839年夏，印第安纳州破产，运河修建被迫中断。1842年，印第安纳州将运河所有权转让给怀特沃特河谷运河公司，运河开凿得以恢复，并于1847年竣工。同年11月，怀特沃特河谷遭受洪水，部分河段被冲毁。10个月后，哈里森以北的河段再次开通，但哈里森和劳伦斯堡之间的河段再未重建。如今，怀特沃特运河可通航河段所剩无几，主要位于梅塔莫拉，印第安纳州部分船闸及劳雷尔引水大坝遗迹依旧可见。这座大坝于20世纪40年代重修，为梅塔莫拉及附近磨坊提供水源。从大坝至布鲁克维尔河段现已改建为怀特沃特运河历史街区，并于1973年列入美国国家历史遗迹名录。这片历史街区重现运河时代的城市风貌，建有博物馆、购物中心、餐馆等设施，可供休闲娱乐。游客置

19th century, with museums, shopping malls and restaurants for entertainment.

身其中，如同穿越在19世纪的运河小镇。

Wiener Neustadt Canal

A canal located in Vienna, Austria. Connecting the Enns River, the Wiener Neustadt Canal was commissioned by the Archduke of Austria and became navigable in 1803. The length of the canal was 56 kilometres in 1803, which was extended to 63 kilometres in 1811. It transported mainly wood, bricks and coal from the area south of the Danube to Vienna. The canal was the only shipping canal in Austria, originally meant to reach Trieste, Italy. Later, private owners primarily pursued railway projects and connected important parts of the waterway to the railway line. The canal shipping began to decline sharply from 1879 onwards and ceased completely before World War I. After World War II, the state of Lower Austria took over the majority of the watercourse, shortened it to 36 kilometres, and made it mainly function as a recreational landscape.

维也纳诺伊施塔特运河

奥地利维也纳市运河。维也纳诺伊施塔特运河受奥地利大公委托而开凿，1803年通航，连通恩斯河。运河初建成时，全长56千米，1811年延伸至63千米，主要用于将多瑙河南部的货物（木材、砖块和煤）运往维也纳。当时，维也纳诺伊施塔特运河是奥地利唯一的通航运河，起初是为了连接维也纳和意大利的里雅斯特市。后私营企业主热衷于铁路工程，将运河主要河段与铁路连接起来。自1879年起，维也纳诺伊施塔特运河航运量开始大幅下滑。至第一次世界大战前，运河全面停航。第二次世界大战后，下奥地利州接管运河大部分航道，航程因此缩短至36千米，主要用于休闲观光。

Wijmerts Canal

A canal located in Friesland, the Netherlands. Also called Bolswarderzeil Canal. The Wijmerts Canal is 8.8 kilometres in length, running from Wijddraai and eventually into the Workum Trek Canal. The part at Bolsward is also called Sneek Canal. It has officially adopted its Frisian name, De Wijmerts, since March 2007.

韦默尔茨运河

荷兰弗里斯兰省运河。亦称博尔斯瓦德宰尔运河。韦默尔茨运河全长8.8千米，始于韦德拉伊河，汇入沃尔克姆拖船运河。博尔斯瓦德河段亦称斯内克运河。自2007年3月起，韦默尔茨运河正式采用其弗里西亚语新名德韦默尔茨。

Wilders Canal

A canal located in the Christian Port, Copenhagen, Denmark. The Wilders Canal is a branch of the Christian Port Canal, connecting Christian Port Canal to the main harbour facing the Søkvæst House. It is spanned by the Wilders Bridge, which leads to the Strand Street. The Wilders Canal is named after father and son, Carl and Lars Wilder, who ran a shipyard in the area north of the canal, where the present-day Wilders Plads is located.

维尔德斯运河

丹麦哥本哈根市运河。维尔德斯运河位于克里斯钦港区，是克里斯钦港运河支线，将克里斯钦港运河和瑟克韦斯屋对面的主港相连。维尔德斯桥横跨维尔德斯运河并通往斯特兰街。维尔德斯运河以卡尔·维尔德和拉尔斯·维尔德父子姓氏命名。此二人曾在运河以北经营一家造船厂，此处现为维尔德斯码头区。

Wilhelmina Canal

A canal located in the province of North Brabant, the Netherlands. The Wilhelmina Canal flows from the South Wilhems Canal to the Amer River, running through the cities including Laarbeek and Geertruidenberg. The 68-kilometre-long canal has an average depth of 2.5 metres and a width of 25 to 42 metres with 56 bridges built on it. The part from Geertruidenberg to Dongen is navigable for ships of 1,350 tons. The remaining part gets considerably narrower, only navigable for those vessels up to 650 tons. Named after Dutch Queen Wilhelmina, the Wilhelmina Canal was constructed in 1910 and officially opened in 1923. The widening and deepening work of the canal will continue until around 2023 so that ships up to 1,350 tons can sail through Tilburg.

威廉敏娜运河

荷兰北布拉班特省运河。威廉敏娜运河始于南威廉斯运河，流经拉尔贝克和海特勒伊登贝赫等城市，最终汇入阿梅尔河。该运河全长68千米，平均水深2.5米，宽25—42米，建有56座桥梁。海特勒伊登贝赫市至栋恩之间的河段可通航1 350吨级船舶。其余河段较为狭窄，仅可通航650吨级船舶。威廉敏娜运河以荷兰女王威廉敏娜的名字命名，1910年开凿，1923年正式通航。运河的拓宽加深工程将持续至2023年，届时一直到蒂尔堡的河段都可容1 350吨级船舶通行。

Willebroek Canal

A canal located in the city of Brussels, Belgium. See Brussels-Schelde Sea Canal.

Willems Canal

A canal located in southern Netherlands. Together with the Scholtens Extension Canal, the Scholtens Canal and the Runde, the Willems Canal connects the Hoogeveen Extension Canal with the Stads Canal.

Wilts and Berks Canal

A canal located in England, the United Kingdom. Running for 84 kilometres, the Wilts and Berks Canal connects the Kennet and the Avon Canal to River Thames at Abingdon. Merged with the North Wilts Canal, it serves as a branch to the Thames and Severn Canal at Latton. The Wilts and Berks Canal was opened in 1810, and officially abandoned in 1914. Either demolished or filled in, most of the course was unnavigable afterwards. To protect and restore the canal, the Wilts and Berks Canal Amenity Group was established in 1977. With their efforts, several locks and bridges have been restored. More than 13 kilometres of the canal route have been re-watered as well.

Windawski Canal

An abandoned canal located in the district of Ši-

维勒布鲁克运河

比利时布鲁塞尔市运河。见布鲁塞尔—斯海尔德通海运河。

威廉斯运河

荷兰南部运河。威廉斯运河与舒尔腾斯扩建运河、舒尔腾斯运河、伦德河一起将弗伦格德霍赫芬扩建运河和斯塔茨运河连通。

威尔茨—伯克斯运河

英国英格兰运河。威尔茨—伯克斯运河全长84千米，在阿宾登镇连通肯尼特—埃文运河和泰晤士河。该运河在拉顿村汇入北威尔茨运河后，成为泰晤士—塞文运河的支线。威尔茨—伯克斯运河于1810年通航，1914年正式被弃用。大部分河段因毁坏或回填而无法通航。为保护并修复运河，威尔茨—伯克斯运河设施集团于1977年成立。在该集团努力下，运河上部分船闸和桥梁得以修复，超过13千米的河道重新引水复用。

温达夫斯基运河

立陶宛希奥利艾区废弃运河。温

auliai, Lithuania. The Windawski Canal was 15 kilometres in length with 20 locks, connecting the Dubysa River to the Venta River. It was a part of the canal system which connects the Vistula River with the Baltic seaport of Ventspils. The canal system was designed and constructed in two sections in the early 19th century. The first section is the Augustów Canal, located in Augustów Province of Poland. The second section is the Windawski Canal, which connected the Neman River, through its tributary the Dubysa River, with the Venta River located in Kovno Province of the then Russian Empire. The construction work was halted due to the unrest caused by the Uprising of 1831 against Russia. The work resumed at the beginning of the 20th century, but was interrupted again by World War I. After the war, there was no need for a canal as Lithuania gained control over the Klaipėda Region and the lower reaches of the Neman River. The Windawski Canal was listed as an engineering monument on Lithuania's Cultural heritage list in April 2005.

达夫斯基运河全长15千米，沿线共建有20座船闸，连通杜比萨河和文塔河，是连接维斯图拉河和波罗的海沿岸文茨皮尔斯市海港运河系统的一部分。19世纪初，该运河系统开始设计和修建，整个工程分两段进行：第一段是奥古斯图夫运河，位于波兰奥古斯图夫省；第二段是温达夫斯基运河，通过杜比萨河连通尼曼河和沙皇俄国时期名为科夫诺省的文塔河。1831年，反抗沙皇统治的起义引发动荡，运河修建工程被迫中断。20世纪初，运河恢复修建，但因第一次世界大战再次停工。战后，立陶宛获得克莱佩达地区和尼曼河下游地区的控制权，已无须再修建运河，该工程从此被废止。2005年4月，温达夫斯基运河作为工程遗迹被列入立陶宛文化遗产名录。

Windsor Locks Canal

温莎洛克斯运河

A canal located in the state of Connecticut, the United States. Also called Enfield Falls Canal. The Windsor Locks Canal has a length of about 8.5 kilometres. It was initially built to enable ships to bypass the Enfield Falls, carrying more cargo at a lower cost. The construction was started in 1827 and completed on 11 November 1829. There is 1 lock at the north end and 3 locks at the south end of the canal, which allow ships of up to 27 metres long and

美国康涅狄格州运河。亦称恩菲尔德福尔斯运河。温莎洛克斯运河全长约8.5千米。修建初衷是方便船只绕过恩菲尔德瀑布，以便提高运力，降低运输成本。温莎洛克斯运河于1827年开凿，1829年11月11日完工。运河北端建有1座船闸，南端建有3座船闸，可通航最长27米、最宽6.1米的船舶。运河设

6.1 metres wide to pass through. The canal has a huge head gate that can precisely control the water level within the lock chambers and the canal. The construction of the canal also influenced the local demographics. A large proportion of the labourers for building the canal came from Ireland. During the thirty years after its completion, the percentage of the Irish population in Windsor Locks increased from 1% to about 20%. In 1844, the Hartford and Springfield Railroad started operation, and the importance of waterway transportation on the Connecticut River is reduced. The canal was listed in the National Register of Historic Places on 22 April 1976, and it is closed by now. The locks of the canal remain, even though they have been idle since the 1970s. The canal is open to hiking and cycling every year from 1 April to 15 November.

有一座大型总闸门，能够准确控制闸室内和运河上的水位。运河的修建对当地人口结构也产生影响，因大量参与运河开凿的劳工来自爱尔兰，运河完工后的30年间，温莎洛克斯镇爱尔兰人口的比例从1%上升到近20%。1844年，因哈特福德—斯普林菲尔德铁路投入使用，康涅狄格河航运的重要性下降。1976年4月22日，温莎洛克斯运河被列入美国国家历史遗迹名录。如今，运河已不再通航。运河船闸自20世纪70年代就已闲置，但依然保存了下来。每年4月1日至11月15日，运河对外开放以供游人远足和骑行。

Winschoten Canal

温斯霍滕运河

A canal located in the province of Groningen, the Netherlands. The Winschoten Canal is 35.5 kilometres long and nearly 100 metres wide. The construction was started in 1618 and completed in 1634. There are 16 bridges and 2 locks as well as many other passages on the canal to pass ships less than 16 metres in breadth. As one of the oldest canals ever built in Groningen, the Winschoten Canal is still in use. There are several ship wharfs in the section between Hoogezand and Waterhuizen. Important watersport activities are held in season at the canal section around Menterwolde.

荷兰格罗宁根省运河。温斯霍滕运河全长35.5千米，宽约100米。该运河于1618年开凿，1634年竣工，沿线共建有16座桥梁和2座船闸及多处可通行宽度小于16米船舶的河道。该运河是格罗宁根省最古老的通航运河之一，至今仍在使用。霍赫赞德镇至霍特惠曾村之间的河段上有多处码头。门特沃德市河段常举办季节性水上竞技活动。

Winsum Canal

A canal located in the province of Groningen, the Netherlands. The Winsum Canal runs from the Boter Canal via the village of Winsum to the Reit Canal near Schaphalsterzijl. The canal was first built in 1759 and widened in 1856 to guarantee better drainage. It is about 6.9 metres in width now. There are 6 bridges along the river with a new one measuring 800 metres open specifically to pedestrians and bicycles since February 2021.

温瑟姆运河

荷兰格罗宁根省运河。温瑟姆运河始于伯特运河，流经温瑟姆村，最后在沙法尔斯特宰尔村附近汇入哈伊特运河。运河于1759年开凿，1856年拓宽，以改善排水功能。温瑟姆运河现宽约6.9米，河上建有6座桥。2021年2月起开通了1座800米长的新桥，专用于行人和自行车通行。

Winter Canal

A canal located in Saint Petersburg, Russia. Originally known as Old Palace Canal. The Winter Canal links up the Great Neva with the Moika River in the neighbourhood of the Winter Palace. The canal was called either the Winter House Canal or the Winter Palace Canal in the 1780s, and it adopted the current name in 1828. As one of the shortest canals in Saint Petersburg, the Winter Canal is 228 metres in length and 20 metres in width. The canal was constructed during 1718 and 1719; the granite embankments were constructed during 1782 and 1784. Three bridges cross the canal, namely the Hermitage Bridge, the First Winter Bridge, and the Second Winter Bridge.

冬运河

俄罗斯圣彼得堡市运河。旧称旧宫殿运河。冬运河连通冬宫附近的大涅瓦河和莫伊卡河。该运河18世纪80年代时称冬宫运河，1828年更名为冬运河。运河全长228米，宽20米，是圣彼得堡市最短的运河之一。冬运河于1718—1719年间修建，1782—1784年间铺设花岗岩堤岸。运河上建有赫尔米蒂奇桥、第一冬桥和第二冬桥共3座桥梁。

Wisbech Canal

An abandoned canal located in Cambridgeshire, England, the United Kingdom. The Winsbech

威斯贝奇运河

英国英格兰剑桥郡废弃运河。威斯贝奇运河全长8.4千米，河上建

Canal ran for 8.4 kilometres with 2 locks. Flowing from River Nene to the Well Creek, it finally connected itself to River Great Ouse. Opened in 1797, the canal fell into disuse in 1926, and was filled in during the 1970s.

有2座船闸。运河始于宁河，与韦尔溪相通，最终汇入大乌斯河。威斯贝奇运河于1797年通航，1926年遭弃用，20世纪70年代被回填。

Wolczkowski Canal

沃尔兹科夫斯基运河

A canal located in Poland. The Wolczkowski Canal is the right tributary of the Gunica and approximately 12 kilometres in length with an average flow of 148 cubic metres per hour. In its basin area of 52 square kilometres, almost half is covered by forests while the other half is meadow and cultivated land. It originates near the village of Wąwelnica and connects with the Gunica near the village of Gunice (now abandoned) in the Police Commune.

波兰运河。沃尔兹科夫斯基运河是古尼察河右岸支流，全长约12千米，每小时平均流量为148立方米。运河流域面积为52平方千米，流域内约50%面积为森林，其余为草地与耕地。沃尔兹科夫斯基运河始于瓦韦尔尼察村附近，在波利采公社的古尼斯村（现已废弃）附近与古尼察河交汇。

Wolfe Island Canal

沃尔夫岛运河

An abandoned canal located in the province of Ontario, Canada. With a length of 2 kilometres, the Wolfe Island Canal connected Maryville with the Bayfield Bay, and cut the Wolfe Island in half. In order to facilitate cargo transportation from Cape Vincent, New York, to Kingston, North Carolina, the construction of the canal was started in 1852 but failed to achieve the intended purpose because the watercourse is neither wide nor deep enough. The Wolfe Island Canal was used for about 20 years but fell into disuse around 1870. It was finally abandoned in 1892. In the 20th century, a local highway was built on a causeway across the canal, cutting off its flow.

加拿大安大略省废弃运河。沃尔夫岛运河全长2千米，从沃尔夫岛中部穿过，连接马里维尔和贝菲尔德湾。为便于在纽约州的开普文森特镇和北卡罗来纳州的金斯敦市之间运输货物，1852年开凿了该运河，但因其航道宽度和深度不足，未能实现预期目标。沃尔夫岛运河通航约20年，于1870年左右停航，最终于1892年被弃用。20世纪时，该运河堤道上修筑起高速公路，运河水流被切断。

Worcester and Birmingham Canal

A canal located in England, the United Kingdom. The Worcester and Birmingham Canal has a length of 47 kilometres, linking Birmingham and Worcester in England. There are altogether 58 locks on the canal. The construction first began from Birmingham in 1792, reaching Selly Oak in 1795, Kings Norton Junction in 1796, and Tardebigge in 1807. The last part of the canal, which is about 26 kilometres in length, was opened in December 1815. The Worcester and Birmingham Canal was mainly used by the Cadbury chocolate factories at Bournville and Blackpole, Worcester.

伍斯特－伯明翰运河

英国英格兰运河。伍斯特－伯明翰运河全长47千米，连接英格兰的伯明翰市和伍斯特市，沿线共建有58座船闸。该运河于1792年从伯明翰开凿，1795年修建至塞利奥克，1796年至金斯诺顿枢纽，1807年至塔迪比格村。运河最后一段长约26千米，于1815年12月通航。伍斯特－伯明翰运河曾主要为伍斯特市的伯恩维尔镇和布莱克波尔镇的吉百利巧克力工厂服务。

Workum Trek Canal

A canal located in the province of Friesland, the Netherlands. The Workum Trek Canal is 15.1 kilometres in length with 1 lock. The canal starts from Workum, runs roughly parallel with Road N359 from the south to the north and finally merges with the Wijmerts near Bolsward.

沃尔克姆拖船运河

荷兰弗里斯兰省运河。沃尔克姆拖船运河全长15.1千米，河上建有1座船闸，始于沃尔克姆市，与N359公路平行，自南向北，最终在博尔斯瓦德市附近与韦默尔茨运河交汇。

Wushen Canal

A canal located in the southeast of China. The Wushen Canal connects the city of Wuhu (Wu for short) in the southeast of Anhui Province and the city of Shanghai (Shen for short). This canal starts at the junction of the Qingyi River and the Yangtze River in Wuhu, passing through the Taihu Lake and connecting with the Huangpu River in Shang-

芜申运河

中国东南部运河。芜申运河连接安徽省东南部城市芜湖市和上海市。运河西起芜湖青弋江与长江交汇处，穿过太湖，连通上海市的黄浦江，横跨安徽省、江苏省和上海市。芜申运河最初只能通行100至200吨级的船舶。2008年12月28

hai. It runs through Anhui, Jiangsu, and Shanghai. Previously, only ships between 100—200 tons could navigate on the Wushen Canal. On 28 December, 2008, the improvement project of the 40.8-kilometre-long Anhui Section was started. Other sections of the canal have also been renovated according to local plans. The renovated Wushen Canal is 271 kilometres in length, more than 3.2 metres in depth with a bottom width of more than 45 metres. After the renovation, the status of the canal has been upgraded from Class V to Restricted Class III to support the navigation of 1,000-tonne ships. It can divert flood from the middle reaches of the Yangtze River. In addition, ships from the upper and middle reaches of the Yangtze River going to Shanghai through the Wushen Canal can shorten their voyage by about 118 kilometres compared with the route through the Yangtze River waterway.

日，全长40.8千米的芜申运河安徽段航道修缮工程开工。除安徽段外，芜申运河的其他河段也根据各省市规划进行了整修。整修后的芜申运河全长271千米，水深3.2米以上，底宽45米以上。整修完成后，该运河航道等级由五级提升为限制性三级，可通行1 000吨级船舶。该运河的修建有助于长江中游地区的洪水分流。长江中上游地区的船舶经芜申运河进入上海，航程可比经长江航道缩短约118千米。

Xerxes Canal

An ancient canal located in northern Greece. The Xerxes Canal was 2 kilometres in length, 30 metres in width, and 3 metres in depth. Starting from the east of Nea Roda, it was in a fairly straight south-westerly direction, and the flow ended in the west of the village Tripiti. The canal, built by King Xerxes I of Persia in the 5th century BC, is one of the few monuments left by the Persian Empire in Europe. Currently, the canal is completely covered by sediments, but its outline is visible by aerophotograph. The land surveys and geophysical investigations in the 20th century have confirmed the existence of the canal.

Xiang-Gui Canal

A canal in planning located in Hunan Province and Guangxi Zhuang Autonomous Region, China. The Xiang-Gui Canal is named after its location. Xiang and Gui are the short forms of Hunan Province and of Guangxi Zhuang Autonomous Region, respectively. The canal will be about 1,260 kilometres in length, with 958 kilometres in Hunan and 302 kilometres in Guangxi. It will be a Class IV waterway, with a minimum depth of 2.5 metres and a minimum width of 40 metres. The proposal for the canal can be traced back to 214 BC, when Qin Shi Huang, the first emperor of Qin Dynasty (221—206 BC) issued the order to construct the Lingqu Canal, which was the primitive form of the Xiang-Gui Canal. It connected the Xiangjiang River with the Lijiang River

薛西斯运河

希腊北部古运河。薛西斯运河全长2千米，宽30米，深3米，始于新罗达村东部，沿西南方向流至特里皮蒂村西部。该运河是波斯帝国在欧洲留下的为数不多的历史遗迹之一，由波斯国王薛西斯一世在公元前5世纪下令开凿。如今，薛西斯运河完全被沉积物覆盖，但从航空摄影中仍然能够看出其旧有轮廓。20世纪开展的土地测量和地理调查均证实了薛西斯运河的存在。

湘桂运河

中国拟建跨境运河。湘桂运河得名于其地理位置，"湘"和"桂"分别为湖南省与广西壮族自治区简称，运河全长将达约1 260千米，其中湖南境内958千米，广西境内302千米。该运河按四级航道标准设计，水深预计2.5米以上，河宽40米以上。开凿湘桂运河的设想可以追溯至公元前214年，当时秦始皇下令修建灵渠（湘桂运河前身），连接湘江和漓江，用以运输粮草。湘桂运河规划包含东西两条线路。其中，西线工程可能会对生态环境造成破坏，且耗资约为东线的两倍，故目前主要规划的是

to transport military supplies. Two contemporary plans have been formulated to construct this canal, namely, the East Line Plan and the West Line Plan. Since the West Line Plan may lead to environmental problems and cost twice as much as that of the East Line Plan, the latter is preferable. According to the East Line Plan, the canal will start from the Pingdao Island located in Yongzhou, Hunan, flow into Daoxian through the Xiaoshui River, and converge with the Yongming River. A 32-kilometre-long artificial canal will be built near the Jiangyong County so as to diverge the river across the watershed. Then the canal will arrive at the Luosi Mountain at the Taochuan Town, flow into the Gongcheng River (a minor form of the Guijiang River), and finally converge with the Guijiang River. The whole plan requires 11 new staircase locks to be built and 6 locks to be renovated, costing 26 billion yuan in total. When finished, the Xiang-Gui Canal will be an inner waterway connecting the Yangtse River and the Xijiang River, running parallel with the Gan-Yue Canal. When the canal is opened, the freight cost will be reduced dramatically and more economic benefits will be produced.

东线工程。东线从湖南省永州市萍岛起，经潇水至道县入永明河，穿桃川镇螺丝岭入桂江支流恭城河，最终汇入桂江。为跨越分水岭，人们还需在江永县城关附近开凿长达32千米的人工运河。东线全程需新建11座梯级船闸，改建6座船闸，总投资估算为人民币260亿元。运河建成后，东线将成为连接长江与西江的内陆航道，与赣粤运河并行。湘桂运河建成通航后，货运成本将大幅降低，并由此产生巨大经济效益。

Xing'an Canal

An inland canal located in Guangxi Zhuang Autonomous Region, China. See Lingqu Canal.

兴安运河

中国广西壮族自治区内陆运河。见灵渠。

Xuhe River

A canal located in the city of Nanjing, Jiangsu Province, China. Also known as Xuxi Canal. The

胥河

中国江苏省南京市运河。亦称胥溪运河。胥河流经高淳区固城镇

Xuhe River flows through Gucheng Town and Dingbu Town of Gaochun County. With a total length of 30.6 kilometres, the canal can be divided into 3 sections, namely, the upper, central and lower reaches. The upper section is connected to the Shuiyangjiang River System, the lower part connects the Taihu Lake System, and the central reach links the two water systems and serves as a watershed. There are two dams built on the canal, namely, the East Dyke and the West Dyke (also known as the Upper Dyke and Lower Dyke, respectively). It is generally believed that the Xuhe River was built by Wu Zixu, a military strategist of the Wu State during the Spring and Autumn Period (770—476 BC). The Xuhe River is also considered as the earliest canal ever built around the world. In 1392, there was a huge dredging project carried out on the canal. In 1849, after a severe flood, the damaged upper and lower dykes were rebuilt, and they were further reinforced the next year. From 1918 to 1920, Sun Yat-sen had a proposal of dredging the Xuhe River to connect the Yangtze River with the Taihu Lake, but it was not realized until the late 1980s. In the summer of 1958, the East Dyke was demolished to divert water from the Gucheng Lake to relieve the drought. From October 1958 to April 1959, the Xuhe River was dredged again, and a new sealing dyke was built around 3.6 kilometres downstream of the site of the former East Dyke in 1959. In the early 1980s, in order to relieve the traffic pressure of the southern Jiangsu section of the Beijing-Hangzhou Grand Canal and the Shanghai-Nanjing Railway, dykes that hindered navigation on the Xuhe

和定埠镇，全长30.6千米，分为上、中、下三个河段。上游河段连通水阳江水系，下游河段连通太湖水系，中游河段则为连通水阳江和太湖水系的分水线。运河上建有东坝和西坝两座水坝，又称上坝和下坝。通常，人们认为胥河由春秋时期吴国军事家伍子胥负责开凿，被视为世界上最古老的运河。1392年，胥河经历一次大型疏浚。1849年，一场特大水灾后，人们重建了胥河东、西两坝，并于次年对其进一步加固。1918—1920年间，孙中山曾提出疏浚利用胥河的设想，以求连通长江与太湖，但直到20世纪80年代末这一设想才得以实现。1958年夏，胥河的东坝被拆除，以便从固城湖中引水用于抗旱。1958年10月至次年4月人们对胥河进行了疏浚，后又于1959年在东坝旧址下游3.6千米处修筑新的封口坝。20世纪80年代初，为减轻京杭大运河苏南段及沪宁铁路的交通压力，胥河上妨碍航行的封口坝和下坝被拆除，新的下坝船闸得以修建。2014年6月，芜申运河南京段改造完成，胥河被纳入其中，成为苏皖之间一条重要的航运通道。

River, namely the sealing dyke and the Lower Dyke, were demolished, and two new locks were built. In June 2014, the reconstruction of the Nanjing section of the Wushen Canal was completed with the Xuhe River included, thus making it an important navigable waterway between the provinces of Jiangsu and Anhui.

Xuxi Canal

A canal located in the city of Nanjing, Jiangsu Province, China. See Xuhe River.

胥溪运河

中国江苏省南京市运河。见胥河。

Yangon Canal

A canal located in the south of Yangon, Myanmar. Also known as Yangon River or Hlaing River. The Yangon Canal joins the Pegu River and the Myitmaka River, which originate from the foothills of the Pegu Mountains near Yangon. As a 37-kilometre-long trumpet-shaped marine estuary, it runs through Yangon City from the northwest and flows southeast into the Gulf of Martaban of the Andaman Sea in the Indian Ocean. The waterway is connected in the west to the mainstream of the Irrawaddy River by the Twante Canal and in the east to the Sittang River system by the Boin Sittang Canal, forming the busiest inland waterway network of Myanmar, with Yangon as its centre. At the intersection of inland waterways and shipping lanes in Myanmar, the canal serves as the main access to Yangon for ocean-going vessels. As a transportation hub for trade, commuting and tourism, it is adjacent to the Port of Yangon, the country's largest seaport in terms of cargo throughput, thus playing a crucial role in Myanmar's socio-economic development.

Yangon River

A canal located in the south of Yangon, Myanmar. See Yangon Canal.

Yatta Canal

A canal located in the Yatta Constituency of Machakos County, Kenya. The Yatta Canal draws water

仰光运河

缅甸仰光市南部运河。亦称仰光河或莱恩河。仰光运河发源于仰光附近的勃固山山麓,连通勃固河和密马加河。运河全长37千米,河道整体呈喇叭状,从仰光西北部向东南方向流动,注入印度洋安达曼海的马达班湾。该运河向西经端迪运河与伊洛瓦底江干流相通,向东通过博因锡当运河与锡当河水系连通,共同构成缅甸以仰光为中心的、最繁忙的内河航道网。仰光运河处于内河航运和海运航线的交汇处,是远洋船舶通往仰光的主要航道。它毗邻缅甸吞吐量最大的海港仰光港,是集贸易运输、市内交通和旅游观光为一体的重要交通枢纽,在缅甸的经济社会发展中发挥着关键作用。

仰光河

缅甸仰光市南部运河。见仰光运河。

亚塔运河

肯尼亚马查科斯县亚塔区运河。亚塔运河全长53千米,水源来自塔

from the Thika River, a tributary of the Tana River, and is 53 kilometres in length. In 1953, the canal excavation at Yatta was commenced to supply water for domestic and livestock use as well as irrigation. In 1958, the project was interrupted. Financed by the African Land Development Board, the project was resumed in 1959. Between 2014 and 2016, the construction work was taken over by the Tanathi Water Services Board under the supervision of the national government, with an investment of more than $20 million. As a major water source for local domestic use and small-scale irrigation, the Yatta Canal is the only water source for this arid and semi-arid region. The flow rate has significantly reduced, especially in dry seasons, due to the increasing water consumption along with the population growth and agricultural activities, which also results in the contamination of the canal. In 2009, the canal dried up because of the environmental degradation in the upstream of the Thika River. The local government is devoted to improving and rehabilitating the Yatta Canal so that the canal can supply more water for domestic use and irrigation and at the same time ensure food security of this region and even the whole country.

娜河的支流锡卡河。该运河开凿于1953年，用来满足日常用水需求以及畜牧业与农作物的供水需求。1958年，运河修建工程中断，1年后，在非洲土地开发委员会的资助下再次启动。2014—2016年间，在国家政府的监管之下，塔纳西水务局开始负责亚塔运河的具体修建工作，耗资2 000余万美元。亚塔运河是当地生活用水和小规模农田灌溉的一个主要水源，也是干旱地区与半干旱地区唯一的水源。人口增长和农业生产导致运河水量显著减少，在旱季尤为明显，同时也造成运河污染。2009年，因锡卡河上游的生态环境恶化，亚塔运河一度干涸。如今，当地政府正致力于改善和修复亚塔运河，保障居民生活用水和农业灌溉用水，进一步确保该地区乃至全国的粮食安全。

Yazoo River

亚祖河

A canalized river located in the states of Louisiana and Mississippi, the United States. The Yazoo River was named by a French explorer in 1682 after the Yazoo tribe living near the river's mouth then. Some people think that the river means the "river of

美国路易斯安那州和密西西比州运河化河流。1682年，一位法国探险家因该河河口附近生活着亚祖族部落而将其命名为亚祖河。有人认为亚祖河的意思为"死亡之

death". The Yazoo River stretches over 300 kilometres and flows generally south and southwest. It is
formed by the confluence of the Tallahatchie River
and the Yalobusha River, and then merges into the
Mississippi River at Vicksburg. The river was diverted into an old river bed by the United States Army
Corps of Engineers in 1902, forming the Yazoo
Diversion Canal. The Yazoo River has seldom been
used for commercial navigation since the 1990s.

河"。亚祖河全长300多千米，由塔
拉哈奇河和亚洛布沙河交汇而成，
大体上呈正南和西南流向，在维克
斯堡汇入密西西比河。1902年，亚
祖河被美国陆军工程兵团改道并
入旧河床，形成了亚祖引水运河。
自20世纪90年代以来，亚祖河很少
用于商业航运。

Yellow River Channel

黄河航道

A canal under construction located in northern
China. Starting from Lanzhou and the Hetao Area
(mainly the Ningxia Hui Autonomous Region,
Inner Mongolia Autonomous Region and Shaanxi
Province) in the upper reaches, the Yellow River
Channel is planned to pass through the provinces
of Shanxi and Henan in the middle reaches and
join the Bohai Sea in Shandong Province. Its total
navigable length will be around 3,000 kilometres.
The development of the Yellow River as a navigable
waterway can be traced back to nearly 3,000 years
ago. In the late West Han Dynasty (202 BC—8
AD), the earliest long-distance water transportation
appeared in the Yellow River from the Huangshui
River basin to Jincheng (present-day Lanzhou).
During the ensuing dynasties (from the early 7th
century to the early 20th century), the Yellow River
witnessed a growing momentum in shipping activities, with wharves and commercial towns prospering alongside. At contemporary times, the water
volume of the Yellow River is declining due to the

中国北方在建运河。黄河航道将
始于上游的兰州市及河套地区（主
要包括宁夏回族自治区、内蒙古自
治区和陕西省），经过中游的山西
省和河南省，在山东省注入渤海。
规划中的可通航河道全长约3 000
千米。黄河航运发展史可以追溯
至近3 000年前。西汉末期，从湟
水流域至金城（今兰州）河段出现
了最早的长途水路运输。在接下
来的唐、宋、元、明、清时期，黄河
漕运发达，码头众多，沿河涌现出
不少商业市镇。在当代，随着黄河
流域地区社会经济发展水平的提
高，用水量不断增加，加之各类水
利工程的兴建，黄河径流出现了大
幅减少的现象，其航运功能也逐
步衰落。目前，黄河只能实现部分
通航。近年来，随着东部地区对西
部煤炭等资源的需求增加，修建黄
河航道已被提上议程，以发挥水

ever-growing need of water consumption in the Yellow River basin along with the rapid economic development in this region, as well as the intervention of various water conservancy projects. This has impacted the navigability of the Yellow River. At present, the Yellow River is partially navigable. In recent years, to meet the increasing demand in the east of China for coal and other resources from the west, the construction of the Yellow River Channel has been put on the agenda. The waterborne transportation of a larger capacity and lower cost will serve as an instrumental complement to the existing road transportation. According to Report on the Navigation of the Yellow River System, by 2030, the entire Yellow River Channel (from Lanzhou to the mouth of the river) will be navigable, and it will be upgraded to a Class IV waterway. The channel will be connected to the Bohai Sea through the Grand Canal, forming a modern waterway that can carry ships of 300 to 500 tons from Zhengzhou to Jinan. After its completion, the total annual cargo volume will reach 45.14 million tons, and the passenger traffic volume 18.644 million. Not only will the waterborne transportation be facilitated by the Yellow River Channel, but also the ecology and people's livelihood, as well as the development of tourism, will be realized, with the view to benefiting the cities alongside.

运运量大、成本低的优势, 补充陆运的不足。根据《黄河水系航运规划报告》, 2030年前, 黄河航道将实现 (兰州至入海口) 全线通航, 航道标准也将提升到四级。该航道将通过大运河与渤海相通, 从郑州至济南形成一条可承载300—500吨级船舶的现代化航道。黄河航道建设完成后的年货运总量将达4 514万吨, 年客运总量将达1864.4万人次。黄河航道的建设将集生态治理、水运发展、旅游开发及民生改善等功能为一体, 为沿线城市带来诸多益处。

Yonne

A canalized river located in the province of Yonne, France. The 292-kilometre-long Yonne River has

约讷河

法国约讷省运河化河流。约讷河从欧塞尔流向蒙特罗, 全长292千

a navigable length of 108 kilometres and 26 locks, running from Auxerre to Montereau. It serves as a part of the Nivernais Canal route in the first 22 kilometres, while the rest of the river forms a part of the Burgundy Canal. Originally, the canalized river was used to transport rafts from the forests of Morvan National Park to Paris. In 1834, Poirée successfully tested his design for a needle weir, which was improved by Thenard in 1839. The canalization of the Yonne River followed then, most of which was started after 1861. Now the Yonne River is an attractive cruising site. Some of the large-sized locks remain on the river but are seldom used for commercial traffic.

米，可通航河段长108千米，建有26座船闸。其中，前22千米的河段是尼韦内运河的一段，余下的河段则属于勃艮第运河。最初，约讷河的主要功能是将莫尔旺国家公园森林中的木排运往巴黎。1834年，工程师普瓦雷设计的栅条堰在约讷河试验成功。1839年，泰纳尔将其进一步改善。人们开始对约讷河进行运河化改造，主体工作始于1861年以后。如今，约讷河是一处景色优美的旅游胜地，河上仍保留一些大型船闸，但几乎不再用于商业航运。

York River

约克河

A canalized river located in eastern Virginia, the United States. Formerly known as Pamunkey River. The name "Pamunkey" is a combination of two lexemes meaning "upland" and "sloping", which describes its high banks by Native North Americans. The York River is approximately 55 kilometres in length, 1.6 kilometres in width at its headwater and 4 kilometres in width at its estuary. Its basin extends from the Piedmont Region all the way to central Virginia, covering around 7,000 square kilometres. The main stream of the river enters the Chesapeake Bay about 8 kilometres east of Yorktown. As an estuary where freshwater and seawater meet, the York River is rich in marine life. Currently, the George P. Coleman Memorial Bridge is the only bridge of the York River that allows vehicular traffic. It is a

美国弗吉尼亚州东部运河化河流。旧称帕芒基河。原语名称包含"高地"和"斜坡"两个词素，北美原住民用来形容河岸之高。约克河全长约55千米，河流上游宽1.6千米，河口宽4千米，流域面积约7 000平方千米，从皮德蒙特地区一直延伸至弗吉尼亚州中部。该河的干流在约克敦以东约8千米处汇入切萨皮克湾。约克河河口处淡水和海水交汇，海洋生物资源十分丰富。目前，约克河上仅乔治·科尔曼纪念桥可供车辆通行。这座双平旋桥建于1952年，连接半岛和潮水活动区域。

double swing bridge built in 1952 to connect the peninsula and the tidewater region.

Youth Canal

A canal located in the southwest of Guangdong Province, China. See Leizhou Youth Canal.

Ypres-Comines Canal

A canal located in the province of West Flanders, Belgium. The Ypres-Comines Canal was meant to form a connection between the Yzer River and the Leie River, and the construction was started in 1864. Due to the unstable subsoil between the Leie basin and the Yzer basin, the tunnel collapsed in 1866 and 1893, and the project came to a standstill. In 1910, a new plan was then conceived and implemented to raise the canal level by 5 metres. However er with the approach of World War I, the plans for the restoration of the Ypres-Comines Canal were shelved.

Ypres-Ijzer Canal

A canal located in the province of West Flanders, Belgium. The Ypres-Ijzer Canal runs from Heuvelland, through the city of Ieper (or Ypres), and flows into the Yser (or Ijzer) at Fort Knokke. The total length of the canal is 17 kilometres. In the 11th century, the Ijzer River was canalized to link the city of Ieper, which thrived on the clothing industry, to the sea. Even in 1842, more than 2,000 ships still

青年运河

中国广东省西南部运河。见雷州青年运河。

伊普尔–科米讷运河

比利时西佛兰德省运河。伊普尔—科米讷运河1864年开凿，最初是为了连通艾泽尔河与莱厄河。但莱厄河与艾泽尔河流域之间底土不稳，1866年与1893年发生两次隧道坍塌，工程陷入停滞。1910年，该运河工程按照新计划开工，将运河水位提高5米。然而，随着第一次世界大战的到来，伊普尔—科米讷运河重建计划被搁置。

伊普尔–艾泽尔运河

比利时西佛兰德省运河。伊普尔—艾泽尔运河始于赫弗兰市，流经伊普尔市，在克诺克堡汇入艾泽尔河，全长17千米。11世纪时，艾泽尔河被改造为运河，使服装业发达的伊普尔市成为一个通海城市。即使在1842年，仍然有超过2 000艘船只通过位于布京厄村的船闸。第

ran through the lock at Boezinge. During World War I, the Ypres-Ijzer Canal was used as a section of the frontline. Now, the waterway is merely used for travelling and recreation.

一次世界大战期间，伊普尔—艾泽尔运河曾是前线的一部分。如今，该运河仅供旅游休闲之用。

Yundu Canal

An ancient canal located in the city of Nanjing, Jiangsu Province, China. The Yundu Canal was situated to the west of the royal court in Jiankang (present-day Nanjing) during the Six Dynasties Period (222—589 AD). Originating from the Qinhuai River in the south, it went north to Cangcheng. It was crossed by 6 bridges and connected to the Chaogou Canal. In history, the Yundu Canal played an essential role in transportation in the city of Nanjing. The canal was constructed in 240 AD, when Sun Quan had dwelled in Nanjing for 12 years as King of Wu during the Three Kingdoms Period (220—280 AD). Xi Jian, an official of Wu, was responsible for supervising the excavation. The water source of the Yundu Canal was the Qinhuai River in the south of the city. The elevation at the northern section of the Yundu Canal was higher than that of its southern section, which made it difficult for the water to flow northwards. Then the food storage and supply in Cangcheng proved to be a challenge. To address the problem, Sun Quan authorized the excavation of the Chaogou Canal, which made the waterway connected with the Qingxi River to replenish the Yundu Canal. In the late Ming Dynasty (1368—1644), along the canal began the accumulation of settlement which encroached the banks of the

运渎运河

中国江苏省南京市古运河。运渎运河地处六朝皇城建康（今南京）西部，南起秦淮河，北连仓城，并与潮沟相通，河上建有6座桥梁。运渎运河曾在都城的交通运输中发挥重要作用。运渎运河开凿于公元240年，当时三国时期东吴开国皇帝孙权已在南京定都12年。左台侍御史都俭负责监督运河开凿。运渎河水来源于城南秦淮河，但由于运渎运河地势北高南低，河水常常难以向北流至仓城，对仓城的粮食储备和供应造成影响。于是孙权又下令开凿潮沟，连通运渎运河和青溪，为运渎运河补充水源。明朝末期，河道被居民区侵占，运渎运河逐渐变得狭窄，仅容小船通行。清朝嘉庆年间，政府曾对运渎运河进行疏浚，但20多年后，河道再次淤塞，导致南京城内洪灾频发。民国时期，运渎运河的水运条件每况愈下，夏季涨潮，冬季干涸。如今，运渎运河的河道已不复存在，仅留下少许遗迹。

channel. The canal gradually became narrower and allowed only small ships to pass through. During the reign of the Jiaqing Emperor of the Qing Dynasty (1616–1911), the Yundu Canal was dredged. Two decades later, the canal silted up again and induced flooding in the city of Nanjing. During the period of the Republic of China (1912–1949), the Yundu Canal continued to deteriorate, flooding in summers and drying up in winters. Today, the Yundu Canal does not exist any longer, and only a few traces of the course can be found.

Yunlianghe River · 运粮河

An ancient inland canal located in Shandong Province, China. See Jiaolai Canal .

中国古代山东省内陆运河。见胶莱运河。

Yunyanhe Canal · 运盐河

A canal located in Shanghai, China. See Pudong Canal.

中国上海运河。见浦东运河。

Zeehaven Canal

A canal located in Delfzijl City, Groningen Province, the Netherlands. The Zeehaven Canal is 6 kilometres in length, 9 metres in depth and 100 metres in width, becoming narrower westwards. With 2 locks on it, the Zeehaven Canal serves as a straight entrance to Delfzijl for freighters reaching the Delfzijl Harbour.

Zhe-Gan Canal

A canal under planning located in Zhejiang Province (Zhe for short) and Jiangxi Province (Gan for short), China. The Zhe-Gan Canal will be one of China's national inland Class III waterways. Several rivers will be canalized along the Xinjiang River to connect the Poyang Lake in Jiangxi with the Qiantang River in Zhejiang and guide the water directly to the East China Sea. The canal will start from Qibao, Hangzhou, Zhejiang Province in the east and reach the Chuxi estuary of the Xinjiang River, Jiangxi Province in the west. It will finally enter the Ganjiang River and the Yangtze River. As planned, the canal will be about 760 kilometres in length, more than 3.2 metres in depth, with a bed width of over 45 metres, navigable for ships with a displacement of 1,000 tons. There will be 7 locks along the line, with an estimated annual cargo capacity of about 25 million tons. At present, the overall planning has been settled. The Xinjiang River section and the Qiantang River section have been completely reconstructed, and the excavation of the

海港运河

荷兰格罗宁根省代尔夫宰尔市运河。海港运河全长6千米, 深9米, 宽100米, 向西逐渐变窄。运河上建有2座船闸, 经代尔夫宰尔港入港的货船可以通过该运河直接驶抵代尔夫宰尔市。

浙赣运河

中国浙江省和江西省拟建运河。按照规划, 浙赣运河是一条内陆三级航道, 从江西鄱阳湖沿信江而上, 通过几条运河化河流与浙江省钱塘江相连, 然后直通东海。该运河东起浙江省杭州市七堡, 西至江西省信江的褚溪河口, 最终注入赣江和长江。建成后, 运河全长可达760千米, 水深3.2米以上, 河底宽45米以上, 可容纳排水量达1 000吨的船只通行。运河沿线将建有7座船闸, 年货运量预计为2 500万吨。目前, 浙赣运河整体规划方案已确定, 信江河段及钱塘江段已改造完毕, 其余运河段预计在2023年左右动工, 建成后将连接京杭大运河和赣粤运河, 成为世界上最长的内陆人工运河, 将极大地便利南北物流运输, 同时有效降低运输成本。

rest parts along the line is expected to start around 2023. After completion, the Zhe-Gan Canal will connect the Beijing-Hangzhou Grand Canal and the Gan-Yue Canal, forming the longest inland artificial canal in the world, which will bring great convenience to north-south logistics and effectively reduce transportation costs.

Ziende Canal

A canal located in the province of South Holland, the Netherlands. The Ziende Canal, 1.47 kilometres long, runs near Zuideinde, connecting the Nieuwkoop's Ponds with the Old Rhine. On the canal is located a lock in Nieuwkoop, 21.5 metres in length and 4.4 metres in width.

Zij Canal C (North Holland)

A canal located in the province of North Holland, the Netherlands. The Zij Canal C connects the Spaarne River and the North Sea Canal. The 3.5-kilometre-long canal is used as important drainage of the Spaarndam pumping station.

Zij Canal C (Zeeland)

A canal located in Zeeland Province, the Netherlands. The Zij Canal C runs from Sluiskil to Sassing in Axel. The 2-kilometre-long canal was excavated in 1825 to facilitate the shipping to Axel and Hulst. The project was later shelved. Nowadays, it is a dead canal and serves as a port of entry. Most of its

辛德运河

荷兰南荷兰省运河。辛德运河长1.47千米，流经祖伊丁德附近，连接尼沃科普湖泊群和旧莱茵河，在尼沃科普附近建有1座长21.5米、宽4.4米的船闸。

塞运河C（北荷兰省）

荷兰北荷兰省运河。塞运河C连通斯帕恩河和北海运河，全长3.5千米，是斯帕伦丹水泵站排水系统的重要组成部分。

塞运河C（泽兰省）

荷兰泽兰省运河。塞运河C从斯勒伊斯基尔流向阿克塞尔的萨辛，全长2千米。该运河开凿于1825年，旨在方便通往阿克塞尔和许尔斯特的水上运输，然而这一水利项目开工不久后即被搁置。如今，塞运

western part has been widened and formed the Yara Port.

河C已废弃不用，仅用作通关港，其西端的大部分河段已拓宽成为现在的雅拉港。

Zijl Canal

宰尔运河

A canal located in the province of Groningen, the Netherlands. The Zijl Canal is a branch of the Lauwers that forms a part of the border between the provinces of Groningen and Friesland.

荷兰格罗宁根省运河。宰尔运河是劳沃斯河的一条支流。劳沃斯河是格罗宁根省和弗里斯兰省边界的一部分。

Zijlroede

宰尔路德运河

A canal located in the province of Friesland, the Netherlands. The Zijlroede was excavated around 1653, with a total length of 1.5 kilometres. It flows westwards from a marina in Joure and joins the North Oudeweg Canal at the Joure Lock. In winter, ice skating has become a popular activity on the Zijlroede.

荷兰弗里斯兰省运河。宰尔路德运河开凿于1653年前后，全长1.5千米，从约勒的一个船坞向西流至约斯船闸，并在此与北奥德韦赫运河相交汇。冬季时，该运河是一处滑冰胜地。

Zuidwending Canal

南文丁运河

A canal located in the province of Groningen, the Netherlands. The Zuidwending Canal is a branch of the Aduard Canal and connects itself with the Hoen Canal.

荷兰格罗宁根省运河。南文丁运河是爱德华德运河的一条支线，与霍恩运河相通。

Zutphen-Enschede Canal

聚特芬－恩斯赫德运河

A canal located in the provinces of Overijssel and Gelderland, the Netherlands. See Twente Canal.

荷兰上艾瑟尔省和海尔德兰省运河。见特文特运河。

Zwolse Canal

A canal located in the province of Flevoland, the Netherlands. The Zwolse Canal is 15 kilometres in lengh, with an elevation of −3 metres. It runs northwest from the Kadoeler Lake through Marknesse, and joins the Urker Canal at Emmeloord.

兹沃尔瑟运河

荷兰弗莱福兰省运河。兹沃尔瑟运河水位低于海平面3米，全长15千米，自卡多埃勒湖向西北流经马克内瑟镇，然后在埃默洛尔德镇汇入厄尔卡运河。

Appendix 1

附录一　世界知名运河组织介绍

Introduction to Major World Canal Organizations

世界运河合作组织（WCCO）

官方网站（Website）：
http://www.whcccco.org/

Founded in 2009, WCCO is a non-profit, non-governmental international organization formed by a number of canal cities and economic or cultural institutions worldwide. Its full official name is World Historic and Cultural Canal Cities Cooperation Organization (abbreviated as WCCO). The Organization has its domicile and Secretariat in Yangzhou, a city on the China Grand Canal in east China's Jiangsu Province.

WCCO's work is oriented around canals. It works to promote the economic and cultural exchanges between canal cities, share their development experience, push for mutually beneficial cooperation, and facilitate common development and prosperity.

Since its founding, WCCO has been dedicated to exploring the conservation and utilization of canals as well as canal-related heritages, seeking the paths of canal-based city development, and pushing for enhanced friendship, cooperation and common advancement between the world's canal cities. It has grown into an influential NGO on inter-city exchanges and cooperation featuring standardized, international operation. A brand event of WCCO is the annually-held World Canal Cities Forum.

世界运河合作组织是由世界各国运河城市和相关经济文化机构自愿结成的非营利性非官方国际组织。世界运河合作组织的全称是世界运河历史文化城市合作组织（英文缩写为WCCO），成立于2009年，目前组织住所和秘书处设在中国江苏省扬州市。

世界运河合作组织的宗旨是：以运河为纽带，促进运河城市间经济文化交流，共享发展经验，推动互利合作，促进运河城市共同发展和繁荣。

自成立以来，世界运河合作组织致力于共同探讨运河及相关文化遗产保护利用之道，寻找运河文化促进城市发展之路，致力于推动世界运河城市增进友谊、加强合作、共同进步，已逐步成长为一家规范化、国际化、有一定影响力的国际间城市交流合作机构。每年举办的世界运河城市论坛是其标志性活动。

On the whole, WCCO is dedicated to the following missions:

Showcasing the history and culture of world canals, and giving full play to their roles in advancing human civilization;

Organizing World Canal Cities Expos and World Canal Cities Forums, sharing development experience, and facilitating mutually beneficial cooperation;

Carrying out cultural and economic exchanges between canal cities worldwide and pushing for common development and prosperity;

Carrying out people to people diplomacy and upgrading the exchanges and cooperation between world canal cities.

总体来说，世界运河合作组织致力于如下几方面的事业：

传播世界运河历史文化，发挥运河文化在促进人类社会文明进步中的作用；

举办运河名城博览会及世界运河城市论坛，共享发展经验，推动互利合作；

以世界运河为纽带，开展经贸和文化交流，促进运河城市共同发展和繁荣；

开展民间外交，促进世界运河城市间的交往与合作。

Inland Waterways International
campaigning for inland waterways worldwide since 1995

内河航道国际组织（IWI）

官方网站（Website）：

http://inlandwaterwaysinternational.org/

Inland Waterways International (abbreviated as IWI) brings together people and organizations who support the conservation, use, development and proper management of inland waterways worldwide. It aims to raise public awareness of the benefits of using waterways for a wide range of activities, from inland water transport to cruising, towpath walking and other recreational uses, as well as appreciating their architectural and landscape values as heritage. It also promotes the restoration, where appropriate, of waterways which have become derelict.

IWI's membership includes leading navigation authorities, as well as voluntary bodies, museums and commercial companies. Individual members include both users and experts in various disciplines. All have a keen interest in both the history and the contemporary significance of inland waterways for commercial carrying and recreational use. Today the membership covers 24 countries from around the world.

IWI's major event is the World Canals Conference (hereafter WCC), held annually and in principle rotates, successive events being held in Europe,

内河航道国际组织（英文缩写为IWI）集合了全世界范围内以各种方式支持内河水道的保护、利用、开发以及管理的人士和机构单位，致力于提高公众对内河航道运输与休闲功能的认识，以及内河航道作为建筑与景观的文化价值的认知。此外，内河航道国际组织也致力于推动有选择性地修复已经部分废弃的河段。

内河航道国际组织的会员单位包括知名的航运管理机构、志愿团体、文博场馆，以及企业单位。个人会员包括各行业的用户和专家。所有会员都对内河航道的历史及其在当代商业航运和休闲娱乐方面的价值表现出极大兴趣。如今，内河航道国际组织的会员分布在全球24个国家。

世界运河大会是内河航道国际组织的年度重要活动，每年在不同的国家及城市举办，至今已在欧洲、北

North America and Asia. Dating back to 1988, the Conference was brought under the aegis of IWI in 2008. Since then, IWI's WCC Site Selection Steering Committee has chosen the site to host the annual conference, from the applications submitted. The event brings together canal enthusiasts, professionals and scholars from around the world to learn about a variety of topics related to canals. Details of the events are available on IWI's WCC page: https://inlandwaterwaysinternational.org/world-canals-conference/.

Other activities include participating in national or regional events organized by members, campaigning to restore abandoned waterways, or promoting the construction of new waterways where feasible. IWI is also a repository of canal information and experts via its website, which includes a bibliography, and through its members. Study tours are organized and frequently form part of the overall programme for the World Canals Conference.

美、亚洲举办过。运河大会最早举办于1988年，从2008年起，内河航道国际组织成为大会的主办方，同时设置选址委员会，每年从申办城市中选出大会的举办地。大会为全世界的运河爱好者和专家学者就运河领域多方面的话题提供了交流平台。可登录内河航道国际组织官方网站浏览世界运河大会相关信息，网址：https://inlandwaterwaysinternational.org/world-canals-conference/。

内河航道国际组织的其他业务活动包括参加会员单位组织的各种全国性或区域性活动、促进废旧内河航道修复通航以及推动新航道开凿。同时，内河航道国际组织也通过官方网站及其会员，建成了一个囊括运河知识和相关学者信息的数据库（其中包含运河领域文献录）。其主办的世界运河大会，也常组织与会者参加各种实地考察活动。

国际水协会（IWA）

官方网站（Website）：
http://www.iwa-network.org/

The International Water Association (abbreviated as IWA) has its roots in the International Water Supply Association (IWSA), established in 1947, and the International Association on Water Quality (IAWQ), which originally formed as the International Association for Water Pollution Research in 1965. The two groups merged in 1999 to form the IWA, creating one international organization focused on the full water cycle.

The IWA is now headquartered in London, with a global secretariat based in the Hague and offices in Beijing, Bangkok, Nairobi, Dakar, Milwaukee, and Singapore. Innovative, solutions and service oriented, the Association works across a range of areas that contribute to achieving a water wise world.

The group's mission is to serve as a worldwide network for water professionals and advance standards and best practices in sustainable water management. The association has four member types: individual, student, corporate, and governing members. There are about 10,000 individual and 500 corporate members, with governing members in approximately 80 countries.

国际水协会由两个较早成立的协会，即1947年成立的国际供水协会和1965年成立的国际水质协会于1999年合并而成，是个关注水资源循环全过程的国际组织。

协会总部目前设在伦敦，其全球秘书处设在海牙，并在北京、曼谷、内罗毕、达喀尔、密尔沃基和新加坡等地设有办事处。协会以创新、提供解决方案和服务为导向，业务工作覆盖一系列有助于促进人类与水共舞的领域。

协会的使命是维持一个全球的水务专业人士的网络，引领可持续水务管理的标准规范和实践。目前，协会的会员分为四类：个人、学者、机构、理事单位。其中，个人会员约有10 000人，机构会员约500个，理事单位分布在全球约80个国家。

The mission of the IWA is to inspire change and service IWA members, the community of professionals concerned with water, external organization and opinion leaders in being the international reference and global source of knowledge, experience and leadership for sustainable urban and basin-related water solutions.

The IWA annually hosts more than 40 specialist conferences and workshops on various aspects of water management. Events organized by the IWA include the World Water Congress & Exhibition and the Water Development Congress & Exhibition.

It brings people of the highest calibre together to share knowledge, experience and know-how about the most pressing water challenges and innovative solutions. It also contributes to water science and technology by stimulating leading-edge science and inventions, helping scientists connect to their peers, publish their latest findings and learn from each other, and offering support and recognition to innovators in the world of water. Moreover, it develops and promotes best practices and international frameworks and standards, supporting transitions to sustainable practices.

协会的工作围绕着促进变革，服务协会会员、水务专家团体、外部组织和意见领袖，为世界城市和流域水务的可持续解决方案提供参考，亦是全球水务知识、经验及领导力的重要来源。

该协会每年围绕水务管理的多个方面举办40多场专家会议或研讨会，其中包括国际水资源大会暨博览会和水资源开发大会暨博览会。

在协会领导下，水务领域的精英人士齐聚一堂，就当前水资源环境领域所面临的最紧迫挑战及创新性解决方案，开展知识、经验、技术等方面的交流分享；通过催生领先的科技发明和促进专家学者成果产出、相互交流、相互学习，对水务领域的创新者提供支持及认可，促进水科学技术的发展；同时，协会通过积累可持续发展的成功实践经验，开发相关国际合作框架及标准，促进水资源的可持续发展。

Appendix 2

附录二　历届世界运河名城博览会概览
(2007—2020)

Overview of the World Canal Cities Expos (2007—2020)

The World Canal Cities Expo is a brand event of the World Historic and Cultural Canal Cities Cooperation Organization (WCCO). The annual event started from 2007, and is normally attended by government officials, scholars, representatives of canal management authorities, and canal enthusiasts of the canal cities worldwide. The Expo is themed on canal-based issues such as tourism in canal cities, protection and utilization of canal heritages, protection of canal environment, and the urban planning of the canal cities, providing a platform for equal, open exchanges of ideas and sharing of experiences.

世界运河名城博览会是世界运河历史文化城市合作组织（WCCO）的一项品牌活动，从2007年开始，每年举办一次，参加者包括世界各运河城市的政府官员、专家学者、运河管理者、运河爱好者等，主要围绕运河城市旅游、运河遗产保护与利用、运河环境保护、运河城市规划设计等主题，进行平等、坦诚、开放的案例展示、观点交流、智慧碰撞。

2007年

World Canal Cities Expo & Mayors Forum

中国·扬州世界运河名城博览会暨市长论坛

Theme:

The Sustainable Development of Canal Cities

主题：

运河城市的可持续发展

Highlights:

The Yangzhou Manifesto on the Sustainable Development of World Canal Cities was agreed and issued. Yangzhou was selected by the State Administration of Cultural Heritage as the leading city in China Grand Canal's bid for UNESCO World Heritage status.

亮点：

共同发布了《世界运河城市可持续发展扬州宣言》。活动期间，扬州还被中国国家文物局正式确定为大运河申报世界遗产项目的牵头城市。

2008年

World Canal Cities Expo & Experts Forum

中国·扬州世界运河名城博览会暨专家论坛

Theme:

Protection and Promotion of Historical & Cultural Heritages of Canal Cities

主题：

运河城市历史文化遗产保护和传承

Highlights:

Those present reached a consensus of "Carrying Forward Canal Culture, Inheriting History and Civilization, and Promoting Lasting and Sustainable Development". The UNESCAP experts panel meeting on "Facilitating Trade and Traffic, Promoting Export Competitiveness" was held in Yangzhou. Ms Noeleen Heyzer, UN Under-Secretary General and Executive Secretary of UNESCAP, and 48 representatives from the experts panel attended the Expo.

亮点：

达成了"弘扬运河文化、传承历史文明、促进永续发展"的共识。联合国亚太经济与社会委员会"提高贸易及交通便利化与促进出口竞争力"专家组会议在扬州召开，联合国副秘书长兼亚太经社会执行秘书诺琳·海泽一行以及专家组会议的48名代表出席了博览会开幕式及有关活动。

2009年

World Canal Cities Expo & Mayors Forum

中国·扬州世界运河名城博览会暨市长论坛

Theme:

Development of Canal Cities' Tourism amid the Global Financial Crisis

主题：

金融危机背景下运河城市旅游业发展

Highlights:

A ceremony was held to lay the foundation stone for the Permanent Venue for World Canal Cities Expo. The World Historic and Cultural Canal Cities Cooperation Organization (WCCO) was formally founded.

亮点：

举行了世界运河名城博览会永久性会址奠基和世界运河历史文化城市合作组织成立仪式，进一步完善了世界运河名城博览会的机制。

2010年

World Canal Cities Expo & Experts Forum

中国·扬州世界运河名城博览会暨专家论坛

Theme:

Developing Low-Carbon Economy in Canal Cities: Significance & Path

主题：

运河城市发展低碳经济的重大意义及其途径

Highlights:

The grand event was attended by 146 guests, including representatives from 15 canal cities worldwide, 9 international organizations, and 3 of the world's top 500 enterprises. A number of intentions on project cooperation and friendly exchanges were reached.

亮点：

146位嘉宾参会，包括国外的15个运河城市、9个国际组织，以及3家世界500强企业。达成了一批项目合作、友好交往意向。

2011年

World Canal Cities Expo & The 1st Global Design Cities Summit

中国·扬州世界运河名城博览会暨首届全球设计城市峰会

Theme:

Updating Canal Cities Through Designing

主题：

设计，提升运河城市

Highlights:

The 1st Global Design Cities Summit was incorporated into this Expo, and representatives from 13 signatory cities to the *Seoul Declaration* met in Yangzhou, giving a boost to Yangzhou's international fame.

亮点：

嵌入式举办首届设计城市峰会，南非开普敦、土耳其安卡拉等13个《首尔宣言》会员城市齐聚扬州，进一步提升了扬州的国际知名度。

2012年

World Canal Cities Expo & The 25th World Canals Conference

中国 · 扬州世界运河名城博览会暨第25届世界运河大会

Theme:

The Grand Canal: A Living Heritage

主题：

大运河 · 活态遗产

Highlights:

The World Canals Conference was held in Yangzhou for the first time. Registration to the Expo and the World Canals Conference on the same website.

亮点：

世界运河大会首次在扬州举办，开通运河博览会暨世界运河大会专题网站，接受网上报名。

2013年

World Canal Cities Expo & Mayors Forum

中国 · 扬州世界运河名城博览会暨市长论坛

Theme:

Water Ecology, Water Civilization, and the Cities

主题：

水生态、水文明与名城

Highlights:

Yangzhou was designated by China's Ministry of Water Resources as the Pilot City for China's Water Ecological Civilization Development.

亮点：

水利部确定扬州为"全国水生态文明建设试点城市"。

2014年

World Canal Cities Expo & Work Conference on the Grand Canal's Protection and Management

中国·扬州世界运河名城博览会暨大运河保护管理工作会议

Theme:

Protection & Utilization of the Grand Canal After Its World Heritage Designation

主题：

大运河成为世界文化遗产后的保护与利用

Highlights:

This Expo was a national event called by China State Administration of Cultural Heritage on the Grand Canal's protection and management after its successful inscription onto the World Heritage List. The Office for the Grand Canal's World Heritage Inscription Application was thus renamed the Grand Canal Protection & Management Office.

亮点：

大运河申遗成功后国家文物局在扬州召开保护管理工作会议，大运河申遗办公室更名为大运河保护管理办公室。

2015年

World Canal Cities Tourism Forum

世界运河名城旅游论坛

Theme:

Interconnective Activities of Canal Tourism within the Framework of the Belt & Road Initiative

主题：

一带一路框架下互联互通的运河旅游业

Highlights:

The event coincided with the 2,500th anniversary of the city of Yangzhou. Among the impressive celebrations was a decorated boat cruise performance in the waters of the Yangzhou section of the Grand Canal.

亮点：

扬州建城2 500周年，扬州古运河花船巡游。

2016年

World Heritage Canals Forum & The General Assembly of World Historic and Cultural Canal Cities Cooperation Organization (WCCO)

世界遗产运河论坛暨世界运河历史文化城市合作组织会员大会

Theme:

Canal Culture Tourism and Sustainable Development

主题：

运河文化旅游与可持续发展

Highlights:

The Secretariat of the World Historic and Cultural Canal Cities Cooperation Organization (WCCO) was launched. *The Charter of WCCO* was ratified after its amendment, and an adjustment was made to the Organization's leadership.

亮点：

世界运河历史文化城市合作组织秘书处揭牌，通过修改后的《合作组织章程》，调整合作组织领导机构成员。

2017年

World Canal Cities Forum

世界运河城市论坛

Theme:

New Opportunities for World Canal Cities Under the Belt & Road Initiative

主题：

运河城市在"一带一路"合作中的新机遇

Highlights:

A Directory of World Canals was formally launched. The World Historic Canal Towns Cooperation Mechanism was founded.

亮点：

《世界运河名录》正式发布。建立世界运河古镇合作机制。

2018年

World Canal Cities Forum	世界运河城市论坛

Theme:

Protection, Inheritance and Utilization of Canal Cities Culture

主题：

运河城市文化保护、传承与利用

Highlights:

The first canal-themed international micro film festival held in Yangzhou.

亮点：

首届运河主题国际微电影展在扬州举办。

2019年

World Canal Cities Forum & World Canals Conference	世界运河城市论坛暨世界运河大会

Theme:

The Preservation, Inheritance and Utilization of Canal Culture

主题：

运河文化的保护传承与利用

Highlights:

The World Canals Conference was held in Yangzhou for the second time. *The Gazetteer of the Canals of China* was formally launched. The Canal Culture Carnival was staged in Yangzhou.

亮点：

世界运河大会第二次在扬州举办。《中国运河志》出版发布揭幕。同期举办运河文化"嘉年华"活动。

2020年

World Canal Cities Forum	**世界运河城市论坛**

Theme:

Sustainable Prosperity and Development of Cultural Tourism Industry of World Canal Cities

主题：

世界运河城市文旅产业持续繁荣发展

Highlights:

2020 Canal Carnival and the 2020 World Canal Cities Food Expo were staged. *The Yangzhou Initiative on the Sustainable Prosperity and Development of Cultural Tourism Industry of Canal Cities* was agreed and issued.

亮点：

举办2020运河嘉年华及2020世界运河城市美食博览会活动。论坛通过《运河城市文旅产业持续繁荣发展扬州倡议》。

List of Major Canal Cities and Towns Worldwide

S/N 序号	CITY 城市	COUNTRY 国家	CONTINENT 大洲
1	Amsterdam 阿姆斯特丹	The Netherlands 荷兰	Europe 欧洲
2	Antwerp 安特卫普	Belgium 比利时	Europe 欧洲

CANAL(S) RELATED 相关运河	**CITY PROFILE** 城市简介

Amsterdam Canals
阿姆斯特丹运河网

Capital of the Netherlands. Amsterdam is also the country's biggest city, and hosts the fourth largest airport in Europe. The system of Amsterdam Canals forms concentric belts around the city, known as the Grachtengordel. This 17th century canal ring was inscribed on the UNESCO World Heritage List in 2010, which earns Amsterdam the fame as the Venice of the North. The canal system of Amsterdam is regarded officially as a symbol of the prosperous economy and culture of Amsterdam during the Dutch Golden Age.

荷兰首都。阿姆斯特丹是荷兰最大城市，欧洲第四大航空港。阿姆斯特丹运河网围绕城市形成了同心环形运河带，即运河环形带。建于17世纪的阿姆斯特丹环形运河带2010年被联合国教科文组织列入世界遗产名录，为阿姆斯特丹市赢得了"北方威尼斯"的美誉。阿姆斯特丹运河网是荷兰黄金时代经济繁荣和文化发展的重要体现。

Albert Canal
阿尔贝特运河

An important industrial city in Belgium, the country's biggest sea port, as well as Europe's second largest and the world's fourth largest sea port. Antwerp is a cultural centre of Europe, and is the birthplace of old master Anthony van Dyck. Antwerp is integrated into Western Europe's inland waterway system via natural rivers as well as the Albert Canal.

比利时重要工业城市、最大港口，欧洲第二大、世界第四大港口。安特卫普是欧洲著名文化中心，著名艺术大师范戴克的诞生地。安特卫普通过天然河道和阿尔贝特运河等与西欧内陆水网相连。

S/N 序号	CITY 城市	COUNTRY 国家	CONTINENT 大洲
3	Beijing 北京	China 中国	Asia 亚洲
4	Bergen op Zoom 贝亨·奥普·佐姆	The Netherlands 荷兰	Europe 欧洲

CANAL(S) RELATED
相关运河

CITY PROFILE
城市简介

Grand Canal (China)
中国大运河

Capital of the People's Republic of China. Beijing is at the northern tip of the Grand Canal, the terminal of the national grain transport system in ancient China. The Grand Canal is of paramount importance to ancient China. It boasts a history of more than 2,500 years. In the Sui Dynasty (581—618 AD), Emperor Yang decided to connect the then existing canals with Luoyang and Zhuojun (known as Beijing today), thus to form one unified system of intra-state communications and transport.

中国首都。北京是中国大运河的最北端，古代漕运的终点。大运河在古代中国的重要性无与伦比，从开凿至今已历经2 500多年。隋朝时，隋炀帝决定将当时的运河贯通至都城洛阳，并与涿郡（今北京）相连，意在打造一条国内交通大动脉。

Schelde–Rhine Canal
斯海尔德 – 莱茵运河

A municipality located in the south of the Netherlands, Bergen op Zoom witnessed a surge in economic growth during the reign of Jan II van Glymes (1417—1494). Large fairs were held twice a year, in spring and autumn, that were known both nationally and internationally. Merchants from all over Europe came to Bergen op Zoom to sell their goods. In the mid-16th century, the city experienced an economic recession due to the poor accessibility of the port caused by several floods in Zeeland and west Brabant. Because of its great reliance on the port, the city's economic growth received a major blow. Currently, the two fairs have been discontinued, but various smaller fairs and events are still held in Bergen op Zoom.

S/N 序号	CITY 城市	COUNTRY 国家	CONTINENT 大洲
5	Bern 伯尔尼	Switzerland 瑞士	Europe 欧洲
6	Bordeaux 波尔多	France 法国	Europe 欧洲

CANAL(S) RELATED 相关运河	CITY PROFILE 城市简介
	荷兰南部自治市。贝亨·奥普·佐姆市在扬二世·范格莱姆斯（1417—1494）统治期间经济迅速增长。每年春季和秋季举办两次大型展览会，在国内外享有盛誉，来自欧洲各地的商人来此出售他们的商品。由于泽兰和北布拉班特西部多次发生洪水，导致港口交通不畅。16世纪中叶，该市经济出现衰退。因对港口高度依赖，该市经济受到沉重打击。目前两大展会已经停办，不过贝亨·奥普·佐姆仍举办各种小型展会和活动。
Nidau-Büren Canal 尼道－比伦运河	Capital of Switzerland, slightly west of the centre of Switzerland. Bern is also the capital of the canton of Bern, where the Nidau-Büren Canal is located. The city is the headquarters of the international postal, railway, and copyright unions. Its industries include the manufacture of printing products, chocolate, machinery, electrical equipment, and chemical and pharmaceutical products. 瑞士首都，位于瑞士中部偏西。伯尔尼同时也是尼道－比伦运河所在地——伯尔尼行政区的首府。万国邮政联盟、国际铁路运输总局、国际版权联盟总部均设于该市。伯尔尼的工业包括印刷业、巧克力加工、机械制造、电器制造、化工及制药业。
Garonne Canal 加龙运河	A port city on the Garonne River in Gironde Department, southwestern France. Bordeaux is known as the world's capital of wine as well as an international tourist destination for its architectural and cultural heritage. The Garonne River connects Bordeaux with Castets-en-Dorthe, and is the end point of the Garonne Canal staring from Toulouse.

S/N 序号	CITY 城市	COUNTRY 国家	CONTINENT 大洲
7	Breda 布雷达	The Netherlands 荷兰	Europe 欧洲
8	Bree 布雷	Belgium 比利时	Europe 欧洲
9	Bruges 布鲁日	Belgium 比利时	Europe 欧洲

CANAL(S) RELATED 相关运河	CITY PROFILE 城市简介
	法国西南部港口城市，位于吉伦特省加龙河畔。波尔多被誉为世界葡萄酒之都，是国际建筑和文化遗产旅游胜地。波尔多通过加龙河与多尔特地区的卡斯泰昂连通，这里也是始于图卢兹的加龙运河的终点。
Aa River 阿河 Wilhelmina Canal 威廉敏娜运河	A city of strategic military and political significance in the Netherlands. The name of the city derived from brede Aa in Dutch (broad Aa), referring to the confluence of the Mark River and the Aa River. 荷兰城市，具有军事和政治双重战略价值。布雷达市名源自荷兰语"宽阔的阿河"，意指马克河与阿河交汇处。
South Willems Canal 南威廉斯运河	A city in the province of Limburg, Belgium. Bree is known as the jewel of the Campine. The South Willems Canal passes through it. 比利时林堡省的城市。布雷被誉为坎皮纳的宝石。南威廉斯运河流经该市。
Canals of Bruges 布鲁日运河网	A renowned medieval city and tourist attraction. Bruges was designated the European Capital of Culture in 2002. The historic centre of Bruges is now a UNESCO World Heritage. The water city is sometimes hailed as "the Venice of the North". Its canal system is largely composed of two interconnected systems. The outer canal circles around the old city just like a moat, while the inner canal comprises a number of waterway sections, each with its own name, flowing largely in a south-to-north direction through the downtown areas of the old city.

S/N 序号	CITY 城市	COUNTRY 国家	CONTINENT 大洲
10	Cangzhou 沧州	China 中国	Asia 亚洲
11	Carcassonne 卡尔卡松	France 法国	Europe 欧洲

CANAL(S) RELATED 相关运河	CITY PROFILE 城市简介
	比利时中世纪名城、旅游胜地，2002年评为欧洲文化之都，布鲁日历史中心城区已列入联合国教科文组织世界遗产名录。布鲁日是一座水城，有"北方威尼斯"的美誉，其运河网大体可分为两个彼此相连的系统：外运河绕城而行，形成古城的护城河；内运河则分为多条河道，每一河段均有自己的名字，大体上为南北流向，流经古城城区。
Grand Canal (China) 中国大运河	A prefecture-level city located in eastern Hebei Province, China. Among all prefectural cities along the Grand Canal, Cangzhou has the longest section of the canal (215 kilometres) within its territory. The city is now a petrochemical industrial base, pipeline production base, and a vital land-sea transportation hub in northern China. Cangzhou is renowned as a centre for Chinese martial arts and the birthplace of Chinese acrobatics. 中国河北省东部地级市。沧州是京杭大运河流经里程最长的地级城市，全长215公里。该市是中国北方石油化工基地、管道生产基地、重要陆海交通枢纽，以武术、杂技闻名于世。
Midi Canal 米迪运河	A city in the south of France, about 80 kilometres east of Toulouse. Carcassonne boasts a strategically important location between the Atlantic Ocean and the Mediterranean Sea. The city derives a considerable part of its income from the tourism connected to the Midi Canal, which flows through it. 卡尔卡松是法国南部城市，距图卢兹东部80千米。该市位于大西洋和地中海之间，战略地位重要。米迪运河穿

S/N 序号	CITY 城市	COUNTRY 国家	CONTINENT 大洲
12	Dinslaken 丁斯拉肯	Germany 德国	Europe 欧洲
13	Dublin 都柏林	Ireland 爱尔兰	Europe 欧洲
14	Dunkirk 敦刻尔克	France 法国	Europe 欧洲

CANAL(S) RELATED 相关运河	CITY PROFILE 城市简介
	过卡尔卡松市，与米迪运河相关的旅游业为该市创造了相当一部分收入。
Rhine River 莱茵河	A town in the Wesel District, North Rhine-Westphalia, Germany. Located in the lower Rhine region, Dinslaken relies more heavily on Rotbach, a tributary of the Rhine in the northern Ruhr area. The cycle path along the Rotbach provides the visitors with a beautiful scenery of the land. 德国北莱茵－威斯特法伦州韦瑟尔区城镇。丁斯拉肯位于莱茵河下游地区，其用水高度依赖莱茵河在鲁尔区北部的支流罗特巴赫河。游客骑行于沿罗特巴赫河沿岸，可以欣赏到丁斯拉肯的美丽风景。
Grand Canal (Ireland) 爱尔兰大运河 Royal Canal 皇家运河	Capital of Ireland, the country's economic, cultural, and political centre, and a world-famous tourist destination. The two biggest canals of the Irish Island, the Grand Canal and the Royal Canal, ring the inner city of Dublin on the south and north side respectively. 爱尔兰首都，同时也是爱尔兰经济、文化、金融中心和世界著名的旅游胜地。爱尔兰岛两大运河：爱尔兰大运河和皇家运河，环绕都柏林的南、北侧流过。
Dunkirk-Escaut Canal 敦刻尔克－埃斯科运河 Veurne-Dunkirk Canal 弗尔讷－敦刻尔克运河 Newport-Dunkirk 新港－敦刻尔克运河	A port city in Nord, northern France. Ten kilometres from the Belgian border, Dunkirk has the third largest French harbour. The city is connected to Mortagne-du-Nord via the Dunkirk-Escaut Canal, to the Belgian coastal town Newport via the Newport-Dunkirk Canal, and to Veurne in western Belgium via the Veurne-Dunkirk Canal.

S/N 序号	CITY 城市	COUNTRY 国家	CONTINENT 大洲
15	Edinburgh 爱丁堡	The United Kingdom 英国	Europe 欧洲
16	Galway 戈尔韦	Ireland 爱尔兰	Europe 欧洲

CANAL(S) RELATED 相关运河	**CITY PROFILE** 城市简介
	法国北部北方省港口城市，距比利时边境10千米。敦刻尔克拥有法国第三大港口，经由敦刻尔克－埃斯科运河与北莫尔塔涅相连，经由新港－敦刻尔克运河与比利时海边城市新港市相连，经由弗尔讷－敦刻尔克运河与比利时西部城市弗尔讷市相连。
Union Canal (the United Kingdom) 联盟运河	Capital of Scotland, one of Britain's cultural centres. The Union Canal opened in the 1850s joins Edinburgh to the Forth and Clyde Canal at Falkirk (where the rotating boat lift Falkirk Wheel is located) which links Scotland's east and west coasts. 苏格兰首府，英国文化中心之一。19世纪50年代，联盟运河建成通航，将爱丁堡与福尔柯克处的福斯－克莱德运河相连，福尔柯克是著名的旋转式轮船电梯福尔柯克轮所在地，福斯－克莱德运河贯穿苏格兰东西海岸。
Eglinton Canal 埃格林顿运河	A county town of County Galway, West of Ireland. Galway lies on the Corrib River between Lough Corrib and Galway Bay. Waterway systems are of great engineering significance in Galway, including the Corrib River, the Cathedral River and the Convent River, etc. Among them the Eglinton Canal connects Lough Corrib to the sea at Galway so that goods could be transported in both directions. The Corrib River and canal systems have over the years provided a number of benefits: navigation, water power, drainage for the Corrib catchment, fisheries and as a source for water supply to Galway city and surrounding areas. 爱尔兰西部戈尔韦郡首府，位于科里布湖和戈尔韦湾

S/N 序号	CITY 城市	COUNTRY 国家	CONTINENT 大洲
17	Geneva 日内瓦	Switzerland 瑞士	Europe 欧洲
18	Ghent 根特	Belgium 比利时	Europe 欧洲
19	Giethoorn 羊角村	The Netherlands 荷兰	Europe 欧洲

CANAL(S) RELATED 相关运河	CITY PROFILE 城市简介
	之间，科里布河穿城而过。包括科里布河、大教堂河和康文特河等在内的戈尔韦水道网具有重要的工程意义。其中，埃格林顿运河在戈尔韦将科里布湖与大西洋连通，促进了两地之间的货物运输。多年来，科里布河及运河网极大促进了城市发展，发展了航海与渔业，提供水力发电，帮助科里布流域排水并为戈尔韦市及周边地区供水。
Rhône 罗讷河	The second most populous city in Switzerland and the most populous city of Romandy, the French-speaking part of Switzerland. It hosts the highest number of international organizations in the world, including the headquarters of many agencies of the United Nations and the Red Cross. Rhône, a canalized cross-border river, flows through the city before it enters France. 瑞士人口第二大城市，瑞士法语区罗曼迪人口第一大城市。日内瓦是世界上数量最多的国际组织所在地，包括联合国多个机构总部和国际红十字会。跨境运河化河流罗讷河流经该市后进入法国境内。
Ghent-Terneunzen Canal 根特－特尔纽曾运河	The second largest city and third largest sea port of Belgium, and capital of East Flanders. Its position as a sea port was most attributable to the opening and expansion of the Ghent-Terneunzen Canal. 比利时第二大城市及第三大港口，东佛兰德省首府。因根特－特尔纽曾运河的开通及扩建，根特成为海港城市。
Beukers-Steenwijk Canal 布克斯－斯滕维克运河	A popular Dutch tourist destination both within the Netherlands and abroad. Giethoorn, without any road

S/N 序号	CITY 城市	COUNTRY 国家	CONTINENT 大洲
20	Groningen 格罗宁根	The Netherlands 荷兰	Europe 欧洲
21	Göteborg 哥德堡	Sweden 瑞典	Europe 欧洲

CANAL(S) RELATED 相关运河	CITY PROFILE 城市简介
	at all, is often referred to as "the Venice of the North" or "the Venice of the Netherlands" for its only full accessibility by boat and canal. 享誉荷兰国内外的旅游胜地。羊角村没有陆路，以运河行船为主要交通方式，有着"北方威尼斯"和"荷兰威尼斯"的美称。
Ems Canal 埃姆斯运河 Ter Apel Canal 泰尔阿珀尔运河 North–Willems Canal 北威廉斯运河	A cultural, industrial, and commercial centre, as well as a waterway and railway traffic hub, of the Netherlands. Groningen hosts one of Europe's oldest university, the University of Groningen. Like many Dutch cities, Groningen has beautiful canals around the centre. These canals give the vibrant city a charming character. 荷兰文化、商贸与工业中心，也是运河、公路和铁路枢纽。格罗宁根拥有欧洲最古老的大学之一格罗宁根大学。荷兰许多城市运河遍布，格罗宁根亦如此，多条风光旖旎的运河环绕格罗宁根市中心，使这座活力城市充满魅力。
Göta Canal 约塔运河	A famous port city on the southwest coast of Sweden, the major port for navigation between Sweden and Western Europe, and the industrial centre of Northern Europe. The Göta Canal connects Göteborg to the Swedish capital Stockholm, forming one of the country's major transport arteries. 瑞典西南部海岸著名港口城市，是瑞典和西欧通航的主要港埠，北欧工业中心。约塔运河连接斯德哥尔摩和哥德堡，是瑞典的交通大动脉之一。

S/N 序号	CITY 城市	COUNTRY 国家	CONTINENT 大洲
22	Guilin 桂林	China 中国	Asia 亚洲
23	Handan 邯郸	China 中国	Asia 亚洲
24	Hangzhou 杭州	China 中国	Asia 亚洲

CANAL(S) RELATED	CITY PROFILE
相关运河	城市简介

Lingqu Canal

灵渠

Ancient Guijiang-Liujiang Canal

古桂柳运河

A city in the northeast of Guangxi Zhuang Autonomous Region, China. Guilin is often acclaimed as "a land with the most beautiful landscape under heaven". The Lingqu Canal connects the Xiangjiang River of the Yangtze River system and the Lijiang River of the Pearl River system. The Ancient Guijiang-Liujiang Canal served as a vital link and transport route between the central government and the ethnic minority groups in southwest China. The two canals had contributed to Guilin's strategic geographical position in ancient China.

中国广西壮族自治区东北部城市。桂林素有山水甲天下之美誉。灵渠连接湘江和漓江，沟通了长江、珠江两大水系，是世界上最古老的运河之一。古桂柳运河是历史上中央政府通过西南重镇桂林联系少数民族地区的纽带和军需通道，沟通了漓江和柳江水系。这两条运河奠定了桂林在古代中国的战略地位。

Grand Canal (China)

中国大运河

A prefecture-level city located in the southwest of Hebei Province, China. The Handan section constitutes one of the earliest sections of the Grand Canal (China).

中国河北省西南部地级市。大运河邯郸段是中国大运河的肇始地之一。

Grand Canal (China)

中国大运河

Capital of Zhejiang Province, China. Hangzhou is the southern terminal point of the Beijing-Hangzhou Grand Canal. Gongchen Bridge is the landmark of the Grand Canal in Hangzhou. China's Beijing-Hangzhou Grand Canal Museum stands near the Gongchen Bridge. It is the first large-scale special museum on the theme

S/N 序号	CITY 城市	COUNTRY 国家	CONTINENT 大洲
25	Huai'an 淮安	China 中国	Asia 亚洲

CANAL(S) RELATED
相关运河

CITY PROFILE
城市简介

of canal culture in China. The museum was officially opened on 1 October 2006. Today, cargo ships still sail on the 39-kilometre-long Hangzhou section of the waterway. Hangzhou is now a vibrant metropolis of e-commerce in China as well as a nodal city in the ecological economic corridor of the Yangtze River Delta region.

中国浙江省省会。杭州是京杭大运河南端终点。拱宸桥是古运河到杭州的终点标志。中国京杭大运河博物馆毗邻拱宸桥，是中国第一座以运河文化为主题的大型专题博物馆，于2006年10月1日向公众开放。目前，长39千米的大运河杭州段仍可通行货船。杭州如今是中国重要的电子商务中心，也是长三角生态经济带节点城市。

Grand Canal (China)
中国大运河

A prefecture-level city in central Jiangsu province, China. As the hometown of Zhou Enlai, the former premier of China, Huai'an is situated on the Grand Canal. Huai'an was the seat of the Caoyun Governor's Office during the Ming and Qing Dynasties. Huai'an, together with Suzhou, Hangzhou and Yangzhou, have been ranked as the four major cities along the Grand Canal in ancient times. The Huai'an section of the Grand Canal, 36 kilometres long, was an important part of the canal inscribed on the list of World Heritage of the UNESCO in 2014. In recent years, the Huai'an Grand Canal Office has made every effort to promote the unified management and maintenance of public facilities along the Inner Canal Cultural Corridor.

中国江苏省中部地级市。淮安地处大运河河畔，是周恩来总理的故乡，明清时期是漕运总督府所在地。淮安与

S/N 序号	CITY 城市	COUNTRY 国家	CONTINENT 大洲
26	Huaibei 淮北	China 中国	Asia 亚洲
27	Inverness 因弗内斯	The United Kingdom 英国	Europe 欧洲

CANAL(S) RELATED 相关运河	CITY PROFILE 城市简介
	苏州、杭州、扬州并称大运河四大古城。2014年，中国大运河被列入联合国教科文组织世界遗产名录，长36千米的大运河淮安段亦包括在内。近年来，淮安市大运河文化带规划建设管理办公室积极致力于里运河文化长廊的统一管理与维护。
Grand Canal (China) 中国大运河	A prefecture-level city in northern Anhui Province, China. Excavations of the Liuzi Relics Site of the Sui-Tang Grand Canal testifies to the accurate path of the ancient Tongji Canal, which was part of the ancient China Grand Canal in the Sui and Tang Dynasties. In early 1976, Huaibei Museum, also known as the Museum of the Sui-Tang Dynasties Grand Canal, was established. As a prominent spreader of China's Grand Canal culture, the museum houses the archeological site of a section of the Grand Canal watercourse. 中国安徽省北部地级市。淮北市柳孜隋唐大运河遗址的考古重大发现证明了通济渠的确切走向。1976年初，淮北博物馆成立，也被称为隋唐大运河博物馆。该馆是传播大运河文化的重要场馆，建在一段大运河水道考古遗址之上。
Caledonian Canal 喀里多尼亚运河	Capital of the Scottish Highlands, a tourist destination in northern Britain, well-known for the Loch Ness. The Caledonian Canal was opened in 1822, linking the area's east and west coasts, and Inverness is situated at the canal's eastern end. 苏格兰高地地区首府，英国北部著名旅游城市，因尼斯湖而闻名。1822年，喀里多尼亚运河通航，将苏格兰北部的东、西海岸连接起来，其中最东端便是因弗内斯。

S/N 序号	CITY 城市	COUNTRY 国家	CONTINENT 大洲
28	Jining 济宁	China 中国	Asia 亚洲
29	Kampong Cham 磅湛	Cambodia 柬埔寨	Asia 亚洲
30	Kiel 基尔	Germany 德国	Europe 欧洲

CANAL(S) RELATED
相关运河

CITY PROFILE
城市简介

Grand Canal (China)
中国大运河

A prefecture-level city in southwestern Shandong Province, China. The highest point and the Nanwang Water Diversion Project is situated in Wenshang, a county-level city under the jurisdiction of Jining. Jining has nurtured the top five sages of the Chinese philosophy, Confucius, Mencius, Zengzi, Yan Hui and Zisi. The Grand Canal that runs through Jining contributed to Jining's commercial prosperity and brought in diverse lifestyles.

中国山东省西南部地级市。中国大运河最高点及南旺分水枢纽位于济宁市汶上县。济宁是中国哲学五圣——孔子、孟子、曾子、颜回和子思的故乡。贯穿济宁的中国大运河促进了该城的商业繁荣，带来了多彩生活。

Mekong River
湄公河

The fourth largest city in Cambodia, located in the central part of Kampong Cham Province, on the west bank of the Mekong River. Kampong Cham has rubber, weaving, brewing, oil extraction, rice milling, and agricultural machinery factories, and is a distribution centre for rice, corn, and tobacco. Located on the Mekong River, it is an important waterway transportation hub in Cambodia.

磅湛市是柬埔寨第四大城市，位于磅湛省中部，湄公河西岸。磅湛市有橡胶、织布、酿酒、榨油、碾米和农机等工厂，是稻米、玉米、烟草等物的集散地。磅湛位于湄公河畔，是柬埔寨重要的水路交通枢纽。

Kiel Canal
基尔运河

A port city in northern Germany. Kiel lies at the Baltic end of the Kiel Canal, and is a railway hub and fishing base. Today, the Kiel Canal remains the safest, cheap-

S/N 序号	CITY 城市	COUNTRY 国家	CONTINENT 大洲
31	Kingston 金斯顿	Canada 加拿大	America 美洲
32	Kratié 桔井	Cambodia 柬埔寨	Asia 亚洲

CANAL(S) RELATED	CITY PROFILE
相关运河	城市简介

est, and the most convenient shipping route between the North Sea and the Baltic Sea. The Kieler Woche (Kiel Week), a festive occasion celebrated in June every year, is the one of the world's most influential sailing tournament.

德国北部港口城市。基尔位于基尔运河注入波罗的海的入海处，是铁路枢纽和渔业基地。目前，基尔运河是北海与波罗的海之间最经济便捷且安全可靠的线路。每年六月的传统节日活动项目"基尔帆船赛"（"基尔周"）是世界最有影响力的帆船比赛项目之一。

Rideau Canal
里多运河

An ancient capital and tourist city of Canada. Kingston's location at the Rideau Canal entrance to Lake Ontario made it the primary military and economic centre of Upper Canada after canal construction was completed in 1832.

加拿大古都，重要旅游城市。金斯顿位于里多运河注入安大略湖入口处。里多运河1832年竣工开通后，金斯顿成为上加拿大地区的军事、经济中心。

Mekong River
湄公河

A city in eastern Cambodia, located along the Mekong River. Kratié is the end point of water transportation on the Mekong River in Cambodia. Therefore, the city is commercially developed and functions as a distribution centre for wood, horns, leather, corn, tobacco, rubber, beans, and kapok.

柬埔寨东部城市，位于湄公河沿岸。桔井市是柬埔寨境内湄公河水运的终点，商业发达，是木材、牛角、皮革、玉米、烟草、橡胶，豆类、木棉等物的集散地。

S/N 序号	CITY 城市	COUNTRY 国家	CONTINENT 大洲
33	La Louvière 拉卢维耶尔	Belgium 比利时	Europe 欧洲
34	Liaocheng 聊城	China 中国	Asia 亚洲
35	Liège 列日	Belgium 比利时	Europe 欧洲

CANAL(S) RELATED 相关运河	CITY PROFILE 城市简介
Central Canal (Belgium) 比利时中央运河	A centre of steel industry in south Belgium. The four boat lifts on the Central Canal are a marvel of the Europe's hydraulic engineering practice in the 19th century, and are collectively inscribed onto the UNESCO World Heritage List. 比利时南部城市，钢铁工业中心。中央运河上的四座船舶升降机是19世纪欧洲水利工程史上的奇迹。它们与周边设施一起被列入联合国教科文组织世界遗产名录。
Grand Canal (China) 中国大运河	A prefecture-level city in western Shandong Province, China. The Yellow River, often called the cradle of Chinese civilization, meets the Grand Canal at Liaocheng. The oldest section of the Grand Canal happens to be at Linqing's port, built in the Yuan Dynasty (1271—1368). Linqing, under the jurisdiction of Liaocheng, was known for its quality bricks. The bricks were transmitted to Beijing via the Grand Canal for building the Forbidden City. Linqing owes its historical prosperity to the Grand Canal traffic. 中国山东省西部地级市。被誉为中国文明摇篮的黄河在聊城与大运河交汇。修建于元朝的临清港是大运河最古老的河段。隶属聊城的临清市以出产优质砖块闻名于世。这些优质砖顺着大运河"漂"至北京，用以建造紫禁城。临清市因大运河而兴盛。
Albert Canal 阿尔贝特运河	One of the major metropolis and industrial centres of Belgium, and the third largest river port in Europe. The site of the Battle of Liège during World War I. The Albert Canal connects the city of Liège to Europe's major sea ports like Antwerp and Rotterdam.

S/N 序号	CITY 城市	COUNTRY 国家	CONTINENT 大洲
36	Lille 里尔	France 法国	Europe 欧洲
37	Liverpool 利物浦	The United Kingdom 英国	Europe 欧洲

CANAL(S) RELATED 相关运河	CITY PROFILE 城市简介
	比利时主要大城市、工业中心之一，欧洲第三大河港，第一次世界大战当中著名的"列日要塞战役"发生地。阿尔贝特运河将列日与安特卫普、鹿特丹等欧洲主要海港相连。
Roubaix Canal 鲁贝运河 Tourcoing Canal 图尔宽运河	One of France's biggest industrial cities. Lille was designated the European Capital of Culture in 2004. The area surrounding Lille boasts the largest concentration of canals in France, including the Roubaix Canal and the Tourcoing Canal, most of which are still navigable today. 法国最大工业城市之一，2004年被评选为欧洲文化之都。里尔地区是法国运河最密集的地区之一，主要运河包括鲁贝运河、图尔宽运河等，大部分运河当前仍可通航。
Leeds and Liverpool Canal 利兹－利物浦运河	A sea port city on the northwest coast of England, the fourth largest city of the UK, and one of the country's major areas of Industrial Revolution. The Leeds and Liverpool Canal, opened in 1816, linked Liverpool to another industrializing city Leeds, the production and trading centre of wool and an inland traffic hub, and served as a transport artery of raw materials in the Industrial Revolution era. 英格兰西北部港口城市，英国第四大城市，工业革命主要地区之一。1816年，利兹－利物浦运河正式通航，将利物浦与英格兰内地的另一座工业革命城市、羊毛生产和贸易中心、交通枢纽利兹相连，成为英国工业革命时代一条原材料运输大动脉。

S/N 序号	CITY 城市	COUNTRY 国家	CONTINENT 大洲
38	Llangollen 兰戈伦	The United Kingdom 英国	Europe 欧洲
39	Luoyang 洛阳	China 中国	Asia 亚洲

CANAL(S) RELATED	CITY PROFILE
相关运河	城市简介

Llangollen Canal
兰戈伦运河

A British memory of the era of Industrial Revolution. Llangollen is the site of UNESCO World Heritage Pontcysyllte Aqueduct and Canal, which carries the Llangollen Canal across River Dee in northeastern Wales. The Pontcysyllte Aqueduct and Canal are recognized as an innovative ensemble that inspired many projects all over the world.

保有英国工业革命时代遗迹的城市。兰戈伦是联合国教科文组织世界遗产旁特塞斯特渡槽和运河所在地。旁特塞斯特渡槽使得兰戈伦运河跨越威尔士东北部的迪河，工程富有创意，受人瞩目，为后世诸多工程所效仿。

Grand Canal (China)
中国大运河

A prefecture-level city in the west of Henan Province, China. Luoyang was important in history as the capital of nine dynasties and as a Buddhist centre. In the Sui Dynasty (581–618 AD), Emperor Yang ordered the construction of the Grand Canal. The Grand Canal was centred at Luoyang. The canal became the main artery for traffic between north and south at that time, and consequently Luoyang developed more prosperously. The Grand Canal was added to UNESCO's World Heritage list in 2014, and two Grand Canal heritage sites are located in Luoyang.

中国河南省西部地级市。洛阳曾是九朝之都和佛教中心。隋朝时，隋炀帝下令开凿大运河，即以洛阳为中心。大运河后成为贯通南北的交通大动脉，洛阳城也因此繁荣起来。2014年，中国大运河成功入选世界遗产名录。大运河有两处遗址位于洛阳。

S/N 序号	CITY 城市	COUNTRY 国家	CONTINENT 大洲
40	Maaseik 马塞克	Belgium 比利时	Europe 欧洲
41	Manchester 曼彻斯特	The United Kingdom 英国	Europe 欧洲
42	Milan 米兰	Italy 意大利	Europe 欧洲

CANAL(S) RELATED
相关运河

CITY PROFILE
城市简介

Maas
马斯河

The 8th largest municipality in Limburg, Belgium, known as the assumed birthplace of the famous Flemish painters Jan and Hubert van Eyck. The Maas (also called the Meuse), which flows through Masseik, is an essential part of navigation in Belgium and serves as the border between Belgium and the Netherlands.

比利时林堡省第八大市镇，著名画家范艾克兄弟相传出生于此。马斯河，亦称默兹河，流经马塞克镇，是比利时航运系统的重要组成部分，构成比利时和荷兰的边界。

Manchester Ship Canal
曼彻斯特通海运河

An important traffic hub and commercial, industrial and cultural centre of Great Britain. Manchester is the world's first industrialized city. Initially an inland city, Manchester became a sea port thanks to the opening of the Manchester Ship Canal in the 1890s, which greatly bolstered its position in Britain's foreign trade geography.

英国重要交通枢纽与商业、工业、文化中心。曼彻斯特是世界上第一座工业化城市。该城本为内陆城市，19世纪90年代，曼彻斯特通海运河开凿通航，曼彻斯特成为海港城市，大大提高了曼彻斯特市在英国外贸格局中的地位。

Grand Canal (Italy)
米兰大运河

The second largest metropolis of Italy, and one of the Europe's four economic centres. In 1258 the Grand Canal reached Milan, and the whole canal was finally navigable in 1272. The Grand Canal is one of the largest post-medieval engineering projects, which contributed significantly to the development of commerce, transport and agriculture.

S/N 序号	CITY 城市	COUNTRY 国家	CONTINENT 大洲
43	Milwaukee 密尔沃基	The United States 美国	America 美洲
44	Moscow 莫斯科	Russia 俄罗斯	Europe 欧洲

CANAL(S) RELATED
相关运河

CITY PROFILE
城市简介

意大利第二大城市，欧洲四大经济中心之一。1258年，米兰大运河连通米兰。1272年，运河实现全线通航。米兰大运河是中世纪以来最宏大的水利工程之一，为当时的商业、交通以及农业发展做出了巨大贡献。

Burnham Canal
伯纳姆运河

The largest city in the state of Wisconsin and an important port city of the United States. Milwaukee lies along the shores of Lake Michigan at the confluence of three rivers: the Menomonee, the Kinnickinnic, and the Milwaukee. Because of its easy access to Lake Michigan and other waterways, Milwaukee's Menomonee Valley has historically been home to manufacturing, rendering plants, shipping, and other heavy industries. Canals of Milwaukee includes the Holtons Canal, the South Menomonee Canal, the Burnham Canal, etc.

美国威斯康星州最大城市和重要港口城市。密尔沃基毗邻密歇根湖，三条河流，即梅诺莫尼河、基尼基尼克河与密尔沃基河在此交汇。由于靠近多个水道，密尔沃基的梅诺莫尼河谷地区在历史上一直是制造业、提炼厂、航运和其他重工业所在地。密尔沃基市内有霍尔顿斯运河、南梅诺莫尼运河、伯纳姆运河等。

Moscow Canal
莫斯科运河

Capital of Russia, the country's political, economic, cultural, financial, and transport centre. The Moscow Canal links the city to the Volga River. Direct water traffic to the sea from Moscow was thus made possible. Moscow becomes a "port of five seas" connecting the White Sea, the Baltic Sea, the Caspian Sea, the Black Sea and the Sea of Azov.

S/N 序号	CITY 城市	COUNTRY 国家	CONTINENT 大洲
45	New York 纽约	The United States 美国	America 美洲
46	Ningbo 宁波	China 中国	Asia 亚洲
47	Offenbach 美因河畔奥芬巴赫	Germany 德国	Europe 欧洲

CANAL(S) RELATED 相关运河	CITY PROFILE 城市简介
	俄罗斯首都，也是该国政治、经济、文化、金融、交通中心。莫斯科运河将莫斯科与伏尔加河直接相连，使得水上交通可以直通大海，莫斯科也由此成为"五海之港"，连接白海、波罗的海、里海、黑海、亚速海。
Erie Canal 伊利运河	The biggest metropolis and port city of the United States, and the world's most influential financial centre. The Erie Canal and the Hudson River connect the Great Lakes areas to the city of New York. New York's prosperity as a port city was, to a very large extent, attributable to the opening of the Erie Canal in the late 19th century. 美国第一大城市和第一大港口，世界第一大经济中心。伊利运河通过哈得孙河将北美五大湖与纽约市连接起来。纽约得益于19世纪末期伊利运河的开通，迅速成为繁荣的港口城市。
Grand Canal (China) 中国大运河	A sub-provincial city in Zhejiang Province, China. Ningbo is the junction between the Grand Canal and the Maritime Silk Road. In view of this fact, the Grand Canal is not only a water passage connecting China's north and south, but also a major channel connecting the world. 中国浙江省副省级城市。宁波是大运河与海上丝绸之路的连接点城市。可以说，大运河不仅是贯通中国南北的水道，也是连通世界的重要航道。
Mein 美因河	A central German city with the highest proportion of foreigners and an important industrial and service city in Germany. Offenbach is located on the southeast bank of the Main River and borders Frankfurt. Commercial activities and trade exhibitions have been very devel-

S/N 序号	CITY 城市	COUNTRY 国家	CONTINENT 大洲
48	Orleans 奥尔良	France 法国	Europe 欧洲
49	Otaru 小樽	Japan 日本	Asia 亚洲

CANAL(S) RELATED 相关运河	CITY PROFILE 城市简介

oped in the past 100 years, and the leather industry is world-renowned. The Offenbach Barrage was built in Offenbach's Main River section to further promote the canalization of the Main River to Offenbach.

德国中部城市，外籍人口占比最高的德国城市，也是德国重要的工业与服务业城市。奥芬巴赫坐落于美因河东南岸，毗邻法兰克福。近百年来，该地区的商业活动、贸易展览十分发达，皮革工业更是享誉全球。美因河的奥芬巴赫段建有奥芬巴赫拦河坝，进一步提高了美因河到奥芬巴赫的运河化程度。

Orleans Canal
奥尔良运河

A city in north-central France. Located about 120 kilometres southwest of Paris, Orleans is the capital of the Loiret department and of the Centre-Val de Loire region. Orleans has benefited from the decentralization of Paris during World War II, and has developed new industries such as textiles, food processing, and the manufacture of machinery. Near the town centre is the Orleans Canal, which links the Loire River at Orleans.

法国中北部城市，中央大区的首府，卢瓦尔省省会，距巴黎120千米。第二次世界大战期间，巴黎工业疏散分布，受益于此，奥尔良市发展了纺织、食品加工、机械制造等新工业。奥尔良运河从奥尔良市中心附近穿过，并在此连通卢瓦尔河。

Otaru Canal
小樽运河

A port city near Sapporo, Japan. Otaru is an economic centre of the west coast of Hokkaido. The Otaru Canal is the city's representative tourist attraction. Its beautifully preserved canal area and interesting herring mansions make Otaru a pleasant travel destination.

S/N 序号	CITY 城市	COUNTRY 国家	CONTINENT 大洲
50	Ottawa 渥太华	Canada 加拿大	America 美洲
51	Palembang 巨港	Indonesia 印度尼西亚	Asia 亚洲
52	Panama City 巴拿马	Panama 巴拿马	America 美洲

CANAL(S) RELATED 相关运河	CITY PROFILE 城市简介
	日本札幌的外港城市。小樽是北海道西海岸经济中心。该城因其保存完好的运河区与独具特色的鲱御殿成为令人神往的旅游胜地。
Rideau Canal 里多运河	Capital of Canada. The Rideau Canal flows north to south through downtown Ottawa. It is an important tourist attraction as well as the oldest continuously operating canal in North America. 加拿大首都。里多运河由北向南穿越渥太华市区，是这座首都城市重要的旅游资源，也是北美洲历史最久而仍在使用的运河。
Sekanak Canal 塞卡纳克运河	Capital of South Sumatra Province, Indonesia, and the largest port and trade centre in southern Sumatra. Many modern commercial centres in Palembang stand on both sides of the Sekanak Canal, and the canal has become one of the most popular tourist attractions in the city. 印度尼西亚南苏门答腊省首府，苏门答腊岛南部最大港口与贸易中心。巨港市的许多现代商业中心分布于塞卡纳克运河两岸，塞卡纳克运河由此成为该市最受欢迎的旅游景点之一。
Panama Canal 巴拿马运河	Capital of the Republic of Panama. Panama City is situated at the Pacific end of the Panama Canal. The canal traverses the Isthmus of Panama, connecting the Pacific Ocean and the Atlantic Ocean, and is a strategic navigation channel for the world. 巴拿马共和国首都。巴拿马位于巴拿马运河太平洋端的入口。巴拿马运河横穿巴拿马地峡，连接太平洋和大西洋，是世界航运的战略要道。

S/N 序号	CITY 城市	COUNTRY 国家	CONTINENT 大洲
53	Port Said 塞得港	Egypt 埃及	Africa 非洲
54	Rimini 里米尼	Italy 意大利	Europe 欧洲
55	Rotterdam 鹿特丹	The Netherlands 荷兰	Europe 欧洲

CANAL(S) RELATED 相关运河	CITY PROFILE 城市简介
Suez Canal 苏伊士运河	A port city located at the northern end of the Suez Canal. Port Said is a major port in Egypt, serving ships and vessels traveling to and from the canal and for the expor of Egyptian products. It was founded in 1859 at the beginning of the construction of the Suez Canal. 苏伊士运河北端港口城市。塞得港是埃及主要港口，往来船只经此往返于苏伊士运河，埃及商品经此港出口。1859年，苏伊士运河修建之初，该城设立。
Port Canal 港口运河	A city in northern Italy, one of the most notable seaside resorts in Europe. Rimini sprawls along the Adriatic Sea with a coastline of 15 kilometres between the Marecchia River and the Ausa River. Revenues from both internal and international tourism form a significant portion of the city's economy. 意大利北部城市，欧洲最著名的海滨度假地之一。里米尼位于亚得里亚海海滨，在马雷基亚河和奥萨河之间，拥有15千米沙滩海岸线。国内和国际旅游收入构成该市经济的重要组成部分。
Delfshaven Schie Canal 斯希运河代尔夫斯哈芬段 Delft Schie Canal 斯希运河代尔夫特段 Oranje Canal 奥拉涅运河	The second largest city and municipality in the Netherlands. Rotterdam is located at the mouth of the New Maas Channel leading into the Rhine–Meuse–Schelde delta at the North Sea. Rotterdam is the largest port in Europe, with the Maas River and the Rhine River providing excellent access to the hinterland upstream reaching Basel, Switzerland and France. The port's main activities are petrochemical industries and general cargo handling and transshipment. The harbour functions as an important transit point for bulk materi-

S/N 序号	CITY 城市	COUNTRY 国家	CONTINENT 大洲
56	San Antonio 圣安东尼奥	The United States 美国	America 美洲
57	Stockholm 斯德哥尔摩	Sweden 瑞典	Europe 欧洲

CANAL(S) RELATED 相关运河	CITY PROFILE 城市简介
	als between the European continent and overseas. The extensive distribution system including rail, roads, and waterways has earned Rotterdam the reputation as the "Gateway to Europe" and "Gateway to the World". 荷兰第二大城市和自治市，位于通往北海莱茵-默兹-斯海尔德三角洲的新马斯海峡入海口。鹿特丹是欧洲最大的港口，马斯河和莱茵河为通往腹地上游的瑞士巴塞尔和法国提供了绝佳的便利通道。该港口主要提供石化工业和一般货物的装卸和转运服务，是欧洲大陆与海外之间大宗物品的重要中转站。包括铁路、公路和水路在内的大范围配送系统为鹿特丹赢得了"欧洲之门"和"世界之门"的美誉。
San Antonio Canal 圣安东尼奥运河	The seventh most populous city of the United States. The San Antonio Canal was initially opened for drainage and flood control purposes in the 1930s. However, the ingenious and successful development of the lands along the canal has made the city of San Antonio one of the top tourist destinations in the country. 美国人口第七多城市。圣安东尼奥运河原本是20世纪30年代为治理洪水而开凿，因运河沿线的旅游开发非常成功，很有特色，圣安东尼奥进而成为全美旅游最热门的旅游胜地之一。
Göta Canal 约塔运河	Capital and the largest metropolis of Sweden, and the seat of the national government, parliament, and royal palaces. The Göta Canal links Stockholm and Goteborg, playing a significant role in the development of Sweden's domestic trade. 瑞典首都和第一大城市，瑞典国家政府、国会以及皇

S/N 序号	CITY 城市	COUNTRY 国家	CONTINENT 大洲
58	Strasbourg 斯特拉斯堡	France 法国	Europe 欧洲
59	Terneuzen 特尔纽曾	The Netherlands 荷兰	Europe 欧洲
60	Tianjin 天津	China 中国	Asia 亚洲

CANAL(S) RELATED 相关运河	CITY PROFILE 城市简介
	室宫殿所在地。约塔运河是连接斯德哥尔摩和哥德堡之间的水路纽带，对促进瑞典国内贸易的发展起到了巨大作用。
Marne-Rhine Canal 马恩－莱茵运河 Rhône-Rhine Canal 罗讷－莱茵运河	The biggest border city of France, the headquarters of many European institutions, including the European Council, European Parliament, and European Court of Human Rights. Strasbourg is therefore known as the "Capital of Europe". The city is the starting point of the Marne-Rhine Canal and the Rhône-Rhine Canal, making itself a hub for France's trade with Europe's heartland. 法国最大边境城市，欧盟多个重要机构，如欧洲委员会、欧洲议会、欧洲人权法院等，均在此设立总部，因而被称作"欧洲首都"。马恩－莱茵运河和罗纳－莱茵运河均始于斯特拉斯堡，使该市成为法国与欧洲腹地贸易的枢纽。
Ghent-Terneuzen Canal 根特－特尔纽曾运河	The most populous municipality of the province of Zeeland, the southwestern Netherlands. Terneuzen is located on the southern shore of the Western Schelde estuary. The port of Terneuzen is the third largest in the Netherlands, only next to those of Rotterdam and Amsterdam. 特尔纽曾是荷兰西南部西兰省人口最多的城市，位于西斯海尔德河口的南岸。特尔纽曾港是荷兰第三大港口，仅次于鹿特丹和阿姆斯特丹。
Grand Canal (China) 中国大运河	One of the four municipalities of China. Tianjin is now the economic centre of the Bohai Economic Rim. His-

S/N 序号	CITY 城市	COUNTRY 国家	CONTINENT 大洲
61	Toulouse 图卢兹	France 法国	Europe 欧洲
62	Venice 威尼斯	Italy 意大利	Europe 欧洲

CANAL(S) RELATED 相关运河	CITY PROFILE 城市简介
	torically, Tianjin was a ferry terminal for transporting grain and silk from southern to northern China. As a folk saying goes, Tianjin is a city that has been carried by the Grand Canal. 中国四大直辖市之一，环渤海地区经济中心。历史上的天津是南方粮食和丝绸北运的水路码头，民间有"天津是大运河载来的城市"的说法。
Midi Canal 米迪运河	The fourth largest city of France, centre of Europe's aerospace industry, and the headquarters of Airbus, the Galileo positioning system. The Midi Canal and the Garonne River converge at Toulouse, and the French's centuries-old dream of a direct navigation from the Mediterranean Sea to the Atlantic Ocean came true. 法国第四大城市，欧洲航空航天工业中心，是空中客车、伽利略卫星定位系统的总部所在地。米迪运河和加龙河在此交汇，使法国数百年来连通大西洋和地中海的梦想成真。
Grand Canal (Venice) 威尼斯大运河	Capital of Veneto, a famous tourist and industrial city in northeast Italy. Venice's transport network is mainly built along the Grand Canal. As one of the city's main waterway corridors, the canal is famous for the centuries-old buildings on the banks in Romanesque, Gothic, and Renaissance styles. 意大利威尼托地区首府，该国东北部著名的旅游与工业城市。威尼斯全市大部分交通网络皆沿大运河修建。作为威尼斯水上交通要道之一，该运河因其两岸的建筑而闻名，这些建筑大多有数百年历史，风格各异，包括罗马式、哥特式和文艺复兴式等。

S/N 序号	CITY 城市	COUNTRY 国家	CONTINENT 大洲
63	Volgograd 伏尔加格勒	Russia 俄罗斯	Europe 欧洲
64	Wuxi 无锡	China 中国	Asia 亚洲
65	Yangon 仰光	Myanmar 缅甸	Asia 亚洲

CANAL(S) RELATED	CITY PROFILE
相关运河	城市简介

Volga-Don Ship Canal
伏尔加－顿河通海运河

One of Russia's oldest cities and an important industrial centre. Volgagrad lies on the Volga River, and is hailed the granary of southern Russia. The Volga-Don Ship Canal links the lower streams of the Volga River to the Don River, flowing into the Azov Sea. The city was renamed during the Soviet era to Stalingrad, a focus for contention on the Soviet-German battlefield during World War II.

俄罗斯历史古城，重要工业中心。伏尔加格勒位于伏尔加河畔，被誉为俄罗斯"南部粮仓"。伏尔加－顿河通海运河连接伏尔加河下游河段与顿河，最终注入亚速海。苏联时期，该城曾改名斯大林格勒，并以第二次世界大战时期苏德战场上的斯大林格勒战役闻名于世。

Grand Canal (China)
中国大运河

A prefecture-level city in southern Jiangsu Province, China. The Grand Canal flows for around 40 kilometres through the entire city of Wuxi. The Wuxi section of the Grand Canal is an intact section of the canal. It witnessed Wuxi's economic development.

中国江苏省南部地级市。大运河无锡段纵贯无锡城区，全长逾40千米，是大运河中保存最完整的一段，见证了无锡的经济发展。

Yangon Canal
仰光运河

Old capital of Myanmar, with Yangon Port, the largest port in Myanmar and one of the largest ports in Southeast Asia. The Yangon Canal is the main channel to Yangon. It can be used for ocean-going ships and is adjacent to the Yangon Port. It plays a key role in the economic and social development of Myanmar and has become an important transportation hub integrat-

768 · List of Major Canal Cities and Towns Worldwide

S/N 序号	CITY 城市	COUNTRY 国家	CONTINENT 大洲
66	Yangzhou 扬州	China 中国	Asia 亚洲

CANAL(S) RELATED	CITY PROFILE
相关运河	城市简介

ing trade transportation, urban traffic and tourism.

缅甸故都，拥有缅甸最大港口、东南亚最大港口之一的仰光港。仰光运河是通往仰光的主要通道，可供远洋船舶航行，且毗邻仰光港，在缅甸经济社会发展中发挥着关键作用，成为集贸易运输、市内交通和旅游观光为一体的重要交通枢纽。

Grand Canal (China)
中国大运河

A prefecture-level city in central Jiangsu Province, China. Yangzhou is the leading city on the Grand Canal. The Hangou Ancient Canal, the earliest section of the Grand Canal, was opened in Yangzhou in the late Spring and Autumn Period (770—476 BC). Thanks to its strategic location at the junction of the Yangtze River and the Grand Canal, which are China's most important waterway transport arteries, Yangzhou retained a prominent position in ancient China's economic geography. The China Grand Canal Museum, located on the bank of the Sanwan section of the ancient canal, was opened to the public on 16 June 2021. It is a museum that fully reflects the history and the current state of the Grand Canal as well as the social life of people along the canal. The exhibitions can be called the "encyclopedia" of the Grand Canal.

中国江苏省中部地级市。扬州有着"中国运河第一城"的美誉。春秋时期吴王夫差开凿邗沟，在扬州挖下了大运河的第一锹土。由于地处长江和大运河这两条中国水路交通大动脉的交汇点，扬州在中国古代经济地理中地位显著。2021年6月16日，坐落于三湾古运河畔的扬州中国大运河博物馆向公众开放。该馆旨在全方位展示大运河历史、现状与风土人情，堪称中国大运河的"百科全书"。

S/N 序号	CITY 城市	COUNTRY 国家	CONTINENT 大洲
67	Zhengzhou 郑州	China 中国	Asia 亚洲
68	Zhitomir 日托米尔	Ukraine 乌克兰	Europe 欧洲

CANAL(S) RELATED
相关运河

CITY PROFILE
城市简介

Grand Canal (China)
中国大运河

Capital of Henan Province, China. During the Sui and Tang Dynasties, Zhengzhou was a major transport and trading hub for its geographically central position in China. It was linked with the rest of China by a complex network of canals, one of which was the Tongji Canal, the western extension of the Grand Canal. Currently, Zhengzhou is designated one of China's national central cities.

中国河南省省会城市。隋唐时期，郑州因其地处中原成为重要的交通和贸易中心。凭借复杂的运河网，古时的郑州得以与其他地区相连通，其中包括大运河西侧延伸河段通济渠。如今，郑州已被列为国家中心城市。

Teteriv River
捷捷列夫河

The administrative centre of Zhitomir Province in the northwest of Ukraine. Zhitomir is also the industrial and cultural centre of this region. Enterprises in the city feature glass, metal fabrication, fabrics and others. The city lies on the banks of the Teteriv River, a tributary of the Dnieper River, and is a traffic junction connecting Warsaw, Kyiv, Minsk, Izmail, and several major cities of Ukraine. Zhitomir enjoys a superior natural environment, surrounded by forests on all sides through which flow several rivers. The city is also rich in city parks and squares.

乌克兰西北部日托米尔州首府。日托米尔也是这一区域的工业中心和文化中心。当地发展玻璃、金属制造、织物等产业。日托米尔坐落于第聂伯河支流捷捷列夫河畔，是连接华沙、基辅、明斯克、伊兹梅尔及乌克兰多个主要城市的交通枢纽。日托米尔自然环境优越，四面森林环绕，河流穿行于森林之中，城内公园广场林立。

Multilingual Glossary of World Canals

SOURCE NAME 原文名称	ENGLISH NAME 英语名称
Aarkanaal	Aar Canal
Aduarderdiep	Aduard Canal
A.G. Wildervanckkanaal	A.G. Wildervanck Canal
Albertkanaal	Albert Canal
Ålkistan	Ålkistan
Allerkanal	Aller Canal
Amstel-Drechtkanaal	Amstel-Drecht Canal
Amsterdam-Rijnkanaal	Amsterdam-Rhine Canal
Annerveenschekanaal	Annerveen Canal
Apeldoorns Kanaal	Apeldoorn Canal
Arembergergracht	Aremberger Canal
Balgzandkanaal	Balgzand Canal
Bảo Định Hà	Bảo Định Canal
Baťův Kanál	Bata Canal
Beatrixkanaal	Beatrix Canal
Bederkesa-Geeste-Kanal	Bederkesa-Geeste Canal
Beemsterringvaart	Beemster Ring Canal
Beerkanaal	Beer Canal
Bergsche Maas	Bergen Maas Canal
Berlikumerwijd	Berlikum Canal
Berlin-Spandauer Schifffahrtskanal	Berlin-Spandau Ship Canal
Besheersdiep	Besheers Canal
Beukersgracht	Beukers Canal
Bijlands Kanaal	Bijlands Canal
Bijleveld Kanaal	Bijleveld Canal
Biwako Sosui	Lake Biwa Canal

CHINESE NAME 中文名称	COUNTRY 所在国家	CONTINENT 所在洲
阿尔运河	荷兰	欧洲
爱德华德运河	荷兰	欧洲
维尔德万克运河	荷兰	欧洲
阿尔贝特运河	比利时	欧洲
阿尔希斯坦运河	瑞典	欧洲
阿勒尔运河	德国	欧洲
阿姆斯特尔－德雷赫特运河	荷兰	欧洲
阿姆斯特丹－莱茵运河	荷兰	亚洲
安纳芬运河	荷兰	欧洲
阿珀尔多伦运河	荷兰	欧洲
阿伦贝赫尔运河	荷兰	欧洲
巴尔赞德运河	荷兰	欧洲
保定运河	越南	亚洲
巴塔运河	捷克	欧洲
贝娅特丽克丝运河	荷兰	欧洲
贝德凯萨－盖斯特运河	德国	欧洲
贝姆斯特环形运河	荷兰	欧洲
贝尔运河	荷兰	欧洲
贝亨马斯运河	荷兰	欧洲
贝利克姆运河	荷兰	欧洲
柏林－施潘道通海运河	德国	欧洲
贝希尔斯运河	荷兰	欧洲
布克斯运河	荷兰	欧洲
白兰茨运河	荷兰	欧洲
拜勒费尔德运河	荷兰	欧洲
琵琶湖运河	日本	亚洲

SOURCE NAME 原文名称	ENGLISH NAME 英语名称
Bladderswijk	Bladder Canal
B.L. Tijdenskanaal	B. L. Tijdens Canal
Bobotski Kanal	Bobota Canal
Bolswardertrekvaart	Bolsward Trek Canal
Boterdiep	Boter Canal
Boudewijnkanaal	Boudewin Canal
Brandenburger Stadtkanal	Brandenburg City Canal
Breevaart	Bree Canal
Britzer Verbindungskanal	Britz Canal
Britzer Zweigkanal	Britz Branch Canal
Brugge-Oostende Kanal	Bruges-Ostend Canal
Buiten Ringvaart	Buiten Ring Canal
Burāla Branch	Burala Branch
Burumervaart	Burum Canal
Bützow-Güstrow Kanal	Bützow-Güstrow Canal

Calandkanaal	Caland Canal
Canal Baussengue	Baussengue Canal
Canal d'Aire	Aire Canal
Canal d'Aire à la Bassée	Aire-la Bassée Canal
Canal d'Arles à Fos	Arles-Fos Canal
Canal d'Asagni	Asagny Canal
Canal d'Assinie	Assinie Canal
Canal de Beaucaire	Beaucaire Canal
Canal de Bergues	Bergues Canal
Canal de Berry	Berry Canal
Canal de Beuvry	Beuvry Canal

CHINESE NAME 中文名称	COUNTRY 所在国家	CONTINENT 所在洲
布莱德运河	荷兰	欧洲
蒂登运河	荷兰	欧洲
博博塔运河	克罗地亚	欧洲
博尔斯瓦德拖船运河	荷兰	欧洲
伯特运河	荷兰	欧洲
鲍德温运河	比利时	欧洲
勃兰登堡市运河	德国	欧洲
布雷运河	荷兰	欧洲
布里茨运河	德国	欧洲
布里茨支线运河	德国	欧洲
布鲁日－奥斯坦德运河	比利时	欧洲
布登环形运河	荷兰	欧洲
布拉拉河支流	巴基斯坦	亚洲
布鲁默运河	荷兰	欧洲
比措－居斯特罗运河	德国	欧洲
卡兰运河	荷兰	欧洲
布桑格运河	法国	欧洲
艾尔河运河	法国	欧洲
艾尔－拉巴塞运河	法国	欧洲
阿尔勒－福斯运河	法国	欧洲
阿萨格尼运河	科特迪瓦	非洲
阿西尼运河	科特迪瓦	非洲
博凯尔运河	法国	欧洲
贝尔格运河	荷兰、法国	欧洲
贝里运河	法国	欧洲
伯夫里运河	法国	欧洲

SOURCE NAME 原文名称	ENGLISH NAME 英语名称
Canal de Bouc à Martigues	Bouc-Martigues Canal
Canal de Bourbourg	Bourbourg Canal
Canal de Bourgogne	Burgundy Canal
Canal de Briare	Briare Canal
Canal de Brienne	Brienne Canal
Canal de Brouage	Brouage Canal
Canal de Caen	Caen Canal
Canal de Calais	Calais Canal
Canal de Castilla	Castile Canal
Canal de Cazaux à la Teste	Cazaux-Teste Canal
Canal de Charleroi à Bruxelles	Charleroi-Brussels Canal
Canal de Chelles	Chelles Canal
Canal de Dunkerque à Veurne	Veurne-Dunkirk Canal
Canal de Furnes	Furnes Canal
Canal de Gallifet	Gallifet Canal
Canal de Garonne	Garonne Canal
Canal de Gieselau (Gieselaukanal)	Gieselau Canal
Canal de Givors	Givors Canal
Canal de Groguida	Groguida Canal
Canal de Haccourt à Visé	Haccourt-Visé Canal
Canal de Huningue	Huningue Canal
Canal de Jouy à Metz	Jouy-Metz Canal
Canal de la Basse Colme	Lower Colme Canal
Canal de la Bridoire	Bridoire Canal
Canal de la Bruche	Bruche Canal
Canal de la Charente à la Seudre	Charente-Seudre Canal
Canal de Lachine	Lachine Canal

CHINESE NAME 中文名称	COUNTRY 所在国家	CONTINENT 所在洲
布克－马蒂格运河	法国	欧洲
布尔堡运河	法国	欧洲
勃艮第运河	法国	欧洲
布里亚尔运河	法国	欧洲
布里耶纳运河	法国	欧洲
布鲁瓦日运河	法国	欧洲
卡昂运河	法国	欧洲
加莱运河	法国	欧洲
卡斯蒂亚利运河	西班牙	欧洲
卡佐泰斯特运河	法国	欧洲
沙勒罗瓦－布鲁塞尔运河	比利时	欧洲
谢勒运河	法国	欧洲
弗尔讷－敦刻尔克运河	跨国	欧洲
弗尔讷运河	法国	欧洲
加利费运河	法国	欧洲
加龙运河	法国	欧洲
吉塞劳运河	德国	欧洲
日沃尔运河	法国	欧洲
格罗吉达运河	科特迪瓦	非洲
哈库特－维塞运河	比利时	欧洲
于南格运河	法国	欧洲
茹伊－梅斯运河	法国	欧洲
科尔莫下游运河	跨国	欧洲
布里多瓦运河	法国	欧洲
布吕什运河	法国	欧洲
夏朗德－瑟德尔运河	法国	欧洲
拉欣运河	加拿大	美洲

SOURCE NAME 原文名称	ENGLISH NAME 英语名称
Canal de la Colme	Colme Canal
Canal de la Deûle	Deûle Canal
Canal de la Haute Colme	Upper Colme Canal
Canal de la Haute-Seine	Upper Seine Canal
Canal de l'Aisne	Aisne Canal
Canal de l'Aisne à la Marne	Aisne-Marne Canal
Canal de la Jeune Autize	Young Autize Canal
Canal de Lalinde	Lalinde Canal
Canal de la Marne à la Saône	Saône-Marne Canal
Canal de la Marne au Rhin	Marne-Rhine Canal
Canal de la Meuse	Meuse Canal
Canal de Lanaye	Lanaye Canal
Canal de la Nieppe	Nieppe Canal
Canal de la Robine	Robine Canal
Canal de la Rochelle	Rochelle Canal
Canal de la Sambre à l'Oise	Sambre-Oise Canal
Canal de la Sarre	Sarre Canal
Canal de la Sensée	Sensée Canal
Canal de la Souchez	Souchez Canal
Canal de la Vielle Autize	Old Autize Canal
Canal del Bío Bío	Bío-Bío Canal
Canal del Dique	Dique Canal
Canal de Lens	Lens Canal
Canal de l'Escaut	Escaut Canal
Canal de l'Espierres	Espierres Canal
Canal de l'Est	East Canal
Canal de l'Oise à l'Aisne	Oise-Aisne Canal

CHINESE NAME 中文名称	COUNTRY 所在国家	CONTINENT 所在洲
科尔莫运河	比利时、法国	欧洲
德勒运河	法国	欧洲
科尔莫上游运河	法国	欧洲
塞纳河上游运河	法国	欧洲
埃纳河运河	法国	欧洲
埃纳－马恩运河	法国	欧洲
新欧蒂兹运河	法国	欧洲
拉兰德运河	法国	欧洲
索恩－马恩运河	法国	欧洲
马恩－莱茵运河	法国	欧洲
默兹运河	法国	欧洲
拉奈运河	比利时、荷兰	欧洲
涅普运河	法国	欧洲
罗比纳运河	法国	欧洲
罗谢尔运河	法国	欧洲
桑布尔－瓦兹运河	跨国	欧洲
萨尔运河	法国	欧洲
桑塞运河	法国	欧洲
苏谢运河	法国	欧洲
旧欧蒂兹河运河	法国	欧洲
比奥－比奥运河	智利	美洲
狄克运河	哥伦比亚	美洲
朗斯运河	法国	欧洲
埃斯科运河	法国	欧洲
埃斯皮埃尔运河	比利时	欧洲
东方运河	法国	欧洲
瓦兹－埃纳运河	法国	欧洲

SOURCE NAME 原文名称	ENGLISH NAME 英语名称
Canal de l'Ourcq	Ourcq Canal
Canal de Marans	Marans Canal
Canal de Marans à la Rochelle	Marans-Rochelle Canal
Canal de Marseille au Rhône	Marseille-Rhône Canal
Canal de Meaux à Chalifert	Meaux-Chalifert Canal
Canal de Mines de Fer de la Moselle	Moselle Iron Mines Canal
Canal de Montech	Montech Canal
Canal de Nantes à Brest	Nantes-Brest Canal
Canal de Neufossé	Neufossé Canal
Canal de Pommerœul à Condé	Pommeroeul-Condé Canal
Canal de Pont-de-Vaux	Pont-de-Vaux Canal
Canal de Roanne à Digoin	Roanne-Digoin Canal
Canal de Rompsay	Rompsay Canal
Canal de Roubaix	Roubaix Canal
Canal de Saint-Maurice	Saint-Maurice Canal
Canal de Saint-Pierre	Saint-Pierre Canal
Canal de Saint-Quentin	Saint-Quentin Canal
Canal de São Roque	Saint Roque's Canal
Canal des Ardennes	Ardennes Canal
Canal de Savières	Savières Canal
Canal des Étangs	Étangs Canal
Canal des Houillères de la Sarr	Saar-Coal Canal
Canal des Landes	Landes Canal
Canal des Mines de Nœux	Nœux Coalmine Canal
Canal des Pangalanes	Pangalanes Canal
Canal des Vosges	Vosges Canal
Canal de Tancarville	Tancarville Canal

CHINESE NAME 中文名称	COUNTRY 所在国家	CONTINENT 所在洲
乌尔克河运河	法国	欧洲
马朗运河	法国	欧洲
马朗－罗谢尔运河	法国	欧洲
马赛－罗讷运河	法国	欧洲
莫－查理菲尔运河	法国	欧洲
摩泽尔铁矿运河	法国	欧洲
蒙泰什运河	法国	欧洲
南特－布雷斯特运河	法国	欧洲
诺福塞运河	法国	欧洲
波默勒尔－孔代运河	跨国	欧洲
蓬德沃运河	法国	欧洲
罗阿讷－迪关运河	法国	欧洲
罗姆赛运河	法国	欧洲
鲁贝运河	跨国	欧洲
圣莫里斯运河	法国	欧洲
圣皮埃尔运河	法国	欧洲
圣康坦运河	跨国	欧洲
圣罗克运河	葡萄牙	欧洲
阿登运河	法国	欧洲
萨维耶尔运河	法国	欧洲
埃唐运河	法国	欧洲
萨尔－科尔运河	跨国	欧洲
朗德运河	法国	欧洲
讷克斯煤矿运河	法国	欧洲
潘加兰运河	马达加斯加	非洲
孚日运河	法国	欧洲
唐卡维尔运河	法国	欧洲

SOURCE NAME 原文名称	ENGLISH NAME 英语名称
Canal de Vaires	Vaires Canal
Canal d'Ille-et-Rance	Ille and Rance Canal
Canal do Cojo	Côjo Canal
Canal d'Orléans	Orleans Canal
Canal du Blavet	Blavet Canal
Canal du Centre	Central Canal (Belgium)
Canal du Centre	Central France Canal
Canal du Charollais	Charollais Canal
Canal du Cher	Cher Canal
Canal du Clignon	Clignon Canal
Canal du Duc de Berry	Duke Berry Canal
Canal du Faux-Rempar	Faux-Rempart Canal
Canal du Grand Morin	Grand Morin Canal
Canal du Havre à Tancarville	Havre-Tancarville Canal
Canal du Loing	Loing Canal
Canal du Midi	Midi Canal
Canal du Mignon	Mignon Canal
Canal du Mussel-Aa	Mussel-Aa Canal
Canal du Nivernais	Nivernais Canal
Canal Dunkerque-Escaut	Dunkirk-Escaut Canal
Canal du Nord	North Canal
Canal du Rhône à Fos	Rhône-Fos Canal
Canal du Rhône à Sète	Rhône-Sète Canal
Canal du Rhône au Rhin	Rhône-Rhine Canal
Canale Boicelli	Boicelli Canal
Canale della Giudecca	Giudecca Canal
Canal entre Champagne et Bourgogne	Champagne-Burgundy Canal

CHINESE NAME 中文名称	COUNTRY 所在国家	CONTINENT 所在洲
威尔运河	法国	欧洲
伊勒－朗斯运河	法国	欧洲
科约运河	葡萄牙	欧洲
奥尔良运河	法国	欧洲
布拉韦运河	法国	欧洲
中央运河（比利时）	比利时	欧洲
法国中部运河	法国	欧洲
沙罗勒运河	法国	欧洲
谢尔运河	法国	欧洲
克利尼翁运河	法国	欧洲
贝里公爵运河	法国	欧洲
福－朗帕运河	法国	欧洲
大莫兰运河	法国	欧洲
阿弗尔－唐卡维尔运河	法国	欧洲
卢万运河	法国	欧洲
米迪运河	法国	欧洲
米尼翁运河	法国	欧洲
米瑟尔－阿河运河	荷兰	欧洲
尼韦内运河	法国	欧洲
敦刻尔克－埃斯科运河	法国	欧洲
北方运河	法国	欧洲
罗讷－福斯运河	法国	欧洲
罗讷－塞特运河	法国	欧洲
罗讷－莱茵运河	法国	欧洲
博采里运河	意大利	欧洲
朱代卡运河	意大利	欧洲
香槟－勃艮第运河	法国	欧洲

SOURCE NAME 原文名称	ENGLISH NAME 英语名称
Canal Henri IV	Henri IV Canal
Canal Latéral à l'Aisne	Aisne Lateral Canal
Canal Latéral à la Loire	Loire Lateral Canal
Canal Latéral à la Marne	Marne Lateral Canal
Canal Latéral à l'Oise	Oise Lateral Canal
Canal Latéral de la Garonne	Garonne Lateral Canal
Canal Maritime Bruxelles-Rupel	Brussels-Rupel Maritime Canal
Canal Maritime de Bruxelles à l'Escaut	Brussels-Schelde Maritime Canal
Canal Maritime de Marans	Marans Ship Canal
Canal Maritime du Brault	Brault Maritime Canal
Canal Nieuport–Dunkerque	Dunkirk-Newport Canal
Canal Plassendale	Plassendale Canal
Canal Saint-Denis	Saint-Denis Canal
Canal Saint-Louis	Saint-Louis Canal
Canal Saint-Martin	Saint-Martin Canal
Canal Saint-Sébastie	Saint-Sébastien Canal
Canal Seine-Nord Europe	Seine-North Europe Canal
Canal Shire-Zambezi	Shire-Zambezi Canal
Canalul Bega	Bega Canal
Canalul Colector Criş	Criş Collector Canal
Canalul Corector Tămaşda	Tămaşda Collector Canal
Canalul Coşteiu - Chizătău	Coşteiu-Chizătău Canal
Canalul Dunăre–Marea Neagră	Danube-Black Sea Canal
Canalul Morilor	Morilor Canal
Canalul Vadu Crişului - Aştileu	Vadu Crişului-Aştileu Canal
Canaux d'Hazebrouck	Hazebrouck Canals
Čertovka	Devil's Canal

CHINESE NAME 中文名称	COUNTRY 所在国家	CONTINENT 所在洲
亨利四世运河	法国	欧洲
埃纳旁侧运河	法国	欧洲
卢瓦尔旁侧运河	法国	欧洲
马恩河旁侧运河	法国	欧洲
瓦兹河旁侧运河	法国	欧洲
加龙河旁侧运河	法国	欧洲
布鲁塞尔－鲁佩尔通海运河	法国	欧洲
布鲁塞尔－斯海尔德通海运河	比利时	欧洲
马朗通海运河	法国	欧洲
布劳特通海运河	法国	欧洲
敦刻尔克－新港运河	跨国	欧洲
普拉森达勒运河	比利时	欧洲
圣但尼运河	法国	欧洲
圣路易斯运河	法国	欧洲
圣马丁运河	法国	欧洲
圣塞巴斯蒂安运河	法国	欧洲
塞纳－北欧运河	法国	欧洲
夏尔－赞比西运河	跨国	非洲
贝加运河	罗马尼亚、塞尔维亚	欧洲
克里什集流运河	罗马尼亚	欧洲
塔马斯达集流运河	罗马尼亚	欧洲
库斯蒂尤－智扎塔瓦运河	罗马尼亚	欧洲
多瑙－黑海运河	罗马尼亚	欧洲
莫瑞勒运河	罗马尼亚	欧洲
克里什河畔瓦杜－阿什蒂莱乌运河	罗马尼亚	欧洲
阿兹布鲁克运河网	法国	欧洲
魔鬼运河	捷克	欧洲

SOURCE NAME 原文名称	ENGLISH NAME 英语名称
Charlottenburger Verbindungskanal	Charlottenburg Canal
Christianshavns Kanal	Christian Port Canal
Dalslands Kanal	Dalsland Canal
Damse Vaart	Damme Canal
Damsterdiep	Damster Canal
Danube-Bucharest Canal	Danube-Bucharest Canal
Datteln-Hamm Kanal	Datteln-Hamm Canal
De Blankenbergse Vaart	Blankenberg Canal
De Geau	Geeuw
De Lits Canal	De Lits Canal
Dedemsvaart	Dedems Canal
Delftse Schie Kanaal	Delft Schie Canal
Delftse Vliet Kanaal	Delft-Vliet Canal
Diezekanaal	Dieze Canal
Dneprovsko-Bugsky Kanal	Dnieper-Bug Canal
Dokkumergrootdiep	Dokkum Grand Canal
Dokkummertrekvaart	Dokkum Trek Canal
Dommerskanaal	Dommers Canal
Donau-Oder-Elbe-Kanal	Danube-Oder-Elbe Canal
Donau-Oder-Kanal	Danube-Oder Canal
Doorslagkanaal	Doorslag Canal
Dortmund-Ems-Kanal	Dortmund-Ems Canal
Dragets Kanal	Draget Canal
Drentsche Hoofdvaart	Drenthe Grand Canal
Eemskanaal	Ems Canal

CHINESE NAME 中文名称	COUNTRY 所在国家	CONTINENT 所在洲
夏洛滕堡运河	德国	欧洲
克里斯钦港运河	丹麦	欧洲
达尔斯兰运河	瑞典	欧洲
达默运河	比利时	欧洲
达姆斯特运河	荷兰	欧洲
多瑙－布加勒斯特运河	罗马尼亚	欧洲
达特尔恩－哈姆运河	德国	欧洲
布兰肯贝赫运河	比利时	欧洲
黑伍运河	荷兰	欧洲
德利茨运河	荷兰	欧洲
代德姆斯运河	荷兰	欧洲
斯希运河代尔夫特段	荷兰	欧洲
代尔夫特－弗利特运河	荷兰	欧洲
迪兹运河	荷兰	欧洲
第聂伯－布格运河	白俄罗斯	欧洲
多克默大运河	荷兰	欧洲
多克默拖船运河	荷兰	欧洲
多默斯运河	荷兰	欧洲
多瑙－奥得－易北运河	塞尔维亚	欧洲
多瑙－奥得运河	跨国	欧洲
多斯拉赫运河	荷兰	欧洲
多特蒙德－埃姆斯运河	德国	欧洲
德拉戈特运河	瑞典	欧洲
德伦特大运河	荷兰	欧洲
埃姆斯运河	荷兰	欧洲

SOURCE NAME 原文名称	ENGLISH NAME 英语名称
Eendrachtskanaal	Eendrachts Canal
Elbe-Havel-Kanal	Elbe-Havel Canal
Elbe-Lübeck-Kanal	Elbe-Lübeck Canal
Elbe-Seitenkanal	Elbe Lateral Canal
Elbe-Trave-Kanal	Elbe-Trave Canal
Elbe-Weser-Schifffahrtsweg	Elbe-Weser Waterway
Elisabethfehnkanal	Elisabethfehn Canal
Embranchement de Croix	Croix Branch
Embranchement de La Nouvelle	New Branch
Embranchement de Montauban	Montauban Branch
Ems-Jade-Kanal	Ems-Jade Canal
Ems-Vechte-Kanal	Ems-Vecht Canal
Enservaart	Enser Canal
Espelervaart	Espel Canal

Falsterbokanalen	Falsterbo Canal
Finowkanal	Finow Canal
Franekervaart	Franeker Canal

Ganzendiep	Ganzen Canal
Geldersegracht	Gelderse Canal
Geuzensloot	Geuzen Canal
Gosener Kanal	Gosen Canal
Göta Kanal	Göta Canal
Grand Canal d'Alsace	Grand Alsace Canal
Grevelingskanaal	Grevelings Canal
Griebnitzkanal	Griebnitz Canal

CHINESE NAME 中文名称	COUNTRY 所在国家	CONTINENT 所在洲
团结运河	荷兰	欧洲
易北－哈弗尔运河	德国	欧洲
易北－吕贝克运河	德国	欧洲
易北河旁侧运河	德国	欧洲
易北－特拉沃运河	德国	欧洲
易北－威悉航道	德国	欧洲
伊丽莎白费恩运河	德国	欧洲
克鲁瓦支线运河	法国	欧洲
新运河支线	法国	欧洲
蒙托邦支线运河	法国	欧洲
埃姆斯－亚德运河	德国	欧洲
埃姆斯－费赫特运河	德国	欧洲
恩瑟运河	荷兰	欧洲
埃斯珀尔运河	荷兰	欧洲
法尔斯特布运河	瑞典	欧洲
菲诺运河	德国	欧洲
弗拉讷克运河	荷兰	欧洲
汉森运河	荷兰	欧洲
海尔德瑟运河	荷兰	欧洲
荷森运河	荷兰	欧洲
格森运河	德国	欧洲
约塔运河	瑞典	欧洲
阿尔萨斯大运河	法国	欧洲
赫弗宁斯运河	荷兰	欧洲
格里布尼茨运河	德国	欧洲

SOURCE NAME 原文名称	ENGLISH NAME 英语名称
Groeve Kanaal	Groeve Canal
Grootfontein-Omatako-Kanal	Grootfontein-Omatako Canal
Haarlemmertrekvaart	Haarlem Trek Canal
Hadelner Kanal	Hadeln Canal
Haldenkanalen	Halden Canal
Haren-Ruitenbrockerkanal	Haren-Ruitenbrock
Harlingertrekvaart	Harlingen Trek Canal
Harlingervaart	Harlingen Canal
Havelkanal	Havel Canal
Heinoomsvaart	Heinooms Canal
Helomavaart	Heloma Canal
Herengracht	Heren Canal
Heusdensch Kanaal	Heusden Canal
Hilversumsch Kanaal	Hilversum Canal
Hjälmare Kanal	Hjälmare Canal
Hoendiep	Hoen Canal
Hoge Dwarsvaart	Hoge Dwars Canal
Hoge Vaart	Hoge Canal
Hohenzollernkanal	Hohenzollern Canal
Hoogeveense Vaart	Hoogeveen Canal
Hoornse Vaart	Hoorn Canal
Huigenvaart	Huigen Canal
Hunsingokanaal	Hunsingo Canal
Hunsingokanaal	Hunsingo Drainage Canal
Hunte-Ems-Kanal	Hunte-Ems Canal
Hunze of Oostermoerse Vaart	Oostermoerse Canal

CHINESE NAME 中文名称	COUNTRY 所在国家	CONTINENT 所在洲
赫鲁夫运河	荷兰	欧洲
格鲁特方丹－奥玛塔科运河	纳米比亚	非洲
哈勒姆拖船运河	荷兰	欧洲
哈德尔恩运河	德国	欧洲
哈尔登运河	挪威	欧洲
哈伦－吕滕布罗克运河	德国	欧洲
哈灵根拖船运河	荷兰	欧洲
哈灵根运河	荷兰	欧洲
哈弗尔运河	德国	欧洲
海诺姆斯运河	荷兰	欧洲
黑洛玛运河	荷兰	欧洲
绅士运河	荷兰	欧洲
赫斯登运河	荷兰	欧洲
希佛萨姆运河	荷兰	欧洲
耶尔马运河	瑞士	欧洲
霍恩运河	荷兰	欧洲
霍赫杜瓦希运河	荷兰	欧洲
霍赫运河	荷兰	欧洲
霍亨索伦运河	德国	欧洲
霍赫芬运河	荷兰	欧洲
霍伦运河	荷兰	欧洲
惠根运河	荷兰	欧洲
亨辛豪运河	荷兰	欧洲
亨辛豪排水运河	荷兰	欧洲
洪特－埃姆斯运河	德国	欧洲
奥斯特莫尔斯运河	荷兰	欧洲

SOURCE NAME 原文名称	ENGLISH NAME 英语名称
Hunze Rivier	Hunze River
Ibrahimiyya-Kanal	Ibrahimiya Canal
Idrovia Ferrarese	Waterway of Ferrara
Interlaken Schiffskanal	Interlaken Ship Canal
Isabellakanaal	Isabella Canal
Johan Frisokanaal	Johan Friso Canal
Jonkersvaart	Jonkers Canal
Julianakanaal	Juliana Canal
Kaiser-Wilhelm-Kanal	Kaiser Wilhelm Canal
Kakatiya-Kanal	Kakatiya Canal
Kammerkanal	Kammer Canal
Kanaal Alkmaar-Kolhorn	Alkmaar-Kolhorn Canal
Kanaal Almelo-De Haandrik	Almelo-De Haandrik Canal
Kanaal Baflo-Mensingeweer	Baflo-Mensingeweer Canal
Kanaal Beukers-Steenwijk	Beukers-Steenwijk Canal
Kanaal Blaton-Aat	Blaton-Aat Canal
Kanaal Bocholt-Herentals	Bocholt-Herentals Canal
Kanaal Bossuit - Kortrijk	Bossuit-Kortrijk Canal
Kanaal Briegden-Neerharen	Briegden-Neerharen Canal
Kanaal Brugge-Sluis	Bruges-Sluis Canal
Kanaal Dessel-Kwaadmechelen	Dessel-Kwaadmechelen Canal
Kanaal Dessel-Turnhout-Schoten	Dessel-Turnhout-Schoten Canal
Kanaal door Walcheren	Walcheren Canal
Kanaal door Zuid-Beveland	South Beveland Canal

CHINESE NAME 中文名称	COUNTRY 所在国家	CONTINENT 所在洲
浑泽河	荷兰	欧洲
伊布拉希米亚运河	埃及	非洲
费拉拉航道	意大利	欧洲
因特拉肯通海运河	瑞士	欧洲
伊莎贝拉运河	跨国	欧洲
约翰－费里索运河	荷兰	欧洲
约恩克斯运河	荷兰	欧洲
朱莉安娜运河	荷兰	欧洲
皇帝威廉运河	德国	欧洲
卡卡提亚运河	印度	亚洲
卡默运河	德国	欧洲
阿尔克马尔－科尔霍恩运河	荷兰	欧洲
阿尔默洛－德·汉德里克运河	荷兰	欧洲
巴夫洛－门辛赫韦尔运河	荷兰	欧洲
布克斯－斯滕韦克运河	荷兰	欧洲
布拉通－艾特运河	比利时	欧洲
博霍尔特－海伦塔尔斯运河	比利时	欧洲
博斯奥特－科特赖克运河	比利时	欧洲
比利赫登－尼尔哈伦运河	比利时	欧洲
布鲁日－斯勒伊斯运河	跨国	欧洲
代瑟尔－克瓦德梅赫伦运河	比利时	欧洲
代瑟尔－蒂伦豪特－斯霍滕运河	比利时	欧洲
瓦尔赫伦运河	荷兰	欧洲
南贝弗兰运河	荷兰	欧洲

SOURCE NAME 原文名称	ENGLISH NAME 英语名称
Kanaal Gent-Terneuzen	Ghent-Terneuzen Canal
Kanaal Ieper-IJzer	Ypres-IJzer Canal
Kanaal Ieper-Komen	Ypres-Comines Canal
Kanaal Leuven-Dijle	Leuven-Dyle Canal
Kanaal naar Beverlo	Beverlo Canal
Kanaal Nieuwpoort-Duinkerke	Newport-Dunkirk Canal
Kanaal Nimy-Blaton-Péronnes	Nimy-Blaton-Péronnes Canal
Kanaal Plassendale-Nieuwpoort	Plassendale-Newport Canal
Kanaal Pommeroeul-Antoing	Pommeroeul-Antoing Canal
Kanaal Roeselare-Leie	Roeselare-Leie Canal
Kanaal Schagen-Kolhorn	Schagen-Kolhorn Canal
Kanaal Steenwijk	Steenwijk Canal
Kanaal Steenwijk-Ossenzijl	Steenwijk-Ossenzijl Canal
Kanaal Stolpen-Kolhorn	Stolpen-Kolhorn Canal
Kanaal Stolpen-Schagen	Stolpen-Schagen Canal
Kanaal van Eeklo	Eeklo Canal
Kanaal van Gent naar Oostende	Ghent-Ostend Canal
Kanaal van Monsin	Monsin Canal
Kanaal van St. Andries	St. Andries Canal
Kanaal van Steenenhoek	Steenenhoek Canal
Kanaal van Stekene	Stekene Canal
Kanaal van Ternaaie	Ternaaien Canal
Kanaal van Corbulo	Corbulo Canal
Kanaal Wessem-Nederweert	Wessem-Nederweert Canal
Kanaal Zutphen - Enschede	Zutphen-Enschede Canal
Kanał Augustowski; Аўгустоўскі канал	Augustów Canal
Kanal Banjir	Banjir Canal

CHINESE NAME 中文名称	COUNTRY 所在国家	CONTINENT 所在洲
根特－特尔纽曾运河	跨国	欧洲
伊普尔－艾泽尔运河	比利时	欧洲
伊普尔－科米讷运河	比利时	欧洲
鲁汶－迪乐运河	比利时	欧洲
贝弗洛运河	比利时	欧洲
新港－敦刻尔克运河	跨国	欧洲
尼米－布拉通－佩罗讷运河	比利时	欧洲
普拉森达勒－新港运河	比利时	欧洲
波默勒尔－昂图万运河	比利时	欧洲
鲁瑟拉勒－莱厄运河	比利时	欧洲
斯哈亨－科尔霍恩运河	荷兰	欧洲
斯滕韦克运河	荷兰	欧洲
斯滕韦克－奥森宰尔运河	荷兰	欧洲
斯托尔彭－科尔霍恩运河	荷兰	欧洲
斯托尔彭－斯哈亨运河	荷兰	欧洲
埃克洛运河	比利时	欧洲
根特－奥斯坦德运河	比利时	欧洲
蒙辛运河	比利时	美洲
圣安德烈斯运河	荷兰	欧洲
斯蒂嫩胡克运河	荷兰	欧洲
斯泰克讷运河	比利时	欧洲
特尔奈恩运河	跨国	欧洲
科布洛运河	荷兰	欧洲
韦瑟姆－下韦尔特运河	荷兰	欧洲
聚特芬－恩斯赫德运河	荷兰	欧洲
奥古斯图夫运河	波兰、白俄罗斯	欧洲
班吉尔运河	印度尼西亚	亚洲

SOURCE NAME 原文名称	ENGLISH NAME 英语名称
Kanal Banjir Kali Malang	Banjir Kali Malang Canal
Kanał Bydgoski	Bydgoszcz Canal
Kanał Bystry	Bystry Canal
Kanal Dunav-Tisa-Dunav	Danube-Tisa-Danube Canal
Kanał Elbląski	Elbląg Canal
Kanał Gliwicki	Gliwice Canal
Kanal Istanbul	Istanbul Canal
Kanał Kłodnicki	Klodnica Canal
Kanał Królewski	Royal Canal
Kanał Mosiński	Mosiński Canal
Kanal Omval-Kolhorn	Omval-Kolhorn Canal
Kanal Wolczkowski	Wolczkowski Canal
Karlbergskanalen	Karlberg Canal
Karl-Heine-Kanal	Karl Heine Canal
Keitele Kanal	Keitele Canal
Keizersgracht	Kaiser Canal
Kênh Tàu Hủ	Tàu Hù Canal
Kênh Vũng Gù	Vũng Gù Canal
Kerkvaart	Kerk Canal
Keulse Vaart	Keulse Canal
Kieldiep	Kiel Canal
Kliefsloot	Klief Canal
Klodnitzkanal	Klodnitz Canal
Knollendammervaart	Knollendam Canal
Kolonelsdiep	Kolonels Canal
Korte Vlietkanaal	Korte Canal
Kubaardervaart	Kubaard Canal

CHINESE NAME 中文名称	COUNTRY 所在国家	CONTINENT 所在洲
班吉尔卡利玛琅泄洪运河	印度尼西亚	亚洲
比得哥什运河	波兰	欧洲
贝斯特雷运河	波兰	欧洲
多瑙河－蒂萨－多瑙运河	塞尔维亚	欧洲
埃尔布隆格运河	波兰	欧洲
格利维采运河	波兰	欧洲
伊斯坦布尔运河	土耳其	亚洲
克罗迪尼卡运河	波兰	欧洲
国王运河	白俄罗斯	欧洲
莫辛斯基运河	波兰	欧洲
奥姆瓦尔－科尔霍恩运河	荷兰	欧洲
沃尔兹科夫斯基运河	波兰	欧洲
卡尔伯格运河	瑞典	欧洲
卡尔海涅运河	德国	欧洲
凯泰莱运河	芬兰	欧洲
皇帝运河	荷兰	欧洲
头胡运河	越南	亚洲
万古运河	越南	亚洲
凯尔克运河	荷兰	欧洲
科尔瑟运河	荷兰	欧洲
基尔运河	荷兰	欧洲
克里夫运河	荷兰	欧洲
克罗迪尼兹运河	波兰	欧洲
克诺兰达默运河	荷兰	欧洲
科洛奈尔运河	荷兰	欧洲
科特运河	荷兰	欧洲
库巴德运河	荷兰	欧洲

SOURCE NAME 原文名称	ENGLISH NAME 英语名称
Kuikhornstervaart	Kuikhorne Canal
Kukonharjun kanavan	Kukonharju Canal
Küstenkanal	Küsten Canal
Kutveleen kanava	Kutvele Canal
Lage Dwarsvaart	Lage Dwars Canal
Lage Vaart	Lage Canal
Landwehrkanal	Landwehr Canal
Langerhanskanal	Langerhans Canal
Larservaart	Larsen Canal
Lathumervaart	Lathum Canal
La Voie Maritime du Saint-Laurent	Saint Lawrence Seaway
Le Canal de Lo	Lo Canal
Leemvaart	Leem Canal
Leermenstermaar	Leermens Canal
Leidsevaart	Leiden Trek Canal
Lekkanaal	Lek Canal
Lemstervaart	Lemster Canal
Leopoldkanaal	Leopold Canal
Leuvense vaart	Leuven Canal
Liaison Rhône-Fos-Bouc-Marseille	Rhône-Fos-Bouc-Marseille Liaison
L'Orne et Le Canal Maritime	Orne and Caen Maritime Canal
Losdorpermaar	Losdorp Canal
Ludwigskanal	Ludwig Canal
Luttelgeestervaart	Luttelgeester Canal
Maas-Waalkanaal	Maas-Waal Canal

CHINESE NAME 中文名称	COUNTRY 所在国家	CONTINENT 所在洲
库伊霍恩运河	荷兰	欧洲
库康纳鸠运河	芬兰	欧洲
屈斯滕运河	德国	欧洲
库特瓦勒运河	芬兰	欧洲
拉赫杜瓦希运河	荷兰	欧洲
拉赫运河	荷兰	欧洲
兰韦尔运河	德国	欧洲
朗格汉斯运河	德国	欧洲
拉森运河	荷兰	欧洲
拉土姆运河	荷兰	欧洲
圣劳伦斯海道	跨国	欧洲
罗运河	比利时	欧洲
莱姆运河	荷兰	欧洲
利尔曼斯运河	荷兰	欧洲
莱顿拖船运河	荷兰	欧洲
莱克运河	荷兰	欧洲
莱姆斯特运河	荷兰	欧洲
利奥波德运河	比利时	欧洲
鲁汶运河	比利时	欧洲
罗讷－福斯－布克－马赛运河网	法国	欧洲
奥恩－卡昂通海运河	法国	欧洲
洛斯多普运河	荷兰	欧洲
路德维希运河	德国	欧洲
吕特尔海斯特运河	荷兰	欧洲
马斯－瓦尔运河	荷兰	欧洲

SOURCE NAME 原文名称	ENGLISH NAME 英语名称
Maas-Moezel Kanal	Maas-Moezel Canal
Maas-Schelde-Kanal	Maas-Schelde Canal
Main-Donau Kanal	Main-Danube Canal
Makkumervaart	Makkum Canal
Markkanaal	Mark Canal
Marknesservaart	Marknesse Canal
Mark-Vlietkanaal	Mark-Vliet Canal
Máximakanaal	Máxima Canal
Meedendiep	Meeden Canal
Mensingeweersterloopdiep	Mensingeweer Canal
Meppelerdiep	Meppel Canal
Merwedekanaal	Merwede Canal
Middenkanaal	Midden Canal
Mittellandkanal	Mittelland Canal
Moervaart	Moer Canal
Munnekezijlsterriet	Munnekezijl Canal
Müritz-Elde-Wasserstraße	Müritz-Elde Waterway
Musselkanaal	Mussel Canal
Naardertrekvaart	Naarden Trek Canal
Nagelervaart	Nagele Canal
Nauernaschevaart	Nauernasche Canal
Naviglio di Bereguardo	Bereguardo Canal
Naviglio di Padern	Paderno Canal
Naviglio Grande	Grand Canal
Naviglio Martesana	Martesana Canal
Naviglio Pavese	Pavese Canal

CHINESE NAME 中文名称	COUNTRY 所在国家	CONTINENT 所在洲
马斯－摩泽尔运河	跨国	欧洲
马斯－斯海尔德运河	比利时	欧洲
美因－多瑙运河	德国	欧洲
马库默运河	荷兰	欧洲
马克运河	荷兰	欧洲
马克内瑟运河	荷兰	欧洲
马克－弗利特运河	荷兰	欧洲
马西玛运河	荷兰	欧洲
梅登运河	荷兰	欧洲
门辛赫韦尔运河	荷兰	欧洲
梅珀尔运河	荷兰	欧洲
梅尔韦德运河	荷兰	欧洲
米登运河	荷兰	欧洲
中部运河	德国	欧洲
莫尔运河	比利时	欧洲
穆纳科宰尔运河	荷兰	欧洲
米里茨－埃尔德航道	德国	欧洲
米瑟尔运河	荷兰	欧洲
纳尔登拖船运河	荷兰	欧洲
纳赫勒运河	荷兰	欧洲
瑙尔纳什运河	荷兰	欧洲
贝雷瓜尔多运河	意大利	欧洲
帕代诺运河	意大利	欧洲
米兰大运河	意大利	欧洲
马尔特萨纳运河	意大利	欧洲
帕维亚运河	意大利	欧洲

SOURCE NAME 原文名称	ENGLISH NAME 英语名称
Neuköllner Schifffahrtskanal	Neukölln Ship Canal
Neuköllnerkanal	Neukölln Canal
Nieuwe Vaart	New Canal
Nieuwe Vecht	New Vecht
Nieuwe Waterweg	New Waterway
Noorder Oudeweg	North Oudeweg Canal
Noordervaart	Noord Canal
Noordhollandsch Kanaal	North Holland Canal
Noord-Willemskanaal	North Willems Canal
Noordzeekanaal	North Sea Canal
Nordgeorgsfehn Kanal	Nordgeorgsfehn Canal
Nord-Ostsee-Kanal	Kiel Canal
Notte-Kanal	Notte Canal
Nymphenburg Kanal	Nymphenburg Canal
Obere Havel-Wasserstraße	Upper Havel Waterway
Obere Spree-Wasserstraße	Upper Spree Waterway
Oder-Havel-Kanal	Havel-Oder Waterway
Oegstgeesterkanaal	Oegstgeest Canal
Oldehoofskanaal	Oldehove Canal
Oostervaart	Ooster Canal
Oosterwijtwerdermaar	Eastern Wijtwerd Canal
Oostsingelgracht	East Singel Canal
Opeindervaart	Opeinde Canal
Opsterlandse Compagnonsvaart	Opsterland Compagnons Canal
Oranjekanaal	Oranje Canal
Oude Eemskanaal	Old Ems Canal

CHINESE NAME 中文名称	COUNTRY 所在国家	CONTINENT 所在洲
新克尔恩通海运河	德国	欧洲
新克尔恩运河	德国	欧洲
新运河	荷兰	欧洲
新费赫特运河	荷兰	欧洲
新航道运河	荷兰	欧洲
北奥德韦赫运河	荷兰	欧洲
诺德运河	荷兰	欧洲
北荷兰运河	荷兰	欧洲
北威廉斯运河	荷兰	欧洲
北海运河	荷兰	欧洲
诺德乔治斯运河	德国	欧洲
基尔运河	德国	欧洲
诺特运河	德国	欧洲
宁芬堡运河	德国	欧洲
哈弗尔河上游航道	德国	欧洲
施普雷河上游航道	德国	欧洲
哈弗尔－奥德河航道	德国	欧洲
乌赫斯特海斯特运河	荷兰	欧洲
奥尔德霍弗运河	荷兰	欧洲
奥斯特运河	荷兰	欧洲
东维特维德运河	荷兰	欧洲
东辛厄尔运河	荷兰	欧洲
奥潘德运河	荷兰	欧洲
奥普斯特朗－康帕尼翁运河	荷兰	欧洲
奥拉涅运河	荷兰	欧洲
旧埃姆斯运河	荷兰	欧洲

SOURCE NAME 原文名称	ENGLISH NAME 英语名称
Oudvaart	Old Canal
Ourthekanaal	Ourthe Canal
Pannerdensche Kanaal	Pannerden Canal
Pasing-Nympenburg Kanal	Pasing-Nympenburg Canal
Peizerdiep	Peizer Canal
Polderhoofdkanaal	Polder Main Canal
Prinsengracht	Prinse Canal
Prinses Margrietkanaal	Prinses Margriet Canal
Prinz-Friedrich-Leopold-Kanal	Prince Friedrich Leopold Canal
Purmerringvaart	Purmer Ring Canal
Qanat al-Jaish	Army Canal
Rangersdiep	Rengers Canal
Rasquerdermaar	Rasquert Canal
Reitdiep	Reit Canal
Rhein-Herne-Kanal	Rhine-Herne Canal
Rijn Schiekanaal	Rhine-Schie Canal
Rijstervaart	Ryster Feart
Ringvaart	Ring Canal
Roosendaalsche Vliet	Roosendaal Canal
Rüdesdorfer Gewässer	Rüdesdorf Waterway
Ruiten-Aa Kanaal	Ruiten-Aa Canal
Ruitenbrockkanaal	Ruitenbrock Canal
Ruppiner Gewässer	Ruppin Waterway
Ruttense Vaart	Rutten Canal

CHINESE NAME 中文名称	COUNTRY 所在国家	CONTINENT 所在洲
旧运河	荷兰	欧洲
乌尔特运河	跨国	欧洲
潘讷登运河	荷兰	欧洲
帕辛－宁芬堡运河	德国	欧洲
派泽运河	荷兰	欧洲
波尔德主运河	荷兰	欧洲
王子运河	荷兰	欧洲
玛格丽特公主运河	荷兰	欧洲
弗里德里希·莱奥波德王子运河	德国	欧洲
皮尔默环形运河	荷兰	欧洲
军队运河	伊拉克	亚州
伦格斯运河	荷兰	欧洲
拉斯奎尔特运河	荷兰	欧洲
哈伊特运河	荷兰	欧洲
莱茵－黑尔讷运河	德国	欧洲
莱茵－斯希运河	荷兰	欧洲
赖斯特费尔特运河	荷兰	欧洲
环形运河	比利时	欧洲
罗森达尔运河	比利时	欧洲
吕德斯多夫航道	德国	欧洲
吕滕－阿河运河	荷兰	欧洲
吕滕布罗克运河	跨国	欧洲
鲁平航道	德国	欧洲
吕滕运河	荷兰	欧洲

SOURCE NAME 原文名称	ENGLISH NAME 英语名称
Sacrow-Paretzer-Kanal	Sacrow-Paretz Canal
Saima Kanal	Saimaa Canal
Schagen-Kolhornkanaal	Schagen-Kolhorn Canal
Schelde-Rijnkanaal	Schelde-Rhine Canal
Schermerringvaart	Schermer Ring Canal
Schiffahrtskanal von Hurden	Hurden Ship Canal
Schipdonkkanaal	Schipdonk Canal
Schloss-Kanal	Schloss Canal
Scholtenskanaal	Scholtens Canal
Schöninghsdorf-Hoogeveenkanaal	Schöninghsdorf-Hoogeveen Canal
Seddinsee-Gosener Kanal	Seddin Lake-Gosen Canal
's-Gravelandsevaart	's-Graveland Canal
Shah Nahar	Royal Canal
Shaṭṭ al-Ḥayy; Shaṭṭ al-Gharrāf	Al-Gharraf River
Silokanal	Silo Canal
Slochterdiep	Slochteren Canal
Slootvaart	Sloot Canal
Slotsholmen Kanal	Castle Islet Canal
Smildervaart	Smilde Canal
Sneeker Oudvaart	Sneek Old Canal
Södertälje Kanal	Södertälje Canal
Sootkanalen	Soot Canal
Spijkstermaar	Spijk Canal
Spoykanal	Spoy Canal
Stads-Compascuumkanaal	Stads-Compascuum Canal
Stadskanaal	Stads Canal
Stecknitzkanal	Strecknitz Canal

CHINESE NAME 中文名称	COUNTRY 所在国家	CONTINENT 所在洲
萨克罗－帕雷茨运河	德国	欧洲
塞马运河	跨国	欧洲
斯哈亨－科尔霍恩运河	荷兰	欧洲
斯海尔德－莱茵运河	跨国	欧洲
斯海默环形运河	荷兰	欧洲
赫登通海运河	瑞士	欧洲
斯希普顿克运河	比利时	欧洲
施洛斯运河	德国	欧洲
舒尔腾斯运河	荷兰	欧洲
舍宁斯多夫－霍赫芬运河	跨国	欧洲
塞丁湖－格森运河	德国	欧洲
斯赫拉弗兰运河	荷兰	欧洲
皇家运河	巴基斯坦	亚洲
阿尔－盖拉夫河	伊拉克	亚洲
西洛运河	德国	欧洲
斯洛赫特伦运河	荷兰	欧洲
斯洛特运河	荷兰	欧洲
城堡岛运河	丹麦	欧洲
斯米尔德运河	荷兰	欧洲
斯内克旧运河	荷兰	欧洲
南泰利耶运河	瑞典	欧洲
苏特运河	挪威	欧洲
斯派克运河	荷兰	欧洲
斯波伊运河	德国	欧洲
斯塔茨－孔帕斯屈姆运河	荷兰	欧洲
斯塔茨运河	荷兰	欧洲
斯特雷克尼茨运河	德国	欧洲

SOURCE NAME 原文名称	ENGLISH NAME 英语名称
Stichkanal Osnabrück	Osnabrück Canal
Stieltjeskanaal	Stieltjes Canal
Storkower Kanal	Storkow Rafting Canal
Stör-Wasserstraße	Stör Waterway
Strömma Kanal	Strömma Canal
Strömsholms Kanal	Strömsholm Canal
Stroobossertrekvaart	Stroobos Trek Canal
Suvorovin sotakanavat	Suvorov Military Canals
Swiftervaart	Swifter Canal
Taivallahden kanavan	Taivallahti Canal
Telemarkskanalen	Telemark Canal
Teltowkanal	Teltow Canal
TemplinerGewässer	Templin Waters
Ter Apelkanaal	Ter Apel Canal
Termunterzijldiep	Termunterzijl Canal
Thuner Schiffskanal	Thun Ship Canal
Trekvaart Haarlem-Leiden	Haarlem-Leiden Trek Canal
Trollhätte Kanal	Trollhätte Canal
Twentekanaal	Twente Canal
Tzummervaart	Tzum Canal
Urkervaart	Urker Canal
Ursemmervaart	Ursem Canal
Usquerdermaar	Usquert Canal
Vaarweg van Franeker naar Berlikum	Franeker-Berlikum Canal

CHINESE NAME 中文名称	COUNTRY 所在国家	CONTINENT 所在洲
奥斯纳布吕克运河	德国	欧洲
斯蒂尔切斯运河	荷兰	欧洲
施托尔科排筏运河	德国	欧洲
施特尔航道	德国	欧洲
斯特伦玛运河	瑞典	欧洲
斯特伦斯霍尔姆运河	瑞典	欧洲
斯特罗博斯拖船运河	荷兰	欧洲
苏沃洛夫军事运河网	芬兰	欧洲
斯威夫特运河	荷兰	欧洲
泰瓦拉蒂运河	芬兰	欧洲
泰勒马克运河	挪威	欧洲
泰尔托运河	德国	欧洲
滕普林水域	德国	欧洲
泰尔阿珀尔运河	荷兰	欧洲
泰尔蒙特宰尔运河	荷兰	欧洲
图恩通海运河	瑞士	欧洲
哈勒姆－莱顿拖船运河	荷兰	欧洲
特罗尔海特运河	瑞典	欧洲
特文特运河	荷兰	欧洲
曲姆运河	荷兰	欧洲
厄尔卡运河	荷兰	欧洲
乌尔塞姆运河	荷兰	欧洲
于斯奎特运河	荷兰	欧洲
弗拉讷克－贝利克姆运河	荷兰	欧洲

SOURCE NAME 原文名称	ENGLISH NAME 英语名称
Van Harinxmakanaal	Van Harinxma Canal
Van Panhuyskanaal	Van Panhuys Canal
Van Starkenborghkanaal	Van Starkenborgh Canal
Varistaipaleen kanavan	Varistaipale Canal
Veendiep	Veen Canal
Veltener Stichkanal	Velten Stich Canal
Ventos–Dubysos Kanalas	Windawski Canal
Verbindingskanaal	Verbindings Canal
Verlengde Hoogeveense Vaart	Hoogeveen Extension Canal
Verlengde Scholtenskanaal	Scholtens Extension Canal
Veurnevaart	Veurne Canal
Visvlieterdiep	Visvliet Canal
Voedingskanaal	Voedings Canal
Vollenhover Kanaal	Vollenhove Canal
Waardkanaal	Waard Canal
Wantij en Otterkanaal	Wantij and Otter Canal
Warffumermaar	Warffum Canal
Warfhuisterloopdiep	Warfhuister Canal
Weesper Trekvaart	Weesp Trek Canal
Werbellinkanal	Werbellin Canal
Wesel-Datteln-Kanal	Wesel-Datteln Canal
Westhafenkanal	Westhafen Canal
Wiener Neustädter Kanal	Wiener Neustadt Canal
Wilders Kanal	Wilders Canal
Wilhelminakanaal	Wilhelmina Canal
Willebroekvaart	Willebroek Canal

CHINESE NAME 中文名称	COUNTRY 所在国家	CONTINENT 所在洲
范哈林克斯马运河	荷兰	欧洲
范班豪斯运河	荷兰	欧洲
范斯塔肯博赫运河	荷兰	欧洲
瓦里斯泰佩勒运河	芬兰	欧洲
芬运河	荷兰	欧洲
费尔滕支渠	德国	欧洲
温达夫斯基运河	立陶宛	欧洲
韦尔宾丁斯运河	荷兰	欧洲
霍赫芬扩建运河	荷兰	欧洲
舒尔腾斯扩建运河	荷兰	欧洲
弗尔讷运河	跨国	欧洲
费斯夫利特运河	荷兰	欧洲
沃丁斯运河	荷兰	欧洲
福伦霍弗运河	荷兰	欧洲
瓦德运河	荷兰	欧洲
万泰－奥特运河	荷兰	欧洲
瓦尔弗姆运河	荷兰	欧洲
瓦尔夫赫伊斯特运河	荷兰	欧洲
韦斯普拖船运河	荷兰	欧洲
韦尔贝林运河	德国	欧洲
韦瑟尔－达特尔恩运河	德国	欧洲
韦斯特哈芬运河	德国	欧洲
维也纳诺伊施塔特运河	奥地利	欧洲
维尔德斯运河	丹麦	欧洲
威廉敏娜运河	荷兰	欧洲
维勒布鲁克运河	荷兰	欧洲

SOURCE NAME 原文名称	ENGLISH NAME 英语名称
Willemsvaart	Willems Canal
Winschoterdiep	Winschoten Canal
Winsumerdiep	Winsum Canal
Workumertrekvaart	Workum Trek Canal
Zeehavenkanaal	Zeehaven Canal
Ziendevaart	Ziende Canal
Zijkanaal C	Zij Canal C
Zijldiep	Zijl Canal
Zuid-Willemsvaart	South Willems Canal
Zwanendiep	Zwanen Canal
Zwolsevaart	Zwolse Canal

CHINESE NAME 中文名称	COUNTRY 所在国家	CONTINENT 所在洲
威廉斯运河	荷兰	欧洲
温斯霍滕运河	荷兰	欧洲
温瑟姆运河	荷兰	欧洲
沃尔克姆拖船运河	荷兰	欧洲
海港运河	荷兰	欧洲
辛德运河	荷兰	欧洲
塞运河C	荷兰	欧洲
宰尔运河	荷兰	欧洲
南威廉斯运河	跨国	欧洲
天鹅运河	荷兰	欧洲
兹沃尔瑟运河	荷兰	欧洲

BIBLIOGRAPHY

参考文献

BLAIR J. Waterways and canal-building in medieval England [M]. Oxford: Oxford University Press, 2007.

BURTON A. The canal pioneers: canal construction from 2,500 BC to the early 20th century [M]. Barnsley: Pen & Sword Books Ltd., 2017.

BUSBY L, BROAD D D. Inland waterways of the Netherlands [M]. 2nd ed. Cambridgeshire: Imray, Laurie, Norie & Wilson Ltd., 2016.

FISHER S. The canals of Britain: the comprehensive guide [M]. London: Bloomsbury Publishing, 2017.

HARLOW A F. Old towpaths: the story of the American canal era [M]. Port Washington, NY: Kennikat Press, 1964.

JEFFERSON D. Through the French canals [M].13th ed. London: Bloomsbury Publishing, 2014.

JONES J. Inland waterways of Belgium [M]. Cambridgeshire: Imray, Laurie, Norie & Wilson Ltd., 2005.

SHAW R E. Canals for a nation: the canal era in the United States, 1790—1860 [M]. Lexington: The University of Kentucky Press, 2014.

ZHANG W, ZHOU K. Canal and navigation lock [C]//HUA J, FENG L. (eds). Thirty Great Inventions of China. Singapore: Spring Nature Singapore Pte Ltd. , 2020.

上海社会科学院生态与可持续发展研究所，世界运河历史文化城市合作组织. 世界运河古镇绿色发展报告[M].上海：上海社会科学院出版社，2020.

王金铨，等. 世界遗产运河的保护与传承:大运河文化带的视角[M].北京：社会科学文献出版社，2020.

魏向清，邓清，郭启新，等. 世界运河名录（英汉对照简明版）[M].南京：南京大学出版社，2017.

中国人民共和国住房和城乡建设部、中华人民共和国国家质量监督检验检疫总局. 中华人民共和国国家标准·内河通航标准：GB 50139-2014 [S]，2014.

网站资源（检索时间：2019年1月—2021年7月）：

http://inlandwaterwaysinternational.org/

http://shtong.gov.cn/

http://stlawrencepiks.com/

http://touringohio.com/

http://www.alluringworld.com/

http://www.bjnews.com.cn/news/

http://www.dili360.com/

http://www.iwa-network.org/

http://www.kunene.riverawarenesskit.com/

http://www.shelbycountyhistory.org/

http://www.stellingwerven.dds.nl/

http://www.stroudwater.co.uk/

http://www.visit-plus.com/

http://www.whcccco.org/

https://allaboutvenice.com/

https://americancanalsociety.org/

https://baike.baidu.com/

https://biwakososui-museum.city.kyoto.lg.jp/

https://brussels.en-academic.com/

https://canalplan.uk/

https://coflein.gov.uk/en/site/

https://commons.wikimedia.org/

https://de-academic.com/

https://discovery.nationalarchives.gov.uk/

https://edepot.wur.nl/

https://en.citizendium.org/

https://europeforvisitors.com/

https://france-world-heritage.com/

https://galwaywaterways.ie/

https://gewaesser.rudern.de/

https://irishwaterwayshistory.com/

https://mapcarta.com/

https://neworleanshistorical.org/

https://nomadicniko.com/

https://roanokecanal.com/

https://savharen.de/

https://sotoncs.org.uk/

https://tropter.com/en/

https://vayla.fi/en/waterways/

https://waterways.org.uk/

https://www.amazingczechia.com/

https://www.britannica.com/

https://www.carolana.com/NC/Transportation/

https://www.dutchdredging.nl/

https://www.eurocanals.com/

https://www.europeanwaterways.com/

https://www.french-waterways.com/

https://www.geheugenvandrenthe.nl/

https://www.gotakanal.se/en/

https://www.hmdb.org/

https://www.jonathanahill.com/

https://www.leipzig.travel/en

https://www.mindat.org/

https://www.mypacer.com/routes/

https://www.newindianexpress.com/

https://www.nkytribune.com/

https://www.pasty.com/

https://www.pc.gc.ca/en/lhn-nhs/qc/chambly

https://www.researchgate.net/

https://www.rijkswaterstaat.nl/

https://www.sardarsarovardam.org/

https://www.skipperguide.de/

https://www.stromsholmskanal.se/sv/

https://www.tameside.gov.uk/canal/

https://www.thecanadianencyclopedia.ca/

https://www.thefreedictionary.com/

https://www.ukwaterwaysguide.co.uk/

https://www.u-s-history.com/

https://www.vastsverige.com/

https://www.visithenrycounty.com/

https://www.water-ways.net/

https://www.wikipedia.org/

Index 1

World Canals in English

A

B

C

D

E

F

G

H

I

J

K

L

M

N

O

P

Q

R

S

T

U

V

W

X

Y

Z

World Canals in Chinese

A

B

C

D

E

F

G

H

J

K

L

M

N

O

P

Q

R

S

T

W

X

Y

Z

Index 3

World Canals by Continent in English

Africa

America

Asia

Europe

Oceania

大洋洲

非洲

美洲

欧洲

亚洲

World Canals by Country in English

Cambodia

Canada

Chile

China

Lishui River	350
Liugongzhen Canal	352
Nanmao Canal	407
New Grand Canal	417
New Qinhuai River	423
North Canal (China)	431
North Jiaolai River	434
Pinglu Canal	481
Pogangdu Canal	483
Pudong Canal	494
Punan Canal	495
Rouge River	523
Shangxin River	555
Songliao Canal	564
South Canal	568
South Jiaolai River	570
Tainan Canal	597
Tongnan Canal	611
Wushen Canal	669
Xiang-Gui Canal	673
Xing'an Canal	674
Xuhe River	674
Xuxi Canal	676
Yellow River Channel	681
Youth Canal	684
Yundu Canal	685
Yunlianghe River	686
Yunyanhe River	686
Zhe-Gan Canal	689

Colombia

Dike Canal	170
Dique Canal	171
Levee Canal	348

Côte d'Ivoire

Asagny Canal	030
Assinie Canal	031
Groguida Canal	248
Vridi Canal	644

Croatia

Bobota Canal	066

Czech Republic

Bata Canal	045
Devil's Canal	170

Denmark

Egypt

Finland

France

Germany

Greece

Guyana

India

Bambawali-Ravi-Bedian Canal	041
Kakatiya Canal	307
Kollam Canal	320
Munak Canal	400
Narmada Canal	410
National Waterway No. 3	411
Paravur Canal	474
Parvati Puthannar	475
Quilon Canal	499
Soundane Cut	567
Sri Ram Sagar Canal	574
Sutlej-Yamuna Link Canal	592
Thiruvananthapuram-Shoranur Canal	609
West Coast Canal	657

Indonesia

Banjir Canal	042
Banjir Kali Malang Canal	042
East Flood Canal	187
Indragiri River	285
Mahakam	366
Sekanak Canal	551
West Flood Canal	658

Iraq

Army Canal	029
Glory River	230
Hayy River	260
Naru Kabari	411
Prosperity Canal	494
Shaal Gharraf	554
Shatt-en-Nil	557

Ireland

Eglinton Canal	190
Grand Canal (Ireland)	236
Jamestown Canal	295
Lecarrow Canal	339
Tralee Ship Canal	612

Italy

Japan

Kenya

Korea

Lithuania

Madagascar

Myanmar

Namibia

Naura

Netherlands

Panama

Philippines

Poland

Portugal

Romania

Sweden

Switzerland

Thailand

Togo

Turkey

Turkmenistan

Ukraine

United Arab Emirates

United Kingdom

United States

River Don Navigation	517
Rochdale Canal	519
Sankey Canal	538
Seeswood Canal	548
Shropshire Union Canal	558
Southwick Canal	570
Southwick Ship Canal	570
Staffordshire and Worcestershire Canal	575
Stainforth and Keadby Canal	576
Stourbridge Canal	581
Stourbridge Extension Canal	582
Stratford-upon-Avon Canal	584
Swansea Canal	594
Tennant Canal	603
Thames and Severn Canal	608
Trent and Mersey Canal	613
Union Canal (the United Kingdom)	621
Uttoxeter Canal	629
Wilts and Berks Canal	664
Wisbech Canal	667
Worcester and Birmingham Canal	669

Adams Creek-Core Creek Canal	004
Albemarle and Chesapeake Canal	008
Aldebaran Canal	010
Alexandria Canal	012
Allegheny River	014
Altair Canal	017
Appomattox Canal	022
Appomattox River Navigation	022
Arkansas River Navigation System	028
Arnot Canal	030
Atlantic Intracoastal Waterway	031
Augusta Canal	032
Barkley Canal	044
Bean Shoals Canal	046
Beaver and Erie Canal	048
Black River Canal	061
Blackstone Canal	062
Bricktown Canal	075
Brunswick-Altamara Canal	083
Cabrillo Canal	095
Caloosahatchee River	097
Cal-Sag Channel	098
Calumet-Sag Channel	100
Canaveral Barge Canal	102
Cape Cod Canal	103
Cape May Canal	104
Carondelet Canal	106
Cayuga-Seneca Canal	108

Vietnam

Transnational Canals

Africa

Asia

America

Europe

World Canals by Country in Chinese

巴基斯坦

巴拿马

白俄罗斯

比利时

波兰

丹麦

德国

多哥

俄罗斯

法国

菲律宾

芬兰

哥伦比亚

圭亚那

韩国

荷兰

加拿大

柬埔寨

捷克

科特迪瓦

克罗地亚

肯尼亚

立陶宛

罗马尼亚

马达加斯加

美国

孟加拉国

缅甸

纳米比亚

瑙鲁

尼加拉瓜

挪威

葡萄牙

日本

瑞典

瑞士

塞尔维亚

沙特阿拉伯

泰国

意大利

印度

印度尼西亚

英国

越南

智利

中国

跨国运河

非洲

美洲

欧洲

亚洲

图书在版编目（CIP）数据

世界运河辞典 = A Concise English-Chinese Dictionary of World Canals：简明英汉对照版 /
魏向清, 郭启新, 邓清主编. -- 南京：南京大学出版社, 2021.12

ISBN 978-7-305-24276-2

Ⅰ.①世… Ⅱ.①魏… ②郭… ③邓… Ⅲ.①运河－世界－词典－英、汉 Ⅳ.①U621-61

中国版本图书馆CIP数据核字（2021）第047335号

出版发行 南京大学出版社
社　　址 南京市汉口路22号　　**邮编** 210093
出 版 人 金鑫荣

书　　名 世界运河辞典：简明英汉对照版
　　　　　A Concise English-Chinese Dictionary of World Canals
主　　编 魏向清　郭启新　邓清
责任编辑 张淑文　　**编辑热线** 025（83592401）
书籍设计 吉　雨

印　　刷 南京爱德印刷有限公司
开　　本 718×1000　1/16　**印张** 63.5　**字数** 1173 千
版　　次 2021年12月第1版　2021年12月第1次印刷
　　　　　ISBN 978-7-305-24276-2
定　　价 598.00元

网址：www.njupco.com
官方微博：http://weibo.com/njupco
微信服务号：njuyuexue
销售咨询热线：(025)83594756